Imagination and Language

Imagination and Language

Collected essays on Constant, Baudelaire, Nerval and Flaubert

ALISON FAIRLIE

Fellow of Girton College and Professor of French in the University of Cambridge

EDITED BY MALCOLM BOWIE

Professor of French, Queen Mary College, London

CAMBRIDGE UNIVERSITY PRESS

CAMBRIDGE
LONDON NEW YORK NEW ROCHELLE
MELBOURNE SYDNEY

Published by the Press Syndicate of the University of Cambridge
The Pitt Building, Trumpington Street, Cambridge CB2 1RP
32 East 57th Street, New York, NY 10022, USA
296 Beaconsfield Parade, Middle Park, Melbourne 3206, Australia

First published 1981

Printed in Malta by Interprint Ltd

British Library Cataloguing in Publication Data

Fairlie, Alison
Imagination and language.
1. French literature – 19th century – History and
criticism
I. Title   II. Bowie, Malcolm
840′.9′007   PQ281   80-40307

ISBN 0 521 23291 0

Contents

Part Three: Nerval

Part Four: Flaubert

* *Note*: Dates in parentheses are those of first publication.
In the case of essays which were originally delivered as
conference papers, date and place of delivery will be found
in the first endnote. Full publishing details for each essay
are to be found in the bibliography.

Editor's note

For years it has seemed to a number of Alison Fairlie's friends and colleagues that her essays on nineteenth-century French literature should be made available in book form. It seemed especially unfortunate that criticism of this high order should remain dispersed in journals and collective volumes – and thus largely inaccessible to students and general readers of the period – at a time when supposed 'market forces' were filling library shelves with potboiling introductory manuals and near-duplicate 'critical' studies. Besides, the first three essays on Constant's *Adolphe* were conceived as a single, unified study and should clearly have been a book long ago; the essays on Nerval, Baudelaire and Flaubert, though produced in response to a variety of isolated academic occasions and given titles which often promised no more than a series of 'remarks', 'observations', 'reflections' or 'aspects', fell into sharply characterized groups, each centred upon a set of recurrent critical problems; and the entire sequence of essays, to those who knew all or most of them, formed an *univers imaginaire* of exceptional depth and coherence. But these good reasons for the publication of the present book repeatedly met with resistance when placed before its author, and an extended campaign of argument and subterfuge was necessary before this resistance could be overcome. Alison Fairlie shrank with characteristic modesty and self-doubt from the idea that a large book on four major authors could reasonably bear her name, and found difficulty in believing what to the campaigners had been obvious from the start – that such a book would offer immediate practical help and intellectual stimulus to a wide international readership of students, fellow researchers and enthusiasts for French literature.

The qualities of her critical writing are well known and will quickly become apparent to those who are introduced to her work by the following pages. If I now recall certain of those qualities, I do so in order to express, on behalf of her colleagues and former pupils, the gratitude they all feel for the complex sense of intellectual and imaginative aliveness which her writing and her teaching impart.

Her manner is often one of questioning and speculation. But the questions she asks and the hypotheses she ventures invariably take their cue from the words on the author's page and, far from clothing the literary text in interpretative fantasies, seek to bring the reader back with clearer sight and a renewed power of enjoyment to its central riches. She writes with precision about ambiguity in literature, and especially about those ambiguities which have a main, informing role in the works of art chosen for discussion. During a period when criticism has suffered from severe factional narrowness and ill-temper – factions defining themselves all too often by their promotion of this or that single aspect of literature – Alison Fairlie is one of the saving few who have remained generously plural in their interests and approach. While attending closely to the formal and expressive properties of the individual literary work she is scrupulously aware that many things lying beyond that work – manuscripts, variant readings or 'sources', the author's personal relationships or his letters – may prompt the literary scholar to valuable new kinds of critical perception. And perhaps most important of all, the language she herself uses is, in its attunement to the subjects discussed, its economy and its discreet inventiveness, a lesson to all those critics who, by their luxuriant verbal displays, seek to outwit and outwrite their writers.

The present volume, together with her extended study of Leconte de Lisle and her monographs on *Les Fleurs du Mal* and *Madame Bovary*, constitute an outstanding corpus of critical writing. There could be no better *Festschrift* for Alison Fairlie than this collection of her own work.

M.M.B.

Acknowledgements

It is a pleasure to express, however incompletely, a deep sense of gratitude for the stimulus and the kindness, both intellectual and practical, so generously given by colleagues, friends and students over the long years represented by these studies.

To enjoy, as an undergraduate at St Hugh's College, Oxford, lectures or tutorials by such scholars as Gustave Rudler, Will G. Moore, Enid Starkie, E. A. Francis, Cécile Hugon (especially on French painting), Rhoda Sutherland (then Miss Clarke), L. A. Bisson and H. J. Hunt provided multiple opportunities for discussion and discovery. To Gustave Rudler's constant initiating of new critical approaches, as to the intellectual and practical care he devoted to all research students, I owe more than can adequately be expressed.

Debts to still earlier influences are many: to grandparents and parents who delighted in reading and discussion, in experiments in writing, and in contrasts between countries and their languages; to the Scottish school system which in the 1920s taught children from age eight to enjoy reading and writing inventive if simple tales in French; to Penrhos College, Colwyn Bay, not only for scholarships but especially for the enjoyment of a wide range of teaching where examination pressures never protruded; to the redoubtable Isabelle H. Clarke both for seeing Oxford as a goal and for suggesting not set-text selection but the widest personal reading across the centuries of French literature.

As a naive newcomer to a College post in Cambridge (after wartime research in Paris and Oxford, and war-work of various kinds – to colleagues at Bletchley I owe many insights into essential problems in the handling of language), I learned from K. T. Butler, then Mistress of Girton, and from Henriette Bibas, Director of

Studies in Modern Languages, both how personal research and discussion with undergraduates may vitally and essentially combine, and the pleasure of free experimentation with many methods of teaching. Later, a University post fell vacant; I recall with gratitude F. C. Green and L. C. Harmer as Heads of Department concerned to further that same combination of interests in newly-appointed lecturers. To another colleague from early years, May Graham Wallas of Newnham College, I am grateful for many quietly penetrating remarks on intellectual or aesthetic issues.

Space makes it impossible to acknowledge here by name all those contemporaries who have given very valuable time to organizing conferences, colloquia and presentation volumes, and to editing the results; to all (individually remembered) I express my gratitude for the discipline of deadlines – often benevolently interpreted – for incitement to concision, and especially for opportunities to engage in interim discussion which others may refute or revise. My debts to the skill and help of expert librarians (in Cambridge, London, Oxford, Paris, Rouen, Geneva, Lausanne, Brussels, Mariemont) must similarly be generally acknowledged; I recall with warm thanks many instances of professional advice and personal kindness. For financial help with research, apart from generosity acknowledged in earlier works, I am indebted to grants from the University of Cambridge.

Two senior colleagues, over recent years, have provided the inspiration not only of their outstanding writings but of a friendship which encourages new enterprises: Jean Hytier and Jean Seznec. To lifelong discussion with friends of my own generation, with research students initiating discoveries and with undergraduates posing and renewing fundamental questions, I owe debts individually recalled if not rehearsed in detail here.

To two Cambridge contemporaries I express especial thanks: Odette de Mourgues, with her exceptional originality in analysis and evaluation of sixteenth- and seventeenth-century poets, drama- tists and *moralistes*; and Lloyd J. Austin, with his breadth of scholar- ship and judgement, his clarity and sensibility in studies and editions of Baudelaire, Mallarmé, Valéry and the writers of their period. Both have given much precious time to reading and discuss- ing articles included in the present volume. To Lloyd Austin as Drapers Professor of French, I, like many members of his Department, owe particularly generous encouragement to research, and many opportunities for wide international contacts.

Not least among my debts of gratitude is that to those who have devoted precious time to reading the proofs of articles originally published in periodicals with varying printers' conventions; to Malcolm Bowie as the most patient and efficient of editors, and to two colleagues as expert in proof-reading as they are generous in friendship: L. J. Austin and I.D. McFarlane.

For permission to reprint the articles collected in this volume I am grateful to the editors and publishers of *Modern Language Review, Forum for Modern Language Studies, French Studies, Europe, Australian Journal of French Studies, Revue des sciences humaines, Annales de la Faculté des Lettres et Sciences Humaines de Nice, Times Literary Supplement, Cahiers de l'Association Internationale des Études françaises, Essays in French Literature*, and to the following publishers: Éditions Droz, Leicester University Press, Oxford: The Clarendon Press, Manchester University Press, Éditions de la Baconnière, Basil Blackwell, Methuen, Éditions Nizet. Warm thanks are also due to James Austin who supplied the photographs for plates 23 to 26 and gave much other valuable help with illustrations.

A.A.B.F.

Introduction

The studies here collected date from many different moments over the last twenty-five years. They stem from personal reactions to particular works. With the exception of the opening three articles on Constant they arose as contributions requested on specific occasions – to special issues of journals, to colloquia, or to presentation volumes – occasions where, within a chosen focus, wide and welcome freedom was left to contributors.

Each study was envisaged, not as establishing a particular theoretical view, but as contributing to a continuing debate. Each owes to the published works of predecessors debts which will be obvious to all readers as well as less immediately definable reasons for gratitude: ranging from those early university teachers who posed quietly persistent questions and rejoiced in the command of words, to the challenge of discussion with colleagues within and across disciplines, or, especially, with generations of undergraduates creatively querying unexamined assumptions.

Over these twenty-five years, for the four authors here discussed, criticism has increasingly queried all such assumptions; scholarship has provided a wealth of new material. Important manuscripts have been brought to light; widely scattered writings have been collected; above all, faulty editions have been brilliantly revised, or are in course of revision. The main hope of the present collection of articles would be to serve in suggesting how much remains to be done. Constant is no longer artificially divided between author of *Adolphe*, politician and diarist (or hastily forced into an uneasy amalgam of the three); his art as novelist, political orator and dissector of personality will need to be more sharply analysed as ideas, feelings and expression are more fully integrated with reactions to eighteenth-century background and to the immense influence of the

Groupe de Coppet. In Baudelaire, the understanding of the *Fleurs du Mal* may be enriched by examining how they interpenetrate with the prose poems, the *Paradis artificiels*, the unfinished projects in many *genres*, and especially the writings on the visual arts; in all of these, the means of expression are coming to be more closely analysed. That same interpenetration of multiple parallel themes and projects is being increasingly traced in Nerval, as is the degree of his lucid self-questioning, his awareness of readers' expectations, and his creative command of structure and expression. Flaubert above all has recently provoked fundamental reinvestigation both of the nature of the novel and of the relation of literature to the reader's preconceptions (on the latter point all three of the other authors had highly penetrating and disquieting insights); the gradual publication of his complex and revealing rough drafts has still to be fully drawn on to illuminate his individual control of construction and style.

An invigorating interest in the theory of criticism is typical of today. Debates between the 'naively biographical' and the 'obdurately immanent' have outlived their time, and literature rightly claims its *nil a me alienum* ... Broadening of fields and recourse to technical terminology have not always made it easy to think of criticism as still an art – until one re-reads those contemporaries for whom, as for the great authors, the way of saying a thing may be essential to what is said. One basic wish links the present short studies: the desire to hand on the joy of reading, interpreting and arguing, all inextricably linked with the love of using language.

To those who suggested the present volume and have given precious time and care to collecting its contents I express my deep gratitude. Their courtesy in consultation precludes any falling back on the delightful distant fiction of the pirated work published without its author's knowledge. Their generosity of mind and skill in argument overcame authorial recalcitrance. In agreement between author and editor, it was decided (apart from correction of misprints and the cutting of an occasional sentence) to produce articles and references exactly as they stood on publication at the dates concerned.

PART ONE

Constant

1

The art of Constant's *Adolphe*:
I. The stylization of experience
(1967)[1]

Against the rich background of recent discoveries in the papers of
Constant and his circle,[2] critics have gradually become aware of the
need for a new study of the art of *Adolphe*, that most quietly
disruptive of all French novels. Constant himself wrote trenchantly,
if disingenuously, of those who read it as a *roman à clefs*: 'chercher
des allusions dans un roman, c'est substituer le commérage à l'étude
du cœur humain' (p. 5). His own personality, and those of the men
and women to whom he wrote, were so particularly endowed with
keen sensibility, unusual lucidity, and fluent or epigrammatic powers of expression, that critics for a century and a half have found
matter for thoughtful 'études du cœur humain' in relating *Adolphe* to
the biographical material which surrounds it. If many valuable
studies have, intentionally or less consciously, been concerned primarily with the problems of Constant the man, others have also
been interested in the relation between experience and creation,
between the raw material of facts and the shaping by the selective
imagination of the artist.[3] Now that much new material has been
assimilated, there is still a need to look afresh at what this novel does
express, and at the skill and subtlety of its means of expression. The
purpose of this article is to suggest briefly a number of lines of
approach, some of which may touch on familiar points needing
perhaps further development, others of which will, it is hoped, be
new. It will centre on the fact that Constant's selection and ordering
of the raw material of reality is not a mere result of the requirements
of personal confession or discreet disguise, but a conscious art,
governed by the logic of the creative imagination. I shall hope to
show in particular how Constant through his characters probes
suggestively into questions of what constitutes authenticity of experience and authenticity of expression, and into the relation between experience and expression.

Constant's 'autobiographical' works, on very different levels, all show him as the conscious artist, sifting events with a particular focus in mind, choosing exactly the tone appropriate to this purpose. The *Journaux intimes* attempt to give as directly as possible the immediate and unsorted product of daily experience with all its contradictions and vacillations. Even here, at his most uninhibited, Constant is aware of the difficulty of direct transposition of the truth, of the temptation to play to the gallery.[4] It is no doubt logical that, combining a sense of the complexity of reality with a need to master it in firm classifications, he should eventually take to the extreme of the 'computer-diary', choosing seventeen figures to represent in a combination of fixed variables the repeated and shifting essentials of his experience.[5] In his letters, he shows even from childhood a brilliant sense of how to select events and adapt tone to the character of the recipient.[6] The analysis of himself or others is worked out in many different modes. The *Cahier Rouge* represents a more developed choice and shaping of memories, and here Constant chooses a unified tone of amused retrospective irony, an incisive comic indulgence. The commemorative articles on Julie Talma and Mme de Staël select in a serious tone and with an elegant critical faculty those intellectual and personal qualities in his subjects which exemplify his own scale of values. *Cécile*, though in so many details close to the facts of biography, yet chooses from the tangled reality a linear narrative of year-long tergiversation between two women only.

Adolphe is obviously at a very different level of stylization from any of these. In characters, events, and expression, the *Journaux* abundantly show how truth is more melodramatic than fiction. The contrast between the submissive, dogged devotion of the patient Charlotte and the clamorous intellectual stimulus of the domineering yet genuinely suffering Mme de Staël, the prolonged vacillation of Constant between countless women, in turn and contemporaneously goad and obstacle to his intellectual and political ambitions, are credible only in the detail of attested fact, and would appear schematized or pathological in any direct transposition into a novel. Mme de Staël's pursuit across the countryside to fling herself, with trailing hair and clothes in disorder, upon the staircase[7] or the frequently brandished threat of suicide by the convenient phial of laudanum, might savour of the *roman noir*. Most important of all is the expression, which in the *Journaux* is often the immediate throwing on to paper of momentary feeling in its ulcerated rawness, violently absolute or tritely derivative in vocabulary. *Adolphe* will tone down the flamboyant or petulant reality, the ranting and inflation, to a controlled and quiet concentration more adequate to suggestion of feeling. It is in daily life that Constant speaks of the possessive woman in terms that belong to melodrama: 'cette furie qui me poursuit, l'écume à la bouche et le poignard à la main', that his exasperation invents a *bestiaire* of insults: 'serpent', 'harpie', 'vipère', 'sangsue', 'diablesse', 'monstre', 'furie', or a meteorology of images: 'l'ouragan va fondre sur moi', 'tous les volcans sont moins flamboyants qu'elle', 'tempête et océan furieux', 'l'ébranlement de l'univers et le mouvement du chaos', 'ce fléau que l'enfer a vomi ...'.[8] The novel will find its own means of conveying harsh exasperation or deadly weariness without the overworn and exaggerated imagery in which immediate experience so naturally throws off the spume of separate moments. And even in less startling transpositions, concentration and discretion are at work: the cry of Charlotte noted in the *Journal*: 'Cette voix, cette voix, c'est la voix qui fait du mal. Cet homme m'a tuée' becomes simply: 'Quel est ce bruit? c'est la voix qui m'a fait du mal'.[9]

Cécile, in its only faintly disguised treatment of Mme de Staël and Charlotte, is obviously very much nearer to the facts of real life than is *Adolphe*. Yet much of the complexity of events and motives has been left aside: its intelligent and subtle analyses seem almost directed as a 'plaidoyer' to his second wife. If on the one hand it lacks some of the sharp sting of the diaries' sensitive and self-critical cynicism, on the other it seems flat and dilute by the side of the suggestive concentration and meticulous structure of *Adolphe*.[10] This concentration, with its sacrifice of still further elements from reality, was achieved in part because the artist consciously tried experiments on his public before finishing the novel. A variant discovered by Rudler shows how he had wished in *Adolphe* also to show a hero between two women: it is on reading parts of the work aloud that he concludes: 'Cette lecture m'a prouvé que je ne pouvais rien faire de cet ouvrage en y mêlant une autre épisode de femme.'[11] *Adolphe*, then, takes one man and one woman to represent the growth and the disintegration of passion, followed by the persistence of an indestructible bond combining exasperation with tenderness. Through their central dilemma questions may be raised on three levels: are the mobility of the man and the possessiveness of the woman to be attributed to their individual characters, to the background of their age and a social situation which precludes marriage, or to the basic nature of man and woman?

Where the *Cahier Rouge* flickered with biting gaiety across the early formation of a character,[12] *Adolphe* takes the focus and tone of quiet but penetrating tragedy. Three central things might be noted here. First, tragedy involves the insoluble situation, from which, once the characters are engaged, there can be no 'right' way out. (The satisfaction we derive from the tragic spectacle lies not in any moral solution, but in seeing how the human mind may face, analyse, bear with dignity or express with adequacy what it may neither cure nor solve.) Once Adolphe and Ellénore are fully involved, irreparable hurt will be caused whether he goes or stays: 'Sa position et celle d'Ellénore étaient sans ressource', wrote Constant, 'et c'est précisément ce que j'ai voulu' (p. 8). Secondly, tragedy at its most ironical may involve the destruction of a character not simply by an obvious flaw, but also by the potentially finest qualities:[13] in Adolphe lucidity and pity; in Ellénore devotion ('la noble et dangereuse faculté de vivre dans un autre et pour un autre' (p. 6)) and her own form of sporadic and corrosive lucidity, giving destructive insight into Adolphe's feelings. Finally, the tensest tragedy implies an exact counterpoise between the outer pressures which crush the character (fate, society, heredity) and an ineradic-able conviction of inner responsibility. If outer pressure alone is stressed, the result may be mere pathos; concentration on inner guilt alone may become pathological. Two lines from *Phèdre* best repre-sent this razor-edge balance between consciousness of outer pressure and inner responsibility:

> Objet infortuné des vengeances célestes,
> Je m'abhorre encor plus que tu ne me détestes.

Adolphe and Ellénore, products and victims of a given society, are no romantic innocents up against a simply evil outside agency, nor are they instruments for a facile attack on its faults. Social pressures, like the Gods elsewhere,[14] merely intensify what is in-herent in the individual: 'la société s'arme de tout ce qu'il y a de mauvais dans le cœur de l'homme' (p. 147). Moreover, the urge to be accepted by society and to contribute to it is presented in double terms: at once a personal ambition and a genuine need for noble activity.[15] *Adolphe*, then, is neither the condemnation nor the self-justification of a central figure, nor, as it is sometimes presented, the simple indictment of a society or a generation, but the probing presentation of certain tragic dilemmas.

If the serious tone of *Adolphe* differs profoundly from that of the *Cahier Rouge*, yet in the *Cahier Rouge* there is a gaily recounted anecdote which bears on the question central to *Adolphe*'s meaning and art. The young Constant is attempting to seduce an English lady who refuses to admit into their relationship the compromising word Love; he wastes the hour and his opportunity by arguing over her offer of Friendship, ironically unaware that she had obviously not intended a mere matter of the choice of terminology to affect the outcome.

This lightly-treated insinuation on the connexion between vocabulary and experience leads to what is perhaps the most suggestive phrase in *Adolphe*:

Les sentiments de l'homme sont confus et mélangés; ils se composent d'une multitude d'impressions variées qui échappent à l'observation; et la parole, toujours trop grossière et trop générale, peut bien servir à les désigner, mais ne sert jamais à les définir. (p. 30)

That this problem is central to Constant's experience becomes clear from the repeated and sharp expression it is given in many different works: in *De la Religion* (p. 1415):

Tous nos sentiments intimes semblent se jouer des efforts du langage: la parole rebelle, par cela seule qu'elle généralise ce qu'elle exprime, sert à désigner, à distinguer, plutôt qu'à définir,

in the *Principes de Politique* (p. 1220):

je demanderais comment on définit avec précision cette partie vague et profonde de nos sensations morales, qui par sa nature même défie tous les efforts du langage,

in his attack on Schelling's system as 'arrangements de mots pris pour des choses' (*Jnx.*, p. 298), and in many other reflections on words in diaries and letters.[16] This question of the relation between experience and expression has of course become one of the main preoccupations of our century: one thinks ahead to Proust's analysis of how certain mental habits 'amassent au-dessus de nos impressions vraies, pour nous les cacher entièrement, les nomenclatures ... que nous appelons faussement la vie' (III, p. 896 – see the whole passage), to Valéry's pursuit of a 'nettoyage de la situation verbale', or even to the linguistic philosophers' attempt to examine the conditioning of modes of thinking by unrecognized assumptions inherent in the traditional forms of verbalization. Constant's particular attitude to the way in which words may distort experience has several important results in *Adolphe*.

A complex state of feelings while still unexpressed retains its full and fluid potentialities: words select, simplify, intensify and perpetuate, giving to the subtleties of feeling a false rigidity and a frightening irrevocability. They are dangerous in two ways, and incidents in every chapter bring alive one or other of these. On the one hand, one may hypnotize oneself or another into a feeling through the effect of persuasive expressions:

Il y a dans la simple habitude d'emprunter le langage de l'amour ... un danger ... L'on ne sait ce qu'on s'expose à éprouver ... (p. 5).

or again:

échauffé d'ailleurs que j'étais par mon propre style, je ressentais, en finissant d'écrire ... (p. 39)[17]

or:

nous sommes des créatures tellement mobiles, que, les sentiments que nous feignons, nous finissons par les éprouver, (p. 86).

At intervals, Ellénore, 'avide de se tromper elle-même', consoles herself with Adolphe's words when the substance behind them has disappeared:

Ces simples paroles, démenties par tant de paroles précédentes, rendirent Ellénore à la vie et à la confiance; elle me les fit répéter plusieurs fois (p. 89)

or even

peut-être trouvait-elle une sorte de consolation à s'entendre répéter [by others] des expressions d'amour que depuis longtemps je ne prononçais plus. (p. 118)

On the other hand, words may crystallize a dangerous truth, may destroy what might have persisted, or fix irrevocably one side only of a complex of feelings. Once pronounced, they cannot be unsaid, and they stiffen and simplify the conflicting or indefinable elements of reality: 'Nous avions prononcé tous deux des mots irréparables; nous pouvions les taire, mais non les oublier' (p. 65). Ellénore's forcing of a definition at the end of Chapter v is a pivot in the progress towards destruction: 'Pourquoi prononça-t-elle ces mots ...?' Adolphe's one attempt to define his contradictory emotions to a third person in Chapter viii (pp. 111–12) shows the resulting only half-true interpretation and forms another 'pas irréparable'. It is fitting that the contrast between words and actions should form the climax of Ellénore's last letter: 'Vos actions sont nobles et dévouées: mais quelles actions effaceraient vos paroles? Ces paroles acérées retentissent autour de moi ... elles flétrissent tout ce que vous faites' (p. 144).

If words, and in particular general terms – love, vanity, weakness – are useful highest common factors in communication, but crude and blunt instruments by the side of the subtlety and fluidity of individual experience, it follows that to sum up Adolphe, as is sometimes done, as 'a man incapable of loving' or 'a weak procrastinator' is to beg the question which the novel constantly investigates: just what unexpected combinations of feeling may lie beneath these labels? Adolphe's own most trenchant formulae applied to himself: 'un homme faible, reconnaissant et dominé' (p. 71) are constantly set at odds with others: 's'ils veulent dompter *ce que par habitude ils nomment faiblesse* ... ils froissent ce qu'il y a de généreux, ils brisent ce qu'il y a de fidèle, ils tuent ce qu'il y a de bon' (p. 8), or 'elle vit de la générosité dans ce que j'appelais de la faiblesse' (p. 111). The word 'amour' is not simply used in statements, but is accompanied, on key occasions, by phrases investigating the strange qualities which together may form its presence or its absence. We are moreover given many different layers: what Adolphe felt, how he judged (or misjudged) himself at the time, how he judges himself later, how others in the story judge (or misjudge) him, and the final conflicting reflections of the letters by two outside judges at the end.

The novel, then, brings alive an individual and fluctuating experience which cannot adequately be reduced to conventional categories or conceptual summaries. Verbal generalization and qualitative judgement, whether by others, or even sometimes by the self, are shown, in networks of ironical suggestion, as being constantly beside the point. Individual experience can be understood only if brought alive in the detail of its complexity and strangeness: *bizarre* is a key-word in Constant, underlining a sense of the puzzling and paradoxical.[18]

Yet this is a novel which is constantly directed towards precision and conclusiveness in ideas and expression. Few authors have at the same time so challenged the criteria of abstract judgment and yet exercised judgment so relentlessly, have more mistrusted general terms, yet been more irresistibly drawn to the maxim, the epigram, the precise formula.[19] A *florilège* of maxims from *Adolphe* would provide not only a cautionary handbook for lovers, but a precise and telling distillation of wider human experience. In fact, the interplay between two urges (each of particular intensity and subtlety) – a startled sense of what is indefinable and illogical in human behaviour; a demand for the intellectual and aesthetic pleasure of firm conceptual definition – this interplay is at the centre of Constant's art.[20]

Constant, then, deliberately decomposes into unexpected components, and suggestively re-defines, such terms as love, vanity, weakness. Again like Proust later, having anatomized the detail of contradiction and flux beneath apparently simple concepts, he will still attempt 'd'en décrire la courbe et d'en dégager la loi'. In looking more closely at his shaping of his material, we may start from the concept of love, with its three stages: the falling in love; the brief period of genuine delight; finally, what Gide was to call 'la lente décristallisation de l'amour'.

Falling in love is no 'coup de foudre': individual experience is shaped by three forces prevalent in any developed society. One remembers of course La Rochefoucauld's: 'Il y a des gens qui n'auraient jamais été amoureux s'ils n'avaient jamais entendu parler de l'amour.' Inherited idealism and inherited cynicism (emulation of a friend in love, 'ses transports et l'excès de sa joie';[21] a previous generation's assumption that women may be enjoyed and left without regret or responsibility),[22] these join with the search for prestige in a relationship 'qui pût flatter mon amour-propre'.

But if the normal process of ruthless analysis is to lay bare beneath the superstructure of feeling the less easily avowable motives of calculation and vanity, Constant has both used this process and gone on to reverse it:

Il y avait dans ce besoin beaucoup de vanité sans doute, mais il n'y avait pas uniquement de la vanité; il y en avait peut-être moins que je ne le croyais moi-même. (p. 30)

Self-deception, instead of garbing the hero as a man of all virtues, may take the opposite turn, that of a false sophistication, and make him mistakenly pride himself on being the clever seducer:[23]

Presque toujours, pour vivre en repos avec nous-mêmes, nous travestissons en calculs et en systèmes nos impuissances ou nos faiblesses (p. 38);

this partly distorted vision of himself blinds him to the genuine needs and feelings which are imperceptibly taking hold of him and which, later, even if they change their nature, cannot be wholly uprooted. Where some critics stress Adolphe as imagining feelings in which he is deficient, his own narrative brings out rather the opposite side: the danger of imagining the cold calculation of a Don Juan or a Valmont while, insidiously, feelings difficult to recognize or define are taking an insinuating hold. This is, of course, the insight of the later Adolphe, in the light of experience to come. At the time, his self-analysis played him false: 'Je portais au fond de mon cœur un besoin de sensibilité dont je ne m'apercevais pas' (p. 22). And not only may self-analysis be mistaken in its findings, but by its very existence it may distort the feelings it sets out to analyse: 'Cette analyse perpétuelle, qui place une arrière-pensée à côté de tous les sentiments, et par là les corrompt dès leur naissance.'[24]

The difficulty of defining the growth of feeling is brought out by the deliberate choice of such words as 'charme', 'magie', 'grâce inexplicable'. They are not used as mere vague, emotional counters: they serve to give a sense at the same time of compulsion and of uncertainty, for they are set in the undertones of a later doubt: '*J'attribuais* à son charme ...', '*me semblait* revêtu d'une grâce inexplicable'. Having suggested in this way the strength and the strangeness of the feelings which underlie apparently cold calculation, Constant looks further into the conflicting components of these feelings.

The central stimulus is one which will be given ironical variations throughout the novel: the galvanizing of potential (or, later, flagging) emotion by the obstacle. Where self-analysis may throw doubts on the genuineness of 'Love', frustration and pain strike home with an immediacy that makes them seem elemental certainties. The need to conquer the obstacle provides an all-absorbing aim, 'un but', doubts recede, and there is temporarily a total involvement in an experience felt at the time as authentic, 'de bonne foi'.[25]

The logic and illogic of pain will form counterpoints in this novel. Logic, because if his own pain is a criterion of authentic experience to Adolphe, so his inability to leave Ellénore later is founded on the impossibility of bearing the sight or thought of her pain, and the final summing-up of the book stands in the phrase: 'La grande question dans la vie, c'est la douleur que l'on cause' (p. 149) (to many others in his age the last phrase would have read 'que l'on éprouve'). Illogic because of the puzzlement of the lucid intellect at the disproportion between cause and effect, and at the startling discontinuity between successive states of mind. If it is Proust one above all thinks of as anatomizing 'les intermittences du cœur', here they are already brought alive in lapidary form:

J'étais étonné moi-même de ce que je souffrais. Ma mémoire me retraçait les instants ou je m'étais dit que je n'aspirais qu'à un succès; que ce n'était qu'une tentative à laquelle je renoncerais sans peine. *Je ne concevais rien* à la douleur violente, indomptable, qui déchirait mon cœur. (p. 40)

Or again:

Je m'étais levé, ce jour-là même, ne songeant plus à Ellénore: une heure après ... j'avais la fièvre de la crainte de ne pas la voir. (p. 42)

Later in the book they will prove equally startling in reversed order:

A peine fus-je éloigné d'Ellénore qu'une douleur profonde remplaça ma colère. Je me trouvai dans une espèce de stupeur ... Je me répétais mes paroles avec étonnement; je ne concevais pas ma conduite. (p. 80)

Still further doubts are raised on the insoluble question whether the effort to avoid causing pain by remaining together does not cause still more pain.

The origins of a passion have been gradually developed. At the end of Chapter III and beginning of Chapter IV, a genuine experience of love is characterized with a care which has not always been sufficiently examined. This is a momentary experience, but one which transfigures past and future:

L'amour supplée aux longs souvenirs, par une sorte de magie ... L'amour n'est qu'un point lumineux, et néanmoins il semble s'emparer du temps ... tant qu'il existe, il répand sa clarté ... (pp. 51–2)[26]

The famous paragraph at the beginning of Chapter IV (p. 57) gives in its brief compass an extraordinarily rich analysis and evocation of a genuine experience of love. It is no vague inflated hymn to romantic 'indescriptibles félicités', but, within simple and apparently almost random phrases, a positive analysis of central and suggestive effects: the human fulfilment of having found the one fitting person, the metaphysical sense of understanding the purpose of life, the everyday transformation, making significant the most trivial circumstances; sudden gaiety and constant tenderness; joy in presence and hope during absence; the feeling of being both above the ordinary world and protected from it; a swift understanding of each thought or feeling without need for words. The passage is short, in keeping perhaps with Constant's own remark in the *Réflexions sur la Tragédie*: 'la peinture du bonheur ne doit pas être prolongée, sous peine d'être monotone', in keeping too with the paragraph's opening and closing sentences on the theme of 'Charme de l'amour, qui pourrait vous peindre';[27] it leaves in the mind its most evocative phrase:

ces heures rapides, dont tous les détails échappent au souvenir par leur douceur même, et qui ne laissent dans notre âme qu'une longue trace de bonheur.

This is very far from a novel on the inability to love.

The ability to prolong this experience is however another matter.[28] And the very terms in which the state of joy has been expressed suggest the forces which will destroy it. This was, in the precise sense of the word, an ecstatic state, giving a sense of absolute sufficiency set apart from contingency, and blotting out three normally intrusive forces – self-observation, the claims of society, the consciousness of inevitable time and change.[29] Neither Adolphe nor Ellénore can later admit as love anything less than the total, isolated, self-sufficient ecstasy.[30] This involves two problems: absorption and continuity. The total absorption in the moment of experience can be stimulated by the intervention of an obstacle or the sense of an approaching end. But the basic problem is not that of experiencing passion but that of prolonging it: 'incapable de suite, de dévouement soutenu, de générosité calme . . . cette pitié passagère . . . sans autre direction que le caprice, sans autre force que l'irritation' (p. 304; pp. 149–50).

The ecstasy Adolphe has experienced; in the second half of the book, mingled with exasperation or desire for freedom, he will know other aspects: tenderness, the terror of hurting, the sheer inability to live without someone who has become interwoven with all memories. These may be part of the old age of love, but for Adolphe and Ellénore love implies the all-consuming ecstasy; when inevitably the demands of time, society, and self-examination move back into consciousness, the *décristallisation* begins.

This too is made up of many threads where the pattern of experience may be misjudged if any one is artificially isolated. Imperceptibly but very rapidly a change occurs. Yet it is not any sudden switch to selfishness or satiety: it is at first their very closeness and confidence which cause strains when they have to be apart, their tenderness which makes Adolphe hate to hurt. Ellénore's devotion becomes an obstacle to freedom in society, and now that she withholds nothing, the all-absorbing aim has been removed: 'elle n'était plus un but: elle était devenue un lien' (p. 59). Set against the desire to escape is a series of emergencies, each providing a period of renewed absorption in an aim (now that of protecting Ellénore), each concentrating feeling into the present only, so that time, society, and self-analysis are blotted out by the immediate and

self-sufficient absorption. Here the galvanism by the obstacle provides again experiences deliberately defined as genuine feeling, as at
the end of Chapter iv, and particularly at the end of Chapter v (p.
82): 'Je l'aimais plus que je ne l'avais jamais aimée … L'amour
était rentré tout entier dans mon âme.' As always, Constant does
not simply make the general statement, but briefly characterizes
those elements, physical, emotional, and intellectual, of which 'Je
l'aimais' is composed:

Tout mon cœur était revenu à elle: j'étais fier de la protéger. J'étais avide
de la tenir dans mes brás … J'éprouvais une fièvre de tête, de cœur, de sens
… (p. 82)

The feeling is genuine at the moment of experience, but the
narrator's technique has subtly suggested other undertones already at
the end of Chapter iv: '*J'attribuai mes indécisions* à un sentiment de
délicatesse' and

Je n'eus … d'autre pensée que de chasser loin d'elle toute peine, toute
crainte, tout regret, toute incertitude sur mon sentiment. *Pendant que je lui
parlais*, je n'envisageais rien au delà de ce but et j'étais sincère dans mes
promesses. (p. 69)

It is Ellénore who brings the implications bitingly to the fore at the
end of Chapter v: 'Vous croyez avoir de l'amour, et vous n'avez que
de la pitié' (p. 83).

The intense importance of the theme of pity for pain in Constant's
personal experience has been made familiar since Ch. Du Bos's
discussion of his 'Religion de la Douleur'; in the novel itself it would
be worth seeing in detail how pity, constantly coupled with exasperation, is composed of three sides: the physical inability to bear the
sight and sound of Ellénore's pain (e.g. p. 89), the imaginative and
tender apprehension in absence of just how she will react to each
word of a letter (e.g. pp. 77–8), and the pervasive intellectual sense
of the demands of justice and generosity.

The charge of 'faiblesse' in the second half of the novel is brought
against Adolphe not simply by some critics, but also by the
narrator's own overt comments at certain moments. Yet the whole
substance of the narrative brings alive the insolubility of two
problems: the intellectual judgment as to where the 'right' decision
could lie; the relation between will to action and recalcitrant or
ineradicable feelings. It is neither effort nor action which is lacking.
Adolphe makes every conceivable effort to remain 'in love' with
Ellénore – and again the component elements of the concept are
succinctly analysed – but can will govern feeling?

J'appelais à mon aide les souvenirs, l'imagination, la raison même, le sentiment du devoir: efforts inutiles! (p. 75)

Constant is not alone in his discovery that admiration, tenderness, logic, or will cannot create or recreate passion. La Princesse de Clèves, two centuries before, had been faced by the same discovery.[31] But if will cannot govern feeling, it can govern action: when Ellénore is threatened by his father, Adolphe acts swiftly and decisively; he accompanies her into distant lands; he fights a duel unhesitatingly: 'Vos actions sont nobles et dévouées.'[32] This contrast between action and feeling is bitterly ironical; still more so is the question raised by the impossibility of one final action: a break with Ellénore.

For if the self-sufficient ecstasy of an all-absorbing love cannot be recreated by will-power, there remains another side, sometimes insufficiently stressed or seen by critics or readers. If in one sense the book is a study in the impermanence and mobility of passion, it is even more strongly a study in the terrifying permanence of shared memories which it is impossible to uproot. If it had to be seen as a cautionary tale, the caution might be less against the insufficiencies of feeling than against the easy embarking on feelings which it becomes impossible totally to destroy: 'Dans leur cœur ... se sont enfoncées les racines du sentiment qu'ils ont inspiré' (p. 7). Adolphe is caught, not simply by weakness or pity, but by the whole detailed weight and tenderness of a shared past:

La longue habitude que nous avions l'un de l'autre, les circonstances variées que nous avions parcourues ensemble avaient rattaché à chaque parole, presque à chaque geste, des souvenirs qui nous replaçaient tout à coup dans le passé et nous remplissaient d'un attendrissement involontaire ... Nous vivions, pour ainsi dire, d'une espèce de mémoire du cœur ... (p. 94)[33]

or again:

Il y a dans les liaisons qui se prolongent quelque chose de si profond! Elles deviennent à notre insu une partie si intime de notre existence! (p. 76)

The Preface to the third edition sums up: 'Combien sont profondes les racines de l'affection qu'on croyait inspirer sans la partager' (p. 10).

This will lead to the final dramatic irony of the book. Ellénore has throughout been characterized under the term 'dévouement': the need to give happiness to another. Adolphe himself will ironically discover, after her death, that in its own way this same need, or its derivative, the urge to avoid giving pain, had provided him with a purpose:

Naguère toutes mes actions avaient un but; j'étais sûr, par chacune d'elles, d'épargner une peine ou de causer un plaisir. (p. 143)

If the initial aim of conquering Ellénore had long since ceased to be a stimulus, it is found reversed in the unrecognized, irritating, yet persistent aim of responsibility for her joy or despair. Here one of the basic impulses of human nature, rendering irrelevant labels of egoism or altruism, has been sharply characterized. In fact, Adolphe and Ellénore suffer as much for each other as for themselves; and this intensifies the tragedy: lucidity and pity may imagine, but may neither share nor cure this basic human experience.[34]

In this analysis of the growth and death of love, it is not simply the insufficiencies of an individual which are being exposed.[35] The mixture of inherited stereotypes and genuine need which marks the origins, and the combined exasperation, pity and tender habit which surround the end, have wider implications relevant to many long-standing relationships. And, however complex the gradations in origin or disappearance, the effect is to clarify, not to destroy, the concept of love, through self-questioning on the difference between the isolated ecstasy and the need or tenderness which are like yet unlike it. In brief parentheses the word 'love' is analysed;[36] on other occasions its qualities are evoked by the results of its absence (the 'si j'avais eu de l'amour pour Ellénore' (p. 71), or the final tragic distinction regarding his grief at Ellénore's death, p. 138: 'Ce n'était pas les regrets de l'amour, c'était un sentiment plus sombre et plus triste; l'amour s'identifie tellement à l'objet aimé, que ...' etc.) Simplifications are destroyed, but the necessity of valid redefinitions is constantly assumed.

Adolphe is the story of a personal relationship, apparently concentrated into a world of *huis clos*. But within its concentration, it reinvestigates many human problems besides that of love, probing briefly but suggestively into such themes as education, ambition, death, immortality, social conventions, ethical standards. The unsystematic and indulgent education given to a young man of exceptional promise, of whom much is expected but on whom nothing is enforced, leads logically to the conflict between a desire to be free of responsibility and an ingrained sense of obligation. Obligation not simply to an individual, but to the demands of society. In the *Réflexions sur la Tragédie* (p. 937), Constant writes:

Quant aux tragédies qui seraient fondées sur l'action de la société en lutte avec l'homme, opposant des obstacles, non seulement à ses passions, mais à sa nature, ou brisant, non seulement son caractère, ses inclinations personnelles, mais les mouvements qui sont inhérents à tout être humain, je n'en connais aucune qui remplisse complètement l'idée que je conçois.

Once again, it is not just the outer force oppressing the individual, but the inner effect on inherent human qualities which is the focus.[37]

Opinion and *considération* are key-words in Constant.[38] In *Adolphe* the sharply represented society which passes false judgments on every move of Adolphe and Ellénore provides one of the main threads of tragic irony; the urge to win a justified respect by using one's full gifts within a social framework is equally strongly felt.[39] A two-sided response to society is firmly given at the beginning in the phrase 'des convenances factices mais nécessaires'. And, if society misinterprets, the fault is partly that of Adolphe's own ambiguous conduct: 'Telle est la force d'un sentiment vrai, que, lorsqu'il parle, les interprétations fausses et les convenances factices se taisent.' (p. 71)

Unlike many contemporaries, who in a background of growing romanticism assume that to stand apart is to stand above, hymn in facile terms the innocent victims of society, and posit some vague superiority without analysis, Constant gives origins, content and criticism to initial reactions against society. When the young Adolphe, before ever meeting Ellénore, reacts against his background, it is for clearly analysed reasons on different levels: first because of the effect of others on his youth (his father and the older woman in Chapter 1), then through an instinctive, exacerbated recoil from bland complacency:

Lors donc que j'entendais la médiocrité disserter avec complaisance sur des principes bien établis, bien incontestables ... je me sentais poussé à la contredire, non que j'eusse adopté des opinions opposées, mais parce que j'étais impatienté d'une conviction si ferme et si lourde, (pp. 25–6)[40]

and finally from an intellectual rejection of that comforting amalgam of logically irreconcilable elements – ethical, conventional and religious – which forms accepted morality and isolates it safely from the demands of difficult action:[41]

des principes bien établis, bien incontestables en fait de morale, de convenances ou de religion, choses qu'elle met volontiers sur la même ligne ... Les sots font de leur morale une masse compacte et indivisible, pour qu'elle se mêle le moins possible avec leurs actions, et les laisse libres dans tous les détails, (pp. 25–6)[42]

Here again it is the simplified labelling of complex problems which is attacked:

J'avais contracté ... une insurmontable aversion pour toutes les maximes communes et pour toutes les formules dogmatiques.

But the attack is neither abstract nor one-sided; at the same time there is a dry allusive dissection, through brief incidents, of the moody impulses and inexperience of youth, hurt at not fitting in, as well as scornfully unwilling to adapt. Later life will increasingly bring out the inherent urge to fill a fit place in society, seen both as personal ambition and recognized duty ('faire un noble usage de mes facultés', p. 87). The dilemma for Adolphe is exacerbated in that the opinion of father and friends stresses his outstanding capacities, but he has not yet been able to exercise them: the choice is not between Ellénore and a valuable career already embarked on, but between Ellénore and a possibility. In Chapter VII he reflects bitterly on how mediocre contemporaries have now outstripped him 'dans la route de la fortune, de la considération et de la gloire',[43] and suggests how both longing and guilt are exacerbated by the unproved evidence and the unchannelled desire:

Ce n'était pas une carrière seule que je regrettais: comme je n'avais essayé d'aucune, je les regrettais toutes. N'ayant jamais employé mes forces, je les imaginais sans bornes, et je les maudissais; j'aurais voulu . . . me préserver au moins du remords de me dégrader volontairement. Toute louange, toute approbation pour mon esprit ou mes connaissances, me semblaient un reproche insupportable. (p. 102)

While experience (when the Baron de T. entrusts him with adminis-trative activities) indicates his real capacities, the framing material of Prologue and Letters by others at the end is made ironically to show that once freed from the obstacle, Ellénore, he achieves nothing. This is very different both from Constant's personal po-sition at the time of writing and from the eventual outcome of Constant's life, though it does represent a sifting out in artistic form of a pause for self-assessment, when his later political career is still in embryo. The main result is to balance sympathy with strong critical detachment. Right and wrong are inextricably mingled in society as in the self. Adolphe may scorn society but both his ambition and his sense of duty mean he cannot live cut off from it: society misjudges, but it does so because of some flaw in the conduct of the individual.

The themes of personal and social commitment run parallel with a wider, metaphysical problem. In the first chapter there is a trenchant analysis of how adolescence is haunted by the thought of inevitable death as a determining factor in its scheme of values. Faced with the idea of 'la brièveté de la vie humaine', the early Adolphe finds that 'aucun but ne valait la peine d'aucun effort'. He is struck by the paradoxical fact that with advancing age this reaction tends to disappear. Again this is no moral lesson, but at the same time a valid psychological observation and a provoking question: is the change a result of narrowing into blinkered practical aims, or of the disappearance of an adolescent morbidity? does the sense of aim stem from maturity or illusion? *Adolphe* is certainly far from a consoling *Bildungsroman*: it traces the changes worked by age, and leaves open the constantly posed question of judgments and values.

Later in the novel, this haunting idea of the inevitability of death provides a further reaction. Adolphe, at a pitch of insoluble tensions, escapes in Chapter VII into the deserted countryside by night, and finds in the thought of the prevalence and ineluctability of death a means of loosening the taut struggle towards immediate decision, a reason for living each day as it comes. Since will-power could not force feeling, nor arrive at the choice of a 'right' decision, it is momentarily abandoned. Here Constant's involvement, at recurrent periods of emotional crisis, with 'quietist' groups, given in daily detail of superstition and doubt in the *Journaux*, analysed at some length in the abstract meditations of *Cécile*,[44] is concentrated and transposed into a personal experience of relaxation and calm. It is the physical details of the countryside by night and the distant lights of a cottage window which are made to suggest both enveloping peace and the idea of a death-agony, which must come to all. Taking up, after an interval, the sense of death as the end suggested in the first chapter, this late chapter evokes a feeling of the fruitless pain of striving, an impulse to live 'au jour le jour', a fatalism and a concentration on the moment as it comes, which in other works of Constant are discussed as philosophical or religious entities, but here become an intimate part of the memories and desires of an individual.

The death of Ellénore adds other dimensions:[45] a stunned sense of the gap between the conventional ritual and the reality of experience; wider general reflections on how death's disrupting of connexions between physical and mental bears on the problem of immortality; above all, the close welding of these into a personal tragedy, ironical, paradoxical, and far from the stereotyped scene of deathbed regret.

Outside the narrative itself (p. 304, notes for Preface), Constant comments on the representative value of Adolphe's experience as sharing 'une des principales maladies morales de notre siècle'. In a time of 'la décrépitude de la civilisation', the weary satiety handed on by past generations gives rise to a corrosive self-analysis, a mistrust of all spontaneous enthusiasm, and, most serious of all, an 'impuissance d'impressions morales'. In a story of personal feelings[46] he has analysed a tendency which he feels to have wide implications in religious or political contexts:

La fidélité en amour est une force comme la croyance religieuse, comme l'enthousiasme de la liberté. Or ... nous ne savons plus aimer, ni croire, ni vouloir. Chacun doute de la vérité de ce qu'il dit, sourit de la véhémence de ce qu'il affirme, et pressent la fin de ce qu'il éprouve ... L'histoire dira l'influence de cette disposition d'âme sur d'autres objets. Car, encore une fois, tout se tient. Ce qui fait qu'on est dur ou léger envers l'affection, fait aussi qu'on est indifférent à tout avenir au delà de ce monde, et vil envers toutes les puissances qui se succèdent, et qu'on nomme légitimes tant qu'elles subsistent. (pp. 304–5)

But if Adolphe's nature echoes the problems of a generation particularly involved in political reassessment and instability, particularly conscious across the whole of Europe of the 'here today and gone tomorrow' position of régimes, dynasties, or governments, it does not do so from direct meditation on these problems. The breadth of implications behind the novel rises always from rigorous analysis of individuals in personal relationships. And the widest meaning of all echoes from the phrase in the introduction:

J'ai voulu peindre le mal que font éprouver même aux cœurs arides les souffrances qu'ils causent, et cette illusion qui les porte à se croire plus légers ou plus corrompus qu'ils ne le sont. (p. 10)

to another in the conclusion: 'La grande question dans la vie, c'est la douleur que l'on cause.' Constant looked to his readers not for condemnation or admiration of a schematic hero, but for understanding of the complexities of a tragic dilemma; as he once wrote: 'Il est encore beaucoup plus doux d'être entendu qu'approuvé.[47]

The present article has been concerned with some of the main themes (youth, love, ambition, indecision, society, age, death) suggested through Constant's central character. But the worth of the novel lies in far more than Constant's analytical insight into general problems raised through one focal figure. Because of the very richness of these problems, *Adolphe* is sometimes discussed as if it were no more than this; Ellénore is looked on as either a patchwork from 'biographical' sources or an abstract foil to the hero, while the secondary characters are taken as mere pivots to narrative. In two further articles I have discussed how Constant's analytical skill is an intimate part of his creation of character, and how structure and expression contribute to his imaginative shaping of experience. From the endless detail of everyday life he has sifted out a representative tragic situation and the probing general comments or questions of the 'moraliste'. But he has in so doing created suggestive figures, products not of careful copy, direct personal confession or discreet disguise, but of the detailed logic of the imagination working within his tragic theme. And he, who both demolished and delighted in the play of definition and epigram, has discovered a means of expression which can combine the insinuation of indefinability with the 'don de la formule'. It is through these further forms of stylization that the themes outlined above are brought alive in a novel exceptional for its brevity, conviction, and suggestion.

NOTES

1 This article was written as the first of three; the two which complete it appeared earlier: 'The Art of Constant's *Adolphe*: Creation of character', in *Forum for Modern Language Studies*, 2 (1966), pp. 253–63; 'The Art of Constant's *Adolphe*: Structure and style', in *French Studies*, 20 (1966), pp. 226–42. These, reprinted below on pp. 28–42 and pp. 43–60, will be referred to in subsequent notes as Art. II and Art. III. Page references to *Adolphe* will be J.-H. Bornecque's edition (1955). For Constant's other works, page references will be to the *Œuvres* (ed. A. Roulin, 1957).

2 In particular, of course, the completely new material contained in A. Roulin and Ch. Roth's edition of the *Journaux intimes* (1952) and in *Cécile* (ed. A. Roulin, 1951) (both reproduced in the *Œuvres*, 1957). See also Benjamin et Rosalie de Constant, *Correspondance* (ed. A.. et S. Roulin, 1955); Benjamin Constant et Mme de Staël, *Lettres à un ami* (ed. J. Mistler, Neuchâtel, 1949). For detailed bibliographies of the work available in editions, critical articles, and full studies, see the excellent 'État présent des Études sur Benjamin Constant' by Pierre Deguise in *L'Information littéraire*, 10 (1958), No. 4, pp. 139–50, and C. Cordié's edition of *Adolphe* (Naples, 1963), pp. 47–64.

3 G. Rudler, to whom Constant studies owe so much, made in his editions of 1919 and 1935 (Manchester) and in his study in the 'Grands Événements Littéraires' series (Société française d'éditions littéraires et techniques) many suggestive remarks, though concerned mainly to relate incidents from the novel to their biographical sources. His point of view is summed up in: 'Constant (non sans dommage) a préservé sa liberté à l'égard de sa matière; il a reconstruit et stylisé la réalité, a éloigné son œuvre de la biographie, l'a rapprochée du roman (ou de l'histoire romancée) et de l'art.' Discussions with F. Baldensperger and A. Monglond centred on the problem of models from real life. With the appearance of new biographical material, a number of important articles tackled a reassessment, attributing differing degrees of importance to particular 'sources' and generally stressing the art of fusion and

decantation; for the most part, however, a useful detailed study of genesis still predominates over an analysis of the finished work. Stimulating suggestions emerging from such genetic studies will be found particularly in P. Bénichou, 'La Genèse d'*Adolphe*', *Revue d'Histoire Littéraire de la France*, 54 (1954), pp. 332–56; P. Deguise, '*Adolphe* et les *Journaux intimes* de Benjamin Constant', *Revue des Sciences humaines*, 21 (1956) pp. 125–51; and J.-H. Bornecque's Introduction to his 1955 edition. C. Pellegrini's 'Benjamin Constant: Dall' Autobiografia al Romanzo', *Rivista di Letterature moderne e comparative*, 9 (1956), pp. 165–79 and 272–96, outlines many important points for a study of the art; C. Cordié's preface to his 1963 edition (Naples) stresses again the need to examine *Adolphe* as a literary work, though does not give space to doing so. J. Mistler in his 1954 edition (Monaco) concludes that '*Adolphe* est une biographie psychologique plutôt qu'un roman'. W. H. Holdheim, in *Benjamin Constant* (1961), briefly treats the problem of biography and art but has little space for close discussion of *Adolphe*. J. Hytier's penetrating chapter on *Adolphe* in *Les Romans de l'Individu* (1928) was already concerned with the inner coherence and the narrative techniques, and attacked some pervasive misconceptions.

Much of the most suggestive work on Constant has of course been concerned primarily with his complex personality in his works as a whole, and illuminates *Adolphe* against this background. All critics will owe a debt, for example, to Ch. Du Bos's *Grandeur et Misère de Benjamin Constant* (1946) and to the particularly penetrating article of G. Poulet in *Études sur le Temps humain* (1950).

4 See particularly *Jnx.*, p. 428.

5 Of necessity, in a novel at this date, two dimensions of this experience, frankly exposed in the diaries, must be left aside: the complex relation between physical needs and the emotional or intellectual aspects of different loves; and the details of political hesitations.

6 Even the earliest letters to his grandmother show a particular fusion of genuine need for feeling, sophisticated self-mockery, and sense of how to use the occasion, expressed with special clarity and subtlety. Later, his periodical indulgence in a prolonged re-reading of the letters of others which he had kept provided an intense stimulus to tragic reflection on problems of personality, fidelity, time, death. – See especially in *Lettres à sa famille* (ed. J. H. Menos, 1932), early letters and pp. 271–2, and the very fine letter to Prosper de Barante (*Revue des deux Mondes*, 34 (1906), 255 ff.).

7 *Lettres à sa famille*, ed. Menos, p. 41.

8 Many more variations on the themes of 'orage', 'tempête', 'torrent', 'convulsions' might be cited. Constant writes to Rosalie that he is pursued by 'des lettres telles qu'on n'en écrirait pas à un assassin de grande route' (B. et R. de Constant, *Corr.*, ed. A. et S. Roulin (1955), p. 60). Yet his own awareness that his expressions of fury at particular provocations do not represent the whole complex of feeling comes strongly and recurrently to the fore. See in particular *Jnx.*, pp. 448 and 459: 'Quoi que je dise, et que j'écrive souvent dans ce journal, je sens ...', 'Quoi que je dise, ou même que j'éprouve souvent ...'

9 *Jnx.*, p. 672. *Adolphe*, p. 133.

10 The art of *Cécile* requires a separate study. Several of the works quoted above (note 3) suggest points of judgment. On the unsolved question of the connexions between *Adolphe* and *Cécile* at the time of initial composition (summarized, with further conjectures, by A. R. Pugh, in *R.H.L.F.*, 63 (1963), pp. 418–23), has it been noted that the last page of *Adolphe* deliberately suggests a possible sequel?: 'de nouveaux détails' dont j'ignore encore si je ferai quelque usage' (p. 150; see also p. 148; 'ces lettres qui vous instruiront du sort d'Adolphe'). (See 'Framework as a suggestive art in Constant's *Adolphe*', below pp. 96–107).

11 *Jnx.*, p. 603. Constant uses *épisode* in the feminine.

12 Brief suggestions on humour, paradox, wit, and irony are raised by F. P. Bowman in 'Benjamin Constant, Humour and Self-awareness', *Yale French Studies*, 23 (1959).

13 'puni de ses qualités plus encore que de ses défauts' (p. 148).

14 Cf. in *Réflexions sur la Tragédie* (p. 952): 'L'ordre social, l'action de la société sur l'individu ... sont tout à fait équivalents à la fatalité des anciens.'

15 See below, pp. 16 ff.

16 See especially the letter to Prosper de Barante (*R.D.M.*, 34 (1906), p. 266); the letter to Rosalie preferring painting to literature, as painting is not distorted by the instrument of words (B. et R. de Constant, *Corr.*, p. 143); the reflection in the Wallstein article (p. 901): 'il n'y a point de paroles pour mettre en commun ce qui jamais n'est qu'individuel.' There is an interesting passage at the beginning of Mme de Charrière's *Cécile (Lettres écrites de Lausanne*, p. 2 in the edition by P. Godet, Geneva, 1907) where she mocks at the paradoxes involved by the general terms in which writers seek to sum up character.

17 Marivaux, in *Le Paysan Parvenu* (p. 92 in the edition by Fr. Deloffre, 1959), has a scene which analyses the same phenomenon in a lighter vein. Later there will be the closing scene between Frédéric Moreau and Mme Arnoux in the *Éducation sentimentale*: 'Frédéric, se grisant par ses paroles, arrivait à croire ce qu'il disait.'

18 p. 73: 'par une inconséquence bizarre ...'; p. 76; 'telle est la bizarrerie de notre cœur misérable ...'; p. 146: 'ce bizarre et malheureux Adolphe'. See also pp. 23, 35, 47, 59. The word echoes very frequently in *Cécile* and in the diaries and letters.

19 The core of the whole novel is given in the balanced maxim of Chapter V (p. 75): 'C'est un affreux malheur de n'être pas aimé quand on aime; mais c'en est un bien grand d'être aimé avec passion quand on n'aime plus.' – The placing and framing of generalization and epigram in *Adolphe* are discussed in more detail in Art. III.

20 A central discussion in the *Réflexions sur la Tragédie* (see especially p. 943) contrasts the stylization and coherence of character demanded by the French tradition with the German tendency to create 'un être ondoyant ... ondoyant comme les caractères réels'. See also pp. 901–3; and, in the letters to Prosper de Barante, *R.D.M.*, 34 (1906), p. 249, a similar discussion ('Je ne connais de naturel en tout que les *nuances*'). P. Deguise has an interesting passage in his article in the *Revue des Sciences Humaines*, 21 (1956), p. 150, extending into different genres the two sides which

attracted Constant: narrative versus analysis, historical versus philosophical method.

21 The expression here may suggest that background of preromantic or
romantic stress on an often febrile intensity of emotion, against which a
more analytical mind may easily be driven either to artificial forcing of
emotion or to accusing the self of insufficient strength of feeling.

22 The theme of how inherited preconceptions, whether those of idealism
or of disillusion, distort the sensibility, before direct experience can make
its impact, is more often in the nineteenth century (and in earlier
satirical works) treated in terms of falsification by literary models, by
reading (Flaubert's *Madame Bovary* or Bourget's definition: 'intoxication
littéraire'). Constant treats it through personal contacts – influence of
father, elderly woman, friend in love. This enhances the importance of
the secondary characters.

23 The irony of: 'J'en aurais joui plus complètement encore [de son
charme] sans l'engagement que j'avais pris envers mon amour-propre'
(and see the rest of this passage on p. 37) points forward to similar
paradoxical situations at the outset of the love-affairs of Stendhal's
Julien Sorel and Lucien Leuwen.

24 This theme of how the mere act of observation distorts what is observed
will have wide repercussions, whether in arts or sciences, in the nineteenth and twentieth centuries. It is typical of Constant's two-
sidedness that a letter to Prosper de Barante (*R.D.M.*, 34 (1906), p. 263)
strongly stresses another conclusion: 'Je suis la preuve qu'on peut
analyser ce qu'on éprouve sans que l'analyse détruise la sensation.'

25 'Un but' of course becomes a key-expression, and is further discussed in
Arts. II and III. The frustration provides the stab which forces a
concentration of energy in place of the indifference or apathy basic to a
given kind of character. In *Adolphe*, Chapter I: 'tout en ne m'intéressant
qu'à moi, je m'intéressais faiblement à moi-même' (p. 22). In Constant
himself this note recurs constantly (e.g. *Jnx.*, p. 395: 'je ne m'intéresse
guère plus à moi qu'aux autres'; pp. 290–1: 'je ne suis pas tout à fait un
être réel', etc., etc.). This lack of a sharp sense of significance and
involvement may be critically seen by Constant as a disturbing factor in
the self, or may become a sporadic means of consolation: B. et R. de
Constant, *Corr.*, p. 231 'N'avoir point de but personnel et ne prendre
guère d'intérêt à soi est un admirable moyen de tranquillité'; this
attitude leads to the moment of 'quietism' in Chapter VII of *Adolphe*
(discussed below, p. 19).

The theme of the stimulus by the obstacle will of course run through great
novelists from Mme de La Fayette to Proust. One recalls in *La Princesse de
Clèves* 'je crois même que les obstacles ont fait votre constance' (*Romans et
Nouvelles*, ed. É. Magne, s.d., p. 387) or 'pour être son mari, il ne laissa pas
d'être son amant, parce qu'il avait toujours quelque chose à souhaiter au
delà de sa possession' (p. 260). Mme de Charrière's *Cécile* has an
epigrammatic summing up of the paradox: 'N'est-il pas étrange qu'on ne se
soucie d'être aimé que quand on croit ne le pas être; qu'on sente tant la
privation, et si peu la jouissance; qu'on se joue du bien qu'on a, et qu'on

l'estime dès qu'on ne l'a plus.' (*Lettres écrites de Lausanne*, ed. Ph. Godet, Geneva (1907), p. 82).

26 The passage recalls the wording of the same idea in a letter from Mme de Staël to Hochet, 23 January 1804 (B.C. et Mme de Staël: *Lettres à un Ami*, ed. J. Mistler, Neuchâtel (1949), p. 67): 'il n'y a que l'amour qui supplée au temps: il n'a pas plus de passé que d'avenir.' Constant uses a later phrase of hers from a letter to Hochet (p. 222), 'un souvenir lumineux'.

27 Stendhal later will be preoccupied with the difficulty of conserving or rendering the *detail* of happiness in memory (*Souvenirs d'Égotisme*, etc.) and will find original solutions.

28 Cf. *Cécile* (p. 213): 'Ma fausseté ne consistait point à feindre une sensibilité plus grande que celle [que] j'avais, mais à laisser croire que cette sensibilité aurait des suites qu'elle ne devait pas avoir.' On this theme see the remarks of G. Poulet in *Études sur le Temps humain* (1950).

29 The phrase 'Malheur à l'homme qui ...' in the last paragraph of Chapter III may be misinterpreted. I take it as showing the narrator comparing the disillusioned foresight which later experience will cause, with an initial stage at which it did *not* exist. The sense would be: 'Alas for the man who ... *But* I did not then feel ...' and would lead into 'J'aimai, je respectai mille fois plus Ellénore' and the delight of Chapter IV.

30 Cf. Adolphe's definition of love when he attempts to tell Ellénore it has disappeared: 'l'amour, ce transport des sens, cette ivresse involontaire, cet oubli de tous les intérêts, de tous les devoirs' (p. 88). Compare also the longing in Chapter I for 'ces impressions primitives et fougueuses qui jettent l'âme hors de la sphère commune, et lui inspirent le dédain de tous les objets qui l'environnent'.

31 'Elle se faisait un crime de ne pas avoir eu de la passion pour lui, comme si c'eût été une chose qui eût été en son pouvoir' (ed. É. Magne, p. 377). See also the early discussion (p. 258) between Mme de Clèves and her husband, where all that should logically contribute to love (admiration, tenderness, physical disturbance) yet does not produce the final spark of feeling.

32 In a letter of 26 February 1807 (*Les Nouvelles littéraires*, 6 June 1963), Constant writes wryly of how women reacted to readings of his novel. 'Elles disent toutes qu'il [Adolphe] devrait aimer, comme si aimer, et surtout aimer toujours, était chose simple et facile, et parce que le pauvre diable n'aime plus, on ne lui sait aucun gré de ce qu'il fait ou de ce qu'il sacrifie.'

33 If, in the biographical background, it is the past shared with Mme de Staël which is obviously most deeply ingrained, yet the renewal of liaisons (or the marriage with Charlotte), because they vitally stir memories of a past stage, occurs again and again. (G. Poulet gives interesting illustrations.) In the past shared with Mme de Staël it is worth noting (*Jnx.*, 324–5) the part played by her particular stimulus to his literary activities; on other occasions he may find her enthusiasm uncritical, yet 'J'ai dans le caractère une partie découragée que Minette

seule relève, et si mon esprit peut se passer de tout le monde, cette partie de mon caractère ne le peut pas' (p. 514). With Ellénore, the memories shared are made generally suggestive, not specific.

34 There is in *La Princesse de Clèves* and her husband a similar tender and tormented sense of each other's dilemma.

35 Preface to second edition: 'Je l'ai montré tourmenté parce qu'il n'aimait que faiblement Ellénore: mais il n'eût pas été moins tourmenté, s'il l'eût aimé advantage.' (p. 8)

36 See above, p. 14, and p. 25, note 30; see also Art. III.

37 See above p. 6. Compare *Réflexions sur la Tragédie*, p. 944: 'Il est évident que cette action de la société est ce qu'il y a de plus important dans la vie humaine ... Cette action de la société décide de la manière dont la force morale de l'homme s'agite et se déploie' (etc.).

38 The importance of public opinion in *Adolphe* has been noted by a number of commentators; it figures in J.-H. Bornecque's preface, and is strongly expressed by, e.g., Ph. Garcia, *Cahiers du Sud*, No. 295 (1949), pp. 451–64: 'il y a dans ce livre un personnage encore, l'opinion'; and C. J. Greshoff, *Forum for Modern Language Studies*, 1 (1965), pp. 30–6; 'Society in *Adolphe* assumes the proportions of a third character.' The balance of elements involved would merit further study. In Constant's life the intense care for reputation (*Jnx.*, 333; 'je préfère la gloire littéraire au bonheur'; Letter to Rosalie (p. 300): 'Je n'ai conservé qu'une chimère, celle de laisser après moi quelque célébrité, et je ne sais devant Dieu pourquoi. Mais c'est une habitude d'enfance') is affected both by public judgments and by the expectations of family. In *Adolphe* the sensitivity to widely scattered family judgments has been concentrated into the one relationship with the father.
Other detailed aspects of the place of *l'opinion* in *Adolphe* are discussed in Art. II.

39 Where C. J. Greshoff (p. 36) says that 'he wants no longer defy, but to conform', I should add, with a very different stress, 'and to contribute'. Moreover, we are perhaps inclined to misjudge undertones to the theme of ambition in many works of the past, for lack of a historical perspective on the assumptions of the times. In the seventeenth century the urge to take one's rightful place at the head of society may be a sign of inborn nobility or admirable duty, not simply of self-seeking; even in the nineteenth century men of substance and talent may take for granted that this is their rightful and expected role. In *Adolphe* there are no diatribes of idealism, but (p. 103) the critical acceptance, as a natural urge, of 'un désir impatient de reprendre dans ma patrie ... la place qui m'était due' (associated with 'J'imaginais la joie de mon père'). See also p. 87: 'Il était temps enfin d'entrer dans une carrière, de commencer une vie active, d'acquérir quelques titres à l'estime des hommes, de faire un noble usage de mes facultés.'

40 Compare Flaubert, *Corr.*, III, 153–4: 'Il y a ainsi une foule de sujets qui m'embêtent également par n'importe quel bout on les prend ... Ainsi Voltaire, le magnétisme, Napoléon, la révolution, le catholicisme, etc., qu'on en dise du bien ou du mal, j'en suis mêmement irrité. La conclusion, la plupart du temps, me semble acte de bêtise.'

41 Compare p. 10 on the astonishment of children at the discrepancy between rules of conduct and cynical witticisms, making principles appear no more than 'des formules banales'.

42 Constant uses much the same formulation at the end of a subtle discussion of axiomatic morality in his article on Mme de Staël, *Œuvres*, p. 868: 'Et ferait-on ainsi de la morale une masse compacte et indivisible, pour qu'elle se mêlât le moins possible aux intérêts journaliers, et laissât plus de liberté dans les détails?'

43 A theme to be given another personal development in the figure of Martinon in Flaubert's *Éducation sentimentale*.

44 The letter of 27 July 1808 to Prosper de Barante (*R.D.M.*, 34 (1906), especially pp. 262 ff.) gives one of Constant's most developed analyses of this state of mind.

45 These points are further discussed in Arts. II and III.

46 He indicates that to study directly the political implications relevant to the personal standards of conduct would have been difficult at the time: 'J'ai peint une petite partie du tableau, la seule qui fût ... sans danger pour le peintre.' (p. 305).

47 *Lettres à sa famille*, ed. Menos, p. 412.

2

The art of Constant's *Adolphe*:
II. Creation of character (1966)

The concentration and complexity of Constant's *Adolphe*,[1] and its relation to a particularly stimulating biographical background, have meant that critical attention has been focussed on the main character. The minor characters have generally been considered as simply a means of externalising his inner dilemma. Ellénore, more developed, is yet seen mainly as a foil: either a patchwork of reminiscences from different real women, therefore criticised as shifting too suddenly from the tender to the shrewish; or a composite abstraction, presenting the essentials of Constant's reactions to many women, but hardly an individual in her own right.[2] Biographical background, often highly illuminating, but sometimes inadequately distinguished from artistic result, has at times tended to bedevil interpretation of the work as it stands. Because Constant draws so largely on personal material, it has been taken for granted that he lacks creative imagination in the treatment of any character other than his own.

The 'classical' qualities, involving a penetrating selection of only those points which will most tellingly bear on a central dilemma, are abundantly obvious. Perhaps in fact it is precisely because the most essential factor in Adolphe's character is his hypersensitivity to the hurts or the judgments of other human beings ('la grande question dans la vie, c'est la douleur que l'on cause') that these others appear in the novel not just as abstractions, foils or pivots, but, however briefly, as people in their own right. In the present article I shall be concerned primarily not with their origins in reality, but with the degree of coherence, conviction and individuality to be found in them if one simply reads the text as it stands. A fuller study, comparing the novel with its biographical origins, far from concluding that Constant produced an ill-welded mosaic, a close 'calque' or a purely abstract epitome of direct experience, would bring out, in contrast with the reality, precisely those qualities which most matter to creative imagination: the choice, from a multiplicity or a morass of conflicting incidents and reactions, of the suggestive essential; the logical extension of this in a patterned crescendo of detail; the capacity, above all, for clinching expression.

Ellénore is neither incoherently composite adjunct nor lifeless schematic abstraction. When Constant tried out his novel by reading aloud in the salons, and rejected the idea of giving Adolphe a second love affair nearer to the conflicting realities of his own experience, he did so not only because 'le héros serait odieux', but because 'Ellénore cesserait d'intéresser' (p. 603). She is a character in her own right, created from the beginning to have those qualities which will with ineluctable logic destroy her by slow stages, as well as those which will create the tension between exasperation and tenderness in Adolphe. Those qualities, too, which will enable two characters of equal stature most closely to understand, and most blindly to misinterpret, each other, as each in turn hopes against hope for a solution, or lucidly realises the tragic impossibility.

Ellénore's development throughout the novel will be influenced by three sides: her basic nature as a woman, her social position as caused by the circumstances of her past, and her individual temperament. The dramatic complexities which these may cause have been deliberately suggested from the start. Her central quality is that *dévouement* which Constant sees as the focus of woman's energy, denied other outlets (Preface to the second edition, p. 6: 'n'ayant de vie réelle que dans le cœur, d'intérêt profond que dans l'affection, sans activité qui les occupe, et sans carrière qui les commande'). It is this which will lead to her final realisation (p. 135): 'J'ai voulu ce qui n'était pas possible. L'amour était toute ma vie: il ne pouvait être la vôtre.'[3] In itself a two-sided quality, 'la noble et dangereuse faculté de vivre dans un autre et pour un autre', this capacity for devotion will both attract and weary Adolphe; in his own way he will ironically echo it both in his inability to cause the pain of a break, and in his bitter realisation after Ellénore's death that 'naguère toutes mes actions avaient un but; j'étais sûr, par chacune d'elles, d'épargner une peine ou de causer un plaisir' (p. 143).

As to her intelligence, the famous phrase 'Ellénore n'avait qu'un esprit ordinaire' (p. 33), often assumed to be a sop to prevent Mme de Staël recognizing herself, might better be seen as an integral part of the tragic pattern. That she is not the exceptional or superior rebel against society, with inner resources in her own originality, intensifies her dependence on Adolphe and his sense of guilt at the prospect of abandoning her. Yet she is given 'idées justes ...

expressions, toujours simples ... quelquefois frappantes par la noblesse et l'élévation de ses sentiments' (pp. 33–4) which will lead to
her destructive lucidity in laying bare Adolphe's later efforts to
console and placate. An additional touch conveys the charm of her
way of speech, as a foreigner: attracting Adolphe because it breaks
through the trite or affected formulae of convention, giving something live, graceful, novel.[4]

In every detail from the beginning she is presented not as the
meek ideal who will later inexplicably change, but as a complex
character where each potentiality for the future is sharply delineated. From the very outset we are shown 'la fierté qui faisait une
partie très remarquable de son caractère' (p. 33); and the word *fierté*
is taken up throughout the book. Her pride and her lack of
rebellious intellect make her long for a place within the stability of an
accepted social and religious code; her long years of devotion to the
Comte de P. have won only a precarious condescension. Before she
becomes involved with Adolphe, we are given the basic conflict within
her:

Cette opposition entre ses sentiments et la place qu'elle occupait dans le
monde avait rendu son humeur fort inégale. (p. 35)

In turn taciturn and dreamy, passionate and impetuous, she has
'quelque chose de fougueux et d'inattendu' and is summed up as the
'bel orage'. Her intense but troubled relationship with her children
is characterized. Her anxiety at an hour's absence from them will be
transposed to her feeling for Adolphe in Ch. iv. The difference in
age between herself and Adolphe[5] needs only the slightest allusion at
the start, and brief, cruel mention by le Baron de T. in Chapter viii;
Constant need not make explicit the undertones of fear, effort to
placate, gratitude and suppressed resentment that will follow in the
woman who has risked everything for a younger lover.

It is therefore no sudden change owed to some different 'model'
that takes place in Ellénore; but the implacable workings of an
ironical logic within a deliberately constructed character. Her firm
efforts at dignified resistance gradually give way to the joy of
conferring happiness on another, in keeping with the two factors of
pride and devotion picked out from the start. Faced by the fear of
loss (ironically brought about by the over-intensity of these very
qualities) her pride and devotion become possessive and domineering, and, when driven to despair, shrewish and tormenting. Clear-
sighted yet 'avide de se tromper elle-même', she is made yet more

desperate by the knowledge of how Adolphe's lack of response is forcing her into harshness. This crescendo is constantly punctuated by the tender or terrified submissiveness and inherent gentleness which lead to the resignation of the final scenes. Each sacrifice adds to his irritation, each sign of irritation to his remorse and her bitterness. However diverse the origins of individual incidents, there is no patchwork here. Constant has given Ellénore precisely the details of mind, feeling and situation which will best intensify a logical and insoluble dilemma for both his characters.

To show the conscious and coherent construction of Ellénore's character, three particular examples from among many might be more closely examined – taken from beginning, middle and end of novel. First, there is the skill with which every detail (planned and unplanned) of Adolphe's campaign to win her (Chs. II & III)[6] works insidiously on precisely those qualities which most matter to her individual nature. He appeals to her pity for suffering and her startled gratitude at an eloquent expression of a devotion very different from the condescending, practical attitude of the Comte de P.; he calls on her sense of justice ('Vous avez laissé naître et se former cette douce habitude' (p. 47)); he doubly bears on her desire for unblemished reputation by threatening an outbreak in public if she will not see him in private, and by wounding her through the accusation of frivolity; he shifts suddenly into the tender evocation of what their hidden friendship could offer; above all, in every detail of their relationship, he brings home to her the pride and peace she finds in preventing another's pain or making another happy. The final deciding factor is the 'charme secret que répandait dans son âme *la vue du bonheur que je lui devais*' (p. 45). In each detail of her reaction to letters and conversations there is traced the outcome of her desire to 'se trouver à la fois généreuse, sensible et prudente' (p. 48). Ironically, in the second half of the book, it will be the desire to spare pain, give happiness and avoid scandal which will motivate Adolphe in turn.

The example from the middle of the novel I have taken as one among many proofs that Constant, far from being exclusively concerned with the self-analysis of Adolphe, investigates with understanding and through Adolphe's own imaginative sympathy, the motives behind other individual conduct. In Ch. VIII (pp. 114–19) Ellénore will attempt to provoke jealousy in Adolphe. Briefly and pointedly there is given a suggestive insight into three motives that contribute to her allowing the attentions of others. The main cause is the effort, undertaken too late, at a planned provocation to Adolphe's feeling. Here all the components of her character as seen in Ch. II are deliberately taken up: 'fierté' and 'inquiétude', 'impétuosité', determination to be respected in society and the combination of 'esprit ordinaire' with 'idées justes', so that the miscalculation of her plans is now motivated and understood in a few phrases:

Elle avait l'esprit juste, mais peu étendu; la justesse de son esprit était dénaturée par l'emportement de son caractère, et son peu d'étendue l'empêchait d'apercevoir la ligne la plus habile, et de saisir des nuances délicates. (p. 115)

The second motive, unrecognized by herself, is 'quelque vanité de femme' (p. 118) in a deeply wounded and ageing woman who 'voulait se prouver à elle-même qu'elle avait encore des moyens de plaire'. Third, and most suggestive, there is the need for the reassurance of those words which habit had made so intimate a part of a lost experience:

Peut-être enfin ... trouvait-elle une sorte de consolation à s'entendre répéter des expressions d'amour que depuis longtemps je ne prononçais plus.[7]

The insight into Ellénore stems also from applying to her, with logic, irony and sympathy, the same laws of human behaviour which have activated Adolphe. The galvanism by the obstacle has often been at the centre of his hurt or his actions: he sees all too clearly how, once he begins to move away from Ellénore, she in turn will be caught in the same mechanism:

Elle n'avait pas le temps de se refroidir à mon égard, parce que tout son temps et toutes ses forces étaient employés à me conserver. (p. 66)

It is in the scenes of Ellénore's death that it would be most fruitful to compare closely the deliberate stylisation of the novel with the direct experience as given in the diary.[8] Here Constant has not only concentrated the prolonged metaphysical reflections provoked in him by the death of a very different woman, fitting them succinctly and easily to the necessity of narrative, but has also re-shaped the details to suit exactly the individual nature of the Ellénore whom the novel had created (see *Jnx*, mai 1805, pp. 515–21).

During the long days he spent attempting to help the dying Julie Talma, Constant was haunted by the problem of the connection between the physical and mental, from two opposite points of view.

He observed the shocking reversal of almost all the qualities of personality under physical strain, and yet was struck by how eventually something essential remains recognizable and unimpaired even to the point of death. In the novel, what in the diary was spread over weeks, and meditated on in the abstract, is given only a few lines: the contrasting observations are set immediately side by side. Sometimes the same terms are used, but sifted, concentrated, and directed to a particular effect. The bitter and everyday details on how the generous Julie, with her gay combination of impulse and self-control, has become 'inquiète, minutieuse, avide' are left aside, while the same anguished question:

Qu'est-ce que cette âme qui ... lorsque les organes s'affaiblissent ... change d'inclinations et comme de nature morale? ...

is applied to Ellénore:

Je vis, spectacle humiliant et déplorable, ce caractère énergique et fier recevoir de la souffrance physique mille impressions confuses et incohérentes, comme si ... l'âme, froissée par le corps, se métamorphosait en tous sens pour se plier avec moins de peine à la dégradation des organes. (p. 138).

Set against this is the survival at the last of the essential quality in personality. In Julie this had been a witty intelligence:

de l'esprit, de la mémoire, de la grâce, de la gaîté, la même vivacité dans ses opinions ... a partie intellectuelle.

In the Ellénore who 'n'avait qu'un esprit ordinaire' a different quality remains indestructible as other faculties decay:

Un seul sentiment ne varia jamais dans le cœur d'Ellénore: ce fut sa tendresse pour moi.

The intellectual Julie was quite without religious beliefs; Ellénore has been shown from the beginning as adhering to those very religious codes which might condemn her conduct. This hitherto unstated part of the sacrifice she made to Adolphe is given now in the quietest of terms:[9]

'Laissez-moi me livrer à présent, me dit-elle, aux devoirs de ma religion; j'ai bien des fautes à expier.'

In the diary it was in the later incident of Julie's funeral that Constant felt the grim gap between the mechanical ritual of ceremony and the terrifying reality of feeling: in the novel this is transposed to the climax where the dying woman receives the last sacraments. That thirst for lucid contemplation of experience which after Julie's death he called a 'bizarre, avide et sombre curiosité' becomes here the 'curiosité involontaire' of the kneeling Adolphe, integrating what in the diary are developed religious discussions into one personal moment fittingly related to the character of Ellénore:

J'entendais ces hommes répéter machinalement les paroles funèbres, comme si eux aussi n'eussent pas dû ... mourir un jour. J'étais loin cependant de dédaigner ces pratiques ... Elles rendaient du calme à Ellénore: elles l'aidaient à franchir ce pas terrible ... Ma surprise n'est pas que l'homme ait besoin d'une religion; ce qui m'étonne, c'est qu'il se croie jamais assez fort, assez à l'abri du malheur pour oser en rejeter une. .. (pp. 140–1)

Finally, in both diary and novel, the watcher sees the death agony as a physical battle with an almost personified outer force. The picture of the body after death, treated with stunned honesty in the diary, could not be used in a novel so long before the death of Emma Bovary, but Ellénore is given no conventionally peaceful end. Shaken by a 'tremblement convulsif ... Elle se relevait, elle retombait, elle s'efforçait de fuir', and there is conveyed the animal-like threat of the power which has tenaciously seized her 'pour l'achever'. As with Julie, we see the appeal for help in her eyes; this deliberately recalls those many moments in the story where understanding or alienation have been conveyed by a swift glance, gay and comprehending, or timid, beseeching, pathetic and exasperating. The failing of the faculties, given more scattered expression in the diary, reaches its bare and balanced epitome in the novel:

Elle voulut pleurer, il n'y avait plus de larmes; elle voulut parler, il n'y avait plus de voix.

The last moments sum up the core of a personality: for Julie

cette intelligence qui ressemblait à un général vaincu donnant encore des ordres à une armée en déroute,

for Ellénore the very different note of tender resignation already so suggestively conveyed in the last walk in a frosty sunlit garden: now

Elle laissa tomber, comme résignée, sa tête sur le bras qui l'appuyait... quelques instants après elle n'était plus.

The letter found after her death combines her submissive devotion ('est-il une retraite où je ne me cache pour vivre auprès de vous, sans être un fardeau?'), her fear ('timide et tremblante, car vous m'avez glacée d'effroi'), her lucid insight into his pity, and her last sense of the tragic dilemma to which there is no solution.[10]

The novel of just one character? No. There is, I think, nothing incoherent, shadowy or subsidiary in this portrait. It is perhaps rare for a novel written in the first person to give such equal status, such compassionate and detailed understanding, to the figure who is the source of the narrator's tragedy. In the double tragedy of Adolphe and Ellénore, the other characters are of course secondary. Yet what is surprising in so brief and concentrated a narrative is how often they are brought alive in that flash of individuality which goes beyond any schematic function as foils to self-revelation, pivots to narrative, or mere symbolic pawns.

Adolphe's father serves primarily to explain in depth the origin of impulses and inhibitions in the central figure, but a suggestive understanding of the father's individual nature is created in careful touches and with deliberate progression. High expectations and unsystematic indulgence educate an 'infant prodigy' into ambition for renown (to which Ellénore is to prove an obstacle) and into irresponsibility ('Il ne m'avait jamais laissé souffrir des suites de [mes] fautes'). The father's conviction of the unimportance of the passing love-affair contributes to Adolphe's initial involvement in feelings which cannot so easily be cast aside; his sense of the seriousness of marriage will be part of the background to Adolphe's struggle. But what comes most individually alive is the analysis of how the cold, caustic, ironical surface covers a deep affection rendered incommunicable by that most stifling form of timidity, family inarticulacy: the inability, within the close and awkward relationship, to express feelings, so that they are distorted into dry or biting phrases.[11] Here as always it is the combination of abstract analysis and live detail which succeeds.

First there is the summary, in personal terms, of the contrast between affectionate and thoughtful letters and the gap between generations in uneasy speech. Then the piercing general analysis:

la timidité . . . qui . . . dénature dans notre bouche tout ce que nous essayons de dire, et ne nous permet de nous exprimer que par des mots vagues ou une ironie plus ou moins amère, comme si nous voulions nous venger sur nos sentiments mêmes de la douleur que nous éprouvons à ne pouvoir les faire connaître. (p. 20–21).

The novel gives persuasive detail not simply to his fruitless efforts to guide his son, whether by advice which leaves Adolphe free, or by one sudden moment of compulsion, but also to the theme of deep affection frustrated by the problem of expression. In Ch. iv his permissiveness is merely briefly stated. In Ch. v two hard, constrained sentences announce a decision, followed by a gesture refusing further discussion. This strangled led conversation contrasts with the relatively long direct quotation from a letter in Ch. VI, combining pride in his son's capacities, insight into his nature, will to practical help and firm warnings, with the personal bitterness insinuated in a passing phrase:

'je n'exercerai pas contre vous une autorité qui touche à son terme, et dont je n'ai jamais fait usage.' (p. 84)

Each of these elements is taken up again in the still more developed letter at the beginning of Ch. VII, culminating with a still more bitterly allusive sentence:

'N'y voyez au moins qu'une preuve de mon zèle, et nullement une atteinte à l'indépendance que vous avez toujours su défendre ... contre votre père.' (p. 97)

Finally, it is through his letters to the Baron de T., not those directly to his son, that he is able to express, and that Adolphe finally realises, the extent of his father's 'affliction bien plus vive que je ne l'avais supposée' (p. 126). If it is his effect on Adolphe (provoking rebellion and affection, cynicism and remorse, respect and mistrust for accepted values) which is his central function, yet he comes alive in his own right through minimal but carefully varied means, as a sharply delineated character.[12]

The Comte de P. plays his necessary part in the narrative through his matter-of-fact appreciation of Ellénore's past devotion, his efforts to have her accepted socially, so that he welcomes Adolphe in his salon, yet his coldness of nature which strengthens her joy in Adolphe's early worship. But even this thumbnail-sketch of a character is given his moment where he moves beyond the mere necessities of plot to be seen in an individual flash from within. In Ch. IV he stands by the fireside discussing Adolphe's approaching departure, and lets fall one of those remarks about 'some people' provoked by bitter resentment:

'Au reste, ajouta-t-il en regardant Ellénore, tout le monde peut-être ne pense pas ici comme moi.' (p. 63)

One might look further at the old woman in Chapter I, necessary as an influence on Adolphe's early sense of the vanity of things, but aphoristically characterized in a way which goes beyond this necessity, or the tiny moments when Ellénore's children are shown in puzzled surprise before the passions of adults,[13] or even the undertones as regards the friend of Ellénore in whom Adolphe confides in Ch. VIII. But the most triumphant study of a secondary character is certainly that of the Baron de T. in the last chapters. To dismiss him as an exteriorisation of Adolphe's inner desires is to miss the savour of a quiet but virulent analysis.[14]

This is the skilful diplomat, used to manœuvres on a large scale, now exercising the same talents on the minor task of inculcating conventional commonsense into the erring son of an old friend. His mixture of apparent frankness, professional eloquence, and exact timing of each stage of the campaign is conveyed in the detail of ideas, letters, speech and gestures. He manœuvres, deflates, flatters and appeals, saying never a word too much, but leaving these words to echo at planned intervals. On Adolphe's first visit (Ch. VII, p. 97) he shows a well-calculated combination of outspokenness, good-fellowship and penetration. First, 'Je vais vous parler avec franchise'; then 'we have all known these trying situations, and no woman dies of them';[15] then an appeal to Adolphe's ambition for a worth-while career; next, the biting observation that if Adolphe came to see him, it was in the hope of hearing such advice; the assertion that to leave Ellénore would be for her own good; the further practical considerations on what age will bring; the climax in an eloquent peroration on Adolphe's infinite prospects, blocked only by Ellénore. Two chapters go by, while he leaves his speech to echo, then action takes the place of oratory. Leaving the subject of contention completely aside, he induces Adolphe to taste success in society, then entrusts him with responsible administrative work. Once confidence has been established, he encourages veiled discussion of the possessiveness of women, or drops a remark about those who cannot be received in society. After the preparation of intimate dinners, he arranges the climax of a larger reception, first leaving Adolphe to the horrors of public gossip tattling and whispering around him, then at the strategic moment taking him under his wing to show what power a respected reputation can exercise. Briefly he draws the moral at the end of the evening, appealing in crescendo to the essentials of reputation, family affection and, above all, Adolphe's inability to make Ellénore happy whatever his sacrifices. Finally, when even this persuasion cannot break through Adolphe's indecision, he sees with the practised eye of the diplomat the devastating use that can be made of the partly false implication of the documents in the case. Here, within the necessities of plot, is a sharp and balanced study of the type most suggestively outlined in the general sentence, with its quietly telling adverb:

un vieux ministre, dont l'âme était usée, et qui se rappelait vaguement que, dans sa jeunesse, il avait aussi été tourmenté par des intrigues d'amour. (p. 124)

The outer observer, however penetrating, sees only a simplified part of the real experience, ignores one dimension of it. If this is true of the Baron de T., it is still more so of the whole cloud of anonymous witnesses who form the background. In this novel of only a hundred pages, it is astonishing how the irony of constant misjudgments or piercing half-truths is given range and variety, not as abstract statement or as diatribe against society, but in the detail of everyday life. The respectable judge complacently or maliciously; the scandal-mongers rejoice in any fragment of gossip; the 'sensible' see easy solutions; the would-be seducers seek to profit from the situation; well-meaning friends by their sympathy falsify the real issue. Each change in the relationship between Adolphe and Ellénore gives more sharply pointed instances: two relatives of the Count who had been forced by him to live on good terms with Ellénore are, once she turns to Adolphe, able to use moral principles as a cloak for their spiteful joy in breaking with her; her children provide another stimulus to conventional judgment; the men who frequent her salon become insultingly familiar, but also find it necessary to provide specious excuses for their presence; serious opinion judges Adolphe as frivolous and cynical precisely when he is attempting to achieve fidelity and tenderness; the young cynics envy him his position when he is most weary of it.[16] Drawing-room or death-bed are ringed round by the pressing presence of others, giving in flashes of detail the sense of convention, criticism, mistaken sympathy, or surmise.

Of certain fixed literary theories ('des formes convenues') Constant wrote in his *Journaux* (p. 459) that they may contain truths, but that they 'demandent à être modifiées et incarnées dans chaque détail'. So perhaps with the novelist's ideas on human behaviour. Through the interplay between his central characters and their relationships with counsellors or observers, he has modified, re-defined, or simply questioned preconceptions around such subjects as love, vanity, ambition, devotion, giving the insight of a *moraliste* into their complex components, part self-sacrifice, part self-seeking, part self-deception. But he is novelist as well as *moraliste*: his characters, within his concise and selective technique, are 'incarnés dans chaque détail'. This article has had space to deal with only some aspects of the art which brings them alive: it remains to re-set them in the patterns of the narrative as a whole, and to study more closely Constant's varied handling of the instrument 'of words through which he defines or suggests them, or makes them directly express themselves. Structure and style will therefore form the subject of another article.

NOTES

1 Page references throughout this article refer, for *Adolphe*, to the Garnier edition by J.-H. Bornecque (1955) and, for other works, to the Pléiade *Œuvres*, ed. A. Roulin (1957). Further points are dealt with in two other articles on the Art of *Adolphe*: 'The Stylisation of Experience' (see above pp. 3–27) and 'Structure and Style' (see below, pp. 43–60). These will be referred to below as Art. I and Art. III. (I discuss Adolphe himself mainly in I.)

2 Battles between the partisans of different women as the 'main' source have died down. Different analyses attribute differing degrees of importance to the very many who may have been drawn on in varying ways: Germaine de Staël, Anna Lindsay, Charlotte de Hardenberg, Mme de Charrière, Julie Talma, Wilhelmina von Cramm, or early loves mentioned in the *Cahier Rouge*. (The *Journaux intimes* give in 1807 [p. 633] a personal summing-up of some of the 'passionnées ... ne me quittant que parce que je les y forçais' and a consequent self-criticism.) Recent criticism has tended to see Ellénore as a synthesis of Constant's experience of the essential nature of woman (see Bornecque p. civ; for further bibliography and discussion see in particular the articles of P. Deguise in *R.H.L.F.* 1954, pp. 125–51 and in *L'Information littéraire*, 1958, pp. 139–50; P. Bénichou in *R.H.L.F.* 1954, pp. 332–56; C. Pellegrini in *Rivista di letterature moderne e comparative*, 1956, pp. 165–79 and 272–96, and C. Cordié's edition, Naples, 1963). In this connection it would be valuable to collect passages on 'les femmes' and 'toutes les femmes' from the *Journaux* and elsewhere (pp. 601 and 700 in the *Jnx.*, and the *Lettre sur Julie*, p. 844, taking up the famous 'but:lien' theme, are obviously vital).

Yet the idea of the secondary importance and colourlessness of Ellénore persists. To take only one or two far-separated examples – G. Rudler in 1935: 'Il n'y a pas d'héroïne dans *Adolphe*; il n'y a qu'un héros, Constant ... Ellénore est un caractère consistant mais sans couleur et sans vie'; J. Mistler, 1945: 'La figure d'Ellénore n'existe qu'en fonction du héros'; C. J. Greshoff, 1965 (*F.M.L.S.* pp. 30–36): 'a shadow in the background ... this slightly marginal presence of Ellénore'. On the other hand, M. Levaillant (*Les Amours de Benjamin Constant*, Hachette, 1958, p. 96) finds it miraculous that from the mixture of such different sources 'Benjamin ait réussi à en composer un être admirablement vivant'. Many critics, from Balzac's Dinah Piédefer (quoted in Bornecque's introduction) onwards, have been able to take for granted the coherence and convincingness of Ellénore; J. Hytier in his brief article in *Les Romans de l'individu* (Les Arts et le Livre, 1928) picked out one or two examples of Constant's art in constructing her character. It seems worth looking further into what has been ably but briefly suggested by a few, and queried or ignored by many other commentators.

3 The distinction between man and woman may well recall Letter cxxx from *Les Liaisons dangereuses*: 'L'homme jouit du bonheur qu'il ressent, et la femme de celui qu'elle procure' and many of the penetrating questions raised round Mme de Tourvel. If Laclos shows in Mme de Merteuil a woman who attempts to safeguard herself from the consequences of this distinction, Constant studies, both in *Adolphe* and the *Journaux*, a man to whom a sense of 'le bonheur des autres' is an inescapable if infuriating determinant in personality.

4 A minor echo to the theme of how words enhance or falsify experience, which I discuss in Art i. The novel itself, perhaps fortunately, does not make any attempt to convey directly the 'foreignness' of Ellénore's mode of speech as Balzac will do with e.g. Schmucke.

5 Not a biographical fact in any of Constant's main relationships, except that with Mme de Charrière early in life; he abandoned her with the ease of youth. Possibly retrospective pity for the ageing woman may have contributed to the novel; possibly the reproaches later of women closer in age to himself, yet feeling no future was left. In the novel, the difference in age has been deliberately stressed, intensifying Adolphe's responsibility and Ellénore's desperation.

6 These chapters also provide, as has been suggested by J. Hytier (op. cit.), an 'art of seduction' in general. As so often, Constant combines the insight of the *moraliste* with the detailed creation of individual situation and character.

7 Certainly the original impulse behind this passage (part of which was omitted on first publication) may have been to analyse some of the reasons which prevented a break with Mme de Staël despite relatives' and friends' criticisms of her conduct with other men, and of himself for not using this as a reason for a break. (One notes also, in *Jnx.* p. 226: 'Germaine a besoin du langage de l'amour'.) But whatever the origins, the details are completely integrated into the impulsive character of Ellénore and her growing despair, and serve to intensify the struggle between Adolphe's apparently justified right to freedom and his increased understanding of the hurt he has caused.

8 The material on the death of Julie Talma from the *Journaux*, and the *Lettre sur Julie*, have often been quoted in part in relation to *Adolphe*; some extracts are usefully given in appendices to the text of the novel by such editors as Bornecque and Cordié. I know of no close comparisons between these passages and the novel (though J. Hytier makes one or two suggestive points) which show exactly how Constant has used and modified the real experience. His reflexions on the artist's lucid and uncompromising analysis of personal contact with death might be compared with those in Flaubert's *Correspondance*.

9 Compare the grandiloquent end of Chateaubriand's *Atala*: 'J'aurais

désiré que cette divinité se fût anéantie, pourvu que, serrée dans tes bras, j'eusse roulé d'abîme en abîme avec les débris de Dieu et du monde!', or the death scene in *Jocelyn*:

> Et dans mes yeux mourants son image est si belle,
> Que j'aime mieux l'enfer qu'un paradis sans elle,

with the bare and quiet phrases: 'mon amour pour vous fut peut-être une faute; je ne le croirais pourtant pas, si cet amour avait pu vous rendre heureux' (p. 140).

10 The present article deals only with the main features of Ellénore as a coherent character. Further details will be found in Art. III.

11 Once again, the problem of words is brought to the fore. Cf. Art. I.

12 The bitter epigrammatic sentence on p. 96: 'Je ne puis que vous plaindre de ce qu'avec votre esprit d'indépendance, vous faites toujours ce que vous ne voulez pas' is distilled from many of Constant's recurring reflections on himself in the diaries. See in particular p. 673: 'Jadis, je murmurais contre les rapports de père et de fils, comme dépendance. Je l'ai joliment atteint, ce but d'indépendance que je désirais par-dessus tout.' On the conflicting influences exercised by the extraordinary Juste de Constant, see particularly the *Cahier Rouge*, in the *Journaux* especially pp. 333 and 395, and a letter to Rosalie (B. et R. de Constant, *Corr.*, Gallimard, 1955, p. 161). Phrases in the *Journaux* suggest in abstract terms the tone of bitter insinuation in his father's letters: 'une aigreur et un mécontentement secret' (347); 'dans son style quelque chose qui me blesse toujours' (485) or (in Menos, *Lettres à sa famille*, Stock, 1932 p. 303) 'un ton d'insinuation et de mécontentement'. The novel gives not just the abstract summary of tone, but recurring and direct expressions aphoristically conveying the father's ambition for his son, indulgence, practicality, bitterness, and frustrated affection. On the theme of the inadequacy of words, see Art. I, pp. 7 sqq.

13 p. 63: 'portant sur leurs visages cet étonnement de l'enfance lorsqu'elle remarque une agitation dont elle ne soupçonne pas la cause'.

14 He is perhaps the only character in *Adolphe* for whom no obvious biographical source has been proposed. A very general resemblance with M. de Maltigues in *Corinne* has been suggested. His function, with obvious differences in treatment, might be compared with that of Œnone in Racine's *Phèdre*.

15 The Baron de T. is not simply 'the voice of reason' (Greshoff, art. cit., p. 36): Ellénore does die. Nor even 'the voice of the most real, but the most hidden, desires of the tempted'. His estimate is proved wrong, in the outcome, both for Ellénore's death and for Adolphe's future. Constant's experience in real life may have shown that women live on and that the urge to a career follows its course. In the novel itself it is precisely the imaginative sympathy for another character than that of the narrator which makes of death the symbol for intolerable suffering, or the destruction of any sense of value in continued existence. This self-reproach is of course underlined by a further form of ironical self-criticism in the third Preface: how far may remorse for suffering supposedly caused rest on 'je ne sais quelle satisfaction de fatuité'?

16 See Constant's remarks on how the chorus in the tragedy of the ancients is replaced by the use of 'personnages secondaires' (pp. 907–9 and 956). For other important functions performed by these representatives of *opinion* see Art. I, pp. 16–18. Few novelists before Sartre have so virulently brought alive in such small compass, if with different emphasis, several sides to the theme of 'l'enfer c'est les autres'.

3

The art of Constant's *Adolphe*:
III. Structure and style (1966)[1]

Adolphe stands in the memory as a miracle of concision. It combines
to a particular degree simplicity of outline with complexity of effect.
From a distance, one tends to think of it as a smooth, unilinear,
abstract account, in the first person, of an obsessive indecision. It
has even been called 'un roman où il n'y a ni descriptions, ni
dialogues'.[2] To look more closely is to realize more and more how
deliberate an art has gone to creating, below the apparently
straightforward surface, the echoes and reversals of themes, the
variety and pattern of detail.

Even the bare outlines of the structure show the careful control of
proportion, balance, suspense. There are ten chapters: three trace
the origins of feeling, and at the beginning of the fourth comes the
pivot on which it turns to weariness. The obsessive indecision which
now takes over might, as indeed it did in real life, become mono-
tonously repetitive: Constant has chosen his incidents with a very sure
sense of progression and climax. The change in feeling is for a time
not fully conscious. Ellénore's first voicing of destructive insight
('Vous croyez avoir de l'amour, et vous n'avez que de la pitié')
comes just before the middle of the book, at the end of Ch. v,
balanced early in Ch. vi by Adolphe's attempt at a similar moment
of truth ('L'amour ... Ellénore, je ne l'ai plus'). Subsequent efforts
at self-persuasion or compromise are cut across by a secondary
revelation, to Ellénore's friend, placed halfway between the central
climax and the end.

This book gives in ten brief chapters a particular effect of the
weight of time and change. There is at the same time a sense of
rapid movement across the years and an illusion of pausing over and
living with the characters' closest thoughts. The sense of inexorable
development is given in three ways. First, in the brief phrases which

firmly point to each scene as a new and irreversible step: 'un premier coup était porté: une première barrière était franchie'; 'pour la première fois de la vie . . .'; 'C'est un grand pas, c'est un pas irréparable, quand . . .'; 'c'était . . . une barrière de plus'. Across these run the momentary evocations of a dead past: 'Autrefois', says Ellénore, 'Autrefois je ne m'adressais à personne pour arriver jusqu'à votre cœur' (p. 113). Secondly, in the choice and progression of the successive crises which force Adolphe to remain with Ellénore. In the first part, her need for his material protection is increased by each successive sacrifice she makes; in the second half her external fortune and position grow assured: this progressively exacerbates Adolphe's dilemma, as the outer reasons for remaining diminish, yet her inner need intensifies.

Third and most important is the crescendo in alternating tension and relief. The Ellénore who near the beginning bore a six months' absence and wrote humbly of

vivre . . . auprès de moi . . . dans une retraite ignorée . . . Elle n'exigeait d'autre prix de ses sacrifices que de m'attendre comme une humble esclave, de passer chaque jour avec moi quelques minutes, de jouir des moments que je pourrais lui donner. (pp. 78–9)

comes by logical stages to express harsh suspicion and domineering demands in the most cutting of terms, expression as well as feeling showing the progression and contrast:

Si je pouvais me faire illusion sur vous, je consentirais peut-être à une absence . . . Je ne veux pas m'y exposer . . . je ne veux pas braver . . . (pp. 90–91)

The moments of reconciliation and tranquillity are first provoked by inner responses of gratitude and tenderness; later they are to be found only in the outer distraction of travel (p. 94), or in the ironical achievement of avoiding discussing feelings at all:

Comme nous avions l'un dans l'autre une confiance sans bornes, excepté sur nos sentiments intimes, nous mettions les observations et les faits à la place de ces sentiments, et nos conversations avaient repris quelque charme. (pp. 115–16)

When finally Adolphe and Ellénore are unable any longer to find moments of precarious peace together, the dramatic alternation between torment and momentary relief still continues, as Adolphe experiences a wider sense of tranquillity, of abandoning decision and taking no thought for the morrow, in that escape to night and space which in Ch. VII precedes the working out of the climax. As the

climax approaches, two intensified moments of a still stranger peace
and tenderness occur. Having promised the Baron that he will break
with Ellénore within three days, Adolphe, as so often before, is
stimulated to a deep regret for what he is about to lose, made
paradoxically precious by impermanence:[3]

Je fixais mes regards sur Ellénore, comme sur un être que j'allais perdre . . .
je jouissais de ses expressions d'amour, naguère importunes, précieuses
maintenant, comme pouvant chaque fois être les dernières. (pp. 130–1)

Ellénore, in face of death, achieves the quiet resignation of the
garden scene. But the relief is short-lived. Adolphe renews his efforts
to console:

Tout le passé ne nous est-il pas commun? . . . commençons en ce jour une
nouvelle époque, rappelons les heures du bonheur et de l'amour; (p. 135)

but they immediately dissolve in temporization as Ellénore reminds
him of what stands between them, and she is forced back to the
blank realization that 'J'ai voulu ce qui n'était pas possible', as is
Adolphe to the knowledge that 'ce n'étaient pas les regrets de
l'amour, c'était un sentiment plus sombre et plus triste'.

Across this progression, certain themes and phrases echo in
ironical interplay. Adolphe is stifled by Ellénore's devotion, yet it is
his own devotion which holds him to her ('Son bonheur m'était
nécessaire, et je me savais nécessaire à son bonheur'). Each makes
sacrifices to the other, realizes that these sacrifices must be hidden,
yet is wounded when the other does not recognize feelings which
such an effort has been made to hide. 'Je tâchai par un effort bizarre
de l'attendrir sur le malheur que j'éprouvais en restant près d'elle'
(p. 92 and cf. p. 60). At first it is the very frankness of love which
ironically brings about its change:

elle était avec moi dans une parfaite aisance . . . Mais il résultait de son abandon
complet avec moi, qu'elle ne me déguisait aucun de ses mouvements . . . (p. 60)

Later, pretence is seen as the most destructive force, and later again,
lucidity and truth become still more destructive. The theme of the
galvanizing of feeling by the pursuit of an all-absorbing aim is taken
up in ironic reversals: Ellénore by Ch. IV 'n'était plus un but: elle
était devenue un lien' (p. 59), but after her death Adolphe is to
realize that his weary devotion had in itself provided another aim:

Naguère toutes mes actions avaient un but; j'étais sûr, par chacune d'elles,
d'épargner une peine ou de causer un plaisir. (p. 143)

For Ellénore on the other hand, the very violence of the pursuit of the aim prevents the means of achieving it: 'elle avait un but; et comme elle se précipitait vers ce but, elle le manquait' (p. 115; cf. also p. 66). A recurring theme, used with intertwining ironies, is that of the illogical gap between what the intellect can foresee or imagine and the experience as it really is. The shock of astonishment strikes Adolphe both before the growth of feeling, and before the pain of its disappearance (see pp. 40, 42 and 80, discussed in Art. i); it occurs once again as he contemplates death, that fact of which he had been so conscious in his youth and at later intervals, but which now he is unable to absorb or explain:

La conviction de sa mort n'avait pas encore pénétré dans mon âme; mes yeux contemplaient avec un étonnement stupide ce corps inanimé. (p. 142)

Two of the major ironies are expressed in the barest phrases of all. The first is that of Adolphe's statement at the beginning of Ch. iii:

Cet amour que vous repoussez est indestructible. (p. 46)

The other echoes across the book from the early letter:

Ellénore, lui écrivais-je un jour, vous ne savez pas tout ce que je souffre. (p. 52)

to Ellénore's words in the last chapter:

Adolphe, Adolphe, j'ai été violente, j'ai pu vous offenser; mais vous ne savez pas ce que j'ai souffert. (p. 134)

Constant's narrative gives a sense both of inexorable speed of movement and of weary prolongation through wastes of time. It is certainly not set abstractly outside time; very exact notations are given: a month, six weeks, six months, three years, the ages of the characters.[4] Yet it is psychological time which counts. A brief phrase may stride across a whole stretch, suggesting the menacing speed of unused time:

La première année de notre séjour à Caden avait atteint son terme, sans que rien changeât dans notre situation (p. 92)

while others will fragmentate time into its endless, separate and hurtful moments:

Ne l'éprouvons-nous pas chaque jour en détail et goutte à goutte, cette douleur? (p. 64)

or:

en entassant péniblement les jours sur les jours. (p. 79)

There is a highly original allocation of proportion in narrative. The account of moments of crisis is bare, brief, almost breathless, each phrase cut off sharply and consisting of nothing much more than subject, verb, complement, hinged on a past historic. One might cite the crisis of the dinner-scene:

Elle ne put achever sa phrase. Je pressai sa main de mon bras; nous nous mîmes à table (p. 44)

or the next turning point:

Alors se modifièrent rapidement les règles sévères qu'elle m'avait prescrites. Elle me permit de peindre mon amour; elle se familiarisa par degrés avec ce langage: bientôt elle m'avoua qu'elle m'aimait. (pp. 50–1)

The duel is an outstanding example:

Nous nous battîmes; je le blessai dangereusement, je fus blessé moi-même. (p. 74)

The strength of impact comes from all that has been created beforehand to bring into play the snap of the spring, and from all that the moment will lead to. Constant in fact devotes the subtlety of his analysis to the causes and consequences of actions: the actions themselves, as with Ellénore's 'Elle se donna enfin tout entière', need only one brief phrase.[5]

Constant's technique makes changes in feeling both insinuatingly imperceptible and logically inevitable. The height of his achievement here comes at the beginning of Ch. IV.[6] The first paragraph opens with the phrase 'Charme de l'amour, qui pourra vous peindre', and closes, after the analysis of enchantment, with a variant echo on these words. The framing question moves significantly from future to past tense. Where one might for the final phrase have expected some such wording as 'Celui qui vous a une fois éprouvé ne saurait vous peindre', there is the sharp cut of 'Qui vous éprouva . . .' with its bare monosyllable and its past historic, drawing in one stroke a line beneath the delight. Then, whereas straightforward narrative technique might have gone on: 'Ellénore and I were in love . . . until I began to feel . . .', Constant moves imperceptibly into the next stage by simply recounting an absorption and devotion which should have been part of the joy, yet gradually builds up, in one paragraph only, an increasing sense of oppression:

Elle ne me laissait jamais la quitter sans essayer de me retenir ... Elle fixait
avec une précision inquiète l'instant de mon retour ...⁷ (p. 58)

The claims of love grow imperceptibly and ironically out of the
ecstasy itself, and linger in the repetitive imperfect: only one page
after the delight we have passed through weeks of mounting exasperation to the epigrammatic pin-pointing of the sudden cruel conclusion: 'Elle n'était plus un but; elle était devenue un lien.'

Four main elements, perhaps, contribute to the ease and compulsion of movement in Constant's narrative. Two have already
been touched on: first, the preparation for events by the direct
details of dialogue, letter and gesture as well as by the more abstract
analysis of meaning or tone; second, the recounting of events
themselves in bare, brief phrases which indicate the outer happening
in one sudden stroke. These are often followed by two ways of both
clinching and broadening the significance of what has been acted
out in detail. A piercing and epigrammatic phrase sums up the new
development in the dilemma of individuals; finally, a lapidary
statement concentrates this individual experience into a biting and
balanced epigram of general import. The force of the final maxim
lies not just in its probing and succinct stab into human experience
in general, but in its being placed at a culminating point, where one
has moved by way of the detailed desperation of individuals at a
pitch of tension, through the concentrated summing-up of the
essentials of their particular experience, to come finally to a still
wider thrust into central paradoxes of human nature. It is only after
the exposing of Adolphe's inextricable entanglement of scheming,
timidity, attraction, indignation and self-persuasion that we come to
the general remark:

Presque toujours, pour vivre en repos avec nous-mêmes, nous travestissons
en calculs et en systèmes nos impuissances ou nos faiblesses, (p. 38)

only when we have seen in detail the youth who seems at once cold
seducer and worshipping lover that Constant hits home with his
central point: 'Il n'y a point d'unité complète dans l'homme ...' (p.
39). We are involved, not in a handbook of isolated maxims, but in
a novel; a novel which gives to a particular degree the natural
broadening of reflection around a representative individual
experience.

As an epitome of the fourfold movement, one might take the scene
in the middle of Ch. iv where Adolphe tells Ellénore the outcome of
his father's letter. The preparation for crisis comes first in an

abstract analysis of his own conflicting reactions, then in the cut-
and-thrust of argument between two characters, in direct speech,
dry, hard, allusive:

Je reste encore six mois ... Vous m'annoncez cette nouvelle bien sèchement
– C'est que je crains beaucoup les conséquences... Il me semble que pour vous
du moins ... Vous savez fort bien, Ellénore, que ... (p. 64)

One sentence, carrying the undertones of all that has gone before, is
enough for each thrust, and each is a renewed and lapidary
statement of the hurts that lie between them. Direct speech then
moves into indirect summary, in which are conveyed four bitter
accusations from Ellénore, three reproaches from Adolphe. It is only
after the force of feeling has been revealed in detailed analysis and direct
speech that the second stage, that of action, momentarily takes over:

Je vis son visage couvert tout à coup de pleurs: je m'arrêtai, je revins sur
mes pas, je désavouai, j'expliquai. Nous nous embrassâmes ... (p. 65)

The scene concludes first with the concentrated formulation of a
dramatic turning-point for two individuals:

Nous avions prononcé tous deux des mots irréparables; nous pouvions nous
taire, main non les oublier,

then with the wider generalization in one of the most telling maxims
for lovers ever coined:

Il y a des choses qu'on est longtemps sans se dire, mais quand une fois elles
sont dites, on ne cesse jamais de les répéter.

These main means of narration move imperceptibly in and out of
each other, none developed for too long, each exactly placed and
proportioned. Framing them is a particular skill in the art of the
first-person narrative with the insinuations it may carry in retrospect. Adolphe may use just one word ('je *crus* l'éprouver avec
fureur') or one phrase ('*Pendant que je lui parlais* j'étais sincère dans
mes promesses') to suggest the difference between the imagined and
the 'real', the sporadic and the persistent.[8] A phrase normally used
to convey conviction may in context serve as a perfidious hint of
doubt: 'Je me sentais, *de la meilleure foi du monde*, véritablement
amoureux' (p. 46). His own narrative sets at odds the inner feeling
and the detached judgement, provoking a particular interplay
between critical conclusion and imaginative sharing of experience.

The world of *Adolphe* is predominantly mental, but the discreet
presence and suggestive use of the physical has not always been

sufficiently realized. Concentration and obsession give an atmosphere of *huis clos*. Neither Poland nor any of the journeys are described, and the dinner party of Ch. II is indeed different from La Vaubyessard, but this is no exclusively abstract universe. Two scenes in particular break out into the natural world. In neither is there description for description's sake, but an evocative use of physical detail as a means of suggesting or intensifying mood and meaning.

At the end of Ch. VII, Adolphe, at a climax of tension, moves almost blindly across the countryside. For long he is still entirely shut in his own bitter reflections, at first those of despair and fury at all that Ellénore prevents his attaining, then those of the imagined ideal marriage and career; finally he is overcome by a sudden flood of childhood memories, made hallucinatingly strong by the pressures of tension. These are not described in any extended detail, but used to stress the strange sharpness and nostalgia of a sudden resurgence:

Les plus petits détails, les plus petits objets se retraçaient à ma mémoire; je revoyais l'antique château que j'avais habité avec mon père, les bois qui l'entouraient, la rivière qui baignait le pied de ses murailles, les montagnes qui bordaient son horizon; toutes ces choses me paraissaient tellement présentes, pleines d'une telle vie, qu'elles me causaient un frémissement que j'avais peine à supporter.[9] (p. 105)

It is only after this physical recollection that he becomes conscious of the real countryside around him, and for the rest of the chapter it intimately influences and echoes his mood.

The falling of night is given in bare, quiet words: and followed without comment by its mental equivalent:

Le jour s'affaiblissait: le ciel était serein; la campagne devenait déserte ...
Mes pensées prirent graduellement une teinte plus grave. (pp. 105–6)

Gradually deepening shadows, an enveloping silence intensified by the few faint and distant sounds, the stretch of the immense and fading horizon, give 'un sentiment plus calme et plus solennel ... la sensation de l'immensité', and the sense of escape from prolonged, narrowing and stifling preoccupations. Adolphe breathes in a physical and a mental sense of space, tranquillity and calm. The meditations that follow, on the inevitability of death and therefore on the need to take each day as it comes, to abandon the taut struggle of the will, are no mere abstract development, but occur as across the still countryside he sees, late in the night, the glimmering light of some distant cottage suggesting a watch over the sick or dying. His sense of tranquillity is made one with the physical weariness as his night of wandering ends. Finally, two bare sentences note the approach of dawn and his gradual distinguishing of objects, as consciousness of Ellénore's suffering returns.

That suffering broadens into its own scene of tranquil resignation in the garden of the last chapter where the gentle rays of the winter sun falling on the soft grey countryside and on the crackling frost of the blades of grass underfoot echo the sense of pity, resignation and sorrowful serenity before the advancing cold of death. Here every detail of the outer world is implicated in the experience of suffering human beings, and every detail counts in an art of quiet and very lovely suggestion.

Of everyday objects there is obviously very little: an occasional detail of salon or fireside. Yet they sometimes come to the fore for a moment: precisely when stress of feeling most alienates the human being from them, and gives a startled awareness. Ellénore gazes wildly and blankly at the objects that surround her, after Adolphe's harshest revelation, unable to recognize them in a world dislocated by shock (p. 88). Adolphe in the early chapters feels the threat of familiar things to nerves on edge with suspense, as he hardly dares turn the door-handle and finds in every outer object a potential enemy (pp. 53–4).

In the scenes between the characters, there is a discreet but frequently recalled sense of physical presence. When Ellénore comes to tell Adolphe that she has left the Count, it is 'd'un air à la fois content et timide, cherchant à lire dans mes yeux mon impression' (p. 68). Elsewhere she speaks 'en saisissant mon bras avec une violence qui me fit frémir' (p. 67). When Adolphe tries to tell her he no longer loves her, he feels the icy cold touch of her hand, and hears her words echo in an almost primeval despair: 'seule ... seule ... seule ... fini ... fini ... laissez-moi, quittez-moi' (pp. 88–9). Above all, the importance of Adolphe's voice to Ellénore is recalled at the end: 'cette voix que j'ai tant aimée ... qui retentissait au fond de mon cœur'.[10] The expression of the eyes in particular, without anything strained or symbolic,[11] recurs in key scenes, from the shared glances of gaiety and understanding that mark the beginning of love:

Lorsque j'arrivais, j'apercevais dans les regards d'Ellénore une expression de plaisir. Quand elle s'amusait dans la conversation, ses yeux se tournaient naturellement vers moi (p. 49)

through the uncertain, beseeching or desperate gaze, to the bare fall of the last sentence 'que vous ne daignez plus récompenser d'un regard'.

Constant's expression of mental pain has an individual relationship to the physical world, conditioned in part by the period in
which he is writing. Merely to pick out images of rending, piercing,
stifling, uprooting would be to give a false impression. Expressions
like 'respirer sans peine' or 'une douleur déchirante' had obviously
become accepted counters for abstract states of mind, with little or
no physical meaning. Yet at times Constant's way of using them
connects them with something more directly physical, so that they
take on more than their token value. A language mainly of quiet
dignity and bare precision in the analysis of abstractions can also,
through slight variation and placing of familiar phrases, indicate
other levels of distress. One might take for example three sentences
from Ch. II:

L'impatience me dévorait; à tous les instants je consultais ma montre. J'étais
obligé d'ouvrir la fenêtre pour respirer; mon sang me brûlait en circulant
dans mes veines. (p. 42).

In the first and last, *dévorer* and *brûler* are used in no literal sense. Yet
between them come two gestures in the physical world, and the
effect is to give back something of the physical undertones once
implicit in the other expressions. Mostly, these semi-physical expressions are placed in phrases so brief, or so deliberately devoid of
rhetorical flow, that they can be used without any sense of forcing
the note, and seem sharply adequate. In a passage like this:

J'étais pénétré d'affection, j'étais déchiré de remords.
La difficulté ... la certitude ... je ne sais quelle révolte ... me dévoraient
intérieurement (p. 75)

everything is placed so as to direct attention primarily and centrally
to the complexity of the feelings; the intellect is held taut following
out the relations between affection, remorse, difficulty, certainty and
anger and it is only as a minor accompaniment that the senses of
'pierced', 'torn' and 'eaten away' are conveying a subsidiary suggestive undertone. In this half-abstract, half-physical way, the theme of
stifling and breathing forms a constant undertone to Adolphe's sense
of alternating oppression and escape. It is used no doubt conventionally enough in an early phrase to Ellénore: 'Je cherche en
vain un air qui pénètre dans ma poitrine oppressée' (p. 53), but takes
on a fresh physical force when their love reaches its climax:

Je marchais avec orgueil au milieu des hommes; je promenais sur eux un
regard dominateur. L'air que je respirais était à lui seul une jouissance. (p.
56)[12]

Compressed and stifled for most of the book, Adolphe will experience an intense sense of air and space in the escape of Ch. VII.[13]

Precision and placing – these are perhaps the central qualities in Constant's choice and use of words. When he reads the works of others, one of his first impulses is to pick out and reject the trite or conventional phrase: 'des tours de phrase qui ont été trop souvent employés pour paraître neufs',[14] or those expressions which are at once affected and 'triviales à force d'être usées'; writing of Lucien Bonaparte, he gives examples worthy of Flaubert's Homais or *Dictionnaire des Idées reçues* ('Il ne peut s'endormir sans *se jeter dans les bras du sommeil* . . . Parle-t-il d'une fête: *la folie y agite ses grelots*').[15] Against the sentimental and declamatory effect of many fashionable novels of his time, and the much more intelligent but far from controlled works of Mme de Staël, two of the correspondents most closely associated with him in both life and literature contribute to and show clearly the development of his firm reaction. Mme de Charrière urges simplicity as opposed to the exaggerations of the present day;[16] Julie Talma remarks that 'l'extrême simplicité du style donne peut-être à la vérité une plus grande puissance' or wittily anatomizes weaknesses in Mme de Staël's admired *Delphine*:

Je voudrais aussi que le style fût plus mesuré, qu'il nous laissât quelques instants de repos. C'est une étrange maladresse que de fatiguer du Beau même . . . Comment un esprit supérieur ne sent-il pas le charme de la simplicité . . . Chaque plainte d'une infortunée, quelque éloquente qu'elle soit, diminue l'intérêt qu'elle inspire.[17]

Of Constant's own letters she had written: 'Comment faites-vous pour dire *en une ligne* des choses qui donnent tant à penser et à dire!' When, after her death, Constant sums up Julie's way of writing, he praises a 'naturel, sans emphase ni pédanterie', and a 'style pur, précis, rapide et léger' (p. 843). But perhaps his most telling comment on expression is made to another correspondent, Prosper de Barante:

Le style m'en a plu souvent, on voit que vous sentez plus que vous ne dites, et c'est le premier mérite du style à mon avis.[18]

Precision in the choice of abstract terms is evident on every page of *Adolphe*. But there is also the less immediately obvious precision in the smallest details of speech or letter. After showing in Chapter I how the inexperienced young Adolphe unintentionally provokes conventional society in a small principality, Constant in the last sentence chooses the two expressions which best bring alive the set phrases in which such a society describes him: *un homme immoral, un homme peu sûr,* before pointedly characterizing the undertones: 'deux épithètes heureusement inventées pour insinuer les faits qu'on ignore, et laisser deviner ce qu'on ne sait pas' (p. 28). Or again, the ambiguous tone of Adolphe's letters to Ellénore when he longs to convey the truth, yet fears to hurt, is not simply indicated in general, but given in exact phrases: first 'Je me félicitais quand j'avais pu substituer les mots d'affection, d'amitié, de dévouement, à celui d'amour' (p. 76), then in the still more telling insinuations of 'Je lui marquais vaguement que je serais toujours charmé de la savoir, puis j'ajoutais, de la rendre heureuse' (p. 78).

If the characters are scarcely differentiated from each other in their modes of speech, yet in their conversations strong and subtle contrasts of feeling and tone depend on the choice of words and rhythms – now clipped and cutting: 'Vous croyez sans doute avoir fait beaucoup pour moi; je suis forcé de vous dire que vous vous trompez', now quiet and tender: 'Chère Ellénore ... l'amitié n'a-t-elle pas ses secrets? N'est-elle pas ombrageuse et timide au milieu du bruit et de la foule? ...'; sometimes developed into a resounding and eloquent art of persuasion (whether in Adolphe's appeals to Ellénore at the beginning or in the Count's exhortations at the end); sometimes concentrated into that bare simplicity which is still more persuasive: 'Je suis horriblement malheureux ... je ne veux que vous voir ...'

It is of course in the welding of words into pointed epigrammatic statements that Constant achieves some of his strongest effects.[19] He comments in the *Cahier Rouge*[20] on his 'esprit qui avait une tournure épigrammatique' from his youth. Yet he is well aware of the dangers of epigram and antithesis which, wrongly used, may produce admiration for ingenuity rather than a compelling sense of aptness and insight.[21] In writing of Julie Talma's capacity to generalize incisively, Constant admires the effect of unstrained and natural discovery:

les observations générales qu'elle exprime en une ligne, parce qu'elles se présentaient à elle, et non parce qu'elle les cherchait.

Earlier in this article it has been noted how his own most general aphorisms on human behaviour take on their full point and conviction precisely because they follow so naturally, with an impression of inevitability, from the close analysis of detail.[22]

Constant is master of the concentrated sentence which either nails home months of repetitive experience:

Nous savions si bien . . . ce que nous allions nous dire que nous nous taisions pour ne pas l'entendre (p. 93)

or in a bare passing phrase clinches a basic irony:

Son amour, qu'elle prenait pour le nôtre. (p. 89)

In some of his most piercing phrases he clamps together epigrammatically the paradox of two irreconcilable needs:

J'aurais voulu qu'elle me devinât, mais qu'elle me devinât sans s'affliger (p. 76),

or:

cette vie . . . je l'aurais mille fois donnée pour qu'elle fût heureuse sans moi (p. 75)

or exposes another type of sorrowful paradox:

Nous parlions d'amour de peur de nous parler d'autre chose (p. 73)

or:

Je me reposais, pour ainsi dire, dans l'indifférence des autres, de la fatigue de son amour. (p. 77)

The expected or the possible are reversed, but in expression and context there is nothing to give an effect of clever affectation; rather a concise and sardonic insight into the workings of human illogic.

Perhaps the core of Constant's achievement lies in the particularly suggestive construction of certain of his most insinuating phrases. The Baron de T., exercising persuasion on Adolphe, might have been expected to say: 'Ellénore is an obstacle between you and your career.' Constant's phrase achieves a quite different effect:

Vous êtes fait pour aller à tout: [*encouragement and temptation*], mais souvenez-vous bien [*pause for admonition*] qu'il y a, entre vous et tous les genres de succès, un obstacle insurmontable [*suspense, and absolute expression balancing the* 'aller à tout'], et que cet obstacle [*renewed suspense*] est Ellénore. (p. 100)

The words themselves are simple enough, but their precision, choice and placing carry brilliantly the flattery, the hesitation and the final devastating thrust, leaving the last phrase to echo in Adolphe's mind as it does some pages later. Still more central and suggestive to the whole meaning of the book is the sentence in which Adolphe tries to tell Ellénore that he no longer loves her. Instead of the straightforward 'je ne vous aime plus', something very different is constructed. The very concept of the word 'love' makes Adolphe pause, as always, to search for a definition of what it can mean and of why his persistent affection differs from that momentary delight involving forgetfulness of both calculation and commitment, of both egoistic practicality and social duty. He pauses again on her name, which sounds as a last appeal to shared understanding, postpones until it can be put off no longer the fact that must at last be stated, then is forced to it in the shortest words of all:

Mais l'amour, ce transport des sens, cette ivresse involontaire, cet oubli de tous les intérêts, de tous les devoirs, Ellénore, je ne l'ai plus. (p. 88)

A key word among critics defining the particular tone of *Adolphe* has been aridity (and Constant himself provided it in the 'même aux cœurs arides' of his Preface): aridity of both feeling and expression. On the side of feeling, however biting Constant's analyses, their function is not to blot out the emotions, but rather, sometimes quietly and allusively, sometimes directly and forcefully, to stress their intensity and individuality. Of his youth Adolphe writes:

Je ne demandais alors qu'à me livrer à ces impressions primitives et fougueuses qui jettent l'âme hors de la sphère commune,

and:

Je portais au fond de mon cœur un besoin de sensibilité dont je ne m'apercevais pas. (pp. 20 and 22)

The intense pain of frustration or of suspense is given incisive expression:

Je ne concevais rien à la douleur violente, indomptable, qui déchirait mon cœur; (p. 40)
J'avais la fièvre de la crainte de ne pas la voir; (p. 42)
Je n'avais jamais éprouvé de contraction si violente. (p. 44)

The 'magie' and 'enchantement' of an all-absorbing experience of shared passion are conveyed not only in the 'Charme de l'amour' passage of Chapter IV, with its 'gaieté folâtre', 'valeur attachée aux moindres circonstances', 'plaisir', 'espoir', 'intelligence mutuelle' (p. 57), but in the earlier passage from Chapter III where Ellénore is asked to tell again and again the stages by which her love grew (p. 51). The gradual death of love is shown in scenes briefly suggesting a Racinian intensity:

Une fureur insensée s'empara de nous: tout ménagement fut abjuré, toute délicatesse oubliée. On eût dit que nous étions poussés l'un contre l'autre par des furies. Tout ce que la haine la plus implacable avait inventé contre nous, nous nous l'appliquions mutuellement, et ces deux êtres malheureux qui seuls se connaissaient sur la terre, qui seuls pouvaient se rendre justice, se comprendre et se consoler, semblaient deux ennemis irréconciliables, acharnés à se déchirer. (p. 80, see also p. 121)

Even here, in the very violence of their battle, the strength and persistence of their feeling for each other is made ineradicable.

If strength of vocabulary or balance of phrase make for one kind of conviction of feeling, another is still more subtly conveyed by softly suggestive sentences which do not define but with a quiet music imply prolonged undertones of delight or pain; for delight:

ces heures rapides, dont tous les détails échappent au souvenir par leur douceur même, et qui ne laissent dans notre âme qu'une longue trace de bonheur; (p. 57)

for pain: 'nos cœurs défiants et blessés ne se recontraient plus' (p. 93) or 'la source des longs entretiens était tarie' (p. 114). And if the physical world is one of grey plains and wintry landscape, it too is something other than arid in the discreet, sharp and gently musical touches that bring it alive:

Le ciel était serein; mais les arbres étaient sans feuilles; ... tout était immobile, et le seul bruit qui se fit entendre était celui de l'herbe glacée qui se brisait sous nos pas. (p. 136)

Adolphe may convey a note of desolation, but neither feeling nor words are fundamentally arid; the very discretion in expression heightens the strength and complexity of experience.

Mistrust of words as general terms was one of the origins of *Adolphe*. Ability to investigate, through the imaginative creation of chosen detail in human lives, the complexities that lie behind these shifting counters, and to offer a sharp definition or a piercing question on human values, marks the achievement of this work. Here I have picked out only a few sides. It probes, with language which is precise and subtle, into the mingling of exasperation and tenderness, mobility and permanence, self-seeking and self-sacrifice which compose many long-standing relationships, into the difficulty of deciding which motives are the real and which the rationalized, yet posits the ineradicable need, beneath complexity of experience and uncertainty of words, for self-knowledge, self-judgment and exact expression.

NOTES

1 Page references throughout this article will be, for *Adolphe*, to the Garnier edition, ed. J.-H. Bornecque, 1955, and, for the other main works, to the Pléiade edition, ed. A. Roulin, 1957.

   I raise further points regarding the art of *Adolphe* in two other articles: 'The Stylisation of experience' (see above, pp. 3–27) and 'Creation of character' (see above pp. 28–42). These will be referred to below as Art. I and Art. II.

2 J. Mistler in *Bibliothèque mondiale*, 15/6/53, pp. 8–11. Cf. recently C. J. Greshoff in *Forum for Modern Language Studies*, January 1965, p. 35: 'there is not one description in the entire novel.' The opposite extreme: 'Adolphe annonce plus Balzac que le roman «psychologique»' is suggested by Raymond Queneau in a light article without much substantiation ('Sur *Adolphe* et la Vie de Benjamin Constant' in the edition of *Adolphe* and other works, Éditions d'art Lucien Mazenod, pp. 213–22). J. Hytier in *Les Romans de l'Individu* (Les Arts et le livre, 1928, p. 29) briefly shows how mistaken were Bourget's remarks on the absence of background, of the physical, and particularly of dialogue.

3 The last and strangest example of the theme of how feeling is galvanized by fear of loss, discussed in Art. I. On time and impermanence in *Adolphe*, see of course the excellent article of G. Poulet in *Études sur le Temps humain*, Plon, 1950.

4 These carefully worked-out details, which do not usually correspond to time-sequences in Constant's own life, fit coherently together; cp. the slips in chronology which have been unearthed in for example *Mme Bovary*.

5 Here I disagree with part of the interesting article of P. Deguise (*Revue des sciences humaines*, 1956, pp. 125–51: '*Adolphe* et les *Journaux intimes* de Benjamin Constant') who (p. 139) sees in the narrative sudden leaps rather than evolution, and of the phrase 'Bientôt elle m'avoua qu'elle m'aimait' remarks 'C'est aller un peu vite, même pour un analyste du cœur.' In Art. II I analyse briefly the different weapons of persuasion used by Adolphe to win Ellénore: each detail of conversation, letter, social gathering brings out the gradual movement of her mind and feelings, fully motivating the climax given in one sharp sentence.

6 The pages between the admission of love and its fulfilment would also be worth analysis for the detail of their restless frustration leading to almost a paroxysm of worship, and for their expression of the age-old lament 'Et si je vous avais connu plus tôt . . .' If that lament is particularly often voiced in Constant's letters to Anna Lindsay, it is a basic human reaction to the circumstances, with many possibilities of irony. Flaubert will give his own treatment to its obligatory recurrences in *Mme Bovary*. For a further discussion of the opening to Chapter VI see Art. I, p. 12.

7 One is reminded of Baudelaire's brilliant treatment of the fourth woman in 'Portraits de Maîtresses' (*Petits Poèmes en Prose*, XLII) where every detail overtly constructs and stresses the woman's perfection, while each detail of that perfection, so unreproachfully reproaching, leads logically to the climax where love has become a 'cauchemar accablant' and to

the sardonic account of her murder. Mme de Charrière's *Mistriss Henley* (read of course by Constant) wittily shows the destruction of a consciously imperfect wife by an all-too-perfect husband.

8 Constantly at issue is the question: what then is the difference between feeling that one loves and 'really' loving? (See Art. I.) This question is to be central in Nerval, who several times shows that *Adolphe* was one of the books which haunted him (see below, pp. 88–90, 287 n. 12, 293).

9 Other authors have noticed the strange resurgence of forgotten memories when strain is followed by a moment of relief. One thinks of the scraps of song that float in Julien Sorel's mind in prison. In *Adolphe* the thought of childhood is logically connected with his meditations, but the sudden sharpness of the detailed vision goes beyond a logical calling-up of voluntary memories.

10 One recalls many passages from *Journaux* and letters on the physical impact of Mme de Staël's grief 'comme sortie de dessous terre'. Constant writes of 'je ne sais quelle faiblesse du cœur qui me rend toujours susceptible d'émotion à la voix d'un être que j'ai aimé' (p. 438; here again it is the intensity of a retrospective emotion). See also pp. 184, 231, and, in the letters to Rosalie (ed. A. & S. Roulin, Gallimard, 1955), p. 36.

11 P. Deguise, art. cit., p. 147, possibly overstrains his interpretation of certain details to make them fit a Sartrean framework where the analogies, of general interest, do not always seem applicable to the individual instances cited.

12 After completing this article, I read Norman J. Shapiro's note on 'The Symmetry of Benjamin Constant's *Adolphe*' in *The French Review*, December 1960, pp. 186–8. He discusses how, in two key passages, Constant uses the theme of breathing to convey the 'high and low points of his spiritual adventure'. There is also a note on how it is Ellénore who gives Adolphe a sense of identity and meaning.

13 A critic reviewing *Adolphe* in the *Constitutionnel* in 1816 remarked that 'l'un des secrets du langage *romantique* est de rapporter ce qu'ils appellent «les phénomènes du monde intellectuel» aux «phénomènes du monde visible»', and attacked Constant for some of his 'romantic' images. Several other articles of the day attack him for affectation and strangeness of style; often it is obvious that political or moral considerations have dictated objection at all costs, but some remarks on details of language are interesting. See E. Eggli and P. Martino, *Le Débat romantique en France*, 1933, Vol. I. Some extracts from this are given in the Bornecque edition of *Adolphe*, and a fuller selection in C. Cordié's edition, Naples, 1963.

14 *Lettres à sa Famille*, ed. Menos, Stock, 1932, p. 158.

15 *Mémoires de Mme Récamier*, in *Œuvres*, p. 975. For other examples of criticism of 'tournures trop usées' see *Journaux*, p. 326 ('le tourbillon des plaisirs' etc.).

16 See a letter quoted in G. de Pourtalès, *De Hamlet à Swann*, Crès, 1924, p. 149: 'Aujourd'hui la langue s'abâtardit. ... Tout est gigantesque à la fois et mesquin. La boursouflure et la trivialité se succèdent ...' Her own skill with words would be worth study.

17 *Lettres de Julie Talma à Benjamin Constant*, publiées par la Baronne Constant de Rebecque, Paris, Plon 1933, pp. 102, 104, 150. These letters are not only among the most interesting background documents to Constant, but a work of literary value in its own right. Constant himself called Julie Talma 'l'esprit le plus analogue au mien'.

18 *Revue des Deux Mondes*, 1906, XXXIV, p. 258. There are of course in *Adolphe* occasional sentences where, when he is stressing rather than analysing feeling, a declamatory phrase in the style of his day remains ('Je la vis se lever pâle et prophétique'; 'j'arrosais de mes larmes le pied des arbres'; 'une lave brûlante qui, tombant goutte à goutte sur mon cœur, m'arrachait des cris'). But these are rare, and see Art. I on how he has modified the often violent expressions of the diaries to achieve the quiet intensity of the novel.

19 Comparisons with La Rochefoucauld have often been drawn. To those already made by others might be added the bitter summing up of how age looks back at the disillusionment of youth: 'Nous ne sommes plus surpris alors que de notre ancienne surprise' (p. 27) – cf. La Rochefoucauld: 'Il ne faudrait s'étonner que de pouvoir encore s'étonner.' The parallels are those of similar minds rather than any direct debt.

20 *Œuvres*, pp. 129 and 132.

21 See *Lettre sur Julie*, in *Œuvres*, p. 843, on the disadvantages of the epigram in conversation, and *Journaux*, p. 382, on La Harpe's abuse of antithesis.

22 Some of the most telling generalizations in the novel recur, with slight variations of expression, in very different works of Constant. To trace these is to realize their importance to his thought as a whole, the care he gave to their formulation, and the skill with which they have been integrated into the detail of narrative. The following are some examples: *Adolphe*, p. 6, 'les sots font de leur morale ...' – cf. article on Mme de Staël, p. 868. *Adolphe*, p. 30, 'la parole, toujours trop grossière ...' – Cf. *De la Religion*, p. 1415 (and see Art. I for other references). *Adolphe*, p. 34, 'des préjugés en sens inverse de son intérêt' – Cf. *Journaux*, p. 344. *Adolphe*, p. 59, 'but ... lien ...' Cf. *Lettre sur Julie*, pp. 844–5. *Adolphe*, p. 9, 'le sanctuaire intime de ma pensée ...' Cf. *De l'Esprit de Conquête*, p. 1039.

4

Constant romancier:
le problème de l'expression (1968)[1]

La difficulté que j'éprouve à parler immédiatement après la communication si riche de M. Poulet[2] n'est pas sans rapport avec le sujet que je voudrais traiter ce matin.

Qui d'entre nous n'aurait pas voulu à ses heures établir entre les cerveaux humains un moyen de communication électronique qui se passerait des mots, ces outils qui tantôt manquent de précision, tantôt imposent aux complexités de notre expérience une précision fausse et simplificatrice? En tant que moyen de communication entre les hommes, les mots portent nécessairement sur ce qu'il y a de plus général dans l'expérience: comment leur faire atteindre la particularité de toute vie individuelle? Si ce problème existe pour tout grand écrivain, Constant en est particulièrement conscient. Devant sa propre conduite, d'ailleurs, sa famille, ses amis et lui-même ne cessent de prononcer, ahuris, le terme qui, à l'époque, portait une nuance fort péjorative: «bizarre», «bizarrerie». Baser un roman sur l'analyse de réactions que d'autres risquent de trouver presque inconcevables, et cela à une époque où le vocabulaire pour qualifier sentiments ou jugements reste en grande partie abstrait et traditionnel, cette entreprise comporte pour un esprit subtil de sérieux problèmes. Je me propose aujourd'hui de suggérer brièvement quelques aspects seulement de la victoire artistique remportée par Constant aux prises avec ce dilemme.[3]

D'abord, quatre exemples de ses réactions contre ces catégories verbales qui, de différentes façons, faussent la réalité de nos sentiments ou de nos idées. Le premier, vu à travers le prisme de l'humour. Au jeune Constant du *Cahier Rouge*, la brave Mme Trevor offre ce qu'elle appelle «la plus tendre amitié»: lui de «[se] rouler par terre et [se] frapper la tête contre la muraille sur ce malheureux mot d'amitié» là où il aurait voulu «amour», et de laisser la dame, après quatre heures, «très ennuyée d'un amant qui *disputait sur un synonyme*» (p. 130).

Le second, d'ordre stylistique: dans les *Fragments des Mémoires de Mme Récamier*, nous notons la joie avec laquelle Constant s'attaque aux clichés:

expressions qui sont triviales à force d'être usées. Il [Lucien Bonaparte] ne peut s'endormir sans *se jeter dans les bras du sommeil* ... Parle-t-il d'une fête, *la folie y agite ses grelots*.[4]

Dommage peut-être que Constant ne se soit pas essayé au genre de roman où il aurait pu créer son propre Homais avant la lettre. (Entre parenthèses, un des charmes d'Ellénore, c'est la gracieuse imperfection avec laquelle, en tant qu'étrangère, elle parle français, car «les idiomes étrangers rajeunissent les pensées et les débarrassent de ces tournures qui les font paraître tour à tour communes et affectées». Puisse la même indulgence m'être accordée.)

Troisième exemple, d'ordre psychologique, caractérisant avec finesse chez le père d'Adolphe, et chez le narrateur lui-même

la timidité, cette souffrance intérieure ... qui glace nos paroles, qui dénature dans notre bouche tout ce que nous essayons de dire, et ne nous permet de nous exprimer que par des mots vagues ou une ironie plus ou moins amère, comme si nous voulions nous venger sur nos sentiments mêmes de la douleur que nous éprouvons à ne pouvoir les faire connaître.

Quatrième et dernier exemple, remarque d'une portée plus générale, encore au début d'*Adolphe*, où le héros éprouve

une insurmontable aversion pour toutes les maximes communes et pour toutes les formules dogmatiques ... ces axiomes généraux si exempts de toute restriction, si purs de toute nuance.

Maximes et formules sans restriction et sans nuance: cela nous amène à une des phrases les plus essentielles du roman:

Les sentiments de l'homme sont confus et mélangés: ils se composent d'une multitude d'impressions variées qui échappent à l'observation; et la parole, toujours trop grossière et trop générale, peut bien servir à les désigner mais ne sert jamais à les définir,

phrase qui trouve son écho dans *De la Religion*:

Tous nos sentiments intimes semblent se jouer des efforts du langage: la parole rebelle, par cela seul qu'elle généralise ce qu'elle exprime, sert à désigner, à distinguer, plutôt qu'à définir[5]

et dans les *Principes de Politique*:

Je demanderais comment on définit avec précision cette partie vague et profonde de nos sensations morales, qui par sa nature même défie tous les efforts du langage.[6]

Entre ces trois phrases, notons que c'est celle d'*Adolphe* qui, par un heureux paradoxe, met le plus de précision, de concision, de force et de forme équilibrée à exprimer l'impossibilité d'atteindre les qualités mêmes dont elle fait preuve.

Mais quelles sont, pour l'originalité de Constant romancier, les conséquences de ces variations sur le thème de l'insuffisance des mots? Je n'en indiquerai pour l'instant que les deux principales.

D'abord, la constatation, à travers les détails d'expériences personnelles, du danger des mots – thème qui court comme un refrain à travers *Adolphe* et reparaît parfois en sourdine dans *Cécile*. Triple danger. A la pleine complexité et aux libres possibilités de développement que retiennent des sentiments encore informulés, les mots imposent par leur nature d'instruments généralisants un choix et une simplification, figeant, rendant rigide et irrévocable ce qui aurait pu contenir de tout autres possibilités. D'un côté se manifeste l'auto-hypnotisme qui crée, par l'effet de l'expression, des sentiments factices mais envahissants: pour Adolphe,

échauffé que j'étais par mon propre style, je ressentais, en finissant d'écrire ...

pour Ellénore:

ces simples paroles, démenties par tant de paroles précédentes, rendirent à Ellénore la vie et la confiance

(et même elle éprouve une pathétique consolation en entendant répéter par d'autres «des expressions que depuis longtemps je ne prononçais plus»); pour l'homme en général:

Nous sommes des créatures tellement mobiles que les sentiments que nous feignons, nous finissons par les éprouver.

Mais si les mots tissent de façon perfide leurs fausses créations, ils deviennent aussi, en n'exprimant encore qu'une partie de la vérité complexe, l'instrument d'une destruction irrévocable:

Nous avions prononcé tous deux des mots irréparables; nous pouvions nous taire, mais non les oublier.

Quand Ellénore, dans un moment de lucidité incomplète et tragique, définit le sentiment d'Adolphe comme étant non pas l'amour mais la pitié, Adolphe de se demander: «Pourquoi prononça-t-elle ces mots?»; quand lui-même essaie de définir devant une amie une partie de ce qu'il éprouve, cette formulation même constitue encore un «pas irréparable».

Et dans *Cécile,* comme dans les lettres d'Adolphe pendant l'absence d'Ellénore, se voit une troisième perfidie: en vain essaie-t-on de se servir de mots persuasifs pour déguiser sa pensée, sous les mots traîtres s'insinue ce qu'on cache. Pour se ménager encore quelques mois avec Mme de Malbée, le narrateur tâche de convaincre Cécile de la nécessité d'un délai dans leurs projets de mariage; étant donné les nécessités pratiques du divorce, ce qu'il dit est d'une logique inattaquable, mais:

mon langage se ressentit de ma pensée secrète, et Cécile lut facilement au fond de mon âme.

Dangers multiples, donc, des mots pour les personnages. Mais, seconde conséquence, et encore plus importante pour ce qui est de l'effet esthétique, danger des termes généraux qui serviraient de résumé ou de jugement de la part de l'auteur ou du lecteur. Quelle serait la vérité insaisissable cachée sous des termes comme «amour», «faiblesse», «vanité», «volonté»? De ces abstractions, certes, Constant se sert souvent, mais rien de plus fallacieux que d'arracher à son contexte une formule en apparence absolue, telle: «Je n'étais qu'un homme faible, reconnaissant et dominé.» L'art du roman consiste d'abord à mettre perpétuellement en doute, à travers un savant contrepoint de réactions variées, la validité de ces jugements tranchants. La phrase: «Je n'étais qu'un homme faible» se trouve cernée par la réaction d'une amie: «elle vit de la générosité dans ce que j'appelais faiblesse», ou par les observations de la préface:

s'ils veulent dompter *ce que par habitude ils nomment faiblesse* ... ils froissent ce qu'il y a de généreux, ils brisent ce qu'il y a de fidèle, ils tuent ce qu'il y a de bon.

Surtout, le roman entier est construit exprès de façon à rendre impossibles des jugements ou des catégories simplistes. Toutes les nuances contradictoires de lettres, de conversations, d'intentions et d'actions sont agencées de façon à demander impérativement au lecteur une nouvelle prise de conscience à l'égard des catégories en apparence les plus simples.

Tomber amoureux: concept apparemment clair, et pourtant quelles sont les proportions de satisfaction, d'amour-propre, d'émulation devant les stéréotypes idéalistes ou cyniques que nous lèguent nos prédécesseurs ou nos contemporains, de subtils calculs de séducteur attitré et de soudaines gaucheries de novice, de galvanisme par l'obstacle et de «sincère besoin de sensibilité», d'ahurissement devant l'illogique, les douleurs et les terreurs incontestables qu'apportent les «intermittences du cœur», et d'extase devant les moments exceptionnels analysés avec une finesse toute particulière au début du quatrième chapitre?

Décristallisation de l'amour: mais les origines de cette lente décristallisation naissent imperceptiblement de l'entente même entre les deux amants, du dévouement d'Ellénore et de la crainte chez Adolphe de «la douleur que l'on cause», partagé qu'il est entre un âcre besoin d'indépendance, avec ses ambitions en même temps nobles et égoïstes, et l'impossibilité de déraciner la vive tendresse résultant d'années partagées: tendresse qui comporte une pitié pour l'autre également intellectuelle, affective et physique.

Faiblesse du héros? Ses actions sont pourtant décisives: il se bat en duel, ou part sans hésiter s'il s'agit de protéger Ellénore menacée. S'il ne peut lui infliger la rupture finale, c'est que trois éléments de son être le plus profond s'y refusent: réactions physiques devant la stupeur de sa douleur à elle; «mémoire du cœur» qui conserve tout ce qui les a liés ensemble; intelligence qui en appelle à la justice en reconnaissant les droits conférés par les sacrifices qu'elle a faits (mais qui, en contrepoint ironique, rappelle ses sacrifices à lui).[7]

A la fin de chaque analyse pourrait donc figurer la phrase lapidaire:

Il n'y a point d'unité complète dans l'homme, et presque jamais personne n'est tout à fait sincère ni tout à fait de mauvaise foi.

Et de cette constatation naissent certaines conséquences pour le style de Constant romancier. D'abord la subtilité de son art d'insinuation. Pour glisser le doute dans une affirmation où subsiste pourtant toute la force apparente d'une expérience instantanée, un seul verbe peut suffire:

L'amour, qu'une heure auparavant je m'applaudissais de feindre, *je crus* tout à coup l'éprouver avec fureur.

L'insertion ironique d'une expression qui normalement indiquerait une sincérité totale peut porter les mêmes indications:

Je me sentais, de la meilleure foi du monde, véritablement amoureux.

Seconde conséquence: Constant se sert rarement d'un terme

abstrait sans y ajouter presque imperceptiblement une analyse des qualités que comporterait pour lui une définition du mot (comme Pascal, il voudrait adopter la méthode idéale – accompagner la définition du défini). La phrase: «L'amour était rentré tout entier dans mon âme» se prolonge pour trouver sa définition:

J'étais fier de la protéger. J'étais avide de la tenir dans mes bras. J'éprouvais une fièvre de tête, de cœur, de sens.

Et – exemple des plus suggestifs pour la définition de l'amour qui sous-tend la texture du roman – au moment où Adolphe essaie de dire à Ellénore que tout est fini, au lieu de constater un fait simple, il s'arrête, en même temps devant la complexité du fait et devant la douleur humaine, pour rechercher une définition précise de cette entité subtile dont l'essentiel s'est peu à peu perdu:

Mais l'amour, ce transport des sens, cette ivresse involontaire, cet oubli de tous les intérêts, de tous les devoirs, Ellénore, je ne l'ai plus.

Du même sentiment, d'autres définitions pourraient exister: la précision de celle-ci servira de souveraine explication (mais pour Adolphe l'explication n'est jamais confondue avec l'excuse).

Après avoir montré ce qui est pour Constant l'insuffisance des mots, je viens pourtant de parler de la précision d'une définition. Et il serait temps de voir l'autre face de son art. Si peu d'auteurs se sont à ce point méfiés des généralisations et des jugements absolus imposés par les catégories ou les étiquettes conventionnelles, pourtant aucun romancier peut-être n'a été plus irrésistiblement attiré vers l'art de la maxime, vers le plaisir esthétique de formules équilibrées, concises, précises, épigrammatiques, ni ne s'est senti plus hanté par le besoin de prononcer un jugement sur les phénomènes qu'il dissèque.[5] L'art original d'*Adolphe* est basé sur la tension et l'équilibre entre deux impulsions également intenses: l'une attirant l'auteur vers ce qui, dans la nature de l'homme, est indéfinissable, «ondoyant» (mot qu'il affectionne), illogique; l'autre réclamant de façon péremptoire la satisfaction intellectuelle et esthétique que fournit le «don de la formule».

Ces deux exigences se réunissent pour former une technique dont l'apparente simplicité dans la narration mériterait une analyse plus serrée que ne le permettent les limites d'une courte communication. Les événements et les faits sont racontés avec une brièveté qui tient du tour de force:

Nous nous battîmes; je le blessai dangereusement, je fus blessé moi-même.

ou «Elle se donna enfin tout entière». Ce qui compte, c'est le détail infiniment complexe des causes et des conséquences de ces faits et de ces actions. Là il y a une étonnante variété (d'autant plus étonnante dans un roman limité à une centaine de pages, d'atmosphère «classique») dans les ressources stylistiques qui sont déployées avec une concision subtile: lettres et conversations, gestes physiques et analyses abstraites, figurent tantôt en style direct, tantôt par le résumé du ton essentiel. C'est seulement en guise de conclusion, après les détails vivants de scènes entre des individus, que figure le prolongement sous forme épigrammatique résumant ces débats d'êtres ulcérés:

Nous avions prononcé des mots irréparables; nous pouvions nous taire, mais non les oublier.

L'aphorisme final, riche de conséquences pour l'homme en général, suit avec une logique imperceptible et inéluctable:

Il y a des choses qu'on est longtemps sans se dire, mais quand une fois elles sont dites, on ne cesse jamais de les répéter.

Ces maximes prennent leur force du fait qu'elles s'intègrent si naturellement dans des tourments d'individus. De par leur concision et leur équilibre ironique elles unissent un aperçu pénétrant sur ce qu'il y a de foncièrement illogique ou d'insaisissable dans la conduite humaine, avec la seule et souveraine victoire sur le plan artistique: celle de cerner et d'exprimer d'une façon lapidaire ce qu'il y a de possibilités, soit tragiques, soit comiques, soit troublantes et suggestives dans les complexités de nos réactions. De courtes phrases concentrent l'amertume et le paradoxe de besoins irréconciliables:

j'aurais voulu qu'elle me devinât, mais qu'elle devinât sans s'affliger,

de désirs foncièrement illogiques mais obsédants:

cette vie … je l'aurais mille fois donnée pour qu'elle fût heureuse sans moi,

ou d'un renversement ironique des réactions traditionnelles:

je me reposais, pour ainsi dire, dans l'indifférence des autres, de la fatigue de son amour.

Et la plus courte de toutes est peut-être la plus poignante: «Son amour qu'elle prenait pour le nôtre.»

A chaque aphorisme analytique font inéluctablement pendant les détails choisis qui l'individualisent. Adolphe ne caractérise pas simplement en termes abstraits le «langage embarrassé» de ses lettres pendant l'absence d'Ellénore, où il désirerait et pourtant craindrait qu'elle comprenne son refroidissement; il rend son embarras à lui dans le détail de ses expressions:

Je lui marquais vaguement que je serais toujours charmé de la savoir, puis j'ajoutais, de la rendre heureuse.

L'amertume du père affectueux ou l'habileté du diplomate plein de bon sens pratique mais borné du côté des sentiments trouvent dans les lettres du premier et dans les éloquentes conversations et les fertiles manœuvres de l'autre une existence complexe, authentique et suggestive.

Quant au langage du narrateur lui-même, on a peut-être eu trop tendance à lui imposer la catégorie simpliste qui tombe sous les vocables «sécheresse, aridité». L'unité de ton de ce très court roman comporte cependant toute une gamme de variations sous-jacentes: une ironie dont la virulence touche exprès à la plus haute comédie:

Je tâchai, par un effort bizarre, de l'attendrir sur le malheur que j'éprouvais en restant près d'elle;

une tristesse sourde et pleine de tendresse:

nos cœurs défiants et blessés ne se rencontraient plus;

un sens indéracinable de la persistance entre deux êtres humains, qui ont partagé de longues années, d'une «espèce de mémoire du cœur»; une férocité toute racinienne pour caractériser ce que ces deux êtres sont capables de s'infliger l'un à l'autre de souffrances atroces; la tranquillité mélancolique des moments de répit et d'expansion (Adolphe la nuit dans la campagne, ou Ellénore dans la délicate scène où le soleil d'hiver tombe comme un symbole de résignation sur les brins d'herbe glacés qui craquent sous les pieds des deux personnages, liés par le regret, les souvenirs et la pitié qu'ils ont l'un de l'autre). Et s'il n'y a aucune sécheresse dans les passages qui soulignent leurs souffrances, il y a une puissance toute particulière dans l'art de la suggestion au moment où est évoqué leur bonheur:

ce heures rapides, dont tous les détails échappent au souvenir par leur douceur même, et qui ne laissent dans notre âme qu'une longue trace de bonheur.

J'ai très peu cité *Cécile*, où les questions de technique me paraissent tout autres.[8] Dans *Adolphe*, Constant a décanté, à partir d'hésitations pathologiques qui ont leurs origines dans sa biographie, des éléments qui, tout en s'individualisant de par une logique imaginative et esthétique, atteignent à une portée très générale. Dans *Cécile*, malgré tout ce qu'il omet des complexités de son expérience personnelle, les deux femmes qu'il voudrait analyser sont chacune exceptionnelle: Mme de Malbée en tant que phénomène intellectuel et dans ses exigences affectives, Cécile en tant que Grisélidis éternellement soumise, «patience on a monument». Nous suivons les péripéties de cette histoire, analyse intelligente et passionnante de certains aspects d'un étrange fait réel; nous n'y accordons pas le même élément d'identification instinctive que suscite *Adolphe*. Dans *Cécile*, d'ailleurs, la simple narration des événements semble prendre souvent le pas et sur la représentation de scènes où seraient individualisés les personnages, et sur la technique d'élargissement par des aphorismes. Dans *Adolphe*, maximes d'une portée générale (mais intimement imbriquées dans l'histoire de deux individus) à toutes les pages: dans *Cécile*, absence presque totale de cette impulsion généralisatrice.

Mon point de départ a été la façon dont Constant se rend compte de l'insuffisance des mots pour quiconque voudrait exprimer la complexité des sentiments humains. C'est en même temps en se méfiant de ces outils si facilement traîtres, et en cherchant à leur faire exprimer avec une nouvelle précision des problèmes d'une portée générale qu'il a remporté sa victoire la plus éclatante. Victoire qui demanderait une analyse stylistique systématique et serrée, que je n'ai pas essayé de faire aujourd'hui. Victoire qui en appelle finalement à la pénétration du lecteur, capable de saisir bien des nuances. Comme disait Constant lui-même à Prosper de Barante:

On voit que vous sentez plus que vous ne dites, et c'est le premier mérite du style à mon avis.[9]

Ce sera peut-être toujours et le défaut et le mérite des amis de Constant que de sentir plus de choses qu'ils n'en sauraient exprimer.

NOTES

1 Texte d'une communication faite au congrès de Lausanne et publiée dans *Benjamin Constant. Actes du congrès de Lausanne* (octobre 1967), Genève: Droz, 1968, pp. 161–69.
2 Voir les *Actes du congrès de Lausanne*, pp. 153–9.

3 Ne voulant pas alourdir d'un appareil de notes la présente contribution, destinée à fournir une très simple offrande à l'occasion du deuxième centenaire, je signale au lecteur trois articles que j'ai publiés en anglais, où se trouvent des précisions bibliographiques sur les critiques précédentes et des développements plus détaillés sur les problèmes esquissés ici (voir ci-dessus pp. 3–60).

Les références que je donne ici se rapportent (sauf autre indication) à l'édition de la Pléiade: Benjamin Constant: *Œuvres*, Texte présenté et annoté par Alfred Roulin, 1957.

— Dans les citations, sauf celle du quatrième paragraphe, c'est moi qui souligne et qui abrège.

4 Voir aussi *Lettres à sa Famille*, ed. J. Menos, Stock, 1932, pp. 158, 242–243.

5 p. 1415.

6 p. 1220.

7 P. Deguise, dans son excellent article: «*Adolphe* et les *Journaux intimes* de Benjamin Constant», *Revue des Sciences humaines*, 21, 1956, pp. 125–51, a déjà caractérisé d'autres aspects de cette même dualité chez Constant.

8 La communication de Frank Bowman hier était d'ailleurs, comme je m'y attendais, si riche de suggestions qu'elle provoquera sans doute des discussions et des réflexions fort utiles (voir les *Actes du congrès de Lausanne*, pp. 97–108).

9 *Revue des Deux Mondes*, 1906, XXXIV, p. 258.

5

L'Individu et l'ordre social
dans *Adolphe* (1968)

Dans *Adolphe*, ce miracle de concision, de clarté et de complexité,
Constant choisit exprès la situation tragique par excellence – celle
où il n'y a pas de solution:

Sa position et celle d'Ellénore étaient sans ressource, et c'est précisément ce
que j'ai voulu.

Devant ces situations sans issue, comme l'a noté Flaubert, le
lecteur aura pourtant toujours tendance à se demander: «à qui la
faute?» Le roman sera-t-il simplement l'analyse des défauts
tragiques de deux individus, l'exposé des insuffisances d'une
situation sociale à une époque donnée, ou la constatation de
l'éternelle insuffisance de la nature des choses? Dans *Adolphe* ces trois
aspects, étroitement imbriqués l'un dans l'autre, trouvent un
équilibre particulièrement subtil.

Pour l'instant je me propose d'isoler l'élément social. Dans ses
Réflexions sur la Tragédie Constant notera que:

l'ordre social, l'action de la société sur l'individu ... ce réseau d'institutions
et de conventions qui nous enveloppe dès notre naissance ... sont tout à fait
équivalents à la fatalité des anciens ... Notre public sera plus ému de ce
combat de l'individu contre l'ordre social qui le dépouille ou qui le garrotte,
que d'Œdipe poursuivi par le Destin ou d'Oreste par les Furies (pp. 952–
3).[1]

«Les conventions, l'ordre social qui le dépouille ou qui le
garrotte»: le début d'*Adolphe* fait vivre ce problème à travers un
individu, un jeune homme sur le seuil de sa carrière. Là où trop de
contemporains ou de successeurs ne feront qu'affirmer en vagues
termes lyriques la supériorité d'un héros en lutte avec la société,
Constant analyse de près les origines d'un malaise. Recul d'abord
purement instinctif devant la suffisance de ceux qui ne se sont jamais
posé de questions sur leurs croyances simplistes:

Lors donc que j'entendais la médiocrité disserter avec complaisance sur des principes bien établis, bien incontestables ... je me sentais poussé à la contredire, non que j'eusse adopté des opinions opposées, mais parce que j'étais impatienté d'une conviction si ferme et si lourde.[2]

Refus intellectuel de l'amalgame illogique et réconfortant d'éléments hétéroclites dont est composée la morale conventionnelle:

des principes bien établis, bien incontestables en fait de morale, de convenances ou de religion, choses qu'elle [la médiocrité] met volontiers sur la même ligne ... Les sots font de leur morale une masse compacte et indivisible, pour qu'elle se mêle le moins possible avec leurs actions, et les laisse libres dans tous les détails.

Critique donc et des idées reçues et des expressions usées:

J'avais contracté ... une insurmontable aversion pour toutes les maximes communes et pour toutes les formules dogmatiques.

Au cœur du roman sera le thème que les jugements d'autrui, soit bien intentionnés, soit malveillants, ne réussiront jamais à pénétrer jusqu'à la vérité complexe de réactions et de mobiles individuels. Constant a noté ailleurs que le chœur des tragédies anciennes est remplacé dans la tragédie allemande de son temps par «une quantité de personnages subalternes» destinés à représenter «l'opinion publique personnifiée» et à faire que l'auditoire soit «pénétré de cette impression, pour ainsi dire, abstraite, et de l'empire de l'ordre social sur tous» (pp. 907–9, 956). Dans *Adolphe* cette fonction est remplie par une foule de témoins anonymes, mais là où le chœur ancien représentait la droiture de jugements collectifs, ici les commentateurs sont destinés à rester inéluctablement et ironiquement à côté de la question. Dans ce si court roman, le réseau de leurs incompréhensions est tissé avec maîtrise. Les gens «respectables» étalent leur complaisance ou leur pharisaïsme; les mauvaises langues échangent avec joie leurs racontars; les représentants du «bon sens» voient des solutions faciles. Deux parentes du Comte de P., forcées par lui à vivre en bons termes avec Ellénore, transforment en principes «moraux» la joie maligne qu'elles éprouvent à pouvoir rompre avec elle; d'autres s'attendrissent sur le sort de ses enfants; les séducteurs attitrés des salons cherchent à profiter de sa situation irrégulière. Avec une ironie cinglante, les gens d'opinions plus pondérées condamnent Adolphe comme frivole et cynique précisément à l'époque où il cherche désespérément à protéger la femme qu'il n'aime plus en lui offrant fidélité et tendresse, tandis que la jeunesse réellement cynique lui envie ses droits d'amant au moment où il en est le plus las. Que ce soit dans la vie mondaine des salons ou devant le lit de mort et les obsèques d'Ellénore, les conjectures erronées, les jugements conventionnels, les sympathies mal placées et les conseils simplistes fourmillent, s'entrecroisent et se contredisent.[3]

D'autres personnages, développés avec plus de détail, montrent comment le lourd héritage qui compose l'*opinion* ne cessera de déformer chez Adolphe toute réaction spontanée et d'empêcher qu'il reconnaisse à temps certains de ses besoins les plus profonds. Le père, tour à tour trop indulgent («Il ne m'avait jamais laissé souffrir des suites de [mes] fautes») et trop amer, profère les épigrammes d'une génération pour qui les femmes peuvent «sans inconvénient être prises, puis être quittées» («Cela leur fait si peu de mal, et à nous tant de plaisir»), faussant ainsi toute perception initiale et des conséquences que comporte l'action, et de la nature essentielle d'une personnalité où gisait «au fond [du] cœur un besoin de sensibilité dont je ne m'apercevais pas». Les «transports» d'un ami, amoureux selon la mode conventionnelle, lui font chercher, par esprit d'imitation, «une liaison de femme qui pût flatter mon amour-propre.» Cynisme et idéalisme d'emprunt déforment donc le contact initial avec la vie. Et à la fin du roman, la voix de l'*opinion* s'exprime à travers une étude brillante et minutieuse des manœuvres conduites par le Baron de T., vieux diplomate expérimenté, pour amener une rupture entre Adolphe et Ellénore, rupture justifée selon le «bon sens», et pourtant funeste pour l'une et pour l'autre.

Quant à la position d'Ellénore vis-à-vis de la société, c'est dans la Préface de la seconde édition que se trouvent des généralisations sur la vie de certaines femmes dans la société de l'époque:

des êtres faibles, n'ayant de vie réelle que dans le cœur, d'intérêt profond que dans l'affection, sans activité qui les occupe, et sans carrière qui les commande ... sentant que leur seule existence est de se livrer sans réserve à un protecteur, et entraînées sans cesse à confondre le besoin d'appui et le besoin d'amour ... Cette société implacable, ... semble avoir trouvé du plaisir à placer les femmes sur un abîme pour les condamner, si elles y tombent.

Pour celles qui refuseraient de se plier aux convenances, elles seront comme la femme âgée du premier chapitre, «n'ayant que son esprit pour ressource ... et envisageant la mort toujours pour terme de tout».

De ce genre de considérations ressort un réquisitoire formidable contre les pressions sociales, et qui rappelle ces réflexions de

Constant dans un article de critique littéraire:

Quant aux tragédies qui seraient fondées sur l'action de la société en lutte avec l'homme, opposant des obstacles, non seulement à ses passions, mais à sa nature, ou brisant, non seulement son caractère, ses inclinations personnelles, mais les mouvements qui sont inhérents à tout être humain, je n'en connais aucune qui remplisse complètement l'idée que j'en conçois (p. 937).

C'est surtout dans les Notes pour une Préface d'*Adolphe*, restées inédites de son vivant, qu'il souligne les rapports profonds qui existent entre la conduite de son héros et les traits généraux de l'époque où il vit.[4] Après la fameuse «J'ai voulu peindre dans Adolphe une des principales maladies morales de notre siècle», ayant résumé sur le plan personnel et dans quelques phrases implacables l'incertitude, l'absence de force et de suite chez son héros, il attribue ces tendances à une génération d'hommes qui «en pensant s'éclairer par l'expérience de leurs pères ... ont hérité de leur satiété», pour enfin tirer des conclusions politiques:

La fidélité en amour est une force comme la croyance religieuse, comme l'enthousiasme de la liberté ... Car, encore une fois, tout se tient. Ce qui fait qu'on est dur ou léger envers l'affection, fait aussi qu'on est indifférent à tout avenir au-delà de ce monde, et vil envers toutes les puissances qui se succèdent, et qu'on nomme légitimes tant qu'elles subsistent.

Conclusions qui ne figurent pas de façon explicite dans le roman, où «j'ai peint une petite partie du tableau, la seule qui fût, non sans tristesse, mais sans danger pour le peintre».

Inculpation donc et d'une époque minée par ses compromissions politiques et des convenances qui régissent toute société artificielle. Mais si dans toute tragédie nous contemplons le spectacle de l'individu aux prises avec de vastes pressions extérieures, la plus haute tragédie exige un équilibre où nous soyons convaincus en même temps que la force extérieure est irrésistible et que l'individu se sent profondément responsable. Si le blâme se porte exclusivement sur les puissances extérieures, qui écrasent une victime innocente, nous en arrivons à un poncif pathétique (poncif cher à bien des romantiques et dérivant de certains courants de la «sensibilité» au 18ᵉ siècle); s'il n'entre en jeu que la culpabilité de l'individu, nous risquons de retomber dans l'étroite étude pathologique d'où la dignité tragique serait absente. Pour ce qui est des auteurs classiques devant le problème du destin, deux vers de

Phèdre représentent l'équilibre miraculeux des deux éléments:

> Object infortuné des vengeances célestes,
> Je m'abhorre encor plus que tu ne me détestes.

Au 19ᵉ siècle, où la société va remplacer le destin comme force extérieure, Constant garde ce même équilibre. Le héros ne sera pas un simple être innocent qui s'oppose à des forces corrompues, car ces forces, comme les Dieux chez Racine, se manifestent à travers sa propre nature. «La société s'arme de tout ce qu'il y a de mauvais dans le cœur de l'homme».[5]

Pourtant, certains effets tragiques, et des plus poignants, ressortent de situations où les personnages, une fois pris dans l'engrenage de pressions extérieures et de tentations intérieures, se démolissent eux-mêmes et se détruisent l'un l'autre non pas uniquement à cause de leurs défauts, mais par les résultats ironiques de leurs qualités mêmes. Chez Racine une Athalie minée par la crainte, la cruauté et la cupidité, mais se perdant finalement quand elle devient «sensible à la pitié». Chez Adolphe et chez Ellénore les potentiels d'intelligence et de sensibilité s'entrecroisent de façon ironique pour n'aboutir qu'à l'impasse tragique. Lucidité désespérante, d'abord chez Adolphe sur la mort de l'amour-passion, ensuite chez Ellénore («Vous croyez avoir de l'amour, et vous n'avez que de la pitié»); dévouement, d'abord chez Ellénore, pour qui c'est le mot-clé, mais qui fait que plus elle se sacrifie pour Adolphe plus elle l'exaspère, l'éloigne, l'étouffe; ensuite chez Adolphe qui, en cherchant à la protéger, lui inflige des douleurs prolongées. S'il est incapable de la quitter, le mot «faiblesse» est pourtant un qualificatif beaucoup trop simpliste. Sous l'effet du galvanisme renouvelé par chaque obstacle, chaque crise, ses actions sont décisives et fermes: il enlève Ellénore pour la protéger devant son père à lui, l'accompagne en Pologne, se bat en duel.[6] Derrière ses longues indécisions se distinguent trois niveaux de réactions, se rapportant toutes au problème de «la douleur que l'on cause»: impossibilité physique de supporter le spectacle de la souffrance; sens intellectuel de la justice devant les sacrifices qu'elle a faits; finalement (et c'est sans doute le plus important dans ce roman qu'on voit souvent comme une étude de la mobilité des passions, et ce qui ressort avec le plus de force) effrayante permanence, après la mort de l'amour, des liens créés non seulement par le devoir mais par une tendresse indéracinable.

Chez les individus, donc, «défauts» et «qualités» s'interpénètrent étroitement et créent comme un réseau de tragiques ironies. Pour la société aussi le point de vue est double, et plein de nuances suggestives. Aucun poncif qui la présente uniquement comme influence néfaste, contre laquelle se profileraient de nobles révoltés. La vieille amie du premier chapitre a résisté à des convenances «factices *mais nécessaires*». Ellénore, après une «faute» initiale, cherche surtout à se faire respecter par la société. C'est une partie de sa fierté et de sa dignité, en même temps que de ses limites intellectuelles, qu'elle n'a aucunement la tournure d'esprit d'une rebelle.[7] Une des pires tortures d'Adolphe sera de voir lentement détruire la *considération* qu'on lui avait accordée.

Opinion et *considération*: ces deux mots-clé qui parsèment (dans leurs acceptions négatives et positives) les écrits personnels de Constant représentent deux tons dans la voix de la société. Et si toutes les susceptibiliriés de ses nerfs, de ses émotions et de son intelligence se hérissent contre les erreurs et les simplifications que fait l'opinion, Adolphe est pourtant marqué par le besoin essentiel de gagner et de mériter une juste considération. Il se sent des talents qui lui imposent et des ambitions et des devoirs; talents qui ne sont nullement illusoires ni vaguement postulés, car ils se mettent en évidence dès que le Baron de T. lui confie quelques tâches administratives. Sa liaison avec Ellénore l'empêche «d'entrer dans une carrière, de commencer une vie active, d'acquérir quelques titres à l'estime des hommes, de faire un noble usage de [ses] facultés». Comme toute autre passion chez Adolphe, l'ambition a deux faces: possibilités d'égoïsme ou de cruauté envers les autres, élans vers une sorte de dévouement social.[8]

Dans la vie de Constant, vie pleine d'obsessions mobiles, la plus permanente des hantises était peut-être celle de laisser à ses contemporains et à la postérité un apport mémorable. *Adolphe* concentre cette hantise dans trois points de vue: celui de son père qui avait conçu pour lui «des espérances probablement fort exagérées», représentant ces pressions familiales et intimes qui forment le complexe de l'enfant prodige; celui du Baron de T., représentant une société pratique, plein de «bon sens» mais fermé aux nuances des douleurs et des obligations personnelles; celui d'Adolphe lui-même quand, la nuit, à la campagne, il rêve à la vie qu'il désirerait mener, pense à ce qu'il pourrait apporter à la société et envisage la joie du père qui a toujours voulu pour lui un avenir utile et glorieux.

Dans le roman, analyse d'un analyste qui se trompe en partie sur sa propre nature et ses propres besoins, la mort de cette Ellénore qui, au quatrième chapitre, «n'était plus un but ... était devenue un lien», enlève à Adolphe de façon ironique ce qui, pendant de longues années et sans qu'il le reconnaisse, avait été aussi un but:

Naguère toutes mes actions avaient un but; j'étais sûr, par chacune d'elles, d'épargner une peine ou de causer un plaisir.

Le choc devant le vide que cause cette liberté ironique et devant ses réflexions sur son passé empêche toute réalisation de ses talents politiques et clot le cercle tragique. Pour l'homme Constant, évidemment, les peines déchirantes de liaisons prolongées et rompues ont été surmontées d'une autre manière.

Je n'ai esquissé qu'un aspect très limité des richesses infinies d'*Adolphe*. Même en ce qui concerne ce problème assez simple, trois côtés d'une réussite exceptionnelle se dégagent nettement. D'abord, devant ce qui sera le poncif par excellence des 19e et 20e siècles – le problème de l'individu d'exception victime d'une société défectueuse – Constant refuse de mettre tous les torts d'un côté, mais tisse un réseau de suggestions complexes et de subtiles ironies. Ensuite, il se refuse tout vague lyrisme, toute rhétorique ampoulée, se confinant au détail convaincant de vies intimes pour insinuer le jeu complexe et réciproque de qualités et de défauts chez l'individu et de forces constructives et destructives dans la société. Conversations, lettres, gestes, impressions physiques de salons, de jardins ou de campagne, chaque mot compte, chaque phrase exigerait une analyse. Finalement, derrière ces individus qui se profilent avec une netteté particulière, derrière les situations sociales où est mise en cause une époque, se placent des maximes sur la nature humaine.[9] Maximes impliquant comme contrepoint à la mobilité personnelle ou sociale une certaine permanence de phénomènes et de jugements. Maximes qui tirent leur force du fait qu'elles ne sont nullement des généralisations isolées, mais sont placées de façon à résumer, à la fin d'un incident ou d'un épisode, les découvertes déjà entrevues à travers les personnages. Maximes sardoniques:

Presque toujours, pour vivre en repos avec nous-mêmes, nous travestissons en calculs et en systèmes nos impuissances ou nos faiblesses: cela satisfait cette portion de nous qui est, pour ainsi dire, spectatrice de l'autre,

ou, à la fin d'une scène déchirante:

Il y a des choses qu'on est longtemps sans se dire, mais quand une fois elles sont dites, on ne cesse jamais de les répéter.

Maximes généreuses:

L'amour s'identifie tellement à l'objet aimé que dans son désespoir même il y a quelque charme,

ou:

La grande question dans la vie, c'est la douleur que l'on cause.

Maximes qui montrent surtout l'ambiguïté de toute réaction humaine:

Il n'y a point d'unité complète dans l'homme, et presque jamais personne n'est tout à fait sincère, ni tout à fait de mauvaise foi,

et de tout effort pour appliquer à cette ambiguïté des catégories verbales généralisatrices, simplificatrices et insuffisantes:

Les sentiments de l'homme sont confus et mélangés; ils se composent d'une multitude d'impressions variées qui échappent à l'observation; et la parole, toujours trop grossière et trop générale, peut bien servir à les désigner, mais ne sert jamais à les définir.

C'est parce qu'il ressent en même temps l'insuffisance de tout un héritage (conventions, religion, politique, formules verbales) et les impulsions irréductibles qui exigent que devant ces phénomènes on arrive à un jugement, à une compréhension et à une définition que Constant a écrit dans les cent pages d'*Adolphe* un livre dont aucun critique n'épuisera les multiples significations.

NOTES

1 Les références que je donne ici se rapportent (sauf autre indication) à l'édition de la Pléiade – Benjamin Constant: *Œuvres*. Texte présenté et annoté par Alfred Roulin, Gallimard, 1957. Les exigences de l'espace ne me permettant pas de discuter de près bien des observations des maîtres de la critique qui ont analysé *Adolphe*, je me permets de signaler que le lecteur trouvera des renseignements bibliographiques détaillés dans les notes de trois articles figurant dans des revues anglaises, articles où j'ai traité plus à fond l'art d'*Adolphe*: I. «The Art of Constant's *Adolphe*: the Stylisation of Experience», *Modern Language Review*, Vol. 62, No 1, Jan. 1967, pp. 31–47; II, «The Art of Constant's *Adolphe*: Creation of Character», *Forum for Modern Language Studies*, Vol. II, No 3, July 1966, pp. 253–63; III. «The Art of Constant's *Adolphe*: Structure and Style, *French Studies*, Vol. 20, 1966, pp. 226–42. Une communication sur «Constant romancier: le problème de l'expression» sera publiée dans les actes du Congrès tenu à Lausanne en Octobre 1967 (voir ci-dessus, pp. 61–70).

2 Voir les mêmes réactions chez Flaubert, *Correspondance*, éd. Conard, Vol. III, pp. 153–4: «Il y a ainsi une foule de sujets qui m'embêtent également par n'importe quel bout on les prend ... Ainsi, Voltaire, le magnétisme, Napoléon, la révolution, le catholicisme, etc., qu'on en dise du bien ou du mal, j'en suis mêmement irrité».

3 A propos de l'amie qui «vit de la générosité dans ce que j'appelais de la faiblesse», Adolphe fait remarquer que «le cœur seul peut plaider sa cause: il sonde seul ses blessures; tout intermédiaire devient un juge; il analyse, il transige, il conçoit l'indifférence; il l'admet comme possible, il le reconnaît pour inévitable, et l'indifférence se trouve ainsi, à sa grande surprise, légitime à ses propres yeux».

4 Edition d'*Adolphe* par J.-H. Bornecque (Garnier), pp. 303–5.

5 Voir aussi dans *Réflexions sur la Tragédie*: «Cette action de la société décide de la manière dont la force morale de l'homme s'agite et se déploie». Même n'y aurait-il pas la possibilité pour certains de vaincre cette société? Adolphe fait remarquer que «Telle est la force d'un sentiment vrai, que, lorsqu'il parle, les interprétations fausses et les convenances factices se taisent».

6 «J'aurais dû ...; je l'essayais aussi, mais que peut, pour ranimer un sentiment qui s'éteint, une résolution prise par devoir»? Voir aussi une lettre du 26/2/1807 (*Les Nouvelles littéraires*, 6/6/1963) où Constant se plaint de la réaction de ses lectrices: «Elles disent toutes qu'il [Adolphe] devrait aimer, comme si aimer, et surtout aimer toujours, était chose simple et facile, et parce que le pauvre diable n'aime plus, on ne lui sait aucun gré de ce qu'il fait ou de ce qu'il sacrifie».

7 J'ai discuté dans l'article de *Forum* (voir ci-dessus, pp. 28–42) la façon dont, en utilisant quantité de détails ayant rapport à la mort de cette amie d'une intelligence exceptionnelle, Julie Talma, Constant les a tous modifiés pour qu'ils conviennent à la nature toute différente d'Ellénore, telle qu'il l'avait définie dès le début du roman, en tant que femme ayant des sentiments nobles mais un «esprit ordinaire», cherchant à se conformer aux conventions sociales et religieuses. Ce portrait n'est ni vague ni fait de réminiscences incohérentes; Ellénore est en même temps nettement individualisée et composée de façon à intensifier les responsabilités d'Adolphe.

8 Nos jugements littéraires sur la signification de l'ambition chez quelques auteurs du passé ne seraient-ils pas quelquefois coupables d'anachronisme? le droit divin pouvait conférer à l'ambition du monarque un caractère de devoir; le «noblesse oblige» pouvait être autre chose qu'une formule vide.

9 La Préface de la seconde édition suggère la distinction entre hommes et femmes en général qui est un des thèmes du roman: les hommes n'ayant pas «au même degré que les femmes la noble et dangereuse faculté de vivre dans un autre et pour un autre». On pense peut-être au mot des *Liaisons dangereuses*: «L'homme jouit du bonheur qu'il ressent, et la femme de celui qu'elle procure».

6

Constant's *Adolphe* read by Balzac and Nerval (1972)[1]

When and how does a given book achieve its place in the canon of great works?[2] I propose here, not to trace the fortunes of *Adolphe*, but briefly to analyse two examples of fruitful contact between creative minds across a generation. Two great writers of the mid-nineteenth century made of this novel, in very different ways, a part of their mental substance: Balzac and Nerval. Both, in those years between the initial 'succès de scandale' of a supposed 'roman à clefs' and the late nineteenth-century rehabilitation of the 'roman d'analyse', react in a highly individual way to a work not yet part of an obligatory cultural tradition.[3] Both are of course characterized by their voracious use and personal assimilation of an exceptional range of material, whether from 'literature' or 'life'; in isolating one particular thread I shall be concerned less with details of 'sources' than with the interplay of instinctive affinities and critical judgements; and above all with the technique of theme and variations: the deliberate recalling of a past work both to provide a resonant sense of the permanence of human experience, and to serve as groundwork for provocative and personal developments.

Several scholars have made penetrating observations on Balzac's references to *Adolphe*.[4] Space in the present article precludes exhaustive treatment of Balzac's attitude to Constant; I shall add to previous surveys one or two minor points of fact, and shall concentrate on *La Muse du Département*, the novel where Balzac deliberately chose the reading of *Adolphe* as a theme around which his characters were to produce their conflicting reactions.

Before *La Muse*, certain of Balzac's characters found in the reading of *Adolphe* a stimulus and a warning. Camille Maupin in *Béatrix* (1839) opened her career as a novelist by recounting her first tragic love-affair in a work which was 'la contrepartie d'*Adolphe*'.

Her later giving up of the young man she intensely loves stems in part from her being haunted by the terrible lesson of the clinging older woman in Constant's novel.[5] In the *Mémoires de deux jeunes mariées* (1841–2), the young Louise de Chaulieu, fresh from her convent, reads love stories with indiscriminate appetite and finds many wearisome, but remarks that: 'Deux livres cependant m'ont étrangement plu, l'un est *Corinne* et l'autre *Adolphe*.' (I, 143). Balzac's sense of the novel's importance, and the fact that it was not yet automatically a canonical work, emerge from a letter to the publisher Charpentier in 1838: 'N'oubliez pas *Adolphe* dans votre collection.'[6] Brief remarks in Balzac's writings other than his novels bring out the two qualities he admires in *Adolphe*. First, its concentrated analysis of the mainsprings of human feeling: 'je ferai remarquer combien il y a peu de faits chez les romanciers habiles (*Werther, Clarisse, Adolphe, Paul et Virginie*). Le talent éclate dans la peinture des causes qui engendrent les faits, dans les mystères du cœur humain ...'.[7] Second, its symbolizing a vital aspect of the society in which it is set; it chooses not the accidental and temporary aspects, but 'toute une face de cette société ... quelque grand et vaste symbole'.[8] Finally, in the *Avant-Propos* to the *Comédie humaine*, when he thinks of those great characters created by the human imagination to 'faire concurrence à l'état civil', he sets Adolphe among his chosen list (I, 6).

But it is in *La Muse du Département* that he has made of *Adolphe* a vital element in the final structure of his novel, placing his references discreetly, deliberately and suggestively at key moments. He has in a sense used *Adolphe* as the equivalent of the classical authors' treatment of ancient and familiar myth: trebly suggestive in underlining the permanence of certain human experiences, in showing the recurrent struggle to avoid an inevitable outcome, and in setting against the echoes of the past new modes of expression and differing dénouements.

To Madame Hanska he wrote in March 1843: 'J'espère que dans la fin de *la Muse*, on verra le sujet d'*Adolphe*, traité du côté réel,'[9] and the fourth part of his story was originally given the heading *Commentaires sur 'l'Adolphe' de Benjamin Constant*.[10] Dinah Piédefer gladly abandons her position as wife of the impotent M. de Baudraye and the much-attacked 'superior woman' in second-rate provincial society, to become the devoted mistress, in Paris, of the journalist Étienne Lousteau; the theme of how devotion may become a deadly and stifling tie will emerge only in the second half of the novel. But, from the beginning, references to *Adolphe* serve as an omen pointing to the sinister inevitability of breakdown and bitterness in the relationship. First, in the predominantly comic scene where Lousteau and Bianchon, guests in the provincial salon, try, through terrifying anecdotes on adultery, to discover whether Dinah has yet been unfaithful to her dwarfish husband. Discussion brings to the fore a highly Balzacian theme: 'Les inventions des romanciers et des dramaturges sautent aussi souvent de leurs livres et de leurs pièces dans la vie réelle que les événements de la vie réelle montent sur le théâtre et se prélassent dans les livres.' (IV, 114.) Examples are quoted, culminating in: 'Et la tragi-comédie d'*Adolphe* par Benjamin Constant se joue à toute heure, s'écria Lousteau.' (It has been suggested that this insertion is meant to stress the 'banalité' of the theme; less so, I think, than the menacing inevitability of its outcome; it is also in keeping with Lousteau's character that he should see *Adolphe* as a 'tragi-*comédie*'.) *Adolphe* is again used as an omen of what is to come in one of those scenes of multiple *sous-entendus* in which Balzac so excels. Dinah has arrived, unannounced and pregnant, to join her lover in Paris, thus irrupting into his plans for a profitable marriage; he asks Bixiou to come and press him to that marriage, so that Dinah from the next room will overhear and sacrifice herself. Bixiou stresses the blank prospects of an illicit relationship between Dinah and Lousteau in the bare phrases: 'La Société, mon cher, pèsera sur vous, tôt ou tard. Relis *Adolphe*' (IV, 166).

This deliberate use of the portent reflects Balzac's preoccupation with structure. The classical theatre had used dreams or oracles to make the end implicit in the beginning, to convey a sense of inescapable menace and of ironical struggle. Balzac, discussing Stendhal's technique of construction in *La Chartreuse*, may also have been struck by Stendhal's use, in his different novels, of the ambiguous omen. That the first, and highly suggestive, reference to *Adolphe* in *La Muse* is inserted as late as the *Furne corrigé* version shows him deliberately highlighting the effect planned much earlier in the 1843 letter.[11] The fact too that *La Muse* was written under special pressure and made use in the first part of much material from previous writings, may have made Balzac particularly keen, when revising, to stress its coherent construction.

But portents are a long-term matter, not immediately fulfilled. Lousteau decides to accept Dinah's devotion (speculating in part on her soon becoming a rich widow), and for a time they share a new 'lune de miel': here Balzac pauses to contrast their circumstances with those of Constant's novel:

Un des traits les plus saillants de la Nouvelle due à Benjamin Constant, et
l'une des explications de l'abandon d'Ellénore est ce défaut d'intimité
journalière ou nocturne, si vous voulez, entre elle et Adolphe. Chacun des
deux amants a son chez soi, l'un et l'autre ont obéi au monde, ils ont gardé
les apparences. Ellénore, périodiquement quittée, est obligée à d'énormes
travaux de tendresse pour chasser les pensées de liberté qui saisissent
Adolphe au dehors. Le perpétuel échange des regards et des pensées dans la
vie en commun donne de telles armes aux femmes que, pour les abandonner, un homme doit objecter des raisons majeures qu'elles ne lui fournissent
jamais tant qu'elles aiment (IV, 183).

These reflections would be true only of the first half of *Adolphe*; they
suggest how closely Balzac interweaves his reactions to a seminal
text, his deductions from personal experience, and his imaginative
creation.

From the omen we move to the reaction. In face of all portents,
Balzac's active characters set out to conquer their fate, to run
counter to their reading. For Dinah: 'Le roman d'*Adolphe* était sa
Bible, elle l'étudiait; car, par-dessus toutes choses, elle ne voulait pas
être Ellénore' (IV, 192). From Furetière to Flaubert and beyond,
deluded girls have attempted to copy fictional models with disastrous results; Balzac rejoices in presenting a reaction against the
model, a reaction which ironically may prove equally disastrous.
Dinah is no Emma Bovary to identify herself with each heroine in
narcissistic pathos; she sets out to 'ne pas être Ellénore', to excise
every trace of reproach or tears (IV, 193).[12] To no effect. Both
she and Lousteau cite their personal interpretations of the book
as weapons in their intimate struggle. Dinah has seen its analysis
of 'le cœur humain', Lousteau its presentation of 'toute une face
de la société'. When her patience is at last exhausted, Lousteau
retorts:

Vous avez beaucoup lu le livre de Benjamin Constant ... mais vous ne
l'avez lu qu'avec des yeux de femme ... Ce qui tue ce pauvre garçon, ma
chère, c'est d'avoir perdu son avenir pour une femme; de ne pouvoir rien
être de ce qu'il serait devenu, ni ambassadeur, ni ministre, ni chambellan,
ni poète, ni riche (IV, 197–8).

The crescendo here reflects the character expressing judgement, as it
moves from social prospects to artistic success and culminates in the
telling 'ni riche'; Lousteau's view of Adolphe both indicates, in
certain turns of phrase, his own superficiality and vulgarity ('un
Allemand blondasse', 'une jupe qu'on devance') and shows something of the swift if limited perceptiveness of the journalist: 'Adolphe

[est] ... un cœur aristocrate qui veut rentrer dans la voie des honneurs, et rattraper sa dot sociale, sa considération compromise' (IV, 198).[13]

The end is both an echo and a reversal of *Adolphe*, and Lousteau is made to underline this: 'Vous jouez en ce moment à la fois les deux personnages.' Dinah reproaches him with the social stigma brought on her, but finds the strength to break decisively: 'Votre Ellénore ne meurt pas'; and she returns to husband and high position.[14] Both novels, in very different tones, have their bitter postscript. Adolphe after Ellénore's death discovers how much he depended on those very bonds he longed to be rid of. Dinah, outwardly reconciled with respectable society, suffers from 'une tristesse cachée mais profonde', finds that 'Parfois les souvenirs de ses misères revenaient mêlés au souvenir de voluptés dévorantes' (IV, 202) and briefly gives in once more to her past lover. Later variants intensify the sardonic allusions implicit in her return to the fold.

Differences in tone and technique are too obvious to require extended comment. Constant has at his command the subtlest resources of retrospective analysis in the first person, reduces external events and settings to the minimum, achieves a unified tone of quiet tragic irony, and rounds off intolerable suffering by the stylized epitome of death. For Balzac, 'Dans la nature, ces sortes de situations violentes ne se terminent pas, comme dans les livres, par la mort ou par des catastrophes habilement arrangées; elles finissent beaucoup moins poétiquement par le dégoût, par la vulgarité des habitudes ...' (IV, 194). Balzac rings Dinah's destiny about with the rich comic detail of provincial pretentiousness, her own as well as that of others, and finds objective correlatives for the prospect of seduction in the difference between a silk and an organdie dress if crumpled in a carriage, and for the shared joy of lovers in elegant *toilettes* displayed at the Opéra, or for the irony of devotion in the drab black worn from self-sacrificial economy but provoking the disgust of the weary lover.

Beneath these differences lies for both authors a particularly penetrating sense of the complexity of that supposed entity, a human character. If, to recent theorists of experimental techniques for presenting the fluctuations of personality, Flaubert has at last been recognized as an ancestor rather than an Aunt Sally, yet preconceptions regarding the Balzacian 'type' still die hard. In *La Muse du Département*, the interventions, explanations or digressions of the author are, for Balzac, unusually few (is there here a reflection of Constant's art of concentration?); we are invited to form for ourselves cumulative conclusions around two main characters who combine, as so often in Balzac, the mathematically and aesthetically satisfying patterns of a basic inner logic with that unpredictable interplay resulting from the reaction of human complexity to fluctuating circumstance. To both Dinah and Lousteau might well be applied Adolphe's fundamental dictum: 'Il n'y a point d'unité complète dans l'homme, et presque jamais personne n'est tout à fait sincère ni tout à fait de mauvaise foi' (p. 57).[15]

The Dinah of the middle of the book is the devoted victim of Lousteau. But where Constant had emphasized the tragic dependence of Ellénore and her lack of inner resources by giving her only an 'esprit ordinaire', Dinah has intellectual, artistic and practical gifts – and above all strong personal ambition. In the early chapters she 'se convertissait par ambition' (IV, 94). If she flies to join her lover in Paris, it is in part because the capital city has long been the loadstone of her frustrated desires.[16] When she leaves Lousteau it is for a husband who has with insect tenacity wormed his way to the highest honours, and her key moment of decision, part that of the victim at last turning on the faithless lover, part that of the woman reverting to conventional values, is poised on the unregenerate reflection that now she can lord it over the schoolfriend whose scorn has so often wounded her: 'Je suis comtesse, j'aurai sur ma voiture le manteau bleu de la pairie, et dans mon salon les sommités de la politique et de la littérature ... je la regarderai, moi! ... Cette petite jouissance pesa de tout son poids au moment de la conversion' (IV, 196). Like others of Balzac's survivorcharacters, she moves from her own form of haunting 'recherche de l'absolu' to learn to 'se contenter de l'à peu près', but to the end, vanity and practicality, tenderness and sensuality recur and interact.

If Lousteau is the cynical profiteer and the drifting 'velléitaire', we are yet made to see moments of fleeting sincerity or suggestive suffering. Like Adolphe, he embarks on seduction as a challenging exercise in technique, and is caught, as an already perceptive Dinah had threatened, in his own trap. Where to Adolphe the thought of a happy and respected marriage is no more than a late nostalgic dream (p. 92), Lousteau has a brilliant prospect, brought hallucinatingly alive in all its practical detail, snatched from him at the moment of achievement. Impulses of admiration or regret for suffering run sporadically beneath his calculating hold on Dinah.[17]

His unsuccessful efforts in writing convey something of the torments of the artist, however ineffectual, faced by 'les affres du style'.[18] And, although he has nothing of Adolphe's tragic dignity, he is at times made to represent that central problem in Constant: the difficulty of distinguishing between different levels of scheming, rhetoric, self-persuasion, and immediate feeling.[19]

The cry of Camille Maupin in *Béatrix* is frequently quoted by critics: 'Adolphe, cet épouvantable livre de Benjamin Constant, ne nous a dit que les douleurs d'Adolphe; mais celles de la femme? hein! Il ne les a pas assez observées pour nous les peindre; et quelle femme oserait les révéler?' But *La Muse* shows Balzac aware of Constant's two-sidedness, and is itself far from being written simply to take the woman's part. Each author has his own allusive technique. Adolphe's retrospective analysis sets the reader as much within Ellénore as within himself; Balzac, who has rejoiced in a reversal of roles, making the woman and the provincial finally stronger than the man and the Parisian, regards Dinah with a sardonic as well as an understanding eye. The balance between the two sides is held in Constant's tragedy by a desolate and critical sympathy for both, in Balzac's tragi-comedy by a fascinated contemplation of two opponents engaged in a struggle for survival.

One important aspect of Balzac's variations remains to be discussed. When Dinah studies *Adolphe* as her Bible she decides to avoid all those reproachful tears 'si savamment décrites par le critique auquel on doit l'analyse de cette œuvre poignante, et dont la glose paraissait à Dinah presque supérieure au livre. Aussi relisait-elle souvent le magnifique article du seul critique qu'ait eu la Revue des Deux-Mondes, et qui se trouve en tête de la nouvelle édition d'Adolphe' (IV, 192). When Lousteau hurls his parting reproaches, he too refers to this article. Gustave Planche (who was mentioned by name in the first version of Dinah's remarks) had published it in the *Revue des Deux Mondes* in 1834 and included it in his *Portraits littéraires* of 1836; it was then placed in the Charpentier edition of *Adolphe* in 1839, republished in 1843, and continued to figure in Charpentier editions up till 1930. Several scholars have pointed out that Balzac is here indirectly attacking Sainte-Beuve, and have discussed the probable importance of Planche in recalling Balzac's attention to *Adolphe*, in 1839 (*Béatrix*) and 1843 (*La Muse*).[20] It is highly likely that Balzac read the article on its first publication in 1834; to the evidence other critics have adduced on possible contacts in 1839 and 1843 must now be added the letter (quoted above, p. 81) where

Balzac in 1838 suggests the Charpentier edition, here without mention of Planche.[21]

On Balzac's direct use of Planche, two further points are important. First that in the vital passage where Dinah decides to be the opposite of Ellénore (a passage which, as B. Guyon has shown, directly quotes not *Adolphe*, but Planche), Balzac uses one of the very few paragraphs from that critic which directly capture the spirit and mode of expression of Constant's book. For Planche's highly personal piece of criticism, while at the beginning excellently characterizing the subtlety of the work, is a thinly-disguised confessional, proceeding to a series of emotional elaborations on the supposed experience of Adolphe and Ellénore, where the critic startlingly endows the text with his own inapposite memories, rhetoric and moral conclusions. (Adolphe in youth is made to dream of the tears and trailing tresses of lovely women wiping the sweat from his brow; Ellénore sees in sleep the ghost of her father with furrowed cheek reproaching her degradation; Adolphe is shameful because he 'essuie sur les lèvres de sa maîtresse les baisers d'une autre bouche', and Ellénore 'avilie' in forgiving him his waning love.)[22] The passage Balzac has selected is however a telling synthesis of the stage of Ellénore's growing reproaches. And, secondly, although he lets Dinah quote Planche almost word for word, the few changes Balzac makes are stylistically highly significant: he compresses the passage still further, and in particular rewords the clumsily comic phrase: 'Dès qu'il fait un pas, il trouve devant lui un œil curieux qui attend sa réponse.'[23]

Lousteau is made to accuse Planche of seeing only the woman's side. This is hardly a tenable accusation, but from Lousteau's further remarks there comes a lapidary comment: 'Ce livre, ma chère, a les deux sexes ... Dans *Adolphe*, les femmes ne voient qu'Ellénore, les jeunes gens y voient Adolphe, les hommes faits y voient Ellénore et Adolphe, les politiques y voient la vie sociale!' (IV, 198.) The network of society, with its intrigues, its interventions, its *idées reçues* and its false judgements, exercises to a particular degree its ineluctable pressures on representative individuals in both *Adolphe* and *La Muse*.[24]

Adolphe, then, is plainly no 'source' in the ordinary sense, but a counter deliberately used. Its importance is twofold. First, in the skilled art by which it becomes an allusive groundwork for Balzac's own vigorous variations: references are placed at structurally significant turning-points, and each also casts a revealing sidelight on the

character who utters it. Second, beneath the very obvious differences of treatment or temperament, in the surprising, or merely
natural, affinities which unite two creative minds, each intrigued or
haunted by the contradictions and ambiguities that underlie any
stereotyped conception of 'character'.

Nerval makes no such use of *Adolphe* as an overt theme or structural
device. But his scattered, yet very significant, references to the novel
show a still more personal response to what are perhaps its two most
fundamental suggestions.[25] Where so many critics, from the time of
publication to our own day, have stressed in Adolphe the inconstant
weakling, incapable of 'real love', Nerval notes in his *Carnet de
Dolbreuse* the essential passage from Chapter III (p. 64) which both
characterizes the delight of dawning love and points forward to the
years when Adolphe will be tied to Ellénore, not merely in weariness
or weakness, but in a prolonged tenderness as persistent as his
sporadic ambition or exasperation. Nerval's notes, as transcribed by
Jean Richer, read: 'L'amour supplée aux longs souv*enirs* par une
sorte de magie. Toutes les autres aff*ections* ont bes*oin* d'un passé, lui
nous d*onne* la consc*ience* d'av*oir* vécu av*ec* un être nag*uère* étranger.
B.C.'[26] No theme could be more central to Nerval's own works than
the search, beneath fluctuating and conflicting encounters and
obsessions, for the means of uniting disparate experience whether
from 'literature' or from 'life' within the converging parallels and
consoling permanence of a shared past. Where Constant will distil
from a multiplicity of real women one infinitely suggestive figure,
Nerval's tales or sonnets will create three archetypes to represent his
longings: the queen or saint as the ideal; the siren or actress as the
fascinating and fallacious echo of that ideal in the real world; the
fairy of naïve legend to suggest in a lovely and traditional countryside a possible but constantly elusive reconciliation with the
nature of things. Behind all three is set the illuminating and shifting
magic, constantly subject to disillusion and to re-creation, of a
double past: historical and personal. That Nerval should note in
Constant the analysis of the 'magic' means by which dawning love
evokes imaginative memories is proof less of a 'source' than of a
recognition of creative affinities.

　　Nerval's note on Chapter III of *Adolphe* stops at 'naguère étranger',
but the next phrases, with their sense at the same time of ecstasy and
of impermanence, have obviously bitten into his memory. Constant

had written: 'L'amour n'est qu'un point lumineux, et néanmoins il
semble s'emparer du temps. Il y a peu de jours qu'il n'existait pas,
bientôt il n'existera plus ...' (p. 64). In the *Lettres à Jenny Colon*
Nerval distinguishes between two levels of love, and of the more
moderate, which he longs to transcend, says: 'C'est un point lumineux dans l'existence qui ne tarde pas à pâlir et à s'éteindre.'[27]

In *Adolphe* the magic of the 'point lumineux' is followed by the
crescendo of irreparable errors. The theme of an obscure and
haunting guilt is fundamental in the works of Nerval, and finds
many individual means of suggestion.[28] That Constant's expression of
a parallel obsession has worked its way into his sensibility emerges
all the more clearly from the quiet allusions made in journalistic
articles to these pivotal phrases from Chapter iv of *Adolphe*: 'Nous
avions prononcé tous deux des mots irréparables; nous pouvions nous
taire, mais non les oublier. Il y a des choses qu'on est longtemps sans
se dire, mais quand une fois elles sont dites, on ne cesse jamais de les
répéter.' (p. 71.) An article on a production at the Opéra, where
Nerval discusses a husband's smug and scheming treatment of his
wife, remarks: 'N'y a-t-il pas, d'ailleurs, dans les blessures de
l'amour-propre, ce quelque chose d'*irréparable* que l'auteur d'*Adolphe*
peignit si bien?'[29] The break with the charming slave-girl of *Les
Femmes du Caire* is prefaced by the phrase: 'Il s'était dit entre nous un
de ces mots *irréparables* dont a parlé l'auteur d'*Adolphe*.'[30]

Beyond specific allusions, certain affinities link particularly closely, despite differences, the temperaments of Constant and of
Nerval. First, their penetrating analysis of the artist's fundamental
problem: that of words. For Constant: 'Tous nos sentiments intimes
semblent se jouer des efforts du langage: la parole rebelle, par cela
seul qu'elle généralise ce qu'elle exprime, sert à désigner, à distinguer, plutôt qu'à définir' (p. 1415), while for Nerval: 'Il y a des
années de rêves, de projets, d'angoisses qui voudraient se presser
dans une phrase, dans un mot.'[31] Second, a kind of instinctive
physical retraction before the evidence of suffering in others: the
Adolphe who, whatever his harshness in absence, is rendered power-
less or momentarily tender when faced by the blank and shivering
despair of a living woman, might be summed up by Nerval's phrase
on Rétif: 'une espèce de crispation nerveuse que lui fait éprouver le
spectacle de la souffrance.'[32] Third, and most important, the fundamental questioning of the 'reality' of any emotional experience.
Both suffer from that 'dédoublement' which will become so much a
part of nineteenth-century experience; each feels and expresses it

with a particular and personal intensity. To Constant 'cette analyse perpétuelle, qui place une arrière-pensée à côté de tous les sentiments, et qui par là les corrompt dès leur naissance'[33] is primarily intellectual: a product of the ratiocination drawn from both collective and personal experience. To Nerval, the threat is that of the imagination: the artist, unconsciously seeking to mould both others and the self to the demands of a stylized creation, meets either the stinging retort of the other: 'Vous ne m'aimez pas! Vous cherchez un drame, voilà tout, et le dénouement vous échappe,'[34] or his own dawning realization:

Nous ne vivons pas, nous! nous analysons la vie!... Suis-je bien sûr moi-même d'avoir aimé?... Nous ne voyons partout que des modèles à décrire, des passions à rendre, et tous ceux qui se mêlent à notre vie sont victimes de notre égoïsme, comme nous le sommes de notre imagination! (II, 1072).

Other affinities could well be traced.[35] For both Constant and Nerval the analysis of an individual love consciously, if discreetly, carries the widest suggestions relating to the political, sociological or metaphysical assumptions of an age. Constant's comments on the wider implications of *Adolphe* remained unpublished in his life-time; he had noted in a projected preface that 'J'ai peint une petite partie du tableau, le seule qui fût non sans tristesse, mais sans danger pour le peintre' and had gone on to draw parallels between inconstancy or aridity in personal emotions and the political and metaphysical causes and results of such a division of the self.[36] Nerval, in *Sylvie*,[37] is able more directly to characterize the implications of the 'époque étrange' of his youth, one of those 'époques de rénovation ou de décadence' in which, as in *Adolphe*, against a background where systems so rapidly rise and fall, where all values are set at odds and questioned, inherited idealism and inherited cynicism find in personal destinies the concentration and the echo of the problems of society as a whole.

This brief article has suggested only a few points of comparison and contrast; many more might be investigated. Both Balzac and Nerval, rather than 'borrowing' from Constant, have recognized in *Adolphe* themes which form part of their own most fundamental preoccupations. Balzac uses as a structural device the main outlines of its situation and dilemmas, then plays on them through parallels, reversals, and interpretations by individuals: his central concern is, as always, with a play of forces. Nerval's fewer references are those of one who has more intimately absorbed details of analysis and expression; the details he recalls are those most vital to the delight and the despair at the centre of Adolphe's experience.

French literature is perhaps particularly characterized, throughout the centuries, by the joy, which both author and reader share, in an ability consciously to play on the resonances of the most suggestive authors of the past, while creating around them original variations and interpretations. To both Balzac and Nerval, countless other authors from many countries and ages will provide stimulus and substance. The individual reactions of these two writers to *Adolphe*, at a time before it was fully established in the canon of great works, suggest both their immediacy of response to subtleties of content and expression, and their own irreducible originality.

NOTES

1 Page references in the text will be to Benjamin Constant, *Œuvres*, ed. Alfred Roulin (Bibliothèque de la Pléiade, 1957); Balzac, *La Comédie humaine*, ed. Marcel Bouteron (Bibliothèque de la Pléiade, 1951); Gérard de Nerval, *Œuvres*, ed. Albert Béguin and Jean Richer (Bibliothèque de la Pléiade, vol. I, 1966, vol. II, 1956.)

2 Stimulating observations on different aspects of this question are made by A. M. Boase, 'Tradition and Revaluation in the French Anthology, 1692–1960' in *Essays presented to C. M. Girdlestone* (1960), pp. 49–63, and T. J. B. Spencer, 'Shakespeare the International Author' in *The Future of the Modern Humanities*, ed. J. C. Laidlaw (*The Modern Humanities Research Association*, 1969), pp. 31–50.

3 A selection of comments by critics, from the date of publication onwards, may be found in E. Eggli and P. Martino, *Le Débat romantique en France, 1813–1830*, vol. I (Paris, Garnier, 1933); J.-H. Bornecque, *Adolphe* (Paris, Garnier, 1955); C. Cordié, *Adolphe* (Naples, 1963). Contemporary comments were strongly swayed by political considerations.

4 J.-H. Bornecque, *ed. cit.*, quotes as 'un jugement étonnamment peu connu' two passages from the discussion between Dinah and Lousteau in *La Muse du Département*. H. J. Hunt in *Balzac's 'Comédie humaine'* (1959), p. 351, comments succinctly and suggestively on the unusual angle from which Lousteau is made to judge *Adolphe* and notes that references to Constant's novel occur here and there throughout *La Muse*. Jean Pommier in '*La Muse du Département* et le thème de la femme mal mariée chez Balzac, Mérimée et Flaubert', *Année Balz.* (1961), pp. 191–221, provides, as always, basic and seminal discussion. Geneviève Delattre, *Les Opinions littéraires de Balzac* (Paris, 1961), gives an able summary of Balzac's main references to Constant (including his appearance in person in *Illusions perdues*) and briefly discusses the tone of *La Muse*. See also her excellent article 'L'Imagination balzacienne au travail: la

lecture créatrice' in *Cahiers de l'Association internationale des Études françaises*, No. 15 (1963), 395–406. The present article will show why, while appreciating the penetrating and suggestive remarks of Mme Delattre, I should see differently her 'tristes pantins', 'cet échec', 'simple avilissement des personnages'. B. Guyon's '*Adolphe, Béatrix* et *La Muse du Département*' in *Année Balz.* (1963), pp. 149–75, provides a mine of information. On attitudes to *Adolphe* over 150 years, see the thorough conspectus by Paul Delbouille, '*Adolphe* sur le chemin de la gloire' in *Benjamin Constant: Actes du Congrès de Lausanne* (1967) (Genève, 1968), pp. 171–80 and the third part of his *Genèse, Structure et Destin d'«Adolphe»* (Paris, Société d'Édition 'les Belles Lettres', 1971).

5 For a fuller discussion of the references in *Béatrix* see the critical studies mentioned in the preceding note. The tragic possibilities of the theme of the woman older than her lover are common to *Adolphe* and to many of Balzac's works. This particular form of intensification is less important in *La Muse.*

6 *Corr.*, 1391, vol. III, p. 470; letter dated [28 novembre, 1838]. I shall discuss below (pp. 86–7) the importance of this letter (published after J. Pommier's and B. Guyon's articles) to the question of Gustave Planche's influence on Balzac's reading of *Adolphe*. Another letter refers to Constant: that from Louis Desnoyers (*Corr.*, 1693, vol. IV, p. 26) querying among 'dangerous' phrases that on an 'orateur d'une finesse voisine de celle de Benjamin Constant'. In the original publication of *Pierrette* in *Le Siècle* it was replaced by 'une finesse à la Walpole', but the phrase was later restored (III, 740).

7 'Lettres sur la Littérature, le Théâtre et les Arts' published unsigned in the *Revue parisienne* (1840). *L'Œuvre de Balzac*, sous la direction d'Albert Béguin et de Jean A. Ducourneau (Club français du livre, XIV, 1964), p. 1053 (cf. also p. 1132).

8 *ibid.*, p. 1149.

9 *L.H.*, vol. II, p. 179.

10 see Pommier, *art. cit.*, and Guyon, *art. cit.*

11 Pommier, *art. cit.*, called attention to the late stage at which this variant occurs. See also Guyon, *art. cit.,* for the different stages of insertion of references to *Adolphe* in *Béatrix.*

12 'Bel exemple d'influence négative', writes Pommier, *art. cit.* The recurring treatment in Balzac of the 'Ne pas être X' as applied to literary models would merit further treatment. An interesting example, combining omen, future reversal, and other suggestive undertones, occurs early in the *Mémoires de deux jeunes mariées*, where Louise, before her passionate involvement with her Hispano-Moorish adorer, reacts against Shakespeare's Desdemona (I, 161).

13 'Considération' is indeed a key-word in *Adolphe*. For discussion of the aspect of *Adolphe* which is here given lapidary form by Balzac, see above 'The Art of Constant's *Adolphe*: The stylisation of experience' (pp. 3–27) and 'L'Individu et l'ordre social dans *Adolphe*' (pp. 71–79).

It would be interesting to analyse closely the cut-and-thrust of literary discussion between Lousteau, Bianchon and Dinah in the early salon scene; the bemused provincials ('On nous regarde! sourions comme si nous comprenions', IV, 123) in an atmosphere of pre-Verdurin display of cultural fashion, hear an analysis of the difference between the 'contour net' of the 'littérature de l'Empire' and the modern desire to 'faire chatoyer les mots'. Critical insights, modish clichés and personal prejudices or pretensions are skilfully and satirically interwoven. See also the comparison between Lousteau and Claude Vignon ('la distance qui sépare le Métier de l'Art'), IV, 178.

14 Both irony and the art of construction are stressed when, speaking of her husband's new position and power, the devoted Clagny remarks (IV, 196): 'Il satisfait tous les désirs que vous formiez à vingt ans.'

15 H. J. Hunt, *op. cit.*, p. 350, has a valuable discussion of the problem of coherence of character.

16 Sexual frustration in the first half of the book finds the *dérivatifs* of furniture-collecting (cf. Pons) and of literary leanings. Frustration of ambitions for her lover's success turns to the *dérivatif* of would-be maternal feeling for him (cf. Bette).

17 Faced by the humility of his proposed pregnant bride, Félicie Cardot, 'Lousteau fut ému, tant il y avait de choses dans le regard, dans l'accent, dans l'attitude' (IV, 158). On Dinah's tears at his cruel reception of her arrival in Paris, 'Lousteau ne put résister à cette explosion, il serra la baronne dans ses bras, et l'embrassa', etc. (IV, 162). He marvels at her love: 'je suis donc aimé pour la première fois de ma vie! s'écriait Lousteau' (IV, 171); like the early Adolphe he feels a woman can be easily cast aside when the moment suits, yet 'Aussi Lousteau conçut-il pour elle une involontaire estime' (IV, 181). Later, facing her grief, he is 'atteint au cœur par cette vivacité de sensitive' and provides a virulent self-analysis: 'Je suis, littérairement parlant, un homme très secondaire ... nous autres danseurs de corde ...', etc. (IV, 188).

18 see IV, 151, 175, 177, 188, 205, and compare the treatment of such characters as Wenceslas Steinbock and Lucien de Rubempré.

19 Pommier's article raises possible parallels with *Madame Bovary*. For passages where the skilled use of both rhetoric and sensuality fore-shadows Rodolphe Boulanger see IV, 118, 141, 149, 154, 157; cf. especially the real but egoistic regrets at a break which he had hoped for, 199. The selfish schemer predominates. But by the side of Constant's most probing passages on the power of self-persuasion through words, the difficulty of estimating degrees of sincerity, might be put the following: 'Il y a des hommes ... qui naissent un peu singes, chez qui l'imitation des plus charmantes choses du sentiment est si naturelle, que le comé-dien ne se sent plus' (IV, 177), or, after the fine rhetorical flourish in his last appeal ('Une goutte d'eau dans le désert, et ... par la main d'un ange'), the comment 'Ce fut dit moitié plaisanterie et moitié attendrisse-ment.' (IV, 207.)

20 See Pommier, *art. cit.*, and Guyon, *art. cit.*, and their references to M. Regard. For a penetrating study of Balzac and Sainte-Beuve, see J. Hytier, *Questions de littérature* (Geneva, 1967), pp. 111–40.

21 Guyon points out that in both 1839 and 1843 Planche's edition of *Adolphe* appeared later than the relevant work of Balzac, but the two

authors were in close contact. Balzac's letter to Charpentier notes (in view of the brevity of *Adolphe*) that it should be combined in one volume with a novel by some other author, and promises to reflect on what this should be. The eventual Charpentier edition added, instead, other works by Constant, and the Planche article.

22 Ellénore's relation to the Comte de P., so quietly evoked with its insufficiencies in Constant, gives rise to such imaginings as: 'Elle avait conquis l'amour d'un homme, elle avait posé sa tête sur son épaule, et dans ses rêves elle avait surpris le murmure de son nom; elle était fière et glorieuse . . .', etc. There is an extended evocation of a sobbing Adolphe scorned for his tears by a dominant and dry-eyed Ellénore, etc.

23 Guyon quotes the relevant paragraphs from Planche, *art. cit.*, p. 167. Cf. IV, 193.

24 Cf. the ironical detail of society's false judgments in *Adolphe* (discussed above pp. 16–18 and pp. 38, 71–9) with for example Bianchon's comment on 'les tragédies qui se jouent derrière le rideau du ménage' – 'je trouve la justice humaine malvenue à juger des crimes entre époux; . . . elle n'y entend rien dans ses prétentions à l'équité.'

25 I have not attempted here an exhaustive survey of Nerval's references to Constant.

26 *Gérard de Nerval: Carnet de Dolbreuse*. Essai de lecture par Jean Richer (Athens, 1967), p. 91. This note corrects the faulty transcription given in the text, p. 65. (See also pp. 7 and 27, and Jean Richer: *Nerval. Expérience et Création* (Paris, 1963), p. 325.) The italics represent Richer's expansion of Nerval's abbreviations.

27 *Œuvres*, vol. I, p. 771.

28 Cf. the standard works of criticism on Nerval, and some brief remarks in my 'Le Mythe d'Orphée dans l'œuvre de Gérard de Nerval' (see below pp. 308–21).

29 *Œuvres complémentaires de Gérard de Nerval*, vol. II, *La Vie du Théâtre*, textes réunis et presentés par Jean Richer (Paris, 1961), p. 655. A passing reference to *Adolphe* is also found in vol. I (1959), p. 153.

30 *Œuvres*, vol. II, p. 286.

31 *ibid.*, vol. I, p. 754.

32 *ibid.*, vol. II, p. 1100.

33 Fragments of projected preface, see J.-H. Bornecque's edition of *Adolphe*, *op. cit.*, p. 304.

34 *Œuvres*, vol. I, p. 271. Nerval's frequent mockery at literary habits which demand either marriage or death as a *dénouement* (vol. II, p. 338, vol. I, pp. 79–80, etc.) might be compared with Balzac's observation quoted above, p. 84.

35 Both comment on how differences of language may seem to break through stereotypes, Constant in the passage: 'Elle parlait plusieurs langues, imparfaitement . . . Ses idées semblaient se faire jour à travers les obstacles, et sortir de cette lutte plus agréables, plus naïves et plus neuves; car les idiomes étrangers rajeunissent les pensées, et les débarrassent de ces tournures qui les font paraître . . . communes et affectées.' (p. 56); Nerval in the remark: 'Il y a quelque chose de très séduisant dans une femme d'un pays lointain et singulier, qui parle une langue inconnue, . . . et

qui enfin n'a rien de ces vulgarités de détail que l'habitude nous révèle chez les femmes de notre patrie.' To Constant what counts is the apparent revivifying of ideas; to Nerval the stimulus of the unknown, allowing the imagination to weave its own dream. Both are brought back to the reality.

36 *Adolphe*, ed. J.-H. Bornecque, p. 305.
37 *Œuvres*, vol. I, pp. 242–3.

7

Framework as a suggestive art in Constant's *Adolphe* (with remarks on its relation to Chateaubriand's *René*) (1979)

The deliberately constructed pattern of conflicting misjudgements that underlies Adolphe's narrative – misjudgements of self by others, of others by self, of past self by partial self-analysis – is framed at beginning and end by three imagined 'documents'.[1] The introductory 'Avis de l'Éditeur' was there from the earliest known manuscript; the concluding 'Lettre à l'Éditeur' and 'Réponse' were added at some time between the 1810 manuscript and publication in 1816. Recent interest in narrative techniques has called attention to certain functions of this framework; in the present brief article I hope to suggest one or two further questions around Constant's highly original adaptation of contemporary conventions.[2]

The time-honoured and prevalent device of a supposed editor's discovery of a manuscript, often in intriguing circumstances, may once have served both as useful disclaimer of authorial responsibility and as means of insisting that 'all is true' to those naïve enough to accept its assertions;[3] by the early nineteenth century such functions were clearly outworn. Constant has made of it an integral and essential part of the patterns of suggestion within the novel itself. The bleak vision of a purposeless, rootless, morose wanderer, sketched in a few phrases of deliberately laconic dialogue and minimal description, is deeply different in tone from the suggestive sorrows or mighty melancholy indicated by a third-person narrator at the opening of a *Corinne* or a *René*. It is as if Flaubert had placed at the outset of *L'Éducation sentimentale* the dry and desolate sequence of 'Il voyagea ... il revint'. The tragedy has reached its appointed end before the story begins. And all Adolphe's ambitions for the life he would lead if once freed of Ellénore, all his dreams of the ideal marriage which would reconcile him with family and society, must irrevocably be set by the reader in ironical contrast to what we know from the beginning to have become of him once he is free of all ties. These initial facts speak more loudly than would any direct judgement by the first-person narrator, both on Adolphe's incapacity to use the freedom he thought he desired, and on the ironically lasting grief (in one who initially assumed no feeling lasted) at the loss of what had most irked him.

To certain commentators, judging from a generally existentialist standpoint, the tragic focus of the narrative as a whole implies *mauvaise foi* in attributing to fate an outcome where the narrator is insufficiently aware of personal responsibility. Others, while arguing ably against this assumption, have considered that the retrospective first-person narrative in itself, founded on informed hindsight, necessarily selects just those items which will lead to a predestined end. It might be suggested that, to very many authors in the nineteenth century, as before, the postulation of the apparently predetermined end, far from either philosophically or aesthetically closing the issue, may serve deliberately to provoke a basic questioning of causality or responsibility. The Baudelaire obstinately investigating the origins of perversion in 'Mademoiselle Bistouri' ('Peux-tu te souvenir de l'époque et de l'occasion où est née en toi cette passion si particulière?'), the Flaubert who rings with ambiguity the phrase: 'C'est la faute de la fatalité' are close to the Constant who at centre asks: 'Comment se fait-il que ...?' (D, p. 186). To each, in different proportions, the fundamental conflict between outer pressure and inner responsibility remains central. Constant's two concluding letters will make this outstandingly clear.

The initial version of the 'Avis de l'Éditeur' was at some stage corrected so as to lead on to these final letters.[4] The corrections in themselves show a vital development in treatment of literary convention. The initial pseudo-realistic yet melodramatic device (manuscript found in a chest whose false bottom concealed diamonds; editor's attempt to trace the owner) gives way to a quite different presentation: two individuals, each with partial knowledge of the participants, exchange views on the story and on possible reasons for publication.

Many commentators (myself included) have from time to time picked out this or that phrase from these concluding letters, taking it out of context and not fully realising the intricate planning of this double coda to the narrative. It serves multiple functions, which I shall first sum up and later discuss separately. First, anecdotal – in suggesting future extensions to the facts here recounted. Second, psychological – in the creation of two further characters, with personal reasons for their conflicting opinions. Third, moral – in the ironical interplay and unexpected parallelism of these apparently opposed judgements. Fourth (and most surprising perhaps in this period), there are suggestions bearing on fundamental aesthetic theories. Finally, of course, the skill in aphoristic summary both sets the two letters in patterns of parallel and contrast, and relates them in detail to the complex suggestions of the narrative itself.[5]

One or two brief comments on that narrative must suffice here to lead up to the points at issue in the two final letters. The society which in part misjudges Adolphe is no vague evil entity provoking equally vague self-righteous 'alienation'. Adolphe and Ellénore encounter clearly defined sections of contemporary opinion: first, the claustrophobic court of a minor German princeling, its strengths and weaknesses analysed in perceptive detail; later, the group of *émigrés*, doubly hidebound in their adherence to tradition during their exile; finally, both the newly-restored Polish aristocracy and the conventional diplomatic circle in Poland. Each ironical mis-judgement is motivated in detail.

Moreover, it is no mere case of misjudgement by the malevolent. The sympathetic may equally well be wrong.[6] The outer observer, severe or indulgent, merciful or malignant, self-seeking or sensitive, can see only a simplified part of the inner experience, can judge only according to 'les faits' as opposed to 'les nuances'.[7] Further, outer judgement is not necessarily wholly wrong, it may be the more exasperating for containing a mere half-truth. Letters from Adolphe's father or from the Baron de T. constantly repeat the 'you know yourself that ...' refrain. Their partial misjudgement stems from their inability to see more than *one* side of Adolphe's inner conflicts.[8]

Yet, if others have misjudged Adolphe (as much through in-dulgence as through severity), the narrator has constantly suggested his own initial misjudgements of the self. I have deliberately used the word 'initial'. Certain recent commentators have rightly seen that the lucidity for which the novel has often been praised does not apply to the young Adolphe experiencing, but to the retrospective narrator investigating experience. Two consequent points would deserve further stress. First, the extent to which it is unrecognized need for feeling rather than 'aridity' or self-analysis, which causes the initial self-deception. Second, that attempts today to apply conceptions of the 'unreliable narrator' may be anachronistic or dubious. While hyper-sophisticated readers may tend to interpret overt self-criticism as yet another form of *captatio benevolentiae,* or scrutinize potential contradiction in the narrator's attitudes, I should suggest that the narrator here functions as a relatively straightforward, 'transparent' means of investigating in Adolphe's past those basic complexities and paradoxes which the two final letters concentrate and extend.

In working out these two letters, so concise and so rich in implications, Constant had, I suggest, a model in mind – but a model which provoked him to creative contradiction.[9] Chateaubriand's *René* was a narrative delivered to two hearers: the totally sympathetic Chactas ('une indulgence aimable') and the morally uncompromising Père Souël ('une extrême sévérité'). Here, the author's emphasis is made still more clear than had already been done in the epic sweep and tone of the first-person narrative, by the proportion and placing of the two commentators' views. There is only one intervention in the course of the narrative: Chactas's brief speech with, at its centre:

Si tu souffres plus qu'un autre des choses de la vie, il ne faut pas t'en étonner; une grande âme doit contenir plus de douleur qu'une petite (pp. 42–3).

At the end, where the two hearers pronounce in turn, there is first the sudden and, after the tone of the main narrative, disconcerting condemnation from Le Père Souël:

on n'est point, monsieur, un homme supérieur parce qu'on aperçoit le monde sous un jour odieux (p. 74).

But Chateaubriand gives the last word to Chactas. René's two hearers may unite in a message of would-be reconciliation with society (eventually unfulfilled), Le Père Souël in remarking that 'Quiconque a reçu des forces doit les consacrer au service de ses semblables', Chactas in his regretful 'Il n'y a de bonheur que dans les voies communes'; but we are left with Chactas's epic vision of the flooding Mississippi which refuses any such boundaries. Beneath overt intellectual judgements it is clear, both from the tone of the main narrative and from the placing and expression of the listeners' reactions, just where the author's sympathies lie.

Rudler raised the possibility of some connection between the conclusions of *Adolphe* and of *René,* but found it unlikely that Constant 'se fût souvenu, à dix ans de distance, de son impression première'.[10] That first impression was strong, and bore precisely on the contrast between narrative and subsequent comment. Writing to Mme de Nassau in 1805 Constant comments:

> Je regarde cet ouvrage comme une des plus belles choses qui aient été écrites dans la langue française; mais lorsqu'à la fin du roman je trouve le discours sévère et juste du père, je sais bon gré à l'auteur d'avoir réuni beaucoup de raison à la conception et à la peinture de toute l'exaltation et de tout le vague qui paraissent à la jeunesse au-dessus de la raison: ce contraste rapide fait un effet extrême et d'autant plus grand que le lecteur ne s'attend pas à trouver l'auteur, qui a si bien décrit la rêverie de René, capable de la juger et de l'apprécier suivant les idées communes.[11]

There is of course the sting in the tail:

> Au reste, Chateaubriand a mis si peu de raison, ou plutôt tant de folie, dans le reste de ses cinq volumes, qu'il n'est pas étonnant qu'ayant voulu être raisonnable une fois, il ait trouvé une quantité de bon sens disponible.

What is certain is that Chateaubriand's presentation and formulation stuck in Constant's memory, and became a persistent household word in diaries ('le bonheur n'est-il donc que dans les voies communes?' Pl. p. 574) and letters: 'si bonheur il y a, et comme dit Chateaubriand, ce qu'on nomme ainsi ne se trouve que dans les voies communes' (1806); 'le bonheur, dit Chateaubriand, est dans les voies communes' (1809); for Mme de Staël also this is obviously a familiar reflection:

> il y a quelque chose de bien sévère dans l'existence quand elle sort *des voies communes*, comme dit Chateaubriand (1812).[12]

The initial impact of *René*, the repeated references, and the handling of the two final letters make it highly likely that this mode of framing was suggested by Chateaubriand – and then used by Constant to achieve very different effects.

To look now more closely at the five possible functions of Constant's final letters: the first, the anecdotal, raises a minor but intriguing suggestion. The friend in Germany, who knew both Adolphe and Ellénore, has sent to the editor a collection of letters 'qui vous instruiront du sort d'Adolphe; vous le verrez dans bien des circonstances diverses . . .', and the reply refers to these 'nouveaux détails, dont j'ignore encore si je ferai quelque usage'. *Adolphe*, as we know, had originated as an *épisode* in a plan for a longer novel; its relation to the unfinished *Cécile* remains problematic. But at least it is clear that Constant here deliberately indicates that he may later publish a further narrative.

The two letter-writers present, on the face of it, opposing natures and points of view; if both judge Adolphe severely, it is for very different reasons and in very different tones. The first, as a friend of Ellénore, had tried to make her break with Adolphe, who caused her suffering and death. Yet, precisely because of his friendship, he reflects her own ulcerated yet tender sense of Adolphe's divided nature and personal sufferings. Each epithet of condemnation is accompanied by one of comprehension: 'être malfaisant ... non moins misérable qu'elle', 'ce mélange d'égoïsme et de sensibilité', 'tour à tour le plus dévoué et le plus dur des hommes'. The focus of blame bears centrally on society: 'La société est trop puissante, ... elle mêle trop d'amertumes à l'amour qu'elle n'a pas sanctionné'; a biting summary of the destruction wrought by moralistic meddlers is combined with a warning to woman, perforce the victim, and with the suggestion that Adolphe 'en se rendant bien digne de blâme, ... s'est rendu aussi digne de pitié'.

This representative of 'indulgence' (already more penetrating in insights and less sweeping in expression than Chateaubriand's Chactas) will be followed by the mouthpiece of 'extrême sévérité'; Constant has significantly reversed the order of the two voices, so as to refuse any final note of complicity.

The 'Éditeur', in his reply, has no personal cause for attenuating sympathy. He rejects uncompromisingly the appeal to social pressures as an excuse:

Les circonstances sont bien peu de chose, le caractère est tout.

A searching and virulent analysis sees Adolphe's conduct as dependent on the caprice of the moment or the stimulus of the obstacle. The worst twist of the knife comes in a phrase sometimes conveniently overlooked by those who attack Constant's *mauvaise foi*; here the commentator is keenly aware of the dangers and distortions of self-analysis:

Je hais d'ailleurs cette fatuité d'un esprit qui croit excuser ce qu'il explique; je hais cette vanité qui s'occupe d'elle-même en racontant le mal qu'elle a fait, qui a la prétention de se faire plaindre en se décrivant, et qui ... s'analyse au lieu de se repentir.

At the centre remains the fundamental principle:

La grande question dans la vie, c'est la douleur que l'on cause.[13]

Comprehension versus condemnation: yet the interdependence of the two letters is suggestive: the writers are being used to raise fundamentally open questions. In the first, outer pressures may seem in part to exonerate; in the second, inner flaw totally to condemn. But if the first writer stresses the outer force, yet he sees it as working through 'tout ce qu'il y a de mauvais dans le cœur de l'homme'; if the second insists on the inner flaw, he yet suggests that the qualities Adolphe lacked: 'la fermeté, la fidélité, la bonté', rather than being achievable by personal effort, are 'les dons qu'il faut demander au ciel'. Taken together, the two represent man's double sense of being caught by ineluctable forces (inheritance, social conventions, inner pressures) and yet of being finally and personally responsible for both 'son malheur et celui des autres' (D, p. 196). Their interplay of judgements is subtle and continuous: the first writer warns woman; the second replies that 'c'est aux hommes que cette leçon s'adresse'; the first picks out the young Adolphe's unrecognized emotional impulses ('puni de ses qualitiés plus encore que de ses défauts, parce que ses qualités prenaient leur source dans ses émotions, et non dans ses principes'), while the second selects the insufficiencies of the intellectual superstructure ('cet esprit, dont on est si fier, ne sert ni à trouver du bonheur ni à en donner'). Their conflicting and concurring analyses both raise and leave open a series of fundamental questions around the bases of any potential judgement.

They raise too, almost imperceptibly in passing, but with Constant's probing ability to touch on suggestive problems, a vital æsthetic issue which was to come to the fore later in the century: that of *l'art utile* versus *l'art pour l'art*. The first writer, in keeping with his function as representative of a particular level of empathy, holds that the narrative should be published as a moral tale which will be of use to others: 'Vous devriez, monsieur, publier cette anecdote. Elle ... ne serait pas sans utilité. Le malheur d'Ellénore prouve que ... L'exemple d'Adolphe ne sera pas moins instructif ...'. The second (though momentarily willing to suggest a contradictory 'leçon instructive') observes sardonically that one can learn only from one's own individual experience: 'chacun ne s'instruit qu'à ses dépens dans ce monde'. His blank rejection of utilitarian aim both underlines the narrator's constant suggestion that no observer – sympathetic or severe – can adequately share a complex experience, and bears on an æsthetic problem that had interested Constant from years earlier. In the *Journal* of 1804 he had been intrigued (after discussions with Henry Crabbe Robinson on Schelling and Kant) by ideas summarized as:

L'art pour l'art, et sans but; tout but dénature l'art. Mais l'art atteint au but qu'il n'a pas. (Pl. p. 266).[14]

The second writer here dismisses any facile or immediate moral effect; if he publishes the book, it will be simply as 'une histoire assez vraie de la misère du cœur humain'. In the interplay between the two letters, Constant has skilfully managed at the same time to meet the persistent conventional requirement for the fulfilling of a moral aim (while yet suggesting the conflicting moral conclusions which might be drawn) and quietly to assert the autonomy of the artist's expression of experience in its own right.

Aphoristic skill, whether in brief, biting phrases, or within balanced periods, reaches its heights in these two summarizing letters. Some readers have seen a potential contradiction between Adolphe's 'aversion pour toutes les maximes communes et pour toutes les formules dogmatiques' (D. p. 114) and his own delight in the firm clinching formula. Yet, even within the story, these formulæ are either deliberately set in contradiction to each other, or, more often, made to suggest in themselves not the simplicity but the complexity of human experience:

Il n'y a point d'unité complète dans l'homme, et presque jamais personne n'est tout à fait sincère ni tout à fait de mauvaise foi. (D. pp. 123–4).

To an enhanced degree, in the concluding letters, epigrammatic phrases clamp together contradictions in the behaviour of others:

les indifférents ... tracassiers au nom de la morale, et nuisibles par zèle pour la vertu,

or in the nature of Adolphe:

ce mélange d'égoïsme et de sensibilité
prévoyant le mal avant de le faire, et reculant avec désespoir après l'avoir fait.

These letters offer a particular opportunity for setting at odds the firmest pronouncements:

puni de ses qualités plus encore que de ses défauts/puni de son caractère par son caractère même
la société est trop puissante / le caractère est tout

In so doing, they suggest not only the basic problems of imaginative comprehension (Constant remarked elsewhere: 'la même action, commise par deux individus dans deux circonstances, n'a jamais une valeur uniforme') but also, as so often in the narrative itself, the need to redefine the terms in which we seek to sum up behaviour:[15] here

je n'appelle pas bonté cette pitié passagère qui . . . .

Both letters end with firm overt condemnation; in the first: 'n'ayant ainsi laissé de traces que de ses torts' and in the second: 'l'on se trouve seulement avoir ajouté des remords aux regrets et des fautes aux souffrances'; there is a final appropriate ironical balance in the fact that the last word of the 'sympathetic' commentator should be *torts*, and that of the 'severe' (the last word too of the book) *souffrances*.

Later, in his two Prefaces and the important variants to them, Constant was to express more fully and explicitly the suggestions he had concentrated into his skilled framework. He was to stress how an artificial and hypocritical society encourages an irresponsible beginning and ironically applauds a bitter end; to analyse more fully the social and personal causes of possessiveness and suffering in Ellénore and of initial blindness in Adolphe (unable to foresee the lasting grip of both pity and need for the other); to note sardonically the potential vanity and self-deception inherent in self-analysis; to query the very terms in which we express our experience ('emprunter le langage de l'amour', 'ce que par habitude ils nomment faiblesse'). It would be worth analysing chronologically, and in their relation to circumstances, these future developments – but that is another story. The two concluding letters already contain in germ each of these later expansions – and, in turning attention back to the rootless wanderer of the beginning,[16] form part of a fundamental principle to be stressed in all Constant's main works. The first writer reflects that Adolphe 'n'a fait aucun usage d'une liberté reconquise au prix de tant de douleurs et de tant de larmes', and the second that 'il n'a suivi aucune route fixe, rempli aucune carrière utile . . .'. The Constant who repeatedly insists that 'Tout se tient' in a threefold parallelism between political principles, metaphysical beliefs, personal fidelity, has here again suggested their interpenetration.[17]

In the tricky circumstances of first publication, well aware of the ways in which readers might interpret, or misinterpret, personal allusions, Constant found in his framing technique a means of prolonging and enhancing the open questions and the patterns of irony which interweave in the narrative itself, without the necessity of prefacing in his own voice.[18] From devices familiar in his time he has evolved a particularly original, suggestive and concentrated means of multiplying angles of vision around basic problems of imaginative comprehension.

NOTES

1 Paul Delbouille's critical edition of *Adolphe* for Les Textes Français, Paris, Les Belles Lettres, 1977, incorporates the hitherto only partially available variants and many useful notes. In the following article, page references have not been included for quotations from the introductory 'Avis' or from the concluding 'Lettres'. For other references, D indicates Delbouille's edition of *Adolphe*, and Pl. the *Œuvres* of Constant, edited by Alfred Roulin, Paris, Gallimard, Bibliothèque de la Pléiade, 1957. Page references to Chateaubriand's *René* refer to the critical edition by J. M. Gautier, Geneva, Droz, 1970.

2 Restrictions of space will prevent detailed reference to all critics who have discussed problems here raised. Paul Delbouille's *Genèse, Structure et Destin d'«Adolphe»* Paris, Les Belles Lettres, 1971, provides an exceptionally thorough bibliography of works up to that date. See also D, pp. 89–96. I. W. Alexander's thoughtful monograph on *Adolphe* (London, Edward Arnold, 1973) both adds interesting personal observations and calls attention, in its Bibliographical Note, to later stimulating discussions (see especially Marian Hobson: 'Theme and Structure in *Adolphe*', in *MLR*, January 1971, and Jeannine Jallat: '*Adolphe*: la parole et l'autre', *Littérature*, May 1971). Subsequent studies, where careful hypotheses might merit closer discussion than is possible here, include H. Verhoeff's '*Adolphe*' *et Constant*, Paris, Klincksieck, 1976, and G. Mercken-Spaas's *Alienation in Constant's 'Adolphe'*, Bern, Lang, 1977. A different kind of 'framing', in a work well known to Constant, is discussed by J. Starobinski in his suggestive article 'Les *Lettres écrites de Lausanne* de Mme de Charrière', in *Roman et lumières au dix-huitième siècle*, Colloque sous la présidence de W. Krauss, R. Pomeau, R. Garaudy et J. Fabre, Paris, Éditions Sociales, 1970.

3 Cf. D, p. 218, and fuller discussion in his *Genèse*.

4 On examining the variants in MS 1, on the time-lapse between 'discovery' of the narrative and its publication by the editor, I reached the same hypotheses as are raised in the succinct and convincing note in D, p. 219, n. 7. The initial 25 years seems an arbitrary figure; its correction to 3 years in MS 1 would suggest first revision (3 years after 1806), and the final 10 years would correspond to publication in 1816.

5 I. W. Alexander, *op. cit.*, p. 17, rightly suggests, in a summarizing sentence, that the framing documents 'extend and in some degree qualify [the reflective function] of the narrator'.

6 Cf. D, pp. 179–80, the intervention of the well-meaning friend of Ellénore, 'celle qui croyait la défendre', and the subtle analysis of how

such attempts at understanding may culminate in distortion. Cf. also, in Chs VIII and IX, the well-intended manœuvres of the Baron de T.

7 Constant's letters and diaries often oppose 'les faits' to 'les nuances' in suggesting the difficulty or impossibility of fully sharing inner experience, e.g.: 'La plupart des hommes, ou même tous, car ce n'est pas un défaut dans l'amitié ou la compréhension, mais une loi de la nature, voient ce qui intéresse les autres d'une manière nette et tranchée, parce qu'ils n'en saisissent que les faits, et que les faits sont la partie la moins importante de nos douleurs'. Cf. D, p. 171, the Baron's 'les faits sont positifs . . .', 'des nuances que l'opinion n'approfondit pas'.

8 For the father, cf. D. p. 161: 'Je m'étais dit cent fois ce qu'il me disait', etc.; for the Baron de T., cf. D. pp. 170–2: 'Vous n'avez pas été fâché d'entendre de ma bouche des raisonnements que vous vous répétez sans cesse à vous-même'.

9 The rôle of creative contradiction in many authors' use of 'sources' would deserve further analysis. I raise an example from Flaubert in my 'La Contradiction créatrice' (see below, pp. 437–60).

10 Cf. his outstanding critical edition of *Adolphe*, Manchester University Press, 1919, pp. lvi sqq. Delbouille, *Genèse*, p. 138, rightly remarks on the difference between Chateaubriand and Constant in the narrative itself, but does not discuss details from the concluding letters.

11 *Journal intime de Benjamin Constant et Lettres à sa famille et à ses amis*, précédés d'une introduction par D. Melegari, Paris, Ollendorff, 1895, pp. 348–9. As always, in assessing material from Constant's letters, one has to bear in mind the effect he intends to present to the recipient, in a particular context. When Constant writes to the aunt with whose opinion he is anxious to coincide: 'Nous sommes tout à fait du même avis sur *René*', we do not possess the letter to which he is replying. The undertones of 'selon les idées communes' are important. For 'toute l'exaltation et . . . tout le vague qui paraissent à la jeunesse au-dessus de la raison', cf. *Adolphe*, D, p. 110: 'je ne demandais alors qu'à me livrer à ces impressions primitives et fougueuses qui jettent l'âme hors de la sphère commune, et lui inspirent le dédain de tous les objets qui l'environnent'. Already, in 1805, conflicting attitudes are subtly set at odds.

12 Benjamin Constant et Madame de Staël: *Lettres à un Ami*, publiées avec une introduction et des notes par Jean Mistler, Neuchâtel, à la Baconnière, 1949, pp. 204–5.

13 This phrase and the passage which follows are used as an epigraph to the second-last chapter of George Eliot's *Felix Holt*. Cf. also her reflections on the 'man of maxims', very close to the end of Ch. I in *Adolphe*: 'The mysterious complexity of our life is not to be embraced by maxims. . . . The man of maxims is the popular representation of the minds that are guided in their judgements solely by general rules, thinking that those will lead them to justice by a ready-made patent method.'

14 For interesting new information about the interplay of influences around ideas on *l'art pour l'art*, see the article by Ernst Behler in *Le Groupe de Coppet*, ed. S. Balayé and J.-D. Candaux, Genève, Slatkine; Paris, Champion, 1977.

15 For discussion of the vital problem of mistrust of words in *Adolphe*, cf.
   above pp. 7–10, 53–7 and 61–9, and T. Todorov, 'La Parole selon Constant',
   Critique, 1968, pp. 765–71.
16 I have deliberately not discussed here possible relations between *Adolphe*
   and its biographical origins. But, contrary to those who have seen in it a
   kind of 'wish-fulfilment' seeking to be rid of Germaine de Staël, I should
   suggest that the *Avis de L'Éditeur* and the two final letters stem rather
   from two nerve-points in Constant's continuous self-analysis. First,
   despite his urge to mobility and transience, there is the recurring sense
   of blank depression at any break with the past (Cf. *Journaux* and letters
   regarding his first wife, Mme de Charrière, Anna Lindsay, etc.). The
   diaries reflectively repeat the incisive judgement of Julie Talma (whose
   penetrating correspondence – *Lettres de Julie Talma à Benjamin Constant*,
   Paris, Plon, 1933, deserves further analysis): 'Vous ne quittez jamais et
   vous prenez toujours', p. 235, significantly reversing the stress, to bear
   on 'je ne quitte jamais' (Pl. pp. 442 and 447). Second, there is his
   awareness, 'Quoi que je dise et même que j'éprouve' (Pl. pp. 448, 514,
   etc.), of the essential literary and political stimulus drawn from Mme de
   Staël: 'J'ai dans le caractère une partie découragée que Minette seule
   relève, et si mon esprit peut se passer de tout le monde, cette partie de
   mon caractère ne le peut pas'. Whether prophecy or later reflection on
   the outcome, the 'Avis' relates fundamentally to these apprehensions.
17 See D, p. 247, for the repeated 'tout se tient' in projected preface. The
   threefold headings to human activity (political, metaphysical, personal)
   are particularly evident in Constant's articles on Julie Talma and on
   Mme de Staël: the sense of their interpenetration frequently recurs in
   many other works.
18 Delbouille (D. pp. 214, and 239) wonders whether possibly the concluding letters arose from attempts to plan a Preface in May 1816. The
   suggestion seems to me valuable.

8

The shaping of *Adolphe*: some remarks on variants (1979)

Now that the earliest known manuscript of *Adolphe* has at last been made available for consultation, and that Paul Delbouille has produced his indispensable critical edition covering all available variants from MSS and editions,[1] it seems worth looking again at what we know or may deduce about the processes which gradually brought about this novel's exceptional blend of complexity and concision. Now, too, that criticism has ceased to be primarily or exclusively concerned with biographical 'keys', it may be possible to re-assess some of the reasons for, and results of, Constant's revision or rejection of factual details. In the final *Adolphe*, an interplay of conflicting impulses between two characters is deliberately organised, both in its crescendo of effects and in its patterns of reflective and ironical allusions backwards and forwards across ten chapters. How did Constant arrive at this exceptional simplicity of outline and his exceptional concentration of complex suggestions?

The present article can be no more than a modest contribution to one small part of the problem. But familiar and newly-discovered variants, if re-examined together in context, may suggest something of both the external and the internal pressures which shape Constant's art. I shall not here re-open the necessarily inconclusive debate about the chronological relationship with *Cécile*; I assume (though the question of course remains open) that Constant, at the end of October, 1806, set forth on a novel which was to recount his re-discovery of Charlotte, and that the 'épisode' which eventually became *Adolphe* was first undertaken as background or prologue to this future discovery of a solution. I shall here suggest one or two general hypotheses which seem to me to result from Delbouille's careful examination of M 1. My main intention is to re-examine side by side the detailed variants, some familiar since Rudler's outstanding edition of 1919, some only recently revealed. Such brief passages are sometimes thought of as 'minimal' or 'purely stylistic'. I hope above all to show that in Constant substance and style are inseparable in import and impact.

Two external influences helped to bring about a particular concentration in Constant's novel. The second I shall leave till the end of this article. The first is the effect of his reading his draft aloud, from the very earliest stages of composition, to friends or groups; he notes his hearers' reactions, is often startled by them, and at times revises accordingly.[2] In themselves, these readings mean that the novel (unlike many prolonged episodic productions typical of the times) has to be concentrated into what an audience could hear in an evening: in length the equivalent of a performance at the theatre. Has any novel ever had so many pre-publication readings, to so many audiences, in so many countries? *Journaux* and Letters give evidence on how seriously, in the early stages, the presentation of both Adolphe and Ellénore was revised after reflection on readers' responses; some ten years later, at the point of publication in 1816, Constant is still deferring to individual comments.

He is fully aware of the cloud of witnesses which, especially since 1794 on his meeting with Mme de Staël, continuously produces its incisive and differing judgments: the international network of Coppet; the widespread and distinctly differing members of his own family; the wider public from whose sometimes ironically misconceived *opinion* he would wish to wrest a deserved *considération*. Some will condemn the desire to break a long liaison as cruel cynicism or even near-sacrilege;[3] others will see the inability to break as spineless or self-interested subjection. The still more fluctuating and complex inner urges will be obsessively revealed in the *Journaux*. If, in Adolphe, Constant had initially hoped (*Jnx.* 28/5/07) to 'faire comprendre mon caractère', he was faced by a challenge comparable in the personal realm to that posed elsewhere by the *plaidoyers* of his political career, demanding the same capacity to analyse in swift and subtle terms both the shifting surface and the serious substructure which will underlie both personal and political commitments.[4]

Several major variants between the 1810 MS and the editions of 1816 or 1824 have long been familiar: the alteration to Ellénore's early life, introduced just before publication; the addition, in 1816, of the 'Charme de l'amour' passage which opens Ch. IV, and of the final 'Lettre à l'Éditeur' and 'Réponse';[5] the omission, in 1816, of a long passage in Ch. VIII. These will be briefly re-discussed in their context below.

The recently freed Lausanne MS (M 1) has been shown by Delbouille both to be the source of the 1810 copy (M 2) and, equally clearly, not to be Constant's first version. Constant must have given an earlier version to his *copiste*; on some pages he has inserted small corrections, whereas he has re-written important sections in his own hand (again occasionally making subsequent changes to details). Delbouille has skilfully and convincingly deduced that the pages in Constant's hand may indicate the parts of his novel which demanded most care in revision or extension. Of those listed by Delbouille, there are certain shorter passages covering key points in the narrative (first assessment of Ellénore, 121–2; reflections provoked by the night in the countryside, 172–4, 178; opening pages of Chs. VIII and IX – intervention of Ellénore's friend, 179–82; second visit to the Baron de T., 188–9). But the two most extended revisions concern first, the second half of Ch. II and all of Ch. III (from Adolphe's first meeting with Ellénore to the climax of their love) and, second, most of Ch. IX and all of Ch. X (from the events causing Ellénore's death to the end of the narrative). Specially important is Delbouille's discovery that what is now Ch. IV was originally Ch. III (with consequent re-numbering of subsequent chapters). So, whether by splitting what, as he re-wrote it, was becoming a very long Ch. II, or by introducing a new section, Constant created an extra chapter, devoted to the growth of feeling.

These facts, meticulously laid out in Delbouille's edition, suggest, in my opinion, a hypothesis about the gradual creative development of the novel. It would seem that *Adolphe* originally centred on those middle chapters (IV–VIII) which analyse the interplay of exasperation, pity, and power of a shared past in the will to break and the reasons for recurrent reluctance. The re-writing of Chs. II and III in M 1 allows more space and status to the origins of feeling – to the analysis of the 'intermittences' and of the stimulus by obstacles, to the joys and ironies of the platonic pause, and to the precarious sense of timeless delight. Their whole movement leads up, completely logically, to the much-discussed 'Charme de l'amour' opening to Ch. IV, introduced in 1816. Whatever its biographical origins, it is certainly far from the mere irrelevant 'couplet lyrique' which many critics have suggested, but is rather one of the most skilled and concentrated analyses ever attempted of that sense of ecstasy menaced by time and change to which Ch. III leads and from which

Ch. IV will, in one vertiginously ironical succeeding paragraph, fall away. As for the re-writing of Chs. IX and X, Constant notes very early in his *Journaux* that 'la maladie est amenée trop brusquement'. His re-writing of these scenes in his own hand in M 1 presumably enables him to develop the causes and consequences of Ellénore's illness and death, so as to achieve those logical and ironical patterns which deliberately recall and reverse phrases and feelings from previous chapters, and in particular from Chs. II and III.

The result, in these two re-worked sections from near beginning and end, is to give more prominence and dignity to the figure of Ellénore. Yet, perhaps partly because these important passages have been redone in M 1, further detailed changes regarding her (though some, as we shall later see, are important) are less frequent than those which immediately affect Adolphe. So I shall first examine the main ways in which alterations of detail influence the presentation of Adolphe himself, and shall later look at variants concerning Ellénore.

Ch. I sums up the influences (father, elderly woman, society in general) which are the seeds of Adolphe's state of mind when he meets Ellénore. M 1 has one or two marginal hesitations, sorted out in M 2. Did Adolphe's father cherish for his son 'des espérances probablement fort exagérées' or simply 'de grandes espérances'? Constant has retained the more self-critical version. It is gradually that he has worked out the importance and individuality of the father's role. The 'quelque chose de contraint que je ne pouvais m'expliquer' (110), now part of the father's nature, had once been attributed to the self: 'Malheureusement il y avait dans mon caractère qqe chose à la fois de contraint et de violent que je ne m'expliquois pas . . .' Similarly, in Ch. II, Constant had hesitated about whether to attribute the inheritance of a past century's cynicism regarding rapid liaisons to a general social background or to an individual influence. The decision to concentrate this in the father (118a) fits the carefully planned recurrence of the father's role in the course of the novel: ironically indulgent when he should be severe, severe when this serves only to provoke resistance (160), he will yet create in the background increasingly recognised claims – whether of family likeness and affection, of duty to career, or of the part-pretexts these provide.

Ch. I, after analysing the influence of the father, had turned to the disillusioned elderly woman whose spirit and wit had so directed the young Adolphe's thoughts towards the insignificance of life and society in face of the brevity imposed by death. Two tiny but significant alterations between MSS and publications change what had been presented as a kind of tutelage into a shared attitude: 'dans *ses* conversations inépuisables, *elle m'avait présenté* la vie sous toutes ses faces' becomes 'dans *nos* conversations inépuisables, *nous avions envisagé* la vie ... (112).[6]

The end of Ch. I tackles in serious vein a point which Constant has expressed in satirical and other tones in the *Cahier Rouge* and elsewhere: the ironical judgments passed on a clumsy youth whose passive boredom in face of a stereotyped society is falsely attributed to active or personal hatred or malice. The initial phrases: 'beaucoup de gens m'ennuyaient' in M 1 becomes the blanker sense that 'peu de gens m'inspiraient de l'intérêt', while in the margin there is added the clinching generalisation:

or les hommes se blessent de l'indifférence, ils l'attribuent à la malveillance ou à l'affectation; ils ne veulent pas croire qu'on s'ennuie avec eux naturellement (113).[7]

This attitude connects with the passage in Ch. II (118), on how youth is naively astounded by the gap between the cynical maxims and the conventional rules of conduct of its elders; and with certain passages on Ellénore's children.

The first meeting between Adolphe and Ellénore is deliberately constructed to suggest how need, chance and the stimulus of the moment may combine to produce intense feeling. It is brought about by the Comte de P., her protector who is keen to surround her by a socially respectable circle.[8] Constant's original version (M 1): 'Il me témoigna beaucoup d'amitié. Il m'invita fortement à venir chez lui' is changed, so as to reduce any sense of obligation, to the neutral: 'Il me proposa de venir le voir' (119).

That first meeting contains in M 1 (then crossed out) a transparently autobiographical allusion. After the exclamation 'Malheureuse visite!' (119) there appeared the phrase: 'qui a empoisonné les huit plus belles années de toute ma vie!' This, I suggest, is an echo of Constant's weary reflection in his *Journal* for 12/8/06 (shortly before he embarks on his novel):

Journée douloureuse et perdue. Il n'y a pas moins de huit ans que cela dure.

The carefully organised time-scheme of the novel will move far from any such association with protracted facts: it covers a period of some four years, with Adolphe as the naive youth of twenty-two at the outset, significantly reaching in the second half the then legal age of majority (twenty-five) which necessarily enhances his awareness of obligations to career and family.[9]

Another brief but suggestive deletion, when Adolphe is about to meet Ellénore, is that of the phrase from M 1 on his previous physical experience (117b):

J'avais partagé les plaisirs faciles et peu glorieux de mes camarades.

The tone of the times may be responsible for two later removals of overtly sexual allusions: in Ch. III (134) impatience with 'un amour séparé des sens' is changed to 'un tel amour'; and in Ch. IV (146) there is the removal of Ellénore's statement about the Count: 'Depuis longtemps tout rapport intime a cessé entre cet homme et moi'.[10] Yet, despite such surface concessions, moments of open challenge will remain. When, at the end of Ch. III, Ellénore 'se donna enfin toute entière', we have the outspoken reflection:

Ce n'est pas le plaisir, ce n'est pas la nature, ce ne sont pas les sens qui sont corrupteurs: ce sont les calculs auxquels la société nous accoutume et les réflexions que l'expérience fait naître (137).

Parts of the first meeting with Ellénore were re-written in Constant's own hand in M 1. Even so, a vital addition occurs in the margin. The MS, after outlining her personality, had opened a new paragraph with: 'Telle que je viens de la peindre, Ellénore me parut une conquête digne de moi'. The phrase which now precedes (a marginal addition in M 1), both in its balance of motives and in the order it gives them, provides a quite different range of suggestions:

Offerte à mes regards dans un moment où mon cœur avoit besoin d'amour, ma vanité de succès, Ellénore ... (121).

From here to the end of Ch. III, Constant re-wrote M 1. In these scenes of involvement and *intermittences*, one or two later corrections show his care for the slightest detail. The persuasive effect of Adolphe's words on his feelings in his letter to Ellénore had at first taken place 'en écrivant', but now occurs 'en finissant d'écrire'. Ellénore's reaction to his letter is not just to see him as ten years younger than herself, but to think of 'le *transport passager* d'un homme qui ...' (124). The sudden switch in feeling when, after Adolphe's anguish at Ellénore's absence, the Count tells him she is to return, undergoes a series of changes. Constant had first written (M 1): 'Je sentis ma douleur s'appaiser graduellement. Mon sentiment diminuait par là-même.' He then deleted from 's'appaiser' onwards. A few lines later, where, after 'et je repris ma vie habituelle' (changed to 'mais j'avais repris'), he had originally written 'l'angoisse que j'avais éprouvée ne me parut bientôt plus qu'un songe', he alters this intense insistence on mutability, first to 'l'angoisse ... se dissipa', then to 'se dissipait graduellement', to arrive finally at the phrase which will allow the last traces to subsist: 'achevoit de se dissiper' (126). At the same time, the sudden recrudescence of feeling is given added complexity by his transferring to an earlier place in the paragraph the phrase: 'Mon amour-propre s'y mêloit',[11] and added intensity by the marginal addition of 'son image erroit devant mes yeux, régnoit sur mon cœur ...'.

It is this sense of total if temporary involvement which is to be brought to the fore in Ch. III, opening with a vital marginal addition to M1:

Il n'étoit plus question dans mon âme ni de calculs[12] ni de projets. Je me sentais, de la meilleure foi du monde, véritablement amoureux. Ce n'étoit plus l'espoir du succès qui me fesait agir: c'étoit le besoin de voir celle que j'aimais, de jouïr de sa présence, qui me dominoit exclusivement.

This tone, with its concomitant analysis of both causes and concentration of feeling, will dominate the chapter: 'Sa résistance avait exalté toutes mes sensations, toutes mes idées ... Mon amour tenait du culte ...', will lead up to the joy of its concluding phrases and to the later opening of Ch. IV. Yet, in the central and often quoted passage on how 'l'amour crée, comme par enchantement, un passé dont il nous entoure' (134), two almost imperceptible changes point forward to the future. Constant had originally written (M 1):

L'amour est un point lumineux qui s'empare du temps;

on the same manuscript he changes his phrase to the more restrictive and dubitative:

L'amour n'est qu'un point lumineux, et néanmoins il *semble* s'emparer du temps.[13]

The delight of achievement is followed, with grim immediacy, by the demands of devotion, in the long and suggestive second paragraph of Ch. IV. It is here that Constant adds in the margin of M 1 one of the key phrases of the whole novel: 'Ellénore étoit sans doute un vif plaisir dans mon existence: mais elle n'étoit plus un but; elle étoit devenue un lien.' The parallel phrase in the *Lettre sur Julie* (completed in March 1807 though projected earlier) has often been noted;[14] which work echoes the other it is impossible to say. Other epigrammatic phrases in the novel would deserve further investigation.[15]

The next major change comes in Ch. VI where, summing up the situation at the end of the year in Caden, Constant deleted in M 1 a series of brief and general factual statements, to replace them by the long marginal insertion in which the complex interplay of hurt, reproach, irritation and guilt is fully defined, and its expression through veiled insinuations, indirect allusions and vague self-justification is much more pointedly brought alive (166). The last phrase, originally the stark 'Nos cœurs ne se rencontraient plus', takes on a different resonance from the addition of the two adjectives: 'Nos cœurs défiants et blessés . . .'. (Cf. n. 11).

Ch. VII brings a small but highly suggestive marginal addition (M 1) in the Baron de T.'s central speech to Adolphe. The tempting outline of Adolphe's high promise for any future career had not originally included the phrase: 'Vous pouvez aspirer aux plus illustres alliances.' Its insertion in M 1 leads on to Adolphe's meditations as he wanders through dusk and night in the peace of the countryside. After reflecting on how patient plodders whom he once scorned have outpaced him 'dans la route de la fortune, de la considération et de la gloire',[16] and experiencing renewed 'accès de fureur' against Ellénore as obstacle to possible career ('fureur' has on two occasions replaced the initial, more absolute, term 'haine', 174), Adolphe, recalling the Baron's phrase, imagines the ideal marriage which would reconcile him with family and society. He had originally written 'me créer l'idéal d'une compagne chérie'; the removal of 'chérie' helps to keep the dream on the ideal plane. But as that dream continued, M 1 momentarily allowed it to come too close to the facts of the author's own existence, to those recurrent consultations over long years with self, with family or with friends in the search for that perfect wife who would provide the means to personal peace, uninterrupted work, conventional respectability, as well as to a compelling reason for a break with the exasperations and the deeply-rooted ties of the past. M 1 originally read: 'L'établissement qu'on me proposait', 'la compagne qui s'offrait à moi s'associait sans peine à tous mes devoirs' – obvious allusions to quite specific offers of or from a possible partner. Corrections in M 1 bring the passage back to the plane of a purely imagined contrast with the present: 'La compagne que mon imagination m'avoit soudain créée . . . s'associait à tous mes devoirs' (175: 'soudain' is a particularly significant insertion).[17] Finally, after a further vision of his childhood home and surroundings graced by the imagined 'créature innocente et jeune qui les embellissait, qui les animait par l'espérance', M 1 had continued in a highly emotional and syntactically involved passage:

> qui doublait leur charme comme un ange entouré d'une lumière éthérée, qui, prenant pitié du voyageur perdu dans la nuit sombre, lui ferait soudain reconnaître à la lueur d'un flambeau céleste, la rive désirée et l'azyle dont il se croyait encore éloigné.

Was there in this climax a trace of what was hoped for from Charlotte? – in any case, fortunately, this uncharacteristic piece of inflated style is already crossed out in M 1.

Another passage is cut towards the end of the same chapter. Adolphe had achieved for a brief space a mood of calm resignation (178), with, in M 1, a momentary exception:

> La volonté de mon père me tourmentait encore. Mais je me flattais de l'appaiser par des assurances d'affection, par la promesse mille fois réitérée de quitter Ellénore dès qu'elle serait moins malheureuse.

This passage disappears, partly perhaps because its suggestion of conscious duplicity would not fit well with the serious family memories which precede it, or simply so as to leave an impression of unimpaired if fleeting tranquillity.

The long cut in the 1816 version of Ch. VIII will be discussed below in relation to Ellénore. In Ch. IX, when the Baron de T., skilled diplomat, begins his campaign for winning over Adolphe, one or two brief phrases are deleted from M 1, which, after 'mes visites chez lui se multiplièrent' (189) had first read:

> Je l'accompagnais souvent à cheval. Je fus de toutes ses réunions, de toutes ses fêtes. Je l'accompagnais dans ses promenades.

These phrases disappear: what is to count is not the sharing of pleasures, but Adolphe's being entrusted with diplomatic responsibilities: he now neglects Ellénore not for personal enjoyment but for the central temptation of an honourable, socially valuable, and socially acceptable career.

Later in the same chapter, Adolphe's outburst of exasperation at the arrival of Ellénore's letter of clamant summons, ironically instrumental in bringing about the end, is intensified by the addition, after the MSS, of the phrase (191) 'Je ne puis respirer une heure en paix'.

The irony of the end is brought fully to the fore at the beginning of Ch. X. Here, a long marginal addition in M 1 (retained in successive versions, and running from 'Tous mes efforts pour obtenir le temps que je voulais ...' to 'le cruel avait trop bien calculé qu'Ellénore y verrait un arrêt irrévocable' (196) re-defines and expands what had been suggested at the end of the previous chapter. Whereas Ch. ix had critically analysed the tergiversations underlying Adolphe's letter of excuses to the Baron for delay in carrying out his promise ('comme il est naturel aux caractères faibles de le faire, j'entassai dans ma lettre mille raisonnements pour justifier mon retard ...' 193), this new passage is centred on one of the most basic experiences and ironies of the book: that the possibility of a break, since it removes the prospect of unending exasperation, brings moments of paradoxical peace, renewed tenderness, lasting memories, deep-rooted regrets. So here, the 'promesses de l'abandonner ... n'avaient été dictées que par le désir de rester plus longtemps près d'elle'. For the rest, the chapter, already re-worked in M 1, turns to the tragedy of death.

One detail remains. Ellénore had sought in vain, just before her death, for a letter she had written to Adolphe, and had made him promise that if it should be found he would not read it. Yet it is essential to the book's many patterns of irony that it should conclude with this letter, where Ellénore, so often seen as 'avide de se tromper elle-même', incisively sums up Adolphe's strengths and weaknesses, and even longs for him to have the decisiveness to put an end to their torment. Adolphe must therefore find the letter. But the initial version, where he too easily read it, contrary to his promise ('Elle étoit de sa main: elle m'étoit adressée: elle étoit ouverte'), is changed in M 1 so as to make his beginning to read accidental or unavoidable:

Je ne la reconnus pas d'abord. Elle était sans adresse. Elle était ouverte (204).

The conclusion has brought us back to the role of Ellénore. It is at the very early stages of writing and reading aloud that Constant (28/12/06) makes his first, well-known, simplification of reality: Adolphe, rather than vacillating between two women, shall be involved with Ellénore only. This drastic reduction to two central characters has one fundamental result: Ellénore's hurt is never dependent on jealousy of another love-affair, but rises from less conventional and possibly more deep-rooted sources of suffering: the lover's weariness at the claims of day-to-day devotion; his urge above all towards a career to which she remains an obstacle.[18]

A second, again well-known, simplification occurs some ten years

later, just before publication, and here as a result of the reactions of
those to whom the novel is read aloud: the changes made in
Ellénore's early life before she met Adolphe.[19] The initial account,
though brief and general, had been closer to the facts of an Anna
Lindsay;[20] now, in a very brief space, Constant makes several highly
important readjustments. In the MS version, Ellénore, exiled from
childhood alone with her mother, had had 'une avanture d'éclat,
dont les détails me sont restés inconnus'; shortly afterwards, her
mother had died, and Ellénore had found a protector in the Comte
de P., to whom she had totally devoted her practical abilities during
his trials as an *émigré*. The suggested alternative motives for her first
(now deleted) love-affair had been 'soit imprudence, soit passion, soit
malheur de circonstances'. In the final version, where her sole
attachment is to the Comte de P., suppositions are confined to 'la
fatalité de sa situation ou l'inexpérience de son âge', and her
mother's death, leaving her alone in the world, takes place before
this one last remaining recourse. One other tiny but vital verbal
change occurs. The MSS, while leading on to Ellénore's exemplary
aid in furthering the Count's recovery of his fortune, had begun
with the phrase 'l' on avait pu croire dans les premiers momens, que
c'était calcul. Mais ...'. The even momentary intrusion of that
slighting word *calcul* – which serves, throughout Constant's personal
and political works, with its connotations of conscious self-interest,
as one of the most strongly pejorative – has been removed.

If it is the demands of contemporary convention that have
suppressed Ellénore's earlier love-affair, the result is to concentrate
her total dependence on Adolphe; the Count, despite his efforts to
have her accepted in society, has still made her feel her subservience;
Adolphe's initial adoration will contrast with the Count's veiled
condescension. While removing, at the last moment before publication, the phrase (136): 'Son premier amant l'avoit entraînée
lorsqu'elle étoit très jeune, et l'avoit cruellement abandonnée',
Constant has overlooked the occasional trace of the initial circumstances: for example, the reference (134) to 'ses fautes', or the
perceptive and ironical analysis in Ch. IV (141) of how the contrast
between constrained past and confident present leads to Ellénore's
spontaneous claims on Adolphe's every moment, including the
phrase 'dans ses relations précédentes'.

Another brief change in the first description of Ellénore has not
yet, I believe, been discussed, yet has its place in the closely-knit
economy of the narrative. Already in the MSS her attitude to her

two children by the Comte de P. has served to suggest her longing
for social respectability and her rejection of her past.[21] Two phrases,
added later and placed at separate intervals, now enhance both her
positive and her negative reactions:

On eût dit quelquefois qu'une révolte secrète se mêlait parfois à
l'attachement plutôt passionné que tendre qu'elle leur montrait, et les lui
rendait en quelque sorte importuns;

whereas

Mais le moindre danger, une heure d'absence, la ramenait à eux avec une
anxiété où l'on démêlait une espèce de remords, et le désir de leur donner
par ses caresses le bonheur qu'elle n'y trouvait pas elle-même. (121)

However minor the children's role, they have a double function in
Constant's narrative. First, in a novel apparently so strictly pared
down to the dilemmas of two central figures only, mentions of the
children are recurrent and deliberately placed (pp. 115, 121, 140,
146, 149, 155, 162, 164–5): they become an essential counter in the
interplay of sacrifices and in the effect on public opinion. Secondly,
they exemplify in action Adolphe's general reflection in Ch. I, on
'l'étonnement de la jeunesse, à l'aspect d'une société si factice et si
travaillée' (115): at a moment of crisis between himself, Ellénore and
the Count, there appear

les deux enfants au fond de la chambre, ne jouant pas, et portant sur leurs
visages cet étonnement de l'enfance lorsqu'elle remarque une agitation dont
elle ne soupçonne pas la cause. (143)

Constant re-wrote in M 1 the initial pages on Adolphe's first
meeting with Ellénore (121–2). After tracing the interplay of emotional need, vanity and chance that causes the moment of attraction, he analyses the qualities that create around Ellénore an
illusory magic; prominent among these is the deceptive originality of
a foreign mode of speech:

Les idiomes étrangers rajeunissent les pensées, et les débarrassent de ces
tournures [rebattues, deleted later] qui les font paraître tour à tour
communes et affectées.

Many other comments of Constant will show his preoccupation with
avoiding these two extremes in expression: flat cliché and self-
conscious artifice. Here, language is an important part of illusory
first impressions.

Detailed variants regarding Ellénore herself are few in the middle chapters of the book: one or two, however brief, are significant. In Ch. III she tells Adolphe how, when he was pursuing her, she joined in social gatherings 'pour concilier le penchant de son cœur avec la prudence'; in the explanation of the reasons, there is a very different shade of meaning when 'par quel calcul' becomes 'par quelle défiance d'elle-même' (134). In Ch. VI, unwilling to leave for Poland without Adolphe, she had originally said: 'Je ne suis plus . . . dans l'âge où l'on forme des liens nouveaux': the suggestion of possible love-affairs is removed when the phrase is softened into 'l'âge où l'âme s'ouvre à des impressions nouvelles' (164). In the same chapter there are two brief cuts. Where the final version of Ellénore's speech reads simply: 'Si je pouvais me faire illusion sur vous, je consentirais peut-être à une absence . . .' (165), the original had inserted after 'sur vous': 'si vous aviez pour moi de l'amour'; later in the same paragraph, Constant has also deleted from the MS versions the sentences: 'au point où nous sommes, toute séparation entre nous serait une séparation éternelle. Vous n'êtes retenu près de moi que par la crainte de ma douleur.' If these analyses, telling in themselves, had been left, they would have repeated that heightened moment at the end of Ch. V (the exact centre of the book), where Ellénore, in the face of Adolphe's protective devotion, insists with sudden insight: 'Vous croyez avoir de l'amour, et vous n'avez que de la pitié.' In the final novel, that moment of penetration is to be echoed only in the letter found after her death.

In the central chapters, the crescendo of unwanted sacrifices has stemmed from fundamental moments in Constant's own experience – transformed in various ways to fit the inner coherence of the two representative characters. First, the turning-point at the end of Ch. V, when Adolphe's father brings about Ellénore's banishment and Adolphe unhesitatingly accompanies her: one is bound to recall the repeated exile of Mme de Staël at the hands of Napoleon. There is, incidentally, no attempt to explain the father's means of having Ellénore cast out; as throughout the novel, it is not the details of events, but their psychological causes and ironical results that matter. Here, Adolphe's reactions are intense: at the prospect of her suffering: 'Je l'aimais plus que je ne l'avais jamais aimée: tout mon cœur était revenu à elle: j'étais fier de la protéger.' That very intensity recalls another occasion on which diaries and letters show Constant's exceptionally strong involvement in sharing Germaine's grief: the moment when he hears of Necker's death while she is absent both from her father and from himself and he rushes to be with her. Ellénore, of course, has not even seen her father since childhood, but her postponement of going to join him, and her absence at his death, add yet further to her sense of sacrifice, of guilt and of reproach to Adolphe – undertones suggestive both bio-graphically and aesthetically.[22]

Thirdly, the long passage towards the end of Ch. viii (184–7) on Ellénore's attempts to provoke Adolphe's jealousy, present in both MSS, removed in 1816 and restored only after Mme de Staël's death, is one of the most subtle in its suggestive insights into two characters and into the ironical judgments others pass on them.[23] Adolphe is well aware that 'c'est ici surtout que l'on m'accusera de faiblesse', but, whatever the misapprehensions of those who see him as condoning Ellénore's apparent infidelities, he interprets her be-haviour as a pathetically misconceived effort to restimulate his love, from an aging woman seeking also to prove that she can still attract, and longing to hear that 'langage de l'amour' which he no longer speaks. His sense of responsibility is heightened yet again.

When, in 1816, Constant temporarily removes this over-allusive passage, he constructs a skilled transition to lead to the end of the chapter. The retreat into solitude is made because of society's malicious misjudgments in general, and has nothing to do with love-affairs, real or imagined. He therefore removes the succinct phrase which had both virulently scorned Ellénore's suitors and yet sought to comprehend her motives:

un mot fit disparaître cette tourbe d'adorateurs qu'elle n'avait appelés que pour me faire craindre sa perte (186),

transfers from the full version certain phrases on how his many sacrifices had been judged, and sums up:

un mot me suffit pour bouleverser de nouveau la situation de la mal-heureuse Ellénore. Nous rentrâmes dans la solitude. Mais j'avais exigé ce sacrifice,

thus intensifying his responsibility and his pity before reintroducing the original epigrammatic culmination on 'nouveaux droits, nouvelles chaînes'.

The last paragraph of this chapter, representing a climax of bitterness, was retained; two small but important alterations were made. Ellénore's phrase which in the MSS read: 'Dieu vous par-donne le mal que vous me faites' is changed to the direct and simple: 'Vous ne savez pas le mal que vous faites' (187) – leading back ironically to Adolphe's exclamation in Ch. iii: 'Ellénore, vous ne savez pas tout ce que je souffre' (134), and forward to Ellénore's in Ch. x: 'Adolphe, Adolphe, vous ne savez pas ce que j'ai souffert' (197). The end of the chapter, though still of an over-lofty tone unusual in Constant, was partly lightened by the removal in M 1 of four final phrases:

Je voudrais abréger ce fatal récit. Le remords me déchire et de lugubres images m'assiègent. Mais une tâche cruelle me reste. Il faut la remplir.

Did these initially serve as an excuse at the stage when Constant felt his conclusion was over-rapid, and were they thought to be no longer required when Chapters ix and x were re-worked?

These last two chapters, from M 1 onwards, form a skilled and balanced tissue of ironies interlinked with all that has preceded, and, both through Ellénore's last walk in the garden and through her illness and death, endow her in the end with resignation, fidelity and dignity. Later verbal alterations concerning her are very few, comprising first the change in her exclamation when she hears Adolphe's voice, from: 'Qu'entends-je? c'est là le son qui m'a fait du mal', to: 'Quel est ce bruit? c'est la voix qui m'a fait du mal' (196), and, later, the realisation that the last rites restore to her not 'de la force' but the more appropriate 'du calme'.

In an article where the necessary plethora of comparative detail already demands apology, I have attempted not to cover all variants, but to pick out those mainly affecting presentation of Adolphe and of Ellénore. Others would deserve discussion. A slight change makes of the description 'inutile et facile' the balanced and alliterative 'frivole et facile' (115), in keeping with Constant's delight in that kind of mnemonic concentration which clamps together contrast and echo (cf., 184: 'ne repoussent ... que pour retenir; plutôt l'indécision que l'indifférence, et des retards que des refus'). Various revisions show the excision of tautologous adjectives (e.g., 'nuit obscure', 167, etc.), or the substitution of more exact expressions for those initially less appropriate ('être heureux' becomes 'réussir', 123; 'embrasser [toutes les religions]' becomes 'invoquer', 202; etc.). Is it because of Constant's habit of self-analysis in letters, or of his reading of epistolary novels, that at one point Adolphe had addressed his readers in the second person: 'Vous devinez facilement ...' – then changed to 'On devine ...' (146)?

I left to the end a second external cause of the novel's particular art of concentration. Some passages (which remained unpublished), from Constant's draft Preface to the 'second' edition, develop his lasting conviction, under the repeated key-phrase 'tout se tient', that the three most vital sides of human experience – political, religious, personal – are intimately interrelated:

L'inconstance ou la fatigue en amour, l'incrédulité en religion . . . la servilité en politique sont des symptômes contemporains (248).

In the years 1806–9, political circumstances prevented any intrusion into the novel of the Stendhalian 'coup de pistolet dans un salon'.

J'ai peint une petite partie du tableau, la seule qui fût non sans tristesse, mais sans danger pour le peintre (247).

Adolphe, in its origins and development, was of necessity focussed on personal feeling, and its long-standing value has lain in its exceptional insight into the ironical complexities underlying both individual conduct and social judgments. Had any political career been open to Constant in the period around 1806 would he ever have written a novel? Yet his Preface, part published and part projected, ten years after the initial version, is no mere *post facto* attempt to suggest an irrelevant political significance: his other writings of the same period as *Adolphe* show him constantly preoccupied by the threefold parallels between personal, religious and political aspirations and frustrations (cf. in particular the *Lettre sur Julie* and *Wallstein*). Both these parallels, and the very detailed variants to his projected preface, would deserve further investigation.

To the novel itself he gave, at intervals over ten years, the utmost care in revising shades of meaning. Personal experience is repeatedly both drawn on and transposed, repeatedly indicating what renders mistaken, irrelevant or over-simplified all attempts at categorical judgments. In this suggestive process there is no such thing as a 'purely stylistic' variant: substance and style are necessarily at one.

NOTES

1 When Paul Delbouille made a close examination of variants in his *Genèse, Structure et Destin d'«Adolphe»* (Paris, Belles Lettres, 1961), the Lausanne MS was not open to consultation; he was able, however, to make available to scholars for the first time certain (valuable but incomplete) notes on its variants taken by the late Pierre Kohler. Delbouille's recent critical edition of *Adolphe* (Belles Lettres, 1977) corrects and completes the transcription of all available variants. Page

references to the novel in the present article will refer to this edition. I have consulted all MSS, and give here Constant's spelling and punctuation (interspersed with those of his *copiste*, hence some variations); I have normalised accents. The following abbreviations will be used: M 1 = the MS in the Bibliothèque Cantonale et Universitaire de Lausanne, Co R1; M 2 = the 1810 copy in the Bibliothèque Nationale in Paris, N.a.f. 14358; 1816 = first edition, London; 1824 = 'Third' edition, Paris. Quotations from the *Journaux* are from the Pléiade edition, ed. Alfred Roulin, 1957. Italics in quotations are mine.

2 For details of these readings, cf. *Journaux*, and the helpful summaries in Delbouille's edition, pp. 14 sqq and 46 sqq.

3 For 'near sacrilege' as seen by Schlegel, cf. Benjamin Constant et Madame de Staël, *Lettres à un Ami*, ed. Jean Mistler (Neuchâtel, à la Baconnière, 1949; hereinafter referred to as 'Hochet letters'), p. 128.

4 I hope elsewhere to examine Constant's style as political orator.

5 An article discussing the 'Avis de l'Éditeur' and the concluding letters appears above, pp. 96–107.

6 The different portraits Constant draws of Mme de Charrière (in the *Cahier Rouge*, *Journaux* and letters), and the differing degrees of responsibility he attributes to her influence, would deserve examination. C. P. Courtney and Roland Mortier have re-investigated some sides of their relationship, in recent articles.

7 'à la malveillance ou' has been added to the original 'à l'affectation'. Multiple passages, from diaries, letters or the *Cahier Rouge*, might be compared with this concentrated passage.

8 In the description of the Comte de P.'s circle, Constant removes in M 1 the over-provocative term 'quelques *nobles*'; his characterization of *émigré* society remains scathing (122).

9 Here, I cannot agree with critics who consider that the novel has welded unsatisfactorily too many widely-spread stages of Constant's experience. His care for coherence of inner chronology would deserve further discussion.

10 Cf., in Delbouille's *Genèse*, the section on 'Une pudeur extrême'. Constant's outspoken expression in the *Journaux* of problems of physical satisfaction and frustration is excluded not merely from *Adolphe*, but also, largely, from *Cécile*; the latter novel is still too often seen as the autobiographical contrast to the stylisation of the former. *Cécile* may be one stage nearer to personal experience; it remains a highly selective presentation, deserving further re-assessment.

11 The adjectives 'inquiet et blessé' are now cut.

12 Constant's opposition between *calcul* and *bonne foi* would deserve further discussion than space here allows. Cf. one or two brief references below.

13 Many parallel passages elsewhere are of interest. Cf., for example, G. Poulet's reference to Mme de Staël (*Benjamin Constant par lui-même*, pp. 151–2); see also Hochet letters, p. 67 and p. 222.

14 Cf. Pléiade, p. 844. (In quoting earlier phrases from this passage, Delbouille, 238, has, like Bornecque, omitted 'bien' from the remark: 'presque toutes les femmes parlent bien sur l'amour'). On the various versions of the *Lettre sur Julie* cf. the fine article by P. Deguise in RHLF, 1967, pp. 100–11.

15 Cf. for example, in Constant's *Publiciste* articles on *Corinne*, phrases appearing on pp. 86 and 89–90 of the Harpaz edition (Benjamin Constant: *Recueil d'articles* 1795–1817, ed. Éphraïm Harpaz, Droz, 1979). These articles have been ably discussed by Simone Balayé in *Actes du Congrès de Lausanne*, pp. 189 sqq.

16 Cf. Flaubert in *L'Éducation sentimentale* (Garnier, 1961, p. 62): 'Rien n'est humiliant comme de voir les sots réussir dans les entreprises où l'on échoue'.

17 The function of this dream in the narrative is one of the few points on which I might differ from I. W. Alexander in his thoughtful study of *Adolphe* (Arnold, 1973); various levels of irony would seem to surround the apparent idealism. Cf., also, in the Harpaz edition referred to in note 15, above, pp. 90–1, Constant's important discussion of Lucile in *Corinne*.

18 Over recent years, Ellénore has come to be seen as synthesis rather than as patchwork creation. We need a further study of her function in patterns of irony.

19 See Delbouille edn., 222, on Lady Charlotte Campbell's dramatic intervention; to the references he gives to Rudler, add, from Rudler's 1919 edition, pp. 19 and 29. I suggest, however, that Constant first removed the passage in Ch. II concerning Ellénore's 'premier faux-pas', and that the note where he reminds himself to write to the publisher about cutting the phrase in Ch. III on 'son premier amant' was a consequence, rather than *vice versa*.

20 One notes that, in such events as run parallel with Anna Lindsay's life, Constant has selected the least melodramatic.

21 The involvement of the children during the novel is, again, less melodramatic than such reported scenes from biography as Mme de Staël's calling her children to witness the harm that would be done to the family by her marriage with Constant. The reply to the Baron's question about marriage in Ch. VII: 'Non, sans doute, elle-même ne l'a jamais désiré', fits the logic both of Ellénore's ten extra years and of her recurrently submissive and sacrificial nature; it is necessarily based on very different postulates from those of the biographical background.

22 For Constant's insight into the complexities of Mme de Staël's relationship with her father, cf. *Journaux*, Hochet letters, and *Mémoires de Mme Récamier*.

23 In *Adolphe*, these 'infidelities' appear as no more than superficial social flirtations, but their deeper motives are penetratingly analysed, especially in the effect of verbalisation on feeling. The dilemma as regards the narrator's own motives (protective duty and guilt, or vanity and 'fatuité' in imagining Ellénore's need) is expressed mainly through the Baron de T. (170) – who is proved wrong in the outcome. Cf. also a sardonic passage on readers who think they share Adolphe's experience, Preface to Third Edition, 105–6.

PART TWO

Baudelaire

9

Some remarks on Baudelaire's *Poème du Haschisch* (1952)

The place generally assigned to the *Paradis artificiels* in Baudelaire's experience might be summed up by some such phrase as 'the escape that failed'. The theme of escape into paradise and the subsequent condemnation of the means used to achieve it are of course clearly present and provide a large measure of justification for this point of view. But other aspects seem to have been underestimated, and on the whole, in comparison with Baudelaire's other works, the *Paradis artificiels* generally receive rather hasty treatment. Baudelaire's debt to De Quincey and his personal contribution in *Un Mangeur d'Opium* have been scrupulously examined by Professor Clapton[1] and I shall not here be concerned with that part of the work. With the hashish section one is on considerably more uncertain ground as regards the sources, whether personal or literary, of the material: I do not propose to discuss the biographical problem of how far Baudelaire was here drawing on his first-hand experience.[2] The main points which these brief remarks will seek to substantiate are three. The first that (whether Baudelaire is using his own experiences of the effects of the drug, observations made on acquaintances, or those taken from his reading) his account of the effects of hashish shows significant differences from the descriptions to be found in certain contemporary writings on the subject, differences due above all to the preoccupations of the artist and the *moraliste*. The second that, although many penetrating and valuable observations have been made[3] on the metaphysical implications of the tempting escape offered by drugs and Baudelaire's condemnation of that means, it is worth stressing to what an extent he is haunted as much by the artistic as by the metaphysical problems involved. The drug is seen as a means of heightening the artistic state of mind, as an instrument of self-observation by the artist; the final condemnation of the instrument is not simply on the metaphysical grounds already so thoroughly discussed but because in the end it hampers the production of a work of art. Finally, and this will form the main body of these remarks, that, since the drug is merely an instrument for heightening the latent tendencies of the poet, and since the observations it gives rise to have been placed in a carefully chosen order by Baudelaire, we have in the concluding sections of the *Poème du Haschisch* a pattern and sequence of experience which forms an interesting comparison with the outline of the much-discussed 'architecture' of the *Fleurs du Mal*, and may serve to suggest further reflections on the significance of the order of the poems.

I would, in fact, suggest that the *Poème du Haschisch*, although in some respects the account of a particular instance of an escape that fails, may also be taken as a kind of allegorical commentary on the whole sequence of human experience traced by the *Fleurs du Mal*; that it follows the same main stages, the drug merely playing the same part in the prose work as Baudelaire's particular brand of poetic sensitivity does in the poetry. In the carefully arranged scheme of a poet's experience which composes the volume of poems, the parallels with the *Paradis artificiels* do not seem to be limited simply to the section *Le Vin*[4] nor even to the many analogies which have been drawn between separate poems and the sensations provoked by drugs. What I wish to consider briefly is the possible parallel in the sequence of experience between the outline of the volume of poems as Baudelaire presented it in the second edition and that of a crucial section of the *Paradis artificiels*, namely parts iv and v of *Le Poème du Haschisch*. To do so, apart from bringing out more clearly certain implications of the arrangement of the *Fleurs du Mal*, may serve in part to answer a question asked by Vivier and perhaps implicit in the relative silence of many critics as regards the *Paradis artificiels*: 'Il faudrait bientôt se demander pourquoi le poète a consacré tant de son temps et de ses forces à reprendre, à transposer, à développer, une matière qui n'était pas la sienne . . .'[5]

First comes the question of Baudelaire's particular originality in his presentation of the effects of the drug. In the Opium section he was, of course, following closely on De Quincey, but he himself remarks that 'La première partie de ce livre est entièrement de moi: c'est le *Poème du Haschisch*'.[6] The main contemporary works which he is considered likely to have known[7] are those of Brierre de Boismont[8] and Moreau (de Tours);[9] whether or not he was making use of them, two important points emerge from a comparison of his account with theirs. These works comprise in part medical comment and theorizing, and in part a compendium of individual experiences provoked by hashish. Baudelaire's earlier article, *Du Vin et du Hachish*,[10] and the earlier chapters of the *Poème du Haschisch*, make use of a variety of anecdotes and reflections in much the same way, but when we come to the concluding sections he has adopted a very different technique. Instead of giving disjointed experiences, he proposes to represent the results of the drug as a sequence occurring to a representative individual: 'concentrer tous les rayons dans un cercle unique, cercle tragique' (i. 304, Pléiade, ed. Le Dantec, 1938).

It is not only in his having chosen this representative figure (to whose qualities we shall return later) that Baudelaire shows his desire for an artistically satisfying pattern, but in his organization of the experiences undergone by that individual. Even the separate accounts in the first person quoted by Moreau or Brierre de Boismont are lively and picturesque precisely because of the capricious and disconnected effect of the succession of experiences; one might refer, for example, to the account given on pp. 371–82 in Brierre de Boismont's first edition. Gautier,[11] no doubt, does loosely distinguish between different stages in the onset of the effect, and Moreau in drawing his analogies between hashish and mental derangement tries to trace eight stages of progression, but in neither does one have the deliberate organization of each detail, to lead up with a sense of inevitability to a final culmination, which we shall see in a detailed examination of the last two chapters of the *Poème du Haschisch*. And in none of these accounts, although certain emotional effects may be briefly mentioned (joy, pride, anger, etc.), does one find them analysed and fitted into a logical sequence leading to a climax as they are in Baudelaire. This is the second important contribution: the place given to the moral rather than to the physical experiences. He himself refers to his work as 'un livre non pas de pure physiologie, mais surtout de morale',[12] and this applies not merely to the conclusion but to every stage in the account. The whole difference between the *Fleurs du Mal* and the *Émaux et Camées* is implicit if one compares Gautier's account of his own experience of hashish with that given by Baudelaire. Gautier's sparkles with rich, strange, and ingenious transformations of objects from the physical world; the hashish he has swallowed becomes a many-faceted emerald, his eyelids fine gold threads turning on tiny ivory wheels;[13] gigantic flowers burst like fireworks; strange creatures with trunks expanding into leafy branches or hands like fins jostle with a railway engine stretching the neck of a swan; he himself becomes the Queen of Sheba's parrot, and so on. The *préciosité* of the world of the *Émaux et Camées*, a world full of subtlety but safely limited so that few disquieting metaphysical elements can enter, is echoed in this experience, and it is only in an introductory reflection on *le désir de l'idéal* and perhaps in the illusion of the immensity of time that anything beyond the purely physical intrudes. Even the passage which reminds one of the *correspondances* – 'j'entendais le bruit des couleurs' – stands as no more than part of a delightful fantasy, an absurdity like the strange flowers or beasts, with no troublous significance.

Baudelaire's original contribution is to arrange his sequence so that the sensuous effects come first, and lead on to his main concern, the moral complexities. Gautier's Paradise is composed simply of pleasurable arabesques on the impressions of the senses, whereas Baudelaire can achieve ecstasy only when all the most contradictory and tormenting sides of his nature have been deliberately faced, transmuted, and satisfactorily fitted into the final synthesis. But even when he is tracing the effect on the senses there is something vitally different in his treatment: all the strange associations which produce the synaesthesia are not merely capricious ornamental fragments but have an intense conviction of significance, a significance that immediately stretches into aesthetic and metaphysical problems.

Baudelaire's preoccupation with the effect on the moral side of man's nature, especially in connexion with the sense of sin and remorse, to be transformed by hashish into pride, can be seen in passing in one of the earlier chapters from the *Poème du Haschisch* where he comments on a woman's account[14] of her experiences (pp. 295–9). Having described her illusion of being in a vast cage she gives one brief sentence, 'Je rêvai de *Belle au bois dormant*, d'expiation à subir, de future délivrance', and passes on immediately to talk of tropical birds and the sound of their song. Baudelaire cannot resist the opportunity at the same time to suggest his views on the nature of the female and to stress the moral effect of the drug, so he picks out for particular comment this 'hallucination morale: le sujet se croit soumis à une expiation', and remarks that as 'le tempérament féminin est peu propre à l'analyse' she has not been able to trace the subtle way in which she has almost *côtoyé le remords*, transformed by hashish into a delight.

A recurring note in the various accounts of the effect of the drug is that of the subject's violent desire to be able to explain his ecstasy but of his inability to do so, for he can do no more than utter exclamations of delight. Baudelaire has contrived to communicate the content of this otherwise inexpressible ecstasy by the method he has chosen. He chooses a climax – that of self-deification – and he makes every detail in the subtly analysed sequence of stages, each delight and each obstacle, point forward and lead logically to this culmination. Here (as in the order of the *Fleurs du Mal*) he is holding to his own principle: 'Je suis un de ceux (et nous sommes bien rares) qui croient que toute composition littéraire, même critique, doit être faite et manœuvrée en vue d'un dénouement.'[15]

The deliberate pattern and the analysis of moral development are, then, the outstanding characteristics of Baudelaire's treatment of the hashish dream. His constant interest in both of these appears in certain remarks on Hoffmann: at the beginning of the *Paradis artificiels* he mentions Hoffmann's *baromètre spirituel* and in *Du Vin et du Haschisch* (Pléiade, 1938, I. 246–7) he tells how 'Hoffmann avait dressé un singulier baromètre psychologique destiné à lui représenter les différentes températures et les phénomènes atmosphériques de son âme', adding the significant remark: 'Il va sans dire que les divisions du baromètre moral d'Hoffmann étaient fixées suivant leur ordre de génération.'[16] It is something of this kind that he himself is tracing in the concluding sections of *Le Poème du Haschisch*, with the drug as his instrument.

This conception of the instrument is important. Baudelaire may be telling of an attempted escape into paradise, but constantly implicit is the idea of the drug as a deliberate means of magnifying for examination the material from which poetry can be created. First, what is his conception of the ideal state which he is seeking to achieve by means of the drug? Stimulants, as he explains at the beginning of the *Paradis artificiels*, are one of three possible means of achieving an ideal mood which the poet constantly seeks and which is expressed again and again in parallel passages in his other works. In the article on the *Exposition universelle de 1855* (Pléiade, 1938, II. 164) he writes:

Sans avoir recours à l'opium, qui n'a connu ces admirables heures, véritables fêtes du cerveau, où les sens plus attentifs perçoivent des sensations plus retentissantes, où le ciel d'un azur plus transparent s'enfonce comme un abîme plus infini, où les sons tintent musicalement, où les couleurs parlent, où les parfums racontent des mondes d'idées?

In *Fusées* (II. 634):

Dans certains états de l'âme presque surnaturels, la profondeur de la vie se révèle tout entière dans le spectacle, si ordinaire qu'il soit, qu'on a sous les yeux. Il en devient le Symbole.

In the *Paradis artificiels* (I. 273) this 'état exceptionnel de l'esprit et des sens, que je puis sans exagération appeler paradisiaque, si je le compare aux lourdes ténèbres de l'existence ... journalière' is fully discussed. What critics do not seem to have stressed sufficiently is that, just as in the 'Notes nouvelles sur Edgar Poe'[17] he speaks of 'ces états de santé *poétique*, si rares et si précieux', here too he is seeking not simply a mystical experience but the state which produces a work of art: 'L'homme gratifié de cette béatitude, malheureusement rare et passagère, se sent à la fois *plus artiste* et plus juste, plus noble.' (The italics are mine.)

There are three possible ways in which this state may be achieved. It may come as an undeserved and unpredictable grace from heaven (I. 273). It ought, no doubt, to be possible to attain it by 'l'exercice journalier de notre volonté', but Baudelaire seems to stress the difficulty and uncertainty of this means in the expressions 'nous *devrions* tirer' and 'l'*espérance* d'y atteindre'. And since the moments when it appears gratuitously from heaven are so rare, and moreover by some *loi absurde* occur often 'après de coupables orgies de l'imagination' rather than as a reward for virtuous effort, the temptation of the third means, to provoke it deliberately by stimulants, must needs be strong.

The interest of hashish in particular lies precisely in the fact that it adds nothing whatever to the essential nature of the person affected by it; in fact, it can give him no mystical revelation. The *Paradis artificiels* are doomed to failure if the object is a metaphysical conquest; but Baudelaire is quite clear about this from the outset:

Dans l'ivresse du haschisch ... nous ne sortirons pas du rêve naturel ... l'homme ... n'est que le même homme augmenté ... Rien que le naturel excessif ... Le haschisch sera, pour les impressions et les pensées familières de l'homme, un miroir grossissant, mais un pur miroir (p. 282). Le haschisch ne révèle à l'individu rien que l'individu lui-même (p. 316).

Contemporary works on hashish are in agreement on this point: one of the subjects quoted by Brierre de Boismont remarks: 'Cet état d'aberration a donné une impulsion plus vive à mes idées mais n'a rien ajouté aux connaissances que j'avais.'[18]

Moreover Moreau chooses to experiment on himself with hashish precisely because le haschisch laisse à celui qui se commet à son étrange influence le pouvoir d'étudier sur lui-même les désordres moraux qui caractérisent la folie ... En désorganisant les divers pouvoirs intellectuels, il en est un qu'il n'atteint pas ... c'est la conscience de soi-même, le sentiment intime de son individualité;[19]

while Brierre de Boismont also points out that 'le sentiment de la personnalité est conservé'.[20] Baudelaire, who writes at the end of *Du Vin et du Hachish* (I. 267) 'Les grands poètes ... sont des êtres qui par le pur et libre exercice de la volonté, parviennent à un état où ils sont à la fois cause et effet, sujet et objet', the Baudelaire of *L'Héautontimorouménos*, is bound to be attracted to the magnifying mirror of hashish as another means to this end. Mystically it may offer no new revelation, but can it not be a tool to the artist?

The basic fact that hashish does no more than intensify for observation all the latent tendencies present in the artist is, then, made quite plain from the beginning, and throughout his account, as we shall see, Baudelaire is stressing the parallel between the experiences provoked by the drug and those of the poet in ordinary life. In studying the sequence of experience under hashish, then, the poet will simply be turning a magnifying glass on his own nature and experience – the whole subject of the *Fleurs du Mal*. With his passion for allegories and analogies of every kind, it is natural, perhaps, that Baudelaire should be attracted not merely to re-semblances of detail but to likenesses in the whole pattern and sequence of experience. The *Poème du Haschisch*, published in the *Revue Contemporaine* of 30 September 1858, is of course an expanded and revised version of the section on hashish from *Du Vin et du Hachish* of 1851, and it is in the second version that Baudelaire makes the important modification announced at the end of his first chapter: 'je fondrai ces documents variés en une sorte de mono-graphie, choisissant une âme, facile d'ailleurs à expliquer et à définir, comme type propre aux expériences de cette nature' (I. 276). The rewriting takes place in the months closely following the first edition of the *Fleurs du Mal*[21] at a stage when Baudelaire is thinking of how to fit new poems into the *cadre* of the volume of poetry for the second edition to be published in 1861. A parallel in pattern between the two is thus made more likely.

Any detailed examination of the order of the *Fleurs du Mal* must, of course, make fairly clear that the work, to use the words of Vivier,[22] at the same time as being a *grande construction allégorique et narrative* has risen out of a *gerbe de poésies éparses*, that the placing of certain poems has been a delicate business, and that it is difficult and often misleading to try to erect a rigorous scheme in which each individual poem marks a logical step forward in an argument.[23] But what emerges from the passages usually quoted[24] to show Baudelaire's insistence on the importance of the 'Architecture' is the stress he lays on the outline of the framework. The famous remark to Vigny: 'Le seul éloge que je sollicite pour ce livre est qu'on reconnaisse qu'il n'est pas un pur album et qu'il a un commencement et une fin'[25] is followed by the statement that all the poems added in the second edition 'ont été faits pour être adaptés à un cadre singulier que j'avais choisi'; and this insistence on the *cadre* is repeated in a letter to Laprade: '35 morceaux nouveaux adaptés au cadre général'.[26] In the following remarks, therefore, I shall be concerned mainly with the general outline of the *Fleurs du Mal* rather than with details on separate poems whose placing might give rise to lengthy arguments.

In the *Poème du Haschisch*, as we have seen, Baudelaire has decided to represent the experiences provoked by the drug in the form of a sequence occurring to a representative individual, so that he may 'concentrer tous les rayons dans un cercle unique ... cercle tragique'. This individual stands for *l'homme sensible moderne*. He is to have 'un tempérament moitié nerveux, moitié bilieux', to be cultured and versed in artistic subjects, to have 'un cœur tendre, fatigué par le malheur, mais encore prêt au rajeunissement', with a sense of past faults and of time wasted, an interest in metaphysical problems, a love of idealized virtue inculcated in childhood, and above all 'une grande finesse de sens'. He is, in fact, as has several times been noticed, the man whose experiences are given in the *Fleurs du Mal*.

Baudelaire, whose desire to plan in view of a denouement has already been quoted, gives from the beginning the key to what that climax is to be: 'Suivons cette procession de l'imagination humaine jusqu'à la croyance en sa propre divinité' (I. 305). The experience has been carefully arranged so as to give first the effects of the drug on the senses, leading, through the complex results this may produce, to reflections on love and on the individual's reactions to things and people external to himself. After this come reactions to the memories and moral problems of his own past and his own nature, and the complex sophistry which integrates these into the pride that will lead to self-deification and revolt. After each step forward into bliss there is a dramatic thrust back into the world of reality and remorse until the final climax when all is fused into a sense of being God and hence of revolt against any other god who may exist. Finally of course comes *Le Lendemain*. The *Fleurs du Mal* also proceed in general from sensuous delights through the tempting perversities of love to problems of remorse, turn to the external world in the *Tableaux parisiens*, move swiftly towards self-deification in *Le Vin*, are hurled violently back in *Les Fleurs du Mal*, and combine the results of all these in the climax of *La Révolte*, the last stage before that of Death. But a more careful examination is called for.

In the *Paradis artificiels* there is a brief initial stage before the stimulant has completely gripped the subject, in which his main feelings, apart from causeless laughter, are those of sympathetic understanding for his fellows undergoing the same experience and of immense and ironical superiority to those who stand in the world of ordinary reason outside it. Although I should not care to overstress the analogy, this might be set side by side with the 'Hypocrite lecteur, mon semblable, mon frère' of the introductory poem and with the theme of superiority occurring in some of the early poems on the subject of the poet, and more particularly in *Don Juan aux Enfers* and *Châtiment de l'Orgueil* (xv, xvi). In the *Paradis artificiels* it is firmly suggested as an initial trace of the satanic temptations which will lead later to the self-deification of the climax: 'l'idée de sa supériorité commence à poindre à l'horizon de son intellect. Bientôt elle grandira, grossira et éclatera comme un météore.' (i. 285).

More important is the *phase essentiellement voluptueuse et sensuelle* which follows, and which corresponds to much of the 'Idéal' section which opens *Spleen et Idéal*. First, 'votre amour inné de la forme et de la couleur trouvera . . . une pâture immense. Les couleurs prendront une énergie inaccoutumée et entreront dans le cerveau avec une intensité victorieuse.' Any sight on which the eyes fall will become charged with splendid significance in

cet état mystérieux et temporaire . . . où la profondeur de la vie . . . se révèle tout entière dans le spectacle, si naturel et si trivial qu'il soit, qu'on a sous les yeux, — où le premier objet venu devient symbole parlant. Fourier et Sweden-borg, l'un avec ses *analogies*, l'autre avec ses *correspondances*, se sont incarnés dans le végétal et l'animal qui tombent sous votre regard.[27] (i. 305–6)

This, says Baudelaire, marks the restoration of allegory to its legitimate importance, and he pauses to draw the analogy with poetry, just as earlier in the same work (p. 293) he has pointed out that for sounds to clothe themselves in colour, for colour to contain music, is not a process confined to drug-taking, but normal in poetry; 'mais j'ai déjà averti le lecteur qu'il n'y avait rien de positivement surnaturel dans l'ivresse du haschisch; seulement, ces analogies revêtent alors une vivacité inaccoutumée'. In keeping with the beginning, *Élévation* and *Correspondances* appear as the third and fourth poems in the *Fleurs du Mal*.

The intensification and the significance of colour, shape, and sound give a sense of solemnity and of the deepening of time and space:

Il [the central figure] regarde avec un certain délice mélancolique à travers les années profondes et s'enfonce audacieusement dans d'infinies perspectives ... paysages dentelés, horizons fuyants, perspectives de villes blanchies par la lividité cadavéreuse de l'orage ou illuminées par les ardeurs concentrées des soleils couchants, – profondeur de l'espace, allégorie de la profondeur du temps;

and together with this comes the influence of music and the fascination of water. *La Vie antérieure* (XII) echoes very closely the whole atmosphere of this passage, and *L'Homme et la Mer* has also been placed early among the poems (XIV). It is at this stage too that paintings on the walls, figures from legend or history, seem to come alive: 'les nymphes aux chairs éclatantes vous regardent avec de grands yeux ... les personnages de l'antiquité, affublés de leurs costumes sacerdotaux ou militaires, échangent avec vous par le simple regard de solennelles confidences', and the placing of such poems as V, VI, XIII, XV, XVI, XIX, XX corresponds in its way to these observations.

In part, of course, phrases from this stage of the *Paradis artificiels* will have significance for the whole of Baudelaire's poetry and they are often vividly illuminating, as with the remark: 'la sinuosité des lignes est un langage définitivement clair où vous lisez l'agitation et le désir des âmes', recalling particularly from the earlier poems *Le Serpent qui Danse* (XXVIII), or the following sentence: 'Les mots ressuscitent revêtus de chair et d'os, le substantif, dans sa majesté substantielle, l'adjectif, vêtement transparent qui l'habille et le colore comme un glacis, et le verbe, ange du mouvement, qui donne le branle à la phrase.'

Certain specific theories about beauty are however placed at this stage in both *Paradis artificiels* and *Fleurs du Mal*. In this sensuous phase, says Baudelaire: 'l'idée de beauté doit naturellement s'emparer d'une place vaste dans un tempérament spirituel tel que je l'ai supposé. L'harmonie, le balancement des lignes, l'eurythmie dans les mouvements, apparaissent au rêveur comme des nécessités.' So far so good; the more normally acceptable idea of beauty has found its place. But gradually by the sophistry of hashish other elements enter. Again Baudelaire is careful to draw the parallel with ordinary experience: 'Il en est de même sans doute dans maints cas de la vie ordinaire, mais ici avec combien plus d'ardeur et de subtilité!' Little by little consciousness of ugliness is transformed into yet another kind of beauty. The fact that he appreciates and longs for true beauty and his capacity to express this desire come to convince him of the beauty of his own imperfections: 'La beauté morale et sa puissance, la grâce et ses séductions, l'éloquence et ses prouesses, toutes ces idées se présentent bientôt comme des correctifs d'une laideur indiscrète, puis comme des consolateurs, enfin comme des adulateurs parfaits d'un sceptre imaginaire.' The poems on Beauty, whether ideal or terrible (XVII, XXI), are placed in the same position in the *Fleurs du Mal.*

Beauty has led imperceptibly from sensuous joy to moral complexity, and love, which immediately follows in the *Paradis* as in the poems, is to play the same part. On the physical side Baudelaire dismisses with scorn the vulgar conception that hashish gives rise to orgies involving any ordinary consummation: 'L'atonie est le résultat ordinaire de l'abus que les hommes font de leurs nerfs et des substances propres à les exciter.' Yet the immensely heightened tension of nerves and senses may mean that the slightest impression brings complete ecstasy. The problem of Baudelaire's delight in contemplation rather than in complete possession, so often discussed in connexion with the poems, has its parallel here too.

But other elements begin to enter, and now complexities and bitternesses are to be fused with the pure delights, for the essential of the whole experience is to bring strange joys out of each successive aspect of human nature. 'Le goût de la protection, un sentiment de paternité ardente et dévouée peuvent se mêler à une sensualité coupable; . . . le besoin de pardon rend l'imagination plus habile et plus suppliante, et le remords lui-même . . . peut agir comme excitant.' It is hardly necessary to point out in detail how the different love-cycles in the poems move from their initial ecstasies to introduce these subtleties.[28]

Remorse is introduced first as a *singulier ingrédient du plaisir*, as indeed it figures in the poems; rapidly its nature changes and it comes to be 'noyé dans la délicieuse contemplation du remords, dans une espèce d'analyse voluptueuse. . . . Il *admire* son remords et il se glorifie, pendant qu'il est en train de perdre sa liberté.' Here is the parallel with so many of the 'Spleen' poems, culminating in *Alchimie de la Douleur, Horreur sympathique, L'Héautontimorouménos,* and *L'Irrémédiable*:

> Soulagement et gloire uniques,
> – La Conscience dans le Mal!

There is another element present among the mental reactions analysed at this stage in the *Paradis*, and this, I would suggest, corresponds in its way to the *Tableaux parisiens* which come next in the poems. Baudelaire speaks, as an interpolation into his considerations on the relationship with another being in love, of other partly similar relationships in which one feels 'une bienveillance singulière appliquée même aux inconnus, une espèce de philanthropie plutôt faite de pitié que d'amour'. There is perhaps some relation between this and the stage of *objectivité*, of merging one's identity with objects outside oneself, which has been analysed in an earlier passage from the *Poème du Haschisch*: 'la contemplation des objets extérieurs vous fait oublier votre propre existence, et ... vous vous confondez bientôt avec eux'. Yet though this figures both in *Du Vin et du Hachish* and in section iii of the *Poème du Haschisch*, Baudelaire has not introduced it into the sequence regarding his chosen individual and this is perhaps significant. The retention of consciousness of self is necessary to the process he is tracing and is nearer to the *Fleurs du Mal*. Here instead we are leading up to the burst of self-glorification at the capacity to participate in the experience of others: 'Pour moi, l'humanité a travaillé, a été martyrisée, immolée, – pour servir de pâture ... à mon implacable appétit d'émotion ...', and Baudelaire is fulfilling his passionate desire to 'vivre plusieurs vies d'homme en l'espace d'une heure'. One thinks immediately of such passages from the poems as that in *Les Petites Vieilles*:

> Mon cœur multiplié jouit de tous vos vices!
> Mon âme resplendit de toutes vos vertus!

and remembers perhaps a phrase from the De Quincey article: 'La jouissance en question ... pourrait s'appeler le dilettantisme dans la charité' (I. 348). In the *Paradis artificiels* Baudelaire is no more indulgent to this form of desire than to any of the others; his hatred of any form of social sentimentality and his irony constantly turned against himself would probably have caused him to smile bitterly at many expressions of admiration for the human sympathy of these poems. This is not to deny that they may possess something of that quality, but they have perhaps other origins and functions. At all events, in the *Paradis* development, this is but one more stage in the temptation which leads to self-deification, for after the phrase 'philanthropie plutôt faite de pitié que d'amour' Baudelaire adds, 'C'est ici que se montre le premier germe de l'esprit satanique qui se développera d'une manière extraordinaire', and one remembers perhaps the Epilogue to the *Spleen de Paris*:

> Tu sais bien, ô Satan, patron de ma détresse,
> Que je n'allais pas là pour répandre un vain pleur;
> Mais comme un vieux paillard . . .

Seen in these connexions, the *Tableaux parisiens*, I would suggest, are placed where they are in the *Fleurs du Mal* not as an attempt to move into human kindness but as a further step in satanic temptation.

Now Baudelaire is precipitating his chosen figure rapidly to the culminating point of the drama, at which, as he has pointed out with a sense of inevitability from the beginning, he will come to consider himself divine and to revolt against God. The crisis is pointed in the *Paradis* by a phrase which deliberately pauses to sum up: 'Voilà . . . mon homme supposé, l'esprit de mon choix, arrivé à ce degré où . . .' He is led to the point of self-deification and revolt by the culmination of the features we have already seen (the glories of significant sense-impressions persuading him he comprehends the essentials of the universe, the delight and superiority he draws from the feeling that others are but a food to his appetite for multiplied experience), all implicit tendencies brought out by the stimulant. At this stage in the *Fleurs du Mal* Baudelaire leads up to his crisis by the section *Le Vin*, showing how that particular stimulant may both foster rebellious pride and give a sense of godlike ecstasy. Wine is no gift of God but an invention of man oppressed by the deity (CV). Under its influence the murderer defies God (CVI). It gives to man 'l'orgueil . . . Qui nous rend triomphants et semblables aux Dieux' (CVII), and in the last poem of this section it provides the ecstatic flight into heaven (CVIII). Similarly at this point in the *Paradis* all other stages have led up to that where 'Tout est matière à jouissance. La plénitude de sa vie actuelle lui inspire un orgueil démesuré.'

But – there comes in the *Paradis* a dramatic pause on a new thought. 'Cependant nous pouvons supposer que de temps à autre un souvenir mordant traverse et corrompe ce bonheur.' Man has thought himself a king and now his hideous, stupid, or vile past comes to his mind. In just the same way the concluding ecstasies of

Le Vin in the poems are followed by the section entitled *Fleurs du Mal* where the culmination of horror is reached. Yet in the *Paradis* this is but one final paradoxical means of leading man to self-deification and revolt, for he reflects on 'cette action ridicule, lâche ou vile' and decides that 'le soin inquisitorial avec lequel je l'analyse et je la juge, prouve mes hautes aptitudes pour la vertu'; and so he has 'tiré de sa condamnation une nouvelle pâture pour son orgueil'. And calling together all that has led him up to this moment, he comes to believe himself God. Moreover, 'si par hasard un vague souvenir se glisse dans l'âme de ce déplorable bienheureux: N'y aurait-il pas un autre Dieu? croyez qu'il se redressera devant *celui-là*, qu'il discutera ses volontés et qu'il l'affrontera sans terreur.' And in the volume of poems *La Révolte* follows *Les Fleurs du Mal*.

The sequence has been the same; the culmination in the two works is in some ways different. The chosen figure in the *Paradis* achieves his ecstasy where the *Fleurs du Mal* can offer only death, and the immediately preceding sections do differ in tone in keeping with their respective climax. The transformation of sin into pride, so evident in the last poems of the *Spleen et Idéal* section, is less explicit in the section entitled *Fleurs du Mal*; despair and even humility (at the end of the *Voyage à Cythère*) are more evident; and wretchedness is one of the main components of *La Révolte*. The figure from the *Paradis* 'confond complètement le rêve avec l'action' where the poet is left to 'un monde où l'action n'est pas la sœur du rêve'. Yet in the end the conclusions are more similar than might appear, and typical of the whole two-sidedness of Baudelaire's nature. In the *Paradis* there follows at last 'le lendemain! le terrible lendemain!' And just as in the *Paradis* there comes the phrase, with its reminiscence of an outstanding passage from *La Peau de Chagrin* (constantly at the back of Baudelaire's mind when desire and destruction are at stake):[29] 'La hideuse nature, dépouillée de son illumination de la veille, ressemble aux mélancoliques débris d'une fête', so in *Le Voyage*, which ends the poems,

> L'Imagination qui dresse son orgie
> Ne trouve qu'un récif aux clartés du matin.

And on the other hand *Le Voyage* itself concludes with a paean of pride which still hopes to achieve its ecstasy even if only in death.

Other differences might perhaps be raised. It may seem, for example, that the above attempt to trace a parallel has perhaps unduly ignored some of the 'Spleen' poems. In part, of course, they may correspond to the terrible depression of 'Le Lendemain'. But there is also Baudelaire's insistence in the earlier chapters of the *Paradis* on the fact that the progress towards bliss is always interrupted by momentary intrusions of the everyday world. These must be attenuated by avoiding surroundings likely to provoke them, for 'cette inquiétude, ce souvenir d'un devoir qui réclame votre volonté et votre attention ... viendraient sonner comme un glas à travers votre ivresse... L'inquiétude deviendrait angoisse, le chagrin torture';[30] but whatever one's efforts to exclude such interruptions, there are bound to come moments when, for example, one examines the clock and realizes that the sense of the immensity of time was no more than an illusion.[31]

No doubt the poet of the *Fleurs du Mal* has not found it as easy as has the *haschischin* to transform automatically his sense of guilt into perverted pride. The condemning comments, the return to terrible reality, and the desperate call on an ebbing will-power which in the *Paradis* are often external to the figure undergoing the experience, introduced as comment from outside or felt separately afterwards, form more of an integral recurring part of the central experience of the *Fleurs du Mal*.

Even with these reservations, however, I would suggest that the parallel I have tried to trace is too striking to be a mere matter of accident. Baudelaire himself towards the end of the *Paradis* again draws the deliberate comparison: 'Il est facile de saisir le rapport qui existe entre les créations sataniques des poètes et les créatures vivantes qui se sont vouées aux excitants. L'homme a voulu être Dieu, et bientôt le voilà, en vertu d'une loi morale incontrôlable, tombé plus bas que sa nature réelle.' The progress in the *Fleurs du Mal* and in the *Paradis* follows the same course, sensitivity of imagination in the one playing the same part as the artificial stimulant in the other. The end of the *Paradis* is uncompromising in its condemnation of the drug as a means of attaining the object set; but on the way through the analysis it has not been simply the means Baudelaire has condemned, for he is constantly drawing analogies between the experience of the *haschischin* and that of the artist or sensitive being in ordinary life. What Baudelaire has called the *orgies de l'imagination* will be fundamentally much the same as those produced by the stimulant, and the *Poème du Haschisch* provides its own kind of allegorical commentary on the insatiable ambition of the human imagination, constantly flung back into reality. In this carefully constructed sequence Baudelaire has provided his own

reflections on, and from a moral point of view his own condemnation of, the pilgrim's or rake's progress traced in the *Fleurs du
Mal*. There have been penetrating requisitories directed against his
spiritual attitude, but none condemns more roundly than he himself
by implication and parallel.[32]

But what of his rejection of hashish in the concluding section? On
moral grounds the drug must be condemned because it implies the
adopting of immediate and infallible 'magic' means, where the
conditions of man's existence are such that redemption can be
achieved only by submitting himself to work and to time. But one
sees immediately how Baudelaire moves from considering the success
or failure of an attempt at metaphysical bliss to come back to the
problems of the artist. If such a state of bliss in dream is infallibly at
his beck and call man will produce nothing. And the aftermath of
hashish is 'l'impossibilité de s'appliquer à un travail suivi... La
volonté est attaquée, de toutes les facultés la plus précieuse.'[33] Here
occurs the anecdote of how Balzac, to whom Baudelaire constantly
refers as the epitome of *la volonté*, refused, in spite of a fascinated
curiosity, to abdicate his will-power to hashish.[34] This *volonté* so
passionately insisted on stands no doubt for human free-will and
dignity, but even these Baudelaire would be prepared to sacrifice if
the artistic results were sure. In the end hashish is condemned not
because it is an infallible and magic means, but because it impairs
rather than furthers the capacity to produce the work of art. 'Si
encore, au prix de sa dignité, de son honnêteté et de son libre
arbitre, l'homme pouvait ... en faire un instrument fécond?' is the
question, and the answer: 'Cette espérance est un cercle vicieux:
admettons un instant que le haschisch donne, ou du moins augmente le génie, ... il est de la nature du haschisch de diminuer la
volonté, et ... ainsi il accorde d'un côté ce qu'il retire de l'autre,
c'est-à-dire l'imagination sans la faculté d'en profiter.' To one in
search merely of mystical satisfaction the artistic production would
be irrelevant, whereas the fundamental problem of Baudelaire's life
as it emerges from his correspondence is that of one who described
himself as a writer 'qui n'accouche qu'avec des forceps' to provide
the visible achievement as opposed to the dream which satisfies
without expression. Hashish attracted him as a possible means of
emerging from this struggle: as Brierre de Boismont was to express
it:

certains stimulants, lorsqu'ils ne dépassent pas la mesure, donnent de la
plasticité aux idées, ou, suivant nous, leur rendent les signes sensibles. Les

phénomènes énumérés, tels que le sentiment de bien-être, l'activité plus grande des idées, leur spiritualité, leur revivification, la rapidité du retour des souvenirs, la force de la mémoire, le pouvoir de créer, les horizons infinis de l'esprit, son détachement des choses terrestres, l'oubli du temps et de l'espace, loin d'être des signes de folie, sont pour nous les conditions, les ferments nécessaires, pour les créations de l'esprit.[35]

He attacked it finally because it intensified the struggle between the need to express and the incapacity to give disciplined work to the means of expression. Yet paradoxically it is from his very sense of oppression and impotence that some of the finest poems arise. And the *Poème du Haschisch* itself as a work of art might well receive more thorough treatment than it has yet had or than the scope of these remarks has permitted.[36]

NOTES

1 G. T. Clapton, *Baudelaire et De Quincey*, Les Belles Lettres, 1931.

2 Indications of the available evidence may be found in Crépet's edition of the *Paradis artificiels*, Conard, 1928, pp. 283 et sqq. See also A. Ferran, *L'Esthétique de Baudelaire*, Hachette, 1933, pp. 44 et sqq.

3 See particularly G. Blin, *Baudelaire*, Gallimard, 1939, part II, ch. III, and in G. Blin, *Le Sadisme de Baudelaire*, Corti, 1948, 'Recours de Baudelaire à la Sorcellerie', and the works referred to in note 32 below.

4 Cf. Crépet et Blin, *Les Fleurs du Mal*, Corti, 1942, p. 262: '*Le Vin* représente ici les *Paradis artificiels* tout comme les *Tableaux [parisiens]* renvoyaient au *Spleen de Paris*.'

5 R. Vivier, *L'Originalité de Baudelaire*, Bruxelles, 1926, pp. 260 et seqq.

6 In the notes for a Brussels lecture, published by E. Henriot in *Le Temps* 27.2.1923 and quoted in a note to Crépet's edition of the *P.A.*, p. 319.

7 See Crépet's notes to his edition of the *P.A.*, pp. 284 et sqq., and J. Pommier, *Dans les Chemins de Baudelaire*, Corti, 1945.

8 A. Brierre de Boismont, *Des Hallucinations*, Paris (Germer Baillière), 1845. Revised editions were published in 1852 and 1862. Crépet and Pommier both refer to the second edition, that of 1852. It is perhaps worth noting that in the 1862 edition Brierre de Boismont, who in the previous editions has referred to and quoted the adaptation of De Quincey by A. D. M[usset] (see p. 364 in the 1845 edition, p. 425 in the 1852 edition), has now become acquainted with Baudelaire's opium articles. On p. 183 he uses without acknowledgement some of Baudelaire's phrases: 'Malheureusement cette ivresse dont l'auteur fait une séduisante description chez les lettrés, les imaginations cultivées, prématurément labourées par la *fertilisante douleur*, chez les cerveaux marqués par la rêverie, *touched with pensiveness*, est suivie chez ceux-ci des tortures les plus cruelles.' (His italics. Cf. p. 321 in the 1938 Pléiade edition of the *P.A.*.) He then mentions Baudelaire by name: 'les visions de l'opium, celles des premières années, que M. Baudelaire dans son

étude sur le livre de Th. de Quincey a si bien nommées les *enchantements* d'un mangeur d'opium.' On p. 189 he adds to the note on Musset: 'On peut lire sur cet intéressant sujet les extraits et les réflexions de M. Charles Baudelaire, intitulés *Enchantements et tortures d'un mangeur d'opium* dans la *Revue Contemporaine* des 15 et 31 janvier 1860.' He does not make any reference to Baudelaire's study on hashish (published first in the *Revue Contemporaine* 30.9.1858).

9 J. Moreau (de Tours), *Du Hachisch et de l'Aliénation mentale*, Paris, 1845.
10 Published in *Le Messager de l'Assemblée*, March 1851.
11 Quoted in Brierre de Boismont, pp. 378 et sqq. of the 1845 edition and repeated in the 1852 edition. Also quoted in Moreau, pp. 20 et sqq.
12 Same source as that given in note 6 above.
13 The effect here could be compared with lines from *Far Niente*, l. 26 in *Poésies complètes*, ed. R. Jasinski, Firmin-Didot, s.d.
14 Moreau, p. 14, and Brierre de Boismont (p. 199 in 1862 edition) give an amusing first-hand account also by a woman; it is different from that given by Baudelaire.
15 *Correspondance*, ed. Crépet, II. 256, Cf. also 'Notes nouvelles sur Edgar Poe', p. 64 in *Selected Critical Studies of Baudelaire*, ed. Parmée, Cambridge University Press, 1949.
16 One might note certain possible similarities in the sequence of moods given as Hoffmann's and parts of the *Paradis artificiels*. At the outset there is an 'esprit légèrement ironique tempéré d'indulgence' (cf. in *Vin et Hachish*, p. 259 'hilarité', 'bienveillance,' 'ironie' and *Paradis*, pp. 284–5 'De temps en temps vous riez de vous-même, de votre niaiserie et de votre folie, et vos camarades, si vous en avez, rient également de votre état et du leur; mais, comme ils sont sans malice, vous êtes sans rancune'), going on to an 'esprit de solitude avec profond contentement de moi-même' (*V.H.* p. 260: 'dès lors l'idée de supériorité pointe à l'horizon de votre intellect' and *P.A.* 'cette jouissance suprême de se sentir plein de vie et de se croire plein de génie', etc.), followed by a crescendo in the delights of the senses, then by a burst of sarcasm, culminating in a desire for escape from the limitations of self.
17 p. 63 in *Selected Critical Studies*, ed. Parmée.
18 pp. 375 et sqq. in 1845 edition. See also 1852 edition, p. 438.
19 p. 34.
20 See p. 438 of 1852 edition.
21 See Crépet's edition of the *Paradis artificiels*, pp. 238 et sqq.
22 Quoted in Crépet and Blin's edition of the *Fleurs du Mal*, Corti, 1942, p. 248, n.3.
23 For the main discussions on the 'architecture' of the *Fleurs du Mal* see M. Ruff, 'Sur l'architecture des *Fleurs du Mal*', in the *Revue d'Histoire Littéraire*, jan.–mars and juill.–sept. 1930; A. Feuillerat, 'L'Architecture des *Fleurs du Mal*', in *Studies by Members of the French Department*, New Haven, Yale University Press, No. XVIII, 1941; and the summing up in Crépet and Blin's edition, pp. 246–67.
24 Letter of 9.12.1856. Letter of 7.4.1855, and the passages quoted below.
25 Letter of Dec. 1861, *Corr.* IV, p. 9.
26 23.12.1861. *Corr.* IV, p. 14.
27 Cf. the passages quoted above, pp. 133–4.

28 Cf. in particular XXXII, XXXVI, XXXVIII, XLII, XLIII, XLIV, XLVI, LIII, LIV, LV, LVII, LVIII.

29 Many valuable comparisons between Balzac and Baudelaire have been brought forward (see in particular the works of Vivier and Pommier quoted above and Crépet and Blin's notes). It is not always easy, of course, to distinguish between what may have affected Baudelaire from such works as *Séraphita* and *Louis Lambert* and what is part of the general atmosphere of the day; there is also to be reckoned with the influence of Maturin (see G. T. Clapton, 'Balzac, Baudelaire and Maturin', in the *French Quarterly*, 1930, XII. 66–84 and 97–115). But resemblances with *La Peau de Chagrin*, which Baudelaire mentions specifically as an analogy in *Du Vin et du Hachish* (p. 262), would be well worth tracing, and the following brief indications may prove useful.

'On vit plusieurs vies d'homme en l'espace d'une heure', says Baudelaire in *Du Vin et du Hachish*. 'C'est bien là le sujet de la *Peau de Chagrin*', and in the novel (p. 83 in the Calmann-Lévy edition) we have 'nous vivons plus en un jour qu'une bonne bourgeoise en dix ans' and (p. 95) 'un privilège accordé aux passions qui leur donne le pouvoir d'anéantir l'espace et le temps'. 'J'aurai connu, épuisé, dévoré mille existences' (p. 56). Again very close to Baudelaire are exclamations from p. 44: 'Par delà les bornes du monde, pour nous verser sur les plages inconnues! Que les âmes montent dans les cieux ou se plongent dans la boue … peu m'importe! … Je commande à ce pouvoir sinistre de me fondre toutes les joies dans une joie.'

Balzac's hero has set out by magic means to enhance the intensity of life, and those means carry with them their inevitable and terrible price; to both the end is tragic and inescapable, yet preferable to the tedium of a life without vast ambitions. Both have by the means they adopt created a disproportion between their powers and reality. The account of Raphaël's desire for intense experience begins with that of sensuous delights, leading to the semi-hallucinations and bitter pleasures in the wine-fumes of the banquet; then follows his experience of a sterile love in his adoration for Fœdora, who fascinates him although he knows her to be icy and heartless; he proves the uselessness of science to solve the fundamental human problems in a way which cannot but have appealed to Baudelaire with his hatred of 'le Progrès'; caught in the dilemma between desire and death he seeks to annihilate his desire and lives in a state of 'atonie' close enough to Baudelaire's 'Spleen'. As we approach the end there comes the summing-up: 'La possession du pouvoir, quelque immense qu'il pût être, ne donnait pas la science de s'en servir' (p. 316), recalling Baudelaire's 'le haschisch … accorde l'imagination sans la faculté d'en profiter'. As Raphael's death draws near he has for a brief space a sense of returning to the life of childhood with its 'bien-être extraordinaire' and in this state, contemplating the natural world, 'il en avait saisi l'âme et pénétré les secrets' (see pp. 324–5 – fuller comparisons with some of Baudelaire's remarks on childhood could be made here). Restored with a shock to real life he is reduced to opium as a final resort. But at the last he dies of yet one more desire – the desire for Pauline, the Ideal, just as in *Le Voyage* the search for *le nouveau* is pursued through death.

In Balzac's allegory as in Baudelaire's *Paradis* there is as we have noted the moral of the magic means which is evil because it involves the abandonment of human effort and because it does not carry with it the capacity to use profitably the power it gives. But there is also the wider dilemma of the superior being who in the world as it is risks having to destroy those desires which mark his superiority or having his tranquillity and his life itself destroyed by them. To both, the desire for unachievable perfection is at once the proof of man's greatness and the source of his destruction.

Other points of detail might be noted. Among the many contributions to the theme of the *correspondances* and to the *Spleen* and *Tableaux parisiens* poems might be placed a passage (pp. 111–17) where Raphaël in his garret finds a strange significance in all the ordinary objects surrounding him and in the lights of the sunset. Speaking of Fœdora, Raphaël (p. 122) remarks on his love for 'tout ce qu'il y a de factice et de moins femme dans la femme'; and the comparison of the outline of her face with the line of hills softened by sunlight on the horizon (p. 138) recalls such poems as L or the beginning of LV from the *Fleurs du Mal*. Rastignac's defence of debauchery (p. 201) is of particular interest in connexion with the *Paradis*: 'La débauche est certainement un art comme la poésie... Pour en saisir les mystères, pour en savourer la beauté, un homme doit en quelque sorte s'adonner à de consciencieuses études... Tous les excès sont frères... Ces monstruosités sociales possèdent la puissance des abîmes... La pensée de l'infini existe peut-être dans ces précipices, peut-être renferment-ils quelque grande flatterie pour l'homme... Le dissipateur a troqué sa mort contre toutes les jouissances de la vie ... la débauche n'est-elle pas une sorte d'impôt que le génie paye au mal?' The introductory scenes may possibly have been remembered for *Les Joueurs* in the *Fleurs du Mal*. And is it going too far to notice in connexion with the various suggestions offered as to the early title *Les Limbes* (see Crépet and Blin, p. 275) the phrase from p. 74, 'les convives se roulaient au sein de ces limbes délicieux où les lumières de l'esprit s'éteignent, où le corps, délivré de son tyran, s'abandonne aux joies délirantes de la liberté'?

30 The accounts given by Moreau and Brierre de Boismont stress the recurrence of lucid intervals. See Moreau, p. 132, and Gautier's account (p. 382 in Br. de B.): 'Ce qu'il y a de particulier dans l'ivresse du haschisch, c'est qu'elle n'est pas continue; elle vous prend et vous quitte, vous monte au ciel et vous remet sur terre sans transition; – comme dans la folie, on a des moments lucides.'

31 Gautier's account stresses the shock of looking at the clock after the illusion of the expansion of time. Moreau (p. 124) gives an account of the terror which can be caused by the sound of a bell.

32 Professor G. T. Clapton, in *Baudelaire the Tragic Sophist*, Oliver & Boyd, London & Edinburgh, 1934, quotes from the *Paradis* certain passages on remorse and pride, and shows how they could serve as a criticism of the tenets of the poet. Without differing from the essentials of Professor Clapton's argument I am suggesting that the parallel is more extensive and more deliberate than his remarks have space to indicate. Any

contemporary criticism of Baudelaire's spiritual position is bound to acknowledge the important contributions made by Sartre (*Baudelaire*, Gallimard, 1947), Blin (see above, n. 3), and Pommier (*La Mystique de Baudelaire*, Les Belles Lettres, 1932). The present article is of course approaching the *Paradis* from a slightly different angle, and considerations of space have forced me to assume familiarity with their arguments where sometimes I should have liked to make further detailed comparison and reference.

33 One might note here the remarks of Brierre de Boismont, p. 375 in the 1845 edition: 'La perte momentanée de la raison, quoique librement consentie, n'est-elle pas d'ailleurs un spectacle douloureux?' To Baudelaire it is not the abdication of reason but that of will-power, namely the quality which leads to production, which matters most.

34 There is an interesting note in another work of Moreau: *La Psychologie morbide dans ses rapports avec la philosophie de l'histoire*, Masson, 1849, regarding Balzac's reactions to hashish. 'Ces phénomènes psychologiques' (those which give the illusion of genius to the *haschischin* whose conduct more closely resembles that of one deranged) 'avaient vivement frappé un écrivain célèbre dont le monde littéraire déplore la perte encore récente, de Balzac. Le lendemain d'une *fantasia* à laquelle il avait pris part, Balzac m'écrivait de Passy une lettre où il me communique les réflexions que lui avaient suggérées les effets du haschisch observés sur lui-même' (this incidentally seems to show that Balzac did not always adopt the position in which Baudelaire shows him). 'Balzac ... va – nous n'oserions assurément le suivre jusque-là – jusqu'à émettre l'idée «qu'il y aurait une belle expérience à faire, et à laquelle il a pensé depuis 20 ans: ce serait de refaire (à l'aide du haschisch) un cerveau à un crétin, de savoir si l'on peut créer un appareil à pensées, en en développant les rudiments».' Moreau adds: 'Je conserve précieusement cette lettre qui est fort longue et intéressante à plus d'un titre. Je la tiens à la disposition de quiconque, parmi les nombreux admirateurs du grand écrivain, voudrait en prendre connaissance' (pp. 414–15).

35 p. 205 in the 1862 edition.

36 In his *Connaissance de Baudelaire*, Corti, 1951, p. 135, Professor H. Peyre, making suggestions for future work on Baudelaire, writes: 'On n'a pas accordé toute l'attention qu'ils méritent à d'autres écrits de Baudelaire, et notamment à celui que nous mettrions peut-être au premier rang de tous: *Les Paradis artificiels*.'

10

Observations sur les
Petits poèmes en prose (1967)[1]

Comme l'a signalé M. Claude Pichois dans son *État présent* de 1958, les *Petits poèmes en prose* ont suscité bien moins de commentaires que les autres œuvres de Baudelaire.[2] Depuis, l'excellente édition de M. Henri Lemaitre a indiqué aux fervents bien des richesses et bien des problèmes.[3] Amateurs et critiques des *Petits poèmes* ont toujours trouvé particulièrement difficile d'expliquer pleinement pourquoi ces œuvres hantent tellement l'esprit de tout lecteur sensible à leur qualité spéciale. Fait peut-être significatif en soi: les ouvrages littéraires les plus troublants et les plus originaux nous laissent souvent avec ce sentiment d'impuissance à exprimer nos impressions que traduit si bien le jeune Marcel du roman de Proust, brandissant son parapluie avec un «Zut, zut, zut, zut!» enthousiaste et insuffisant devant une impression étrangement significative qu'il n'arrivait pas encore à analyser. Si j'espère aller un peu plus loin qu'un simple balbutiement d'enthousiasme, je ne pourrai aujourd'hui ajouter aux importants travaux qui existent déjà que quelques modestes remarques personnelles.[4]

Ce recueil a eu, bien entendu, ses détracteurs. Déchéance d'un grand talent, tentatives intéressantes mais avortées – les appréciations de ce genre ne manquent pas. Mais s'il va sans dire que les *Fleurs du Mal* marquent l'apogée de la carrière artistique de Baudelaire, les *Petits poèmes en prose* formeront toujours une sorte de «somme baudelairienne» où, à mi-chemin entre poésie d'une part, critique et documents personnels d'autre part, se trouvent des complexités de tempérament et d'expression qui avaient besoin d'une forme autre que la poésie traditionnelle.

Je n'ai pas l'intention d'examiner les sources indiquées ou par Baudelaire lui-même ou par les critiques, bien qu'elles soient d'une importance exemplaire, surtout comme contraste avec ce qui fait l'originalité du genre tel que Baudelaire l'a créé. Je prends comme point de départ un document supplémentaire. C'est dans les *Notes nouvelles sur Edgar Poe* (1857) que nous trouverons (empruntées, sans guillemets, à Poe lui-même, comme l'a récemment démontré M. Melvin Zimmerman[5]) des méditations qui seraient peut-être à l'origine de la forme des *Petits poèmes en prose*. Baudelaire explique la distinction entre la nouvelle et le poème: le poème cherche une beauté pure, par le moyen du rythme; la nouvelle se dirige vers les détails complexes de la vérité, par le mélange des tons:

Le rythme est nécessaire au développement de l'idée de beauté, qui est le but le plus grand et le plus noble du poème. Or, les artifices du rythme sont un obstacle insurmontable à ce développement minutieux de pensées et d'expressions qui a pour objet la *vérité* ... L'auteur d'une nouvelle a à sa disposition une multitude de tons, de nuances de langage, le ton raisonneur, le sarcastique, l'humoristique, que répudie la poésie, et qui sont comme des dissonances, des outrages à l'idée de beauté pure. Et c'est aussi ce qui fait que l'auteur qui poursuit dans une nouvelle un simple but de beauté, ne travaille qu'à son grand désavantage, privé qu'il est de l'instrument le plus utile, le rythme.[6]

Unir les exigences d'une vérité multiforme et récalcitrante, qui demanderait un troublant mélange de tons, avec celles d'une beauté faite d'harmonie et de régularité: de ces deux considérations naît peut-être le rêve bien connu qu'exprime Baudelaire dans sa lettre-dédicace: créer:

le miracle d'une prose poétique, musicale sans rythme et sans rime, assez souple et assez heurtée pour s'adapter aux mouvements lyriques de l'âme, aux ondulations de la rêverie, aux soubresauts de la conscience.

D'une part «musicale, souple, ondulations» – les qualités harmonieuses qu'il faut créer sans les ressources traditionnelles du vers (en y substituant des sonorités moins régulières et tout aussi subtiles, des échos lointains, des refrains avec variations); d'autre part une prose «heurtée» et susceptible de «soubresauts», donc ayant des dissonances et des dislocations voulues, de brusques changements de ton qui détonneraient dans la poésie traditionnelle mais qui ici renforcent le sérieux, au lieu de risquer de le détruire.

Il est évident que Baudelaire avait déjà dans les *Fleurs du Mal* pris des objets appartenant au monde quotidien, considérés traditionnellement comme «prosaïques», pour leur conférer les prestiges de la magie suggestive. Et il avait tiré beaucoup des plus beaux effets de sa poésie en vers d'une expression dépourvue de toute rhétorique, volontairement atténuée et d'autant plus évocatrice. Toutefois, les œuvres de poètes plus récents – un Apollinaire chez qui les avions côtoieront au ciel les anges et les prophètes, un Péguy chez qui les besognes les plus serviles et les objets les plus prosaïques (balai et torchon de la ménagère, boîtes de conserves et appareil photographique) fusionneront avec les doctrines religieuses les plus ferventes – ces œuvres révèlent ce qu'elles doivent à Baudelaire et nous montrent en même temps ce qu'il était impossible de faire dans la poésie proprement dite à son époque. Aussi est-ce avec mesure et discrétion, malgré certains effets de choc, que Baudelaire a employé le mélange de tons dans les *Fleurs du Mal.* Dans les *Poèmes en prose* il peut s'essayer à des dissonances de ton plus poussées, entrelacer les extrêmes du fantastique et du terre-à-terre, introduire le ton de la conversation courante ou de la raillerie sardonique dans la texture d'une envolée lyrique, unir l'anecdote mordante à la réflexion générale, l'aphorisme provocant à la rêverie lente et réfléchie. L'odeur des frites à la fête foraine ferait un effet bizarre dans le ton des *Fleurs du Mal*; quelque cruel que le poète puisse être envers sa maîtresse en la confrontant avec une charogne puante ou en lui lançant dans le cœur les sept épées douloureuses, il ne juge pas à propos de l'y comparer avec une jeune grenouille; et le poème en vers, «Crépuscule du Soir», malgré ses évocations détaillées d'une atmosphère de complicité et de cruauté, ne pouvait guère aller jusqu'à inclure l'histoire d'un ami qui, sous l'effet de la tension nerveuse, jetait à la tête du maître d'hôtel son poulet rôti. Il y aura toujours des critiques qui chercheront à juger le poème en prose d'après des critères rigides que Flaubert aurait qualifiés de Pohhhétiques avec plusieurs H comminatoires, et qui trouveront ces détails déplacés; d'autres sembleraient parfois vouloir plutôt éliminer les effets rythmiques, selon eux trop visibles. Il faudrait peut-être se souvenir de trois choses: d'abord des riches suggestions psychologiques que Baudelaire tire de ses détails les plus terre-à-terre; ensuite de la maîtrise avec laquelle il sait évoquer le côté sensuel et suggestif de certaines impulsions instinctives rarement jusqu'à lui reconnues ou caractérisées; finalement des transitions qu'il opère entre les prétendus «style noble» et «style trivial», les unissant pour produire en même temps un courant de résonance poétique et un interrupteur critique qui, en empêchant brusquement toute complicité sentimentale de la part du lecteur, ne fait que prolonger chez lui des réflexions multiples.

Si multiples que puissent être ces réflexions, nous sommes, comme les pauvres fées du vingtième poème, «soumis à la terrible loi du

Temps» (ou plutôt, et Baudelaire aurait aimé cette ambiguïté, l'auditoire est protégé par cette même loi contre les abus possibles de la part de l'orateur), de sorte que je ne pourrai isoler que quelques aspects principaux de ce problème – rapports entre la vérité et la beauté: vérités complexes; harmonie subtile, – que j'ai pris comme point de départ. Avant de les choisir, je tiens à souligner, ce qui n'est que trop évident, que l'intérêt intrinsèque des thèmes ne serait rien sans l'expression; comme le dit Baudelaire à une autre occasion:

Dans la composition tout entière, il ne doit pas se glisser un seul mot qui ne soit une intention, qui ne tende, directement ou indirectement, à parfaire le dessein prémédité.

Fond et forme s'imbriquant nécessairement l'un dans l'autre, ces deux aspects de l'originalité des *Petits poèmes en prose* seront, dans la mesure du possible, discutés ensemble. Et, quelle que soit la complexité des idées, c'est la perfection de la forme, résultat d'une maîtrise de chaque vocable, qui compte surtout dans cet art, si peu assujetti aux règles habituelles, et pourtant si savamment organisé.

Les vérités que cherche Baudelaire ne se trouveront pas, on le sait, dans une simple transcription de la réalité mais dans une transfiguration opérée par une imagination avide, cherchant à exercer et à analyser ses propres puissances:

Qu'importe ce que peut être la réalité placée hors de moi, si elle m'a aidé à vivre, à sentir que je suis et ce que je suis?

L'Étranger du premier poème refuse tout ce que lui offre le monde pour ne contempler que les nuages, image des possibilités changeantes et impondérables qu'il pourra façonner à son gré. Sur un thème très voisin de «Bénédiction» dans les *Fleurs du Mal*, Baudelaire substitue ici à une rhétorique riche et soutenue, des questions et réponses brèves, nues, minimes, des ellipses tranchantes ou des litotes qui ne sont qu'un murmure, pour finir par une phrase dont le mouvement ascendant nous emporte imperceptiblement et fait écho au sens: «J'aime les nuages ... les nuages qui passent ... là-bas ... là-bas ... les merveilleux nuages!»

Serait-ce donc dans les rêves que se trouverait la «vérité»? Les *Petits poèmes en prose* en contiennent de très beaux. Dans «L'Invitation au Voyage», par contraste avec le poème en vers, les refrains ne sont d'abord qu'à moitié perceptibles; on passe de la troisième personne («une vieille amie») au «vous», puis, au point culminant du rêve, au «tu» intense et intime; des phrases minuscules et douces s'entrelacent peu à peu, se modulent, s'écartent, reprennent encore, à mesure que les échos principaux reviennent à des intervalles irréguliers mais non sans une certaine symétrie: «Un pays de Cocagne; Chine de l'Europe; un pays où tout vous ressemble; Chine occidentale; c'est là qu'il faut aller vivre ... mourir ... fleurir ... respirer ...» tandis que s'égrènent presque imperceptiblement les mots-clé très simples: beau, riche, tranquille, honnête, luxe, ordre. Dans «Les Projets», Baudelaire évoque trois mondes imaginés comme décor pour la femme aimée, et les deux premiers sont ceux de rêves grandioses et exotiques: un vaste palais aux escaliers en marbre, avec ses pelouses et ses bassins; une case au bord d'une mer tropicale, ombreuse et parfumée, avec «le chant plaintif des arbres à musique, des mélancoliques filaos». Mais c'est le troisième rêve qui tire sa splendeur des éléments d'une humble réalité, chaque épithète restrictive rehaussant à son tour la sensation de joie:

Le plaisir et le bonheur sont dans la première auberge venue, dans l'auberge du hasard ... Un grand feu, des faïences voyantes, un souper passable, un vin rude, et un lit très large avec des draps un peu âpres, mais frais; quoi de mieux?

De même, dans «L'Invitation au Voyage», parmi les paysages, les fleurs ou les meubles exotiques, la séduction et la tendresse trouvent leur plus haut point dans des métaphores qui unissent les sentiments abstraits aux objets les plus prosaïques de l'art culinaire: «la cuisine elle-même est poétique, grasse et excitante à la fois – où tout vous ressemble», et surtout dans la plus belle phrase de toutes, où des épithètes d'ordre physique: «riche, propre, luisant», sont hardiment appliquées à la notion abstraite d'une conscience nette, puis cette conscience est transposée dans la batterie reluisant de marmites en cuivre pendues au mur, et se révèle comme le produit d'humbles soins quotidiens qui donnent une patine de beauté:

un vrai pays de Cocagne ... où tout est riche, propre et luisant, comme une belle conscience, comme une magnifique batterie de cuisine ...

Le rêve d'ailleurs tire sa valeur du fait même qu'il est implacablement cerné par la réalité, qu'il est reconnu comme étant une conquête difficile et momentanée. Dans «La Chambre double», après une évocation envoûtante de la sensation de s'évader hors du temps et d'accéder à l'éternité, où encore une fois concret et abstrait s'unissent d'une façon étonnante – l'éternité «que je *savoure* minute par minute, seconde par seconde», – après le «bain de paresse, *aromatisé* par le regret et le désir», le «coup terrible, lourd» retentit à la porte et «il m'a semblé que je recevais un coup de pioche dans l'estomac». Existe-t-il d'évocation plus étonnante à la fois du dégoût physique et de l'angoisse abstraite que celle qui résulte des mots et des rythmes de ces phrases:

ce parfum d'un autre monde ... hélas, il est remplacé par une fétide odeur de tabac mêlée à je ne sais quelle *nauséabonde moisissure.* On respire / ici / maintenant / *le ranci de la désolation.*

Mots et rythme changent de nouveau et le poème se termine par l'évocation du poète fouetté par le Temps en un refrain familier, spasmodique, implacable: «Et hue donc! bourrique! Sue donc! esclave! Vis donc! damné!» Retour à une dure vérité.

Vérité qui peut être évoquée par la femme aimée, surtout parce que, frivole ou égoïste, elle refuse de regarder la réalité en face. «Les Yeux des pauvres», dans un café Second Empire avec ses fresques prétentieuses aux murs représentant «toute l'histoire et toute la mythologie mises au service de la goinfrerie», oppose à la pitié et à la honte que ressent le narrateur devant les yeux du père en guenilles et de ses enfants, abasourdis par trois convoitises différentes, la mauvaise humeur d'enfant gâtée de sa compagne qui ne veut que faire éloigner «ces gens insupportables avec leurs yeux ouverts comme des portes cochères». Et «La Femme sauvage et la petite-maîtresse» prend pour ainsi dire au collet cette maîtresse frivole et dolente pour lui montrer que ses pleurnicheries pour mendier des consolations ne sont que de vides affectations devant la férocité et l'angoisse de la réalité. Dans les *Fleurs du Mal,* «Une Charogne» avait imposé à la femme un spectacle suffisamment répugnant, mais sans l'horreur sinistre et grotesque élaborée ici – la femme sauvage et poilue de la foire, exhibée dans une cage par son mari, battue, et déchirant à belles dents les boyaux dévidés de lapins vivants et de volailles piaillantes. Les résonances de ce poème sont multiples. Il offre le contraste apparent de la maîtresse plaintive qui se cramponne: «Aimez-moi bien! j'en ai tant besoin! Consolez-moi par-ci, caressez-moi par-là!» avec l'être simiesque en cage, mais aussi l'insinuation qu'elles ont en commun leur féminité essentielle. Quant à la captive, Baudelaire, tout en évoquant par l'horreur même du tableau une pitié indignée que ne détruiront aucunement d'autres suggestions, ne s'attendrit sur elle avec aucune sentimentalité; il suggère même, chez elle, un orgueil perverti à être livrée en spectacle, la possibilité d'éprouver «les jouissances titillantes de la gloire» (cette gloire qui, de tous les appâts offerts dans «Les Tentations», attirera le plus Baudelaire lui-même). Puis un mouvement d'élargissement introduit d'autres formes d'angoisse ignorées par sa maîtresse, d'abord avec des exemples précis, ensuite dans une phrase volontairement dépouillée (faisant penser au «bien d'autres encor» du «Cygne»): «Il y a des malheurs... irrémédiables, et sans compensation». Finalement, retour à la situation personnelle: la femme affectée et bovaresque est pittoresquement et ironiquement évoquée:

A vous voir ainsi, ma belle délicate, les pieds dans la fange et les yeux tournés vaporeusement vers le ciel, ... on dirait vraisemblablement une jeune grenouille qui invoquerait l'idéal.

Avec une concision remarquable dans l'allusion, l'image de la grenouille suggère la fable des grenouilles mécontentes de La Fontaine qui rejettent le roi Soliveau et sont dévorées par le roi Cigogne: cette femme l'a méprisé comme un soliveau inerte parce qu'il ne répond pas à ses désirs physiques, et il la menace dans une phrase qui commence avec une allitération douce et ironique et finit par une métaphore brutale et prosaïque:

Si vous me fatiguez trop souvent de vos *précieuses* pleurnicheries, ... je vous jetterai par la fenêtre, comme une bouteille vide.

Ce poème brosse un tableau grotesque et chargé d'humour sardonique, mais le centre en est profondément sérieux: devant le «joli enfer» de la femme frivole «il me prend quelquefois envie de vous apprendre ce qu'est le vrai malheur».

Si la femme aimée symbolise le refus de regarder la réalité en face, quelles sont donc les «vérités» que le poète tire lui-même de cette réalité? Lui-même peut refuser de l'accepter. Dans «Laquelle est la vraie?» la belle maîtresse du poète, Benedicta, meurt et de sa tombe s'élève une personne grossière et violente qui s'écrie: «la vraie Benedicta! C'est moi, *une fameuse canaille*! Et pour la punition de ta folie et de ton aveuglement, tu m'aimeras *telle que je suis!*». Le poète frappe furieusement la terre du pied dans un geste de refus et reste avec un pied pris pour toujours dans la fosse de l'idéal.

Mais s'il possédait cet idéal? Thème et expression dans «Portraits de Maîtresses» sont d'une complexité tout autre. Le style crée brillamment le ton d'une conversation de fumoir; quatre hommes dissertent sur leur expérience des femmes. Les trois premiers décrivent, avec des détails mordants, la femme autoritaire, la femme frigide, la femme gloutonne. Puis le quatrième évoque une femme parfaite à tous égards, et pourtant chaque phrase est si subtilement ambiguë que les détails de sa perfection constituent un reproche involontaire, paradoxal et insupportable: à la fin, avec une logique calme, ironique et pleine de componction, il la tue: «Que vouliez-vous que je fisse d'elle, *puisqu'elle était parfaite?*» Boutade, évidemment, application amusante d'une tactique de choc, mais qui ne s'arrête nullement là. Comme certains poèmes adressés à Madame Sabatier dans les *Fleurs du Mal*, ce poème en prose suggère comment l'imperfection aime et déteste à la fois une perfection qui se dresse en un contraste plein de reproches devant ses propres fautes; il insinue également que même si l'idéal existait (et la perfection ne manquerait-elle pas par définition des qualités que seules peuvent créer ou comprendre l'imperfection et la souffrance?),[7] l'homme resterait toujours insatisfait, chercherait quelque chose au-delà.

D'ailleurs, ne faut-il pas reconnaître, et accepter, comme dans «Les Dons des Fées», «la logique de l'Absurde»? Ce conte de fées, thème en apparence si mince, s'élargit pour embrasser des légendes millénaires, pose d'une touche légère et allusive le problème du destin, et met en jeu d'une manière vive et savoureuse les mots et les gestes de la vie quotidienne. Les marraines bienveillantes ont au début l'entière majesté de la Fable antique: «ces antiques et capricieuses Sœurs du Destin, ces Mères bizarres de la joie et de la douleur». Au centre du conte, elles sont réduites à un état de précipitation comme des hommes politiques surmenés ou des employés du Mont-de-Piété aux heures d'affluence, et leurs dons abstraits s'empilent sur une table, comme les prix sur l'estrade dans une distribution de prix; puis l'angle de vision se déplace de nouveau lorsqu'elles deviennent des créations pittoresques et diaphanes de légendes gracieuses et magiques: Sylphides, Sylphes, Nixes, Ondines. Ces incarnations changeantes font ressortir le thème central: le caractère arbitraire de la Fortune; autour de ce thème, des syllabes et des mots légers dansent selon de savantes onomatopées – «capricieuses, bizarres, d'un air folâtre et malin» ou bien une phrase analytique transperce la trame du récit avec une insinuation ironique:

Les Dons n'étaient pas la récompense d'un effort, mais tout au contraire une grâce accordée à celui qui n'avait pas encore vécu, une grâce pouvant déterminer sa destinée.

J'ai dit «l'arbitraire de la Fortune» et j'ai évité exprès la locution plus relevée «injustice du Sort». Car il ne s'agit pas de vides invectives contre le cours inéquitable des choses. Baudelaire traite son thème avec plus de détachement et il provoque aussi des résonances plus suggestives par sa justification ironique des pauvres Fées, distribuant leurs dons de façon précipitée sous la pression de la «terrible loi du Temps»; la comparaison avec des fonctionnaires humains comporte à la fois une critique et une compréhension sardonique du juge qui expédie son jugement à cause de ses pantoufles qui l'attendent au coin du feu. C'est ainsi que les problèmes métaphysiques du temps et du hasard sont associés ici aux problèmes psychologiques de la faillibilité de la justice et du jugement humains. Finalement il y a le père petit boutiquier de la fin. Symbole de l'homme qui demandera toujours quelque chose de plus au destin, mais aussi l'éternel petit bourgeois pratique avec ses expressions comiquement familières lorsqu'il empoigne la robe de la Fée: «Eh! Madame! vous nous oubliez! il y a encore mon petit! je ne veux pas être venu pour rien.» Dans son philistinisme il ne sait apprécier à sa juste valeur le meilleur lot de tous, donné par hasard à son enfant: «le don de plaire». «Mais plaire comment? plaire? ... plaire pourquoi?» Voilà l'ironie la plus forte et la moins appuyée de toutes – c'est la question célèbre posée à propos de la tragédie racinienne «Qu'est-ce que cela prouve?» Et la fée de mépriser cet esprit positif «incapable de s'élever jusqu'à la logique de l'Absurde».

Il y a donc des moments où le poète, au lieu de refuser l'imperfection des choses, accepte avec une tendresse amusée le monde réel, comme dans «La Soupe et les Nuages», où il est rappelé de ses rêveries par «une voix rauque et charmante, une voix hystérique et comme enrouée par l'eau-de-vie ... qui disait: «Allez-vous bientôt manger votre soupe, sacré bougre de marchand de nuages?» Ramené sur terre, et sans ambages: il n'en reste pas moins qu'il s'agit d'une voix charmante, «la voix de ma chère petite bien-aimée», «la petite folle monstrueuse aux yeux verts».

Il peut même essayer d'intervenir de façon pratique dans ce monde réel, comme dans «Assommons les Pauvres». Tactique de choc encore une fois, mais avec une signification sérieuse. La râclée qu'il donne au pauvre est évoquée par des sensations physiques violentes et aiguës et un comique virulent, mais on a eu peut-être trop tendance à souligner le «sadisme» sans voir que, rejetant l'idéalisme des utopistes politiques, le poète provoque chez le mendiant l'orgueil, le respect de soi et la volonté.

Mais, pour ce qui est de l'attitude fondamentale, je voudrais surtout attirer l'attention sur une analyse capitale, dans l'effrayant poème «La Corde», où Baudelaire découvre dans un enfant un désespoir hideux, dans les voisins une curiosité sadique et morbide, dans la mère une cupidité sans cœur:

Quand l'illusion disparaît, c'est-à-dire quand nous voyons l'être ou le fait tel qu'il existe en dehors de nous, nous éprouvons un bizarre sentiment, compliqué moitié de regret pour le fantôme disparu, moitié de surprise agréable devant la nouveauté, devant le fait réel.

La découverte de cette vérité a beau être atroce, elle n'en est pas moins une sorte de conquête qui répond à deux besoins profonds de l'esprit humain: l'impulsion scientifique qui pousse à isoler et à examiner les faits quels qu'ils soient; le sens esthétique ou mathématique qui dans la complexité de la psychologie humaine découvre de nouvelles lois, des symétries nouvelles. Proust a un sentiment analogue du moment de détachement esthétique même devant la pire découverte:

tout en souffrant au point de croire qu'il ne pourrait supporter longtemps une pareille douleur, il se disait: «La vie est vraiment étonnante et réserve de belles surprises.»[8]

Car, au centre de l'expérience des *Petits poèmes en prose* est ce mot-clé de Baudelaire, *la curiosité* – mot qui n'a ici aucun sens frivole, mais la même gravité que comportait au moyen âge son acception théologique. Atteindre l'Arbre de Science; dépasser les limites de sa propre personnalité, être, de par les prestiges de l'imagination, un autre ou une multitude d'autres, essayer surtout de comprendre les causes et les origines des délices et des aberrations qu'offre la vérité, voilà l'ambition fondamentale. Comme toute ambition chez Baudelaire, pour qui toutes les impulsions humaines ont des possibilités doubles, elle est également analysée comme une dangereuse tentation. Baudelaire ne fait pas avec condescendance un tour charitable des taudis, il ne fait pas au tableau noir la démonstration des vérités sociales, bien que la participation qui fait équilibre avec le détachement puisse être d'autant plus forte qu'elle ne s'exprime pas de façon explicite. Dans «Le Mauvais Vitrier», là où encore on n'a souvent souligné que le sadisme, une sympathie inexprimée mais intense sourd à travers la simple évocation physique de la fragilité délicate et de la destruction brutale des marchandises. Mais Baudelaire cherche évidemment moins à plaindre les éclopés de la vie qu'à se scruter lui-même, portant en lui comme chaque homme selon Montaigne «la forme entière de l'humaine condition». A travers les autres, ce qu'il cherche, c'est la vérité sur sa propre nature en tant que poète. Dans «Les Foules» il analyse, dans des phrases d'abord tranchantes, ensuite légères et rythmiques, les impulsions complexes qui poussent certains hommes à «prendre un bain de multitude», à «faire, aux dépens du genre humain, une ribote de vitalité», et à connaître «cette sainte prostitution de l'âme qui se donne tout entière, poésie et charité, à l'imprévu qui se montre, à l'inconnu qui passe». Dans «Les Tentations», le Diable offre comme appât «le plaisir, sans cesse renaissant, de *sortir de toi-même pour t'oublier* dans autrui», mais le poète, tiraillé entre les deux pôles du désir humain – la consolante perte de la conscience individuelle, et l'intensification de cette conscience, riposte: «Bien que j'aie quelque honte à me souvenir, je ne veux rien oublier.» Apparemment aux antipodes du poète ou du missionnaire, le Prince cruel dans «Une Mort héroïque», essayant d'échapper à l'ennui en titillant ses nerfs blasés, est pourtant aussi l'emblème du savant et du chercheur d'une vérité cachée: il veut «faire une expérience physiologique d'un intérêt *capital*», découvrir quelles sont les extrêmes possibilités de l'être humain qui se dévoue à son art lorsqu'il se sait condamné à une mort imminente et inéluctable. De même, on pourrait, nous dit Baudelaire, excuser en une certaine mesure celui qui donne à un mendiant une fausse monnaie s'il se livrait consciemment à une expérience pour analyser réactions et conséquences; ce qui est impardonnable, au contraire (et ici Baudelaire égrène un chapelet d'épigrammes équilibrées et sardoniques), c'est de vouloir

faire à la fois la charité et une bonne affaire; gagner quarante sols et le cœur de Dieu; emporter le Paradis économiquement; enfin attraper gratis un brevet d'homme charitable.

Car, entre les vices qu'offre le spectacle de la réalité, la stupidité béatement suffisante est le plus impardonnable, et des maximes mordantes en témoignent:

on n'est jamais excusable d'être méchant, mais il y a quelque mérite à savoir qu'on l'est; et le plus irréparable des vices est de faire le mal par bêtise.

(L'on pense aux vers capitaux des *Fleurs du Mal*:

Soulagement et gloire uniques,
La conscience dans le Mal!)

S'il veut voir clair dans les vérités que présente la nature humaine, si atroces soient-elles, c'est que Baudelaire est hanté par le mystère des causes et des origines de ces complexités. Dans «Le Mauvais Vitrier», à travers des anecdotes sur la joie bizarre que trouve dans un acte subit, absurde et décisif un homme pathologiquement timide ou léthargique (le cyclothymique caractérisé avant la lettre?) il allègue sept ou huit causes possibles (y compris le *simplement pour voir* qui est l'impulsion de la curiosité), confronte les explications médicales, psychologiques et religieuses, et laisse au lecteur le soin de trancher la question. Mais le passage essentiel se trouve dans «Mademoiselle Bistouri». La vie fourmille de «monstres innocents», et Baudelaire devant une des plus perverties dirige vers le créateur ses questions angoissées:

Seigneur, ayez pitié, ayez pitié des fous et des folles! O Créateur! peut-il exister des monstres aux yeux de Celui-là seul qui sait pourquoi ils existent, comment ils *se sont faits* et comment ils auraient pu *ne pas se faire*?

Quiconque s'est jamais trouvé imperceptiblement et inéluctablement vaincu par une tare qui à l'origine avait paru anodine, reconnaîtra ici la question qu'il se posera sans cesse: à quel moment exact les choses sont-elles devenues inévitables; comment et quand auraient-elles pu se passer autrement? On se souviendra des vers de «L'Irrémédiable»:

Un navire pris dans le pôle,
Comme en un piège de cristal,
Cherchant par quel détroit fatal
Il est tombé dans cette geôle.

Dans le poème en prose aussi sens et rythme s'unissent pour exprimer, avec une angoisse que souligne la nudité du vocabulaire, le problème des origines et des fins:

comment ils *se sont faits* et comment ils auraient pu *ne pas se faire*.

J'ai laissé de côté bien de mes poèmes en prose préférés; j'ai d'ailleurs commenté surtout ceux où Baudelaire dissèque les insuffisances de la réalité. Je voudrais terminer par une des plus belles évocations des richesses de cette réalité, illuminée par l'imagination. Les quatre enfants des «Vocations» représentent bien entendu quatre aspects de cette imagination: les aspects mimétique, mystique, voluptueux et suggestif. Ne pouvant ici analyser en détail les mots et les rythmes par lesquels Baudelaire exprime la fraîcheur et l'émerveillement du monde de l'enfant avec la précision et la résonance de l'artiste, je me borne à rappeler l'essentiel de ce qu'il en tire. D'abord l'aspect mimétique: la joie de devenir autrui, d'entrer dans l'univers de l'artiste où les choses sont ordonnées selon une solennité significative plus vaste et plus simple que la vie réelle, et qui pourtant illumine cette vie par la majesté de ses vérités; puis l'aspect mystique: l'élan humain vers une extase toujours insaisissable, vers l'illusion d'une communion avec le créateur; ensuite, l'aspect voluptueux: la découverte ravie des délices du corps, en une image d'une délicatesse extraordinaire: «la peau si douce, si douce qu'on dirait du papier à lettre ou du papier de soie»; enfin l'aspect suggestif: l'attrait de l'incertain, le besoin d'errer comme les bohémiens de ces gravures de Callot que Baudelaire aimait tant, libres, sans encombre et sans entraves, se délectant dans la mobilité et dans la recherche de nouvelles sensations. Ce quatrième enfant n'est pas parti, retenu qu'il l'est, comme le poète, par la paresse et le manque de volonté, mais c'est chez lui surtout, avec ses rêves inquiets, que Baudelaire reconnaît «un frère à moi-même inconnu». Frère aussi de ce Fancioulle qui, dans «Une Mort héroïque», remportera la victoire essentielle, en prouvant (et la force des adjectifs est ici souveraine) en prouvant

d'une manière *péremptoire, irréfutable*, que l'ivresse de l'Art est plus apte que toute autre à voiler les terreurs du gouffre.

Je n'ai pu que très sommairement indiquer quelques moments où, dans ce recueil, les exigences de la «vérité» et de la «beauté», telles que Baudelaire les définissait dans la citation qui fut mon point de départ, ont créé une forme pleinement satisfaisante et très originale, unissant par des transitions subtiles une riche variété de tons: pensée pénétrante, grâce délicate; humour sardonique, tournures épigrammatiques; structures musicales dans leur harmonie et dans leurs dissonances voulues. J'aurais voulu pouvoir examiner plus à loisir les subtiles merveilles de l'expression. Dans ce monde où l'action n'est pas la sœur du rêve, les lacunes qu'aura laissées mon acte de parole vous auront peut-être fait rêver sur les infinies possibilités offertes par ce recueil. Si je reviens en terminant aux deux postulations: vérité, beauté, c'est une citation d'un des poèmes en prose, citation où Baudelaire évoque la joie d'une fête troublante et solennelle, qui servira le mieux à résumer son propre ouvrage, et qui sera ma conclusion:

Cela était doublement vrai, d'abord par la magie du luxe étalé, ensuite par l'intérêt moral et mystérieux qui y était caché.

NOTES

1 Texte d'une communication faite au Colloque Baudelaire de l'Institut Français du Royaume-Uni, à Londres, en février 1967, et qui vise moins à apporter des découvertes dans le domaine de l'érudition qu'à signaler en toute simplicité quelques-unes des possibilités offertes par un ouvrage qui attend toujours des commentaires détaillés.

2 *L'Information littéraire*, janvier–février 1958, pp. 8–17.

3 Garnier, 1958. Les editions de M. Zimmerman (Manchester U. P., 1968) et de R. Kopp (Corti, 1969) ont paru depuis la date de la présente communication.

4 L'article le plus riche et le plus pénétrant est évidemment celui de Georges Blin: «Introduction aux *Petits poèmes en prose*», dans *Le Sadisme de Baudelaire*, Corti, 1948. Voir aussi J.-H. Bornecque: «Les poèmes en prose de Baudelaire» (*L'Information littéraire*, novembre–décembre 1953) et R. Guiette: «Baudelaire et le poème en prose» (*Revue belge de philologie et d'histoire*, 1964, n° 3, pp. 843–52). J'ai discuté ailleurs – dans un compte rendu, *French Studies*, XII, 1968, pp. 348–50, et dans une communication dans les *Actes du Colloque Baudelaire de Nice, mai 1967*, Minard, 1968, pp. 89–97 (voir ci-dessous, pp. 164–75) – le point de vue de Charles Mauron dans *Le dernier Baudelaire* (Corti, 1967). Deux études ont paru depuis la date de la présente communication: l'excellent article de Jean Starobinski: «Sur quelques répondants allégoriques du poète» (*R.H.L.F.*, avril-juin 1967, numéro spécial sur Baudelaire) et l'étude pénétrante de Max Milner: *Baudelaire, Enfer ou Ciel qu'importe?* (Plon, 1967).

5 *Revue de littérature comparée*, juillet-septembre 1965, pp. 448–50.

6 Edgar Allan Poe: *Histoires*, traduction de Charles Baudelaire, texte établi et annoté par Y.-G. Le Dantec, Gallimard, Pléiade, 1932, pp. 707–8.

7 Cf. «Réversibilité» dans *Les Fleurs du Mal*.

8 *A la recherche du temps perdu*, Gallimard, Bibliothèque de la Pléiade, 1954, I, p. 366.

11

Quelques remarques sur les *Petits poèmes en prose* (1968)[1]

«La fantaisie est d'autant plus dangereuse qu'elle est plus facile et plus ouverte; dangereuse comme la poésie en prose».[2]

C'est dans le *Salon de 1859* que Baudelaire laisse tomber cette remarque révélatrice. Et il ajoute: «dangereuse comme toute liberté absolue». Dans les «Notes nouvelles sur Edgar Poe» il s'attarde un instant sur le désir de réunir les qualités qui sont propres à la poésie à celles qui appartiennent à la prose, et il insère la remarque que voici: «Je ne serais pas éloigné de croire que ... ces tentations héroïques vinssent d'un désespoir».[3] Tentations héroïques – celle d'une forme dont la facilité apparente comporte pour l'auteur – et pour le lecteur – des gageures particulièrement subtiles.

Sensible aujourd'hui à l'honneur de parler devant un auditoire choisi, de suivre de très loin notre Président «dans les chemins de Baudelaire» et d'être accueillie dans cette belle région qui aurait pu figurer parmi les climats paradisiaques évoqués dans les rêves d'«Any where out of the world», je voudrais en toute simplicité rappeler aux connaisseurs que, malgré certaines études très pénétrantes (l'article séminal de M. Blin[4] comprimant magistralement en un espace restreint des réflexions riches de conséquences, l'édition de M. Lemaitre[5] fournissant dans sa préface et ses notes un fort utile instrument de travail, et celle de M. Ruff, qui vient de sortir,[6] nous montrant qu'«aucun écrit de Baudelaire ... ne dénude aussi complètement sa personnalité») et malgré des commentaires suggestifs dans des ouvrages ne se limitant pas aux *Petits poèmes*, on aurait encore besoin d'un examen approfondi de l'art des *Petits poèmes en prose*. Nous attendons d'ailleurs avec impatience deux éditions qui doivent sortir prochainement: celles de M. Melvin Zimmerman travaillant sous la direction de M. Bandy, et de M. Kopp, sous la direction de M. Pichois.

Jusqu'à présent, même ceux qui ont illuminé notre compréhension de ce texte ont quelquefois eu trop tendance à y voir
les indices de la dilution ou la déchéance d'un talent poétique. Je
voudrais donc signaler, à partir de quelques exemples seulement
(tâchant, comme les Fées-marraines bousculées, dans un des morceaux les plus réussis, de me conformer à la «terrible loi du Temps»)
signaler certains aspects d'abord de la richesse de l'imagination
et ensuite de la maîtrise de l'expression que renferme ce recueil
qui en font comme une somme baudelairienne.

Richesse de l'imagination. D'abord dans le simple choix des
anecdotes ou des symboles qui serviront à clouer dans la mémoire
du lecteur un thème riche de conséquences. Pour les questions en
même temps angoissées et ridiculement bornées de l'homme moyen
devant «la logique de l'absurde», les fées-marraines présidant à leur
distribution de prix bien-intentionnée et gênée par les nécessités
pratiques de la nature des choses; pour les cruautés et les paradoxes
de la lutte sociale, les yeux des pauvres vus à travers la vitre d'un
restaurant cossu, la bataille sanguinaire où deux enfants réduisent
en miettes inutiles ce pain convoité qu'ils appellent gâteau, le rat en
cage qu'envie l'enfant du riche, ou la raclée vivifiante
d'«Assommons les pauvres»; pour les rapports entre les sexes, la
misère et la férocité de la femme sauvage exhibée à la foire devant
l'égoïsme plaintif de la petite maîtresse, ou les quatre «Portraits de
Maîtresses», burinés de façon sardonique; pour la vision d'un
«monde où l'action n'est pas la sœur du rêve», le tableau grotesque
du poète, la jambe enfoncée jusqu'au genou dans la fosse de l'idéal,
ou l'apologue succint et suggestif de «La Soupe et les nuages». J'en
passe, et des meilleurs... Mais cette capacité de choisir des symboles
variés, dont l'effet est en même temps immédiat et riche de
conséquences ultérieures, n'est-elle pas le premier signe d'une forte
puissance imaginative?

La vraie richesse de l'imagination, cependant, se montre dans
l'extraordinaire faisceau d'analogies qui se groupent autour du
symbole initial. «L'imagination» a dit Baudelaire «est une faculté
quasi divine qui perçoit ... les rapports intimes et secrets des choses,
les correspondances et les analogies».[7] Dans «La fausse Monnaie»,
«ma fantaisie allait son train, ... tirant toutes les déductions possibles de toutes les hypothèses possibles».[8] Cette prolifération de
possibilités parallèles autour de chaque thème est une seconde
source de richesse. On a souvent signalé que «Le Thyrse» est comme
l'emblème de tout le volume: le bâton roide autour duquel

s'entortillent tiges et fleurs symbolise, dit Baudelaire en s'adressant à l'artiste, «votre volonté, droite, ferme et inébranlable» et «la promenade de votre fantaisie autour de votre volonté». On n'a peut-être pas pleinement analysé la façon dont le poème même groupe autour du thème central un faisceau d'analogies prises dans les domaines les plus divers des expériences intellectuelles et sensorielles. Dédié à Liszt, il évoque le jeu entre thème et variations dans la musique; par des associations en même temps historiques et kinésiques il suggère les bacchanales de l'antiquité où un instinct élémentaire trouvait son exutoire dans les mouvements complexes de la danse; il joue sur des parallèles plus abstraits avec le contraste entre les principes masculin et féminin, ou entre des formes géométriques qui auraient été dotées de mouvement («la ligne courbe et la spirale font leur cour à la ligne droite et dansent autour»), et soulève en passant une question fondamentale concernant les rapports entre fond et forme dans l'œuvre d'art: «Et quel est, cependant, le mortel imprudent qui osera décider si les fleurs et les pampres ont été faits pour le bâton, ou si le bâton n'est que le prétexte pour montrer la beauté des pampres et des fleurs?».

Cette technique qui consiste à construire un faisceau d'analogies montre une très riche capacité de saisir les rapports les plus imprévus et les plus suggestifs entre plusieurs royaumes fondamentaux dans l'expérience humaine. Mais c'est surtout la délicate précision de l'expression qui fait vivre les correspondances entre le symbole physique et les diverses analogies abstraites: des monosyllabes coupants, «sec, dur et droit», suscitent la forme du bâton, emblème de la volonté, tandis que la luxuriance de la fantaisie qui serpente autour est évoquée par toutes les ressources de la sonorité, par une définition précise et onomatopéïque des formes arrondies, (cloches, coupes renversées, corolles, calices) et par une esquisse de mouvements légers et indéfinissables: «dans ces méandres capricieux, se jouent et folâtrent des tiges et des fleurs, celles-ci sinueuses et fuyardes, celles-là penchées comme des cloches ou comme des coupes renversées . . . toutes ces corolles délicates, tous ces calices, explosions de senteurs et de couleurs, exécutent un mystique fandango . . .».

Cette technique qui construit des faisceaux d'analogies à partir d'un symbole en apparence simple, s'organise évidemment autour de deux pôles. Cependant, même les commentateurs les plus avisés n'ont peut-être pas suffisamment indiqué combien les «deux sentiments contradictoires» sont ici «deux postulations simultanées».[9]

On a eu tendance à caractériser une cruauté ou un sadisme foncier compensé par des moments de charité; trop séparer ces deux éléments c'est faire tort à la lancinante complexité de l'analyse baudelairienne.

Dans «Le Mauvais Vitrier» un geste en apparence sadique et gratuit marque le refus désespéré des limites imposées par la réalité: si ce geste atteint «dans une seconde l'infini de la jouissance», c'est pour se dresser contre la menace d'une «éternité de damnation». Geste sadique? pourtant, la façon dont Baudelaire rend l'ascension pénible de l'escalier par le marchand et la fragilité des vitres fracassées suscite sous le ton sardonique une pitié sous-entendue d'autant plus subtile qu'elle n'est pas explicite: «L'homme devait éprouver quelque peine à opérer son ascension et accrocher en maint endroit les angles de sa fragile marchandise... le choc acheva de briser sous son dos toute sa pauvre fortune ambulatoire, qui rendit le bruit éclatant d'un palais de cristal crevé par la foudre».

Geste gratuit? Le début du poème dirige d'*avides conjectures* vers l'analyse de ces «impulsions mystérieuses» qui agitent soudain les «âmes pathologiques et voluptueuses», offre une pléthore d'hypothèses, chacune riche de significations: «pour voir, pour savoir, pour tenter la destinée, pour se contraindre lui-même à faire preuve d'énergie,[10] pour faire le joueur, pour connaître les plaisirs de l'anxiété, pour rien, par caprice, par désœuvrement», dresse l'une en face de l'autre les explications médicales et métaphysiques et laisse ouverte devant l'imagination du lecteur la question des origines de cette «espèce d'énergie qui jaillit de l'ennui et de la rêverie».

De même dans «Une Mort héroïque», les implications ambiguës de chacun des deux personnages s'insinuent de façon si discrète que leur pleine portée risque de passer inaperçue. Le Prince est certes d'un côté le tyran sadique, en proie à l'ennui et aux nerfs blasés, mais il est aussi le symbole de la curiosité intellectuelle, de cette curiosité qui, dans son acception la plus sérieuse, est pour Baudelaire le signe en même temps de la misère et de la grandeur de l'homme: «Il voulait faire une expérience physiologique d'un intérêt *capital*, et vérifier jusqu'à quel point les facultés habituelles d'un artiste pouvaient être altérées ou modifiées par la situation extraordinaire où il se trouvait».[11]

Doué de «facultés plus grandes que ses États... jeune Néron qui étouffe dans des limites trop étroites», ce Prince n'est pas simplement le tyran opposé à l'artiste; il est lui-même l'artiste en puissance. C'est d'ailleurs un tyran chez qui se montrent des possibilités de charité:

chez lui «tout était possible, même la vertu, même la clémence»; mais suit l'insinuation maligne (contrepoint auto-critique) «surtout s'il avait pu espérer y trouver des plaisirs inattendus».[12] Autour des réactions de cet expérimentateur, cherchant à sonder les ressources de l'artiste devant l'ultime épreuve, se tissent une série d'*avides conjectures*: jalousie de l'homme politique devant l'emprise sur le public de l'artiste? déception du sadique qui voit l'impuissance de ses menaces? mécompte du savant dont les prévisions sont démenties par l'expérience? Quant au bouffon Fancioulle, si lui, d'un côté, il meurt du coup de sifflet symbolisant la désapprobation publique, il a déjà remporté la victoire «d'une manière *péremptoire, irréfutable*», en montrant que «l'ivresse de l'Art est plus apte que toute autre à voiler les terreurs du gouffre». Ici aucune opposition simpliste entre le tyran sadique et l'artiste victime: le Prince est lui-même artiste dans sa sérieuse curiosité à l'égard des capacités intellectuelles et nerveuses de l'être humain, et dans la sympathie, mi-charitable, mi-hédoniste, qui l'attire vers l'objet de son expérimentation créatrice; et l'artiste, brutalement assassiné par un moment de désapprobation apparente, a néanmoins créé une victoire souveraine.

Cette irréductible ambiguïté d'effets à travers des thèmes en apparence simples demanderait des analyses très variées. Je ne ferai mention que de trois cas particulièrement suggestifs. D'abord, les rapports avec un autre individu: la quatrième section de «Portraits de Maîtresses», où lentement et doucement s'élabore le portrait de cette femme parfaite à tous égards, qui ne vous reproche rien et à qui on ne peut rien reprocher – et qui devient avec une logique impitoyable et comique le symbole des reproches que l'on se fait à soi-même, méritant ainsi d'être, avec fermeté et avec regret, assassinée. Car l'idéal, s'il existait, ne pourrait comprendre l'être nécessairement imparfait qui le désire; de plus, comme le dit Baudelaire ailleurs, si l'idéal était trouvé, l'homme ne resterait-il pas éternellement insatisfait?[13]

Ensuite les rapports avec la multitude. Si la solitude fournit l'extase dans l'apaisement et pourtant la terreur de l'examen de conscience, d'autre part «prendre un bain de multitude» témoigne en même temps de l'expansion d'une sympathie imaginative et d'une impitoyable autocritique: les poèmes qui évoqueront cette forme de délice rivent ensemble les éléments d'égoïsme et d'altruisme que comporte cette impulsion créatrice: «cette sainte prostitution de l'âme qui se donne tout entière, poésie et charité, à l'inconnu qui passe» . . . «faire, aux dépens du genre humain, une ribote de vitalité». Finalement, les rapports avec soi-même. Déjà à travers le thème de la foule s'est suggérée une tentation qui attire le poète vers deux solutions contradictoires: accroître ou perdre la conscience de sa propre individualité. Des deux côtés, l'intensité d'un instinct primordial se suggère, pour être immédiatement freinée ou nuancée par une impulsion contraire. Même dans le rêve d'un pays d'atonie délicieuse où s'émousseraient dans le néant les tortures de l'individu, Baudelaire laisse subsister juste assez de lucide conscience pour savourer la détente et le répit: dans la monotonie du paysage glacial il y aurait toujours pour nous divertir les gerbes roses et le feu d'artifice de l'aurore boréale, tandis que la sieste tropicale serait «une espèce de mort savoureuse où le dormeur, à demi éveillé, goûte les voluptés de son anéantissement».

Et quand, dans «Les Tentations», on lui offre «le plaisir . . . de sortir de toi-même pour t'oublier dans autrui», il répond: «Bien que j'aie quelque honte à me souvenir, je ne veux rien oublier».

De toutes les «conjectures possibles», celles qui hantent le plus le poète sont peut-être celles qui se rapportent aux origines des choses comme elles sont: comment, et à quel moment exact, s'est formé l'irrémédiable? Pour représenter ce problème, il prend, entre d'autres, le cas le plus extrême: celui de la petite prostituée naïvement obsédée d'instruments de chirurgie et de sang sur le tablier. Avec l'obstination du chercheur qui se demande à lui-même la source de ses tares inhérentes, il lui demande: «Peux-tu te souvenir de l'époque et de l'occasion où est née en toi cette passion si particulière?», mais la pauvre hébétée répond en détournant les yeux: «Je ne sais pas. . . je ne me souviens pas», laissant au poète le refrain angoissé qu'il adresse au créateur, «Peut-il exister des monstres aux yeux de Celui-là seul qui sait . . . comment ils *se sont faits* et comment ils auraient pu *ne pas se faire*?».

Devant «le mystère et l'absurdité» des choses comme ils sont, la réaction de l'imagination créatrice est encore double. Dans «La Corde» sont mis à nu le désespoir d'un enfant, la curiosité macabre de la foule, l'affreuse cupidité d'une mère. Devant ces découvertes, le narrateur note que «Quand l'illusion disparaît, c'est-à-dire quand nous voyons l'être ou le fait réel tel qu'il existe en dehors de nous, nous éprouvons un bizarre sentiment, compliqué moitié de regret pour le fantôme disparu, moitié de surprise agréable devant . . . le fait réel». Car l'acte de voir la complexité de la réalité comporte en même temps une destruction d'illusions et une nouvelle possibilité de création.

Mais si «peu d'hommes sont doués de la faculté de voir» selon Baudelaire, «il y en a moins encore qui possèdent la puissance d'exprimer». Si certains critiques, hantés par des idées préconçues et arbitraires à l'égard de ce que «devrait» être le poème en prose comme genre, ont excommunié comme ou trop rythmiques ou trop prosaïques certains morceaux, d'autres ont très bien vu la puissante originalité de cette forme où l'artiste est pleinement conscient de ses moyens. Il faudrait pourtant une analyse plus poussée servant à montrer non seulement les dissonances voulues, mais les subtiles transitions de ton qui font de chaque morceau une unité puissante et complexe. Je propose simplement quelques indications.

Dans «Le Joueur généreux» les transitions sont particulièrement subtiles, destinées à unir les tons d'une ironie en apparence insouciante, d'une nostalgie souverainement musicale, et d'une parodie critique de cette même nostalgie, pour aboutir à une unité d'effet complexe, effet profondément sérieux sous son comique sardonique. En contraste avec la présentation du Satan des *Fleurs du Mal*, monarque muet des profondeurs de l'Enfer, à qui s'adressent des litanies musicales, mélancoliques, pleines de résonances, le poème en prose s'ouvre sur le ton d'une rencontre de hasard: «Hier, à travers la foule du boulevard...», se poursuit par une conversation d'après-dîner où l'on savoure longuement la fumée des cigares dans une luxueuse maison de jeu souterraine, et où la lutte miltonienne entre le Prince des Ténèbres et son Adversaire divin subit une réduction parodique nuancée de nostalgie: «Je lui demandai des nouvelles de Dieu, et s'il l'avait vu récemment. Il me répondit, avec une insouciance nuancée d'une certaine tristesse: «Nous nous saluons quand nous nous rencontrons, mais comme deux vieux gentilshommes, en qui une politesse innée ne saurait éteindre tout à fait le souvenir d'anciennes rancunes».»

Ici, la perte de l'âme au jeu n'a rien de dramatique; on joue et perd «avec insouciance» et «légèreté» et n'éprouve «qu'un peu moins d'émotion que si j'avais égaré, dans une promenade, ma carte de visite». Et quand le Prince offre de combler les désirs les plus outrecuidants, ces désirs sont représentés sous une forme simpliste et parodique dans sa brutalité; «vous vous soûlerez de voluptés, sans lassitude, dans des pays charmants où il fait toujours chaud et où les femmes sentent aussi bon que les fleurs» pour se terminer en un

brusque dégonflement: «et cætera, et cætera». Pourtant c'est
précisément dans la légèreté du ton que se trouve l'insinuation la
plus sérieuse, bâton droit supportant les multiples variations du
thème central, – car, la puissance du Malin ne se montrant pas de
façon tragique, sa victoire se manifeste insidieusement à travers
l'insouciance de sa victime. Pour l'indiquer, un aphorisme âpre et
nu pénètre comme un dard: «la plus belle des ruses du diable est de
vous persuader qu'il n'existe pas». La conversation a d'ailleurs porté
en passant sur les leurres divers qui trompent l'humanité – que ce
soient les corps académiques ou les théories de la perfectibilité –
«toutes les formes de l'infatuation humaine». Quant au ton de la fin,
où le poète adresse le soir à Dieu une prière fervente: «Seigneur mon
Dieu! faites que le diable me tienne sa parole!», – si un éditeur bien
pensant, choqué par la phrase: «faisant encore ma prière par un
reste d'habitude *imbécile*», a substitué «une *bonne* habitude», c'est
qu'il n'a pas saisi le paradoxe et sérieux et comique: nous ne cessons
pas, imbéciles que nous sommes, de demander avec importunité au
Ciel précisément ces choses qui seraient le plus en contradiction avec
la volonté divine.

Le ton léger et sardonique sert donc à suggérer insidieusement des
questions d'un sérieux profond. Et en même temps dans la trame de
la narration alerte et satirique s'insèrent sans disparate des phrases
qui évoquent par une musique solennelle les nostalgies les plus
invétérées: dans la «béatitude sombre» de la demeure souterraine,
dit le poète: «jamais je ne vis d'yeux brillant plus énergiquement de
l'horreur de l'ennui et du désir immortel de se sentir vivre», et, dans
un des plus beaux passages de tout le recueil, par un jeu
exceptionnellement subtil de réminiscences littéraires, de sons
onomatopéiques et de rythmes obsédants, il évoque la tentation
d'une léthargie paradisiaque:

on y respirait une béatitude sombre, analogue à celle que durent éprouver
les mangeurs de lotus quand, débarquant dans une île enchantée, éclairée
des lueurs d'une éternelle après-midi, ils sentirent naître en eux, aux sons
assoupissants des mélodieuses cascades, le désir de ne jamais revoir leurs
pénates, leurs femmes, leurs enfants, et de ne jamais remonter sur les hautes
lames de la mer.

Cette citation, où s'évoquent des souvenirs millénaires, passant du
mythe d'Homère à travers Tennyson ou De Quincey jusqu'au poète
français, m'amène à un des procédés les plus caractéristiques de
l'imagination baudelairienne: la façon dont il insère presque
imperceptiblement, dans le cadre d'une rencontre ou d'une

méditation, des analogies s'élargissant à travers un passé historique, littéraire, légendaire. Pour l'homme d'une timidité pathologique, les contrôleurs des guichets de théâtre «paraissent investis de la majesté de Minos, d'Éaque et de Radamanthe». Dans les baraques de la foire se pavanent des Hercules; le solitaire déploie les «courageuses vertus de Crusoé»; les pieds de la belle Dorothée rappellent les statues de déesses majestueuses dans les musées; le chantre des bons chiens reçoit sa récompense comme les bergers de Théocrite et de Virgile. Là où d'autres auteurs se servent d'analogies historiques ou légendaires surtout comme moyen ou d'amplification (tel Balzac) ou de dégonflage (tel Flaubert), Baudelaire, à travers des analogies qui unissent de façon voulue la bizarrerie et la logique, évoque une permanence envoûtante reliant passé et présent.[14] La réalité quotidienne lui fournit des exemples d'un comique riche de signification sempiternelle: sur les murs d'un restaurant à la mode s'étalent des fresques où sont représentés:

les pages aux joues rebondies traînés par les chiens en laisse, les dames riant au faucon perché sur leur poing, les nymphes et les déesses portant sur leur tête des fruits ... les Hébés et les Ganymèdes présentant à bras tendu la petite amphore à bavaroises ou l'obélisque bicolore des glaces panachées; *toute l'histoire et toute la mythologie mises au service de la goinfrerie.*[15]

Le rôdeur parisien se promène non pas simplement à travers le Paris de son siècle, mais à travers des souvenirs d'époques éloignées, époques qui s'imbriquent discrètement, par la nostalgie, la terreur de l'obsédé ou le sourire sardonique, dans la durée des impulsions humaines à travers les âges.

Cet élargissement prend toujours son point de départ dans des sensations; sensations rendues avec une netteté et une richesse toute particulière. Si dans *Les Fleurs du Mal* toute la gamme des sensations est évoquée, il y subsiste quand même une certaine hiérarchie quant aux sensations moins «élevées»; cependant que dans les poèmes en prose quelques-uns des moments les plus réussis résultent d'analogies prises dans le domaine le plus quotidien qui soit: l'art culinaire.[16] La nostalgie lyrique de «L'Invitation au voyage» tisse son analogie entre la bien-aimée et la Terre Promise en notant que dans ce pays de Cocagne «la cuisine elle-même est poétique, grasse et excitante à la fois ... tout vous ressemble», et évoque l'atmosphère de «luxe, calme et volupté» par cette image extraordinaire: «un vrai pays de Cocagne ... où tout est riche, propre et luisant, comme une belle conscience, comme une magnifique batterie de cuisine».

Et si l'extase peut se communiquer à travers les sensations

traditionnellement considérées comme les plus humbles, il en est de même pour le tourment – tourment vivifiant: dans «Assommons les pauvres», quand le narrateur rend au misérable le sens de sa propre dignité, c'est parce que «je le battis avec l'énergie obstinée des cuisiniers qui veulent attendrir un beefsteak».

De même, l'odeur des frites à la fête foraine se transforme sans effet disparate en un encens faisant action de grâces pour les deux dons offerts à l'humanité souffrante: explosion de vitalité; moment de répit. Vocabulaire, rythmes, symboles concourent à évoquer la violente énergie et la délicatesse plaintive de ces deux impulsions fondamentales. Dans «Le Vieux Saltimbanque» le crescendo étonnant des verbes «partout s'étalait, se répandait, s'ébaudissait le peuple en vacances ... piaillaient, hurlaient, convulsaient, se prélassaient, sautaient, cabriolaient» est entrelacé avec des substantifs également énergiques et suggestifs: «jubilé, insouciance, détonations de cuivre, explosions de fusées, énormité, lumière, poussière, cris, joie, tumulte». Mais ces éléments isolés ne prennent leur pleine valeur que dans le contexte de phrases où s'unissent sans couture visible le solennel et le quotidien: «les Hercules ... se prélassaient majestueusement sous les maillots lavés la veille pour la circonstance. Les enfants ... se suspendaient aux jupons de leurs mères pour obtenir quelque bâton de sucre, ou montaient sur les épaules de leurs pères pour mieux voir un escamoteur éblouissant comme un dieu».

Et si la vitalité se représente par l'enfant qui se cramponne à son bâton de sucre et ouvre des yeux éblouis devant les dieux de la foire, le répit, lui aussi, s'exprime à travers des sensations subtiles provoquées par les choses de tous les jours:

une senteur infinitésimale ... à laquelle se mêle une très légère humidité, nage dans cette atmosphère, où l'esprit sommeillant est bercé par des sensations de serre-chaude. La mousseline pleut abondamment devant les fenêtres et devant le lit; elle s'épanche en cascades neigeuses;

ou encore: «une heure immobile qui n'est pas marquée sur les horloges et cependant légère comme un soupir, rapide comme un coup d'œil».

Assoupissement, excitation; atonie et victoire de l'imagination: les *Petits poèmes en prose* ont créé une forme qui unit et qui exprime de façon obsédante ces deux impulsions contradictoires et complémentaires de l'esprit humain. Dans «Les Vocations», à travers les rêves de quatre enfants, Baudelaire évoque quatre aspects de la vision de l'artiste: – mimétique, mystique, sensuelle, imaginative. Le «frère inconnu» du poète, c'est le dernier: l'enfant qui représente les ambitions de l'imagination, et c'est lui qui a entendu la complexe musique des bohémiens: «une musique si surprenante qu'elle donne envie tantôt de danser, tantôt de pleurer, ou de faire les deux à la fois ... L'un, en traînant son archet sur son violon, semblait raconter un chagrin, et l'autre, en faisant sautiller son petit marteau sur les cordes d'un petit piano suspendu à son cou par une courroie, avait l'air de se moquer de la plainte de son voisin, tandis que le troisième choquait, de temps à autre, ses cymbales avec une violence extraordinaire».

Quelle meilleure évocation pourrait-on donner de l'entrelacement des tonalités dans les petits poèmes mêmes? Et, comme l'enfant devant cette musique harmonieusement dissonante, le lecteur se sentira sans cesse attiré vers d'éternelles découvertes.[17]

NOTES

1 Texte d'une communication faite au Colloque Baudelaire de Nice, 25–27 Mai 1967, et publiée dans les Actes du Colloque (*Annales de la Faculté des Lettres et Sciences humaines de Nice*, 4–5, 1968, pp. 89–97).

2 *Œuvres complètes*, texte établi et annoté par Y.-G. Le Dantec, édition révisée, complétée et présentée par Claude Pichois, Gallimard, «Bibliothèque de la Pléiade», 1961, p. 1061.

3 Edgar Allan Poe, *Histoires*, traduction de Charles Baudelaire, texte établi et annoté par Y.-G. Le Dantec, Gallimard, 1932, p. 708.

4 *Le Sadisme de Baudelaire*, Corti, 1948: «Introduction aux *Petits poèmes en prose*».

5 Charles Baudelaire: *Petits poèmes en prose*, introduction, notes, bibliographie et choix de variantes par Henri Lemaitre, Garnier, 1958.

6 Charles Baudelaire: *Petits poèmes en prose*, Chronologie et introduction par Marcel Ruff, Garnier-Flammarion, 1957, p. 24.

7 Voir *L'Univers poétique de Baudelaire, symbolique et symbolisme*, par Lloyd James Austin, Mercure de France, 1956, p. 175.

8 Cf. «Les Veuves» (XIII): «c'est surtout vers ces lieux que le poète et le philosophe aiment diriger leurs *avides conjectures*».

9 L'excellent livre de Max Milner, que je n'ai pu consulter qu'après avoir écrit la présente communication (*Baudelaire, Enfer ou Ciel, qu'importe*, Plon, 1967), montre combien «extase de la vie – horreur de la vie ... ces deux mouvements sont moins divergents que solidaires» (p. 152). Mes remarques sur «Le Mauvais Vitrier» et surtout «Une Mort héroïque» montreront que j'y vois d'autres «réseaux» que ceux qu'a indiqués le regretté Charles Mauron dans *Le Dernier Baudelaire*, Corti, 1966.

10 Cf. L. J. Austin, «Baudelaire et l'énergie spirituelle», *Revue des Sciences humaines*, janvier–mars 1957, pp. 35–42.

11 Cf. «La fausse monnaie»: «une pareille conduite ... n'était excusable que par le désir ... de connaître les conséquences diverses ...»; suit tout un faisceau de conjectures autour de ces conséquences.

12 On pense peut-être à la XXIᵉ Lettre des *Liaisons dangereuses.*

13 «Les poètes, les artistes et toute la race humaine seraient bien malheureux, si l'idéal, cette absurdité, cette impossibilité, était trouvé. Qu'est-ce que chacun ferait désormais de son pauvre *moi?*» (Pléiade, 1961, p. 912–13).

14 Pour Balzac, tout Troubert est un Alexandre VI en herbe; pour Flaubert, les amours de Louis XIV se représentent par une assiette peinte dans une auberge de campagne. Le dosage d'amplification et de raillerie chez Baudelaire pourrait se comparer avec un équilibre semblable, relié au sens de la permanence des expériences humaines à travers les siècles, qu'on trouve dans certaines images chez un La Fontaine ou un Proust.

15 Cf. L. J. Austin, *L'Univers poétique de Baudelaire,* p. 201.

16 Dans les Projets de Préface pour *Les Fleurs du Mal* Baudelaire avait déjà rattaché l'effort poétique à l'art de la cuisine.

17 J'ajoute trois références à des études qui ont paru pendant que cette communication était sous presse: l'édition des *Petits poèmes en prose* par Melvin Zimmerman, Manchester University Press, 1968; l'excellent article de Jean Starobinski, «Sur quelques répondants allégoriques du poète», *RHLF,* LXVII, avril–juin, 1967; et mes «Observations sur les *Petits Poèmes en prose*» (voir ci-dessus, pp. 150–63).

12

Aspects of expression in
Baudelaire's art criticism (1972)[1]

The recent discovery of some of Baudelaire's youthful letters gives
two earlier moments of insight than we yet had into his way of
reacting to pictures. At the age of seventeen he describes to his
stepfather a School Visit to Versailles, where an exhibition had been
laid on.[2] Dutifully disclaiming expert knowledge ('Je ne sais si j'ai
raison'), he at once pronounces his own judgement: 'Tous les
tableaux du temps de l'Empire, qu'on dit fort beaux, paraissent
souvent si réguliers, si froids!' and immediately picks an evocative
verb and amusingly opposed similes to convey his reasons in visual
form: 'Leurs personnages sont souvent échelonnés comme des arbres
ou comme des figurants d'opéra.' Due deference to the opinions of
the elderly is interwoven with a reassertion of personal taste and a
provocative reference to its contributory source, namely Gautier's
articles in *La Presse* of 1838:[3] 'Il est sans doute bien ridicule à moi de
parler ainsi des peintres de l'Empire qu'on a tant loués; je parle
peut-être à tort et à travers; mais je ne rends compte que de mes
impressions: peut-être aussi est-ce là le fruit des lectures de la *Presse*
qui porte aux nues Delacroix?' In deliberate provocation he quotes
the pun of a journalist describing their visit in *Le Charivari*: 'après
notre dîner nous étions rassasiés de croûtes'.
   A few months later, he asks his stepfather to substitute, for
training in fencing and horsemanship, lessons on the philosophy of
religion and on 'l'esthétique ou la philosophie des arts'.[4]
   Obviously Baudelaire's judgements on Empire paintings will
change, but here are already signs of the qualities his criticism will so
outstandingly develop. Mistrust of shibboleths; recognition of stimulus from reading; desire to relate artistic enjoyment to wide
intellectual and moral problems; half-mocking modesty regarding
technical competence; belief in 'une critique ... amusante et poé-

tique' (877). At the centre will remain the sense that 'je rends compte de mes impressions', with the joy of expressing physical and mental responses in words at once precise and provocative, subtle and suggestive.

Before a professional audience of art-historians, and coming after many penetrating studies, I shall not today be directly concerned with evaluating Baudelaire's judgements, nor with tackling the charge (whether informed or anachronistic) that he is not always the infallible prophet of present-day modes. My aim is very simple. Since recent research has done the inestimable service of making available in exhibitions and reproductions a wide choice from the pictures he discussed,[5] I want to look at certain selected details which seem to have made a specially immediate or haunting impact on him, and through them to see how he verbally conveys visual sense-impressions, their relation to those of the other senses, and their wider evocative power. 'Peu d'hommes sont doués de la faculté de voir', wrote Baudelaire; 'il y en a moins encore qui possèdent la puissance d'exprimer' (1162). 'La faculté de voir.' When Baudelaire looks at a picture, he shows two special capacities: one for seizing a general impression of the effect made on him by the picture as a whole; the other for picking out the significance of particular details. Where the general impression is concerned, one might ask how far it depends on the associations of the subject, how far on formal values, on execution: as so often with Baudelaire the answer would be two-sided. His hatred of conventional moralizing leads him to attack 'l'art plastique qui a la prétention de remplacer le livre, c'est-à-dire de rivaliser avec l'imprimerie pour enseigner l'histoire, la morale ou la philosophie' (1099),[6] and to assert that torture or eroticism, 's'ils sont savamment dessinés, comportent un genre de plaisir dans les éléments duquel le sujet n'entre pour rien ... Une figure bien dessinée vous pénètre d'un plaisir tout à fait étranger au sujet. Voluptueuse ou terrible, cette figure ne doit son charme qu'à l'arabesque qu'elle découpe dans l'espace' (1124). A keen sense of formal delight for its own sake is evident in the famous passages on judging the harmony of a picture from a distance at which the subject cannot be discerned.[7] Yet Baudelaire will also make the open statement in 1859: 'le sujet fait pour l'artiste une partie du génie, et pour moi, barbare malgré tout, une partie du plaisir' (1084).[8] In both sensation and subject he will discover and analyse the particular fusion of melancholy and delight, of struggle and aspiration, which combine in his definition of '*mon* Beau': 'quelque chose d'ardent et de triste ... laissant carrière à la conjecture' (1255). He will look above all for the artist who can convey the solemnity and the strangeness that are inherent in the everyday and the trivial. To him, the bad artist incongruously attempts to impose these qualities from without, through inapposite conventions; the great artist finds his own fitting expression for the complex nature of things. For artists who seek this two-sided vision, even through uncertain execution, Baudelaire often makes his reservations clear, while rejoicing in the suggestions their work has offered.

'La puissance d'exprimer.' In general Baudelaire eschews technical vocabulary: part modesty about his ᵗraining, part consideration for the general reader, part provocative pose of the *dandy*. Yet he inserts parentheses to show that 'I could an' if I would',[9] and takes steps to inform himself about technical problems.[10] His criticism is no mere impressionistic paraphrase of the plastic in verbal terms: he speaks of himself as wishing 'non pas d'*illustrer* mais d'expliquer le plaisir subtil' (1095). It is constantly informed by analysis and principle, but principle that is suggestive rather than systematic. Just as he demands of the painter not a copy of the real world, but an imaginative illumination of it, through selection, sacrifice, suggestion and synthesis, so his criticism rarely gives a methodical description of the left-to-right, top-to-bottom kind; he selects both central personal impression and revealing details, groups and constructs his effects.

Baudelaire's famous phrase 'transformer ma volupté en connaissance' would apply to all his criticism, and raises three implications. The choice of the strongest word for the immediate response: not just 'plaisir' or 'joie' but 'volupté'; the deliberately personal '*ma* volupté', and the enhancing of the delight by the urge to understand causes and consequences, for 'Jouir est une science, et l'exercice des cinq sens veut une initiation particulière' (874; cf. 814, 913). Late in life he will call himself 'un homme qui, à défaut de connaissances étendues, a l'amour de la peinture jusque dans les nerfs'. Sharp sensuous response; special ability to relate this to basic problems; outstanding capacity to give to both of these suggestive expression: these are the qualities I hope to show in looking at his remarks on some individual pictures. I shall begin and end with certain paintings to which he gives developed discussion; in the middle I shall examine reactions to some particular problems of perspective, of movement and of colour.

I start with a picture where Baudelaire's youthful enthusiasm has been found puzzling: Haussoullier's 'Fontaine de Jouvence'. [1] Why did this odd and stiffly stylized piece provoke his 'éloge violent'? First, I suggest, because the subject itself goes to the roots of his most intense preoccupations. In a later article he imagines a personal museum of works of art representing each shade of eroticism or tenderness (901); in looking at the Haussoullier he at once groups the lovers into representative types (was this the painter's intention?): on the left the platonic, in the centre the sensuous, on the right the festive. The central theme, to which he moves gradually, is one fundamental in Baudelaire – that of re-birth. These are not just young lovers, but 'rajeunis', reborn after sickness and suffering to tranquil delight: 'Dans cette composition l'on aime et l'on boit, – aspect voluptueux – mais l'on boit et l'on aime d'une manière très sérieuse, presque mélancolique. Ce ne sont pas des jeunesses fougueuses et remuantes, mais de secondes jeunesses qui connaissent le prix de la vie et qui en jouissent avec tranquillité' (821). Baudelaire, from early life so personally haunted by apathy and disease, has responded to the theme of miraculous cleansing and renewed vigour; he sees the picture as combining melancholy and joy, and his still somewhat flat and factual evocation points forward to the many moments where he will later define the experience of 'l'âme dans ses belles heures' (1053), when out of weariness or anguish emerges the fresh ecstasy of child, convalescent or poet (349–50, 974, 1158–9, 1257, etc).[11]

He has set out here to justify his enthusiasm by an unusually systematic analysis (the young critic showing his paces). Structure is divided into 'premier plan', 'second plan', background (to which I shall come back); the division of the picture by the central standing figure is noted. On colour, he stresses in a crescendo of adverbs and adjectives the virulence of tone and violence of contrast, praised for boldness, mistrusted for crudity; 'deux femmes vaporeusement, outrageusement blanches', 'la couleur d'une crudité terrible, impitoyable, téméraire même'.[12] That the painter might later grow more subtle is indicated by a remark on 'des alliances de ton heureuses', without attempt to specify. The picture has an assertive self-confidence which appeals to the Baudelaire who so strongly attacked the eclectics and doubters of his day: it is no weak copy of nature. Yet on reflection he warns against the temptations of the derivative (Giovanni Bellini is mentioned) and the over-artificial. Outspoken praise and clear

[1] Haussoullier: 'La Fontaine de Jouvence'

reservations unite in this youthful attempt at careful analysis, conducted with something of the combined boldness and stiffness of the picture itself.

Finally, it is the rendering of the sense-impressions which shows Baudelaire's imaginative ability, as he conveys, more delicately than the picture itself, the objective correlatives for purification and hope, whether in his image for the re-birth: 'une femme nue et à moitié couchée, semble comme une chrysalide, encore enveloppée dans la dernière vapeur de sa métamorphose', or in the evocation of the fountain (even as he admits its air of stage-property in the picture), where his words so well suggest the mobile and wavering semi-transparency of fringes of falling water: 'cette fontaine fabuleuse ... se partage en deux nappes, et se découpe, se fend en franges vacillantes et minces comme l'air'.

I mentioned the background: here Baudelaire picks out a sense-impression whose meaning for him I shall briefly trace in a few further examples. In the top left-hand corner, 'dans un sentier tortueux qui conduit l'œil jusqu'au fond du tableau, arrivent, courbés et barbus, d'heureux sexagénaires'. 'Un sentier tortueux qui conduit l'œil jusqu'au fond du tableau.' The physical device of perspective leading the gaze into the distance he sometimes merely briefly mentions, as with Corot's 'Homère et les bergers' [2] where he pauses to note the value of 'les deux petites figures qui s'en vont causant dans le sentier'. In other works he suggests how the recurring fascination of effects of perspective is intimately related to themes of human limitation and longing.[13] In a letter he had noted how a feeling of endless distance may best be given by framing the sky in a restricting opening; man's aspirations he likewise sees as intensified by the limits which constrain them. The sense of the hemming-in which stimulates a sense of endless expansion is explicitly expressed at the centre of his pleasure in a picture by Penguilly l'Haridon [3]: 'l'azur intense du ciel et de l'eau, deux quartiers de roche qui font une porte ouverte sur l'infini (vous savez que l'infini paraît plus profond quand il est plus resserré) ...' (1070). His reservations about Penguilly's over-precise technique in general had already been indicated through telling images, 'la minutie, la patience ardente et la propreté d'un bibliomane ... Sa peinture a le poli du métal et le tranchant du rasoir'; for this picture, a crescendo of metaphor leaves us with the bold and mobile

[2] Corot: 'Homère et les bergers'

[3] Penguilly L'Haridon: 'Les Petites Mouettes'

impressions of the gulls in space, 'une multitude, une avalanche, une *plaie* d'oiseaux blancs, et la solitude . . .'

He has no reservations about Delacroix's 'Prise de Constantinople par les Croisés' (970) [4]: here, behind the dual central effect swiftly summed up in 'tout y est tumultueux et tranquille, comme la suite d'un grand événement', he turns again to the suggestive perspective in that curving canyon of street leading into infinite distance: 'La ville, échelonnée derrière les Croisés qui viennent de la traverser, s'allonge avec une prestigieuse vérité', and one remembers his own poetic creation of 'les plis sinueux des vieilles capitales'. In the artists who represent Paris, he picks out again effects of perspective, with the interaction of compression and space: in Meryon (to whom I shall return) he stresses 'la profondeur des perspectives augmentée par la pensée de tous les drames qui y sont contenus' (1083) [5], and he finds Constantin Guys 'épris d'espace, de perspective' (1173).[14]

One last example: a Delacroix which Baudelaire specially loved – 'Ovide chez les Scythes' (1053) [6]. Here certainly the subject in itself goes to the roots of Baudelaire's preoccupations; just as in one of his finest poems, 'Le Cygne', he unites, around the theme of exile, Andromache from the ancient world and the negress in the mist and mud of the modern city, so here he recalls Chateaubriand's modern and musical melancholy in evoking the bitter exile of the poet of sensuous love. He gives no detailed description of the picture, simply conveying, in words that combine physical and abstract, a central effect once more of both sorrow and tranquillity: 'Je n'essaierai pas de traduire avec ma plume la volupté si triste qui s'exhale de ce verdoyant exil,' and the personal suggestion of the hypersensitive dreamer, 'couché sur des verdures sauvages, avec une mollesse et une tristesse féminines'. It is above all the sense of stretching distance which is given intense physical expression, and made to broaden into suggestive analogies: 'l'esprit s'y enfonce avec une lente et gourmande volupté, comme dans le ciel, . . . dans des yeux pleins de pensée, dans une sentence féconde et grosse de rêverie'.[15]

These are a very few examples of how Baudelaire, without attempting technical analysis, has drawn from physical reactions to details of perspective certain widely suggestive effects. The sense of movement he thus introduces into the static – 'l'esprit s'y enfonce' – brings me to another sensation that preoccupies him: the effect of mobility. In discussing conventional renderings of battle scenes, he mocks at 'l'immobilité dans la violence et l'épouvantable et froide

[4] Delacroix: 'La Prise de Constantinople par les Croisés'

[5] Meryon: 'Rue des Chantres'

[6] Delacroix: 'Ovide chez les Scythes'

grimace d'une fureur stationnaire'. One odd and amusing example of his close imaginative interpretation of the slightest gesture may be seen in remarks on Delacroix's 'Romeo and Juliet' (897) [7]:

Dans cette étreinte violente de l'adieu, Juliette, les mains posées sur les épaules de son amant, rejette la tête en arrière, comme pour respirer, ou par un mouvement d'orgueil et de passion joyeuse. Cette attitude insolite, – car presque tous les peintres collent les bouches des amoureux l'une contre l'autre, – est néanmoins fort naturelle; – ce mouvement vigoureux de la nuque est particulier aux chiens et aux chats heureux d'être caressés.

To Baudelaire, 'la modernité, c'est le transitoire, le fugitif, le contingent' (1163). In his first *Salon*, he picks out from a whole series by Decamps this means of representing the fugitive and fleeting [8]: 'On reconnaît le génie de Decamps tout pur dans cette ombre volante de l'homme qui enjambe plusieurs marches, et qui reste éternellement suspendu en l'air ... M. Decamps aime prendre la nature sur le fait, par son côté fantastique et réel à la fois – dans son aspect le plus subit et le plus inattendu' (823). I shall not attempt to illustrate the constant fascination for Baudelaire of all that is 'ondoyant' and 'miroitant' in 'le beau multiforme'. The artist who would render this shifting complexity must, he holds, achieve extreme speed in execution; Delacroix is a master here, and in Constantin Guys there is 'une ivresse de crayon, de pinceau, ressemblant presque à une fureur'. The Baudelaire who saw that one might often admire in an artist those qualities one most longs to possess is haunted here by his own struggle to achieve adequate expression before the moment of insight disappears: 'C'est la peur ... de laisser échapper le fantôme avant que la synthèse n'en soit extraite et saisie, c'est cette terrible peur qui possède tous les grands artistes et qui leur fait désirer si ardemment de s'approprier tous les moyens d'expression, pour que jamais les ordres de l'esprit ne soient altérés par les hésitations de la main' (1168). To him, the sharp outline, the over-finished and finical detail, suggest static self-satisfaction rather than the aspiration he demands of Beauty; or else give a painful sense of effort, where effort should give the illusion of ease. (Yet it is the sense of a painful and stylized effort, appealing to his own preoccupation with the struggles of *la volonté*, which makes him find a particular stimulus in Ingres.) He demands, however, not simply spontaneity but synthesis, realizes the dangers of apparent ease in the technique of the 'eau-forte', and is uncompromising in his attacks on works (e.g. some by Diaz) which provide, instead of

[7] Delacroix: 'Roméo et Juliette'

suggestive mobility, only a kaleidoscopic patchwork or the disorder
of limbs that seem scattered by a railway explosion.

One of his most evocative longer passages, all the more significant
in that it runs counter to his mistrust both of the 'mere' sketch and
of the landscape without human focus, finds in Boudin's pastel
sketches of cloudscapes a 'plénitude de jouissance': many passages
from his own creative works where drifting clouds form the emblem
of the shifting moods and dreams of man might obviously be set

[8] Decamps: 'Samson écartant les colonnes du temple'

beside these works of Boudin, 'études si rapidement et si fidèlement croquées d'après ce qu'il y a de plus inconstant, de plus insaisissable dans sa forme et dans sa couleur, d'après des vagues et des nuages' (1082).

Just as the infinite may be sensed through contrasting limitations, so mobility may be most suggestively conveyed through the impression of sharp, defined, geometrical outlines made shifting or impermanent. Masts and rigging of ships, wheels and harness of carriages, provide this challenge. Baudelaire calls up the combined precision and complexity of patterns in Whistler's Thames-side engravings, 'merveilleux fouillis d'agrès, de vergues, de cordages; chaos de brumes, de fourneaux et de fumées tirebouchonnées; poésie profonde ... d'une vaste capitale' (1148, 1150), and, in the article on Guys, analyses the sources of this pleasure:

une voiture, comme un vaisseau, emprunte au mouvement une grâce mystérieuse et complexe très difficile à sténographier. Le plaisir que l'œil de l'artiste en reçoit est tiré, ce semble, de la série de figures géométriques que cet objet, déjà si compliqué, navire ou carrosse, engendre successivement et rapidement dans l'espace (1191; cf. *Fusées* (1261), on man's basic need for both symmetry and complexity).

Some geometrical shapes, even when still, may fascinate by combining a complex loveliness of lines with both the physical and the mental suggestion of their impermanence. This outstanding passage on Meryon shows both the closeness of Baudelaire's contemplation of detail and the vigour and variety of his expression [9, 10]. Each word first stresses the solidity and majesty of ancient buildings, then the violent and twining movement of belching smoke against the angry firmament; finally there stands out the temporary spider-web lace-work of scaffolding, the word *arachnéenne*, added in his revision of the passage, underlining its pattern and its impermanence:

Nous avons rarement vu, représentée avec plus de poésie, la solennité naturelle d'une grande capitale. Les majestés de la pierre accumulée, les *clochers montrant du doigt le ciel*, les obélisques de l'industrie vomissant contre le firmament leurs coalitions de fumée, les prodigieux échafaudages des monuments en réparation, appliquant sur le corps solide de l'architecture leur architecture à jour d'une beauté arachnéenne et paradoxale, le ciel brumeux, chargé de colère et de rancune ... Aucun des éléments complexes dont se compose le douloureux et glorieux décor de la civilisation n'y est oublié (1149; cf. 1083).

The sense of flux and mobility may of course be conveyed by play of light and colour. If Baudelaire is occasionally captivated by bold

[9] Meryon: 'La Tour de l'horloge'

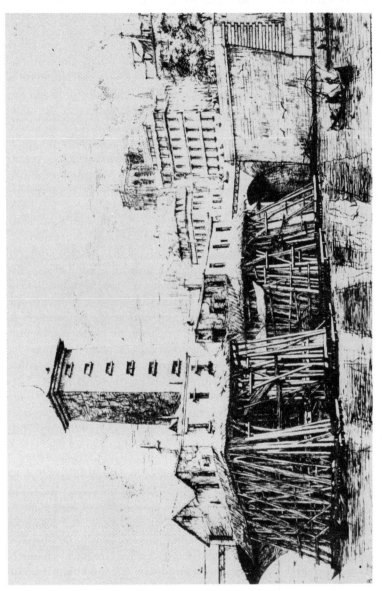

[10] Meryon: 'La Pompe'

contrasts or 'bitter' tones (Haussoullier or Janmot), he elsewhere sees over-rich and violent colouring as the appurtenance of the window-dresser or theatrical costumier, garish as a village scarf; he looks above all for a harmony, a system of relations involving subtle transitions and reflections, and culminating often in a muted effect whose rich subtleties emerge only on close contemplation. In Delacroix's 'Sultan du Maroc', where he hymns the 'prodigieux accord de tons nouveaux, inconnus, délicats, charmants', he stresses that 'Ce tableau est si harmonieux, malgré la splendeur des tons, qu'il en est gris – gris comme la nature – gris comme l'atmosphère de l'été, quand le soleil s'étend comme un crépuscule de poussière tremblante sur chaque objet' (818–19).[16] The *tour de force* passage on colour in the *Salon de 1846* brings out his double preoccupation: with a technical approach analysing relationships between complement-aries, tones, reflections, and with an either expressive or symbolic approach, elsewhere associated with the famous term *correspon-dances*.[17] The second of these will clearly have richer consequences in his own work. What is important, however, is that he does not erect the potential symbolism of colour into any set of fixed, hieroglyphic equivalents. As in his poetry 'Ce qui dit à l'un: Sépulture!/Dit à l'autre: Vie et Splendeur!', so in criticism he draws attention to the infinite variables: 'Tout le monde sait que le jaune, l'orangé, le rouge inspirent des idées de joie, de richesse, de gloire et d'amour; mais il y a des milliers d'atmosphères jaunes ou rouges, et toutes les autres couleurs seront affectées logiquement et dans une quantité proportionnelle par l'atmosphère dominante' (1042).[18]

From his individual responses to colour I shall discuss only one, constantly recurring: his delight· in the combination of red and green. Quite apart from technical or symbolic explanations, this was obviously an immediate reaction of his nerves: 'J'ai eu longtemps devant ma fenêtre un cabaret mi-parti de vert et de rouge crus, qui étaient pour mes yeux une douleur délicieuse.' In early criticism he flourishes the technical term: 'cette *pondération* du vert et du rouge plaît à notre âme' (816). The suggestive possibilities evoked come to centre on a preoccupation we have already seen: the fusion of violence and of peace; countless brief phrases convey the obsessive joy, in every mood from gay to sinister, 'partout, le rouge chante la gloire du vert' (881); 'L'uniforme égaye ici, avec l'ardeur du coquelicot ou du pavot, un vaste océan de verdure' (1061); 'le rouge ... abondait tellement dans ce sombre musée, que c'était une ivresse; quant aux paysages ... ils étaient monotonement, éternelle-

ments verts': 'le rouge, cette couleur si obscure, si épaisse, plus
difficile à pénétrer que les yeux d'un serpent, – le vert, cette couleur
calme et gaie et souriante . . . je les retrouve chantant leur antithèse
mélodique'; and finally 'cette sanglante et farouche désolation,
à peine compensée par le vert sombre de l'espérance' (894).

If Delacroix specially fascinates him here, I want to look at a less
immediately obvious example of how he is haunted by this combination, even when the meaning is implicit rather than specifically
underlined: a passage on David's 'Marat' [11] (868–9). Here incidentally Baudelaire takes David not as an outmoded figure, but as
an early example of what he is looking for in the Painter of Modern
Life: the ability to synthesize from the trivial, the harsh or the ugly
its latent solemnity. The kitchen knife, bare planks, letter, the
famous ugliness of Marat himself; these might, he writes, figure in a
'realistic' novel by Balzac. A miracle of simplicity and speed has
conferred outstanding and appropriate beauty and dignity: 'Cruel
comme la nature, ce tableau a tout le parfum de l'idéal . . . Dans
l'air froid de cette chambre, sur ces murs froids, autour de cette
froide et funèbre baignoire, une âme voltige.' Against the deliberate
bareness, Baudelaire picks out those two colours that haunt him.
The red of violent death is elaborated in each detail, 'L'eau de la
baignoire est rougie de sang, le papier est sanglant; à terre gît un
grand couteau de cuisine trempé de sang.' At the beginning is the
simple mention of 'le pupitre vert placé devant lui', while at the
end, 'tel qu'en lui-même', comes the achievement of peace: 'il repose
dans le calme de sa métamorphose'.[19]

Baudelaire also noted that 'Les grands coloristes savent faire de la
couleur avec un habit noir, une cravate blanche et un fond gris'
(951). This interest in the art of suggestion through minimal means
draws him to contemplation of engravings, woodcuts, etchings.[20] Of
Daumier he writes: 'Ses lithographies et ses dessins sur bois éveillent
des idées de couleur . . . Il fait deviner la couleur comme la pensée'
(1004). His discussion of Daumier's 'Le Choléra' [12] shows the
swiftness with which the black-and-white medium has suggested a
whole range of sensations and reflections; it shows too how deliberately Baudelaire constructs his gradation of effects. He opens
with a pervasive and violent general impression: glowing sensations
beneath the burning sunlight, 'une place publique, inondée, criblée
de lumière et de chaleur . . . le ciel . . . incandescent d'ardeur'
(1004). After the sensation comes the bitter reflection on 'le ciel
parisien, fidèle à son habitude ironique dans les grands fléaux et les

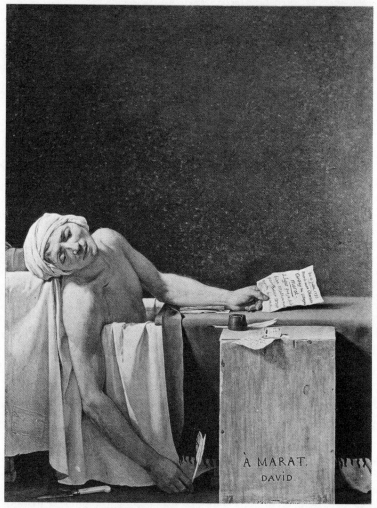

[11]   David: 'Marat'

grands remue-ménages politiques' (we remember the ironical sky of
'Une Charogne' or 'Le Cygne', or the ironical beauty of many
fateful political days throughout the last two centuries). Neither
sensation nor reflection is mere embroidery; they stem from the
observation that the sun's force is conveyed by 'les ombres noires et
nettes'.

Corpse and fleeing woman at the centre are indicated barely,

[12]   Daumier: 'Le Choléra', from *La Némésis médicale*

with one sensorial detail to suggest the horror of the plague: the woman 'se bouchant le nez et la bouche'. We are brought back to the emptiness of the square, set once more against wide memories ('plus désolée qu'une place populeuse dont l'émeute a fait une solitude'); the deep and resonant dignity of despair, 'ce forum de la désolation', is then deliberately narrowed into the sharp delineation of grotesque nags trailing hearses in the distance ('haridelles comiques') and, as the last touch of harsh triviality, the skinny stray dog, each word intensifying its physical misery as it, 'maigre jusqu'aux os, flaire le pavé desséché, la queue serrée entre les jambes'.

In this very simple example, visual evocation is closely interwoven both with other sensorial effects and with wider reflections. I shall not attempt here any systematic examination of the extent to which Baudelaire almost imperceptibly introduces sense-impressions beyond the visual (we have already noted the pervasive cold in David's 'Marat'; in Delacroix's 'Croisés' iridescent flags twisting in the wind convey the sound of their flapping; in Tabar's 'Guerre de Crimée' we breathe the cool scent of autumn sheaves or in Liès's 'Malheurs de la guerre' feel the jolting of conquerors' carts). Having looked rapidly at some individual sense-impressions, I shall now take more generally certain examples of pictures, deliberately chosen to be very different from each other, which show details of Baudelaire's way of looking and expressing.

First, Legros's 'L'Angélus' (1046) [13]: Baudelaire's admiration has pained or puzzled some critics. He realizes that this is a 'modeste toile', and constructs a dialogue between himself and a conventional critic, M. C. . . .; he also insists that good religious painting depends not on faith, but on the power to imagine and render faith. His remarks must be seen in chronological context; what worries his opponent, the conventional M. C. . . ., is that the picture is an example not only of unfashionable religiosity, but of low and trivial 'realism', an ignoble village subject. Whatever Baudelaire's theories on relevance of subject-matter, it is clear that both subject and rendering have called up deeply rooted memories and sensations from his own sensibility. 'Comme les voilà bien revenues et retrouvées, les sensations de rafraîchissement qui habitent les voûtes de l'église catholique.' But what has centrally caught him is the artist's attempt to combine those two sides he himself wishes to see fused in 'la modernité' – a contemplation of the everyday or the grotesque so as to bring out its natural dignity with penetration and tenderness. The triviality of clothes upsets M. C. . . .; Baudelaire picks out the detail of 'coton, indienne, cotonnade, sabots et parapluies' (that most prosaic 19th-century object, boldly in the foreground), and we remember his discussion elsewhere of the problem of rendering 'le tissu, le grain, le pli' of untraditional modern materials. In his description of the characters, creative physical terms evoke a theme of deep personal moment to himself: the cumulative effects of toil and suffering: 'tout voûté par le travail, tout ridé par l'âge, tout

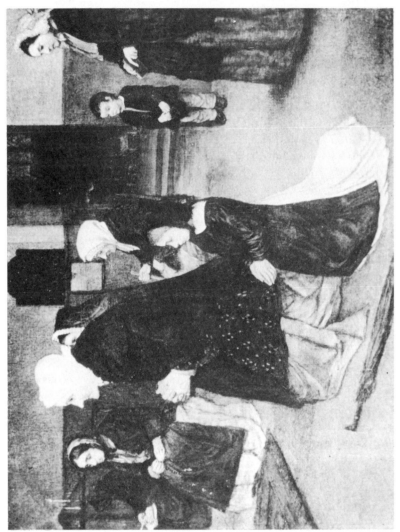

[13] Legros: 'L'Angélus'

parcheminé par la brûlure du chagrin'. He concentrates on the background detail which most suggests to him the effect that may be drawn from the awkward and the ugly: 'l'enfant grotesquement habillé, qui tortille avec gaucherie sa casquette dans le temple de Dieu' (we almost glimpse Charles Bovary); and underlines his meaning by a literary allusion to a moment from the writings of Sterne which haunted him elsewhere – Sterne's loving contemplation of a donkey grotesquely devouring macaroons.[21] The central impression is summed up in 'la trivialité est ici comme un assaisonnement dans la charité et la tendresse'. Remarks on technique are brief, and introduced by 'j'oubliais de dire que', but each relates execution to central effect: 'la couleur un peu triste et la minutie des détails s'harmonisent avec le caractère éternellement *précieux* de la dévotion'. As for M. C...'s objection that perspective is clumsily handled,[22] Baudelaire feels that its very awkwardness, by recalling the primitives, may suit its religious theme, 'ce défaut, je l'avoue, en me rappelant l'ardente naïveté des vieux tableaux, fut pour moi un charme de plus. Dans une œuvre moins intime et moins pénétrante, il n'eût pas été tolérable.'

Through this close contemplation of a partly unskilled work, Baudelaire suggests, whether or not the artist has fully realized them, something of the subtle possibilities of combination of tones that he himself so triumphantly creates in 'Les Petites Vieilles', as he deliberately interweaves *naïveté* and *préciosité* to draw natural dignity from the trivial or the grotesque. This particular picture has to him proved more evocative than the sentimentalities of an Ary Scheffer whom he so uncompromisingly attacks, more suggestive of his own aims than the work of a Millet whose peasants he considers too self-consciously didactic, or a Courbet whom he sees as too unimaginatively close to brute nature. Both his reasons and his reservations are swiftly and allusively handled through the dialogue form.

Another form of suggestively using the most contemporary subjects, of endowing the trivial or the terrible with a momentary beauty or a lasting import, is what Baudelaire brilliantly evokes in Constantin Guys[23]. That Guys has brought to a pitch certain almost mechanical tricks of stylization is recognized as Baudelaire characterizes his swift effects: 'On rencontre souvent l'Empereur des Français, dont il a su réduire la figure, sans nuire à la ressemblance, à un croquis infaillible, et qu'il exécute avec la certitude d'un paraphe ... Quelquefois il est immobile sur un cheval dont les pieds sont aussi assurés que les quatre pieds d'une table ...' (1174) [14].

[14] Guys: 'L'Empereur des Français'

[15]   Guys: 'Trois femmes'

In keeping with the swiftness and multiplicity of Guys's sketches, Baudelaire's article draws a synthesis from many flickering effects rather than pausing in detail over individual works. It picks out as central impression the ability to convey 'le geste et l'attitude solennelle ou grotesque des êtres et leur explosion lumineuse dans l'espace' (1169), and notes the technique for giving swift highlights: 'M. G., traduisant fidèlement ses propres impressions, marque avec une énergie instinctive les points culminants ou lumineux d'un objet' (1166). That Guys's subjects go to the centre of Baudelaire's preoccupations is of course clear. For his personal expression of close reaction to detail I take this one example [15], which first evokes a general background, then moves in to a tiny notation, and finally adds its own grim reflection:

Dans un chaos brumeux et doré ... s'agitent et se convulsent des nymphes macabres et des poupées vivantes dont l'œil enfantin laisse échapper une clarté sinistre; cependant que derrière un comptoir chargé de bouteilles de liqueurs se prélasse une grosse mégère dont la tête, serrée dans un sale foulard qui dessine sur le mur l'ombre de ses pointes sataniques, fait penser que tout ce qui est voué au Mal est condamné à porter des cornes (1189).

Baudelaire's own drawing of a seductive woman with the legend 'Quærens quem devoret' makes the bow around her hair give the same satanic suggestion.[24]

From Baudelaire's reflections on caricature I shall take two examples, again showing his swift personal reaction to the smallest detail, and his virulent expression of both its physical impact and its mental prolongation. Daumier's 'Le Dernier Bain' [16], which he calls a 'caricature sérieuse et lamentable', is a subject obviously near the bone. Baudelaire first forces home the startling geometrical effect, 'sur le parapet d'un quai ... faisant un angle aigu avec la base d'où il se détache comme une statue qui perd son équilibre, un homme se laisse tomber roide ...'. Physical details lead to the ironical reflection: the decisiveness of crossed arms and the enormity of the stone prove that 'ce n'est pas un suicide de poète qui veut être repêché et faire parler de lui'. Each detail of grotesque wretchedness is brought alive in epithets which give to objects a grim personality: 'C'est la redingote chétive et grimaçante qu'il faut voir, sous laquelle tous les os font saillie! Et la cravate maladive et tortillée, et la pomme d'Adam, osseuse et pointue!'[25] Then, an ironical footnote on a background detail: 'Dans le fond, de l'autre côté de la rivière, un bourgeois contemplatif, au ventre rondelet, se livre aux délices innocentes de la pêche.' If the provocative detachment is there in the lines of the picture, the 'ventre rondelet' is Baudelaire's own satirical touch (1003).

Thomas Hood's 'Tell me, my heart, can this be love?' [17] is illustrated by the merest outline of a satirical Cupid; but the subject has provoked Baudelaire not only to translate a passage from *Whims and Oddities*, but to provide his own virulent verbal equivalent (1054–6). Rarely can there have been a more intense debauchery of deflating images, evoking a rich and sensuous disgust, and leading at vertiginous speed to the stab of the climax. We are sick, says Baudelaire, of the conventional 'Cupidon des confiseurs ... un poisson qui s'accommode à toutes les sauces':

ce vieux polisson, ailé comme un insecte, ou comme un canard, que Thomas Hood nous montre accroupi, et, comme un impotent, écrasant de sa molle obésité le nuage qui lui sert de coussin. De sa main gauche il tient en manière de sabre son arc appuyé contre sa cuisse; de la droite il exécute avec sa flèche le commandement: Portez armes! sa chevelure est frisée dru comme une perruque de cocher; ses joues rebondissantes oppriment ses narines et ses yeux; sa chair, ou plutôt sa viande, capitonnée, tubuleuse et soufflée, comme les graisses suspendues aux crochets des bouchers, est sans doute distendue par les soupirs de l'idylle universelle; à son dos montagneux sont accrochées deux ailes de papillon.

Behind this coruscation of satire, we are bound to remember the Goltzius engravings [18] from which Baudelaire drew one of his subtlest, most suggestive and most serious of poems:

> L'Amour est assis sur le crâne
> De l'Humanité,

evoking the distant and lovely flight into infinity of the aspiring, frail, iridescent and transient bubbles, and concluding with his completely personal interpretation:

> Car ce que ta bouche cruelle
> Éparpille en l'air,
> Monstre assassin, c'est ma cervelle,
> Mon sang et ma chair!

I risk the suggestion that both pictures resurrect a complex memory of the picture by Baudelaire's father recently rediscovered and reproduced [19],[26] where on the pedestal of the statue can be glimpsed the opening words of the sinister Virgilian inscription: 'Frigidus, o pueri, fugite hinc, latet anguis in herba' – the threat of the sting that lurks in the delight.

Two last examples, from Baudelaire's lifelong admiration, show

[16] Daumier; 'Le Dernier Bain'

[17] Hood: 'Tell me, my heart, can this be love?', from *Whims and Oddities*

[19] J.-F. Baudelaire: 'La Surprise'

[18] Goltzius: 'Quis evadet?'

even in the briefest passages the combined care for detail and for breadth of suggestion. Each of these two Saint-Sulpice murals of Delacroix is given only a few lines (1109–10); from each Baudelaire has selected and concentrated those details which lie closest both to his personal struggle and to his vision of man. First, Jacob and the Angel [20]. 'Au premier plan, gisent, sur le terrain, les vêtements et les armes dont Jacob s'est débarrassé pour lutter corps à corps.' Reproductions today sometimes rightly pick out this detail in itself as a still-life of unusual beauty.[27] Baudelaire comments only on its meaning (in the final struggle one is stripped of all adventitious aids) yet visually he puts it first. His one sentence on the two wrestlers finds vocabulary and images to stress the rendering of a being bending all his force against the abstract calm of the absolute: 'Jacob incliné en avant comme un bélier et bandant toute sa musculature, l'ange se prêtant complaisamment au combat, calme, doux comme un être qui peut vaincre sans effort des muscles et ne permettant pas à la colère d'altérer la forme divine de ses membres.' Man battling with the transcendent: and opposite it, man transcendentally condemned for guilt. In the Heliodorus mural [21] Baudelaire at the beginning evokes the richness and immensity of the background, and at the end takes the eye back to those watchers from the height of the immense staircase who gaze with those same double feelings he himself so often experiences and creates: 'avec horreur et ravissement'. Nearer the centre are the scourging angels, again suggesting the power and impassivity of transcendent justice as they 'fouettent avec vigueur mais aussi avec l'opiniâtre tranquillité qui convient', and the avenging rider whose dazzling beauty represents 'toute la solennité et tout le calme des cieux'. The focus is made to rest on the hoof of the horse, with a cruel and calm elegance of gesture holding the victim suspended in the endless moment of expiation.[28]

To Baudelaire, the artist rejects conventional 'poncifs', looks at the physical world and transforms it through his individual temperament. Similarly, the critic's means of expression, so constantly broadening into general insights, are rooted in the physical world. Abstract formulae, lapidary in their concision, do constantly stand out strongly: 'L'étude de la nature conduit souvent à un résultat tout différent de la nature' (883); 'Plus on possède d'imagination, mieux il faut posséder le métier pour accompagner celle-ci ... Et mieux on possède son métier, moins il faut s'en prévaloir et le

[20] Delacroix: 'Lutte de Jacob avec l'ange', detail

[21] Delacroix: 'Héliodore chassé du temple', detail

montrer' (1029). But, through the deliberately varied tones of leisurely conversation, sustained evocation of delight, or meditative reflections of a *moraliste*, constantly flash rich, violent or subtle images, not as mere verbal paraphrase, but as a means to provoking personal reaction. Attack is uninhibited: on the huge eyes by Lehmann 'où la prunelle nage comme une huître dans une soupière', on 'les puces de M. Meissonier', on Horace Vernet's 'masturbation agile et fréquente, une irritation de l'épiderme français', on a multitude of purveyors of prettified religiosity: 'ce capharnaüm de faux ex-voto ... cette immense voie lactée de plâtreuses sottises', on the kind of artist who gives 'draperies tubulées et tortillées comme du macaroni', or would be capable of transforming the great tombs of Saint-Denis into cigar-boxes and patterns for shawls.

In this world of sensation and suggestion there are constantly recurring images taken from the art of cooking – for Baudelaire explicitly held that this was a subtle and disciplined art to be set by the side of poetry, music or mathematics – and to the art of tasting. Condiments, seasonings, sauces, pastry decorations: these and many others are used as suggestive images with their both serious and satirical place as a part of the 'correspondances' in a world of harmonious joy for both senses and intellect.

In this expression of praise, two sides of Baudelaire's own nature, as a 'paresseux nerveux', emerge specially strongly. On the one hand, there is the recurring image of explosion, whether for joy, energy, laughter, colour or light. Or flooding energy and a sense of prolonged vibration find strong and varied verbs to convey the resonance of four associated sensations: 'partout où peut resplendir la lumière, retentir la poésie, fourmiller la vie, vibrer la musique' (1162). On the other hand, he evokes the shifting and intangible softness of drifting clouds and vapours: the 'mollesse floconneuse' of skies in Théodore Rousseau, or the Delacroix sky in the Luxembourg ceiling, 'les nuages, délayés et tirés en sens divers comme une gaze qui se déchire'; or suggests the melancholy hypersensitive indolence we have seen in Delacroix's 'Ovide', or the languor of a Commodus, 'jeune, rose, mou et voluptueux, et ... qui a l'air de s'ennuyer'.[29] And in Delacroix's 'Femmes d'Alger', of which he possessed a contemporary copy, beneath a surface appeal 'le plus coquet et le plus fleuri', he reads for himself 'les limbes insondés de la tristesse'.

Fully to examine such means of expression would of course demand a detailed study. I have raised only a very few suggestions.

I have intentionally left aside today all that other scholars have so penetratingly discussed on the suggestive contribution of the plastic arts to *Les Fleurs du mal*. Baudelaire once desperately imagined the artist 'assailli par une émeute de détails, qui tous demandent justice avec la furie d'une foule amoureuse d'égalité absolue' (1167). Against this he set the harmony of selective creation, with its power to call miraculously to life the hidden responses of the human being: before certain pictures he hears a cry of 'Lazare, lève-toi' (1168) or feels 'un petit vent frais qui fait se hérisser le souvenir'. His writings on the visual arts select in a deliberately personal way those details which have what he called a 'resurrectionist' effect on deeply rooted responses. Many readers will find them suggestive principally as a means of insight into his own creative skill; but there remains too his way of making us re-examine the pictures he discusses. He himself paraphrased a line of verse: 'Et le tableau quitté nous tourmente et nous suit' (971). Whether or not we share Baudelaire's personal judgements or aesthetic principles, I have hoped simply to suggest that his way of freshly looking at both general impression and detail, and his gift for sharp and suggestive expression, constantly provoke and enrich our own means of both seeing and enjoying.

As a tailpiece, one example of how Baudelaire expresses himself in water-colour and not in words [22]. Certainly no mere copy of nature; an interpretation at once grotesque and solemn. Correspondences of shape are the first impression: the verticals of the self, of the Colonne Vendôme and of the factory chimneys in the distance; the brim of the hat echoing the top of the column and the huge boots its base. Real proportions are boldly reversed, not so much for perspective, as to make man uncompromisingly the towering centre. The fascination of geometrical shapes is evident again in the stylized rays of the setting sun, bisected as it is in Baudelaire's description of a plate by Rethel where it figures as an emblem of the close of life.[30] In contrast to the stiffness of column and jaggedness of rays is set the opposite sensorial effect, that of the twining clouds of smoke; here it is man who puffs defiantly against the sullen sky those 'coalitions de fumée' echoed by a faint plume from the tiny chimney in the background. Both the stiffness and the spiralling effect of the city clothing are echoed in the column. The face might recall Baudelaire's description of a 'Hamlet' by Delacroix – 'délicat et pâlot ... avec un œil presque atone' (971); what comes most sinisterly alive (and we remember Baudelaire's comment on the tie

[22]   'Baudelaire par lui-même'

twisted round the ankles in Daumier's 'Le Dernier Bain') is those springing shoe-laces. A darting winged object, mysteriously threatening (recalling Meryon or the evil Cupid?), streaks towards him through the sky. Here momentarily Baudelaire has himself schematically suggested something of what he looks for in 'le peintre de la vie moderne'.

NOTES

1 This paper was delivered at a symposium in Manchester (organised by U. Finke), 26–9 November, 1969. Page-references in the text will be to Baudelaire's *Œuvres complètes*, ed. Y.-G. Le Dantec, édition révisée, complétée et présentée par Claude Pichois, Gallimard, Bibliothèque de la Pléiade, 1961. In a brief article of this kind, full reference to excellent previous studies is impossible. See the index of R. T. Cargo, *Baudelaire Criticism 1950–1967*, University of Alabama Press, 1968, and the 'États présents' by Cl. Pichois (*L'Information littéraire*, 1958) and L. J. Austin (*Forum for Modern Language Studies*, III, 4, Oct. 1967). Among articles which have appeared since may be noted: L. J. Austin, 'Baudelaire et Delacroix'; W. Drost, 'De la critique d'art baudelairienne' (both in *Baudelaire: Actes du Colloque de Nice*, Paris, Minard, 1968); G. Poulet, 'Baudelaire précurseur de la critique moderne' in *Journées Baudelaire – Actes du Colloque de Namur*, Brussels, Académie royale de langue et de littérature françaises, 1968; Yoshio Abe, 'Baudelaire face aux artistes de son temps' in *Revue de l'Art*, 1969, 4; J. C. Sloane, 'Baudelaire as Art Critic' in *Bulletin baudelairien*, Nashville, Tennessee, V, 1; D. J. Kelley, 'Deux aspects du *Salon de 1846* de Baudelaire: la dédicace aux bourgeois et la couleur' in *Forum for Modern Language Studies*, V, Oct. 1969.
2 Baudelaire, *Lettres inédites aux siens*, présentées et annotées par Philippe Auserve, Paris, Grasset, 1966, p. 153. Letter of July 1838.
3 See M. C. Spencer, *The Art Criticism of Théophile Gautier*, Geneva, Droz, 1969.
4 *Lettres inédites aux siens*, p. 170 (Feb. 1839).
5 See especially the following: *Les Fleurs du mal, Les Épaves, Sylves*, avec certaines images qui ont pu inspirer le poète, édition établie par Jean Pommier et Claude Pichois (Paris, Club des Libraires de France, 1959, reprinted 1967); Jonathan Mayne, *The Mirror of Art* (London, Phaidon, Anchor, 1955); Jonathan Mayne, *Baudelaire: The Painter of Modern Life and Other Essays* (London, Phaidon, 1964); Jonathan Mayne, *Baudelaire: Art in Paris, 1845–62* (London, Phaidon, 1965); B. Gheerbrandt, *Baudelaire critique d'art* (Paris: Club des Libraires de France, 1956); J. Adhémar's edition of the *Curiosités esthétiques* (Lausanne, Éditions de l'Œil, 1956); G. Poulet and R. Kopp, *Qui était Baudelaire?* (Geneva, Skira, 1969); the Catalogue of the Baudelaire Exhibition at the Petit Palais, 23 Nov. 1968 to 17 March 1969 (Paris, Réunion des Musées Nationaux, 1968); P.-G. Castex, *Baudelaire critique d'Art* (Sedes, 1969).
6 Several passages object to the contamination of one art form by another.

Cf. 'Je désire qu'un artiste soit lettré, mais je souffre quand je le vois cherchant à capter l'imagination par des ressources situées aux extrêmes limites, sinon même au-delà de son art' (1064); see pp. 1008, 1031, etc. Baudelaire's views on allegory, which in the *Salon de 1845* he calls 'un des plus beaux genres dans l'art', on several occasions stress the difference between its generally suggestive function and the dangers of a fixed system of equivalents (over-ingenious, over-rigid, anachronistic) (cf. 1014). Moreover, 'même à l'esprit d'un artiste philosophique, les accessoires s'offrent, non pas avec un caractère littéral et précis, mais avec un caractère poétique, vague et confus, et souvent c'est le traducteur qui invente *les intentions*' (1101–2).

7 'La bonne manière de savoir si un tableau est mélodieux est de le regarder d'assez loin pour n'en comprendre ni le sujet ni les lignes' (883). 'Un tableau de Delacroix, placé à une trop grande distance pour que vous puissiez juger de l'agrément des contours ou de la qualité plus ou moins dramatique du sujet, vous pénètre déjà d'une volupté surnaturelle ... Et l'analyse du sujet, quand vous vous approchez, n'enlèvera rien et n'ajoutera rien à ce plaisir primitif' (1124).

8 Cf. his defence of Balzac's supposed way of looking at pictures (957). W. Drost in the article quoted in note 1, discusses further aspects of Baudelaire's reaction to subject. Baudelaire is of course willing to claim the right to contradiction and to admiring an individual artist contrary to his own general principles. His treatment of Chenavard in painting might be compared with his attitude to Marceline Desbordes-Valmore in poetry.

9 E.g., p. 957.

10 See, quoted in H. Lemaitre's edition of the *Curiosités esthétiques* (Paris, Garnier, 1962), p. 400, Delacroix's letter of 8 Oct. 1861: 'Vous m'avez écrit, il y a deux mois, relativement au procédé que j'emploie pour peindre sur mur.'

11 Here Baudelaire's response should be compared with his very strong reaction to the Baron picture discussed in 1859 (1062).

12 He does not comment specifically on the combination of reds and greens; this must certainly have affected him strongly (see below). Reproductions fail to bring out the sharpness of the green in particular.

13 In certain English painters, 'représentants enthousiastes de l'imagination', he notes the 'profondeurs fuyantes des aquarelles, grandes comme des décors, quoique si petites' (1026). Delacroix above all conveys to him 'l'infini dans le fini' (1053).

14 Cf. also on one of his Athens pictures: 'Tous ces petits personnages ... rendent plus profond l'espace qui les contient' (1173).

15 Cf. on Lavieille: 'une lisière de bois, avec une route qui s'y enfonce ... il y a une volupté élégiaque irrésistible que connaissent tous les amateurs de promenades solitaires' (1080). See also the passage on Delacroix's Luxembourg ceiling: 'Ce paysage circulaire, qui embrasse un espace énorme ... un horizon à souhait *pour le plaisir des yeux*' (896).

16 Cf. also remarks on Corot and Fromentin in particular.

17 For wider aspects of this passage see the article by D. J. Kelley listed in note 1 above.

18 For general remarks on 'le sens moral de la couleur, du contour, du son et du parfum' see especially the discussion on imagination and analogy (1037). Occasional remarks touch on the allusive attributes of particular colours, e.g. 'le rose révélant une idée d'extase dans la frivolité . . . violet couleur affectionnée des chanoinesses)' (1187). The sense of context is always important.

19 Having opened with its cruelty, Baudelaire ends: 'il y a dans cette œuvre quelque chose de tendre et de poignant à la fois'. I discuss below the fusion of the grotesque and tender he finds in Legros. Cf. his remark that the caricatures of Traviès contain 'quelque chose de sérieux et de tendre' (1013).

20 That some of these are commented on more closely than are many paintings is a natural result of their easy accessibility. Baudelaire possessed many himself.

21 Cf., p. 307, 'Les Bons Chiens' and note in R. Kopp's edition of the *Petits poèmes en prose* (Corti, 1969), p. 364.

22 Cf. note in J. Mayne, *Art in Paris*, p. 165, on this point.

23 Gautier's introduction to *Les Fleurs du mal* (Calmann-Lévy, s.d.) has some interesting pages on Baudelaire and Guys (noted by Gustave Geffroy, *Constantin Guys*, Crès, 1920). Gautier remarks that he gave Baudelaire several of Guys' works and analyses some of Baudelaire's reasons for enthusiasm, and reservations. Some passages run closely parallel with parts of Baudelaire's article. For interesting *rapprochements* between the literary and the visual see *Au temps de Baudelaire, Guys et Nadar*, avant-propos de François Boucher, présentation d'Anne d'Eugny en collaboration avec René Coursaget (Éditions du Chêne, 1945).

24 See *Baudelaire, Documents iconographiques*, ed. Cl. Pichois and Fr. Ruchon (Geneva, Cailler, 1960), pl. 122; also reproduced in many other works.

25 Cf. in *Salon de 1846*, on the general problem of representing modern dress, 'les plis grimaçants, jouant comme des serpents autour d'une chair mortifiée, n'ont-ils pas leur grâce mystérieuse?' (951).

26 Reproduced for the first time in *Documents iconographiques* (see above, note 24), pl. 60.

27 See Lee Johnson, *Delacroix*, London, Weidenfeld and Nicolson, 1963, Pl. 67.

28 A different vision of triumphant rider and trampling hoof struck Baudelaire in the Mortimer engraving which inspired the poem 'Une Gravure fantastique'. See F. W. Leakey, 'Baudelaire and Mortimer', in *French Studies*, VII, 2, 1953.

29 Cf. his evocation of Delacroix's *Hamlet* 'tout délicat et pâlot, aux mains blanches et féminines, une nature exquise, mais molle, légèrement indécise, avec un œil presque atone' (971) or of Guérin's Cleopatra, who 'une créole aux nerfs détendus, a plus de parenté avec les premières visions de Chateaubriand qu'avec les conceptions de Virgile . . . son œil humide, noyé dans les vapeurs du Keepsake . . .' etc.

30 See p. 1101. The Rethel plate is given in Mayne, *Painter of Modern Life*, pl. 50.

13

Reflections on the successive versions of 'Une Gravure fantastique' (1973)[1]

[I]
Le spectre a pour toute toilette
Sur son front luisant de squelette
Un noir diadême [sic] de vers
4 Gentiment posé de travers.
        Lariflaflafla
        Larifla fla fla
7   Lariflafla fla.

Sa monture apocalyptique
Est un cheval epileptique [sic]
Qui va reniflant les corps morts
11 Et galope toujours sans mors
        Larifla fla fla.
        Larifla fla fla
14   Larifla fla fla.

Le cavalier porte à sa selle
Une ténébreuse escarcelle.
C'est là qu'il met tous les petits
18 Livrés à ses fiers appétits.
        Larifla fla fla
        Larifla fla fla
21   Larifla fla fla

[II]
Ce fantôme de squelette
    N'a pour toute toilette
Qu'un diadême [sic] de vers
4   Posé tout de travers
        Larifla fla fla
        Larifla fla fla
7   Larifla fla fla

Sa monture fantastique,
Jument épileptique,
Va reniflant les morts,
11 Et galope sans mors.

<pre>
                Larifla flafla.
                Larifla fla fla.
14   Larifla fla fla.
        ─────────────────────
        Le spectre porte à sa selle
            Une vieille escarcelle
        Où il met les petits
18   pour ses grands appétits
                Larifla fla fla.
                Larifla fla fla
21   Larifla fla fla.
</pre>

UNE GRAVURE FANTASTIQUE

Ce spectre singulier n'a pour toute toilette,
Grotesquement campé sur son front de squelette,
Qu'un diadème affreux sentant le carnaval.
Sans éperons, sans fouet, il essouffle un cheval,
5   Fantôme comme lui, rosse apocalyptique,
Qui bave des naseaux comme un épileptique.
Au travers de l'espace ils s'enfoncent tous deux,
Et foulent l'infini d'un sabot hasardeux.
Le cavalier promène un sabre qui flamboie
10 Sur les foules sans nom que sa monture broie,
Et parcourt, comme un prince inspectant sa maison,
Le cimetière immense et froid, sans horizon,
Où gisent, aux lueurs d'un soleil blanc et terne,
Les peuples de l'histoire ancienne et moderne.

For those fascinated by following the detailed transformations through which Baudelaire shapes initial stimulus into final poem, *Une Gravure fantastique* must now occupy a privileged place. In 1953, Felix Leakey reproduced the Haynes engraving of the work of Mortimer which the poem's title, on first publication, had referred to (*Une Gravure de Mortimer*) and, in an article outstanding both for delicate analysis and for firm insight into relations between the poem and the picture, set Baudelaire's lines in the background of the problems and practice of the *transposition d'art*.[2] Then, in 1959, two earlier manuscripts discovered by Claude Pichois were published by himself and Jean Pommier;[3] these have since been included, among the 'Reliquat des *Fleurs du Mal*', at the end of the indispensable Crépet–Blin–Pichois edition.[4]

We therefore have now four versions of this poem: two in manuscript; two published (*Une Gravure de Mortimer* in *Le Présent*, 15 November 1857; *Une Gravure fantastique* in the second edition of the *Fleurs du Mal*, 1861). Within each pair, the variants are few, if significant; between manuscripts and publication there have been large changes. What is exceptional here is that we have a poem where Baudelaire has tried three completely different metres;[5] tone and final meaning are intimately associated with the choice and the exigencies of the rhythm. In this brief article, I shall simply examine some of these 'retouches et variantes', that 'série d'efforts' which Baudelaire himself half-purposed to analyse in his 'Projets de Préface', while grimly reflecting that 'une dizaine d'exemplaires' would suffice for the few who are concerned with 'l'intelligence d'un objet d'art'.[6]

On the relation between the two manuscript versions, Claude Pichois notes:

La version I est écrite au 1er f° v°, la version II au 2e f° r° d'une double feuille ... Écriture de jeunesse; entre 1843 et 1847?[7]

If the order in which the two appear in this manuscript represents the order of composition, it would show Baudelaire moving from stanzas in the traditional form of four octosyllabic lines, to attempt a much more odd and challenging form, involving in each stanza an opening seven-syllable line, followed by three lines of six syllables. One cannot of course be sure which was composed first. The scored-out 'Qu''' at the beginning of line 3 in I might point back to the 'Ne ... que' construction in II as possibly preceding it, and one might suppose that Baudelaire started from the minimal evocation in II, then tried a metre allowing for more expansion in I; the latter would then be a half-way house to the fuller elaboration of the published versions. What matters, in these two versions where there is no change whatever in the material to be conveyed, is the difference in Baudelaire's ways of meeting the exigencies of his experiment with two different forms. In discussing these, I shall speak of 'first' and 'second' versions as referring to their order in the manuscript, leaving open the order of composition.

If in the first version Baudelaire chooses the regular and re-cognised form of octosyllabics, yet it is fitting that the manuscript should have been found among the Hugo papers, for he has clearly set out on an exercise that might be called 'disloquer ce vieux niais d'octosyllabe'. To convey the sinister and frenetic gallop of spectral horse and rider, he varies and shifts stresses and pauses so that they fall disconcertingly and unpredictably, setting the occasional evenly divided line against both the deliberately incongruous dancing movement of the opening, and the hurtling bursts of irregular energy carried by the jerky vigour of the whole.

Of the second version, a note in the Crépet–Blin edition (p. 418), written at a time when all that was available was a sale catalogue's quotation of the first stanza, remarks:

Il serait d'autant plus intéressant de retrouver ce ms. qu'aucun poème ne nous est parvenu où Baudelaire ait fait alterner les vers de six et de sept pieds.[8]

In fact, what has come to light is a still stranger experiment. Crépet's understandable assumption that the metre was 7, 6, 7, 6 depended on reading line three with the 4-syllable division 'di / a / dè / me' (as it might be normal to expect), whereas from the complete manuscript it is clear that the pattern followed in the three stanzas is 7, 6, 6, 6, and that one must scan 'dia / dè / me'. In the other manuscript and in the published versions there is the normal four-syllable reading: possibly Baudelaire resolved his hesitations by consulting the rhyming dictionary which he asked Poulet-Malassis to let him have for proof-correcting in 1857.[9]

The octosyllable is in itself a relatively compressed line, but the metre of version II cuts things to the bare bone, and provides a *gageure* in the art of suggestion through minimal means. A whole range of adjectives, adverbs, nouns and connecting verbs from I is absent ('un *noir* diadème de vers', '*gentiment* posé', '*est un* cheval', 'les *corps* morts'), 'galope *toujours, c'est là qu*'il met *tous* les petits'). From the first line, version II gives a doubly deathly effect in 'Ce fantôme de squelette', and it stresses the note of the grotesque by reducing the lofty 'monture' to 'jument'. Its rhythm is specially suited to conveying a sinister obsession: the rare heptasyllable which opens each stanza, stretching oddly beyond the familiar half-alexandrine yet not attaining the equally familiar octosyllable, serves towards a sense of haunting and unfulfilled effort, then falls with a jerk into the three shorter lines, sharply punctuated by swiftly recurring rhymes, as they hammer out a rapid gallop. Its very bareness and lack of descriptive elaboration achieves a concentrated and compelling effect, fitting the theme of skeletal speed.

The words or phrases quoted above as being absent from II may at first seem otiose or only marginally suggestive, yet each does have a discreet function in version I ('les *corps* morts' stressing the physical, 'gentiment' increasing the irony, 'toujours' and 'tous' stretching out over time). The metre, too, allows for moments of more developed suggestion, whether in the resounding adjective 'apocalyptique' (again extending over the ages, and relating the poem more closely to Mortimer's theme),[10] or in the concluding lines: 'tous les petits / *Livrés* à ses *fiers* appétits'.[11]

When Jean Pommier and Claude Pichois first published these

manuscript versions, they noted that to attribute them, on grounds of handwriting, to the year 1844 'correspond à la période où Baudelaire dut avoir pour Hugo la plus grande admiration ... comme à celle où il cultiva un peu le genre de la chanson'.[12] The very unusual metre of II, and the way of noting the refrain in both, have led me to wonder whether, for either or both versions, Baudelaire may have had a musical setting in mind. The relation of engraving and 'chanson' is bound to recall the charming *format* of the *fascicules* in which, from 1851 onwards, the *Chants et Chansons* of Pierre Dupont were published; each normal *livraison* contained a delicate engraving, a poem, and the music to which it should be sung, and the twentieth *livraison* held Baudelaire's first article on Pierre Dupont. Might these early manuscripts be part of a plan for similarly producing engraving, poem and music together? A minor piece of corroborative evidence subsists in a remark from the preface to the fourth volume of Dupont's collected *Chants et Chansons* (1854):

On y trouvera aussi des chants dont Pierre Dupont n'a composé que la musique et dont la poésie est d'autres auteurs avec lesquels il s'est trouvé en relations de sentiments: Victor Hugo,[13] Gustave Mathieu, Charles Baudelaire, etc.[14]

Nothing came of this, but may it hark back to projects of collaboration of which the first versions of *Une Gravure fantastique* may be an echo?[15]

The engravings that accompany Dupont's songs are of course illustrations to them, whereas the Mortimer-Haynes engraving provided the starting-point to Baudelaire's three poems. In discussing the relations between the picture and the definitive version of the poem, Felix Leakey's fine article traces three different sides: what Baudelaire chose directly from Mortimer; what preoccupations of his own, differing perhaps from the intentions of the artist, he read into it; what details or wider reflections he added. The manuscripts show the same threefold stimulus. From the start, he is gripped by the grotesque contrast between the skeletal face of the rider and the triumphant diadem, but already he introduces his own interpretation. Leakey pointed out that the slight angle at which the crown is set in the engraving is probably simply for an effect of swift movement; in all versions Baudelaire creates a rider at once sinister and rakish, his crookedly placed crown evoked with mocking irony, 'Gentiment posé de travers'.[16] And in the manuscripts that crown is much further from the original picture than it is in the published poems: it is 'Un noir diadème *de vers*'. Deliberate macabre invention, or possible conflation with, for example, the background figure in Dürer's *Ritter, Todt und Teufel*?

The powerfully snorting nostrils of the horse at the centre of the picture again call up an imaginative elaboration from Baudelaire and produce the strongest sense-impression in the manuscripts: 'Qui va reniflant les corps morts', 'Va reniflant les morts'. And the third stanza makes of Death the tyrannical devourer, through an image, which as Pommier and Pichois have noted, is not there in the engraving: the great pouch in which he collects 'tous les petits/ Livrés à ses fiers appétits'. Perhaps the detail was suggested by some other visual source in Baudelaire's collection of engravings on death. Perhaps, however, it did have its origin in the Mortimer-Haynes, where the huge swirl of the cloak streaming out from the skeleton's left shoulder falls in a great pouch-like circle beneath the right arm. But in any case it is abundantly clear that Baudelaire throughout is using the picture not as something to be accurately transposed into words, but simply as the stimulus to his own creation. One remembers how the project of his writing texts to accompany Meryon's engravings was abandoned (instead of allowing 'une occasion d'écrire des rêveries de dix lignes, de vingt ou trente lignes, sur de belles gravures, les rêveries philosophiques d'un flâneur parisien' Meryon insisted that 'Il faut dire: à droite, on voit ceci; à gauche, on voit cela. Il faut chercher des notes dans les vieux bouquins'),[17] or the passage in the *Salon de 1859* where Baudelaire explains that in writing the poem *Danse macabre* around a work by Christophe 'j'ai essayé, non pas d'*illustrer*, mais d'expliquer le plaisir subtil contenu dans cette figurine'.

By the time *Une Gravure de Mortimer* was published in *Le Présent* of 15 November 1857, Baudelaire had given to his 'rêveries' around the engraving a very different form and tone. Since it did not appear in the first edition of the *Fleurs du Mal*, it is perhaps reasonable to suppose that he took up and fundamentally revised his early versions after he had handed over the complete manuscript of the volume in February. When he is preparing the second edition in 1860, he several times mentions it (calling it 'D'après Mortimer'), along with other poems which he will have to fetch from among the batch of papers left with his mother at Honfleur, unless an old copy of *Le Présent* can be found;[18] the last revisions which give it its final form as *Une Gravure fantastique* must have taken place at some date after August 30 1860. In the volume, he placed it (between two other poems on death: *Sépulture* and *Le Mort joyeux*) at the hinge where the theme of love shifts gradually into that of Spleen.

The early versions had been part of a late romantic mode – experiments in sardonic tone where the form calls attention to its own virtuosity and the macabre and sinister subject is deliberately set in the light and mocking metre. The revised versions look for a quite different dignity of effect (that sense of *solennité* potential in every experience, however grotesque or trivial, which becomes increasingly central to Baudelaire's vision of his own art and that of others), and move back to the most traditional of rhythms: the alexandrine in rhyming couplets. In the manuscripts every rhyme had been rich; in the new versions, though Baudelaire keeps most of these rhymes, he adds others less clearly contrived (lines 9 & 10, 13 & 14), and in any case the longer lines allow a more natural effect, not flourishing the same swiftly recurring implacable virtuosity in rhyme. Then, instead of fiercely dislocating the rhythm to make it echo the wild gallop, he chooses to make his alexandrines move particularly slowly and regularly: only in lines 12 and 13 is there an expressive shift in pauses, leading up to the dignity of the last line.

In comparing the final version with the engraving, Felix Leakey picked out two fundamental differences: that in the first half of the poem we may be surprised to see Baudelaire 'suppressing or attenuating the horrific aspects of his engraving' (here Leakey contrasts the result with Baudelaire's own *Danse macabre*); and that in the second half, whereas Mortimer gives to the trampled bodies in the foreground 'an individuality of suffering and subjection', 'narrows down to the single moment and instance of destruction', Baudelaire 'moves away from strict description or even evocation, and towards a wider interpretation and *generalization* of the poem's subject'. Comparison with the manuscripts shows how both tendencies were there from the outset, to be much further developed in the revision.

In the first half, those grisly or fantastic elements in the picture which Leakey notes as absent from the final poem (hollow eye-sockets and claw-like hand of the skeleton, staring eyeballs of the horse, flying reptiles in the black heavens ...) are absent too in the manuscripts. And in the revision, the two most macabre touches of all have been removed: the diadem of worms has disappeared, as has the horse's sniffing of the odour of corpses. Otherwise, in this first half, Baudelaire keeps very close to the details of his early versions, but gives an enhanced precision and intensity. Sinister and sardonic are suggestively fused rather than provocatively contrasted.

And if the specifically macabre is reduced, yet the strong sense impressions are enriched.

Manuscript II cut the material of I to its basic elements; the process of expansion into alexandrines might risk obvious 'padding', but in fact each new expression or modification makes its suggestive contribution. Instead of a shock opening, there is the ironically reflective 'Ce spectre *singulier*' – a word which runs quietly and hauntingly through so many contexts in Baudelaire (for whom 'le beau est toujours bizarre'), and echoes to the end of the *Fleurs du Mal* in 'Et de toi fais-tu dire: Oh! l'homme singulier!' Instead of the macabre diadem of worms, there is the grim mockery of the crown clapped on askew (with the strong physical effect of 'Grotesquement *campé* sur son front de squelette') and looking like some cardboard imitation, inappositely and grimly gay ('sentant le carnaval').[19] In manuscript II, the juxtaposition of the lofty and the humble terms: 'monture' and 'jument' had provided another sardonic touch; the final poem intensifies the incongruity between 'monture' and 'rosse', with the added contrast of 'rosse apocalyptique'. The bridle-less galloping becomes an active and tyrannical pressing of the horse to the last extremes without spurs or whip (made, even through their absence, to evoke goading and lashing); the horse, instead of breathing in the odour of corpses, becomes another victim of the spectral tyrant, with foam slavering from its nostrils.

The second half of the poem is almost entirely new. Yet from the early versions onwards, the basic structure had been the same: developed description, followed by a stanza which moved away from the visual source into an image making of Death the insatiable devourer. But now the proportions are reversed: the greater part of the poem is given to the second section, with its expansion first into infinite space and finally into unending time,[20] and the alexandrine form allows majestic development.

The 'escarcelle' has disappeared. Perhaps simply for logical reasons: in the manuscripts the pouch had hung from the saddle ('selle' and 'escarcelle' incidentally providing another 'rime riche'); if the skeletal rider has neither bridle, spurs nor whip, the saddle would be sadly out of keeping, and is of course not there in the Mortimer. But one further detail from the engraving has been restored: the flaming sword flourished over the anonymous multitudes. And in lines seven to ten the contrasting and elemental sensations of aspiration towards infinite distance, and terror before the threat of piercing, crushing or burning, interplay in phrases pointed by verbs of violence: 'au travers de l'espace ils *s'enfoncent* . . .';[21] 'Et *foulent* l'infini'; '*flamboie*', '*broie*'.

But after that violence come the special tone and movement of the last four lines, the authentically Baudelairean achievement in this poem. A blank and chilling stillness seems to fall, and the seeping sense of Spleen spreads over all the ages. The spectral rider who 'parcourt, comme un prince inspectant sa maison,/Le cimetière immense' already suggests 'le roi d'un pays pluvieux', and his quietly sinister and strangely-lit background holds the grating nervous tension of

> ces jours blancs, tièdes et voilés,
> . . .
> Quand, agités d'un mal inconnu qui les tord,
> Les nerfs trop éveillés raillent l'esprit qui dort.

In giving to the spreading dominion of death both the agelong dignity and the muted and strange sense-impressions that make it a fitting preface to the poems of personal spleen, Baudelaire re-worked each word of his penultimate lines between the 1857 publication in *Le Présent* and the inclusion at the chosen place in the volume of 1861. In 1857, lines 12 and 13 had read:

> Un *triste* cimetière *à l'immense* horizon,
> Où *grouillent*, aux *clartés* d'un soleil *froid* et terne . . .

The pleonastic 'triste' is removed. Space is infinitely extended by first transposing 'immense' from the horizon to the graveyard, then setting the whole against the limitless '*sans* horizon'. The too-positive 'clartés' of the sunlight sink to 'lueurs', and the moving of cold from sun to graveyard makes way for the two flat and haunting monosyllabic adjectives of 'un soleil blanc et terne'. Finally, where Baudelaire, in keeping with the anguished figures of the engraving, trampled by the rider or fleeing in hordes in the background, had first written: 'Où *grouillent* . . . Les peuples de l'histoire', he now substitutes the word where both sense and echoing sound call up the helpless immobility of agelong victims; and the finally shaped lines stretch implacably over endless time and space:

> Le cimetière immense et froid, sans horizon,
> Où gisent, aux lueurs d'un soleil blanc et terne,
> Les peuples de l'histoire ancienne et moderne.

This is not a poem which strikes immediately home by explicitly moving from the visual symbol either to the acute personal experience ('c'est ma cervelle,/Mon sang et ma chair!') or to the bitter general reflection ('Montrer que dans la fosse même/Le sommeil promis n'est pas sûr').[22] In this general sense, it is closer to pictorial art than are most of Baudelaire's poems. Sequential analysis of variants, moreover, will always lay itself open to Baudelaire's own virulent comment as he reflected on his projected preface: 'ne paraît-il pas évident que ce serait là une besogne tout à fait superflue, pour les uns comme pour les autres, puisque les uns savent ou devinent, et que les autres ne comprendront jamais?'[23] Yet perhaps even an incomplete discussion of his deliberate experiment in contrasting forms, and of the unremitting care that culminated in the quiet subtlety of these last lines, may in small measure contribute to his wish for 'un ... travail de critique [qui] aurait sans doute quelques chances d'amuser les esprits amoureux de la rhétorique profonde'.[24]

NOTES

1 The following abbreviations will be used:
   CB: *Les Fleurs du Mal.* Édition critique établie par Jacques Crépet et Georges Blin. Corti, 1942.
   CBP: *Les Fleurs du Mal.* Édition critique Jacques Crépet et Georges Blin, refondue par Georges Blin et Claude Pichois. t. I. Corti, 1968.
   FMPP: *Les Fleurs du Mal, Texte de 1861, Les Épaves, Sylves,* avec certaines images qui ont pu inspirer le poète. Édition établie par Jean Pommier et Claude Pichois. Club des Libraires de France, 1959 [reprinted 1963].
   FS: *French Studies.*
2 *FS,* VII, April 1953, p. 101–15. For further stimulating reflections on Baudelaire's transposition of Mortimer, see in particular L. J. Austin: *L'Univers poétique de Baudelaire,* Mercure de France, 1956, p. 312; Jean Prévost, *Baudelaire,* Mercure de France, 1953, p. 169; and, for penetrating treatment of associated problems, Chapter III of Jean Pommier's *La Mystique de Baudelaire,* Les Belles Lettres, 1932.
3 The texts are given in *FMPP,* p. 166–7, and commented on, p. 15 and 367.
4 *CBP,* p. 374–5. It is this version I reproduce here; see below, note 7.
5 The two published versions are in alexandrines. I have reproduced above the final poem. For the variants of 1857, see *CBP,* p. 138.
6 See *CBP,* p. 369–70, for Baudelaire's insistence on 'le mécanisme des trucs, ... les repentirs, les épreuves barbouillées, bref toutes les horreurs qui composent le sanctuaire de l'art'.
7 *CBP,* p. 374. On first publication in *FMPP,* p. 166–7, the two versions were placed in the opposite order, and the refrain was 'normalised'.

8 Cf. also Crépet's discussion of other deductions about this stanza, in *Œuvres posthumes*, ed. J. Crépet, Conard, t. 1, p. 394.

9 For further evidence of Baudelaire's attention to tricky problems of syllabification, see my article ' "Mène-t-on la foule dans les ateliers?" ' (below, pp. 228–49).

10 Beneath the Haynes engraving was quoted (see Leakey, art. cit., p. 102) the reference to Revelations, VI, 8; Death rides a pale horse and is one of the four horsemen each given power over a fourth part of the earth.

11 L. J. Austin, to whom I am grateful for reading this article in manuscript, called my attention to the phrase from 'Bohémiens en voyage': '*livrant* à leurs *fiers appétits*'.

12 *FMPP*, p. 367.

13 Does the presence of Baudelaire's manuscript among Hugo's papers perhaps fit with the suggestion that both might have agreed to do something with Dupont?

14 *L'Art romantique*, ed. Crépet, p. 503.

15 This question arose from my reading of the first versions of the Baudelaire poem on their publication (*FMPP*) in 1959. An article by Daniel Grojnowski (*Europe*, avril–mai, 1967, p. 228–33; 'Baudelaire et Pierre Dupont: la source d'inspiration de *L'Invitation au voyage*') has since noted the remark from the *Chants et Chansons* Preface to Vol. IV, as quoted by Crépet, and concluded that 'on voit que Baudelaire avait dû s'essayer à écrire des chansons' at a period marked by the popularity of Béranger. M. Grojnowski was unaware of the early versions of *Une Grave fantastique*, and does not mention the engravings that accompany Dupont's songs. For Baudelaire's relations with Dupont, see, besides much material in the notes to *L'Art romantique*, ed. Crépet, and *Œuvres posthumes*. W. T. Bandy and Claude Pichois: *Baudelaire devant ses contemporains*, Monaco, Éditions du Rocher, 1957, and D. Higgins: 'Pierre Dupont, a chansonnier of the 1848 Revolution', *FS*, April 1949, p. 122–36.

16 An early and simple adumbration of the tones that will subtly combine in *Le Joueur généreux* of the *Petits Poèmes en prose*. Baudelaire is often fascinated by geometrical angles as a means of evoking the grimly pitiful in human experience: cf. *Les Sept Vieillards, Les Petites Vieilles*, etc.

17 *Correspondance générale* (Conard), t. III, p. 29. (see below, p. 246 n. 1., for details of this edition).

18 *Correspondance générale* (Conard), t. III, p. 86, 135, 174–5.

19 Here of course he is nearer to Mortimer than in the early versions. And in the engraving, whether intentionally or not, the crown stands out with a startlingly artificial air against the stark violence of the rest.

20 Cf. Leakey's excellent analyses of Baudelaire's process of widening perspectives, both in this poem and many others. Cf. also my article mentioned above in n. 9, and 'Aspects of expression in Baudelaire's art criticism' (above pp. 176–215) (I there also suggest a possible link in Baudelaire's visual memory between the trampling hoof suspended above the overthrown bodies in the Mortimer, and Baudelaire's picking out of the hoof that holds down the body of Heliodorus in Delacroix's *Héliodore chassé du temple*).

21 The change from 'ils galopent' to 'ils *s'enfoncent*' once again intensifies

the sense of distant space and introduces a word that is frequent and significant in Baudelaire's art criticism.

22 Cf. illuminating comments on this aspect in the works mentioned above, note 2.
23 *CBP*, p. 369.
24 Claude Pichois, to whom I am grateful for advice on this article in manuscript, kindly calls my attention to the fact that the manuscript here discussed should be considered in connection with a 'Chanson de croquemort' by Baudelaire mentioned in the *Catalogue des Autographes de Champfleury*. Does this constitute the same manuscript, or rather simply another similar experiment?

14

'Mène-t-on la foule dans les ateliers?' – some remarks on Baudelaire's variants (1973)

Montre-t-on au public ... le mécanisme des trucs? Lui explique-t-on les retouches et les variantes improvisées aux répétitions, et jusqu'à quelle dose l'instinct et la sincérité sont mêlées [*sic*] aux rubriques et au charlatanisme indispensable dans l'amalgame de l'œuvre? (*CBP* 369–70)[1]

How dearly Baudelaire would have liked to do just this. He never completed the projected 'grande préface où j'expliquerai mes trucs et ma méthode et où j'enseignerai à chacun *l'art d'en faire autant*' (*Corr.* IV, 105); but if the pose of weary disdain and the sincerity of deep difficulty alike make him repeatedly put aside[2] this 'sérieuse bouffonnerie' as being useless to the vulgar throng, he would still have wished to 'amuser les esprits amoureux de la rhétorique profonde', whose number he sardonically estimates as requiring a modest 'dizaine d'exemplaires' (*CBP* 369).

For these few, to whom technique is not automatically equated with triviality, or worth with spontaneity,[3] he would have analysed the need for exact command of every detail of rhyme, of rhythm, of syntax, of suggestion (*CBP* 364, 366), would have anatomised that 'série d'efforts' which is the terror and the triumph of the artist:

Les loques, les fards, les poulies, les chaînes, les repentirs, les épreuves barbouillées, bref toutes les horreurs qui composent le sanctuaire de l'art (*CBP* 370).

We have only fragments of that analysis, scattered throughout letters and critical works; but, increasingly, we are able ourselves to look at some of the detailed evidence from which it would have been drawn: the variants to the poems. All too few remain; the rare poems where we do have a rich harvest of successive versions, and also Baudelaire's own famous protestations ('Facilité à concevoir? ou facilité à exprimer? Je n'ai jamais eu ni l'une ni l'autre, et il doit

sauter aux yeux que le peu que j'ai fait est le résultat d'un travail
très douloureux' (*Corr.* v, 36))[4] sufficiently suggest how many must
have been the stages of correction, now lost, to other poems. But
simply to look as a whole at what we do have, now so splendidly
presented by Claude Pichois in the Corti edition, is to be amazed by
the quantity, the range and the value of Baudelaire's meticulous
alterations. Some of the most important, of course, have long been
familiar, and have been tellingly commented on here and there in
general critical works on the poetry;[5] there have also been occasional studies on particular aspects of the variants as such.[6] A
whole book would be needed for this rich subject. In the present
brief article I hope simply to suggest further, from a deliberately
limited choice of examples, how, as an ancillary method, the close
study of variants may offer one of the most stimulating and revealing means to a full delight in that specially subtle simultaneity of
effects which the final poems so firmly and so finely achieve.[7]

It is only on rare, if important, occasions that the central meaning
of a poem has been changed – and then usually in succinct
alterations to a final stanza. The evocation of an experience, with its
divers potentialities, stands as it was throughout the poem; in the
clinching last lines the poet chooses a different emphasis for his flash
of personal retrospect. The outstanding example here is 'Un
Fantôme', where in the manuscript the last three lines of the fourth
sonnet continue the image of Time as destroyer of that delicacy
which the poem has recalled with mingled sorrow and delight:

> Comme un manant ivre, ou comme un soudard
> Qui bat les murs, et salit et coudoie
> Une beauté frêle, en robe de soie.

The very fineness of this initial end, evoking conquering crudity and
defenceless, evanescent grace, and moving to a dying fall like that of
'Le Cygne', suggests the importance of the change from sad and
lovely lament to challenging and bitter victory:

> Noir assassin de la Vie et de l'Art,
> Tu ne tueras jamais dans ma mémoire
> Celle qui fut mon plaisir et ma gloire!

The placing of the poem at the culmination of the Jeanne cycle,
immediately before the magnificent *Exegi monumentum* of 'Je te donne
ces vers', may well have determined the change.[8] The final version is
no abstract proclamation of Eternal Values; simply, a personal sense

of ineradicable and defiant persistence emerges through the ways in which sense and sound unite in disciplined structure. Life and Art are alike threatened by the ravages of Time; the conquest set against them is purely personal: '*ma* mémoire', '*mon* plaisir', '*ma* gloire'. Two sound-patterns interplay: '*noir assassin* ... *Art* ... tue*ras* j*a*mais ... m*a* mém*oire* ... m*a* gl*oire*', and 'T*u* ne tu*e*ras ... Celle qui f*ut*'. To the vast 'Vie' and 'Art' of the first line correspond, in placing, in sound and in sense, the personal equivalents 'plaisir' and 'gloire' of the end, while the loss from which this bitter conquest is drawn stands in the monosyllabic cut of the past historic 'Celle qui *fut* ...'

Minor changes of meaning within the poem may of course be important. The implications of one line may be far-reaching, as when

> L'orbe mystérieux tracé par le bonheur

around the eyes of Sappho becomes

> Le cercle ténébreux tracé par les douleurs (*CBP* 274).

The change of just one letter gives a vitally different tone, as 'Où je traînais mon agonie' becomes 'je traînais mon atonie' (*CBP* 283); and that of one word, in 'Confession' ('cette confidence étrange' becoming 'cette confidence horrible' (*CBP* 99)) gives the full shock of seeing the Ideal reveal a mere plaintive humanity. Or both insinuation and music may be enhanced, as in the line where the sensuously enchanting woman was first destined to 'charmer les loisirs d'un Mécène ou d'un prince', then comes to

> ... charmer les loisirs d'un *p*ontife ou d'un *p*rince (*CBP* 57).[9]

For most of Baudelaire's revisions, whether in manuscript or in proof, are concerned with making each detail of expression still more adequate to the tone and meaning of the whole. And no tiniest detail is irrelevant in his desire for total perfection of material presentation, where spacing, punctuation, capitals, all have their suggestive functions. For each of these, his comments indicate his search for a balance between personal adventure and traditional order, even down to the placing of a comma: as in the two-sided comment: 'est-ce bien ainsi qu'il faut ponctuer? peut-être trouvez-vous que cette ponctuation rend bien la langueur du rythme', concerning the line: 'Suivant un rythme doux, et paresseux, et lent' (*CBP* 110).

His consequent and life-long battles over proofs reveal his vigorous fury at finding his works sometimes published with autant de fautes d'impression qu'il y a de puces dans la poussière d'un fleuve espagnol (*Corr.* III, 42)

(one remembers how 'Tristesse de la lune' became 'Vitesse . . .' or 'Citadins' turned to 'Italiens', *Corr.* I, 115–16, III, 207); his delight in reading Soulary's Sonnet to a Proof-Reader (*Corr.* III, 44); his recurrent conviction that his fundamental honour is at stake in any imperfection (*Corr.* IV, 254, etc.); and his recognition of a factor shared by many others:

Mon infirmité qui ne me permet de juger de la valeur d'une phrase ou d'un mot que typographié (*Corr.* II, 9).[10]

And from his brief comments on proofs, to editors who neglect or contest his corrections, comes a rich sense of the areas of suggestion lying behind the choice of each single word. Of the lines in 'L'Amour du mensonge' where a variant read:

> Le souvenir divin, antique et lourde tour
> La couronne, et son cœur, meurtri comme la pêche,
> Est, comme son corps, mûr pour le savant amour (*CBP* 193),

to become:

> Le souvenir massif, royale et lourde tour
> La couronne, et son cœur, meurtri comme une pêche,
> Est mûr, comme son corps, pour le savant amour,

Baudelaire wrote:

Le mot *royale* facilitera pour le lecteur l'intelligence de cette métaphore qui fait du souvenir une couronne de tours, comme celles qui inclinent le front des déesses de *maturité*, de *fécondité*, et de *sagesse* (*Corr.* III, 71)[11]

– and, if he did not draw attention to the triumphant replacement of the abstract 'divin' by the physically evocative 'massif', to the removal of the over-specific '*la* pêche', or to the change in the last line to give exact balance between 'cœur' and 'corps', yet he commented on the double sense of 'savant amour': 'L'amour (sens et esprit) est niais à 20 ans, et il est savant à 40', adding: 'Tout cela, je vous l'affirme, a été très lentement combiné.' Similarly, when Calonne chose for a line from 'Danse macabre' the wrong set of variants, giving

> Bayadère sans nez, aux yeux pleins d'épouvantes

instead of

> Bayadère sans nez, irrésistible gouge (*CBP* 191),

Baudelaire's reasons for his final version are several. First, since there is a line with 'le gouffre de tes yeux plein d'horribles pensées',

Des yeux pleins d'épouvante font double emploi. J'ai l'air d'être privé d'imagination.

Second, the aptness of the word to the tone of the whole:

Gouge est un excellent mot, mot unique, mot de *vieille* langue, applicable à une *danse macabre,* mot contemporain des *danses macabres.* UNITÉ DE STYLE …

(here follow detailed discussions of the sense of the word). Third, its suggestive range:

Or, la Mort n'est-elle pas la Gouge qui suit en tous lieux la *Grande Armée universelle,* et n'est-elle pas une courtisane dont les embrassements sont *positivement irrésistibles?*

and the conclusion, as before, stresses how one change serves several purposes:

Couleur, antithèse, métaphore, tout est exact (*Corr.* II, 265–6).

If one seeks, however roughly, to group the multiple pre-occupations that may underlie even the slightest alteration, Baudelaire's famous attack on Musset may provide a starting-point:

Je n'ai jamais pu souffrir … son impudence d'enfant gâté qui invoque le ciel et l'enfer pour des aventures de table d'hôte, son torrent bourbeux de fautes de grammaire et de prosodie, enfin son impuissance totale à comprendre le travail par lequel une rêverie devient un objet d'art … le décousu, la banalité et la négligence (*Corr.* III, 38).

Once again Baudelaire is looking for originality within a disciplined and accepted tradition: avoidance of both the banal and the facile; adherence to the laws of language and versification; concentration of effects; and if he rejects what he sees as inapposite juxtaposition of the lofty and the trivial, it is with a sense of that UNITÉ DE STYLE which figured in capitals in the letter to Calonne.

I leave aside here the many small changes made so as to remove repetition, tautology, over-obvious epithet or potential cliché; though each of these adds its own touch of suggestion, as 'sombres chagrins' become 'vastes chagrins', or 'les flèches de l'amour' turn to 'les griffes de l'amour'. Where grammatical purity is concerned, the Baudelaire constantly on the watch for 'des lourdeurs et des violences de style' (*Corr.* III, 66) will remove awkward constructions ('Qu'on dirait que j'emprunte' becoming 'Que j'ai l'air d'emprunter' (*CBP* 54), or 'Et c'est pourquoi l'on peut' turning to 'Et l'on peut pour cela te comparer au vin' (*CBP* 59)); will closely discuss the phrase 'Tel que jamais mortel n'en vit' (*CBP* 199), or the expression 'la couleur noire' ('le noir étant le zéro de la couleur, cela peut-il se dire?' (*CBP* 201)); will find a simple solution, and one that intensifies the tone of longing, to the strange initial error of 'Le Cygne', so that 'Eau quand pleuveras-tu?' becomes 'Eau, quand *donc* pleuvras-tu?'[12] (*CBP* 168).

But one manuscript note is especially significant. On the proof for 'Le Beau Navire' in the first edition, the opening had read:

Je veux te raconter, pour que tu les connaisses
Les diverses beautés qui parent ta jeunesse;

corrected by Baudelaire to 'connaisse', with the remark: 'Violons plutôt la grammaire que la rime' (*CBP* 110).[13] The violation was not left, of course; scored out in its turn, it led to the new supple and suggestive opening:

Je veux te raconter, ô molle enchanteresse! ...

But the primacy of rhyme and rhythm is certain, and the subtlety of Baudelaire's changes to meet their needs causes some of his finest variants.

It is when working on the proofs of the first edition that he writes to Poulet-Malassis:

Si vous pouvez dénicher, dans vos greniers ou armoires un ou deux dictionnaires de rimes, apportez-les-moi. Je n'en ai jamais eu. – Mais ce doit être une chose excellente dans le cas d'épreuves (*Corr.* II, 13).

He has not, then, needed the rhyming dictionary as stimulus, stand-by or stop-gap in the act of composition;[14] and his assurance over rhythm emerges in the angry remark on hiatus:

Je suis incapable de faire un hémistiche tel que celui-ci: '*Pourquoi, heureuse enfant* ...? Ce ne peut être que: 'pourquoi, l'heureuse enfant ...?' (*Corr.* V, 158),

or in the still more justifiable fury with which he finds ('voilà une faute sans cesse répétée') encor/encore confused in the printing of the tremendous line from 'Le Reniement de Saint Pierre'

Les cieux ne s'en sont point encore rassasiés! (*CBP* 238)

But the hesitations on which he wishes to check are often concerned with tricky traditions of diphthongs, in words where the dictionary indicates whether they count as one, two or more syllables; one of his most effective changes, both broadening the sense and prolonging the sound, is in the line from 'Un Voyage à Cythère', originally reading

> Le long fleuve de fiel de mes douleurs anciennes

and finally becoming

> Le long fleuve de fiel des douleurs anciennes (*CBP* 233).[15]

Tiny changes give new sound-patterns: sometimes onomatopœic, as the replacement of 'pleurs' by 'cris' gives the echo of

> Ses cr*is* me déch*i*raient la f*i*bre (*CBP* 212),

or 'les violons mourant' becomes

> Les *vi*olons *vi*brant derrière les coll*i*nes (*CBP* 129);

sometimes simply serving to hold a line more tautly together, as 'Cherchant la jouissance avec férocité' changes to

> É*pr*i*se* du plai*sir* jusqu'à l'atroc*i*té (*CBP* 180);[16]

and just as often moving away from initial imitative harmony, to affect the tone of the whole in a subtler or deeper way: the famous penultimate line of 'Les Phares' at first began 'Que ce cri renaissant', then tried the physically more intense 'Que ce long hurlement', before achieving:

> Que cet ardent sanglot qui roule d'âge en âge . . . (*CBP* 40).

But it is especially in the play of mute 'e's, evoking often the rocking waves of the sea, the skimming flight of birds, or the graceful walk of woman, that the slightest variant tells. The astonishing dance of 'e' mutes in stanzas three and four of 'A celle qui est trop gaie' is heralded when the opening line moves from 'Ta tête, ton geste et ton air' to 'Ta tête, ton geste, ton air' (*CBP* 283); the stress and movement are completely different when in 'Que diras-tu . . .' the line 'Son fantôme en dansant marche comme un flambeau' becomes

> Son fantôm*e* dans l'air dans*e* comme un flambeau (*CBP* 93).

Jean Pommier has finely indicated[17] how in 'La Vie antérieure' the change from

Au milieu de l'azur, des flots et des splendeurs

to

Au milieu de l'azur, des vagues, des splendeurs (*CBP* 47)

suggests in the two syllables of 'vagues' (the first, strong; the second half-absent) the crest and the fall of the wave. The poem where Baudelaire's revisions as a whole achieve the subtlest effects of this kind is 'La Musique'. There the second stanza read, in the first edition:

> La poitrine en avant et gonflant mes poumons
> De toile pesante,
> Je monte et je descends sur le dos des grands monts
> D'eau retentissante (*CBP* 136).

The opening image there is awkward, hard to follow; and the rising and falling movement is merely stated. In the final version:

> La poitrine en avant et les poumons gonflés
> Comme de la toile,
> J'escalade le dos des flots amoncelés
> Que la nuit me voile;

the 'comme' both elucidates the image and sets going a sequence of 'e' sounds, to be echoed in comm*e* d*e*, toil*e*, escalad*e* l*e*, qu*e*, m*e*; instead of the relative ordinariness of 'monte, descends, grands monts', there is the redoubled triumph of 'esc*a*l*a*d*e*', the liquidly echoing sounds of 'le dos des flots amoncelés', and the veiling by night which recalls the 'plafond de brume' and 'pâle étoile' of the opening stanza. For the final stanza, there is a tiny, but a very powerful, change. The poem had ended:

> Le bon vent, la tempête et ses convulsions
> Sur le sombre gouffre
> Me bercent, et parfois le calme, – grand miroir
> De mon désespoir!

The new version:

> Sur l'immense gouffre
> Me bercent. D'autres fois, calme plat, grand miroir
> De mon désespoir!

creates, instead of the quiet and almost imperceptible alternation led into by 'et parfois', an abrupt physical shock. The prolonged sentence which had stretched through four stanzas carrying the delight and terror of the mighty rocking of the waves, is sharply broken off, both at the most unexpected early point of the line (the third syllable) and immediately after the climax of 'Me bercent' – to create, through the pause, the contrast of 'D'autres fois', and the echoing and clinching monosyllable that now follows 'calme': '*calme plat*', the sudden fall into blank and motionless impotence.

Even the briefest attempt to examine rhythmical effects will of course show how inseparable they are from central meaning and tone. For the rest of this discussion, I propose to group one or two main aspects which seem to emerge as one examines Baudelaire's variants. On the one hand, there is the enhancement, by very varied means, of all that contributes to a deliberate dignity and solemnity; on the other, the specially difficult achievement of an apparently effortless, familiar, conversational style – familar but not trivial; seemingly simple, but penetratingly suggestive.

In 'Paysage', poem of his plans for poetry, the 'chants mélodieux' of the bell-towers give way to an expression more telling at once in its meaning, in its sound patterns, and in its contrast with the rest of the line:

Leurs *hymnes solennels* emportés par le vent (*CBP* 161).

Of Baudelaire's many means of deepening this suggestive solemnity, one notices first, perhaps, how he introduces, when revising, classical or literary reminiscences: superficially suspect to the romantic period as artifice or periphrastic stereotype, these may now come to take up once again their traditional and lasting function of succinctly relating individual insight to a wide range of significance in the stretch of time and space. If this sense of suggestive interaction across the ages is clearly inherent in Baudelaire's approach throughout his works, it emerges yet more strongly through his variants, as the haunting spectre of the eighth sinister figure in 'Les Sept Vieillards' becomes at once a

Sosie inexorable, ironique et fatal

and a

Dégoûtant Phénix, fils et père de lui-même (*CBP* 173);

as 'un riche' and 'une catin' in 'L'Imprévu' take the particular and evocative form of Alceste and Célimène dissected in a new light; or, especially, as, in 'Les Litanies de Satan', we follow the threefold transformation from the abstract 'bonheur insolent', through the more specific and contemporary 'un banquier', to an agelong echo enhanced by its placing at the key-point of the line:

Sur le front du Crésus impitoyable et vil (*CBP* 245).[18]

Such changes extend the bounds of time and space. Of all the effects that most strike home when one looks at Baudelaire's variants as a whole, the strongest is probably that of the alterations which intensify a sense of a vast universe, its enhanced immensity serving to stress in turn man's insatiable appetites, recurrent terrors, and brief, bitter, miraculous conquests. In his minor changes, when Baudelaire removes an over-obvious or tautological epithet, it is very frequently to substitute an adjective of undefined extension: 'sombres chagrins' become 'vastes' (*CBP* 32); 'ces beaux yeux', 'ces grands yeux' (*CBP* 86); while adjectives already evocative are changed to add to the sense of stretching space: 'cette vieille nuit' becomes 'cette immense nuit' (*CBP* 73), and in 'La Musique' 'un pur éther' and 'le sombre gouffre' turn to 'un vaste éther' and 'l'immense gouffre' (*CBP* 136).

This is no mechanical process. Where context demands, adjectives of extension have been replaced by others, as in 'Le Cygne', where 'Comme je traversais *ce vaste* Carrousel' (in itself evocative of the demolitions) has given way to the contrast between progress and memory in '*le nouveau* Carrousel' (*CBP* 167). And in 'Brumes et Pluies' the earlier

D'un linceul vaporeux et d'un *vaste* tombeau (*CBP* 198)

was first subjected to the wish to call up both the title and the first half of the line, by the substitution of 'brumeux tombeau', before culminating in the one word where the sense of misty uncertainty, the extension into undefined space, and the echo of sound are united in:

D'un linceul *vaporeux* et d'un *vague* tombeau (*CBP* 198).

Extensions in space are conveyed of course through much more varied means than mere changes of adjective. 'Projette l'illimité' becomes '*allonge* l'illimité' (*CBP* 106), 'Traversant la forêt' is changed to '*parcourant les* forêts (CBP 124); 'Au travers de l'espace ils galopent' is intensified to '*ils s'enfoncent*' (*CBP* 138). Perhaps most suggestive may be the difference between the positive stress on immensity:

Un triste cimetière *à l'immense horizon*

and the blank, negative sense of infinity:

> Le cimetière immense et froid, *sans horizon* (*CBP* 138).

The variants to one of the most deliberately discreet of the poems, 'Je n'ai pas oublié', are perhaps the more significant in that here Baudelaire certainly seeks no rhetorical tone; it is all the more notable that his rewriting of a quiet personal fragment should gently extend personal memories to the breadth and richness of a cosmic background. The first version evokes the separate sunsets of each evening descriptively:

> Et les soleils, le soir, orangés et superbes
> ... Semblaient, au fond du ciel, en témoins curieux ... ;

the second gives lasting generality, richness, and the magnification of the physical image:

> Et le soleil, le soir, ruisselant et superbe,
> ... Semblait, grand œil ouvert dans le ciel curieux,
> Contempler nos dîners longs et silencieux,

while the original variants ('Et versaient doucement', then 'Et versait largement') finally find the expression for the most bountiful sense of stretching space as a benison behind the daily world:

> *Répandant largement* ses beaux reflets de cierge
> Sur la nappe frugale et les rideaux de serge (*CBP* 195).

The sense of time, like that of space, may be intensified, as in 'Un Fantôme', where the generalized opening and the tense of

> De tout ce qui pour nous a flamboyé

move into the brief image, the alliteration, and the cutting off by the past historic:

> De tout le feu qui pour nous flamboya (*CBP* 86),

or in 'Le Reniement de Saint Pierre', where the first version in descriptive imperfect:

> Où tu venais remplir l'éternelle promesse

shifts to separate that past promise ineluctably from the present:

> Où tu vins pour remplir l'éternelle promesse (*CBP* 238).[19]

In these and other lines, variants often stress a sense of inexorability. 'L'homme … Porte souvent le châtiment' in 'Les Hiboux' becomes 'Porte *toujours* le châtiment' (*CBP* 134); the endless wastes of *ennui* find, in place of the flat 'sous le premier poids des neigeuses années' a musically and sensuously evocative image for the softly and insidiously irresistible:

> Quand sous *les lourds flocons* des neigeuses années … (*CBP* 143);

or the already strong 'irrésistible calenture' of 'Le Vin des amants' takes on a harder and more obsessively echoed compulsion as 'une implac*a*ble c*a*lenture' (*CBP* 216). Two poems are specially suggestive here.

In 'La Fontaine de sang', the ebbing blood, which at first had flowed in 'tranquilles sanglots', becomes, seeming to beat with the human pulse, a 'fontaine aux *rythmiques* sanglots'; incidental expressions are changed to give greater strength and dignity, '*j'ai beau me tâter*' becoming '*je me tâte en vain*', and 'le marché' changing to 'la cité'); and finally the lines:

> J'ai demandé souvent à des vins généreux
> D'endormir pour un jour la terreur qui me mine,
> Mais le vin rend la vue et l'oreille plus fine

take on, in the change to highly original adjective, and in the redoubled irony of the last line with its balanced monosyllables, a stranger and sharper threat:

> J'ai demandé souvent à des vins *captieux*
> D'endormir pour un jour la terreur qui me mine;
> *Le vin rend l'œil plus clair* et l'oreille plus fine!

(We have here Baudelaire's own note on 'captieux': the printer had tried to correct it to the epithet that would more normally go with wine: 'capiteux', and he replies:

Mais non! s'il y avait: *captieux*, c'était fort bien; *des vins captieux*, et non pas *capiteux* qui d'ailleurs ne rime pas (*CBP* 226 [the rhyme is with 'oublieux'].)

The last stanza of 'Quand le ciel bas et lourd' (*CBP* 147) moves through a whole sequence of variants, gradually to discover its final magnificent means of conveying at once endlessly prolonged oppression and the sharp stab of anguish. The opening had read successively

> Et de grands [d'anciens] corbillards sans tambours ni musique,
> Passent en foule au fond de mon âme;

before finding its prolonged and rich dignity:

> Et de *longs* corbillards, sans tambours ni musique,
> *Défilent lentement* dans mon âme.

There had then followed:

> et l'Espoir
> Fuyant vers d'autres cieux [Pleurant comme un vaincu], L'An-
> goisse despotique
> Sur mon crâne incliné plante son drapeau noir.

The removal of the 'et' and of the long participial phrases, then the splitting up of the lines, and the placing of 'atroce' in a stressed position, lead up to the sudden piercing movement of the end:

> l'Espoir,
> Vaincu, pleure, et l'Angoisse atroce, despotique,
> Sur mon crâne incliné plante son drapeau noir.

Solemnity and irrevocability contribute to the growing emergence of ritual invocations, whether in 'Crépuscule du soir', where the conversational early line:

> Oui, voilà bien le Soir, le Soir cher à celui ...

is strengthened and intoned:

> O soir, aimable soir, désiré par celui ... (*CBP* 184);

or in 'Les Litanies de Satan', where the already dignified 'Souverain incompris' becomes the still more mighty and litanesque:

> O *Prince de l'exil*, à qui l'on a fait tort.

This last poem, too hastily dismissed by some critics, is a rich example of Baudelaire's close re-writing. The changes sometimes involve only one word, but profoundly affect both sound and sense: the line originally opening 'Et qui toujours vaincu' takes on a different stress and indomitability as it becomes:

> Et qui, vaincu, toujours te redresses plus fort;

Hope becomes not simply the ironically charming daughter of her grim parents ('une fille charmante') but the still more ironically suggestive 'une *folle* charmante'; the treasures hidden in the depths are not just in 'secrets arsenaux' but in '*profonds* arsenaux'; 'l'homme faible' becomes the more suggestive 'l'homme *frêle*'; finally, in the line which at first read

Bâton des exilés, *soutien* des inventeurs,

after first substituting 'torche', Baudelaire finds his stronger symbol

Bâton des exilés, *lampe* des inventeurs.

Meantime there have been more extended changes. In the stanza which first read:

Qui même aux parias, ces animaux maudits,
Donne[s] avec l'amour le goût du Paradis,[20]

the tautology or padding of the first line has been removed, and the deliberate gift of the second has been strengthened:

Toi qui, même aux lépreux, aux parias maudits,
Enseignes par l'amour le goût du Paradis.

The abstract and somewhat flat nobility, and the awkward inversion, in

Aux nobles malheureux, toi qui donnes l'orgueil,
Et les fais sans broncher aller jusqu'au cercueil

give way to a new strength and dignity:

Toi qui fais au proscrit ce regard calme et haut
Qui damne tout un peuple autour d'un échafaud.

The awkward mingling of abstract and concrete in

Toi qui mets un opprobre éternel et sanglant
Sur le front mal fardé du bonheur insolent

becomes, after a number of changes, the sinisterly musical and evocative

Toi qui poses ta marque, ô complice subtil,
Sur le front du Crésus impitoyable et vil.

An in itself physically suggestive phrase

Toi qui frottes de baume et d'huile les vieux os

makes way for a more haunting and prolonged musical effect:

Toi qui, magiquement, assouplis les vieux os.

The stanza, initially near to flat sentimentality,

Toi qui mets dans les yeux et dans le cœur des filles
Un invincible amour des hommes en guenilles

is changed to recall the bitter pondering on the obsessions of Mademoiselle Bistouri in the *Petits Poèmes en Prose:*

> Toi qui mets dans les yeux et dans le cœur des filles
> *Le culte de la plaie* et l'amour des guenilles.

In the final stanza Baudelaire had first written of 'Du ciel d'où tu tombas' [then of 'Des Cieux spirituels'], and of 'L'Enfer où couché [then 'fécond'] tu peuples le silence' [then 'couves le silence'], before achieving his final expression for lost glory and potential creation:

> Gloire et louange à toi, Satan, dans les hauteurs
> Du Ciel, *où tu régnas*, et dans les profondeurs
> De l'enfer, où, *vaincu, tu rêves* en silence.

But most suggestive perhaps are the changes made in a line from the third stanza, which first read:

> Puissant consolateur des souffrances humaines,

then moves through three stages from the pitch of dignity to the subtlety of the familiar. First the 'souffrances' are intensified to 'angoisses', and, at the same time, instead of 'Puissant consolateur', Baudelaire tries another tone, giving

> Aimable médecin des angoisses humaines.

The discrepancy is over-incongruous, and he then finds instead of 'médecin' the term which will fit his atmosphere of litany: 'Guérisseur tout-puissant'. Finally he discovers the means of at last combining the power and the intimacy:

> Toi qui sais tout, grand roi des choses souterraines,
> Guérisseur familier des angoisses humaines . . .

And in poems where conversational intimacy is the predominating tone, it is the achieving of an effect of quiet and total ease that has required Baudelaire's detailed care. The slight changes in the opening lines to one of the best-known poems:

> La servante au grand cœur dont vous étiez jalouse,
> *Dort-elle* son sommeil sous une humble pelouse?
> Nous *aurions déjà dû* lui porter quelques fleurs

remove the rhetorical question, make for a gentle continuous movement, and increase the immediacy:

> La servante au grand cœur dont vous étiez jalouse,
> *Et qui dort* son sommeil sous une humble pelouse,
> Nous *devrions pourtant* lui porter quelques fleurs.

Later the lofty expression for the infinite passing of time 'Et l'éternité fuir' is made the more telling for its reduction in scope and its stranger physical verb: 'Et le siècle couler'. Finally the unspoken reproach of the end is made again the more immediate by substituting for

> si le soir,
> Calme, dans le fauteuil *elle venait* s'asseoir

the one touch

> Calme, dans le fauteuil *je la voyais* s'asseoir.

Outstanding from this point of view is the sonnet 'Le Rêve d'un Curieux' (*CBP* 254) where, to the mighty theme of death and the life after death, Baudelaire has chosen to give no lofty oratory, but the tone and imagery of the most every-day conversation. The opening, originally

> As-tu connu, dis-moi, la douleur savoureuse,
> Et de toi disait-on [changed to 'De toi dit-on souvent']: 'Quel homme singulier!'?

is made less jerky, less dramatic, with the removal of 'Quel', and is given the immediacy of the present tense:

> Connais-tu, comme moi, la douleur savoureuse,
> Et de toi fais-tu dire: 'Oh! l'homme singulier!'

The final lines, at different stages, had read:

> J'étais comme l'Enfance, avide du spectacle,
> Et qui hait le rideau comme on hait un obstacle
> Et puis . . . la vérité froide se révéla

[*Or* Mais voilà qu'une idée étrange me glaça]

> J'étais mort, ô miracle, et la fameuse [terrible] aurore
> Avait lui! 'Quoi! me dis-je alors, ce n'est que ça?'

The abstract 'Enfance' is removed, the present participle 'Haïssant' adds to the immediacy, the 'mais' or 'puis' becomes the cry of 'Enfin'; instead of 'une idée étrange' and the emphatic 'me glaça', there is simply the blank revelation. Further emphatic stresses are removed – 'ô miracle!' and 'avait lui', and so is the diluting 'me dis-je alors'; meantime instead of 'avait lui' the stretching verb in the imperfect has already imperceptibly and completely spread around him. The terror and the simplicity of the realisation have been fully fused:

> J'étais comme l'enfant avide du spectacle,
> Haïssant le rideau comme on hait un obstacle . . .
> Enfin la vérité froide se révéla:
> J'étais mort sans surprise, et la terrible aurore
> M'enveloppait. – Eh quoi! n'est-ce donc que cela?
> La toile était levée et j'attendais encore.

This limited paper has touched on only a few of the many sides where every detail counts. At one end of the scale are changes in one apparently insignificant word: from 'à' to 'vers' in

> Et cependant je sens ma bouche aller vers toi (*CBP* 278);

at the other, broad questions concerning Baudelaire's images: how far are his corrections concerned simply with developing his initial discovery, or how far does he discard or change images once found, as in the first half of 'La Mort des Artistes', with the completely different strength and subtlety of its final version, or in the intriguing case of 'Spleen' ('Pluviôse, irrité') (*CBP* 142) which earlier read

> Mon *chien* sur le carreau cherchant une litière

but substitutes the mangy and wretched cat indoors to lead on to the phantom cry from the roof-top. Above all, the increasingly strong or delicate ways of conveying certain sense-impressions, and effects of rhythm and sound, would need much further investigation, closely related to their context as a whole, than I have been able to give them here.[21]

But I should like to end with a stanza from 'Au Lecteur'. The early version was already very strong in its vocabulary and its effects:

> Dans nos cerveaux malsains, comme un million d'helminthes,
> Grouille, chante et ripaille un peuple de démons,
> Et, quand nous respirons, la mort dans nos poumons
> S'engouffre, comme un fleuve, avec de sourdes plaintes.

But its slow-moving opening lacks the 'attack' of previous stanzas, its 'malsains' is weak by the side of other adjectives and images of condemnation, and 'chante' even in the ironical feasting context, risks being too pleasant in its associations. The final version has a quite different concentration:

> Serré, fourmillant, comme un million d'helminthes,
> Dans nos cerveaux ribote un peuple de Démons,
> Et, quand nous respirons, la Mort dans nos poumons
> Descend, fleuve invisible, avec de sourdes plaintes (*CBP* 22).

Where the first had moved through a regularly divided alexandrine, there is now the unusual division 5/7, isolating 'serré, fourmillant' so that the seething pressures are intensified by the very fact of these words being crammed together in shortened space; and lengthening the effect of the loathly worm-image. The swarming and devouring lead up to the one fierce, colloquial word 'ribote' at the place of strongest stress in the line. And whereas the early version had moved in logical sequence, its opening phrase showing that all is within the brain, the variant first creates the intense sense-impressions of pressure, pullulation, filth and carousal, holding them in suspense until the elucidation of 'un peuple de Démons'.[22]

The last line shows intensification of a different kind. Here, the strongest word was used in the first version: 'S'engouffre, comme un fleuve'. The 'comme' is removed, perhaps so as to avoid a repetition of the first line: then the full terror is suggested, not by the resounding verb, but by the quiet statement of 'Descend', and by the insidious sense of the adjective and its echo in the sound pattern:

> Descend, fleuve invisible, avec de sourdes plaintes.

Here indeed is brought out the force of Baudelaire's own meditation on 'la décence du langage qui augmente la profondeur de l'horreur'.

'Au Lecteur' opened the volume. Among the variants of 'Le Voyage' which so majestically closes it, there is one which may serve as a symbol. Baudelaire began by writing 'Il est, hélas! des âmes sans répit', changed it to 'des Ennuis' and then to 'des martyrs', moving from the over-abstract through the over-romantic or pathetic before reaching the word which discreetly and physically evokes the sense and tone which his stanza, the whole poem and indeed the volume, need:

> 'Il est, hélas, des *coureurs* sans répit'

To Soulary he wrote:

Vous savez imiter les élans de l'âme, la musique de la méditation; *vous aimez l'ordre*; vous dramatisez le sonnet et vous lui donnez un dénouement; vous connaissez la puissance da la réticence (*Corr.* II, 45).

Imagination, music, structure, art of discreet suggestion: he has here defined some of the central qualities behind his own tireless perfecting of a creative balance between Adventure and Order.

NOTES

1 The following abbreviations will be used:
CBP: Charles Baudelaire: *Les Fleurs du Mal*, édition critique Jacques Crépet–Georges Blin, refondue par Georges Blin et Claude Pichois, I, Paris, Corti, 1968. [The new Pléiade two-volume edition of Baudelaire's works (see below pp. 262–7) has, since the first publication of this article, made full variants still more widely available.
CB: Les Fleurs du Mal, édition critique établie par Jacques Crépet et Georges Blin, Paris, Corti, 1942.
Corr.: Correspondance générale, recueillie, classée et annotée par Jacques Crépet [and Cl. Pichois for Vol. VI], Paris, Conard, 1947–53, 6 vols.
Pl.: Œuvres complètes, texte établi par Y.-G. Le Dantec, édition révisée, complétée et présentée par Claude Pichois, Paris, Gallimard (Editions de la Pléiade), 1961.

2 See the four Projets de Préfaces, *CBP* 361–71. The pose (especially p. 370) deliberately recalls Gautier.

3 Cf. (*Pl.* 609) Baudelaire's comments on Dupont's work for the Academy Dictionary and the immense value of the 'gymnastics' involved in discussing grammar, rhetoric, and the 'mot propre': 'Ceci paraîtra peut-être puéril à beaucoup de gens, mais ceux-là ne se sont pas rendu compte du travail successif qui se fait dans l'esprit des écrivains, et de la série des circonstances nécessaires pour créer un poète.' Cf. also *Pl.* 722: 'Parmi les innombrables préjugés dont la France est si fière notons cette idée qui court les rues, et qui naturellement est écrite en tête des préceptes de la critique vulgaire, à savoir qu'un ouvrage *trop bien* écrit *doit* manquer de sentiment'; *Pl.* 746: 'J'ai entendu dire à beaucoup de personnes, fort compétentes d'ailleurs, que le fini, le précieux, la perfection enfin, les rebutaient et les empêchaient d'avoir, pour ainsi dire, *confiance* dans le poète. Cette opinion (singulière pour moi) ...'; and the outstanding passage on 'les rhétoriques et les prosodies' from the *Salon de 1859, Pl.* 1043.

4 Cf. also *Corr.* II, 256, IV, 324, etc.

5 See especially the basic studies by L. J. Austin, F. W. Leakey, J. Prévost, R. Vivier. H. Peyre, *Connaissance de Baudelaire*, Paris, Corti, 1951, pp. 129 et sqq., pointed out how much needed to be examined; there is a pungent remark in R. Kopp and Cl. Pichois, *Les Années Baudelaire*, Neuchâtel, A la Baconnière (Études baudelairiennes, I), 1969, p. 139, on the value of analysing how Baudelaire re-works his own material as compared with what he does with sources or influences.

6 André Guex, *Aspects de l'Art baudelairien*, Lausanne, Imprimerie Centrale, 1934, gives in a 62-page appendix an 'Étude des variantes' – largely useless, as the 1868 edition is taken as the basis, there is no proper apparatus of references, and the variants are forced to fit the headings of the main thesis. There are some interesting comments in the section on variants (pp. 164–95) in Marc Seguin's *Aux Sources vivantes du symbolisme – Génie des 'Fleurs du Mal'*, Paris, Messein, 1938. J. Doucet, 'Quelques variantes de Baudelaire', *Les Études classiques*, 25, 1957, pp. 327–43, somewhat contestable on general points, has some perceptive comments

on detail. Alfred Noyer-Weidner, 'Stilempfindung und Stilentwicklung Baudelaires im Spiegel seiner Varianten', *Linguistic and Literary Studies in Honour of Helmut Hatzfeld*, Washington, 1964, pp. 302–27, provides a thorough and scholarly analysis of some interesting examples, with the merit of setting details in their context and seeking to see how lexical and syntactical changes contribute to poetic value. The most stimulating and sensitive treatment of one set of variants which I have read is that comparing the first and second editions, in J. Pommier, *Autour de l'Édition originale des Fleurs du Mal*, Geneva, Slatkine reprints, 1968, pp. 150–69.

7 Some of my examples will be familiar from previous works, though here set in another framework of discussion. I have left aside some aspects ably discussed in the works mentioned above; I have also left to be discussed on another occasion the multiple variants to three poems in particular: 'Le Vin des Chiffonniers', 'Une Gravure fantastique', and 'Sur Le Tasse en Prison'. I am not here concerned with drawing chronological conclusions about developments in Baudelaire's style at given dates (for suggestions here, see F. W. Leakey, *Baudelaire and Nature*, Manchester University Press, 1969; Professor Leakey was able to use *CBP* for his Chronological Index but not for his text). Where I speak of 'initial' or 'first' version, I mean of course the first *extant* version; many others must have existed.

8 Similarly, the change in the last stanza of 'Le Vin des Chiffonniers', where wine, seen first as the gift of God, becomes the invention of man, fits the function of the section *LE VIN* as leading up to the sections on *FLEURS DU MAL* and *RÉVOLTE*.

9 Cf. also 'Pauvre pendu muet' becoming 'Ridicule pendu' in 'Un Voyage à Cythère' (commented on in Fairlie, *Baudelaire: Les Fleurs du Mal*, London, Arnold, 1960, pp. 31–2); 'grand comme le monde' becoming 'laid comme le monde' in 'L'Imprévu'; etc.

10 For his struggle for total perfection in material presentation see especially *Corr.* II, 38 and III, 94. For grammatical correction, he applied to others the same rigorous standards as to himself: Cf. the firm and tactful letter to Soulary, *Corr.* III, 44–5. He once amusingly over-reached himself in his zeal for such helpful amendment, when he set out to correct the language of Barbey d'Aurevilly's *L'Ensorcelée*, thereby removing all the deliberate 'patois normand' (*Corr.* II, 236).

11 For suggested sources of the classical reminiscences here, see *CB* 473; L. J. Austin, op. cit. p. 248, discusses this variant. The comment on 'maturité' and 'fécondité' suggests the closeness to the complete Du Bellay quotation of which Austin gives a portion: 'Telle que dans son char la Bérécynthienne,/Couronnée de tours et joyeuse d'avoir/Enfanté tant d'enfants.'

12 Cf. also the change at the end of 'Je te donne ces vers'. The second-last line had read:

  Les stupides mortels qui t'appellent leur frère –

the 'te' depending on 'Etre maudit' from five lines earlier. In a poem to a woman, and immediately preceding 'Statue', 'leur frère' stands out oddly and was changed to 'Les stupides mortels qui t'ont jugée amère' (*CBP* 88), adding, too, a new echo of sound in the repeated 'u'. For other important grammatical points, see the articles mentioned in footnote 6 above. See also Jacques Crépet, *Propos sur Baudelaire*, pp. 85–9, for hesitations over 'bétail' and 'satyre'.

13 In the almost impeccable *CBP*, there is an error in the note to line 14 of 'L'Examen de minuit'. In the text this line is given as 'Digne vassal des Démons', and in the note is the variant of the third edition 'Digne vassale des Démons', with an appended [*sic*]. Not only would 'vassal' leave the line short of a syllable, but, when one examines the context, 'vassale' is intended to be feminine, in apposition to 'la brute': the lines read: 'Nous avons, pour plaire à la brute,/Digne vassale des Démons,/ Insulté ce que nous aimons'. [The new Pléiade edition (see below, pp. 262–7) corrects this point.]

14 For a different use of rhyming dictionaries see my 'Nerval et Richelet' (below, pp. 304–07).

15 See J. Crépet, op. cit. p. 88, for examples of hesitation over dividing syllables. Baudelaire corrects 'viande' in 'Le Reniement de Saint Pierre' where 'Comme un tyran gorgé de vian/des et de vins' becomes 'Comme un tyran gorgé de vi/ande et de vins'; but the opposite takes place in the line from 'Bénédiction' which was first 'De génuflexions, de vi/ande et de vins' and becomes the more ringing and balanced 'De génuflexions, de vian/des et de vins'.

16 The change from 'avec' to 'jusqu'à' is of course also significant.

17 J. Pommier, op. cit., p. 157.

18 Cf. also, in 'La Mort des artistes', 'N'ont plus qu'un seul espoir qui souvent les console' which becomes 'N'ont qu'un espoir, étrange et sombre Capitole' (*CBP* 252); 'Le Jet d'eau' with its refrain of 'Phoebé réjouie' in place of 'la lune pâlie' (*CBP* 291); 'Le Couvercle' with its 'riche', 'richard', 'Crésus' (*CBP* 345).

19 For other means of intensifying time, cf. the change from 'Le Temps descend sur moi minute par minute' to '*Et le Temps m'engloutit* minute par minute' (*CBP* 149), or from 'ne connaît pas le nom' to '*n'a jamais su le nom*' (*CBP* 257).

20 *CBP* 244 gives 'Donne' as the variant here, without a *sic*. Scansion and grammar would require 'Donnes'. [This has been corrected in the new Pléiade edition.]

21 Among rhythmical questions, it would be interesting to discuss the variants where Baudelaire gives a new movement to the line by placing on the sixth syllable a word to which tradition would not have allowed that stress (a frequent practice in Leconte de Lisle). Cf. the change from 'Car il est fait, amis, de l'immortel péché' (relatively flat and with an effect of padding at the caesura) to the urgency of 'Car il est fait *avec* l'universel Péché' (*CBP* 319); or from the regular 'Puisqu'il me trouve belle et qu'il veut m'adorer' to 'Puisqu'il me trouve *assez* belle pour m'adorer' (*CBP* 29).

Among other points there emerges Baudelaire's frequent substitution of the personal for the general: 'l'amour' becomes 'votre amour'; 'l'argent' becomes 'ton or'; 'ce carquois' becomes 'mon carquois', etc.

(Though there are occasional examples of the opposite.) In 'Les Petites Vieilles' the hortatory 'Aimez-les' becomes the shared 'aimons-les'.

22 This technique of intense sense-impressions held in suspense to await a later elucidation of their connection and meaning makes one think ahead to Mallarmé. Cf. L. J. Austin, 'Mallarmé et le Réel', in *Modern Miscellany presented to Eugène Vinaver*, Manchester University Press, 1969, p. 17.

15

Baudelaire's correspondence (1974)[1]

How on earth, wonders the sixteen-year-old Baudelaire in 1837, do
people manage in careers which require constant correspondence, if
I find it so intolerably hard to put my ideas on paper, whether at
school or in letters? Behind this reflection on his delay in dutifully
writing to a grown-up step-brother, parental admonitions about
making a way in the world are clearly discernible; far in the future
will come the prose poem, where the arbitrariness of fate is given the
sardonic form of harassed officials misdirecting their prizes or judgements because they are always behind time. Throughout the letters
of thirty-five years, with their desolate and repetitive sequence of
procrastination, debt, illness, remorse, their sudden bursts of mockery, tenderness, confidence, Baudelaire is constantly and consciously at grips with the theme that is the centre of all his works:
the gap between desire and action. As Claude Pichois's introduction
points out, he is no instinctive letter-writer. Yet the very fact that so
many letters are forced from him by circumstances and after long
delay means that he is driven to a specially close analysis of the
inner and outer compulsions that brought this about; it means too
that each letter is carefully shaped to suit its recipient. The raw
material of biography is given a conscious and deliberate form.

Baudelaire himself wanted to draw on correspondence when he
planned *Mon Cœur mis à nu*; in one of his letters he laments that he
had not kept many letters sent to him and lost in his countless
moves. Now at last much scattered material comes together again.
M. Pichois, with his unrivalled knowledge as editor of the Pléiade
Œuvres complètes, and of the sixth volume of the Conard *Correspondance*
undertaken by Jacques Crépet from 1947–53, has produced for the
Pléiade two volumes containing all the known letters of Baudelaire,
and at the same time, in collaboration with his wife, has published

in the series 'Études Baudelairiennes' the surviving letters sent to Baudelaire by more than a hundred correspondents.

Both works will give pleasure to a wide range of readers: the presentation makes it easy to dip at random with profit and enjoyment; the annotation is rich, scholarly and suggestive. It is only a pity that the *Lettres à Baudelaire* could not have been incorporated into the Pléiade edition, in their place in the sequence. To read the two works in conjunction, chronologically, demands some acrobatic page-turning (since the letters to Baudelaire are grouped under names of authors), helped by the editors' careful if not complete system of cross-references; to follow this material as a whole, with the full apparatus of notes, is to find countless new insights into Baudelaire's plans, his finished works, and the whole life of his times.

M. Pichois, seeking in his brief, penetrating and personal introduction to differentiate Baudelaire from nine other great *épistoliers* of his century (one wonders why Mallarmé is missing) has indeed been over-modest about the range and scope of this correspondence. Weariness and vexation of spirit there may be in plenty; rarely have plans and promises been so relentlessly and persuasively reiterated, so remorselessly abandoned; debts and dunning certainly outweigh in space any developed discussion of theories of literature; but the sharp intelligence, the gift for satire, the harsh tenderness, and above all the allusive remarks on psychological, political, philosophical or literary problems – these offer quite other dimensions.

Neither collection is primarily concerned with *inédits*, though both contain letters not hitherto published as a whole or in part. Their outstanding contribution is in bringing together material up till now scattered in different publications, incorporating the most recent discoveries and frequently setting right faulty dates or attributions. Letters attested by internal allusion but now lost are indicated at the appropriate date. Above all, a very high proportion of the texts have been collated with the manuscripts, or occasionally, where these were not available, with photocopies or facsimiles. Some of the most important collectors and dealers in autographs have generously given full access; it is a sad comment on certain contemporary transactions that for only a few of the ninety-five, mainly early, letters first published by Ph. Auserve in 1966, and requiring a good deal of correction or verification, was M. Pichois able to consult a photocopy.

In one of the finest of his prose poems, 'Les Vocations', Baudelaire (who elsewhere suggested that 'le génie, c'est l'enfance retrouvée à volonté') evokes four basic impulses: the child as actor, as mystic visionary, as marvelling worshipper of sensuous delight, and as imaginative wanderer across the face of the world. Sartre, writing long before the recent discovery of the early letters, saw Baudelaire as having 'chosen' his destiny by the age of ten, in reaction to his mother's remarriage. M. Pichois long since destroyed the facile generalizations that clustered round Baudelaire's supposed attitude to his step-father. The early letters now provide a quite exceptional insight into the growth of the tensions that form the material of the artist, expressed by a child and adolescent who is hyper-conscious both of his own puzzling personality and of the effect he wants to produce on each recipient.

An intense appetite for life marks the beginning: an appetite not just for experience, but for contemplating his own consciousness of it, and for seeing that consciousness through the eyes of others. The ten-year-old is not content with simply describing the delights of the coach journey to Lyon: he consciously characterizes the self who is experiencing it: 'moi qui suis toujours en mouvement, toujours sur un pied ou sur l'autre ... gai comme à l'ordinaire', and rejoices in hearing another traveller give him a dramatic entity: 'Voilà ce petit Monsieur qui court en avant, tout seul, sur la grande route' (one thinks of the even more precocious Constant analysing for his grandmother his own febrile moods). To journey for ever would be his ideal – but independently, not stifled in the coach by the paraphernalia of bourgeois comfort, which the child brilliantly evokes in a concatenation of thirty or more heterogeneous objects, from footwarmers to forks, from coverlets to corsets. And to his grown-up step-brother the child presents his mother as the scatter-brain prone to nervous, theatrical outcry; himself as the cool, collected master of circumstance.

A light letter. But the famous later letters – where Baudelaire recalls to his mother, with bitter nostalgia, the idyllic period of exclusive tenderness when mother and child were alone together before her remarriage – have often been taken as the sole centre to psychological explanations of the poet's basic tensions; other impulses and other frustrations are also deep-rooted. The child who clamours so intensely for affection may equally draw back repeatedly from the over-demonstrative and over-demanding: even if to his step-brother he rings round the remarks with 'it is for my own good', yet the occasional pointed phrases on his mother's 'exigence' and 'tendresse excessive' strike home.

That these loving claims on him were often expressed in declamatory or conventional style is plain from the child's reiteration of his duty to make an ageing mother happy before she dies: much later, at the age of forty, he remembers especially sharply and across some ten years her high-flown expression of *idées reçues*, as on an expedition together she cried out at every viewpoint 'Que c'est beau!' – Baudelaire comments 'avec ton emphase habituelle ... et puis tu ajoutais «Mais toi, tu ne sens pas les beautés de la nature, ce n'est pas de ton âge.» – Car c'est ainsi que tu t'exprimes.' The pose of the *dandy*, with his cultivated absence of passion and his scorn of the trite, has perhaps very early origins.

But the claims and strains which most strongly and overtly link this childhood and adolescence with the problems of the later creative artist are those imposed by the unremitting challenge to justification by fame. Strains imposed at once by outer pressure and inner urge. The gifted child, whom his family would wish to see a prodigy, painstakingly reports in letter after letter his exact place in each subject in the gruelling, continuous series of assessments; responds gratefully to his mother's 'refrain' which she has feared might be wearisomely repetitive: 'qu'il faut bien travailler, *qu'il faut être un homme distingué*'; reflects on the prize-giving ceremony: 'C'est vraiment bien beau d'entendre proclamer pour un prix son nom ... sept fois nommé'; 'être couronné à la fin de l'année, devant une grande multitude'. Twenty-five years later, a prose poem was to set side by side three tempter-figures: sensuous delight, riches and fame – *Eros, Plutus et la Gloire* – and find the third the hardest to resist.

His gifts mean that at first he can succeed with little effort, can boast of his last-minute spurts to catch up; the later Baudelaire wrote: 'je ne sors jamais des situations difficiles que par explosion', and analysed in detail and suggested in a multiplicity of subtle images the paradoxes of a sudden upsurge of creative energy or will to action. In adolescence, as sporadic effort proves more and more insufficient, two other moods come to the fore: a pervasive fear of failure, and fits of overpowering lethargy. Fear of moving from Lyon to the famous Louis-le-Grand; fear of the demands of the *classe de rhétorique*; fear at the prospect of having to choose a career: 'trouver une place vide au milieu du monde ... cette lutte avec les autres', fear of disappointing his mother's longing for him to distinguish himself in the *concours général* – his step-father he sees as more indulgent, and at this period it is her tears and her nervous tension that haunt him. The boy of seventeen writes:

Quand je commence à considérer la somme énorme des bienfaits que je te dois, je vois qu'il n'y a pas d'autre moyen de te les payer que par des jouissances d'amour-propre, des succès. Mais ma pauvre mère, si la nature ne m'a pas fait apte à te contenter, si je suis trop pauvre d'esprit pour contenter ton ambition, alors tu mourras donc avant que j'aie pu te récompenser . . .

The extent to which he is echoing her own expectations and expressions can be seen from a letter about him which she wrote to Ancelle twenty-six years later:

Il me faut absolument, avant ma mort, un peu de contentement par lui. . . . Je ne l'aurai jamais. J'aurais pu me consoler dans de grands succès littéraires (trouvant en lui l'étoffe qu'il fallait pour cela), mais là encore, de cruelles déceptions.

The theme of 'ma paresse', cause or consequence of strain, fear and guilt, runs through almost every letter from the age of eleven, taken lightly at first, soon carrying with it 'je confesse ma faute', and culminating in an analysis, at age eighteen, of how it has reached the dimensions of total apathy – no longer 'indolence poétique'; no longer outbursts of joy or anger, urges to good or evil, but the blank emptiness of *ennui*. Here already is the core of 'Enfer ou Ciel, qu'importe?'

Yet, beside their desperate appeals for understanding and above all for sheer physical presence, the early letters are full of zest – for dancing, acting, skating, fencing, travelling; for the remembered elegance of Paris in contrast to the dirt and discomfort of the Lyon boarding-school; full of gratitude to the occasional master who can draw out his personal enthusiasm, and of swift comments on reading, from *Robinson Crusoe* and travellers' tales to Juvenal and Virgil or to the latest 'moderns', Sainte-Beuve's *Volupté* and Hugo's *Marion Delorme*. Already preoccupied by the connexion between physical and mental, he dips into theories of magnetism and wants to investigate comparative religion. He begins writing verse, and asks to see the verse his own father wrote; in later life he was to cherish some of his father's paintings and drawings, in spite of finding them execrably bad. For already the fine arts are becoming a focus of interest, as he reads Gautier's articles in *La Presse* of 1838, articles of glowing praise for Delacroix.

The positive appetite for life and the negative need to escape from the threat of stifling apathy, the desire to excel and to astonish, lead into the years of extravagance, the enforced voyage, the imposition of the Conseil Judiciaire. For the rest of his life, Baudelaire looked back on that imposition as the central catastrophe, deserved in its origins, disastrous in its effects. It left the practical burden of unpaid debts amassing increasing interest, and it permanently wounded his pride by the day-to-day *humiliasseries* of being legally a minor in the eyes of creditors or *concierges*, editors or enemies. For pride is at the centre of the human experience in the *Fleurs du Mal*, the *Paradis artificiels* and the *Petits poèmes en prose*, whether as the urge to transcend the limitations of man's condition or as the source of individual dignity, shown in 'Assommons les Pauvres' to be so different from the mechanical theories of utopian social reformers. A pattern is established, of vast ambitions – 'je suis un esprit à projets, moi: ... un violent désir de tout embrasser' – of endless pro-crastination, remorse, terror, apathy, and sudden explosions of creative activity.

'La terreur qui me mine' sometimes takes specific forms, serious or trivial – fear of individuals or events, fear of opening a letter or of the ringing of the door-bell, fear of the city, of illness, poverty, age or death; but often it is pathologically indefinable and all-embracing: 'une peur perpétuelle et un malheur vague', 'l'état d'angoisse et de terreur nerveuse'; worst of all, it comes to con-centrate on the struggle to create: 'la peur de voir s'user et péricliter et disparaître l'admirable faculté poétique, la netteté des idées, et la puissance d'espérance qui constituent en réalité mon capital, c'est là que gît ma principale frayeur', 'si j'allais sentir mon cerveau dé-périr', 'l'idée folle de mon impuissance littéraire': he compares this malady with that of Gérard de Nerval: 'la peur de ne plus pouvoir penser, ni écrire une ligne'. Once the lines are written, to the end of his life, each time acceptance of an article is delayed or refused, he has the conviction that no one will ever again publish a word of his. The brilliant Fancioulle, in 'Une Mort héroïque', could blot out the threat of death by absorption in his acting, but fell dead when he thought his art had been rejected by the public.

The letters rarely show that 'féconde paresse' evoked in the poems (though one adumbrates the lovely little prose poem 'Le Port'); they analyse, in infinitely varied monotony, the overwhelming sense of apathy: 'engourdissement', 'maussaderie', 'marasme', 'paresse', 'abî-mes d'indolence', 'fainéantise', 'atonie', 'hideuse léthargie', 'A quoi bon?, que m'importe?', 'une absence totale de désirs, une impossibilité de trouver un amusement quelconque, le véritable esprit de spleen . . .' In two ways they go to the roots of tragedy. First in their sense of the interplay of external force and inner flaw – 'par ma faute et sans ma faute'; one or the other may be highlighted at a given moment (as with the persecutions in 'Bénédiction' or the self-disgust of 'L'Examen de Minuit'), but we move between two convictions of equal strength. Secondly, in Baudelaire's probing of the psychosomatic. Again and again he comes back to the vicious circle: 'Est-ce le physique malade qui diminue l'esprit et la volonté, ou est-ce la lâcheté spirituelle qui fatigue le corps?'. The prose poems set medical and metaphysical explanations of man's strangest aberrations side by side and suggest acceptance of the metaphysical; similarly in the letters, seeking to preserve man's most precious faculty, his will-power, from physical determinism, Baudelaire comes back to his persistent belief in a satanic force of evil (as in the famous argument with Flaubert), for Satan the Tempter suggests at least some possibility of resistance to temptation.

And yet . . . as Poulet-Malassis points out to him, in the first version of the *Paradis artificiels* he had called will-power not the most precious of man's faculties, but 'de tous les *organes* le plus précieux'. Baudelaire, agreeing that, grammatically speaking, he was wrong, yet insists that 'j'avais voulu, par cette violation du langage, faire comprendre quelque chose'. The general problem is moreover con-sciously associated with the more specific one of his venereal in-fection; while an early letter to his step-brother treats this in the obligatory 'man-of-the-world' tones, later letters to Poulet-Malassis, repeatedly urging him not to assume himself cured, culminate in the significant reflection: 'Il y a des gens qui vivent soixante ans avec le sang infecté. Mais moi, *cela me fait peur*, ne fût-ce qu'à cause de la mélancolie que cela engendre.'

To pick out such central strains is of course to see only one part of the letters. And one of the values of this collection is that the reader can follow in detail the chronology of Baudelaire's complex develop-ment. If there subsist sadly few letters from some important stages – the years when most of the first *Fleurs du Mal* are being written, or the events of 1848 – other key moments stand out. The discovery of Poe is not that of a disciple in search of a master but the delight of finding an alter ego who proved that from the same sufferings and problems a work of art could be made; it is while translating him that Baudelaire comes more and more to see his own struggles not simply as those of a sinner but as those of a poet.

The great burst of creative energy in which the finest poems for the second edition of the *Fleurs du Mal* were achieved is a reaction to the legal suppression of six poems – for which he substitutes more than thirty, written, he says, 'à tout casser, comme une explosion de gaz chez un vitrier'. For the prolonged moods of stagnation culminate in two kinds of explosive force: sometimes in an almost supernatural sense of rejuvenation, sometimes in an outburst of fury at conventional stupidity; and with the creative renewal comes the renewed reflection on the paradox of how such powers are not the necessary outcome of toil, will-power or virtue.

The multiplicity of plans shows the desire for fame in every genre in favour at the time – short story, novel, theatre, criticism, translations, collected reflections, provocative study of a foreign country; the discussions of the intentions for the play *L'Ivrogne* are among the most suggestive. The 'practical' projects leave one with some intriguing visions of the might-have-been: Baudelaire as a theatre manager (he already aroused enough surprise by suggesting that the Gaîté produce Diderot's *Est-il bon, est-il méchant?* whereas it kept to a safe menu of melodramas); Baudelaire being received into the astounded French Academy; even Baudelaire accompanying Nadar in his balloon from Brussels to Paris (though he is fairly quick to provide a substitute for this expedition).

Behind all this is an allusive but varied and often penetrating insight into a whole period. The world of official and of hand-to-mouth journalism and of publishing is close enough to Balzac's *Illusions perdues*; the shuttle-service or passing-the-buck system for holding off creditors emerges in all its shifts and disastrous ingenuities. The Baudelaire who declared himself depoliticized by the events of 1851 still finds constantly that 'on est contraint de s'intéresser à toutes ces vieilles folies humaines', discusses the flaws and the future of the Second Empire or praises Proudhon as an economist, intends to write a refutation of Napoleon III's preface to *César*, reads and briefly comments on various political works.

Fully developed literary discussions are rare – among the most interesting and important are letters to the minor poet Soulary, to Swinburne and to Flaubert on *Salammbô* –but the choice, from the mass of contemporaries, of his favourite writers is expert: Barbey d'Aurevilly, Gautier, Banville, Flaubert, Leconte de Lisle, Chateaubriand, Balzac, Stendhal, Mérimée, Vigny. Many brief but strong comments on past and present authors and articles are illuminating when set beside their works or Baudelaire's other writings – from his keen and angry advice to Poulet-Malassis on what to include in a series of eighteenth-century authors to his fury at attacks on Heine.

The letters also provide specially valuable evidence in the perennial argument about the 'sincerity' of Baudelaire's critical articles. The genuineness of his admiration for Gautier has been questioned; here he is seen remarking that Gautier is the one candidate 'dont l'élection réhabiliterait l'Académie', persuading Delacroix to read *Mademoiselle de Maupin*, finding 'des beautés étonnantes' in *Le Capitaine Fracasse*, repeatedly returning to Gautier's article on him as the one which best represented his works.

Other problems of sincerity face authors who must write to thank acquaintances for their books: a brilliant example of Baudelaire's sardonic technique is the letter to Feydeau about his novel *Fanny*, as famous in its time as *Madame Bovary*. Far from producing generalized flattery, Baudelaire's letter first picks out, as if Feydeau had possessed them, the qualities he would admire in a contemporary novelist (art of construction, analytical and suggestive treatment of the tensions of the hyper-civilized in the Parisian city background), then devastatingly suggests, beneath a transparent pretence of praise, his own reactions (a novel of veiled hypocrisy, where the lover becomes unintentionally comic); the *coup de grâce* comes, when we remember Baudelaire's antipathies, in an ingenuous parallel with George Sand. The phrase he used about his Hugo article: 'Je n'ai pas menti, j'ai esquivé' fits his reactions to this novel, which he found 'archi-répugnant', in keeping with his lasting hatred for sly pornography; to Sainte-Beuve who wrote for information about erotica published in Belgium he replied that he had never acquired any of these 'livres imbéciles', not even those with fine printing and engravings. Whether in articles or letters, Baudelaire's literary criticism is almost always two-edged, and demands a specially alert reading.

Engravings, fine printing, the whole wide and detailed world of the visual arts is Baudelaire's abiding passion. The letters to him appropriately begin with his early and enormous debts to the dealer Arondel for paintings of doubtful authenticity; throughout his life, even in his most impoverished moments, he acquires paintings, drawings, engravings, porcelain, a lacquer desk, and gives loving and detailed instructions for their restoration, mounting, repair. The beautiful bindings he caused to be created for his books were proverbial among his friends. During his years in Belgium, he longs more and more frequently to be back at peace among 'mes collections', which he had sent in many packing-cases to his mother in Honfleur. His favourite photographic portrait of himself, by Carjat, has as its background a double row of his engravings. His direct relations with Delacroix, Courbet, Meryon, Constantin Guys, Legros, Daumier, Manet, Whistler, Fantin-Latour, Félicien Rops run through many letters; one in this edition includes minor but significant variants to his famous appreciation of Meryon. Asides and plans for further articles are rich in allusive indications both of developing principles and immediate personal reactions. On this aspect of Baudelaire's interests, where so much has been investigated in recent years, much still remains to be discovered or discussed.

The volume of letters addressed to Baudelaire contains a varied cross-section of contemporary reactions: sustained exchanges of serious discussion (Flaubert, Sainte-Beuve, Hugo, Manet, Soulary), practical details of finance and publishing, quarrels and reconciliations with friends and editors, protective friendship from the Lejosne circle or the outspoken and witty Madame Paul Meurice, reproaches from a colonel for his attack on the painter Charlet, praise from a naval administrator for his work on Poe, outpourings of gratitude from Wagner, penetrating observations from Delacroix, Taine's brief remarks on Poe, sensitive and stimulating reflections from Villiers de l'Isle-Adam, and an assortment of heterogeneous tributes from admirers, in prose or verse. With very rare exceptions, the verse offerings make one understand all too well why Baudelaire had no desire for disciples, and why he hated to be thought of as 'Le Prince des Charognes'.

The critical apparatus in these three volumes is outstanding for its clarity and coverage, its succint use of space and choice of moments for more elucidation. The biographical notes sometimes have a personal touch that might have appealed to Baudelaire, giving short shrift to some individuals (Alphonse and Félicité Baudelaire, or E. Deschanel as an academic careerist), moving warmly to the defence of others (Montalembert, or the polyglot *comparatiste* at whose French Baudelaire makes a sharp thrust). Acknowledgements to predecessors, and to younger scholars who have themselves benefited from M. Pichois's advice, are generous; occasionally more detailed references to their works might be added.

With such a multiplicity of varied and valuable information on a whole period, the problem of indexing is particularly important; M. Pichois did not have available here the space for the equivalent of the splendid 'index onomastique et idéologique' that so many scholars appreciated in the Conard edition. To make the maximum of material easy to consult, he has provided in the Pléiade volumes the following: at the beginning, a twenty-five page chronology of Baudelaire's finances written by Jean Ziegler; at the end, a *Répertoire* giving information and brief critical comments on some 170 of the people most often mentioned in the letters, followed by seven separate indexes of names of people and characters, names of places, Baudelaire's addresses, Baudelaire's ways of signing, Baudelaire's works, the works of Poe, titles of periodicals and of works by other authors or artists.

The division between indexes gives rise to some difficulties and some gaps; scholars will be grateful for the amount that has been included, and for the excellent principle that allusions and suppositions, where the name does not figure in the text, should be noted in the indexes, although the principle has not always been put fully into practice. The major disappointment is that it was possible to index only the text and not the great body of important ancillary material in the notes, and that no index could be provided for the *Lettres à Baudelaire*.

The Crépet edition, as Claude and Vincenette Pichois would certainly wish, will continue to be used, both for some of its more extended notes and for the convenience of its index; but the present volumes, with their revised text and datings and the incorporation of so much new material, textual or critical, will be the essential tool. They should rapidly run into re-editions, where certain minor details will be corrected. Among the very occasional slips, Poe's *Gold Bug* has become the *Golden ·Bug*; a note on La Harpe (I, 922) overlooks Baudelaire's deliberate irony. To the letters indicated by allusions should be added one from Constantin Guys in London (I, 670), planning a work on the Venus de Milo and asking Baudelaire to send him a note of all writings and hypotheses on the famous statue.

In the notes there are occasional gaps in the references to the Conard edition and in the system of asterisks; on rare occasions, a date or page reference has been corrected on one occurrence and not in the cross-reference. Points of this kind are exceptionally few in nearly three thousand pages. A sample comparison of a few texts with available facsimiles suggested one or two minimal misreadings: an intrusive *ils* (I, 413, 1.8), *indispensable* instead of 'indiscernable' (note *b* to I, 669), some details in the letters from Flaubert. In a new edition, the problems raised by the texts of one or two poems included in the letters, as compared with the material used in the admirable critical edition of the *Fleurs du Mal*, would need further elucidation.

The present editors, from their exceptional knowledge, provide an edition which it will be, for many, a scholarly necessity and, for still more, a sheer pleasure to possess. Baudelaire himself was a by-word for his meticulous care over the correction and physical presentation of a text. To him, both the meaning and the pleasure afforded by a book depended on its elegance: paper, type-face, spacing on the page, frontispiece and *cul-de-lampe*, binding; discussing these with a publisher in his later years he wrote that 'je ne tire vanité que d'une seule vertu, c'est de l'amour du métier'. To the very end, the letters show in detail the persistence and the vitality of this *conscience professionnelle*, his most fundamental faith.

Throughout, too, they suggest how essential it is to see and interpret even the most often-quoted of Baudelaire's pronouncements in the full context both of chronology and of particular intentions – from the child deliberately half-mocking at his polite adherence to the conventional behaviour of a younger brother to the later 'fin manœuvrier' addressing to mother or friends a searing analysis of his own nature – while consciously directing it so as to achieve quite specific effects at particular moments of crisis. Finally, a comment on a work he admired in 1860 suggests his most fundamental preoccupation: 'C'est partout le Génie qui pactise avec le Destin: «Laisse-moi comprendre *tes lois*, et je te tiens quitte des vulgaires jouissances de la vie, des vides consolations de l'Erreur».'

NOTE

1 This essay originally appeared in the *Times Literary Supplement* as a review of *Correspondance*, Volume I: 1832–1860, 1, 114 pp. Volume II: 1860–1866, 1, 149 pp. Edited by Claude Pichois with Jean Ziegler, Paris: Gallimard, 1973; *Lettres à Charles Baudelaire*, Edited by Claude Pichois with Vincenette Pichois. 408 pp. Neuchâtel: A la Baconnière, 1973.

16

The new Pléiade edition of Baudelaire's Complete Works (1977)[1]

The publication of this fundamentally new Pléiade edition of Baudelaire is a major event. These two volumes are not simply the latest revision of a work which has come to be, in successive versions, both the prized possession of many non-academic readers and a standard text for scholars; they mark a deliberate change in editorial principles.

In 1931, when Baudelaire (then edited by Y.-G. Le Dantec) was the first author to be chosen for the Pléiade, that series was intended to give the general reader, in convenient compass and fine format, a reliable text and variants, with minimal annotation. During the near half-century since, factual and textual discoveries have progressed; critical illuminations (or sometimes obfuscations) have proliferated. Claude Pichois, who from the 1960s has been responsible for succinctly and skilfully incorporating corrections and additions into successive editions, has now undertaken a total revision. While still intending these volumes for 'le grand public', he sets out to provide, for each of Baudelaire's works, a detailed survey of existing knowledge and a personal approach to recent critical judgments.

Clearly a titanic task, and one which requires very tricky decisions as to just what choice from the superabundant material may best fit the needs of those two mythically separated entities – general reader and dedicated scholar. M. Pichois's exceptional breadth of experience qualifies him for the challenge. Over the years, the Pléiade Baudelaire has moved from two volumes to the highly convenient single-volume edition, and now back to two. In Volume I are the main creative works – poems, translations of poems, prose poems; studies on hashish and opium; essays and short stories; plans for the theatre; the so-called diaries and the notebooks; in Volume II, the critical writings on literature, the visual arts and music; the material on Belgium; and finally a selection of newspaper articles. Within the main sections, the order is, as far as possible, chronological. Texts and variants have been collated with all known manuscripts, proofs or editions. If comparisons with facsimiles, or internal evidence, may occasionally suggest slightly different readings, this is certainly, overall, the text which comes closest to Baudelaire's intentions.

One subsidiary but strongly felt protest might be raised by those to whom, as to Baudelaire, visual presentation of the poem on the page affects its impact. In all previous Pléiade editions the principle subsisted that the poems (differently treated from the prose work) should remain free of numerical references to footnotes. The text of the poems now not only bristles with figures and italic letters (at once too large to be unobtrusive and too tiny for rapid consultation); it has also been numbered by fives in the margin, so that in some lines of poetry the last word has had to be skied or dropped. The effect of sudden hiccup this produces, even if one appreciates the editor's problems, and those of coherence within a series, may leave readers nostalgic for the past uncluttered text of the poems.

No one will expect startling discoveries of unknown writings, but this edition adds both some new material and some which up to now could be consulted only in scattered specialist publications; we have, to take a few examples, one or two very early poems; the schoolboy's Latin verses; the intriguing if unsuccessful effort at a prose translation of Longfellow's *Hiawatha*; marginal annotations on books read; notes on literary predecessors for defence at the trial; a complete reading (established jointly with Jean Ziegler) of the *Carnets*; a partly new selection of works attributed to Baudelaire or written in collaboration. This is the only edition to include, at the end of Volume II, examples of the kind of journalism to which Baudelaire contributed in the late 1840s, some scurrilous and frivolous, some of serious political moment. Definite attribution remains hypothetical (as M. Pichois indicates in his thoughtful caveat); the choice gives a sense of the atmosphere and problems of the period. Two additions to past Pléiade volumes are especially welcome. First, the bold innovation of reproducing, complete with its lively illustrations, the *Salon caricatural de 1846* (where again Baudelaire's contribution remains conjectural); second, and most important of all, the inclusion of all Baudelaire's introductions to his Poe translations.

It is of course the new notes which are the nub of this edition.

What were once 300 pages of elucidation have now swelled to over 1,500, providing a treasure-house – and a treasure-hunt. No one will expect M. Pichois to mince words, whether in praise or in blame. Faced by the increasingly intractable problem of choosing from the sheer bulk of Baudelairian bibliography, he has decided to mention only works held to deserve discussion; in a typically elegant and provocative aside he remarks that, given the flood of present publications, authors he omits may feel free to attribute their absence to 'un réel oubli' rather than to intended condemnation.

Very many readers will undoubtedly appreciate the thoughtful and challenging introductions to each section, and, in the notes, the swift, skilful summaries of vast swathes of critical controversy, (eight pages of small print on responses to the Lévi-Strauss/Roman Jakobson dissection of 'Les Chats'; twelve on 'Correspondances', etc). Is there a danger that, precisely because of the richness of annotation (with direct quotation from recent articles running to some length), some may misinterpret the editor's intentions by imagining that he has provided a conveniently predigested compendium of All We Need to Know? His introductions make generous reference to certain major predecessors or contemporaries (Crépet, Pommier, Prévost, Blin, Bandy, Austin, Leakey and others) and to such younger scholars as D. J. Kelley; in selecting salient points, whether from these, from his own critical editions, or from those by his disciples (Robert Kopp on the prose poems, Michèle Stäuble-Lipman Wulf on de Quincey) he has clearly decided not to preempt the full detail offered elsewhere.

The treasure-hunt is guided by six valuable indexes. Four, established by Vincenette Pichois (characters, place-names, periodicals, allegories and personifications), are skilled in the expert indexer's art of catching up allusions where the name itself is not mentioned; an interesting reference to Mallarmé is among a few which have been overlooked. Jean Ziegler lists information on individuals mentioned in the *Carnets*, and M. Pichois himself compiles highly helpful summaries on painters, sculptors and engravers, indicating also where reproductions of their works may be seen in recent studies. Occasional omissions or minor misprints will easily be rectified in future editions – where all readers will fervently hope that the indexes, and the select bibliographies, may be extended to cover the very rich resources of the notes as well as simply Baudelaire's texts.

From these rich resources, what main suggestions emerge?

Baudelaire's creative ambition, rather than the sexual or religious problems so much studied hitherto, is taken as the nodal point; his will to writing as the proof of worth turns to experimentation with widely differing genres in which sudden success had been achieved by contemporaries (short story, theatre, novel, essay, *chanson* ...). Abortive plans and part-failures may often illuminate his greatest works. There is also the need to see him not as our own 'timeless' contemporary but as an individual, subject to changing views, and experimenting with the themes, conventions and vocabulary of his period.

The *Fleurs du Mal* are of course the most fully discussed. In the excellent conclusion to his 'notice' on the poems, after an inspiriting attack on the kind of criticism which assumes an inflated value for its own lucubrations and may smother rather than discover, M. Pichois suggests that what has been most neglected is a proper study of Baudelaire's own thoughts on the deeply-rooted and subtle powers of prosody. The need to sum up existing work, where suppositions about which woman a given poem was 'written for' have waxed so rife (here, a welcome scepticism has been directed at some lingering pseudo-biographical myths) has left relatively little space in the notes for close analysis. Since the first volume of the present Pléiade appeared, there has been much welcome new work on those sound effects which its editor suggests as vital.

'Sources' are out of favour today, but, if M. Pichois pares away some of the wilder suppositions of the past, he goes to no fashionable extremes, but fully realizes both Baudelaire's retentive memory and his love of weaving suggestive variations on inherited themes. There are telling remarks on parallels with Gautier, Nerval, Sainte-Beuve and Hugo, and above all on Baudelaire's pre-Proustian skill in deliberate 'pastiche d'admiration'.

Among very many seminal asides is the observation that foreigners find it easier than the French to appreciate the *Petits Poèmes en Prose* (here given their alternative title *Le Spleen de Paris*). Is this perhaps because foreigners are less tied to the two French traditions: first, of setting new experiments under headings – classicism, romanticism, realism (traces of this intellectual game, skilfully played, survive in this edition) and second, of creating a hierarchy of genres (a tradition which caused Baudelaire himself, both in literature and criticism, some of his most productive struggles)? The startlingly original and disconcertingly varied forms of the *Petits Poèmes en Prose* still await full analysis, as do many sides of Baudelaire's creative art in prose: the hyper-conscious irony in the short story 'La Fanfarlo'; the deceptively informal penetration of the essay on toys; the balance of analytical and evocative power in the *Paradis artificiels*; the intensely individual use of language in the art criticism. The present edition offers constant incitement.

Baudelaire's adaptation of De Quincey is seen as a rare example of how a foreign work may be acclimatized in France – as with Galland's version of the *Arabian Nights*. In the literary criticism, the *Madame Bovary* article is singled out for its art of imaginative identification; we have also a valuable exposition of the facts and pressures behind articles written for a contemporary anthology of poetry. The way is now open, long years after Margaret Gilman's fine study, for a new appreciation of Baudelaire's critical skills as drawing challenge from importunate circumstance: how his persistent and passionate analysis of interaction between author and public determines the means to success, deserved or undeserved; his ability to play subtly on insinuation, irony or pastiche so as to convey pointed reservations without undermining either personal enthusiasm or reflective principle.

The same complexities underlie the art criticism, increasingly seen today as revealing more of Baudelaire than necessarily of the artists concerned. His gradual formulation of ideas around that most slippery of all terms, 'modernité', is reassessed, as are his varying views on major artists (Delacroix, Ingres, Daumier, Courbet, Meryon, Manet), and on individuals, major or minor, to whom the poet attributes the qualities he himself most longs to possess. Traditional surprise subsists around Baudelaire's choice of Constantin Guys: Guys who fascinated him partly through the suggestions inherent in ephemeral modes, partly through command of a swiftly executed and immediately communicative stylization, however dangerously near to stereotype.

In the section on music, the Wagner article, fully set in its background, is shown as focusing and extending Baudelaire's major and manifold preoccupations at a particularly creative period of his life. From early years, two persistent threads interweave in his thinking: the search for underlying unity behind the different art forms, and the deep suspicion of any false or blurring impingements of one on the other.

In the personal notebooks, with their interplay of insight and aggression, principle and paradox, this edition brings out the very different intentions behind Baudelaire's different headings: *Fusées, Mon Cœur mis à nu, Hygiène.* The copious notes for the projected book on Belgium are sifted and explained (for complete details of the newspaper cuttings which Baudelaire collected often as much for style as for substance, the scholar will go back to the Crépet–Pichois edition). If, in this last of Baudelaire's efforts, much spins off as the spume of an exasperated sensibility consciously facing final crisis, yet it holds also the poet's last experiences of fragile tranquillity or renewed aesthetic discovery.

The Pléiade edition has now added multiple concordances to the text. Readers of very different interests will owe a deep debt of gratitude to the editor, whether for the prolonged, patient scholarship which has given us the most complete and accurate existing presentation of the collected texts, or for the vital stimulus to new discussion and discovery offered in his firm personal assessments. This new edition suggests more clearly than ever before both the interdependence of Baudelaire's widespread experiments, and the ways in which his masterpieces typify yet transcend the particular pressures of his times.

NOTE

1 This essay originally appeared in the *Times Literary Supplement* as a review of *Œuvres complètes*, edited by Claude Pichois. Volume 1: 1,604 pp. Volume 2: 1,691 pp. Paris: Gallimard, Bibliothèque de la Pléiade, 1975, 1976.

PART THREE

Nerval

17

An approach to Nerval (1961)

The immensely increasing volume of detailed and often valuable research on Nerval has made it difficult for any but the most impenitent specialist to pretend to an understanding or an appreciation of his works. A generation ago it was easier to enjoy him with a clear conscience, and he was no recognized part of academic studies. Since then he has made a triumphal progress from log cabin to White House, and academic consecration was reached when he became a set author for the Agrégation. Even then, the Sorbonne seemed unhappy about how he might best be approached, for to their list of recommended reading they added the unusual, suggestive and badly-needed cautionary footnote: 'De valeur très inégale.'

When affectionate condescension for the charming minor romantic with a touching love-life and engaging eccentricities gave way to apotheosis, the results were at first chaotic and often unfortunate. The Nerval of the 1940s was often seen as a seer, communicating a gospel of transcendental value. Instead of his lobster on a blue ribbon he now held as obligatory attribute the cross of saints and martyrs, the lore-book of the illuminist, the alchemist's retort or the pack of tarot cards, when he was not reclining on the psychoanalyst's couch. Albert Béguin[1] would have wished to make him a Catholic 'sans le savoir'; Jean Richer[2] in his earlier investigations found a mystical revelation based on occult traditions compounded of neo-platonism, cabbalism, free-masonry, arithmology and even astrology. Under Sébillotte's promising title *Le Secret de Nerval*[3] lay the the conclusion that the real secret was sexual inadequacy. G. Le Breton's discovery[4] of allusions to alchemy and tarot cards forced on *nervaliens* an important 'crise de conscience' which was not always adequately faced: annotators tended simply to allow the possibility that this or that detail might have these associations rather than discussing the consequences to central meaning and value in such a range of reference.

An Étiemble might well have written 'Le Mythe de Nerval'. Myths die hard, but recent criticism has discarded most of the extravagances of pseudo-biographical[5] and occult approach, is trying to appreciate not the man or the seer, but the artist, and is moving away from the position which Jean Prévost so aptly attacked when he wrote: 'Beaucoup adorent en Nerval son mystère plus que son génie; c'est un prétexte à majuscules plutôt qu'un objet d'examen.'[6]

But the first stages in making him an 'objet d'examen' have added to the difficulties of appreciation. The Pléiade edition has amassed some three thousand pages of his writings and is far from complete; the first of seven projected volumes of *Œuvres complémentaires*[7] has appeared. The cross-currents of allusion from one work to another are probably more important in Nerval than in any other author, and the most minor articles he wrote can suddenly illuminate central problems. Yet this new interest brings a new danger. Already a kind of spiritual snobbery, or an honest attachment to the object of much toil, had tended to surround the most 'difficult' works with an aura of suspect supremacy; now it is the hitherto neglected ones which are sometimes given an inflated value. To say, for instance, that the *Histoire de la Reine du Matin* is 'un des sommets de l'œuvre de Nerval, sa véritable expression' is, I think, to confuse representative with artistic value.

Thanks to many patient studies, we now know much more of Nerval's wildly heterogeneous reading and of his affinities with those authors he has 'convertis en sang et nourriture': Goethe, Hoffmann, Apuleius, Rousseau, Rétif de la Bretonne, Scarron, Cazotte and many more. These are not just material for source-grubbing: the resonances Nerval draws from them are an essential part of his meaning.

Precisely because of this abundance of material, the problem of the nature and value of Nerval's art involves a severe 'examen de conscience', an 'examen de conscience' that is perhaps particularly painful for those whose business, or whose pleasure, it is to introduce students to his work. It is not surprising that G. Rouger shudders at the vision of a slender text smothered under a 'débauche d'herméneutique' and retreats as many have done to the suggestion: 'Qu'il nous suffise d'écouter les vers des *Chimères* avec délices, comme de la musique.'[8] Have things come to the stage where Nerval can be appreciated only by two extremes: the dilettante content to let the poem make a lovely sound, or the specialist with a lifetime to give to one author?

The impenitent enjoyers have to find a way out. I should like here, while very conscious of the dangers of over-simplification, and knowing that I shall touch on points which other critics have been aware of in slightly different contexts,[9] to suggest a method of approach to what I consider Nerval's central works: *Les Chimères* and *Sylvie*. For I think it essential, in any honest approach, to see how far, when these works are read closely, in themselves and without apparatus of notes, there emerge a worth-while meaning and an art, a meaning and an art which make Nerval neither just the poet of the music-makers nor the delight of the juggler with cryptograms and crossword-puzzles. After, but only after, this initial impact, the further allusions which research has discovered or has still to discover come to enrich and to underline something which should make its central effect unaided.

First, *Les Chimères*. The challenge of this strange form with its apparently random, dissociated and unelucidated images, and the processes gone through by the reader's mind as he attempts gradually to sort them out, are an essential part of the meaning. The form is not just one way of expressing sense, but forces a re-enactment of that process about which the *Chimères* are written.

Their first impact conveys two impressions: music and dissociated images. The music does not lull or jingle; it has a particular quality (shared perhaps only by Mallarmé and Valéry), rich, closely-knit and haunting, which imprints lines and stanzas in the memory before they have been understood and without conscious learning-by-heart. This, surely, is a first absolute essential for 'obscure' poetry. Why otherwise, unless just as puzzle-solving, idle curiosity or academic habit, should one go further? It is only when the poem has bitten itself inescapably into the mind and become an incantation that it forces conscious intellect and subconscious faculties to follow up its suggestions. Mallarmé's *Le Démon de l'Analogie* offers an allegory of how this kind of poetry works: it is because the musical and apparently meaningless phrase 'la pénultième est morte' echoes infuriatingly in his mind that he is forced to search dictionary meanings, musical associations, imaginative links and elaborations of all kinds until a pattern forms. The search into the allusions of 'obscure' poetry should be neither dutiful nor gratuitous, but simply inescapable because of its echo in the mind and the sensibility, and only a particularly obsessive music can ensure this.

The music of the *Chimères* has not yet been as fully analyzed as it deserves. To mention only one most obvious point, no-one has discussed the astonishing variations on the 'rime riche' and their echoes within the lines; and that no-one has done so is significant. For usually the 'rime riche' makes blatant calls on the attention by its sheer virtuosity or by contrast with the flat or contorted line used to lead up to it. In Nerval the density and suggestiveness of both sound and allusion throughout the sonnets are such that the rhyme passes almost unnoticed as a fitting part of the whole. The delicacy, subtlety and precision of the musical effects in a form so demanding as the sonnet are in themselves a guarantee that Nerval is not the dreamer in a state of automatism but is consciously and lucidly shaping his material.[10]

The first effect is an obsessive incantation; the second the kaleidoscopic shift and play of dissociated images. There have been many efforts to find 'La Clef des Chimères'; I should suggest that one important key not only to their meaning but to their form is to be found not outside but within them, at its clearest in the sequence of five sonnets *Le Christ aux Oliviers*. Vigny's poem on the same subject and taken from the same source is set within the bounds of a human, 'realistic' scene; his Christ takes for granted that a plan exists behind the universe and the reproach is that the Creator has not revealed it. Nerval evokes at its utmost the cosmic terror of being hurled through fantastic spaces to find only purposelessness and chaos. The full meaning of the fourth sonnet which follows has not, I think, been looked at closely. Unable to find God, the absolute good, Christ turns to Judas: His terror of chaos is such that He would be reassured by the existence of absolute evil, for this at least would provide a purpose and a pattern behind things. But that absolute too crumbles: Judas is no mighty criminal but a mere mercenary disgusted with his petty reward, and already beginning to experience bitter remorse. It is no plan which brings about Christ's death: Pilate 'sentant quelque pitié, se tourna *par hasard*'. Nerval has pushed to its pitch the anguished fear of a blind chance ruling a wheeling chaos. Then comes the last sonnet, with its triumphant answer. Christ is yet another in a sequence of sacrificed victims, struggling, cast down and resuscitated in turn. Icarus, Phaeton, Atys, each succeeds the other and the ritual is endlessly repeated. I should stress as vital that the answer is rationally inexplicit. There is no reply to the questions, no logically exposed philosophy and no defined faith; simply the terror of chaos gives way to ordered pattern as the repeated sacrifice – *oublié, perdu, meurtri* – is followed by the rebirth – *remontait, ranime*. After the total disintegration of the universe, the horror of chance and chaos, the one elemental security of an ordered pattern emerges.

Le Christ aux Oliviers is more discursive, more dilute and more explicit than the rest of the *Chimères*. In the others, the form itself is part of the working of the central meaning. Their first impression is of dissociation and mystery; slowly, as they lie in the mind, associations make links and take shape. Constantly the evocation of the random and the chaotic works out into the satisfaction and reassurance of recognizing parallel and repeated patterns. One remembers Valéry's phrase: 'Créer une angoisse pour la résoudre.' The detailed intellectual or associative meanings of the final pattern are secondary. The shift of mood from chaos to pattern, from terror to consolation, is the core of what Nerval has to convey (and he is always lucid and modest enough not to confuse consolation with truth). The content of the pattern may matter less than the fact of its triumphant appearance out of chaos and the new kind of expression given to this basic human need.

Behind the shaping of ritual repetitions in the *Chimères* there are, of course, and are meant to be, many levels of association with their own parallel meanings. Meanings personal to Nerval in his struggles through illusion to lucidity. Meanings that are partly political and run parallel with those of the Parnassians under the Second Empire: the spirit of opposition constantly repressed and constantly about to rise, though the time is not yet ripe. Meanings that call up the central myths of humanity on the hero's descent into hell and the eternal return, on the rebirth of the Golden Age, or Nature myths on the cycle of Spring reborn after Winter. Constancy echoes again and again in the obsessive *encor* and *toujours*, and the verbs press home their reiteration: *rends-moi, rouvert, ressème, recommence, reconnais, reviendront, ramener, se releva, rapporte, reparais* . . .

Even if *El Desdichado* is the best known, it is perhaps worth looking at it as if one had never seen it before, and discovering how it can simply in itself convey a meaning and a value which detailed research does thoroughly enrich but does not alter. Its first effect is deliberately one of dreamlike, unconnected and unelucidated images. But one thing is utterly clear: the syntax. By contrast with Mallarmé, certain simple verbal phrases give a time-sequence and a general sense which works its way out regardless of detailed allusions. '*Je suis* le ténébreux' (present sorrow); 'Toi qui *m'as consolé*' (past comfort); '*Rends-moi*' (desire for renewal); '*Suis-je* Amour ou Phébus?' (hesitation over the nature of self); 'mon front *est rouge encor* du baiser' (persistence of past joy); finally the climax of repeated victories in '*J'ai deux fois* vainqueur ... Modulant sur la lyre ...'. Loss, hesitation, fugitive and strange beauty, renewed consolation and final victory through a song gradually emerge before any detailed elucidation.

Another kind of pattern forms from images showing light suddenly plunged into darkness, darkness giving way miraculously to light. The struggle between despair and ecstasy, the pause in the half-light of dream and hesitation, the reiterated victory are given through the sensuous effect of the intensely rapid shift and play of light and dark.

Many of the images or proper names have general associations that begin to make parallel suggestions. A medieval Prince has lost his kingdom; a lute-player sings of the deprivations of courtly love. His lute is decked with the star that is the symbol of his lady; then it becomes the lyre of Orpheus who descended into the underworld to find a lost love and lost her yet again; Orpheus whose singing magically vanquished the whole world; Orpheus whose lute in legend became a constellation. Lusignan, if less familiar to English ears, would in France call up the legend of the fairy Mélusine, half-woman, half-serpent, so linking with the mermaid in the cavern; an enchantress lost through her lover's own fault; giving strange cries in the night around his castle: all this begins to fit with the theme of the elusive and enchanting – the mermaid, the lost Eurydice, the 'cris de la fée'.

There will be many details which ask for something further, but without any complex apparatus of notes, reiterated themes keep forming: a sequence of loss and consolation; doubt and hesitation shot through by memories of ecstasy; a sense of being alternately consecrated and bewitched, and the repeated conquest by the poet who has shaped a triumphant song out of loss and longing. Jean Richer, looking for an astrological enigma, speaks of this as a poem 'dénué de sens apparent'. One might go to the opposite extreme and see in it two of the best-known themes of the nineteenth century: the pursuit of the 'idéal insaisissable' and the assertion that memory and art triumph over time, change and death. But instead of anecdotal pathos or explicit argument, Nerval has found a form which involves all the reader's perceptions in following the shift from apparently random chaos to reiterated pattern.

Round this theme there are many other undertones. Names and images take on a fuller range of association when we can pick up their echoes from other works of Nerval. A network of reminiscences enriches the suggestive value, but constantly leads back to the same central theme.

The same is true of alchemy and the tarot cards. G. Le Breton has suggestively shown how in Dom Pernetty, whom Nerval read and mentioned in other works, expressions such as *Le ténébreux, le veuf, la nuit du tombeau, la Mer d'Italie, la grotte, la sirène, Achéron* and *Orphée* all stand for terms in the alchemical experiment. One might irreverently remark that if Pernetty could show in detail how Virgil's descent into the underworld was intended as an alchemical treatise, it is perhaps possible *après-coup* to force any literary work into the alchemical retort. Moreover the system of symbols among alchemists is so wildly varied and shifting that at times it seems as if anything may justifiably stand for anything. Yet, though I might disagree on some points of detail in M. Le Breton's analysis, the weight of the evidence certainly does go to show that Nerval is consciously recalling the alchemists. The essential point here is that alchemical symbolism, far from changing the meaning and intention, is simply a parallel way of enriching what I have suggested as the central preoccupation of the *Chimères*. In a sequence of repeated ritual stages the alchemist is seeking to refine crude undifferentiated matter, whose first state he often calls the chaotic, into gold or the elixir of life. He is concerned with the shaping of chaos, and with the struggle between the volatile and the fixed (echoing Nerval's evocation of the elusive and the permanent) and after each failure he sets out again and again on his experiment. To be able to trace in the poem the colour-sequences and the detailed references of alchemy brings a parallel set of suggestive associations to the same central theme: form emerging from chaos; the struggle between the shifting and the constant.

So too for the tarot cards. At the beginning of *El Desdichado* the fifteenth, sixteenth and seventeenth of the symbolic pictures of the fortune-telling pack are perhaps being laid in order before us. If so, and if we recognize them, the associations will again be with chance and hazard moving into some strange order (and we may remember how T. S. Eliot later uses the tarot pack to call up the conflict between the random and the patterned).

In Nerval's world a theme or an image has value perhaps less in itself than because it echoes, catches up and forms parallels and patterns with other themes and other images round the same centre. He is playing on two delights of the human mind – the half-magical and half-mathematical pleasure in the coinciding of patterns, which becomes richer as we recognize more of them. In *El Desdichado* the medieval lute-player, Orpheus, Lusignan the alchemist, Nerval the poet, all take up the same ritual sequence of human experience. *Delfica*, prophesying the rebirth of the past, beats out a variation on the famous prophecy of the Sybil in Virgil: 'Jam redit et Virgo, redeunt Saturnia regna', and weaves through it Goethe's *Kennst du das Land*. When the oppressors become the avengers in *A Madame Ida Dumas*, the figures of archangels, the Goths and Huns at the fall of the Roman Empire, the rebels in Nerval's own century and the poet himself are all associated in the greatest of the songs of the exiles, the Psalm *Super flumina Babylonis*.

To present the sonnets as, for example, a convinced statement of faith in positive religious syncretism, as is often done, is, I think, to simplify and falsify them. It is the sheer pattern of rebirth and not the content of what is reborn which matters to Nerval. And this is where he differs from the Parnassians who also present the succession of religions and the avenger in revolt. Leconte de Lisle and Ménard define explicitly and describe in detail the abstract and the historical qualities of the lost world they recall. In Nerval there rise again 'ces Dieux que tu pleures toujours' and 'l'ordre des anciens jours', but we know no more of them than that. We are made to experience intensely the fascination, consolation and confidence of seeing the traditions of the ages shape to the same ritual. This elemental experience evokes three main moods: timeless persistence, revolt and rebirth, and, in several sonnets, the pause of expectancy, a stilled motionless waiting, for the time is not yet ripe.

The tone of these concise and suggestive poems fuses in a new way the epic and the intimate, the cosmic and the personal. A litany of revolt calls up the avengers of the ages – Antaeus, Cain, Baal . . . – but it starts with a line that is bare, piercing and personal: 'Tu demandes pourquoi j'ai tant de rage au cœur.' In the briefest space the wheeling worlds, the ashes falling round vast horizons after volcanic eruption, the gods and heroes of Egypt, India, Greece or Phoenicia, the races and dynasties of the middle ages, form a background to something gently and almost conversationally intimate: 'Je pense à toi', 'Je sais pourquoi', 'Tu demandes pourquoi', 'Toi qui m'as consolé', 'La connais-tu?', 'protégeant tout seul ma mère', 'ces dieux que tu pleures toujours'. The imagery brings out the contrast and fusion of the elusive and the permanent, the frail and the firm, the tenuous and the solid. Against the immense still dignity of colonnades and arches in *Delfica* ('péristyle immense', 'sévère portique', 'arc de Constantin') are set the most delicate and graceful flowers and shrubs, slight and slender ('l'olivier, le myrte et les saules tremblants'), while past the motionless architecture winds the thread of a song, the lightest song of all, an 'ancienne romance'. The central figures unite implacability with delicacy, tenderness with ferocity, hesitation with persistence as in the graceful and biting line of *Antéros*: 'Et sur un col flexible une tête indomptée.' The conquest of chaos is wrought from human frailty as well as human force.

There are many details of the *Chimères* which have been illuminated by research; many remain mysterious and a challenge. The sense of an unelucidated and private range of reference is perhaps one of the deliberate threads of which the poems are woven; a cosmic and a private fate are being worked out at once, and of the private sense we may be given only glimpses. Some images will have too wide a range of possible associations, others too personal an interpretation to mean much without the most careful elucidation. But, between narrowing and rigidifying interpretations by pseudo-biography or literal belief in syncretism, and the defeatism that abandons everything to incantation, there is, I think, a body of meaning and value to be found in even the most obscure.

I have suggested that to Nerval it is less things in themselves that count than the fascination of echoes and parallels between things. The individual moment matters not for its uniqueness but for its place in a pattern of half-magical coincidence and reassuring permanence. The most basic activity of the human mind in general is of course the search for valid relationships between isolated objects. 'Rapports' is probably the key-word in Nerval's personal writings. In his daily experience the search for connections takes on an obsessional force and omens are read into the slightest event. But he is constantly aware of the dividing line, so difficult to draw, between the rational and the superstitious 'rapport'. The very instinctive and obsessive effect of certain patterns provokes in him an utterly lucid mistrust.[11] His mind tends to work in four stages. First, the bewilderment at the random and the chaotic; second, the weaving of patterns that are haunting but perhaps fallacious (absolute good and absolute evil in *Le Christ aux Oliviers*; the echo of the ideal between Adrienne and Aurélie in *Sylvie*); third, a lucid questioning and a gentle mockery directed at these fallacious patterns, and finally, when they have been undone, the discovery of a persuasive ritual cycle of human experience; a reconciliation with the relative and faulty, but lovely and persistent, nature of things.

The poetry is less concerned with the direct questioning of fallacious patterns (it gives merely the moments of hesitation); the more leisurely prose of *Sylvie* has space for the weaving and undoing of the obsession before the final discovery. Here the obsession is seen as an obsession, not as a truth; the utter lucidity behind the evoking and destroying of a dream is one of the main values of *Sylvie*.

Sylvie used to be read as a delightful country idyll. Reaction set in and it became 'le poème de la fin du monde', a 'bilan de la faillite' – 'Sylvie s'achève en débâcle'. Here I disagree, and think that the undertones of the last chapter have been overlooked, and with them some of the use of themes and form throughout the story.

The outline is simple: the narrator had pursued in the actress Aurélie the reflection of the 'idéal sublime' once seen in the child Adrienne; not only had this reflection of the ideal proved illusory but in its pursuit he had let slip Sylvie, 'la douce réalité'. Summarized in this form, it sounds like an obvious temptation to various kinds of insufferable romanticization: it might either glorify the ideal as a metaphysical super-reality, or twist round to give an equally spurious glorification to the lost Sylvie, or finally exalt loss, anguish and hankering after the impossible as superior values in themselves. And the story is often presented as if Nerval were doing one or other or all of these. Quite the contrary. The obsession by Adrienne and Aurélie is worked out not in supernatural but in human terms, and every detail of background is made to suggest that it is as fallacious as it is gripping and lovely. The narrator is neither psychopath nor prophet; he analyses lucidly the conditions which cause sensitive minds in his generation to set woman on a pedestal and fear to approach her, since feelings have been distorted in the moulds both of inherited idealism and of inherited cynicism.[12] Then, though Adrienne deliberately suggests the archetypal figures of Queen and Saint, Aurélie the Enchantress and the Siren, and Sylvie the strange Fairy, yet the sense of dream and illusion that surrounds them is woven from the live details of an everyday world with its children's games and folk-songs, its plays in the convent or on the Paris stage. The hero is haunted by the idea that Aurélie strangely recalls Adrienne, but the echoes between them are called up in terms of the real world, by suggestive sense-impressions of the two kinds most evocative in Nerval: play of light and modulations of voice. Aurélie sings on the stage as Adrienne had in the garden or the convent play; the stage lighting casts a circle round her head as the moon in the garden or the halo in the mystery-play had done for Adrienne. And constantly the illusory nature of his worship is suggested. From the first sentence he mocks gently at his passion as he sits every night in the theatre 'en grande tenue de soupirant', among a thinly-scattered audience in frumpish clothes, watching his idol in a second-rate play. Adrienne is made mysterious by the half-light of sunset or moonrise, and wreathed in swirls of evening mist; in the convent play her halo is of gilded cardboard. Lucidly and consciously the dream is presented as lovely but a mere imagining: the narrator punctures it with 'Reprenons pied sur le réel', Aurélie with her pointed 'Vous cherchez un drame, voilà tout', and Sylvie, questioned as to any strange connection between Adrienne and Aurélie, with a burst of gay laughter at the very idea.

The pursuit of the ideal proved illusory, and because of it he has lost Sylvie. Here was the opportunity for the large-scale disillusion in romantic terms: Nerval has delicately avoided it. There is no psychological analysis, simply the tiny details of everyday life which the reader must juxtapose with the past: the Sylvie who had never heard of Rousseau now reads *La Nouvelle Héloïse* and sees the countryside in terms of Walter Scott; instead of sitting with her green cushion and lace-bobbins she works in a glove-factory; in her bedroom the old-fashioned 'trumeau' has given place to something more modern; instead of folk-songs she sings fashionable operas in sophisticated style. She had seemed the opposite of Aurélie, but she has followed the same pattern: Aurélie will marry the devoted and useful 'jeune premier ridé' and Sylvie too realizes that 'il faut songer au solide' so is engaged to the village baker. Yet he does not erect her into a lost ideal in her turn: when he reflects on what he might have had it is in the form: 'Là était le bonheur *peut-être, cependant* . . .'

Nerval has refused to inflate either dream or reality, or to confuse the two. His particular sense of irony is vital; an irony quite without bitterness. When the narrator comes back to beg Sylvie to save him from his obsessions, at the key point we have what might have been seen as the Interruption of Fate. But here it is no large-scale incident or dramatic lamentation: simply Sylvie's brother and the baker in a benevolent state of post-ball fuddledness blundering their wavering course through the undergrowth at daybreak, and without recriminations all go home together. When he returns to the scenes of his childhood, there is the dangerous opportunity for the obligatory romantic set-piece. But the two things which survive from the past are not the lofty emotions: they are the intellectual and the touchingly comic. Through the eighteenth-century characters who decked the countryside with their maxims now so out of date comes the realization that '*la soif de connaître* restera éternelle'. And childhood memories are evoked not through lofty symbols but from the odd bits and pieces dug up by the amateur archaeologist, and most of all from a stuffed dog and an ancient parrot who 'me regarda de cet œil rond, bordé d'une peau chargée de rides, qui fait penser au regard expérimenté des vieillards.' The theme of loss and persistence finds an individual dimension in that live comic glance of ancient and friendly irony.

Then there comes, in the last chapter, the very opposite of a 'bilan de la faillite.' As always, Nerval's method is not to analyze feeling or to sum up explicitly (though one sentence, with a graceful apology, brings home the value of experience, even with its bitterness). What he does is to take a series of tiny details, each of which is deliberately directed to calling up something almost unnoticed from earlier in the story, and through both details and tone to convey the rebirth of all that seemed lost, in a cycle of repetitive and satisfying pattern. It is some years later, and now, time after time, the narrator sets out from Paris for the old country inn, arriving in the evening. In his inn room he finds the 'trumeau au-dessus de la glace'. There is no statement, but we must recognize it as that same old-fashioned object which had decked Sylvie's room in childhood and been banished as she grew sophisticated. The odd collection of 'bric-à-brac' recalls that in his own room at the beginning of the story, later given up. He wakes in the morning and sees round the inn window the same flowers that grew round Sylvie's in childhood; looks out over the same countryside with its memories of eighteenth-century thinkers and lovers. Every word contributes not to a sense of failure but to the joy and renewal of a fresh country morning: 'Après avoir rempli mes poumons de l'air si pur, je descends gaiement . . .' His foster-brother greets him with the familiar nicknames of childhood. Sylvie's children play round the ruins of the castle, the 'tours de brique' recalling the background where he first saw Adrienne; they practise for the archery festival which had been part of his own memories at the beginning and was linked with druidical traditions from a further past. The cycle of repetitive pattern has caught up in the present all that seemed to have disappeared. He and Sylvie read together old tales now out of date. Again the tone mixes loveliness with gentle mockery: he and Sylvie are part of a permanent human experience but one that will not take itself melodramatically: 'Je l'appelle quelquefois Lolotte et elle me trouve un peu de ressemblance avec Werther, moins les pistolets, qui ne sont plus de mode.' Nostalgia and mockery have achieved a gentle reconciliation with the world as it is, and out of the elusive, the fallacious, the fragmentary or the lost, has come, as in the *Chimères*, the persistent ritual of human traditions.

Again form as well as theme deliberately evokes a play of opposites, a setting of the elusive and the chaotic against the patterned and the permanent. Memories apparently evoked at random are in fact grouped round a meticulous time-sequence and complex echoes of detail. There is a deliberate sense of inconsequentiality: events which would normally be prepared, stressed and led up to seem to flicker past almost unimportantly; then there come the sudden transformation scenes where we stand outside time and the characters become exemplars: a hushed circle listens to Adrienne singing and 'nous pensions être en Paradis'; or the boy and girl stand dressed up in the old wedding-clothes: 'Nous étions l'époux et l'épouse pour tout un beau matin d'été.'

The whole story has of course created the palimpsest of the past beneath the present. To pick out the extraordinary tissue of allusions to different ages is to make it sound an artificial and strange amalgam: Herculaneum, the Queen of Trebizond, Apuleius, Dante, the neo-platonists and the druids, Virgil and Rousseau, the Tiburtine Sybil and the Song of Solomon, the Carolingian, Valois and Medici monarchs – but all are intimately and relevantly evoked by a fresh and real countryside and a personal experience. If the air of the story is given to the elusive and the fugitive, the accompaniment constantly and irresistibly suggests a timeless world where the present catches up the echoes of the past.

Sylvie obviously takes on a new richness when the reader knows Nerval's other works and Nerval's reading. The theme of the 'double' (here the foster-brother) has all kinds of undertones. Nerval has worked fascinating coincidences between themes suggested by works and authors as startlingly different as the *Pastor Fido*[13] and Rétif de la Bretonne, the *Roman Comique*, the *Songe de Poliphile* and

Wilhelm Meister. To recognize them is to be brought back once again to the coincidence of experience across the ages, the weaving of parallel patterns out of disparate elements.

There is one particular tone that I should suggest is distinctively Nervalian in the world of *Sylvie*. What he has specially picked out from the past are those traditions that stand outside the accepted line of greatness. Sainte-Beuve and Baudelaire had talked of how all the 'great' subjects had already been monopolized, and how beauty must now be drawn from the prosaic, the horrible or the bizarre. Nerval quietly turns to more neglected material. The themes he takes up have stood outside the margin of the great tradition for two opposite reasons: some because they were too mannered and artificial, others for their naivety, simplicity and halting clumsiness. From the outmoded and the neglected Nerval brings a gentle mockery at whatever is odd or stiff or strange, and a sense of the permanent human value so particular in its loveliness and its oddity. So he consciously chooses the note of the Gessner pastoral, the ancient idyll, or the countryside of the pre-romantics with its elaborately natural parks and its deliberately constructed ruins, its sentimental moral maxims carved on temples and trees, its delightful conventionalizing of the ceremonies of antiquity in the stylized engravings of the *Voyage du Jeune Anacharsis*, and all its delicate formality: 'les traces fugitives d'une époque où le naturel était affecté.' And on the other hand the folk-songs attract him because they are limping and irregular, sung by young voices haltingly imitating the quavers of old age. Elsewhere he loves them because they are 'ces mélodies d'un style *suranné*', and even 'des airs anciens *d'un mauvais goût sublime*'.

Loveliness is evoked through the *suranné* and what is outside accepted taste, and is the more penetrating for that. Aurélie shines out from a second-rate play, in a dowdy theatre; Adrienne enchants as a mechanically propelled angel with a cardboard halo; Sylvie dressed up as a bride is all the more charming for the outmoded sleeves, the material yellowed with age, the faded ribbons and tinsel, the 'deux éventails de nacre un peu cassés', and the whole gentle air of the ridiculous of a Greuze village wedding. In the background of this scene stand the portraits of the old aunt and her husband, perhaps the most Nervalian touch of all. No great paintings: the local artist has done his doubtful best in the charming and half-ridiculous conventions of his day, with their mixed stiffness and grace; but through this laborious and well-meant art, and the necessary pose with the obligatory bird on curved finger, there shines the personality of the gay mischievous girl, now a bent old woman, beside the self-consciously pink-and-white martial air of her husband the gamekeeper, and the two come alive again in the boy and girl who borrow their clothes, while the naive, halting country songs the old aunt remembers from her pompous village wedding seem to go back to the tradition of the Song of Solomon. From both the limpingly natural and the elaborately formalized Nerval weaves his sense of tenderness, irony and final persistence.

Nerval wrote of Goethe, 'Le génie n'aperçoit pas un chaos sans qu'il lui prenne envie d'en faire un monde.' The world he himself creates exercises a hallucinatory fascination as the reader moves further into the intertwining suggestions of age-long traditions, whether familiar or strange. The present article has deliberately concentrated on one or two simple points. The reader who has once been captured by Nerval will sooner or later find himself both deeply grateful for the recent research which has made possible the understanding of so many details, and impelled, deliberately or instinctively, to look further at the allusions that have not yet been elucidated.

NOTES

1 *Gérard de Nerval*, Corti, 1945.
2 In *Gérard de Nerval et les doctrines ésotériques*, Editions du Griffon d'or, 1947, and in many articles on points of detail. Béguin and Richer produced jointly the Pléiade edition, and the introduction to Vol. I, 1952, shows how each has modified his earlier point of view. (See p. 12: it would be wrong to 'l'annexer à n'importe quelle doctrine occulte' or to 'supposer chez lui une adhésion chrétienne'.)
3 Corti, 1948. This work is criticized even from the point of view of the psychiatrist by Ch. Mauron, *Cahiers du Sud*, 293, 1949. In so far as biography is relevant, discussions of Nerval's 'ambivalent' relationship with his father do not seem to have considered two more obvious points. No term has yet been invented for the strain imposed on the 'infant prodigy' who is expected to keep up his early dazzling successes. Nerval seemed brilliant at an early age and earned an outstanding reputation in youth for his translation of *Faust*. He is determined to make a name in literature, yet until well on into his life he produces only plans, works in collaboration, the occasional short story or light poem, and the miscellanea of journalism; there is nothing on which a great reputation can be founded. The underlying fear of the loss of the power to write can already be seen in the Preface to the 1840 *Faust*. Like Baudelaire's mother, Nerval's father would have wished for his son a career leading to conventional success and stability. The effort to justify, as about to

bring fame and fortune, a career which has all too visibly as yet produced neither gives to the letters of both Baudelaire and Nerval at times the same note of submerged appeal, bursts of pride, and naive evaluation of prospects. Nerval's letters seem to show abundantly that this desire to justify in the eyes of a loved and practical parent a hand-to-mouth literary career, and the fear of being unable to fulfil early promise, are a very large cause of the tension and the sense of guilt (Letters of 18/9/38; 26/11/39; 30/1/40; 5/3/41; 31/5/54; 19/7/54, etc.).

4 *Fontaine*, 44–5, 1945. Two essential and penetrating articles.

5 The tendency to confuse the prose tales with biography and to 'explain' the *Chimères* in the light of this mixture has been pervasive; as late as 1955 the Hachette selection *Le Rêve et la Vie* opens with a preface where the confusion is pushed to an extraordinary degree. The often quoted: 'Je suis du nombre des écrivains dont la vie tient intimement aux ouvrages qui les ont fait connaître' requires to be set against its neglected counter-statement from a letter where, speaking of the falsity of a contemporary biography, Nerval remarks: 'ce qui prouve que j'ai bien fait de mettre à part ma vie poétique et ma vie réelle.' One welcomes the opening to L. Cellier's *Gérard de Nerval*: 'Imagine-t-on un biographe de Proust retraçant avec une émotion discrète les amours de Marcel et d'Albertine? C'est ce spectacle déconcertant que, toutes proportions gardées, ont donné et donnent encore maints biographes de Nerval, qui, ne sachant pas ce qu'est un roman, ont pris argent comptant de fausses confidences.' Biographers have still not picked out how central in Nerval is the struggle to create and to prove his worth by his writings. (See Pléiade edition, I, 754, 985, 1029, 1034, 1070, etc.)

6 *Baudelaire*, Mercure de France, 1953, p. 11.

7 *Œuvres Complémentaires de Gérard de Nerval*, I, *La Vie des Lettres*, textes recueillis et présentés par Jean Richer, Lettres Modernes, 1959.

8 *Cahiers du Sud*, 292, 1948: 'En marge des *Chimères*.'

9 The most stimulating from among many books and articles have, to my mind, been: G. Poulet, 'Sylvie et la pensée de Nerval', *Cahiers du Sud*, October 1938; O. Nadal, 'Poétique et Poésie des *Chimères*', *Mercure de France*, 1/11/55; M. J. Durry, *Gérard de Nerval et le Mythe*, Flammarion, 1955; L. Cellier, *Gérard de Nerval, l'homme et l'œuvre*, Hatier-Boivin, 1956; J. Gaulmier, *Gérard de Nerval et les Filles du Feu*, Nizet, 1956. The nature and scope of the present article obviously does not allow detailed discussion of the points where I should differ in interpretation and evaluation. Jeanine Moulin's annotated edition of the *Chimères*, Droz, 1949, would require further discussion both of what it takes for granted and of many of its 'explanations'.

10 In an article in the *Revue des Sciences Humaines*, July–September 1958 (see below pp. 304–7), I have examined his use of Richelet's rhyming dictionary. This shows both his lucid consciousness as a craftsman and his use of still another means of stimulating wide and rich associations.

11 See for example Pléiade edition, II, 354. The questioning of fallacious but obsessive patterns is the centre of many other works. Hashish is made a means of evoking them in *Le Calife Hakem*, and *Aurélia* is the study of patterns of significance which intensely seem, yet in the real world are not held to be, truths.

12 Some passages at the beginning of *Sylvie* distinctly recall Constant's *Adolphe*. From several remarks in Nerval's personal writings it is obvious that *Adolphe* made a deep impression on his mind. I hope briefly to investigate this subject on another occasion (See above, pp. 88–90).

13 The *Pastor Fido* is mentioned by Nerval himself as one of the works which had an early influence on him.

18

Aspects of suggestion in Nerval (1965)[1]

At the centre of Nerval's art is a quite exceptional gift for creating
analogies, sudden and surprising or controlled and convincing.
Having caught the infection, I intend to start today by a
part-frivolous, part-serious analogy. For when I began to think out
the sequence of perhaps five basic moods in Nerval's major works,
they seemed to me to correspond oddly closely to the experience of
attending an academic conference. I outline them like this
(deliberately simplifying their impact, and leaving to you the parallels with our present activity): first, the eager appetite, reaching
towards the ideal of 'tout ce bel univers qu'on s'est créé jeune, par
les lectures, par les tableaux et par les rêves' (and here how close
Nerval's 'géographie magique d'une planète inconnue' in the mind
of the child is to Baudelaire's 'Pour l'enfant, amoureux de cartes et
d'estampes,/L'univers est égal à son vaste appétit.'). But already
appetite for the ideal is accompanied by doubt:

Le monde qui se compose ainsi dans la tête des enfants est si riche et si beau
qu'on ne sait s'il est le résultat exageré d'idées apprises . . .

or 'c'est une image que je poursuis, rien de plus.' So, second, there
comes the *Descente aux enfers*, with its two sides: the disillusion of
finding that reality is so far from the ideal; the still more bitter
discovery that one is oneself at fault (and Nerval has subtle
individual ways of conveying all that may be clumsy, pusillanimous,
exaggeratedly demanding or exaggeratedly mistrustful in the urge
towards the impossible ideal and, in particular, of suggesting the
consequent haunting by an undefined sense of guilt, of opportunities
missed and will-o'-the-wisps pursued). It is only after this *Descente
aux enfers* that three different and potentially positive creative moods
may follow. The first is surprised and delighted recognition that,

whatever the insufficiencies of others or of the self, one can still constantly 'se retremper aux sources', 'la fête renouvelée de la jeunesse et du printemps'. The second is the revolt against the tyranny of the immediate past; a revolt which yet takes its place in a long tradition and which sows the seeds of the future. The third combines the preceding threads in a lucid or controlled appreciation of the interplay between overweening desire and relative achievement; it consciously echoes La Fontaine's classic expression of the return from the distant flight to an enhanced appreciation of the 'quotidien'. In the *Voyage en Orient*, Nerval writes at one point: 'J'en ai assez de courir après la poésie; je crois qu'elle est à votre porte', and in the last chapter of *Sylvie*, where dreams have proved abortive, he gathers memories into a quietly renewed cycle of perennial experience. So, too, at the end of *Aurélia*, the insights of personal visions and the assumptions of conventional wisdom are modestly left in continuing dialogue.

A conference may similarly move, we hope, from expectation to doubt about assumptions, from revolt against binding formulae to a sense of the vital, or of the relative and fallible traditions which each individual may catch up and develop for himself. Even so, it is an annual 'crise de conscience', whether for speaker or audience. For speaker, it is no doubt a healthy challenge in the problem of communication. To just whom is he communicating? A small number of experts, and I know there will be several here today, may well have far closer knowledge of the subject than has the supposedly specialised lecturer; others with less factual knowledge of detail will have better judgment and wider range of reference than I. Nerval has defined the speaker's problem for me, when in an article from the recently published *Variétés et Fantaisies* he writes of

cet être complexe qu'on nomme tout le monde, ce personnage vague et coiffé d'un feutre qui s'appelle un particulier.

To that hydra-headed 'être complexe', I shall not seek to present either a bibliographical summary or a complete critical conspectus – limited time would make either depressing and wearisome. Our main problem is surely how to preserve initial enjoyment and informed judgment unimpaired by any crushing sense of inability in present conditions to keep fully abreast of documentary discoveries or stimulating criticism. With Nerval that problem is acute. The Pléiade edition runs to some 3,000 pages, and the *Œuvres complémentaires* are in course of adding several volumes. Even if much of this is day-to-day journalism there flashes frequently the sentence that vitally explains and illuminates the central works. We badly need a critical study of Nerval's art as a journalist, investigating his highly conscious sense of contemporary conventions, and his skill in alternately ridiculing and fulfilling their demands. His own creative works are probably influenced, more often than has been realised, by his assessment of what he considers the French reading public demands: a work in which love and death are the central preoccupations. Much supposed autobiography in the works may more probably stem from this conviction.

As for keeping abreast of critical exegesis, I had better open like Nerval on a personal note and wonder if I am here on false pretences. I began to work on Nerval in the distant years when he was being rediscovered and perhaps over-rapidly presented as the apostle of various creeds (paganism, syncretism, esotericism or Christian redemption). The last ten years have seen in France the production of a number of major books (Léon Cellier, Mme Durry, Jean Gaulmier) bringing sense and sensibility to reassessment, while some of the best work on Nerval has always been done in widely scattered articles: one thinks of the suggestions offered in very different ways by G. Le Breton, F. Constans, Georges Poulet, and Jean-Pierre Richard. Articles are now appearing from all quarters of the globe, from the United States to the Belgian Congo, from Australia to Great Britain. If I mention those I have personally found stimulating (A. Guérard, Brian Juden, Ross Chambers, Norma Rinsler) my choice is, I know, incomplete; there is also work in course by N. Osmond and, no doubt, by several others. The compilers of anthologies often provide probing general comments. In the last year we have seen, at opposite extremes, the evocative and elegant little *Nerval par lui-même* of Raymond Jean, and the 700 pages of Jean Richer's *Nerval, expérience et création*, thick with relevant discoveries, but requiring months of collation before proper conclusions can be drawn from its proliferation of detail. Time and circumstance leave me the half-guilty, half-impenitent amateur. My intention is simply to suggest a number of general problems, to ask one or two perhaps uncomfortable questions around them, and to make some suggestions about future work, as a purely personal provocation to our collective creative activity.

A first problem in Nerval: the different levels of his writing. One might be tempted to divide it into three, setting at opposite extremes the journalistic and the pathological, and isolating the works of art proper in the middle. Yet this would be to falsify. His accounts of books read, plays seen, journeys made in Italy, Germany or the East, still more in the Ile de France or in Paris by night, are often works of creative imagination, with the same structures of fantasy, myth, humour and poetry as his greater works. Symptomatic and documentary interest needs to be further sifted from evocative value. The *Nuits d'octobre* and the *Promenades et Souvenirs* deserve comparison with Baudelaire's *Petits poèmes en prose*; the *Voyage en Orient* and *Les Illuminés* demand further reassessment less as partial autotherapy than in their relation to the literary climate of an age. The relation of the early 'simpler' poems to the *Chimères* is often highly suggestive. For the pathological, one remembers how often Baudelaire remarked that the analysis of what he called (in nineteenth-century terminology) 'hysteria' might contribute to the work of art, showing in heightened form the problems of a complex sensibility. One might, I think, contrast *Pandora* as rather of documentary value, the relatively unsorted chaotic raw material of an exacerbated imagination, with *Aurélia*, which sifts the essentials of that experience through a command of three qualities: a sense of structure, of critical detachment, and, above all, of controlled evocative language. A further point on the question of context; we possess the so-called *Lettres à Jenny Colon* in three states: manuscripts, those published as *Un Roman à faire*, and the central elaboration in *Octavie*. Where and how does the 'biographical' material become art? or indeed was it ever purely biographical? Beside the familiar quotation 'Je suis du nombre d'écrivains dont la vie tient intimement aux ouvrages qui les ont fait connaître'[2] it might be well to remember Nerval's resignedly caustic comments on the biography by Mirecourt which, he says, conventionalises him into an 'héros de roman', 'Ce qui prouve que j'ai bien fait de mettre à part ma vie poétique et ma vie réelle.'

Nerval's subconscious urges have been analysed in Freudian, post-Freudian or phenomenological frameworks, often with considerable subtlety – yet the basic impulses which are so discovered might in expression be either sentimentally indulged or suggestively ordered. In his *conscious* mind, whatever may be the sources of tension, the struggle of the artist to create is the central problem. It may be revealed in three main ways: (1) The letters to his father show the constant obsession with the need to justify himself by literary success. (2) In the *Lettres à Jenny* I would suggest that the knot of the problem, with its violently oscillating moods from pride to guilt, is that of the artist seeking to immortalise the actress through his works (the Dante–Beatrice analogy early haunts him), then desperately doubting his own. (3) In the last years, it is fear of literary sterility which torments him; of his mental crisis he writes: 'Vous savez que l'inquiétude sur mes facultés créatrices était mon plus grand sujet d'abattement', and of his effort to return to creative writing: 'là est le seul espoir de ma guérison.' The terror of losing the power to write went back much further; it is latent in the remark on Goethe in the 1840 preface to *Faust*:

ce puissant génie dont la faculté créatrice s'était éteinte depuis bien des années, quand il essaya de lutter avec lui-même en publiant son dernier ouvrage.

Recent works have made us familiar with his remarks on the struggle to write during his final years: 'je n'arrive pas; c'est déplorable. Cela tient peut-être à vouloir trop bien faire'. Or 'je *perle* trop.' In many works he expresses how two difficulties dog him: *Sylvie* shows the fear of the trite and the derivative:

j'essayai de parler de choses que j'avais dans le cœur, mais je ne sais pourquoi, je ne trouvais que des expressions vulgaires, ou bien tout à coup quelque phrase pompeuse de roman ... Je m'arrêtais alors avec un goût tout classique.

The *Lettres à Jenny*, starting from the same fear, lead to the second, and graver, problem in literary expression: 'N'attendez pas de moi des phrases de roman, ... des lettres éloquentes et ménagées. Il y a des années de rêves, de projets, d'angoisses qui voudraient se presser dans une phrase, dans un mot.' This above all is the problem both of Nerval the artist, and of his reader: the concentration of multifarious suggestions into the briefest compass. And in the *Histoire du Calife Hakem*, when hashish is the instrument of releasing man from his limitations, giving him the illusion of the godlike, it significantly gives to Yousouf this power over words:

'Il me venait des paroles d'une signification immense, *des expressions qui renfermaient des univers de pensées*.' (my italics)

Nerval then is repeatedly and explicitly conscious of the problems of expression. And the theme of the artist's peculiar self-consciousness is central in his works. How far does the artist ever feel directly; how far is he a victim of past stylisations of reality? ('Ceci est la faute de mes lectures' in *Aurélia*) or of his own desire to create a rounded significance different from anything real life can offer?': 'Vous ne m'aimez pas', says Aurélie in *Sylvie*, 'vous cherchez un drame, voilà tout, et le dénouement vous échappe.' The same theme is taken up in *Corilla*, sparks out in the *Voyage en Orient* ('Nous ne vivons pas, nous n'aimons pas. Nous étudions la vie, nous analysons l'amour') and is fully developed in the words attributed to Rétif de la Bretonne in *Les Illuminés*:

Nous ne vivons pas, nous! nous analysons la vie … Suis-je bien sûr moi-même d'avoir aimé? … nous ne voyons partout que des modèles à décrire … et tous ceux qui se mêlent à notre vie sont victimes de notre égoïsme, comme nous le sommes de notre imagination … Sais-tu ce que nous faisons, nous autres, de nos amours? Nous en faisons des livres pour gagner notre vie …

The drama *Léo Burckhart* plays many variations on the theme, including the moment of startled recognition that genuine involvement in feeling need not, after all, be simply 'une invention des poètes'.

This sense of the possible deformation of direct experience by the intrusion of the analytical and artistic consciousness is a theme that slowly grows through the nineteenth century and becomes vital in the twentieth. If a sense of this 'dédoublement de la personnalité' is becoming current in his age, Nerval seems to owe something of his sharp apprehension of it directly to Constant's *Adolphe*. I suggested affinities between them some years ago in a footnote;[3] Richer's latest work provides an *inédit* in which Nerval copies the suggestive passage on 'charme de l'amour'. As always, Nerval takes from an admired author those elements which fit his own mental structure, and which he can creatively develop: in this instance they are perhaps four: the inherited cynicism of the uncle in *Sylvie* which echoes that of the father in *Adolphe*; the sense of love as a 'point lumineux' (Nerval takes over the term) which links the timeless present with all the resources of the past; the terror or guilt arising from a decisive moment which was to become the *irréparable*; and, finally, the creation of a personality who both doubts the authenticity of his own experience because of its self-consciousness, and yet cannot doubt its genuine suffering.

Inherited preconceptions, whether idealistic or cynical, may deform the immediate impact of experience. Yet that experience remains a fact and leaves a problem: 'Je crois être amoureux, ah! je crois être malade n'est-ce pas? Mais, si je crois l'être, je le suis!' (*Voyage en Orient*). Or, more quietly adumbrated in *Sylvie*: 'Ces enthousiasmes … ces rêves, ces pleurs, ces désespoirs et ces

tendresses ... ce n'était donc pas l'amour? Mais où donc est-il?'
This questioning of the borderline between the imagined and the
'authentic' suggested by other nineteenth-century authors and by
Flaubert in particular, is especially acute and probing in Nerval.

From these problems of the artist come certain key-figures and
key-moods in the world Nerval created. Intense ambition and
intense self-questioning combine in the figure of the King unsure of
his royalty, the god uncertain of his divinity, the poet suffering loss,
doubt or torment, but shaping the victory of his song. Within a
recurrent cycle of loss, guilt, renewal, three figures of woman suggest
three basic urges: (1) the saint, queen or goddess who represents the
unattainable ideal, the impulse of worship; (2) the actress, gypsy or
siren, who seems to reflect the ideal yet is fallible and capricious;
symbol of how the two-sided imagination creates both tender
dreams and cynical suspicions; (3) the 'child of nature', an image
whom the narrator lets slip either because she seems too closely tied
to the every-day, or because she loses her initial simplicity.
(Reversals of pattern and inter-reflections between characters bring
shifting angles of vision and prevent any set stereotype figures not
just of Nerval's inner world, but also of contemporary
categorisations: it would be worth comparing them with the four
key-figures of Flaubert's *Éducation sentimentale* (in themselves a
conscious reworking and part-ironical reversal of Balzacian 'types'):
Mme Arnoux as the worshipped ideal; Rosanette and Mme
Dambreuse as two very differing aspects of its fallacious equivalent
in real life; Louise, as the naive childhood companion in the
provinces. The resulting tones are obviously intensely different: some
structural postulates are all the more stimulating.)

Finally, there is the theme of the double, externalising what the
self might have been; again no set stereotype, he is sometimes
portrayed as a sinister usurper, sometimes as a mockingly reproachful epitome of perfection. These figures of the double, which
were more melodramatic or comic in minor works, and were to have
deeply serious implications in *Aurélia*, are in *Sylvie* fined down to a
human scale and left with only undertones of symbolic intent: in the
'jeune premier ridé' who obtains Aurélia and especially in the
foster-brother who marries Sylvie. The cousin who intrudes in the
'Amours de Vienne' is both amusingly and seriously representative
of the reproachful 'might-have-been', opposing to the irresponsible
artist the man charged with the destinies of his country. The
treatment of the *Doppelgänger* in Nerval would deserve further

investigation. In all these themes, future research might trace the parallels both between Nerval's individual works, and between him and his contemporaries, more fully than has yet been done; it might also be concerned to distinguish moments of fantasy from the controlled art of suggestive selection.

I began with analogies. Analogies are obviously the seed of both inspiration and temptation in Nerval's art. Personal memories, literary reminiscences, esoteric lore, historical and mythological figures are linked in a web of unexpected interconnections spanning time and space. The constant suggestion of strange *rapports* is both obsessional and creative. The butchers of Montmartre who asked for an address at the annual festival of the *Bœuf Gras* must have been surprised by the linking of their ceremonies to legends of the dethroning of Saturn; an article mentioning *Lohengrin* moves back from the legend of the Grail to the Golden Fleece and then leaps forward to parallels with the Gold-Rush in nineteenth-century California; another article which suggests that the one infallible phrase to win over a woman is to whisper to her 'vous n'êtes pas comprise' adds immediate references to the riddle of the sphinx. These are part-comic examples, but they bear on an important problem for the artist: the dividing-line between the analogy which is serious, convincing and suggestive, and that which is either ornamental, witty and frivolous, or a product of private superstition and pathology. Once again parallels might be drawn with the deliberate play on dissonant yet unified tones, mythological and mocking, in Baudelaire's *Petits poèmes en prose*.

Nerval can both experience and mock at the ingrained super-stition which looks for omens in the tiniest event, as in the *Voyage en Orient* where he half-seriously tries to deduce his destiny from the progress of a beetle across the sand. His wide if random reading in 'illuminist' works of all kinds offers the tempting picture of a world in which the most insignificant detail would provide a hieroglyph, standing for something significant beyond itself, part of a reassuring pattern behind the universe. His ineradicably sceptical mind, or his awareness of the reader's potential scepticism, refuses to go further than 'il serait consolant de croire ...' or 'des rapports dont je m'exagérais sans doute l'importance'. It is precisely this two-sidedness which enables him, in his best works, to make an imag-inative rather than a metaphysical use of the tempting patterns of analogy: to punctuate in *Sylvie* the hankering after some magic explanation with the narrator's 'reprenons pied sur le réel' or with

Adrienne's and Sylvie's incisive practicality; and in *Aurélia* to draw a clear line of distinction between the ecstatic illusion, with all its suggestive validity, and 'ce que les hommes appellent la raison.'

Nerval belongs to an age, of course, where the story told on two levels, leaving supernatural versus rational explanations to the reader's choice, is familiar: one thinks of Mérimée's *La Vénus d'Ille* or Balzac's *La Peau de Chagrin*. In many of his light works he explains away the apparently mysterious by external devices: the disguise, or two sisters resembling each other. But this technique is a kind of detective-story mechanical demystification, amusingly caricatured in an article where he picks up Hoffmann's anecdote of the bourgeois who found the end of Don Juan highly improbable, but was given a relieved sense of superior understanding on being persuaded that the Statue of the Commander was in fact the Chief of Police who had been keeping an eye on public morals and had roped in Don Juan to a just downfall, conducted on a rational and 'vraisemblable' level. Nerval's lucid scepticism is normally far from reductive. Seeking some more suggestive dimension, he achieves, in his best works, a particularly evocative balance by treating the haunting illusion not as a product of external deception but as an inner faculty or fallacy inherent in the ranging imagination. Different instruments are used to suggest the tempting means of illusion or illumination, constantly doubly questioned: hashish in *Le Calife Hakem* (which deserves closer comparison with Baudelaire's *Paradis artificiels*); the hallucinations of dream or derangement in *Aurélia*; and in *Sylvie* – the most discreet and the most balanced – the interplay between multifold imaginings and temporal shifts in experience.

But the most potent instrument, in the workings of Nerval's 'démon de l'analogie', remains that of literary tradition. Perhaps no great author has ever had so compulsive a faculty for identifying himself with such disparate sources, could more truly say 'je prends mon bien où je le trouve' or has converted odder elements 'en sang et nourriture'. Here, in one sense, his use of analogies is part of a particularly French tradition; it also raises its own particular problems. From Scève or the Pléiade onwards, many great French writers have of course based their art on a catching up of the great works of the past, where an essential part of the aesthetic pleasure lies in the reader's ability to recognise creative variations on a familiar theme, to follow on the score the echoes, the harmonics and the departures from known tradition. A vital part of Ronsard's resonance comes, obviously, from the echoes and contrasts between tradition and individuality, as he revivifies the *Exegi monumentum* or the *Fons Bandusiae*; Racine or Bossuet draw substance from suggestive allusions to a rich past. Much later Apollinaire, Péguy, Giraudoux, Sartre, Beckett 'et bien d'autres encor' have in their very different ways played on the technique of echo and variant where the reader's response to originality depends in part on his recognition of the theme on which the variants are strung. Such a technique may obviously give the serious sense at the same time of persistence throughout the ages and of the excitement of new expression. It may on the other hand be no more than a self-conscious display of erudition or ingenuity in adaptation. Or it may deliberately adopt the mock-heroic parody, as does Nerval in some articles. In his richest works what we have is not just variations on *a* theme, but an extraordinary coincidence, in brief compass and discreet allusion, of a whole sheaf of unexpectedly converging traditions. (Again, one thinks of Baudelaire's techniques in some of the *Petits poèmes en prose*). In 'Delfica', Goethe's Song of Mignon fuses with Virgil's *Jam redit et virgo*; while in 'À Mme Ida Dumas' the greatest Psalm of the Exiles, the *Super Flumina Babylonis*, already resoundingly recalled in one of Bossuet's major *oraisons funèbres*, becomes one with the obsessive music of a 'pantoum malais'; and in 'Erythréa' erudition on the ritual of Isis may be united with memories of Indian dancers in contemporary Paris. In the prose, *Sylvie*, with its surface simplicity of style, is decanted from intertwining allusions – to Apuleius, Dante, Petrarch, the *Songe de Poliphile*, Rousseau, Rétif ... but to start on such an enumeration is utterly insufficient, and painters are as much part of the substance as writers. Recent research, whether in documentation or in criticism, has shown more and more how Nerval draws on an individual choice from traditions which others in his day might have found conflicting: illuminist and esoteric lore; the accepted 'great tradition', and those 'en marge'. His affinities with classical traditions have been well pointed out; one might add much highly interesting evidence from the *Œuvres complémentaires* on Corneille or Sophocles. The marginal authors remain a vital stimulus, leading him into further realms of analogy. A pervasive image is that of Scarron's troupe of strolling players 'cahotés sur les pavés du Mans', accompanied by their sorrowful 'seigneur-poète'; these provide, with the names L'Étoile and Le Destin, and their elaboration in prose texts, a background to 'El Desdichado'; they are linked with the strolling players in *Wilhelm Meister,* and hence made to recall those of *Hamlet,* and is not Hamlet 'Oreste sous d'autres habits?' . . . Here, clearly, a problem occurs. How far will traditional or marginal references be immediately recognisable to later readers? A Bach may *state* at the outset the theme on which he will found his variations; a writer's allusiveness depends on other factors of recognition, constantly changing as the cultural inheritance shifts. (Nerval's range of allusion was always a combination of the traditional and the esoteric: discussion of his immediate impact on readers of differing periods might look more closely at the aesthetic problems involved.)

That Nerval should catch up such multifarious and disparate analogies across the ages already suggests that his art is not that of analysis of the individual. Critics may have been drawn to analyse the phenomenon Nerval; his own works, for all their atmosphere of intimacy, give little *direct* analysis either of the self or of others. Self-consciousness may indeed give rise to an art which eschews certain forms of self-analysis. The sonnets are epic in their expression of moods of despair, victory, revolt, doubt or anticipation: they have something of the absolutism of the ringing epic tragedy of a Garnier in the sixteenth century with his: 'Je suis le malheur même', or 'Pareil aux Dieux je marche'. Even the intimacy of the 'Toi qui m'as consolé' or of the 'Reconnais-tu . . .?' receives no psychological elucidation, and is left as a tonality or a generally suggestive allusion. In *Sylvie,* none of the three women is psychologically characterised in the abstract; simply we see their effect on the narrator, watch their actions and hear what they say (not even that for Adrienne, who is simply a voice singing). The narrator himself, with an occasional moment of self-investigation, recounts his memories, actions, words and sensations rather than analysing the complex of his feelings. The self-revelation of *Aurélia* emerges from no abstract psychological analysis but from the sheer notations of 'I dreamed that . . .' and 'I wondered whether . . .'. In fact this is an art that suggests the subtleties of human feelings not through direct discussion, but through the two extremes of mythological or literary parallel and swiftly suggestive sense-impressions.

And it is to the place of certain sense-impressions in Nerval's art that I want to come now, sense-impressions woven also from various kinds of analogy. It is hyper-evident that the *Chimères* bite themselves into the mind by way of their particular sound-patterns. It is perhaps worth noticing how often Nerval himself is captured by sheer unelucidated patterns of sound, divorced from meaning, as a stimulus to the imagination, calling up rich associations 'Un charme syllabique, une grâce d'intonation [...] qu'on écouterait volontiers des heures sans comprendre' (followed by the disillusioning discovery of meaning) or the fascination of the gypsy seamstress in *Octavie*, with her sudden phrases in an unknown language: 'des syllabes sonores, gutturales, des gazouillements pleins de charme'.

The theme of singing voices runs through Nerval:

Dans les grandes peines, les grands chagrins, les grandes infortunes, il est rare, très rare, que des paroles chantées ne bruissent pas au fond de nous-même et n'accompagnent constamment notre pensée surexcitée et anxieuse;

at different times he is haunted by little snatches 'Là-haut sur les montagnes,/Le monde y vit content,/Le rossignol sauvage/Fait mon contentement', or finds the full sharpness of childhood memory recalled by 'la vieille romance de Garat, *Plaisir d'Amour*' (is this the 'ancienne romance' of 'Delfica'?). In *Sylvie* of course the songs of opera or religious play, and above all of the countryside, echo on almost every page (and Nerval excels in finding the combination of words which can convey the *timbre* of voices inter-relating the approximations of folk-song both to a misty countryside and to the odd conventions of a half-forgotten past). In the *Chimères* the renewal of past splendour or the urge to rebellion is heralded by a song ('Delfica', 'À Mme Ida Dumas') and the return from the *Descente aux enfers* is that of the musician Orpheus. Nerval is, in fact, one in a large line of authors who have been intrigued by one or other of the two sides suggested by this surfacing of a scrap of song clutched at in a moment of crisis (Stendhal's Julien Sorel as he returns to consciousness in prison; one recalls earlier Senancour's *Obermann*, and later the very different uses in Proust of the 'Petit Air de Vinteuil' or in Sartre of 'Some of these days'). The sense-impression may evoke for Nerval both an immediate suggestion of permanent patterns through time, and an intellectual authentification of the artist's ability to seize and use such suggestions of persistence.

I do not propose to run through a solemn classification of the sensations evoked by Nerval, but simply to suggest one or two of the sharpest. That which is most tricky to convey, the olfactory, has a suggestive place. Delight is often associated with 'une fraîcheur et un parfum des premières matinées du printemps'; youth is 'follement enivrée de l'odeur des prés'; later 'j'allais respirer l'odeur des arbres presque effeuillés', while, in *Sylvie*, a vital turning-point is conveyed

through a delicate equivalent of Baudelaire's: 'Le printemps ador-
able a perdu son odeur', in: 'Les plaines étaient couvertes de meules
de foin, dont l'odeur me portait à la tête sans m'enivrer, comme faisait
autrefois la fraîche senteur des bois et des halliers d'épines fleuries'.

A recurring sensation in Nerval is that of the delight of looking
out from some point of vantage over a wide-stretching horizon. In
the last chapter of *Sylvie*, the narrator looking out from his inn
window in the morning 'découvre avec ravissement un horizon vert
de dix lieues où les peupliers se rangent comme des armées'. The
Chimères give in many ways this sense of vast horizons. In a brief
space there is concentrated a whole *Légende des siècles*: the gods of
Greece, Rome, Egypt, Persia, India, Judea, the dynasties and heroes,
the tyrants and the *révoltés* of ancient epic, medieval legend,
Renaissance or nineteenth century play out their roles against a
background of the violence and beauty of the most elemental
processes of nature. Once again, there is no need (and no space in
the sonnets) for abstract analysis of the experiencing 'hero'; the
interplay of elemental forces suffices to suggest terror or delight,
revolt or uncertainty. In 'Le Christ aux Oliviers', the vastness of
space in which wheel the worlds evokes first a past prodigal fertility,
then the terror of random purposeless movement, the advancing
grip of cold on a dying universe, and at centre the huge empty eye-
socket of absence and nothingness. At the opposite extreme 'Vers
Dorés' replies; here there is a thronging world of small material
objects gradually being brought alive, and the tiny shape of the eye
emerges, from the shape of a stone or the knot in the bark of a tree, as
a sign of ritual renewal of life. In other poems we move between the
dark rivers of the underworld, the glittering beauty of a mediter-
ranean landscape and the flaming sunset. Natural forces are, like all
other analogies in Nerval, ambiguous, and each may evoke terror or
loveliness, destruction or creation. Mountains may suggest in turn
the sunlit splendour of Posillipo or the stony, irresistible persistence
of an ancient past where the great rocks of Salzburg covered in snow
recall the white bones of Du Bartas's ancient giants. The shudder of
the elemental forces of destruction is there in the frost and earth-
quakes of the old winter God Kneph; the shiver of potential creation
in 'La terre a tressailli d'un souffle prophétique' and in the eruption
of the volcano. The cavern may be the dream-filled 'grotte où nage
la sirène' or the 'grotte fatale ... Où du dragon vaincu dort l'antique
semence.' Variations are played out on recurring cosmic sense-
impressions: after the eruption of the volcano, dust falls around the

vast horizon ('Et de cendres [or 'de sa poudre'] au loin l'horizon est couvert'); in the same way white roses fall from a flaming sky in 'Artémis', and in 'A Madame Aguado' and 'Erythréa' there are the rain of white butterflies over the sea, the falling veil of the goddess, the strewing of flowers on the streams, the falling snow over the ocean. To those who have followed Nerval's interest in alchemy this recurrent image may suggest how at a critical stage of the experiment the volatile elements which had been set loose float back downwards into the initially chaotic substance to take part in the next ritual stage of creative aspiration. More generally, it evokes the pause in contemplation after the outburst of revolt or of desire. And the cosmic shudder may be followed, as in 'Horus', by the trailing through the heavens of another lovely veil, that of Iris, the rainbow. In 'Le Christ aux Oliviers' the rainbow had seemed an emblem of threat and mystery on the edge of chaos; in 'Horus' it may stand, as in *Aurélia* and by ancient tradition, for the coming of reconciliation: 'Et les cieux *rayonnaient* sous l'écharpe d'Iris'.

Expressed by the two extremes of the cosmic and the intimately sensuous, patterns of analogy between the sonnets add to their inner coherence and to their suggestive meaning. The heroes are physically marked by some sign of destiny: that of delight in 'Mon front est rouge encor du baiser de la reine'; of revolt (the brand of Cain) in 'Antéros'; of some strange consecration in 'Il m'a marqué le front de sa lèvre irrité'; or 'Frappés au flanc tous deux par un double mystère' of 'La Tête Armée'.

To two themes constantly growing in the first half of the nineteenth century Nerval gives his own lapidary and gnomic expression. First, to the sense of a questioning pause before the pregnant possibilities of a still frustrated future (cf., in particular, Hugo's preface to the *Chants du Crépuscule*):

> Cependant la Sibylle au visage latin
> Est endormie encor sous l'arc de Constantin:
> – Et rien n'a dérangé le sévère portique.

or

> Mais le César romain nous a volé la foudre.

But, second, comes the evocation, in cosmic terms, of the sowing of the fertile seeds that will finally and triumphantly spring up – here again one remembers, in Hugo's 'Le Semeur' of the *Contemplations*, the conclusion: 'semble élargir jusqu'aux étoiles/Le geste auguste du semeur' – whether as repeated revolt: 'Je ressème à ses pieds les dents du vieux dragon', or as triumphant renewal of ancient worth: 'L'autre versait au ciel la semence des dieux'.

The art of the *Chimères* is dignified, oracular, and uses for its suggestive sensuous effects the most intense cosmic forces; that of *Sylvie* is based on discreet understatement, on a gentle nostalgia half-mocked at with controlled sophistication, and on the use of a familiar countryside and its everyday objects. Yet it stretches constantly into wider suggestions. In a brief paragraph in the first chapter Nerval characterises the combined idealisation, cynicism and hesitation of a transitional generation in a way that sums up those same ideas as are analysed in the opening to Musset's *Confession d'un Enfant du Siècle*, in Hugo's Preface to the *Chants du Crépuscule*, or re-created in Flaubert's *Éducation sentimentale*. Critics have sometimes seemed to assume that its main meaning might be summed up by the phrase in Ch. XIV 'les illusions tombent l'une après l'autre, comme les écorces d'un fruit'; I should still wish to stress the end of that sentence: 'et le fruit c'est l'expérience. Sa saveur est amère; elle a pourtant quelque chose d'âcre qui fortifie.' There are two sides to the relative and resigned conquest of this world where 'L'action n'est pas la sœur du rêve' – first the joyous renewal and the reconciliation with the nature of things (whatever the underlying hurt or hesitation in the last chapter, which I have analysed elsewhere); second the evocation of those privileged moments of self-sufficient joy in past experience. The scene of Adrienne singing in the castle garden; the scene of the dressing up in the wedding clothes with Sylvie: both are made exemplars of a timeless experience which cannot be destroyed: 'nous pensions être en paradis' and 'nous étions l'époux et l'épouse pour tout un beau matin d'été'. Three things perhaps make for the worth of these moments. First, they are created from sensations sharply observed and expressed (in the Adrienne chapter the brick and stone of the castle warmed by the rays of the setting sun, the drifting patches of evening mist catching on the points of the long grasses, the sheen on the laurel leaves with which she is symbolically crowned; for Sylvie the crumpled and out-of-date finery of the wedding-clothes in which she decks herself, the background sound of crackling frying-pan, the smell of onion soup and the sight and taste of strawberries displayed in bright country pottery). Second, both are presented as a mere *moment* of loveliness; circumscribed by the real world which precedes and follows, they stand out all the more intensely against the sense of impermanence or doubt. It might be worth following up further Proust's suggestion (much discussed, but leaving plenty of space for re-investigation) that he found in *Sylvie* a number of basic laws on human behaviour. By what means in Nerval's finest poems and prose works do certain 'romantic' temptations to melodrama or sadism (cf. the Nero theme in the Preface to *Un Roman à faire*) lose their potential shrillness and exaggeration to be suggestively stylised in the age-long, yet newly-enriched, themes of fertile revolt or questioning part-reconciliation? Command of structure (often deliberately made to appear random); variations on past traditions; skilled control of language; all need further close study. Third, they catch up countless analogies with past traditions, in an exemplary moment of wonderment and worship. Recent criticism has seen that there are in many minor works of Nerval prefigurations of these key-scenes; we still need full discussion, not just of the parallels between the different versions, but of how in *Sylvie* choice of detail and means of expression transform such sketches into a delicately balanced and haunting whole.

In a scathing article on a contemporary, Nerval recalls the Oriental tradition that it is courteous to insert in any work of art some imperfection as a consolation in face of the crushing effect of the perfect. He adds of the author he is discussing the brief but devastating phrase 'Il ne nous a que trop consolé'. This is all too obviously my position today in trying to say anything adequate about a work I so much enjoy. I can only hope that for those who are going to go further into its worth, what I have so briefly suggested will leave them so 'consolés' by its obvious gaps or imperfections, that they will be all the more provoked to further and better work.

NOTES

1 This is the previously unpublished text of a paper, originally entitled 'The Art of Gérard de Nerval', which was delivered to the Society for French Studies at their conference in St Anne's College, Oxford, 27–28 March 1965.
2 For discussion of this remark, see above, p. 286, n. 5.
3 The article in which these affinities were eventually discussed is to be found above on pp. 80–95.

19

Nerval et Richelet (1958)

Est-il besoin de dire d'emblée que je ne prétends nullement donner, après tant d'autres, une «clef des *Chimères*»? Encore moins réduire Nerval à un jongleur dans l'art des bouts-rimés.

C'est lui-même pourtant, dans un poème léger sur le vin, qui m'a mise sur la voie; poussée par la curiosité, j'ai examiné de près un livre moins ésotérique que ceux qui figurent d'habitude parmi les sources de Nerval, et j'en suis venue à la conclusion que, toute proportion gardée, on devrait tenir compte de cet ouvrage lorsqu'on discute la genèse des *Chimères*.

La qualité incantatoire de cette poésie se fait évidemment plus facilement sentir qu'elle ne se laisse analyser. Le spécialiste, d'ailleurs, a peut-être tendance à ne pas assez souligner l'importance de cette musique, qui est au fond une condition *sine qua non* de la poésie obscure ou hermétique. Pour lui, il est tout naturel de poursuivre dans toutes leurs ramifications des allusions complexes. Mais le lecteur qui n'est ni érudit ni adepte de mots croisés, pourquoi choisirait-il d'aller plus loin? Uniquement parce qu'il ne pourra s'en empêcher, que l'incantation du poème se sera fixée dans sa mémoire, que des vers en même temps retentissants et mystérieux auront créé une hantise. C'est à partir de cette impression initiale que, tel Mallarmé obsédé par la phrase musicale et incompréhensible «la pénultième est morte»,[1] il fera travailler toutes les forces de son intelligence, de sa sensibilité et de son inconscient en tâchant d'exorciser cet envoûtement ou d'en pénétrer le secret.

Étant donné cette fonction toute particulière de l'élément musical chez Nerval, il est peut-être étrange qu'on ne trouve pas, à ma connaissance, de commentaire suivi sur l'extrême richesse des rimes dans les sonnets des *Chimères*.[2] Et que cette richesse ne se fasse pas immédiatement remarquer, c'est là un fait significatif. Car trop souvent chez des poètes qui se préoccupent de cette technique la rime riche attire l'attention uniquement par sa virtuosité; elle s'accuse par un contraste saugrenu avec le vers plat et vide qui l'amène, ou par les contorsions qu'a dû subir le vers pour que l'auteur puisse la placer. Chez Nerval, les qualités de densité, d'équilibre et de suggestion, la richesse de sons et d'allusions à l'intérieur de chaque vers, empêchent que la rime riche ne fasse une impression trop éclatante ou forcée.

Cependant, à les regarder de près, ces rimes sont d'une subtilité extraordinaire. Laissons de côté les sonnets du *Christ aux Oliviers*, tout en remarquant que c'est dans un poème où le sens offre fort peu de difficulté que la rime suffisante a la prépondérance. Dans les autres *Chimères*, dans les rares occasions où la rime n'est que suffisante, c'est en général parce qu'elle sort déjà de l'ordinaire par une combinaison insolite où figure un nom propre (Gudule/brûle; Cybèle/appelle). Pour la plupart, les rimes sont non seulement riches mais archi-riches. Le poète fait rimer les voyelles avant la consonne d'appui (un*i*vers, h*i*vers); il donne à toutes les rimes de l'octave, soit masculines, soit féminines, la même assonance (Romance, blancs, tremblants, recommence, immense, dents, imprudents, semence); il joue sur des entrecroisements de voyelles se faisant écho avant la rime (inc*o*ns*o*lé, ab*o*lie, c*o*nstellé, Mélanc*o*lie).

Une énumération risque de devenir fastidieuse et mécanique, et la rime n'est évidemment qu'une partie de l'effet total. Mais ce qui compte, c'est que la «rêverie supernaturaliste» de Nerval s'exprime à travers une forme des plus exigeantes et des plus strictes. Plus on examine la complexité, la délicatesse et la précision de cette musique, plus on voit un effet voulu, résultat non pas du hasard ni d'une vague inspiration, mais d'une étude et d'une discipline. Que Nerval se soit consciemment servi de toutes les aides techniques qui puissent contribuer à cet effet, il n'y a rien là qui fasse tort à sa grandeur, au contraire.

C'est à la fin du petit poème *Gaieté*[3] qu'on trouve les vers:

> Et je n'ai pas de Richelet
> Pour finir ce docte couplet ...
> Et trouver une rime en ampre.

avec la note de Nerval: «Lisez le *Dictionnaire des Rimes*, à l'article AMPRE, vous n'y trouverez que *pampre*; pourquoi ce mot si sonore n'a-t-il pas de rime?». Il s'est donc servi du *Dictionnaire de Rimes*[4] de Richelet, et j'ai suivi son indication. Il est évident que, vu le nombre limité de rimes possibles, la présence dans l'ouvrage de Richelet de certaines rimes dont se sert Nerval ne sera pas en elle-même concluante. Mais, à parcourir les listes et les classifications de Richelet, on est de plus en plus frappé par les possibilités qu'il offre, et surtout par le fait qu'à de très rares exceptions près, les rimes les plus insolites de Nerval s'y trouvent indiquées. A travers ces rimes s'offre tout un monde de suggestions mythologiques et autres.

On peut commencer par les noms propres, car Nerval s'en sert à la rime à un degré impressionnant. J'en ai noté trois qui ne figurent pas dans Richelet: Judée dans *Le Christ aux Oliviers*; Patani dans *Erythréa* (et là Nerval se sert, selon toute probabilité, de réminiscences d'une traduction en vers);[5] Gudule dans *Artémis* (où il faut sans doute tenir compte de souvenirs personnels de l'église Sainte-Gudule à Bruxelles). Autrement tous, même ceux qui demanderaient le plus d'explications du point de vue du sens, se trouvent dans les classifications de Richelet. Pour *El Desdichado*, le Biron tant discuté figure (avec la note *ville de France* et *général français*) à côté d'Achéron (*fleuve de l'Enfer*); et sous FÉE on trouve Fée et Orphée. Pour *Antéros*, Nerval aurait pu trouver ensemble indompté(e) et Antée, dragon et Dagon (*dieu des Philistins*); Cocyte (*fleuve de l'Enfer*) et Amalécite (*peuple de l'Idumée*); dans cette dernière liste figure aussi Baalite, *adorateur de Baal, Bel ou Belus* (cf. «mon aïeul Bélus ou mon père Dagon»). *A Madame Ida Dumas* offre une forme peu habituelle du nom de l'Archange Saint Michel; dans Richelet on trouve dans une même liste: ciel, Gabriel, Israël et les alternatives Michel–Michaël. Pour le quatrième sonnet du *Christ aux Oliviers*, Richelet donne, avec crime, estime, victime, le mot Solyme (*Jérusalem, capitale de Judée*), et fait rimer avec démon et limon Ammon (*surnom de Jupiter*). On pourrait allonger la liste en citant pour *Delfica* latin et Constantin, pour *Horus* Iris et Osiris, pour *Myrtho* agile, argille (*sic*) et Virgile.[6]

Pour les mots autres que les noms propres, je n'indiquerai pas en détail toutes les occasions où les rimes choisies par Nerval figurent dans les listes de Richelet.[7] Il y a cependant trois cas intéressants. Constellé, qui est certes loin d'être un mot usuel, est suivi immédiatement dans Richelet par consolé, et désolé se trouve dans la même liste. Sous la rubrique IÈRE Nerval aurait pu trouver en même temps bière et la fleur étrange d'*Artémis*, la rose trémière. Et si tous les mots de la séquence: aboli(e), mélancolie, Italie, (s')allie se trouvent dans une liste de Richelet, cette liste des mots en LIE s'ouvre par Ancholie (*fleur*). André Rousseaux avait déjà suggéré[8] que si le manuscrit Éluard d'*El Desdichado* porte la note Ancolie c'est que Nerval avait peut-être pensé à l'utiliser à la rime et qu'il y a renoncé.[9]

Il serait évidemment téméraire et vain d'essayer, le Richelet à la main, de tracer dans les détails le processus de création qui a produit les *Chimères*. Dire que Nerval a pu trouver dans Richelet des mots dont il avait besoin pour la rime n'est nullement refuser à ces mots d'autres fonctions plus importantes. Et quiconque ne connaît pas Richelet sera étonné en le feuilletant d'entrer dans une espèce de monde enchanté qui offre non seulement des ressources de sonorité mais, dans le choc de tant de mots étranges bizarrement juxtaposés, un fort stimulant pour une imagination poétique. Cet article ne prétend nullement révolutionner l'interprétation des *Chimères*. Si Richelet a pu fournir un répertoire de suggestions, reste le choix qu'en a fait Nerval, et tout ce que les termes choisis comportent de signification et d'allusion. Mais ne serait-il pas permis de voir, dans le fait qu'il s'adresse à ce manuel technique où s'offrent tant de possibilités diverses, encore une preuve de la lucidité et de la volonté d'un artiste suprêmement conscient?

NOTES

1 Voir *Le Démon de l'Analogie*, éd. de la Pléiade, p. 272.
2 Il existe un article de Y. Le Hir sur «La Versification de Gérard de Nerval», *Les Lettres romanes*, 1956, I, pp. 409–22.
3 Pléiade, I, p. 47.
4 J'ai pu consulter trois éditions: *Dictionnaire de Rimes* par P. Richelet. Nouvelle édition revue, corrigée, augmentée et mise en ordre par M. l'abbé Berthelin. Paris MDCCLI.
  Dictionnaire de Rimes par P. Richelet. Retouché en 1751 par Berthelin. Nouvelle édition, corrigée et considérablement augmentée par les CC. Dewailly, membre de l'Institut national et Dewailly fils aîné. Paris, l'an VII.
  Dictionnaire de Rimes par P. Richelet. Retouché en 1751 par Berthelin. Nouvelle édition, revue, corrigée et considérablement augmentée par M. Barthelemi, Lyon, 1810.
  Les différences, sans avoir une très grande signification, sembleraient indiquer que c'est la plus récente, celle de 1810, que Nerval a dû utiliser.
5 Voir l'art. de Gilb. Rouger «En marge des Chimères», *Cahiers du Sud*, 1948, 292, pp. 430–2.
6 D'autres rimes qu'offre Richelet sous cette rubrique auraient pu contribuer à des résonances secondaires: telles péristyle, sibylle, volatile.
7 Par exemple: enchanteresse, tresse, ivresse, Grèce; Orient, souriant, brillant; univers, pervers, vert, hiver; bouche, couche, farouche, louche; cœur, vainqueur, vengeur, rougeur; génie, tyrannie; romance, immense, semence; prophétique, portique, etc.
8 «Sur trois Manuscrits de Gérard de Nerval», *Domaine français*, 1943, pp. 303–18.
9 La note sur Mausole serait-elle un écho de Mausolée?

20

Le Mythe d'Orphée
dans l'œuvre de Gérard de Nerval (1970)[1]

C'est exprès que j'ai choisi comme titre, non pas «L'Orphisme de Nerval», mais «Le mythe d'Orphée chez Nerval». Le moindre «nettoyage de la situation verbale» suggérerait que le terme «orphisme» risque depuis longtemps de sombrer dans le vague, de devenir un mot passe-partout indiquant soit une inspiration surnaturelle mal définie, soit un don lyrique qu'on admire sans l'analyser. Georges Poulet, cité dans l'introduction du livre de Georges Cattaui, *Orphisme et prophétie chez les poètes français, 1850–1950*, parle de «termes fort équivoques, qui n'offrent plus qu'un sens analogique fort fuyant».[2] Dans une très modeste communication, consciente de grandes dettes envers bien des prédécesseurs, je ne prétendrai ni traiter dans le détail les lectures d'où Nerval tire sa vision d'Orphée (le *Nerval: Expérience et création* de Jean Richer[3] et les multiples ouvrages que signalent les bibliographies de Jean Senelier et de James Villas[4] nous montrent la pleine complexité de ces questions de «sources»), ni apporter des inédits. Je chercherai à souligner deux points. D'abord que Nerval, qui transmue les matériaux les plus hétéroclites en «sang et nourriture» personnels, a toujours cherché à distinguer, avec une lucidité en même temps humble et tranchante, d'un ton tendre ou humoristique, entre le Mythe et la Vie. Ensuite, qu'en dernière analyse ce qui compte pour lui, et ce qui fait la valeur de ses œuvres pour nous, ce n'est pas simplement la portée ou la finesse de ses aperçus sur les problèmes psychologiques, sociologiques ou religieux que soulèvent les mythes, mais sa maîtrise des moyens de l'expression.[5]

Depuis la riche communication faite par Léon Cellier devant cette Association même, en 1957, sur «L'Orphisme des romantiques»,[6] et depuis l'ouvrage de Mme Durry sur *Nerval et le Mythe*[7], les études nervaliennes ont bénéficié de plusieurs œuvres majeures.[8] Deux tendances, d'ailleurs complémentaires, sembleraient se discerner. Certains critiques, retrouvant chez Nerval les éléments du «chamanisme» qui intéresse les anthropologistes ou les psychanalystes, se concentrent sur ses intuitions dans un domaine qui préoccupe divers chercheurs contemporains: celui du primitivisme qui sous-tend nos structures intellectuelles ou qui y sert de contre-point. Si Nerval fait revivre des mythes profondément enracinés dans un inconscient collectif, c'est pourtant en homme de son siècle, en individu, et finalement en artiste qu'il les choisit et qu'il les façonne. En second lieu, une critique thématique nous offre des moyens d'investigation qui, en regroupant certains symboles obsédants, sont riches de conséquences. Ne tendrait-elle pas quelquefois à mettre sur le même niveau des révélations symptomatiques et des réussites dans le domaine de l'esthétique?

Si, pour bien des commentateurs, le mythe d'Orphée sous-tend toute l'œuvre de Nerval,[9] nulle part pourtant Nerval ne l'a développé de façon systématique. Ni conte, ni sonnet, ni article où la légende d'Orphée soit «racontée». Technique faite simplement d'allusions et de sous-entendus. Là où d'autres broderont sur le côté pittoresque, ou développeront le sens philosophique du mythe, Nerval, dans ses œuvres les plus réussies, ne fera qu'insérer les quelques phrases d'une extrême simplicité et d'une obsédante musicalité qui évoquent la substance essentielle d'un mythe familier: «Eurydice! Eurydice! Une seconde fois perdue!» (on pense au «nage vers ton Électre» de Baudelaire) ou:

Et j'ai deux fois vainqueur traversé l'Achéron,
Modulant tour à tour sur la lyre d'Orphée ...

A côté de cette décantation toute classique se trouvent pourtant, à travers l'œuvre en général, des allusions très variées.[10] Quelles sont donc les possibilitiés qu'offre à Nerval le mythe d'Orphée? quel choix a-t-il fait parmi les multiples aspects de la légende? et quels sont les résultats esthétiques qui accompagnent ce choix?

L'apport des siècles peut évidemment suggérer différentes tonalités. «Appel aux profondeurs» mystique; rationalisation; parodie même. Comme l'a dit Mme Eva Kushner, bien des écrivains tâcheront d'«introduire une logique dans le sein du mythe sans le dépoétiser».[11] Logique qui peut porter sur des explications physiques ou psychologiques – mythes solaires, symboles de luttes politiques, analyses de phénomènes produits par l'influence de stimulants ou de crises nerveuses. Au XIXe siècle, mages et médecins, érudits et écrivains sont particulièrement fascinés par ces différentes possibilités. Nerval, lui, d'une multiplicité de parallèles, combinant le sourire devant l'incongruité ou devant l'illusion avec la solennité des résonances, fera ressortir le «retour cyclique», à travers les âges, des souffrances, des désirs et des victoires de l'imagination humaine.

Devant les grandes lignes du mythe d'Orphée, cinq thèmes sembleraient s'offrir. Orphée voyageur, participant à l'expédition des Argonautes. Orphée amant, cherchant ou pleurant une Eurydice perdue. Orphée initié, fondateur de cultes mystiques (rôle que l'érudition lui conteste vigoureusement de nos jours). Orphée poète, dont la puissance magique exerce un charme miraculeux sur toutes les créatures – arbres, rochers, bêtes et oiseaux. Orphée mourant, démembré par les Bacchantes, mais dont la tête surnagera pour chanter, et dont la lyre, qui représenterait l'harmonie des sphères, deviendra une constellation.

De ces cinq possibilités, la première et la dernière figurent peu chez Nerval. La quasi-absence de la mort d'Orphée est en elle-même révélatrice. (Je dis «quasi», car elle figure quand même dans un contexte inattendu, traitée d'un ton humoristique, dans les *Nuits d'Octobre*: près des Halles, un ivrogne s'apprête à dormir, vautré sur les tas de fleurs,

imaginant sans doute être le vieux Silène, et que les Bacchantes lui ont préparé ce lit odorant. Les fleuristes se jettent sur lui, et le voilà bien plutôt exposé au sort d'Orphée (I. 99).

A tout moment, le spectacle le plus quotidien suscite ainsi chez Nerval des réminiscences mythologiques: les deux royaumes s'interpénètrent de la façon la plus naturelle. Aurait-on sous-estimé, en soulignant la gravité des obsessions sérieuses, la façon dont le ton léger peut évoquer la persistance de l'expérience humaine à travers les siècles?) Si le démembrement d'Orphée figure peu chez un auteur qui a tendance à éviter certaines précisions dans la cruauté, et pour qui Orphée représentera moins la victime que le vainqueur, le sort de sa lyre, consacrée, après sa mort, parmi les constellations, ajoutera une dimension importante aux allusions du sonnet «El Desdichado»; le «luth constellé» du début, qui «porte le soleil noir de la mélancolie», devient à la fin cette «lyre d'Orphée» qui, tout en chantant les alternances d'angoisse et d'extase chez un individu, rappellerait aussi l'harmonie finale de la musique des sphères.

L'absence relative de l'Orphée des Argonautes est peut-être, elle aussi, symptomatique. Relative, car la fonction de cet Orphée était de vaincre les sirènes; la tentation par la sirène séductrice, celle qui, de façon fallacieuse, semble réincarner l'idéal, se retrouvera partout chez Nerval, et le poète qui «module sur la lyre d'Orphée ...» a aussi «rêvé dans la grotte où nage la sirène.» Mais la quête d'un idéal chez Nerval s'exprime à travers des symboles plus immédiatement personnels que la recherche épique de la Toison d'Or: Orphée s'associe, non pas aux Argonautes, mais à la recherche d'Eurydice.

Orphée amant a donné lieu à travers les siècles aux interprétations les plus divergentes. Vainqueur des enfers en ce qu'il réussit à en arracher sa bien-aimée; victime en même temps des dieux et de sa propre culpabilité quand il la reperd avant de lui rendre la vie. Les érudits de nos jours distinguent nettement deux traditions: symbole de conquête et symbole de faillite. Nerval, toujours tiraillé entre des contraires, se servira des résonances des deux côtés.

Sur la faute d'Orphée, sur la signification de son geste quand il se retourne vers Eurydice, sur *Le Regard d'Orphée* qu'a évoqué mon collègue et ami M. Barrère dans sa leçon inaugurale de Cambridge,[12] les mystagogues et les artistes ont fourni, à travers les âges, toutes les interprétations possibles et imaginables. L'explication du «trop d'amour» leur semblerait souvent trop simple: entre le débile rimeur de Platon, coupable de ne pas vouloir mourir avec sa bien-aimée, et le représentant de l'inconscient chez les modernes, qui rechercherait sans le savoir la mort de sa femme ou la sienne propre, nous aurons tout vu. Le thème d'une culpabilité obscure est une des hantises de Nerval. Avec son habituelle discrétion personnelle et son sens aigu des besoins de la généralisation esthétique, il réussit à évoquer l'intensité d'un instinct profondément enraciné dans l'homme sans trop l'enserrer dans les précisions anecdotiques. Relisons cette phrase du début d'*Aurélia*:

Peu importent les circonstances de cet événement qui devait avoir une si grande influence sur ma vie. Chacun peut chercher dans ses souvenirs l'émotion la plus navrante, le coup le plus terrible frappé sur l'âme par le destin. (I, 359).

La faute envers la femme aimée revêt d'ailleurs chez lui différentes formes. Il s'agit parfois d'avoir cherché à la «ressusciter» – pendant sa vie mais dans son absence – par des amours faciles avec une autre qui lui ressemble: on pense aux *Lettres à Jenny*, à *Octavie*, à *Sylvie*, et, dans l'article sur Rétif, Nerval attribue précisément à Orphée cette faute qui n'appartient pas à la légende:

Ce souvenir immortel qui le suivait au milieu de ses plus grands égarements, image virginale et pure, impuissante, hélas! à le préserver, fuyant toujours, comme Eurydice, que le destin arrache aux bras du *poète parjure* ... (II, 1088),

comme dans *Octavie* «le fantôme du bonheur n'avait été que le reproche d'un *parjure*» (I, 291).[13]

Mais la faute fondamentale, c'est pour Nerval celle de l'artiste, déchiré entre la vie humaine et les exigences d'une imagination en quête de l'idéal. S'il perd son Eurydice, c'est surtout parce qu'il s'en est servi comme pâture à rêveries, comme moyen de création esthétique.[14] Au centre se trouvent les paroles moqueuses d'Aurélie dans *Sylvie*:

Vous ne m'aimez pas! ... Vous cherchez un drame, voilà tout (1271);

ou de Corilla:

Le seigneur Fabio n'adore en moi que l'actrice peut-être, et son amour a besoin de la distance et de la rampe allumée ... [il est] trop poète (I, 322);

la constatation de Nerval lui-même:

Nous ne vivons pas, nous n'aimons pas. Nous étudions la vie, nous analysons l'amour (II, 61);

ou celle qu'il attribue à Rétif:

Nous ne vivons pas, nous! nous analysons la vie! ... Les autres créatures sont nos jouets éternels. ... Suis-je bien sûr moi-même d'avoir aimé? ... Nous ne voyons partout que des modèles à décrire, des passions à rendre, et tous ceux qui se mêlent à notre vie sont victimes de notre égoïsme, comme nous le sommes de notre imagination (II, 1072).

Les souffrances de celui qui cherche à évoquer une Eurydice perdue, décantation des plus beaux rêves de la jeunesse, n'en sont pas moins vraies:

Ces enthousiasmes bizarres que j'avais ressentis si longtemps, ces rêves, ces pleurs, ces désespoirs et ces tendresses, ... ce n'était donc pas l'amour? Mais où donc est-il? (I, 271),

et trouvent la réponse: «Je crois être amoureux, n'est-ce pas? Mais, si je crois l'être, je le suis» (II, 350; cf. II, 109). De ces incertitudes devant la réalité des sentiments, trois genres de victoire émergeront: le sourire tendre et ironique d'une réconciliation avec la vie quotidienne et imparfaite à la fin de *Sylvie*; la reconquête d'un amour idéal à la fin d'*Aurélia*; la suprême victoire du chant de l'artiste qui résonne dans «El Desdichado».

Orphée amant s'associe étroitement à Orphée initié, dans sa descente aux enfers. Ici se combinent les traditions d'un Orphée fils du soleil avec les multiples interprétations des illuministes. Dans son article sur Quintus Auclair, Nerval cite longuement les commentaires de cet auteur sur les hymnes attribués à Orphée: il a soin cependant de parler des théories de *La Thréicie* («titre qu'il avait emprunté au surnom donné par Virgile à Orphée») comme d' «une pensée qui semble aujourd'hui toucher la folie» et de chercher à en dégager une idée plus immédiatement compréhensible; celle du «retour cyclique des destinées» (II, 1208). Dans son introduction aux *Illuminés*, il pose d'ailleurs la question essentielle:

N'y a-t-il pas quelque chose de raisonnable à tirer même des folies! ne fût-ce que pour se préserver de croire nouveau ce qui est très ancien . . . Analyser les bigarrures de l'âme humaine, c'est de la physiologie morale, – cela vaut bien un travail de naturaliste, de paléographe, ou d'archéologue (II, 938).

L'Orphée des illuministes des XVIIIe et XIXe siècles tirait sa sagesse des traditions de l'Égypte ancienne, et d'une initiation au culte de la déesse Isis. Le chapitre de Nerval sur les Pyramides, dans le *Voyage en Orient*, est on ne peut plus éloigné de tout ton de mystagogue. Partagé lui-même entre un scepticisme rationaliste et la hantise de l'au-delà, il s'attaque aussi à un genre à la mode, où il s'agit de fournir à tout phénomène des explications rationnelles tout en laissant la possibilité d'un frisson surnaturel. Le chef-d'œuvre du genre sera *La Vénus d'Ille* de Mérimée. Sur les Pyramides, Nerval se sert de détails trop saugrenus pour créer un envoûtement; l'Orphée qui subit les épreuves (et dont la femme est subtilisée par des ruses de prêtres) a trop l'air d'un athlète qui échoue aux Jeux Olympiques: il ne réussit pas à saisir certains anneaux de fer et tombe dans le canal.[15] Devant ces explications du mythe, attribuées de façon humoristique à un savant allemand, Nerval ajoute:

Avec ce système, il est possible d'expliquer matériellement toutes les religions. Mais qu'y gagnerons-nous? (II, 231)

et reçoit la réponse: «Rien». La hantise de l'au-delà persiste. D'autres interprétations de croyances surnaturelles seront traitées ailleurs: d'un autre héros, Nerval écrira:

Je n'ai pas dit que Hakem eût fait des prodiges, je n'ai analysé que les sensations de son âme (II, 1345).

Haschisch, alcool, maladie nerveuse, rêve: autant d'angles de vision et de moyens d'analyser le parallèle entre le mythe et les impulsions de l'âme créatrice. Et la noyade bizarre de l'Orphée des Pyramides fera écho à celle, toute naturelle, qui figure parmi les souvenirs d'enfance dans *Sylvie*, conte où le rationalisme et le mystère se rencontreront dans un équilibre parfait.

Le thème de la descente aux enfers tient évidemment une place privilégiée dans l'œuvre de Nerval.[16] Épreuves, initiations et finalement consécration et pardon reçus de la grande déesse syncrétique, déesse qui représente la mère, l'amante, la Vierge Marie, l'idéal longtemps rêvé, il a fait siens ces aspects de la mythologie. Il en tire pourtant moins des révélations ésotériques que des moyens de suggérer et d'analyser certaines impulsions fondamentales de l'imagination humaine. Son livre sur *Les Illuminés* porte le sous-titre *Précurseurs du socialisme*, titre inventé en partie pour les besoins d'une époque (II, 1457), mais répondant aussi au désir éprouvé par tant de héros de Nerval de purifier, après leur descente aux enfers, non seulement l'individu mais la société.[17] Certaines résonances politiques chez Nerval demanderaient une analyse détaillée. Il faudrait aussi une analyse suivie des résonances de symboles portant sur les luttes de forces naturelles (printemps/hiver; neiges/volcans), symboles visibles particulièrement dans «Horus» ou «Quintus Auclair», mais latents partout. La hantise fondamentale qui gouverne la descente aux enfers est pourtant le désir de savoir que rien ne meurt,[18] de retrouver les êtres aimés et les ancêtres les plus éloignés dont l'expérience préfigure la nôtre et contribue à la vision des «splendides villes» de l'avenir. Un autre poète, de notre siècle, chantera l'hymne de ces «temps passés, trépassés, . . . dieux qui me formâtes».

Et nous nous trouvons en face de la dernière et de la plus importante des incarnations d'Orphée: Orphée poète. C'est par le chant que se fait la conquête du royaume des ombres. Inutile de rappeler les innombrables occasions où, pour Nerval, une voix qui chante fournit le rappel le plus instinctif et le plus immédiat des joies de l'enfance, ou d'un passé historique ou légendaire. Les airs qui traversent son œuvre en prose, airs d'opéra et surtout de chanson populaire, ne comportent ni la fine fleur de culture du «petit air de Vinteuil» ni le modernisme du «One of these Days» de Sartre; ils se basent pourtant sur une même intuition de l'emprise particulière du son comme moyen d'imposer au chaos le salut d'une forme. Vers la fin d'*Aurélia*, parmi les visions cosmiques, surgit comme signe de paix la simple chanson des pâtres:

> Là-haut sur les montagnes
> Le monde y vit content;
> Le rossignol sauvage
> Fait mon contentement!

Dans «A Mme Ida Dumas», résonne à travers les âges le plus beau
de tous les chants d'exil, le *Super flumina Babylonis*:

> Et tous deux en rêvant nous pleurions Israël[19]

dans «*Myrtho*», un chant grêle et victorieux unit passé et avenir; dans
des notes de projets, la musique préside à la naissance d'un monde
nouveau.[20]

La richesse musicale des *Chimères*, malgré maintes études d'un
grand intérêt, n'a pas encore reçu l'analyse détaillée qu'elle
mériterait, propre à montrer comment se produit une hantise faite
d'une rare équivalence entre sens, son et suggestion.[21] Il ne serait
même pas frivole de noter combien les vocables *Orphée* et *Eurydice*
(que ce soit en latin, en italien ou en français) se prêtent déjà à des
prolongements poétiques:[22] ce genre de conjonction miraculeuse où
son et sens concourent préoccupera un Valéry. Qu'Eurydice eût
porté un nom moins musical, son destin littéraire aurait-il été le
même?

La musique proprement dite a certainement contribué à la
conception nervalienne d'Orphée. Cherchant lui-même dans l'acte
de voyager, après une de ses crises, une nouvelle remontée des
enfers, ce sont des vers tirés du livret de l'*Orphée* de Gluck que
Nerval cite:

> Laissez-vous toucher par mes pleurs,
> Ombres, larves, spectres terribles,

et Jean Richer a supposé avec vraisemblance que le cri d'*Aurélia*:
«Eurydice! Eurydice!» aurait encore comme source les plaintes
déchirantes et mélodieuses de la version de Gluck. Devant les
théories sur les Pyramides comme lieu d'initiation, théories qu'en
tant que journaliste en voyage, tenu à fournir une copie sémillante,
il traite de façon assez désinvolte, Nerval se prend pourtant à rêver à
ce que donnerait une représentation dans ces monuments séculaires
des épreuves d'un autre initié, en pensant à la *Flûte enchantée* de
Mozart.[23] A-t-on assez dégagé chez lui les résultats de hantises de ce
genre? Dans ses visions de luttes épiques, c'est souvent le *Robert le
Diable* de Meyerbeer qui revient l'obséder. Et le voyageur en Orient,

d'un ton mi-souriant, mi-sérieux, écrit:
Je retrouverai à l'Opéra le Caire véritable, l'Égypte immaculée, l'Orient qui m'échappe.

De mon aperçu sommaire il ressort de plus en plus qu'Orphée, quelles que soient les résonances de son mythe chez Nerval, est loin d'être seul au centre de son œuvre. En fait, il y figure assez rarement, ayant subi de multiples avatars. En tant qu'initié, il s'assimile à Moïse, au Rama des Indiens, au Christ, à Pythagore, à bien d'autres encore. Son nom est évoqué dans les importants chapitres sur la religion des Druses. Poète, amant ou voyageur, il rappelle les personnages les plus hétéroclites – l'acteur Le Destin de Scarron ou Wilhelm Meister, l'Empereur Néron (lui aussi frustré en amour et, «poète ardent», jouant d'un instrument de musique au milieu de catastrophes) ou même, par un jeu de mots, ce Baron Puckler-Moskau qui a «deux fois traversé le lac funeste de Karon», dans l'Égypte (II, 741). Les noms d'autres héros mythiques, d'ailleurs, résonnent à travers les *Chimères* – Icare, Phaëton, Atys, Antéros... Dans les œuvres en prose, d'autres héros qu'Orphée tiendront des rôles plus développés. L'amant qui retrouve dans le paradis du rêve celle qu'il ne peut posséder dans le monde quotidien est évoqué à travers le Polyphile des néo-platoniciens. Le héros-martyr prend la forme de Prométhée. Pour le thème de la descente aux enfers, c'est le *Faust* de Goethe qui donne lieu, dans la seconde *Préface*, a un des passages les plus riches et les plus émouvants; dans maintes autres allusions, nous trouvons plutôt des souvenirs de la descente de Virgile et de Dante ou même de celle d'Alcide, que de celle d'Orphée. Le thème s'étend d'ailleurs pour comprendre les descentes de Nerval lui-même dans les bas-fonds de Paris, dans les recoins oubliés de la province, ou dans les sinuosités des villes orientales. Et à côté de la descente aux enfers se place l'envol vers la lune, à l'instar des héros de l'Arioste. Quand Nerval cherche dans des ouvrages de longue haleine à recréer les épreuves d'un héros à l'affût de l'amour et de la gloire, ce n'est pas Orphée qu'il choisit, mais un Adoniram, amant de la Reine du Matin, ou un Rétif qu'il assimile à sa propre substance, avant de trouver sa vraie voie et d'écrire à la première personne sa descente dans les profondeurs du moi.

Trois conclusions sembleraient se dégager au point de vue esthétique. D'abord l'exceptionnelle complexité du réseau analogique grâce auquel Nerval tisse autour de toute figure mythologique de riches allusions. Je n'en ai indiqué qu'une sélection très restreinte. Mais ensuite, pour le lecteur n'ayant pas à sa disposition la même érudition hétéroclite, ce qui portera la charge poétique la plus immédiate, ce seront les mythes qui font partie d'une tradition séculaire et familière: la suggestion d'une angoisse par le soupir musical du vocable *Eurydice*, ou d'une conquête par le chant qui accompagne victorieusement la double traversée de l'Achéron. Finalement, je reviens à cette lucidité que Baudelaire a soulignée chez Nerval. Si, plus que tout autre, Nerval s'identifie avec les héros les plus étranges de ses lectures ou avec les créatures de son imagination, jamais il ne cesse de distinguer entre le rêve et la réalité, entre ce qu'«il serait consolant de croire», «le monde d'illusions où j'avais quelque temps vécu» et «ce que les hommes appellent la raison.» Toujours chez lui revient le ton en même temps nostalgique et ironique du «peut-être» et du «cependant». Sa descente aux enfers, dans *Aurélia* même, n'est pas celle d'un illuminé rapportant une doctrine «orphique»; c'est celle d'un poète qui, à partir des impulsions, des craintes et des désirs de notre commune humanité, crée de riches visions et les interroge avec une douce modestie. Là, il suit la même courbe que plus tard un Rimbaud: désir d'être Dieu et de renouveler le monde, voyage éperdu à travers d'étranges visions, nostalgie de la terre familière, luttes épiques entre la conviction d'une innocence primordiale et la menace d'une culpabilité indéfinie, retour finalement dans le monde de tous les jours avec «la réalité rugueuse à étreindre».

Dans la musique, a écrit Nerval, certaines mélodies peuvent également se prêter à la plus haute expression tragique, ou à des chants de folie et des chœurs de buveurs.

De même pour le thème d'Orphée. On a tendance, de nos jours, à rechercher partout dans l'œuvre de Nerval les signes avant-coureurs des angoisses de la fin; ne négligerait-on pas trop la fine allégresse et la vive et précise observation que l'on trouve dans des ouvrages tels que les *Nuits d'Octobre* ou les *Promenades et Souvenirs?*[24] Dans sa descente aux enfers à travers les carrières de Montmartre ou les tavernes des Halles la nuit, en même temps qu'il égrène ses propres souvenirs ou ses propres rêves, il esquisse un tableau de son époque d'une saveur exceptionnelle, où, pour des raisons qui mériteraient une analyse suivie, un travail de journaliste devient une œuvre d'art.

Un dernier mot. Prononcez le nom d'Orphée en Angleterre et l'on citera immanquablement:

> Orpheus with his lute made trees
> And the mountain tops that freeze
> Bow themselves when he did sing.

Ce pouvoir magique sur la nature figure comme thème chez Nerval; plus important est son don de l'exercer lui-même en tant qu'artiste. Il se réjouit certes de faire des bêtes les symboles d'une puissance mystérieuse: des oiseaux doués de la parole et soumis aux ordres d'un héros magicien parcourent ses contes fantastiques ou ses rêves. C'est pourtant lorsqu'il amoindrit le côté ésotérique en faveur d'une technique où le mystère de la vie s'exprime à travers le quotidien qu'il atteint la réussite de *Sylvie*; là, souvenirs individuels et traditions séculaires se combinent dans la visite à Ermenonville où Gérard retrouve d'abord le chien empaillé qu'il avait connu vivant («le dernier carlin peut-être», représentant d'un passé royal maintenant perdu mais que le souvenir fait revivre) et ensuite le vieux perroquet dont le regard résume les trois côtés essentiels du monde nervalien, nostalgie, ironie, persistance des choses aimées à travers les âges:

Le perroquet demandait à déjeuner comme en ses plus beaux jours, et me regarda de cet œil rond, bordé d'une peau chargée de rides, qui fait penser au regard expérimenté des vieillards.[25]

Dans le sonnet «Vers dorés», Nerval réexprime les doctrines attribuées à Pythagore sur un univers où tout vit, tout est sensible.[26] Son propre don sera moins celui du mystagogue, marchand d'abstractions, que celui du poète qui, pour faire revivre les mythes séculaires, anime les objets du monde naturel dans toute leur force et toute leur fragilité. Ces rochers que charmait le chant d'Orphée surgissent dans les vers martelés du sonnet «A Mme Sand» pour évoquer physiquement en même temps le thème de la vigueur des ancêtres et celui de la gloire des poètes (tel Du Bartas) qui les célèbrent et les renouvellent à travers les siècles:

> La neige règne au front de leurs pics infranchis,
> Et ce sont, m'a-t-on dit, les ossements blanchis
> Des anciens monts rongés par la mer du Déluge.

Ces arbres qui suivaient les pas d'Orphée (et c'est sans doute par analogie que Nerval a noté la forêt qui semble marcher à la fin de *Macbeth*) sont évoqués dans toute la grâce et la délicatesse d'une végétation qui pousse, meurt et renaît. Sur la surface d'un monde où gisent les rochers indestructibles, symboles d'une permanence à travers les âges, Nerval fait revivre la beauté frêle et éphémère, qui pourtant renaît et persiste – celle des arbres, des arbustes et des fleurs. Sa magie s'exerce à travers les touches les moins appuyées et les plus précises pour évoquer les grains de corail des sorbiers, les limoniers aux feuilles luisantes, les saules aux branches rougeâtres, le tronc blanc du bouleau se détachant du milieu des bruyères, même l'humble asperge avec ses «panaches décorés de perles rouges». Et cette végétation suggère en même temps la complexité et l'unité de tous les phénomènes naturels:

> Toujours, sous les rameaux du laurier de Virgile,
> Le pâle Hortensia s'unit au Myrte vert!

tandis que, pour évoquer le paradis perdu, on pense à

> ... La treille où le Pampre à la Rose s'allie.

L'Orphée du mythe exerçait une puissance magique sur le monde naturel. En dernière analyse, la seule vraie magie, comme Mallarmé l'a dit, consiste en la maîtrise des mots. «La dernière folie qui me restera probablement», disait Nerval, «ce sera de me croire poète.» Et dans le mythe d'Orphée, victime ou vainqueur, mythe qui offre à l'artiste «ce privilège d'exposer à tous un idéal que chacun interprète et réalise à son gré» (II, 191), ce qu'il a surtout vu et ce qu'il a triomphalement renouvelé, c'est le thème du destin du poète.

NOTES

1 Texte d'une communication faite au XXIe Congrès de l'Association Internationale des Études Françaises, le 24 juillet 1969, et publiée dans les *Cahiers* de l'Association, N° 22, 1970, pp. 153–68.
2 Plon, 1965, p. 24.
3 Hachette, 1963.
4 Jean Senelier, *Gérard de Nerval, Essai de Bibliographie*, Nizet, 1959; *Bibliographie nervalienne* (1960–1967), *et compléments antérieurs*, Nizet, 1968, James Villas, *Gérard de Nerval. A Critical Bibliography*, University of Missouri Press, Columbia, Missouri, 1968. Aux références que donne l'index sous le mot *Orphée* devraient s'ajouter les numéros 84, 219, 317. Je n'ai pu, dans une courte communication, examiner dans le détail maints livres ou articles contenant des observations intéressantes.
5 Les chiffres dans le texte renvoient à l'édition de la Pléiade des *Œuvres* de Nerval procurée par A. Béguin et J. Richer (t. I, 4° édition, 1966; t. II, 1956).

6 *Cahiers de l'Association internationale des études françaises*, Numéro 10, mai 1958, pp. 138–157.

7 Marie-Jeanne Durry, *Gérard de Nerval et le Mythe*, Flammarion, 1956.

8 Parmi les récents ouvrages de longue haleine, je signale en particulier Gérard Schaeffer, *Le Voyage en Orient de Nerval, Étude des Structures*, Neuchâtel, La Baconnière, 1967; Kurt Schärer, *Thématique de Nerval ou le monde recomposé*, Minard, 1968; Ross Chambers, *Gérard de Nerval et la poétique du voyage*, Corti, 1969 (Voir surtout pp. 291–304).

9 J. Richer, *op. cit.*, p. 514; G. Schaeffer, *op. cit.*, pp. 10, 25, 33; R. Chambers, *op. cit.*, p. 296.

10 Sur certains aspects des mythes classiques chez Nerval, voir la belle étude d'Albert S. Guérard, «Images, structure et thèmes dans 'El Desdichado'», *Modern Language Review*, LVIII, n° 4 (1963), pp. 507–15, et l'article de Norma Rinsler, «Classical literature in the work of Gérard de Nerval», *Revue de Littérature Comparée*, XXXVII, n° 1 (1963), pp. 5–32.

11 Eva Kushner, *Le Mythe d'Orphée dans la littérature française contemporaine*, Nizet, 1961, p. 76. Le livre de Mme Kushner nous permet de profiter des travaux d'érudits tels que J. Heurgon, I. M. Linforth, etc.

12 Cambridge University Press, 1956.

13 Le thème de la présomption du poète, cherchant à immortaliser la bien-aimée, puis doutant de ses propres capacités, parcourt les Lettres. Pour la faute de l'acteur qui joue mal son rôle, voir en même temps *La Pandora* et, dans la «Lettre à Alexandre Dumas» qui ouvre *Les Filles du Feu*, le développement sur Brisacier et Néron. Dans *Aurélia*, différentes fautes se suivront et se feront enfin pardonner.

14 Le «Malheur à qui me touche!» qu'expriment devant la femme aimée un Hernani ou avant lui un René trouve ici une nouvelle dimension. Bien des auteurs du XIXᵉ siècle ressentiront la division entre l'analyste et l'amant. Nerval a lu de près *Adolphe* et le cite à plusieurs reprises (voir ci-dessus, pp. 80–95). Ce thème est d'ailleurs sans doute un de ceux qui font que Proust reconnaît avec joie chez Nerval certains côtés de sa propre substance.

15 Unir, de façon satisfaisante, l'ironie et le sérieux sera un des problèmes esthétiques de la seconde génération romantique. Le ton humoristique substituera souvent à une ironie créatrice un dégonflement incongru. Ces variations de tonalité, avec leur plus ou moins grande réussite, pourraient se suivre chez un Gautier ou un Musset.

16 Après une des «Nuits d'Octobre», il cite, sans nom d'auteur, un vers d'Auguste Barbier sur Michel-Ange qui a dû le hanter – citation d'ailleurs inexacte, ou comportant une coquille:

Voilà, voilà celui qui [re]vient de l'enfer! (I, 102).

17 Léon Cellier a d'ailleurs noté, *op. cit.*, p. 140, la tradition d'un Orphée «héros plébéien».

18 Voir la seconde Préface du *Faust* de Gœthe. Voir aussi, dans l'édition critique des *Chimères* par Jean Guillaume (Bruxelles, Palais des Académies, 1966) la variante d' «El Desdichado»: «J'ai deux fois *vivant* traversé l'Achéron.»

19 Cf. dans la «Lettre à Jules Janin» qui précède *Lorely* le passage où,

comme consolation après une faillite artistique, «nous serions partis à pied pour l'Allemagne, et une fois là, nous aurions récité en chœur le *super flumina Babylonis!*» Là encore, un auteur classique, avant Nerval, a dans un magnifique développement, tissé ses propres variations sur un thème séculaire: le Bossuet des *Oraisons funèbres*, pour qui les prêtres de son siècle en exil «chantaient hautement les cantiques de Sion dans une terre étrangère».

20 II, 718. Voir aussi les pages sur Liszt dans *Lorely* (II, 788 *et sqq.*).

21 Voir Yves Le Hir, «La Versification de Gérard de Nerval», *Lettres romanes*, X (1956), p. 409–22; Henri Meschonnic, «Essai sur la poétique de Nerval», *Europe*, 353 (1958), pp. 10–33 (quelques aperçus très fins); A. Fairlie: «An approach to Nerval» (voir ci-dessus, pp. 271–87); A. Fairlie: «Nerval et Richelet», *Revue des Sciences Humaine*, 91 (1958), pp. 397–400 (voir ci-dessus, pp. 304–7).

22 Cf. dans les *Cahiers de l'A.I.E.F.*, Numero 18, mars 1966, p. 282, l'intervention de L. J. Austin sur la musicalité suggestive du nom de Piranèse.

23 II, 227. Voir aussi les allusions au *Don Juan* de Mozart.

24 Les *Œuvres complémentaires*, éditées par Jean Richer, fournissent évidemment un précieux apport, dont s'est servi en particulier Kurt Schärer.

25 On se souvient évidemment du perroquet de Flaubert dans *Un Cœur simple*. Symbole qui unit, dans les deux cas, la vie quotidienne du bon bourgeois et les rêves ésotériques ou mystiques.

26 Voir Georges Le Breton, «Le pythagorisme de Nerval et la source des *Vers dorés*», *La Tour Saint-Jacques*, 13–14 (1958), pp. 79–87.

PART FOUR

Flaubert

21

Flaubert et la conscience du réel (1967)

Bouvard (François-Denis-Bartholomé) et Pécuchet (Juste-Romain-Cyrille) sont la double réduction à l'absurde du thème de la conscience humaine aux prises avec cette réalité qu'elle essaie de comprendre, de maîtriser et de façonner. Leurs rêves outrecuidants sont multiples; il y en a un en particulier qui me hante aujourd'hui:[1] «Leur rêve est de faire partie de la société des Antiquaires de Normandie – de lire un mémoire dans un Congrès.»[2] Mais la présence railleuse de ces deux fantômes à nos assises ne va pas sans un grain de consolation. Car, sous la caricature guignolesque de leurs efforts pour interpréter devant un auditoire stupéfait les Immortels Chefs-d'œuvre de la Littérature, (et que fais-je d'autre, devant un tout autre auditoire?) Flaubert a néanmoins affirmé en sourdine certaines valeurs indestructibles, opposant ainsi, en un savant contrepoint, à des négations manifestes, des convictions latentes d'autant plus efficaces qu'elles ne sont pas sans réserves. Voici la phrase-clé: «L'Art, en de certaines occasions, ébranle les esprits médiocres, et des horizons infinis peuvent être révélés par ses interprètes les plus lourds.»[3] Derrière les limites imposées à cette communication par l'horaire, la nécessité du choix, les insuffisances d'un point de vue personnel ou la difficulté de l'expression (problèmes qui se posent à quiconque essaie de décrire n'importe quel aspect du réel), j'ai peut-être donc l'autorisation sardonique de Flaubert si j'espère qu'à travers un interprète des plus lourds, la réalité complexe de son art pourra parler pour elle-même.

Dans ses écrits personnels, Flaubert a exprimé plus fortement peut-être qu'aucun autre écrivain les deux extrêmes qui constituent le dilemme de la conscience créatrice aux prises avec le réel: soumission humble ou émerveillée devant les choses en elles-mêmes; transformation et logique et magique. Ce sont quelques-uns des rapports entre ces deux impulsions également intenses qui feront le centre de ma communication. J'examinerai très brièvement quelques principes, pour en voir ensuite certaines conséquences dans l'œuvre d'art.

La conscience créatrice a une double fonction: celle d'apercevoir et celle de trier et de regrouper les éléments multiples et divers de la réalité. Flaubert, qui trouve fallacieux tant de systèmes adoptés par la conscience pour trier ces éléments selon des attitudes acquises, soulignera toujours avec une intensité toute particulière la valeur positive de la simple perception, de la simple contemplation des faits en eux-mêmes. Préjugés moraux, absolus métaphysiques, théories intellectuelles, arrivisme pratique, narcissisme affectif: tous ces facteurs faussent notre vision et simplifient à l'excès notre perception du réel. Même le grand art du passé peut entraver la perception authentique, lorsque nous essayons dans notre propre vie de mouler une réalité réfractaire pour l'adapter à la stylisation de l'art. Si les personnages de Flaubert découvrent inéluctablement que la réalité n'est ni du Walter Scott ni du Balzac, cette réaction à la culture acquise sera féconde.

Ainsi donc, des raisons d'ordre intellectuel incitent Flaubert à vouloir se soumettre aux faits extérieurs, dépouillés de jugements («l'ineptie consiste à vouloir conclure»),[4] d'explications métaphysiques («Cela est parce que cela est»)[5] ou d'une échelle de valeurs traditionnelles («L'histoire d'un pou peut être plus belle que celle d'Alexandre»).[6] Car la trame de l'expérience quotidienne est faite non de ce qui est manifestement dramatique mais de nuances presque imperceptibles: «La vérité est autant dans les demi-teintes que dans les tons tranchés»,[7] et

Ce ne sont pas les grands malheurs qui font le malheur, ni les grands bonheurs qui font le bonheur, mais c'est le tissu fin et imperceptible de mille circonstances banales, de mille détails ternes qui composent toute une vie de calme radieux ou d'agitation infernale.[8]

Mais ce qui incite à la contemplation impartiale, ce n'est pas seulement l'intellect, mais des impulsions d'ordre affectif et sensoriel.[9] «Aimez les faits pour eux-mêmes: la contemplation peut être pleine de tendresses.»[10] «J'éprouve des sensations voluptueuses rien qu'à voir, mais quand je vois bien»; «voir jusque dans les pores des choses».[11] «A force quelquefois de contempler un caillou . . . je me suis senti y entrer.»[12] «Etre brahme, exister dans cette absorption démesurée.»[13] «Je m'incrusterai dans la couleur de l'objectif et je m'absorberai en lui, avec un amour sans partage.»[14] Surtout «C'est une délicieuse chose que d'écrire, que de ne plus être *soi*, mais de circuler dans toute la création dont on parle ... j'étais les chevaux, les feuilles, le vent.»[15] C'est ainsi que saint Antoine sera ramené des spéculations métaphysiques les plus vastes jusqu'au désir d' «être la matière», et que Bouvard et Pécuchet, après leur pèlerinage encyclopédique à travers les connaissances humaines, devront se heurter à la constatation: «Il n'y a que des phénomènes», se mettant à les copier en une «joie finale» – «ils ont trouvé le bonheur» (et Flaubert de noter: «Plaisir qu'il y a dans l'acte matériel de copier»).[16]

La phrase connue: «Pour qu'une chose soit intéressante, il suffit de la regarder longtemps»[17] nous rappelle évidemment le mot de Baudelaire: «Dans certains états de l'âme presque surnaturels, la profondeur de la vie se révèle tout entière dans le spectacle, si ordinaire qu'il soit, qu'on a sous les yeux. Il en devient le symbole.» Et nous nous trouvons devant cette autre conviction de Flaubert, qui dépasse la simple soumission à l'objet, et qui s'exprime avec autant de force. C'est de la simple contemplation des faits de l'existence que, dès les œuvres de jeunesse, jaillit un éclair d'illumination: «je percevais tout à coup des rapports et des antithèses dont la précision lumineuse m'éblouissait».[18] Ce sera la fonction de l'art de mettre en lumière ces structures, en disposant les éléments de la réalité en des groupements harmonieux et suggestifs. Car «L'art n'est pas la réalité. Quoi qu'on fasse, on est obligé de choisir dans les éléments qu'elle fournit»;[19] «On ne peut faire vrai qu'en choisissant et en exagérant ... exagérer harmonieusement»;[20] «La réalité ne doit être qu'un tremplin»;[21] «Faire vrai ne me paraît pas être la première condition de l'art. Viser au beau est le principal.»[22]

Soumission au réel, transfiguration du réel: ces deux tendances trouvent une synthèse. D'une part, la double hantise de la précision et de la structure fait même prévoir à Flaubert que la littérature de l'avenir pourrait devenir «quelque chose entre l'algèbre et la musique».[23] D'autre part, comme l'a bien remarqué Geneviève Bollème,[24] Flaubert ira «voir, non pour copier, mais pour vérifier» et elle cite sa distinction entre l'observation artistique et l'observation scientifique; celle-là «doit surtout être instinctive et procéder par l'imagination d'abord. Vous concevez un sujet, une couleur, et vous l'affermissez ensuite par des secours étrangers. Le subjectif débute».[25] Mais le plus essentiel, c'est la conviction que la réalité, telle qu'elle est perçue par la conscience individuelle, est purement relative: «Il n'y a de vrai que les «rapports», c'est-à-dire la façon dont nous percevons les objets»;[26] «Il n'y a pas de Vrai! il n'y a que des manières de voir»;[27] et: «La poésie n'est qu'une manière de percevoir les objets extérieurs, un organe spécial qui tamise la matière et qui, sans la changer, la transfigure.»[28]

Quittant maintenant les théories, où je n'ai cherché qu'à rappeler brièvement quelques points évidents, je voudrais examiner quelques-unes des conséquences qui en découlent dans les œuvres. Mes remarques porteront d'abord sur la question de la soumission au réel, ensuite sur celle du choix qu'opère Flaubert en groupant les éléments que lui fournit la réalité, finalement sur les aspects qu'il a omis, ou qu'il est censé avoir omis, en faisant ce choix.

D'abord, la soumission au réel. Certains des personnages de Flaubert ressentent comme leur créateur un désir de s'absorber dans le monde extérieur. La conscience de soi-même, trait si fondamental de tous ses personnages, se manifeste sous deux formes: soit dans des êtres d'une suffisance béate (Homais dans le domaine des idées, Emma dans celui des sentiments), soit dans ceux qui sont dévorés par l'incertitude (Frédéric qui craint l'échec auprès de Mme Arnoux; Emma ou Bouvard et Pécuchet acculés à la désillusion lorsque la réalité reste réfractaire au rêve). Pendant des moments d'absorption totale en quelque chose d'extérieur au moi, les forces trompeuses ou paralysantes de la conscience de soi sont suspendues. Emma, étendue dans la forêt après avoir connu pour la première fois le bonheur des sens avec Rodolphe, Frédéric contemplant Mme Arnoux ou dans les épisodes avec Rosanette à Fontainebleau, Bouvard et Pécuchet dans leurs vagabondages à travers la campagne, se voient tous accorder ces moments parfaits en eux-mêmes où le désir et la crainte, le sentiment du passé et de l'avenir, disparaissent dans le caractère immédiat et harmonieux du présent. Chaque détail, isolé ainsi, semble être rehaussé pour recevoir une signification neuve, magique et multiple, comme dans ce moment-clé à Fontainebleau: «Près de l'auberge, une fille en chapeau de paille tirait des seaux d'un puits; chaque fois qu'ils remontaient, Frédéric écoutait avec une jouissance inexprimable le grincement de la chaîne.»[29]

Inutile de dire que ces instants ne sont nullement idéalisés. Si l'abandon apaisé à un moment de délectation venant du monde extérieur peut contenir en puissance la contemplation esthétique, il peut aussi représenter une sorte de lâcheté et de lassitude devant tout effort. La contemplation esthétique n'existe qu'en puissance chez ces personnages puisque, tel Swann chez Proust, ils ne savent ni pleinement analyser les causes de cet éclair d'illumination ni en tirer les conséquences. Abandon passif devant les choses plutôt que réflexion suivie et féconde. Que l'instant de communion entre la conscience et le monde extérieur s'attache à un objet, à une personne (Frédéric en présence de Mme Arnoux)[30] ou à une idée (Frédéric devant l'élan de la Révolution),[31] Flaubert en disséquera impitoyablement les causes physiques ou affectives, et fera suivre la désillusion inévitable. Cependant l'amère beauté de ces instants, malgré le sentiment lucide de leurs limites, n'en suggère pas moins que «ce sont ces souvenirs-là qui», une fois la vieillesse venue, nous réchauffent et nous «font regretter la vie».[32] Et, entre les différents moyens de sortir de soi, celui qui surgit momentanément comme le plus efficace, c'est l'impulsion créatrice: au cours des efforts de Frédéric pour écrire (efforts vite abandonnés) «peu à peu la sérénité du travail l'apaisa»; et Flaubert de commenter: «En plongeant dans la personnalité des autres, il oublia la sienne, ce qui est la seule manière peut-être de n'en pas souffrir.»[33]

Quant à la transfiguration du réel, de nombreux critiques[34] ont traité, souvent d'une manière remarquable, son art de tirer du monde des structures significatives. Je voudrais attirer ici l'attention sur un point seulement: la façon dont Flaubert, même dans ses romans les plus «réalistes», vise des effets fantastiques, obsédants, vertigineux. Son admiration pour Rabelais entre ici en jeu: il y a une joie analogue à combiner d'innombrables détails précis et authentiques avec un grossissement hallucinatoire. Le fiacre à Rouen, à travers une énumération minutieuse et cacophonique de rues, de ponts, de places, de statues, de quais, de tours et de cimetières réels, file à travers le dédale de la cité dans «une fureur de locomotion» interminable, frénétique, et qui atteint enfin des proportions héroï-comiques. A travers ce même labyrinthe de la ville, réel mais agrandi d'une manière sinistre, se poursuit à diverses reprises le thème de la recherche d'un être perdu ou désiré: Charles cherche Emma à travers Rouen; Frédéric essaie de retrouver Mme Arnoux, avec un degré surajouté de possibilités fantastiques, car il doit, lui, dépister d'abord Regimbart, et alors le chapelet des cafés de Paris, que cette nullité vient justement chaque fois de quitter, se déroule dans le crescendo d'une obsession grandissante.

On pourrait évidemment multiplier les exemples. Je me borne à noter comme particulièrement significatifs deux projets de fins de romans. D'abord, pour *Madame Bovary* (projet finalement écarté). Homais, se regardant au miroir, devait tomber dans le délire, avec des «effets fantastiques», en se demandant s'il était, non pas un être réel, mais la simple création d'un «petit paltoquet d'auteur que j'ai vu naître et qui m'a inventé pour faire croire que je n'existe pas».[35] Ici, dans un beau paradoxe à trois niveaux, l'imaginaire et le réel semblent s'emboîter l'un dans l'autre comme des poupées gigognes. Ensuite, la fin projetée de *Bouvard et Pécuchet* avec ses diverses étapes. L'échec dû à la combinaison de ces trois éléments dont Flaubert forme sa vision des rapports entre la conscience et le monde – la théorie, la pratique, le hasard – cet échec oblige les deux bonshommes à se rabattre sur les délices de copier: d'abord (en une soumission épique au réel) n'importe quel bout de papier, jusqu'aux emballages d'épicier. Pourtant eux aussi, tel Flaubert jeune, découvrent que le simple effort pour copier la réalité mène inévitablement au groupement des détails selon des structures parallèles et antithétiques; ils se débattent ensuite contre l'impossibilité d'imposer un classement adéquat aux éléments réfractaires de la réalité, pour rejeter enfin toute discrimination. Finalement ils trouvent le document qui les classe eux-mêmes, le rapport qui les résume comme «deux imbéciles inoffensifs», lettre qui «doit, pour le lecteur, être la critique du roman».[36] Que faire? ils se mettent à la copier en tant qu'un des éléments constitutifs de la réalité. Dans ces deux dénouements l'auteur change abruptement, pour ne pas dire brutalement, l'angle de vision: il dénude ses personnages devant l'auditoire comme le fait Corneille à la fin de *l'Illusion comique*, et le problème de l'artiste qui crée son illusion se trouve imbriqué dans le roman même, selon une technique qui rappelle le *Roman bourgeois* de Furetière, *Jacques le Fataliste*, et, à partir des *Faux-Monnayeurs*, quantité de romanciers qui jongleront avec le même thème.

Dans *Bouvard et Pécuchet* les deux tendances qui furent mon point de départ – soumission au réel et transfiguration du réel – se rencontrent à leurs extrêmes. Les Scénarios montrent que Flaubert voulait créer des effets comiques en juxtaposant «des morceaux vrais et pastichés».[37] D'une part il y a la conviction que le simple fait de recueillir les documents existants fournirait un monument suffisant des efforts ambitieux et de la bêtise éternelle de l'homme: ces pièces parleraient pour elles-mêmes. D'autre part il y a la caricature créatrice qui souligne l'action exercée sur deux tempéraments par cette documentation. On voit admirablement les deux techniques à l'œuvre dans le chapitre sur les jardins pittoresques, où sont juxtaposés un passage composé d'une mosaïque de citations, déjà groupées de manière à produire un effet d'un comique aigu, et un autre morceau où le résultat des efforts pour réaliser les théories est communiqué en une vision fantasmagorique de formes géométriques abstraites qui se dressent prétentieusement au-dessus d'humbles légumes: «Le tombeau faisait un cube au milieu des épinards, le pont vénitien un accent cironflexe par-dessus les haricots ... la pagode chinoise ... semblait un phare sur le vignot ...» Ce roman marque en même temps l'effort vers le maximum de documentation et vers le maximum de stylisation.

J'en viens à mon troisième point: le problème de ce qui est omis, ou de ce que l'on croit à tort avoir été omis par Flaubert dans le choix qu'il opère entre les éléments de la réalité. On a souvent commenté, parfois sévèrement, le fait qu'il met en scène des personnages «médiocres», et l'on a souligné l'écart qui existe entre ce que la conscience de tels personnages aurait pu éprouver, analyser ou exprimer, et ce que l'auteur lui-même voudrait nous suggérer. Mais ce choix de personnages qui ne savent analyser leurs illusions et qui expriment par des clichés leurs idées reçues, est la base nécessaire de ce que la vision de Flaubert a d'ironique et de positif à la fois. Ce choix sert à deux fins. D'abord à faire réfléchir le lecteur sur les possibilités que les personnages négligent, déforment ou ne font qu'ébaucher dans le rêve désireux ou le souvenir nostalgique. Ensuite, à faire voir des problèmes de la portée la plus générale incarnés dans des êtres rigoureusement distancés de nous-mêmes, ou du moins de nous-mêmes comme nous nous complaisons à nous voir. Autour de ces êtres, toutes les ressources qu'offre le style indirect libre pour exprimer les impulsions informes qu'ils ne sauraient formuler eux-mêmes, toutes les riches suggestions apportées par ce monde matériel qui agit sur eux, nous fournissent des moyens d'une compréhension profonde mais dénuée de toute complicité suspecte.

Car dans ses personnages Flaubert oppose les unes aux autres trois attitudes-types vis-à-vis la réalité, en une sorte de ballet d'idées dont aucune en soi ne constitue une solution satisfaisante: chassé-croisé destiné à «amuser avec des idées», à «faire rêver». A ceux qui acceptent la nature des choses plus ou moins sans réflexion et sans question (un Charles Bovary) sont opposés ceux qui les manipulent pour des fins pratiques et étroites, inébranlables dans leurs préjugés conventionnels et bornés (un Rodolphe ou un Homais), et ceux qui méprisent le réel, pour rêver à une satisfaction absolue et impossible, qu'elle soit métaphysique, sentimentale ou intellectuelle (saint Antoine, Emma, Frédéric, Bouvard et Pécuchet). Dans *Un Cœur simple* il est finalement permis au rêve de se confondre avec la réalité d'une manière particulière: l'illusion touchante et cruellement comique de Félicité sur son lit de mort est néanmoins, dans les limites de sa conscience à elle, une extase totale et que ne menace aucune désillusion ultérieure: cette vision, et le prénom pas uniquement ironique dont Flaubert a doté son héroïne, rappellent une remarque riche de conséquences qu'on trouve déjà dans la première *Éducation sentimentale*: «Puisqu'ils se croyaient heureux, ils l'étaient en effet.»[38] C'est ici surtout qu'est indiquée la relativité des différentes façons possibles «dont nous percevons les objets».

Cette relativité est, bien entendu, au centre de la vision individuelle de l'artiste. Les œuvres de Flaubert expriment avec une intensité rare la fusion des deux attitudes extrêmes de la conscience: le sens de la monotonie intolérable et éternelle d'une réalité qui se répète toujours, et d'autre part le sentiment de la particularité de chaque expérience individuelle. «C'est pourtant toujours la même chose, dit Leporello. Eh! non, ce n'est jamais la même chose», dit Don Juan.[39]

Chaque artiste est appelé à reproduire ce qu'il y a de général dans le monde ... chaque passion, suivant l'homme où elle se produit, rend un son différent.[40]

Et les redites mêmes de la réalité peuvent être transformées, par la conscience qui en saisit les rythmes, en un spectacle plein de dignité et en une source de jouissance:

Il aperçut une symétrie miraculeuse rien que dans le retour périodique des mêmes idées devant les mêmes choses, des mêmes sensations devant les mêmes faits.[41]

Mais, après l'exemple, resté unique, du Jules de la première *Éducation*, ce qui brille surtout par son absence des romans de Flaubert, c'est un personnage qui représenterait directement le centre de sa réalité à lui: le grand artiste. C'est encore une fois par allusion et par contraste que Flaubert évoque cette conscience esthétique. L'homme fermé à l'art est satirisé – dans les jugements didactiques d'un Homais ou d'un Sénécal, et, avec des résonances plus subtiles, dans les réactions envers l'art d'une Emma Bovary ou d'une Veuve Bordin. Celles-ci, même en voulant trouver dans l'œuvre d'art un moyen de dépasser les bornes étroites de leur propre personnalité, ne font que rétrécir la portée de l'œuvre en l'appliquant à leurs besoins immédiats: dans l'opéra *Emma* ne voit qu'un héros idéal qui comblerait ses désirs; Mme Bordin exprime d'une façon plus terre-à-terre la même impulsion quand, devant l'évocation lyrique de Doña Sol par Hernani, elle réfléchit: «cela me ressemble» ou «Ce doit être bien agréable, un monsieur qui vous dit des choses pareilles, – pour tout de bon.» Attitude très humaine, mais qui fait de la lecture une forme d'onanisme sentimental au lieu d'un moyen d'auto-critique ou d'une contemplation de structures révélatrices.[42]

L'homme qui abuse ainsi de l'art est analysé; l'artiste médiocre est caricaturé, et à travers lui sont indiquées, sur un ton à la fois comique et amer, les tentations et les aspirations de Flaubert lui-même. Binet s'épanouit, pleinement heureux dans l'art pour l'art d'un fignoleur de formes insignifiantes et faciles; Pellerin, apôtre et dupe de tant de théories, éprouve l'angoisse physique et mentale des affres du style, exprime souvent des idées que Flaubert a ruminées (par exemple son attaque contre le réalisme) et ne produit, par une application excessive, que des croûtes hideuses, ou, par esprit d'opportunisme, des monstruosités comme son Christ debout sur une locomotive. Il n'y a qu'un seul personnage dans lequel (comme je l'ai suggéré ailleurs)[43] les valeurs de l'artiste soient incarnées, fort indirectement du reste: le docteur Larivière. L'artiste véritable, comme Flaubert l'aurait souhaité, est comme Dieu dans sa création, présence invisible mais dont témoigne pleinement son œuvre.

J'ai jusqu'ici écarté exprès le problème le plus essentiel qui confronte toute conscience dans ses rapports avec le réel: celui de recréer ou d'interpréter l'expérience par l'instrument du langage. En ce sens, il est évident qu'aucune œuvre littéraire ne peut simplement copier la réalité: il faut transformer en symboles linguistiques notre contact initial avec le monde, et la parole, comme le dit Constant, «toujours trop grossière et trop générale» risque de fausser toute expérience par sa généralité ou par son imprécision. Flaubert, dès ses œuvres de jeunesse, est hanté par ce problème: «Avec votre langue châtrée . . . pouvez-vous exprimer tout le parfum d'une fleur, tout le verdoyant d'un pré d'herbe? Me peindrez-vous seulement un tas de fumier ou une goutte d'eau? . . . Voyons donc! avec des mots, des phrases et du style, faites-moi la description bien exacte d'un de vos souvenirs, d'un paysage, d'une masure quelconque.»[44] Et, comme beaucoup d'autres ont dû le faire, il soupire après un moyen immédiat de communication entre les esprits, que ce soit un rapport télépathique ou un système d'une précision équivalente à celle de la musique.

De là la longue contemplation de la valeur représentative, comme son et comme sens, de chaque vocable, et des suggestions qu'ajoute la structure de la phrase. L'analyse de la manière dont Flaubert résoud victorieusement ce problème ne pourra nous retenir aujourd'hui.[45] Mais, avant de terminer, je ne résiste pas à la tentation de faire remarquer comment le détail le plus minime du défi désespéré de la première jeunesse retentissait dans son esprit jusqu'à ce que la petite phrase «me peindrez-vous seulement un tas de fumier?» culminât dans le Rêve de Bouvard devant les possibilités infinies de l'Engrais. Tandis que les Scénarios donnent directement le commentaire satirico-épique («un poète méditant "au bord des mers" n'est pas plus sublime»),[46] le roman laisse parler eux-mêmes des substantifs choisis et ordonnés dans un crescendo pour faire sortir de l'objet le moins poétique de la vie réelle les aspirations les plus démesurées: «il rêvait au bord de la fosse, apercevant dans l'avenir des montagnes de fruits, des débordements de fleurs, des avalanches de légumes».[47]

Et, en dernier lieu, nous remarquerons comment le sentiment qu'éprouve l'artiste devant le problème de l'expression le rapproche le plus de certains de ses personnages dans leurs moments de mutisme ou d'impuissance à s'exprimer. Dans une de ses rares interventions d'auteur, Flaubert défend Emma contre le manque de compréhension de Rodolphe:

> Il ne distinguait pas ... la dissemblance des sentiments sous la parité des expressions ... On en devait rabattre, pensait-il, les discours exagérés cachant les affections médiocres; comme si la plénitude de l'âme ne débordait pas quelquefois par les métaphores les plus vides, puisque personne, jamais, ne peut donner l'exacte mesure de ses besoins, ni de ses conceptions, ni de ses douleurs, et que la parole humaine est comme un chaudron fêlé où nous battons des mélodies à faire danser les ours, quand on voudrait attendrir les étoiles.[48]

Dans les *Œuvres de Jeunesse*, deux personnages se confrontent et «le regard va plus avant que les mots»;[49] dans l'avant-dernier chapitre de *L'Éducation sentimentale* nous partageons le long quart d'heure d'un lourd et tendre silence.

Bouvard et Pécuchet auraient vite fait de résumer les paradoxes inhérents à toute discussion théorique de nos problèmes: «L'application trop exacte du Vrai nuit à la Beauté, et la préoccupation de la Beauté empêche le Vrai. Cependant, sans idéal pas de Vrai; c'est pourquoi les types sont d'une réalité plus continue que les portraits. L'Art d'ailleurs ne traite que la Vraisemblance, mais la Vraisemblance dépend de qui l'observe, est une chose relative ...»[50] Le problème de l'art, comme celui de la réalité, suscitera sans doute toujours des théories qui renouvelleront et qui aiguiseront nos perceptions. Nous n'en reviendrons pas moins au fait que tout dépend de celui qui observe, et de sa façon individuelle de maîtriser les mots; nous nous retrouverons enfin devant la simple existence d'une œuvre complexe et harmonieuse, à travers laquelle «des horizons infinis» peuvent nous être révélés.

NOTES

1 Communication présentée le 31 août 1966 au Xe congrès de la Fédération Internationale des Langues et Littératures Modernes, à Strasbourg. Les limites inhérentes à une communication de ce genre, et la nature du sujet, ne permettent pas de signaler en détail les ouvrages fondamentaux d'éminents érudits ou critiques auxquels tout étudiant de Flaubert est évidemment redevable. Je ne pourrai faire de rapides allusions qu'à des travaux récents qui portent sur certains aspects du problème que j'envisage sommairement ici. L'article sur «Flaubert et le réel», publié par Jean-Jacques Mayoux dans le *Mercure de France*, 15 février 1934, traite le sujet d'un tout autre point de vue.

2 *Bouvard et Pécuchet*, édition critique par Alberto Cento, t. I (Nizet, 1964), p. 189.

3 Ibid., p. 403.

4 *Correspondance* (Conard), t.II, p. 239.

5 Ibid., t.IV, p. 61.

6 Ibid., t.IV, p. 225.

7 Ibid., t.I, p. 417.

8 Ibid., t.II, p. 12; cf. t.II, pp. 41, 289 etc.

9 Voir en particulier les riches observations de J.-P. Richard: *Littérature et sensation* (Le Seuil, 1954) et certaines pages de Geneviève Bollème: *La Leçon de Flaubert* (Julliard, 1964). D'importantes suggestions sont fournies par les travaux de C. Digeon: *Le dernier visage de Flaubert* (Aubier, 1946); M.-J. Durry: *Flaubert et ses projets inédits* (Nizet, 1950) et Jean Bruneau: *Les débuts littéraires de G. Flaubert* (A. Colin, 1962).

10 *Correspondance*, t.IV, p. 399.

11 Ibid., t.I, p. 178; t.II, p. 343.

12 Ibid., t.III, p. 210.

13 Ibid., t.I, p. 427; cf. t.II, p. 290.

14 Ibid., t.I, p. 168.

15 Ibid., t.III, p. 405.

16 *Bouvard et Pécuchet*, p. 73.

17 *Correspondance*, t.i, p. 192.
18 *Œuvres de Jeunesse* (Conard), t.i, p. 173.
19 *Correspondance*, t.vii, p. 224.
20 Ibid., iie volume supplémentaire, p. 118.
21 Ibid., ive volume supplémentaire, p. 25; cf. ibid., t.viii, p. 374.
22 Ibid., t.vii, p. 351.
23 Ibid., t.iii, p. 18.
24 G. Bollème, op. cit., p. 49.
25 *Correspondance*, t.iii, p. 230.
26 Ibid., t.viii, p. 135.
27 Ibid., t.iv, p. 370.
28 Ibid., t.iii, p. 149.
29 Les moments d'extase ou d'assoupissement chez les personnages de Flaubert s'accompagnent souvent d'une sensation rythmique: telle ici la répétition du son de la chaîne qu'on tire (Voir *Œuvres de Jeunesse*, t.i, pp. 538–9). Cf. le mouvement régulier de la marche; *Madame Bovary*, édité par A. Thibaudet et R. Dumesnil (Gallimard, «Pléiade», 1951–2), i, p. 337 – Charles à cheval; etc.
30 *L'Éducation sentimentale*, édité par A. Thibaudet et R. Dumesnil (Gallimard, «Pléiade», 1951–2), ii, p. 304: «C'était une béatitude indéfinie, un tel enivrement, qu'il en oubliait jusqu'à la possibilité d'un bonheur absolu.»
31 Comparer le passage dans *L'Éducation sentimentale*, p. 323: «Le magnétisme des foules enthousiastes l'avait pris ... Il frissonnait sous les effluves d'un immense amour comme si le cœur de l'humanité tout entière avait battu dans sa poitrine» avec celui dans la *Correspondance*, t.iii, p. 150: «La foule ne m̦'a jamais plu que les jours d'émeute, et encore! ... N'importe, en ces jours-là il y a un grand souffle dans l'air. On se sent enivré par une poésie humaine, aussi *large* que celle de la nature, et plus ardente.»
32 *Œuvres de Jeunesse*, t.i, p. 127.
33 *L'Éducation sentimentale*, p. 216.
34 Cf. entre autres l'ouvrage déjà cité de J.-P. Richard, et les articles de Georges Poulet dans *Les Métamorphoses du Cercle* (Plon, 1961), de Jean Rousset dans *Forme et Signification* (Corti, 1962) et de Victor Brombert dans *Flaubert, a collection of critical essays*, edited by Raymond Giraud, (Prentice-Hall, 1964).
35 *Madame Bovary*, nouvelle version précédée des scénarios inédits, par J. Pommier et G. Leleu (Corti, 1949), p. 129.
36 *Bouvard et Pécuchet*, p. 125.
37 Ibid., p. 14.
38 *Œuvres de Jeunesse*, t.iii, p. 121. Thème approfondi par d'autres analystes du cœur humain, dont Constant et Nerval. Cf. en particulier le *Voyage en Orient* de Nerval, *Œuvres*, t.ii (Gallimard, «Pléiade», 1956), p. 350: «Ah! je crois être amoureux, ah! je crois être malade, n'est-ce pas? Mais, si je crois l'être, je le suis!»
39 *Œuvres de Jeunesse*, t.iii, p. 322.
40 Ibid., p. 258.
41 Ibid., p. 245.

42 Comme c'est si souvent le cas chez Flaubert, il y a deux impulsions contraires. Il exprimera souvent dans sa correspondance le sentiment de se reconnaître avec joie dans ce qu'écrivent les grands auteurs du passé, tout en critiquant avec sévérité «cette sympathie personnelle qui n'a rien de commun avec la contemplation désintéressée du véritable artiste» (*Œuvres de Jeunesse*, t.III, p. 144).

43 Alison Fairlie: *Flaubert – Madame Bovary* (Arnold, 1962), p. 76.

44 *Œuvres de Jeunesse*, t.I, p. 96.

45 Inutile de dénombrer ici les ouvrages de base sur les problèmes du style chez Flaubert. Signalons pourtant aux Flaubertistes d'excellentes pages dans un article général par Albert Henry: «L'expressivité du dialogue dans le roman» (*La littérature narrative d'imagination*, Colloque de Strasbourg, 1959 (P.U.F., 1961)).

46 *Bouvard et Pécuchet*, p. 177.

47 Ibid., p. 292; cf. *Madame Bovary*, nouvelle version précédée des scénarios inédits, p. 570; *Correspondance*, t.VIII, p. 397.

48 *Madame Bovary*, Pléiade, I, p. 500.

49 *Œuvres de Jeunesse*, t.III, p. 322.

50 *Bouvard et Pécuchet*, p. 411.

22

Flaubert and the authors of the French Renaissance (1968)[1]

Flaubert would have been the first to look with a sardonic eye at this title. Evidence on his reading is necessarily incomplete, and any mind tinged with his own encyclopaedomania will be aware of the gaps in what we can deduce. Moreover, a critical discussion of his sporadically adumbrated reactions could not but have appeared *HHHénaurme* to one who so often scarified the profession of the critic. From his early notebook ('Voici les choses fort bêtes: 1° la critique littéraire quelle qu'elle soit, bonne ou mauvaise')[2] or the first *Éducation* to *Bouvard et Pécuchet*, there echoes the theme of the insufficiency of aesthetic theories: because first, they use abstract terms in undefined or tautological ways; second, they lay down 'norms' to which every work of art must be fitted; third, they concentrate either on peripheral circumstances or sweeping parallels, rather than on investigating what is irreducibly individual; finally and above all, they cannot explain the genesis of a masterpiece: Bouvard, in his search for the creative principle, is driven back to the fundamental advice: 'inventez des ressorts qui puissent m'attacher', and retorts with the naive but still more basic question: 'Comment inventer des ressorts?' To Flaubert, in fact, past criticism serves mainly to provide instructive and amusing evidence of the frame of mind of the times in which it was written. He would certainly have read with joy the article in which A. M. Boase analyses through anthologies of poetry 'the whirligig of taste'.[3]

Yet Flaubert, on this as on most problems poised between opposite urges, had his own plans for critical works. Two lay in his own century: the preface to the works of Bouilhet, and the introduction to the *Dictionnaire des Idées reçues*. His other main critical projects refer to three sixteenth-century authors: Ronsard, Rabelais and Montaigne. In 1838 he writes:

Je lis toujours Rabelais et j'y ai adjoint Montaigne. Je me propose de faire plus tard sur ces deux hommes une étude spéciale de philosophie et de littérature (C i 29),

and in 1853:

Nous relisons du Ronsard et nous nous enthousiasmons de plus belle. A quelque jour nous en ferons une édition . . . J'y ferais une préface . . . Je dirai l'histoire du *sentiment poétique en France* (C iii 139; see also iii 321).

Except for the very early article on Rabelais (*Œuvres de Jeunesse* i 144–56), no sixteenth-century plan was carried out, but this trinity of authors recurs at intervals throughout his lifetime among the *livres de chevet* which have in different ways been 'convertis en sang et nourriture'.

Of detailed knowledge of other early or late Renaissance authors in France, there is little proof. We may too easily today assume a general reassessment of sixteenth-century poets from the 1830s onwards, after Sainte-Beuve's *Tableau*, Nerval's anthology, and the enthusiasm of individual romantics; scholastic syllabuses continued to make the classical seventeenth century the focus of literary studies, and earlier reading must largely have remained a matter for personal enterprise.[4] Flaubert provides brief mentions of Marot, Régnier, Saint-Amant; the preface to Bouilhet's *Dernières chansons* remarks that Bouilhet was annotating Du Bartas; there are allusions to d'Aubigné and Brantôme, and the joyful discovery, among the later non-classics, of Cyrano de Bergerac.[5] As one might expect, there is nothing on the poets so rewardingly restored to the canon of our own day (Scève, Sponde or others); more surprisingly, perhaps, I have found no mention of Du Bellay.

The present article will first briefly sum up the evidence on Flaubert's reading in the three great authors,[6] and will then discuss what Flaubert's remarks on these 'pères nourriciers'[7] reveal of the mainsprings of his own temperament: of the interplay of satirical scepticism, absorptive enthusiasm and rigorous self-discipline from which his art is wrought.

First, the facts. Ronsard is mentioned in *Par les Champs* (p. 74) of 1840, and in 1842 is being read, with Horace and Rabelais, 'mais peu et rarement, «comme l'on fait de truffes»' (C i 116); a year later Flaubert is again reading 'un peu de Ronsard, de mon grand et beau Ronsard' (C I 145). The stage of prolonged reading and enthusiasm comes in 1852–3; he writes triumphantly:

J'ai un Ronsard complet, 2 vol. in-folio,[8] que j'ai enfin fini par me procurer. Le dimanche nous en lisons à nous défoncer la poitrine. Les extraits des petites éditions courantes en donnent une idée comme toute espèce d'extraits et de traductions, c'est-à-dire que les plus belles choses en sont absentes ... Quel poète! quel poète! quelles ailes! ... Donc nous avons encore pour deux ou trois mois de dimanches enthousiasmés. Cet horizon me fait grand bien et de loin jette un reflet ardent sur mon travail (C II 368–9).

There are frequent references between now and 1854,[9] including a letter (not in the Conard *Correspondance*) of 14 March 1853,[10] relating that 'nous avons hier passé trois heures à lire les hymnes de Ronsard'; at the end of March comes Bouilhet's plan for an edition to which Flaubert would write the Preface, for:

il y a cent belles choses, mille, cent mille, dans les poésies complètes de Ronsard, qu'il faut faire connaître, et puis j'éprouve le besoin de le lire et relire dans une édition commode (C III 139).

After 1854 there is little evidence until 1872, when Flaubert is associated with plans for a monument in Vendôme;[11] he subscribes, intends to write a speech for the opening ceremony, but in a period of strain is too weary to complete it, and finally, at the thought of those who would be his travelling-companions, decides not to attend.

The Preface to Bouilhet's *Dernières Chansons* instances Ronsard as among the outstanding examples of reversal of reputation, for:

la gloire d'un écrivain relève non pas du suffrage universel, mais d'un petit groupe d'intelligences qui à la longue impose son jugement.[12]

And to the end of Flaubert's life attitudes to Ronsard obviously remain a kind of litmus-paper test of literary judgement; in appreciating an article of Maupassant on French poetry in 1877 he regrets that there is no proper praise of Ronsard (C VIII 9), and in the same year he writes of his stay at Chenonceaux:

Mme Pelouze est une personne exquise et très littéraire. On y apporte *Ronsard* à table, au milieu du dessert! (C VIII 44)

Montaigne is quoted by the truculent adolescent in the *Moralité* of *Un Parfum à sentir* of 1836: 'Cecy est un livre de bonne foy: je donne mon advis, non comme bon, mais comme mien', and the 'Que sais-je?' of Montaigne and 'Peut-être' of Rabelais are cited in the

provocative *Moralité* to *Rage et Impuissance*.[13] The project for a special
study of Montaigne and Rabelais occurs in September 1838, but the
real burst of enthusiasm comes in October 1839: 'Je me recrée à lire
le sieur de Montaigne dont je suis plein; c'est là mon homme' (C I
57). Much later he recalls this period 'Je m'en suis bourré [de
Montaigne] toute une année à 18 ans, où je ne lisais *que lui*' (C III
379). The *Voyage aux Pyrénées* (1840) tells how he handled the
manuscript of Montaigne with religious veneration (p. 352) and
discusses (p. 391) the shift in Renaissance spirit from the wild and
gigantic fantasy of Rabelais to the clarity, humanity and consciousness of style in Montaigne. From now on references, brief discussions
and scraps of quotation proliferate.[14] Montaigne is above all a
recourse in times of distress: he comes to mind in a fit of student
wretchedness in 1843 (C I 137), is among the *livres de chevet* in
nervous strain in 1844 (C I 153) and is the author read as Flaubert
watches for the night by the body of his dead sister (C II 3). In
February 1853 he sets out to 'relire Montaigne en entier. C'est une
bonne causerie, le soir avant de s'endormir' (C III 102); this remains
his bedside book through April (III 184) and into October:

C'est singulier comme je suis plein de ce bonhomme-là ... Je suis ébahi ...
de trouver l'analyse très-déliée de mes moindres sentiments! Nous avons
mêmes goûts, mêmes opinions, même manière de vivre, mêmes manies. Il y
a des gens que j'admire plus que lui, mais il n'y en a pas que j'évoquerais
plus volontiers et avec qui je causerai mieux. (C III 379–80)

It is in 1854 that Montaigne is called 'mon père nourricier' (C IV
33). As years go on, he is held up to Flaubert's correspondents as 'un
homme dont vous devriez vous nourrir, et qui vous consolerait'; his
works are made part of the education of Flaubert's niece.[15] Finally,
in 1876, shut off from the outer world, Flaubert is reading each
evening Montaigne and La Bruyère 'pour me retremper dans les
classiques' (C VII 367).

Quotations from Rabelais, as from Montaigne, chosen to be
provocative, are used in the adolescent works of 1836–7.[16] In 1838 a
youthful letter remarks:

Vraiment je n'estime profondément que deux hommes, Rabelais et Byron,
les deux seuls qui aient écrit dans l'intention de nuire au genre humain et de
lui rire à la face (C I 29);

a month later Flaubert is nearing the end of his reading and

Mon Rabelais est tout bourré de notes et commentaires philosophiques,
philologiques, bachiques, etc. (C I 33).

From this stage presumably dates the youthful essay on Rabelais. As J. Bruneau points out (op. cit., p. 263), Rabelais specialists have treated this severely for its enthusiastic and derivative generalizations.[17] Bruneau defends its 'admiration sincère et assez bien motivée' for Rabelais; but it is worth calling special attention to how, at this very early age, Flaubert has through Rabelais shaped an embryo programme for the different sides of his own future work. Rabelais's enigma, crammed with the trivial, the crude and the comic, showing how

l'humanité . . . dépouillée de ses robes de parade et de ses galons mensongers . . . frémit toute nue sous le souffle impur du grotesque

at the same time provides

les aperçus les plus fins sur la nature de l'homme, les nuances les plus délicates du cœur, les analyses les plus vraies.

Imaginative inventiveness and skill with dialogue combine with 'le comique des caractères' and with 'la phrase si bien ciselée en relief'. Other possible attitudes to the human condition (bitter, openly personal, meditative) are compared with the great gust of laughter. Rabelais's successor in a modern age will find his subject in 'cet éternel gouffre béant que l'homme a en lui'; provided he can achieve detachment, 'se dépouiller de toute colère, de toute haine, de toute douleur! . . . son livre serait le plus terrible et le plus sublime qu'on ait fait'. In clumsy but suggestive formulations Flaubert is groping for the detached technique which might treat Romantic despair with Renaissance scale and vigour, might combine satirical sting with subtle analytical insight.

In the next years references and quotations are frequent.[18] Letters from Alfred Le Poittevin show how to both friends Rabelais is a household word, and culminate in a sardonic vision of what it would be like if both ever qualified as pillars of justice: 'Ce serait à désirer que Rabelais revînt, pour faire un nouveau roman.'[19] In 1852–3 the constant discovery of new riches in Rabelais is reiterated (C III 49, 98, 312). He is the Sunday reading, along with *Don Quixote*, towards the end of 1852 (C III 53 and Preface to Bouilhet's *Dernières Chansons*). Other dates when Flaubert goes back to reread 'le sacrosaint, immense et extra-beau Rabelais', 'patriarche de la littérature française depuis trois cents ans' (C VII 319) are September 1861 (C IV 452) and November 1867 (C V 341). When Caroline visits Chinon in 1876 she is to greet Rabelais's supposed house with his 'pensée de respect et d'adoration' (C vII 317); Flaubert is reading him yet again. In his last years, wishing to praise a contemporary, he will write 'Il y a là un souffle à ranimer Rabelais du tombeau', or, consoling Maupassant for accusations of immorality, will recall 'Rabelais, d'où découlent les lettres françaises'.[20]

Flaubert certainly first came to the Renaissance through highly coloured and impressionistic generalizations. From the beginning he attributes to this period four sides deeply rooted in his own nature: a violent demolition of set social and religious systems; a mighty grasp of encyclopaedic detail, ranging from the trivial to the epic; a frank and rich expression of the world of the senses; and finally a vital spirit which, whether through revolt, scepticism, stoicism, hedonism or sheer sense of the comic, moulds a positive reaction to permanent problems.[21]

The spirit of opposition plays a joyous part in his choice of authors. Du Camp speaks of Flaubert's reading while at school: 'lectures que ses maîtres n'eussent pas approuvées, s'occupant plus de Ronsard que de Virgile et plus de Brantôme que de Fénelon'.[22] Letters tilt at the poor taste of the French who prefer to Ronsard 'un pédant comme Malherbe ou un pisse-froid comme Boileau'[23] (C I 145), note that 'Béranger sera toujours plus lu' (C III 139) and scorn Villemain's phrase 'la diction grotesque de Ronsard' (III 264). His projected preface was to be an attack on the stereotyped and orthodox French taste in poetry; the speech for the Ronsard cere-mony in 1872 would have been 'une protestation contre le Panmuflisme moderne' (C VI 382; CS III 33). In the Preface to Bouilhet's *Dernières Chansons* Ronsard is the poet of the few, and in the *Dictionnaire des Idées reçues* the stock view of Ronsard is laconically summed up: 'Ridicule avec ses mots grecs et latins.'[24]

Rabelais in the early article is the great demolisher whose gale of laughter has a destructive force equivalent to that of Luther in the realm of religion or of the French Revolution in the realm of action. 'Mes lectures de Rabelais se mêlent à ma bile sociale' (C III 94). His 'robustes outrances' are set against the petty wit or salacious innuendo of nineteenth-century taste (C II 451; III 31, 39). Like Ronsard, he is unappreciated by the crowd:

D'où vient qu'on est toujours indulgent pour la médiocrité dorée? et qu'on sait Béranger par cœur et pas un vers de Saint-Amant, pas une page de Rabelais? (C v 153)[25]

He provides a fine contrast to contemporary cant, whether in an early comment on a Belgian expurgator (*Par les Champs*, p. 28), in a sardonic aside about what would have been Rabelais's views on Queen Victoria (C iv 227) or in comments on the Préfet of scandalous personal life who banned public lectures on his work (C viii 71, 85, 104).

Montaigne's destruction of conventional beliefs goes still deeper:

Je suis de l'avis de Montaigne ... il me semble que nous ne pouvons jamais être assez méprisés selon notre mérite. J'aime à voir l'humanité et tout ce qu'elle respecte ravalé, bafoué, honni, sifflé. La torpeur moderne vient du respect illimité que l'homme a pour lui-même (C iv 33).[26]

Montaigne lays bare man's presumptuousness, shows how he 'bêle après l'infini' (C ii 414), refuses him heroism in face of physical pain, being 'homme à me mettre sous la peau d'ung veau pour l'éviter' (C iii 358) and finds that 'toutes nos vocations sont farcesques' (C viii 112).[27]

But there is a good deal more in these likings than the joyous opposition to stock literary taste or to illusions about the human condition. Had Flaubert written his prefaces, he intended to make them a safety-valve, a means of exorcising his furies so that no passionate didacticism would intrude into his own literary works (C iii 139–40). We have seen the need for detachment posited in the call for a successor to Rabelais;[28] Montaigne is early made its symbol in this vision of him at the States-General of 1588:

Assis à l'écart ... sans doute qu'il remâchait en lui-même quelque passage de Salluste ou quelques vers de Lucain que les circonstances présentes lui remettaient en mémoire. Sans passions au milieu de toutes ces passions hurlantes, sans croyances à côté de tant de convictions violentes, il était là comme le symbole de ce qui reste à côté de ce qui passe (*Par les Champs*, p. 15).

The Renaissance offers lessons not just in detachment but in delight. Delight first in the sensuous detail of the physical world. As a blessed contrast to the aridities of legal terminology the young Flaubert quotes from Ronsard the stanza:

> *Quand au lit nous serons*
> *Entrelasséz, nous ferons*
> *Les lascifs, selon les guises*
> *Des amants, qui librement*
> *Pratiquent folâtrement*
> *Dans les draps cent mignardises* (C i 116)

and in the *Mémoires d'un Fou* he recalls Marot's

> *Tetin refaict plus blanc qu'un œuf,*
> *Tetin de satin blanc tout neuf.*

A letter to Taine in 1865 discusses the abstract images of the seventeenth century ('appuyons les soupirs', 'couronner la flamme') and asks:

> Pourquoi n'y a-t-il pas une image fausse dans les poètes du XVIe siècle – et peut-être pas une précise ou originale dans ceux du XVIIe? La rage de l'*idée* leur avait enlevé tout sentiment de la *nature*. Leur poétique était antiphysique (CS II 44–5).

To read Ronsard aloud was to experience intense physical sensations:

> une pièce qui m'a fait presque mal nerveusement, tant elle me faisait plaisir. C'était comme si l'on m'eût chatouillé la plante des pieds (C II 369).[29]

From Montaigne he recalls 'un [des baisers] dont parle Montaigne (les âcres baisers de la jeunesse, longs, savoureux, gluants)' (C I 317). The epic treatment of appetite constantly rejoices Flaubert; the passage on Maître Gaster is one he early picks out in Rabelais (C I 33) and he remarks with gusto that 'les héros sont de terribles mangeurs'.[30] Gastronomic images to describe the chosen authors are frequent: he prefers Rabelais to *Gil Blas* because:

> J'aime les viandes plus juteuses . . . les styles où l'on en a plein la bouche (C III 98).

and of Montaigne he writes:

> C'est là mon homme. En littérature, en gastronomie, il est certains fruits qu'on mange à pleine bouche, dont on a le gosier plein, et si succulents que le jus vous entre jusqu'au cœur (C I 57; cf. I 116 on Ronsard).[31]

For he is constantly drawn by a sense of untrammelled vitality. In poetry:

> Depuis la fin du XVIe siècle jusqu'à Hugo, tous les livres, quelque beaux qu'ils soient, sentent la poussière du collège (C III 367). Il n'y a peut-être que Ronsard qui ait été tout simplement un poète, comme on l'était dans l'antiquité et comme on l'est dans les autres pays (C III 68).

Both Rabelais and Montaigne pursue things to the extreme:

> Pour être durable, je crois qu'il faut que la fantaisie soit monstrueuse comme dans Rabelais. Quand on ne fait pas le Parthénon, il faut accumuler des pyramides (C III 31);

while Montaigne takes self-analysis to a pitch where only the most exceptional nature could succeed in his gigantic task (C I 385–6). The Flaubert who signed letters 'l'Excessif' rejoices in a world both of epic stature and of infinite detail, and in writers who were 'des encyclopédies de leur époque' (C IV 52).

But it is precisely these *écrasants livres* of superhuman stature (C III 149) which provide a particular problem for the artist:

> Une chose triste, c'est de voir combien les grands hommes arrivent aisément à l'effet en dehors de l'Art même. Quoi de plus mal bâti que bien des choses de Rabelais ... Mais quels coups de poing subits! ... Vouloir imiter les procédés de ces génies-là, ce serait se perdre (C III 143). Ils n'ont pas besoin de faire du style, ceux-là; ils sont forts en dépit de toutes les fautes et à cause d'elles. Mais nous, les petits, nous ne valons que par l'exécution achevée ... Les très grands hommes écrivent souvent fort mal, et tant mieux pour eux. Ce n'est pas là qu'il faut chercher l'art de la forme, mais chez les seconds (Horace, La Bruyère) (C III 31–2).

To learn one's craft one must turn to close study of a 'génie complètement différent de celui qu'on a, parce qu'on ne peut le copier' (C III 228; cf. II 353 and *L'Éducation* of 1845, p. 256): for this he turns from the exuberance of Rabelais to the controlled precision of La Bruyère. Even so, one must still steep onself in the greatest works, for 'cela s'infiltre à la longue ... le talent se transmet par infusion' (C III 228). They are no guides to technique, but a means to gradual forming of substance:

> Il faut savoir les maîtres par cœur, les idolâtrer, tâcher de penser comme eux, et puis s'en séparer pour toujours.[32]

Above all, they are a means of living on a particular level. Loving the qualities of demolition or exuberance, Flaubert still stresses that the artist transforms them into a strange but pervasive serenity. At its barest, this comes from the refusal of illusion:

> Lisez Rabelais, Montaigne, Horace ou quelque autre gaillard qui ait vu la vie sous un jour plus tranquille, et apprenez une bonne fois pour toutes qu'il ne faut pas demander des oranges aux pommiers ... du bonheur à la vie (C I 98).

In Rabelais 'le rire est le propre de l'homme' and no mere destructive gale of angry satire. Even the very early article, concentrating on the demolition of prejudice, underlines the frank and healthy force of this reaction to human ills, contrasted with bitterness, melancholy or disillusion, and adds the suggestion that behind denunciation and farce 'il a ... que sais-je, entrevu peut-être un monde politique meilleur, une société tout autre'. Later, laughter will be defined as 'le dédain et la compréhension mêlés, et en somme la plus haute manière de voir la vie' (C iv 33). And as with the other authors whose works are pitiless, complex and infinitely troublous in implications, there is yet in Rabelais a prevailing serenity:

Cela est sans fond, infini, multiple. Par de petites ouvertures on aperçoit des précipices; il y a du noir en bas, du vertige. Et cependant quelque chose de singulièrement doux plane sur l'ensemble! C'est l'éclat de la lumière, le sourire du soleil, et c'est calme! c'est calme! (C iii 323).

But Montaigne particularly provides the means to calm:[33]

Je vous recommande d'abord Montaigne. Lisez-le d'un bout à l'autre, et, quand vous aurez fini, recommencez (C iv 197). Je ne connais pas de livre plus calme, et qui ... dispose à plus de sérénité (C iii 184).[34] Lisez Montaigne, lisez-le lentement, posément. *Il vous calmera.* Ne lisez pas ... pour vous amuser, ni ... pour vous instruire. Non, lisez *pour vivre* (C iv 197).

The letter on the night spent watching by the body of his sister (C ii 3) analyses without complacency or sentimentality what such reading can offer. From personal anguish, physical decay, and snoring husband and priest, he turns to reflect on his reading and on the calm splendour of the distant stars through the open window:

Je lisais du Montaigne, ... et je me disais, en contemplant tout cela, que les formes passaient, que l'idée seule restait, et j'avais des tressaillements d'enthousiasme à des coins de phrases de l'écrivain.[35] Puis j'ai songé qu'il passerait aussi;

the stars, too, will pale and disappear, 'tout sera dit; et ce sera plus beau encore'.[36] Whether in face of personal suffering or a wider sense of metaphysical impermanence there is the same recourse:

Rappelle-toi l'arrière-boutique de Montaigne ... et tâche de t'en faire une. ... Est-ce que l'Art ne doit pas consoler de tout? (C i 119)[37].

As a tailpiece to the theme of literature as a way of life, one thinks of the days in May 1877 when Ronsard was read over dessert in the Château de Chenonceaux, this shared enjoyment of one of 'mes chers anciens' taking up across the centuries, in a Renaissance background, Ronsard's own delight in the reading of the ancients in his own countryside.

Flaubert's three sixteenth-century admirations would have to be seen against a wider background than can properly be discussed here. By the side of Shakespeare there are times when all the rest seem dwarfs, and *Don Quixote* 'que je savais par cœur avant de savoir lire' he finds at the root of his whole literary experience; when he recalls it, three aspects predominate which we have seen in his love for the French Renaissance authors: the theme of man's baffled but creative dreams ('cette perpétuelle fusion de l'illusion et de la réalité qui en fait un livre si comique et si poétique'); its sharp sense of everyday physical detail – dusty roads in the sun and the smell of onions; and its final tone of the 'gaîment mélancolique'. On the side of abundance or excess would be set his views on Homer, Apuleius, Aristophanes, Sade, Goethe, Chateaubriand, Hugo; on that of clarity or craftsmanship Horace, La Bruyère, La Fontaine, Boileau, Buffon, Voltaire, Montesquieu. Modern authors are often associated in odd parallels or contrasts with those of the Renaissance. Byron, later to be outgrown, is initially seen as the modern form of Montaigne's self-analysis. To Michelet, whose works Flaubert devoured with enthusiasm in youth, and both admired and sharply criticized later, he writes in 1861: 'je vous serre les mains dans la haine de l'*anti-physis*' (iv 430);[38] in his love of suggestive paradox he is said to have claimed Sade as 'l'incarnation de l'*Antiphysis*, le dernier mot du catholicisme, la haine du corps'.[39] Musset and Béranger are held up with scorn against the touchstone of Rabelais; Hugo, that force of nature, full of flaws and greatness, is frequently compared with the spirit of the Renaissance.

Can any direct results of his 'fréquentation des grands hommes' be traced in Flaubert's own works? Other critics have investigated some aspects in detail; I add only one or two brief suggestions. Ronsard would seem to have been a personal enjoyment rather than of immediate importance to his own art.[40] Montaigne, as the epitome of self-examination and of scepticism (but also as, through the destruction of illusion, finding the personal calm of his *arrière-boutique*) was obviously a permanent 'père nourricier'. If the self-confession of Flaubert's early works is often closer to more romantic models, yet a letter of 1846 (C i 386) shows how closely Montaigne's self-analysis is associated with the urge to draw a great work from direct expression of personal substance, and with the reasons (both of personal humility and of aesthetic purpose) which gradually turn Flaubert to different means of expression.[41] The contribution of Montaigne's mind and style is obviously both pervasive and difficult to pinpoint.[42]

It is Rabelais's influence which is most openly, and often intentionally, to be seen and enjoyed; pastiche, parody, and transposition into modern terms weave deliberate variations on his themes and technique. Early letters elaborate fashionable coruscations around his style; mocking remnants of this mode among the intellectuals of Flaubert's youth will persist in the Hussonnet of *L'Éducation sentimentale*.[43] The comic aggrandizement of the most trivial material object to make it hold an epic significance is one of Flaubert's main delights, reaching its pitch of virtuosity in a letter where the spirit of each century is with a fine fantastic logic symbolized in the rich detail of its different footwear; in *Madame Bovary* a subtler network of variations will be woven on how the shape, material or state of upkeep of this humble object reflect character or mood.

Rabelais's technique of inserting into epic fantasy the details of a comic pseudo-precision has obviously captivated Flaubert's interest in playing with different tones and levels of artistic illusion. Where Rabelais mainly starts from gigantic and fantastic feats, then parodically 'authenticates' them through solemn and exact location and numeration, Flaubert often reverses the effect, setting out from factual precision to produce a crescendo of detail which almost imperceptibly culminates in epic fantasy. On the cab journey of Emma and Léon through Rouen, exact details of streets, squares, docks, parks are strung together in a labyrinthine concatenation widening into a sense of the infinite complexity of the city and the frenetic fulfilment of desire.

Rabelais's amassing of a horde of characters in one festive gathering, where they rub shoulders, declaim paradoxes, and bring alive in vastly heightened form an age and its problems, was, of course, handed on to the nineteenth century through the scene in *La Peau de Chagrin* in which Balzac deliberately sets out to rival the 'propos des Beuveurs' in contemporary terms. Flaubert's equivalents will be many, from the wedding-feast or the *comices agricoles* in *Madame Bovary*, through a series of contrasted celebrations in *L'Éducation sentimentale*, to the receptions at which Bouvard and Pécuchet entertain their neighbours. The arrival of the carriages for the wedding feast in *Madame Bovary* shows a Rabelaisian delight in developing to the last degree the enumeration of every type of current wheeled vehicle, in caricaturing these odd conveyances and their occupants, stylized into stiffened and clumsy puppets by Sunday clothes, cropped hair and razor-slashed skin; they participate in a gargantuan provincial feast, bedecked with nineteenth-century pretentiousness and provincial prettification; cliché and crude jest seethe; then all finishes in an epic *débandade* as unreined vehicles crazily rocket with their drunken owners across the countryside into the night. In *Madame Bovary* the puppet-show with epic extensions is restricted to a provincial background; in *L'Education sentimentale* it spreads over the political experience of a key generation in the capital; the use of precise and trivial detail to culminate in a vertiginous heightening of obsession or ineptitude reaches its epitome in Frédéric's prolonged pursuit of the ever-absent Regimbart from café to café, and in the mad manœuvres at the Club de l'Intelligence.[44] Finally, Bouvard and Pécuchet involve themselves in a wild emulation of the Rabelaisian desire to become 'un abîme de science'. The outcome proves them no giants; the mocking sympathy directed towards them[45] has perhaps a certain affinity with the presentation of the all-too-human Panurge in face of his recurrent dilemmas.

On the sixteenth century Flaubert is obviously neither scholar nor critic proper, though his scattered remarks might well fit Baudelaire's desire for criticism: 'partiale, politique, et qui ouvre le plus d'horizons'. What he says is suggestive much less for its analysis of the authors than for what it reveals of his own mind and art, and of the fruitful contact of minds and forms across the centuries. In this context, his personality shows some of its most positive and generous impulses. If, set against complacency and apathy, 'haïr et admirer' are 'deux rares vertus'[46] (CS IV 208), yet 'la postérité rira de nos dénigrements plutôt que de nos admirations' and 'Comme ça fait du bien d'admirer' (Preface to Bouilhet's *Dernières chansons*, and C III 91). Whatever his scepticism, there is one unwavering conviction:

«Je ne permets pas qu'on touche à mes chers anciens». . . . Cela m'a rappelé Montaigne disant «Insulter Seneca, c'est m'insulter moi-même» (C VI 185).

Finally, he writes of the difference between the authors one respects, those one enjoys in general, and

ceux qui nous prennent à la fois par tous les bouts, et qui nous semblent créés pour notre tempérament. On les hume, ceux-là! on s'en nourrit, ils nous servent à vivre (C IV 416).

Those whose profession and pleasure has been to transmit to successive generations a response to the mind and art of the

Renaissance can find in Flaubert an *amateur* who conveys in his own terms the stimulus of personal delight and the renewal of lasting tradition.

NOTES

1 References will be to the Conard edition unless otherwise stated. I have adopted the abbreviation C for the nine volumes of the *Correspondance* and CS for the four volumes of supplement. Place of publication in references is Paris unless otherwise stated.

2 *Souvenirs, notes et pensées intimes*, ed. L. Chevalley Sabatier (1965), p. 97.

3 'Tradition and Revaluation in the French Anthology, 1692–1960', in *Essays presented to C. M. Girdlestone*, Durham (1960), pp. 49–63.

4 A. M. Boase, art. cit., p. 62, remarks that as late as the Crépet anthology of 1861–2 'it is striking to realise with what serious reservations the Pléiade are still represented ... The prejudices of academic "good taste" ... are revealed as still deeply entrenched in attitudes to the Renaissance.' I possess a delightful *Course of French Literature containing a Critical Review of all the French Authors of Eminence*, by A. D. Doisy, Dublin (1832) – out of 423 pages it devotes two to Rabelais and Montaigne together; one line is given to Marot, and no other sixteenth-century poet is mentioned. (But La Fontaine is surprisingly well analysed in detail.)

On Flaubert's school programmes J. Bruneau, *Les Débuts littéraires de Gustave Flaubert*, provides interesting material, It would be useful to have further studies of syllabuses and textbooks as a background to nineteenth-century authors.

5 Marot is quoted in *Mémoires d'un Fou* (p. 521), mentioned in the *Voyage aux Pyrénées*, 1840 (pp. 392 and 395), and given as evidence of how tastes change in *Par les Champs*, 1840 (p. 74). As J. Bruneau points out (op. cit., p. 246) the quotation may come from the Ledentu edition of Rabelais which Flaubert possessed. For Saint-Amant see *L'Éducation sentimentale* of 1845 (p. 262); Preface to Bouilhet's *Dernières chansons* (in *Œuvres*, ed. Lemerre, 1880, p. 297); Letter to the Municipalité de Rouen (L'Intégrale edition of Flaubert, 1964, II, p. 765); and C V 153, VII 71. Régnier is among Flaubert's *livres de chevet* in 1844 (C I 153), is quoted in a letter of 1846 (C I 370), and mentioned in *Par les Champs* (p. 74), Preface to Bouilhet, p. 294 and C IV 83. In 1853 he has read of D'Aubigné only *Le Baron de Fæneste*, long since and with difficulty (C III 392; see also C VIII 373 and *L'Éducation* of 1845, p. 257). For Brantôme see *L'Éducation* of 1845 (pp. 161 and 257); C VI 405. For Cyrano de Bergerac C II 449, 455, III 4, 34; here there is clearer evidence of enthusiastic reading – 'C'est énorme de fantaisie et souvent de style.'

6 A number of critics have treated excellently certain aspects of the subject. The present article will attempt a synthesis, will use some details from works either not available at the dates when previous studies were published, or not used in them, and will, I hope, have its

own focus. For previous discussions see particularly: J. Boulenger, *Rabelais à travers les âges* (1925); D. M. Frame, *Montaigne en France, 1812–52*, New York (1940); the following articles in the *Revue des Études rabelaisiennes*: H. Patry, 'Rabelais et Flaubert' (1904); L. Larose, 'Rabelais et Flaubert' (1910); J. Plattard, 'Flaubert lecteur de Rabelais' (1912). See also the relevant passages in A. Coleman, *Flaubert's literary development in the light of his 'Mémoires d'un Fou,' 'Novembre' and 'Éducation sentimentale' (version of 1845)* (1914); H. Frejlich, *Flaubert d'après sa correspondance* (1933); E.-L. Ferrère, *L'Esthétique de Flaubert* (1913) (pp. 97 ff.); and for the early years the very full study by J. Bruneau, *Les Débuts littéraires de Gustave Flaubert, 1831–1845* (1962), with his full bibliography.

7 Expression used of Montaigne, C IV 33.

8 This is not the edition mentioned by Bruneau, op. cit., p. 35, as existing in the Croisset library.

9 II 426, III 18, 68, 264, IV 52 (and others discussed below).

10 Published by Jacques Suffel in *Figaro littéraire*, 11 August 1962.

11 C VI 382, 384, 390; CS III 9, 32, 33, 35. Flaubert mentions Blanchemain as 'mon ami', but is unaware that he no longer lives in Paris. The desire to discover which towns commemorate their great men by statues recurs at intervals, not only when the Bouilhet monument is being discussed.

12 See also *Par les Champs*, p. 74: 'le mauvais goût du temps de Ronsard, c'était Marot; du temps de Boileau c'était Ronsard', etc.

13 For Balzac's *La Peau de Chagrin* as a possible source cf. A. Coleman, op. cit., p. 69, and J. Bruneau, op. cit., p. 120.

14 *Par les Champs*, p. 15. *Souvenirs, notes et pensées intimes*, ed. L. Chevalley Sabatier (1965), pp. 64, 70, 80, 107 (the enigmatic remark on p. 70: 'L'esprit de Montaigne est un carré; celui de Voltaire un triangle', may be illuminated by the passage on p. 106 on the geometry of dramatic art: 'le sublime dans Corneille et dans Shakespeare me fait l'effet d'un rectangle'). See also an unpublished letter quoted by J. Bruneau, p. 285; the epigraph to *Novembre*; C I 57, 62, 98, 116, 119, 317, 353, 385–6, II 236, 414, 434, III 228, 341, 358, 409, IV 122, 239, V 197, 250, VI 47, 154, 160, VII 8, VIII 112, 255; CS II 307, CS complémentaire 19, as well as the other passages discussed below.

15 C IV 185, 197, V 167, 206, 208, 209.

16 On the corruption of monarchs preceding *Un secret de Philippe le Prudent*; *Moralité* to *Rage et Impuissance*; epigraph from *Gargantua* to *La Dernière Heure*.

17 I am not, however, sure that the Gargantua, Sancho, Falstaff comparison is as closely derived from the Philarète Chasles article only as J. Bruneau assumes.

18 *Par les Champs* pp. 28, 38; *Éducation* of 1845, p. 257; C I 62, 98, 116, 152, 267, 368 (with misprint 'Panurge fuyait les loups' for 'coups' cp. Index), II 450, III 39, 41, 149, 157, 322, 325, 333, 349.

19 See Alfred Le Poittevin, *Une Promenade de Bélial et Œuvres inédites*, ed. R. Descharmes (1924), p. 177, and also p. 170.

20 For other references see C III 69, 98, 157, 332, 333, 347, 442, IV 22, 33, 96, 422, VII 141, VIII 101, 372; CS II 159.

21 Brief general passages on the Renaissance occur in the Rabelais article,

the *Voyage aux Pyrénées*, pp. 390 ff., *Par les Champs*, pp. 287 ff., and *L'Éducation* of 1845, pp. 257 ff. If early 'morceaux de bravoure' on the Renaissance highlight its picturesque and passionate aspects, by the first *Éducation* the artist-hero has learnt to look beneath the purely picturesque, to mistrust all formulae, to investigate in each individual author the ways in which general and particular are combined to make originality, and to wish to make his own art profit from what is best in all periods.

22 Quoted in preface to L'Intégrale edition, p. 19.

23 Other letters will express admiration for Boileau.

24 Gustave Flaubert, *Dictionnaire des Idées reçues*, Édition diplomatique des trois manuscrits de Rouen par Lea Caminiti (1966), p. 110.

25 See also CS II 159: 'Fr. Baudry, qui a déjeuné chez moi ... m'a avoué que la littérature française était en décadence depuis le XIIe siècle et que Rabelais avait une mauvaise syntaxe. Vous voyez que les idées *chic* ne sont pas mortes en France.' The *Sottisier* contains Lamartine's remark 'Rabelais, ce boueux de l'humanité' (G. Bollème, *Gustave Flaubert: le second volume de Bouvard et Pécuchet* (1966) p. 90). Flaubert might have wished to add the few lines that dispose of Rabelais in the work of A. J. Doisy (1832) mentioned above: 'Rabelais abused his talent, and the gaiety which seems to have been his principal characteristic, by turning all his contemporaries into ridicule; ... nothing, however sacred, escaped his sarcasm' (p. 7).

26 Cf. *Souvenirs, notes et pensées intimes* (1965) p. 64: 'Me parler de la dignité de l'espèce humaine c'est une dérision, j'aime Montaigne et Pascal pour cela.'

27 See also C V 197 on 'cette délicatesse qui est au giron de la mélancolie'.

28 'Qu'il puisse se dépouiller de toute colère, de toute haine, de toute douleur' (*Œuvres de Jeunesse*, II 156).

29 Cf. Baudelaire on the physical effect of his first reading of Gautier (Pléiade edition, 1961, p. 690).

30 One remembers J.-P. Richard's opening sentence: 'On mange beaucoup dans les romans de Flaubert' (*Littérature et sensation*, 1954).

31 Cf. *Souvenirs, notes et pensées intimes* (1965), p. 64: 'Montaigne est le plus délectable de tous les écrivains. Ses phrases ont du jus et de la chair.'

32 One remembers Chénier on the ancients:
   Faire, en s'éloignant d'eux avec un soin jaloux,
   Ce qu'eux-mêmes feraient s'ils vivaient parmi nous
   and, of course, the Pléiade discussions of imitation.

33 He is quoted on 'l'homme [qui] bêle après l'infini' and on 'il nous faut abestir pour nous assagir' (C II 414, I 137).

34 'Le chapitre de Démocrite et Héraclite ... le dernier paragraphe' is singled out.

35 E-L. Ferrère, op. cit., p. 101, presents Flaubert as oddly interested in the man rather than the writer. But here, at a moment of heightened tension, it is the expression that strikes home. D. M. Frame, op. cit., gives a more balanced summing up.

36 One remembers the 'Et ce fut tout' of the second-last chapter in *L'Éducation sentimentale*.

37 No slick pronouncement; Flaubert immediately adds 'Ce qui est facile à dire' ...

38 Many passages in letters summing up what he admired in Michelet are very close in tone to those evoking Rabelais.

39 Reported by the Goncourts, quoted by J. Bruneau, op. cit., p. 33.

40 Flaubert does note as a discovery a point familiar to any student today: 'il y a dans la poétique de Ronsard un curieux précepte: il recommande au poète de s'instruire dans les arts et métiers, forgerons, orfèvres, serruriers, etc., pour y puiser des *métaphores*. C'est là ce qui vous fait, en effet, une langue riche et variée' (C IV 52).

41 A. Coleman, op. cit., pp. 12–15, examines some detailed parallels.

42 *Par les Champs*, p. 287, evokes 'Rabelais qui rit, Shakespeare qui voit, Montaigne qui rêve', three key-points in Flaubert's own art.

43 Scraps of pseudo-sixteenth-century language recur throughout the letters, too numerous to list. Balzac's *Contes drolatiques* were no doubt a contributory influence. See C III 72–5 for a developed piece of this style (discussed by H. Patry in art. cit.). See also VII 337.

44 I have left aside *Salammbô* and *La Tentation* where the multiplicity of sources would require a different kind of discussion.

45 I have discussed some aspects of this in an article on 'Flaubert et la conscience du réel' (see above, pp. 325–37).

46 Saint-Simon, in his *Mémoires*, discussing a weakling unable to hate, remarked that 'le nerf et le principe de la haine et de l'amitié ... est le même' (*Selections*, ed. A. Tilley, Cambridge, 1920, p. 203).

23

Flaubert and some painters of his time (1974)

'Si j'avais été peintre, j'aurais été rudement embêté ...' wrote Flaubert in a letter. He had just been trying to capture in words the countless extraordinary colours shifting on the surface of the sea, and it came naturally to think of the painter's problem, since exact reproduction of this 'truth' is impossible, and if it could be achieved would produce a false effect (*C* ii.210).[1] He often disclaimed any technical knowledge as an art critic, but he reacted strongly and individually to works of art; his responses are perhaps of three main kinds. First, in the context of his reflections on aesthetic problems in general, and of the paradoxes of representation and suggestion in particular, he compares and contrasts the dilemmas of writer and painter. Second, there is what might nowadays be called the sociological approach: his fascinated contemplation of the details which reveal the Taste of the Times, whether he searches for the atmosphere of a past age transfigured by the great masters, or is provoked to a creative 'horreur sacrée' by the spectacle of contemporary adulation for the second-rate. Of course, the terms aesthetician and sociologist would have been anathema to Flaubert;[2] it is his third response which matters most, and was evident, as with Baudelaire, from early childhood: his reaction to pictures as a means of extending and crystallizing his own inherent aspirations and projects.[3]

The wide and varied discoveries, penetrating analyses, and seminal suggestions of Jean Seznec have shown both how rewarding it can be to examine the ways in which Flaubert shaped his initial responses so as to give them suggestive value in his own creative works, and how much new material awaits investigation. I propose here to add two small contributions: by looking first at Flaubert's letter to the art critic Ernest Chesneau in 1868, then at a few of his manuscript notes on artists of the 1840s, notes which he compiled in the 1860s, in preparation for *L'Éducation sentimentale.*

Flaubert thanked other writers, notably Fromentin and Taine, for their books on art.[4] I have chosen his letter to Chesneau for three reasons: first, the previously published versions of the text contain many errors; second, beneath the informal tone and the appearance of taking up Chesneau's views just as they come, Flaubert has initially picked out three basic points of principle, then proceeded to agreement or disagreement on specific artists or problems; finally, to follow his allusions, one needs the kind of commentary provided for the Taine letter in the Supplement to the *Correspondance*, and Chesneau's volume is not easy to come by.

First, the text:

> Croisset.
> Dimanche

[fo. 1ʳ] Non! mon cher ami, votre livre ne «contrarie en rien mes goûts» loin de là! J'ai même été ravi de voir ce que je sens, ce que je pense formulé d'une telle façon.

Votre morceau sur l'École anglaise est à lui seul une œuvre. Et d'abord
5 vous avez très bien signalé son trait saillant, l'absence de composition –
(si vous aviez tenu à noircir du papier vous auriez pu faire un rap-
prochement entre la Peinture & la littérature britannique)

Bien que j'aie lu l'ouvrage de Milsand voilà la première fois que je trouve enfin une définition nette du Préraphaelisme! – La manière dont
10 l'Absolu & le contingent doivent être mêlés dans une œuvre d'art me semble indiquée nettement p. 62. Je pense comme vous. «dès qu'il y a interprétation dans l'œuvre d'un peintre, l'artiste a beau s'en défendre, il fait fonction d'idéaliste» (94) Bref, on n'est idéal qu'à la condition d'être réel & on n'est vrai qu'à force de généraliser. [fo. 1ᵛ] Du reste vous
15 concluez fort bien, en montrant l'inanité des théories par l'exemple des deux écoles Anglaise & Belge arrivant à des résultats divers bien qu'elles soient parties du même principe (89–90)

La limite de la peinture, (ce qu'elle peut et ce qu'elle ne peut pas) est montrée avec une évidence qui crève les yeux, à propos d'un tableau de
20 Pauwels et d'un autre de Comte. Enfin, je n'ose trop vous louer de vos idées parceque ce sont les miennes Donc sur la Religion nous sommes d'accord

Quant aux appréciations particulières (question de nerfs & de tempérament autant que de goût) je vous trouve parfois un peu
25 d'indulgence – Comme pr mon ami H. Bellangé entr'autres. Cela tient peut-être à ce que vous savez beaucoup et que vous êtes sensible à des mérites que je ne vois pas? Cependant j'applaudis sans réserve à tout ce que vous dites sur Ingres & Flandrin (215) Gérôme (221) le sculpteur italien Vela (378) bien d'autres encore! & je vous remercie d'avoir rendu
30 justice à Gustave Moreau – que beaucoup de nos amis n'ont pas selon

moi suffisamment admiré. (mais porquoi dites-vous *le* sphinx. C'est, ici, *la* sphinx – [fo. 2ʳ] Cette infime remarque vous prouvera que je vous ai lu attentivement. Aussi p 124 il y a une faute. «les récits d'hist. romaine d'Augustin Thierry.» vous avez voulu dire «les récits *mérovingiens*
35 d'A. Thierry. les récits d'hist. romaine sont d'Amédée Thierry.

Mais je ne suis nullement de votre opinion quand vous prétendez que «Decamps nous fit un Orient imaginaire» Son Orient n'est pas plus imaginaire que celui de Lord Byron – ni par la brosse ni par la plume personne encore n'a dépassé ces deux là comme *vérité*
40 Vous m'avez souvent remis sous les yeux des tableaux que j'avais oubliés. La description des portraits de l'empereur & de Mme de Ganay sont des pages du meilleur style, achevées, excellentes. – votre article sur l'art Japonnais est d'un critique supérieur où l'on sent le Praticien sous l'esthéticien (pardon du mot) à preuve: vos observations sur les surfaces
45 courbes, la perspective, 420. – cela est creusé. Vous êtes entré au cœur de l'art Japonais il me semble.

Une chicane, cependant. êtes-vous bien sûr que ce soit «le rationalisme étroit & sec de la Chine» qui lui ait fait repousser toute tentative de Progrès Le rationalisme seul en est-il la cause? Je n'en sais rien.
50 [fo. 2ᵛ] En résumé, mon cher Chesneau, votre livre m'a fait grand plaisir & je vous remercie de m'avoir envoyé. Je vous remercie également de l'aimable lettre qui l'accompagnait. Mon nom répété deux fois dans votre volume m'a prouvé votre sympathie. – Croyez bien à la mienne

Je vous serre les deux mains
55 & suis votre
Gᵛᵉ Flaubert
Si vous voyez les De Goncourt priez les donc de m'envoyer leur adresse. rappelez-moi au souvenir de votre patron –.

Enfin, si cela n'est pas inconvenant, présentez tous mes respects à la
60 Princesse –⁵

1.10. 'contingent' is written above a crossed-out word which I have not deciphered but which may simply be an initial mis-spelling.
1.13. the same is true of 'fait'.
1.19. 'montrée' is written above 'exprimée,' crossed out; 'une' has been inserted above the line between 'avec' and 'évidence'; probably in the course of writing Flaubert changed 'exprimée avec évidence' to the stronger 'montrée avec une evidence qui crève les yeux'.
1.36. A word or beginning of word has been crossed out before 'Mais'. Possibly 'Un'?
1.49. After 'Progrès' a phrase of four or five words has been crossed out: it ended 'et que' and led on: 'et que le rationalisme seul en soit la cause?' This has been changed to 'Le rationalisme seul en est-il la cause?'.
1.51. *sic*, for 'de me l'avoir envoyé'.

Chesneau's book: *Peinture – Sculpture. Les Nations rivales dans l'art*, with its voluminous sub-title,⁶ was a survey of contemporary art in many lands as seen at the Paris Exposition Universelle of 1867. If Flaubert, in a list of those obligatory subjects for cliché-conversation which infuriated him, included 'Les expositions universelles',[7] yet, with his customary interplay of encyclopedic appetite and wry criticism, he did attend them, from his journey to the London Exhibition of 1851 onwards,[8] and he had made at least two visits in 1867 (*C* V.299). He presumably knew Chesneau through their common Rouen connections[9] as well as through the circle of Princess Mathilde; the tone of the letter is clearly that of a polite acquaintance rather than a close friend. Chesneau later sent him others of his many works; there survives,[10] inscribed 'A Gustave Flaubert – Bien affectueux hommage – de son constant et fidèle admirateur', a copy of *La Chimère* of 1879, a strange lyrical prose tale, dedicated to Gustave Moreau, so admired by himself and by Flaubert, and with as frontispiece, to symbolize intense aspirations and temptations, a work by Moreau. Chesneau's career had been unconventional; on his parents' refusal to let him train as a painter he joined the army and spent four years in the ranks; after an unsuccessful venture at founding a newspaper in 1857 he gradually won a reputation for articles of art criticism in a variety of periodicals. By 1868 he had published a number of works on French and English painters, was 'rédacteur au Louvre' and 'chargé du rapport officiel du jury des classes des beaux-arts pour l'exposition de 1867'; in 1869 he was to become 'inspecteur des beaux-arts'. His long sequence of books was to continue throughout the 1880s, including his major contribution in *L'Œuvre complet de Delacroix* of 1885.

Flaubert is clearly conscious of producing a *modèle du genre* in the art of the polite thank-you letter, with its balance between wide principles and detail, between disclaimers of expert knowledge and suggestion of good grounds for his own views, between shared enthusiasm and occasional vigorous objection. He no doubt had more reservations about Chesneau's book than he cares to express; one wonders about his reactions to Chesneau's leisurely and repetitive style, and to the obvious gap, at times, between those rational arguments which reject trite conventions and those instinctive preferences in subject-matter where clearly bullfight-watchers or cruel landlords are at a disadvantage as compared to a sweet girl with a dead dove (e.g. pp. 55–6). But Chesneau was seen by others discussing him in the context of his times as eschewing both rigid general theories and cramping specialized technicalities; this approach, and his genuine if not always sustained or informed desire for breadth and variety of vision, gave Flaubert grounds for agreement.

Les Nations rivales opens with an article on contemporary English painters, and recalls the shock to all French standards when some of their works were originally exhibited in Paris in 1855: a shock caused first by violent crudity of colour, then by 'l'absence de toute composition. Ici, pas de centre, une action principale noyée dans l'accessoire' (p. 2; cf. pp. 9, 29, 50). On the other hand, Chesneau stresses that they have a kind of national originality unknown in France since David[11] (except for caricaturists), and that the French, 'trop portés à généraliser', could profit from their meticulous respect for detail. Flaubert, himself so often (and so wrongly) accused of subjecting structure to accessory detail, goes immediately to the importance of *composition*, his initial and lasting preoccupation in each of his novels[12] – and at once draws an analogy with English literature. His letter gives no evidence as to his direct knowledge of English painting – and Chesneau himself had significant difficulties over seeing many pictures: he points out that Rossetti's works have never been exhibited in France and are hard to see in England (p. 40) so must be reported on at second hand;[13] and that it is a pity nothing is known in France of Madox Brown or Jones Burne (*sic*, p. 47). But Flaubert's pleasure at finding in Chesneau a clear definition of Pre-Raphaelitism, after attempting in vain to extract one from Milsand, is neither empty compliment nor name-dropping; among his manuscript notes there exist two foolscap pages of efficient summary and quotation from Milsand's *L'Esthétique anglaise: étude sur John Ruskin.*[14] Chesneau's central point about this school is that 'par un système d'analyse microscopique poussé jusqu'au vertige ... ils voulaient réaliser, épouser étroitement le Vrai, principe et fin de toute morale'; even if this culminated in a 'création quasi-monstrueuse' it is a 'noble erreur' (pp. 14, 26). The sense of 'vertige' inherent in the pursuit, at two related extremes, of abstract truth and concrete exactitude no doubt held Flaubert's attention, as perhaps did the account (p. 22) of Holman Hunt's five years of study and travel in Judaea while preparing his 'Finding of Christ in the Temple'.

Flaubert moves immediately to his second conviction: the falsity of the simplified arguments, so rife at the time, around the ill-defined terms 'realism' and 'idealism'. On p. 62 Chesneau had discussed the way in which the old masters combined the general and the specific; Flaubert relates this to Chesneau's attack (pp. 94 ff.) on Courbet's dogmatic theories of realism, and quotes the clinching sentence: 'Dès qu'il y a interprétation dans l'œuvre d'un peintre ...' His own summing-up, in its lapidary expression of potential paradox: 'Bref, on n'est idéal qu'à la condition d'être réel & on n'est vrai qu'à force de généraliser', points forward to the puzzlement of Bouvard and Pécuchet in their study of aesthetic theories: 'L'application trop exacte du Vrai nuit à la Beauté, et la préoccupation de la Beauté empêche le Vrai. Cependant, sans idéal pas de Vrai; c'est pourquoi les types sont d'une réalité plus continue que les portraits' (*BP*, ed. Cento, p. 411).[15] And indeed here his conclusion, over-vigorously attributed to Chesneau, is, typically, that of 'l'inanité des théories'.[16]

He then takes up a third fundamental conviction: that of the essential separation between the different arts; one remembers his famous refusal to allow illustrations of his novels, since these would limit to one particular angle of vision the author's deliberate and suggestive appeal to the creative imagination of individual readers' responses. Chesneau was frequently concerned with the problem of the anecdotal or the allusive in painting, and with distinguishing between works where gesture and facial expression adequately convey the central suggestion, and those which unjustifiably demand outside knowledge or commentary: on pp. 98–100 he gives detailed examples from three pictures by Pauwels (how, for example, can a picture convey that the woman giving her jewels is doing so in order to save by her heroic magnanimity the populace who had murdered her husband?); much later (pp. 252–3) he looks into the problems involved by Charles Comte's attempt to depict in 'Seigni Joan' the anecdotal and verbal complexities of an incident from Rabelais. Flaubert's grouping of these observations shows that he has indeed 'lu attentivement'. And his interest in this problem, as in his notes on Milsand, shows how strongly he thinks of literature as calling on special resources for selection and interpretation.

Contact with the unfamiliar history or traditions of other nations has suggested the dangers of counting on a shared response to the painter's subject: Chesneau, however, holds that 'la légende biblique et chrétienne échappe seule dans l'ordre historique aux inconvénients que nous venons de signaler', for here the artist is using material familiar to all civilized societies (p. 101). But he also attacks (with all due respect for moral intentions) the stultifying conventions imposed on contemporary painters of church frescoes by well-meaning ecclesiastics who 'se préoccupent beaucoup plus de l'idée religieuse que de l'idée esthétique' (pp. 211–16). Hence Flaubert's 'sur la Religion nous sommes d'accord'.

With the elegant formula 'Je n'ose trop vous louer de vos idées parceque ce sont les miennes',[17] Flaubert turns from theory to appreciation of particular works, stressing that this depends not just on criteria of taste, but on individual and physical response – that of 'nerfs et tempérament'.[18] His comments are skilfully grouped to lead from artists about whom he has reservations to those he wholeheartedly admires, and at the same time to place his queries concerning Chesneau's judgements between passages in which he can stress his partial or complete agreement.

First, a polite doubt. The space and the praise (with only gentle reservations) which Chesneau gives to Hippolyte Bellangé (pp. 228–40), immensely popular in his day (along with Charlet and Raffet) for the combined 'realism' and nostalgia of his paintings and prints of military life in the epic age of Napoleon (his vignettes of the Old Guard – his battle paintings where 'Les deux amis' fall touchingly across each other on the field, each clutching the ribbons given by his beloved; his last rendering of the famous theme, 'La Garde meurt' – both exhibited in 1867), these seem excessive to Flaubert. His polite deference to Chesneau's specialized knowledge suggests perhaps not just Chesneau's technical equipment as an art critic, but the personal reactions produced by four years in the army; Flaubert's own friendship with the late Bellangé does not inhibit his doubts.[19]

Chesneau's criticism of Ingres and Flandrin (pp. 215 ff.) comes in a discussion of religious painting; he sees them as 'esprits intelligents mais limités', marking the culmination of past traditions and devoid of any new stimulus. One remembers Flaubert's derogatory recalling of Ingres's 'Roger délivrant Angélique',[20] or his reaction to 'Françoise de Rimini': 'Détestable, sec, pauvre de couleur; le col du jeune homme qui va pour embrasser Françoise n'en finit';[21] but also his appreciation of Ingres's portraits, when in the moment of intense delight produced by the encounter with a beautiful 'passante' in Rome he dreamed of having her portrait done by a painter summoned from Paris, and the painters he thought of were Ingres and Lehmann.[22] As for Flandrin, Flaubert did more than once remember details from the fresco of Christ's entry into Jerusalem, which he saw in Saint-Germain-des-Prés the day before he left for his journey to the Middle East in 1849.[23]

Chesneau makes Gérôme the occasion for an analysis (pp. 220–3) of how the contemporary public, determined to have value for its money, likes to see each detail minutely rendered, 'prendre le tableau sur ses genoux, l'étudier point par point à la loupe'. On the positive side, he provides an evocative page on Gérôme's skill in rendering the suppleness and substance of folds of material, the fragility and transparency of crystal, the rich touches of gold and silver on the hilt of weapons – sensuous impressionistic effects very close to those which Flaubert captures verbally in *L'Éducation sentimentale*; on the negative side, he attacks Gérôme's trite following of a now outmoded fashion for the caricaturing of antiquity, which 'vient après-coup, comme *Orphée aux Enfers* ou la *Belle Hélène*'. Flaubert was likely to agree with both sides of this appraisal.[24] As for Vincenzo Vela's statue of 'The Last Days of Napoleon' (pp. 377–8), one can imagine Flaubert's mesmerized and ironically reflective contemplation of this masterpiece of *trompe-l'œil* in all the glory of its 'realistically' rendered woollen blanket and intricate lace-work.

But Flaubert's admirations, as so often, outpace his hatreds. Here he chooses one painter who had meant much to his own generation, Decamps, and one who seems to promise much for the future, Gustave Moreau.[25] Decamps, who has obviously been a long-standing stimulus to his own way first of imagining, then of directly experiencing, the Middle East,[26] is defended, in general terms, and with an immediate literary parallel, for the fundamental insight of his vision (once again, it is not superficial accuracy of representation which is the criterion).

Although only two of Gustave Moreau's pictures appeared in the 1867 Exhibition, and he there received no award, Chesneau, considering him 'la personnalité la plus haute parmi les peintres vivants et militants', gave Moreau pride of place (pp. 179–207) and quoted at length his own past discussions of other paintings shown in the *Salons* of 1864, 1865, and 1866. Much of what he says would fit with Flaubert's own temperament and preoccupations: for example, Chesneau's stress on how Gustave Moreau's sudden rise to fame in 1864 was the result of long years of effort and of waiting (against all the arguments of his friends) until he considered his work ready; or on how, out of elements chosen from reality, the painter constructs a compelling unity of effect, intense, haunting and suggestive. Detailed evocations and analyses are given to 'Œdipe et le Sphinx', 'Jason', 'Le Jeune Homme et la Mort', 'Diomède dévoré par ses chevaux', and 'Orphée' (for the last, the theme of the severed head is related in detail to that of John the Baptist);[27] there is also a mention of an enamel exhibited in the *Salon* of 1867, based on Gustave Moreau's 'La Chasse'. Worried perhaps by the idea that these enigmatic paintings may appear to contradict his strictures on the over-allusive or over-literary, Chesneau insists that their value does not depend on precise interpretation of detail, compares their effect with the kind of suggestion to be found in Shakespeare, sees them as representing 'le droit d'échapper à la terre par le rêve, l'imagination', and stresses that they transform any impetus given by fact, idea, emotion, or sensation into its purely pictorial equivalent. Flaubert's enthusiasm for Gustave Moreau (his physical, emotional, and intellectual reactions to problems of the stylization of suffering, represented through intense colour and through a sharp and strange precision where detail is at once hyper-realistic and hyper-symbolic, would deserve further discussion) certainly found here an eloquent advocate for the defence.[28]

Flaubert says nothing of his own reactions to Cabanel's portraits of Napoleon III and Mme de Ganay (Chesneau, pp. 175–6);[29] what he praises is Chesneau's way of writing about them. The merely 'realistic' portrait had always seemed to Flaubert the temptation of the bad painter; what interests him here is the attempt to sift out from peripheral detail certain significant suggestions. Chesneau centred his discussion on what he held to be the 'modernity' of these portraits, where, instead of using the obligatory conventions (Emperor in military accoutrements or mantle of imperial purple; society beauty fashionably corseted), the painter, rejecting the pompous and the prettifying, had chosen to convey the epitome of aristocratic dignity in the man and of complex sensitivity in the woman, not through picturesque symbolic accessories, but through the simple and subtle suggestions of their mere physical appearance as arranged and interpreted by the artist. Late in the day, and beneath a good deal of initial verbiage, Chesneau is here formulating something akin to Baudelaire's ideas on 'le peintre de la vie moderne', 'le dandy', the hyper-civilized woman; Flaubert is perhaps half-ironically praising his 'tour de force' in extracting such ideas from the exigencies of official portraiture. And one thinks ahead to how, on the contrary, Flaubert's aspiring and dismally unsuccessful painter Pellerin, in *L'Éducation sentimentale*, will set out to produce the master-portrait of all time, not by seeking to combine the suggestively representative and the specifically individual in his model, but by surrounding the unfortunate Rosanette with a concatenation of derivative, romanesque and caricatural accessories.

Flaubert, who commented only on what he had himself looked at, left out some sections of Chesneau's work. But, like others in the late nineteenth century, he turns to Japanese art. Chesneau's final article, on 'L'art japonais', once again raised the question of supposedly 'realist' art and of varying conventions, and sought to show that what to French eyes might appear primitive or barbaric was the product of a deliberate and sophisticated technique. The Flaubert who is so drawn to playing in every way on geometrical patterns (whether in plot, in relations between characters, or in description of landscapes), and on suggestive shifts in point of view, has picked out Chesneau's comments both on how the curve of a vase and the angle from which it is seen may affect decorative stylization and on the differences between linear geometrical perspective and 'la perspective du sentiment' (pp. 420–1).

But he objects vigorously to Chesneau's generalizations contrasting Japan and China (pp. 416–17); here the Flaubert in whom some critics of today over-stress the potential absurdist or nihilist refuses to see rationalism qualified as 'étroit et sec' or made an obstacle to progress.[30]

'Vous m'avez souvent remis sous les yeux des tableaux que j'avais oubliés': this is part of Flaubert's thanks to Chesneau. At a period when reproductions as we now know them were unobtainable, and travel to see the originals was much more difficult, the ability of the art critic to give in words either a purely factual, or a physically evocative, description of a painting had an important function, sometimes overlooked today in derogatory remarks on 'descriptive' critics of the nineteenth century. Flaubert's own notes on the paintings which at different stages of his life he contemplated so closely have often a purely mnemonic purpose, designed simply to resuscitate before his own mental vision the slightest detail of the picture, details on which he will later work as he selects and transforms for his own evocative purposes.[31]

He had, however, special reasons in 1868 for being interested in Chesneau's panorama of painters. For at least four years he had been systematically compiling his documentation for *L'Éducation sentimentale*, in which the hero's early, and sporadically renewed, ambition is to be a painter, while the significant figure of Pellerin provides a richly detailed evocation, both sardonic and serious, of the ambitious and contradictory succession of aesthetic theories throughout the period, and that of Arnoux an epitome of the trivializing compromises inherent in the commercial pressures imposed by the popularization of art.

From about 1864 he set out to re-create in his own mind the atmosphere of the years 1840–51, through reading and annotating an encyclopedic range of books and periodicals.[32] Many of course he read primarily for their political background, but the fine arts hold an important place, in several ways.

For the treatment given in this period to the treasures of the past, there is the grim or gleeful study of pompous theoretical aspiration set by the side both of the details of commercial double-dealing, deliberate fraud and forgery, and, still more ironically, of the damage caused to great works of art in State museums whether by the inertia of neglect or by the ill-conceived initiative of clumsy restoration. From *L'Artiste* Flaubert copies a project for a Chair of Aesthetics (to be coveted by the unfortunate Pellerin) as a means of enlightenment in this age of lack of criteria, when mankind is 'égaré par le positivisme': this Chair should be given to one who possesses 'l'entraînement passionné vers l'idéal uni à un sentiment profondément naturel du plastique ... un philosophe ému dont l'éloquence comme celle d'Abélard au Moyen Age parvienne à grouper la multitude éparse ...'.[33] On the commercial dealings that influence reputations or corrupt taste, and on the official failure to preserve the great works, he collects material from many books and articles. His very detailed investigations will be sifted out to give in his novel the brief but virulent suggestions on the one hand of Arnoux's profiteering from Pellerin's ability to paint 'dessus de porte, genre Boucher', of the machinations round Rosanette's portrait or Pellerin's dangerously revolutionary Christ on a Railway Engine, and on the other hand of Pellerin's strictures on some of the damage inflicted in the Louvre.[34]

For the artists of the present, Flaubert takes systematic notes on each year's *Salon*. In these, whether from the eight annual pieces of leisurely gossip by Jules Janin in *L'Artiste* or from the more compressed and forthright two annual articles by Planche in the *Revue des Deux Mondes*, he selects out of a vast number of names the main painters of the year: obviously he has the benefit of hindsight in his choice; obviously too he concentrates, though not exclusively, on the early pages of each series where the critic picks out those who count most at the time; but in any case Flaubert is here concerned not just with choosing his personal preferences, but with pin-pointing the artists who formed the talking-points of the year, destined for representative and allusive use, as in the first scene at Arnoux's where the up-to-date subject is the much-contested Ingres portrait of Cherubini.[35]

The notes on the *Salons* are mainly lists of names – again a simple means of recalling material familiar to Flaubert, and part of the atmosphere he wished to re-create. But there are other notes which bring alive his immediate and personal response as he looks at some of the engravings in which periodicals either reproduced the pictures of the year or provided other examples of popular taste. And if the majority of the notes on the *Salons* are taken from *L'Artiste*, it is no doubt because its two plates for each week provided a visual means of recalling the paintings from twenty-five years earlier. Sometimes there is a brief analysis of pleasure, as for the four charming colour-plates of fancy-dress costumes by Gavarni in *L'Artiste* of 1840: one in particular is 'charmant de grâce et de mouvement'.[36] But the most expressive passages come from the Flaubert 'nauseated and fasci-nated at the same time' by the taste of contemporaries 'who take delight in the bad with edifying tenacity'.[37] *L'Artiste* of 1841 produced an engraving by Perronel of Cassel's 'Nina attendant son bien-aimé' [23] and flanked it with a lyrical description of the elevated grace and charm of this admired painting; the *Salon* article in an earlier issue had seen it as 'noble, gracieux', evincing a 'tristesse de bon goût'. To Flaubert it is 'hideux de mauvais goût', and he contemplates the tiniest details of the clichés which contri-bute to its fearful effect: 'en marquise Pompadour, le coude appuyé sur un rocher, un mouchoir à la main – bouffette au soulier, rubans au corsage, mantelet à dentelles – rêvant – un clocher à l'horizon'.[38] Other works of pious sentimentality – in particular Bourdet's 'Une Petite Fille d'Eve' [24],[39] with its mournful maiden poised in melancholy between a grisly demon and an improbable angel, and Compte-Calix's sugary 'Les Sœurs de lait' [25][40] – rouse the same stupefaction at the spectacle of the *Salon* including works that exemplify 'ineptitude pushed to this degree'.[41]

But there are occasional reflections of another kind – and one in particular proves that Flaubert finds it natural for a painting or engraving to stimulate a literary work. Looking at '«L'Enlèvement», lithographie par M. Alfred de Dreux. Première pensée du tableau – Salon de 1840' [26], he notes: 'A peut-être inspiré la jolie romance dans Éviradnus. Les deux jeunes gens se baisent à la bouche [.] celles des chevaux se cherchent. Crinières au vent – elle s'appuie sur son bras. Les deux chevaux galoppent'.[42]

As always with Flaubert, his documentation was to be sifted and re-sifted. Jean Seznec has shown how[43] in *Madame Bovary* details of the engravings in the Rouen hotel room of Emma's and Léon's last meetings were sacrificed in the final version of the novel; engravings

[23] Cassel: 'Nina attendant son bien-aimé'

which were at the same time savorously representative of popular taste, and deeply suggestive, through ironical parallel or contrast, of the fundamental patterns of impulse underlying the two characters and their situation. We do not know what the huge first manuscript of *L'Éducation sentimentale* may have contained or what may have been deleted from it later. In that country inn beyond

[24] Bourdet: 'Une Petite Fille d'Eve'

[25] Compte-Calix: 'Les Sœurs de lait'

Fontainebleau where Frédéric and Rosanette dined by the river in the evening, in a privileged moment of isolated and illusory delight, did Flaubert originally place on the walls those engravings which he noted in his *carnet* when he selected the auberge 'A la bonne matelotte' at La Plâtrerie for this key scene – engravings comprising a Bellangé caricature and portraits of the men of 1830? They

Alfred del'Dreux

Imp. Béld & Bechauds

[26] Alfred de Dreux: 'L'Enlèvement'

would have given a finely allusive ironical touch as background to the central figures' moment of careless escape from the battles of 1848.[44] Alfred de Dreux at all events survives in the final version of *L'Éducation*. Frédéric's multiple purchases from Arnoux's shop, displayed in the room he shares with Deslauriers, include, beside views of exotic cities (Venice, Naples, Constantinople), 'des sujets équestres d'Alfred de Dreux'.[45] Suggestive enough of Frédéric's aspirations to the world of aristocratic fashion (where Alfred de Dreux's elegant works found a long and steady sale) and of the modish background of Jockey Club and races on the Champ de Mars; but did Flaubert also have at the back of his mind a more specific allusion to 'L'Enlèvement', as evoking Frédéric's dreams of Mme Arnoux, dreams held in common with other lovers borne 'dans un délire parallèle/Vers le paradis de mes rêves'?[46]

I have ended with a question. And the main purpose of this brief article has been to indicate how much remains to be investigated by those to whom Jean Seznec's sensitive scholarship has offered a new and lasting stimulus. To Flaubert 'la plastique, mieux que toutes les rhétoriques du monde, enseigne à celui qui la contemple la gradation des proportions, la fusion des plans, l'harmonie enfin!' (*Par les champs*, p. 299), and he has followed his own counsel (*C* v.302): 'Emplissez-vous la mémoire de statues et de tableaux.'

NOTES

1 Page references below are to the Conard edition unless otherwise stated: I use the following abbreviations: *C*: *Correspondance* (9 vols., 1926–33); *CS*: Four supplementary vols. of *Correspondance inédite*, ed. R. Dumesnil, J. Pommier, Cl. Digeon, 1953; *ES*: *Éducation sentimentale*; *BP*: *Bouvard et Pécuchet*.

For Flaubert's manuscript notes taken in the 1860s, I have consulted, in the Bibliothèque Historique de la Ville de Paris, the Carnets de Lecture (CL) and the Carnets de Voyage (CV); and, in the Bibliothèque municipale de Rouen, the eight dossiers g 226[1-8]. A debt is owed to the work of many scholars who have provided analyses of these documents, or published important material from them. I give here references to the originals.

2 Cf. below, p. 357, his apology for using the word *esthéticien* in the Chesneau letter, and his summing-up of Pellerin as 'un esthétiqueur qui fait le portrait d'un enfant mort' (*CS* II. 172). Cf. also below, p. 365, on the 'chaire d'esthétique'. Cf. his use of *esthéticien* to Fromentin, *C* VII.322.

3 Cf. Jean Seznec, *La Source de l'épisode des dieux dans «La Tentation de Saint*

Antoine» (Vrin, 1940), on the important fact that the visual stimulus may be less an initial source than a means to 'cristalliser des pensées et des rêves encore flottants' (p. 12), and on how it is after he has created his own 'idée d'ensemble' that Flaubert searches for its exemplification in detail (p. 24). Cf. also the same author's *Nouvelles Études sur* «*La Tentation de Saint Antoine»* (London, Warburg Institute, 1949), and his other studies mentioned below. On some other aspects of Flaubert's reaction to the visual arts, cf. Jean Bruneau, 'Les deux voyages de Gustave Flaubert en Italie', in *Connaissance de l'Étranger*, Mélanges offerts à la mémoire de J.-M. Carré (Paris, Didier, 1964), pp. 164–80, and Irma B. Jaffé, 'Flaubert – the novelist as art critic', *Gazette des Beaux-Arts*, May–June 1970, pp. 335–70.

4 *C* VII.321–2 to Fromentin, for *Les Maîtres d'autrefois*; *CS* II.86–90, to Taine for *Voyage en Italie*, *II*, *Florence et Venise*, and *CS* II.160–2 for *Philosophie de l'art dans les Pays-Bas*.

5 I am glad to express here warm thanks to Professor G. Donnay, Conservateur, Musée de Mariemont, for his kindness in letting me have excellent photo-copies of the manuscript and for authorization to publish a corrected version.

The letter appears (without its postscript and with a number of misreadings) in the Conard *Correspondance*, V.379–81. It was exhibited in 1967; see Paul Culot's notes on it in *Trésors inconnus du Musée de Mariemont*, Aut. 366/1. In Dec. 1968 J.-M. Paisse produced in the Bulletin of the *Amis de Flaubert* No. 33, pp. 27–8, a version which restored the postscript and made some other corrections, but cf. below.

Other observations: I have inserted some missing accents, but otherwise followed Flaubert's text exactly. Apart from details of spelling, punctuation, and paragraphing, the following are the main corrections to the Conard version, affecting the sense of the letter:

Restoration of quotation marks indicating that Flaubert is citing Chesneau: ll. 1 and 11–13.*

Corrections to page references: 1. 11, 62 *not* 60*; 1. 17, 89–90 *not* page 550; 1. 28, 215 *not* 315*.

Other corrections: 1. 20, Pauwels *not* Pamvels; 1. 32, prouvera, *not* prouve*; 1. 33, Aussi *not* Ainsi; 1. 34, vous avez voulu dire, *not* vous avez bien voulu dire*; 1. 40, remis *not* mis*; 1. 45, *insert*, 420 *after* perspective; 1. 48, *insert* & sec *after* étroit*; 1. 51, m'avoir *not* me l'avoir*; 1. 55, *insert at end* et suis votre G^{ve} Flaubert; *at end add postscripts*.

On the points indicated by asterisks, J.-M. Paisse's version produced the same corrected readings. But it dislocated the order of Flaubert's comments by placing fo. 2^{r} before instead of after fo. 1^{v}, left some errors uncorrected, and introduced misreadings (1. 17, par. 990 *for* 89–90; 1. 33, je sais [qu'] *for* p. 124; 1. 35, André Thierry *for* Amédée Thierry; 1. 45, etc. *for* 420).

6 *Peinture – Sculpture. Les Nations rivales dans l'art.* Angleterre – Belgique – Hollande – Bavière. Prusse – États du Nord – Danemark – Suède et Norwège – Russie – Autriche – Suisse – Espagne – Portugal – Italie – États Unis d'Amérique – France. L'Art Japonais. De l'Influence des Expositions Internationales sur l'Avenir de l'Art. Par Ernest Chesneau.

Paris. Librairie Académique. Didier et Cie. 1868. Dedicated to Princess Mathilde, Chesneau's book was listed in the Bibliographie de la France on 1 Aug. 1868. I have found no exact evidence for the date of Flaubert's letter of thanks, though it is not likely to be between mid-July and mid-August, when he was away from Croisset on visits to Dieppe, Fontainebleau, Saint-Gratien, and Paris.

7 'Choses qui m'ont embêté, alias: scies'. BMR g 226¹ fo. 277 (quoted by a number of scholars).

8 Cf. Jean Seznec, *Flaubert à l'Exposition de 1851* (Oxford, Clarendon Press, 1951). The notebook which Professor Seznec so impeccably deciphers, and illuminates with his introductory comments, appears to me to be Flaubert's 'fair copy', in more coherent form, of Carnet de Lecture 4, BHVP (where most pages are diagonally crossed out as was Flaubert's habit when he had rewritten). This latter, often very illegible, *carnet* would be the one used on the spot. To set the two versions side by side is to discover an interesting development of 'variants' even in such brief notes. CL 4, fo. 70ᵛ, suggests that in Seznec p. 32 l. 22 *moutons* should read *montans*.

The editors of the Club de l'Honnête Homme *Œuvres* have recently published in Vol. VII the *Carnets de lecture*. As with previous volumes of this edition, the presentation of important material is marred by some serious misreadings. Mme Durry's indispensable volume of material from particular *carnets* is of course familiar to all scholars.

9 Ernest Chesneau (1833–90) was born in Rouen (twelve years after Flaubert); he was at school in Rouen (after Versailles) in 1848.

10 Cf. L. Andrieu's list of books inscribed to Flaubert (*Les Amis de Flaubert*, No. 24 (mai 1964), pp. 3–23) and *C* VIII.332. Chesneau also sent Flaubert his *Peintres et statuaires romantiques* of 1880.

11 Cf. Flaubert on the Empire painters, e.g. in *Voyage en Orient: Italie*, ed. L'Intégrale II.682, 'Peinture à faire périr d'ennui ... il gèle à 36° dans cette école'.

12 Cf. also to Caroline (*C* VIII.290), 'Quant à tes études picturales, tu devrais t'exercer à la composition', and compare with VII.373, 'tu me dois un Vénitien, quelque chose de royal et *d'archicoloré*'. Construction and colour are central to his reactions.

13 Chesneau speaks of a Rossetti exhibition at Russels place [*sic*] in 1857, and of how Georges Pouchet, a friend of Flaubert, on a visit to Darwin, saw a Rossetti painting (pp. 72–3).

14 BMR g 226¹ fo. 165ʳ⁻ᵛ. These careful notes show Flaubert's choice of central problems relating to his own basic preoccupations and would deserve close analysis. They end with: 'Les penseurs qui s'occupent des artistes les engagent sous prétexte de se relever à se dégrader. L'intérêt humain, pathétique, moral, philosophique sont précisément ce que cherche et aime dans un tableau la foule ignorante et les lettrés qui lui demandent les mérites d'un récit ou d'un roman' and also include: 'les lettrés sont incapables d'apprécier les qualités en quelque sorte musicales qui distinguent les tableaux des œuvres peintes'. Joseph Milsand's *L'Esthétique anglaise*, étude sur M. John Ruskin (Paris, 1864), appeared at the time when Flaubert was embarking on his documentation for

L'Éducation sentimentale. Milsand's other works bear on philosophy, religion, politics, education, rather than art. Chesneau mentions his *Esthétique anglaise* on pp. 20, 22, 27. The CHH notes to *ES*, p. 468 (cf. above, n. 8), mention notes by Flaubert on Pre-Raphaelites without including his own reference to Milsand.

15 On the supposed dichotomy between *Le Vrai* and *La Beauté*, see discussions throughout Flaubert's *Correspondance*, and cf. Baudelaire, *Notes nouvelles sur Edgar Poe.*

16 For Chesneau's milder expression of the problem, cf. pp. 88–90 where he sees both the Pre-Raphaelites and the Neo-Germanists as a theoretical return to primitivism but stresses the inferior execution of the former. Cf. also p. 327 on the difference between system and result.

17 Cf. the self-mocking marginal note on political views in a periodical, BMR g 226[4], fo. 117[v]: 'Idées fort sages (c'est à dire les miennes)'.

18 Both terms – *nerfs* and *tempérament* – recall Baudelaire's stress on individual physical response to the work of art. Cf. my article on 'Aspects of expression in Baudelaire's art criticism' (see above pp. 176–215).

19 Flaubert refers to Bellangé as 'mon ami', and must certainly have known him closely. Joseph-Louis-Hippolyte Bellangé (1800–66) was Conservateur au Musée de Rouen from 1837 to 1854; he published a catalogue of the collection in 1846 (O. Popovitch, *Catalogue du Musée des Beaux-Arts de Rouen* (Paris, Arts et Métiers graphiques, 1967), p. 4). Chesneau (quoted in Jules Adeline, *Hippolyte Bellangé et son œuvre*, Paris, A. Quantin, 1880) was at school with his son Louis who died young, and describes Bellangé's picturesque studio which Flaubert presumably knew (Adeline, pp. 14–17). Flaubert recalls how, when he left for Egypt in October 1849, the farewell party included 'le jeune Louis Bellangé qui est mort pendant ma visite' (*Voyage en Orient: Égypte*, ed. L'Intégrale II.550; cf. II.559 where the child is recalled). Cf. M. Mespoulet in *Images et romans* (Paris, Belles Lettres, 1939), p. 108, for Bellangé's representation of a Normandy wedding procession (dating from well before *Madame Bovary*) – this, and a Bellangé portrait of Achille Flaubert, are reproduced in the *Album Flaubert*, ed. Jean Bruneau and A. Ducourneau (Pléiade, 1972), pp. 107 and 69.

Cf. Jean Seznec, 'Flaubert and the Graphic Arts', *Journal of the Warburg and Courtauld Institute*, VIII (1945), (p. 182, n. 1 remarks how Callot and Bellangé are juxtaposed in a note by Flaubert). Were those prints of Napoleonic battles, dear to Henry's bourgeois father in the first *Éducation* (Seznec, p. 176) works by Bellangé? Early in his career, Bellangé had even produced scenes for the decoration of popular china (cf. Jean Seznec, '*Madame Bovary* et la puissance de l'image', *Médecine de France*, VIII (1949), for the china plates with the Louise de la Vallière story which had so influenced Emma). On Bellangé, cf. below, n. 35 and n. 44.

20 *Voyage en Orient: Italie et Suisse*, ed. L'Intégrale, II.463.

21 Ibid., *Italie*, II.682.

22 Ibid., II.698.

23 *Voyage en Orient: Égypte*, ed. L'Intégrale, II.566; cf. *C* II.228.

24 Cf. *C* v.241 'Le Chic ... admirer *Orphée aux Enfers*', and *C* IV.371 on Gluck's *Orphée*: 'une des plus grandes choses que je connaisse'.

25 As regards the future, Flaubert makes no comment on the passages where Chesnéau uneasily combines reproof and real effort at explanation around the startling works of Manet. (Cf. the refusal to pronounce in *C* VIII.279 to Zola: 'Comme je ne comprends goutte à sa peinture, je me récuse'.)

26 Cf. in J. Seznec, art. cit., *Jnl. Warburg and Courtland Inst.*, p. 175, and M. Mespoulet, op. cit., p. 68, references to L. Hourticq's discussion, in *La Vie et les images* (1927), of Decamps in relation to *Salammbô*. Cf. below, n. 35.

27 Cf. also Flaubert's comments on pictures representing Judith and Holophernes.

28 Cf. above, p. 358, for Chesneau's *La Chimère*.

29 Both pictures date from 1865. Alexandre Cabanel (1824–89) won fame in his day particularly for his portraits of society women: he contributed to the decoration of the pre-1870 Hôtel de Ville, and of the Panthéon and the Tuileries. Contemporary critics frequently select, along with the portrait of Mme de Clermont-Tonnerre, the two mentioned here. Flaubert's long-standing attack on the merely 'realistic' portrait painter (cf. the satirical apotheosis of Ternande in the first *Éducation*) now finds an analysis which stresses the suggestive function in portraiture. He knew Cabanel personally; *C* VIII.236.

30 One or two further details from the letter deserve brief comment:
    (i)   In his remark on the gender of 'sphinx' Flaubert is thinking of the female figure in the picture, though the title followed grammatical usage, 'Orphée et le Sphinx'.
    (ii) The correction of the confusion between the two Thierrys recalls his own lifelong reading of historians.
    (iii) The two references to Flaubert in Chesneau's book occur on p. 65 (where a water-colour by Lamont recalls 'l'ennui de Mme Bovary, analysé dans un chef-d'œuvre de Gustave Flaubert') and p. 90 (where Leys's historical paintings are compared with 'l'archaïsme savant et cependant animé, presque vivant' through which Leconte de Lisle and Flaubert restore past civilizations).
    (iv) In the postscript, 'votre patron' is presumably Nieuwerkerke, directeur des musées impériaux, who furthered Chesneau's career. In *C* V.421 Flaubert wonders whether the Goncourts are still at Trouville; he has had no news of them since before August.

31 The process can already be seen if one compares the chapter summaries for *Par les champs et par les grèves* with the developed passages, or the *Notes de voyage* with parallel passages in the *Correspondance*.

32 Much of this documentation subsists in the BMR dossiers g 226[1-8]. See Alberto Cento's careful analysis, made with a view to determining which sections of these dossiers belong to the preparation of *L'Éducation sentimentale*, in his critical edition of *Bouvard et Pécuchet* (Paris, Nizet, 1964), pp. lxiii–iv, and especially his *Il Realismo documentario nell' 'Éducation sentimentale'* (Naples, Liguori, 1967), pp. 73 ff. A few other sections should probably be added to his list, and his dating by the type of paper used (in general useful and valid) may need further investigation in relation to MSS in other collections. The following are

the notes on art (not necessarily for the *ES*) not mentioned in his lists: g 226¹ fos. 125–36 (notes on Winckelmann and Lessing); fo. 165 (notes on Milsand, cf. above, p. 115); g 226⁵, fos. 233–355 (notes on great painters of different schools and nationalities); g 226⁷, fos. 230ᵛ–233 (notes on *Revue des Deux Mondes*, including *Salon*; cf. those in g 226⁴, fo. 105). Many of these notes can be dated through cross-references from the *Correspondance*.

The CHH edition (cf. n. 8 above) published for the first time (in Vol. III) an important selection from this material, but it must be used with caution in view of many misreadings and omissions.

When undertaking his systematic reading of the periodicals of the 1840s, Flaubert often appended to his notes the shelfmark in the Bibliothèque Impériale [Nationale] where he read many of them; cf. *C* v.142, 144, 211, etc.

33 Cf. Flaubert's notes in BMR g 226⁴, fo. 106, and *L'Artiste*, July–Oct. 1847, pp. 1–2, article by Édouard L'Hote, 'De l'enseignement des beaux-arts en France'. Flaubert's hatred of the confusion between philosophy and art, and his insistence on the importance of the individual talent separated from the stereotypes of the crowd, must have made him leap on this passage. The precise sections he quotes are marked by a pencil line in the BN copy of *L'Artiste*; perhaps Flaubert's own marking? (Cf. n. 32, above, for his reading of periodicals there.)

34 Cf. the notes (BMR g 226¹, fos. 153–67), on Henri Rochefort, *Les Petits Mystères de l'Hôtel des Ventes*; Horsin Déon, *De la conservation et de la restauration des tableaux*; Ch. Blanc, *Le Trésor de la curiosité*. Attacks on neglect or restoration in the Louvre were frequent in periodicals: Flaubert takes particularly full notes on examples from *Les Guêpes* by Alphonse Karr (g 226⁴, fo. 111) and from *L'Alliance des Arts* of June 1849 (g 226¹, fo. 148). He also notes at intervals paeans of praise to Daguerre, suggesting Pellerin's final career as photographer. For some aspects of Pellerin's significance in *ES*, see my article 'Pellerin et le thème de l'art' (below pp. 408–21).

35 This figures in his notes on *L'Artiste* of 1842 (BMR g 226¹, fo. 160ᵛ, in a list which also includes Bellangé's 'Maréchal Ferrant'). To give one example of the kind of choice made: from Planche's two *Salon* articles, *RDM* 1847, he picks out the much-discussed 'Portrait de Louis-Philippe et de ses cinq fils' by Horace Vernet (for Flaubert the sadly popular equivalent of Béranger in poetry), Ziegler's 'Judith', Isabey's 'Cérémonie dans l'église de Delft au XVIᵉ siècle', Gérôme's 'Combat de coqs', Pradier's 'Pietà', one or two busts – and joyously copies Planche's scandalized comments on Clésinger's 'Femme piquée par un serpent' (g 226⁴, fo. 105). Works by Delacroix and Decamps are specially noted whenever they occur.

36 g 226¹, fo. 159. On Gavarni, cf. M. Mespoulet, op. cit., p. 68 (also p. 54). In g. 226⁴, fo. 116 there are notes on costumes for *Bals masqués* by Gavarni from *Le Charivari*, 1841, mingling, as at Rosanette's ball, the most incongruous and picturesquely wild contrasts – 'un général étranger', 'les débardeurs', 'un insulaire de n'importe où, une tête suspendue à la ceinture'.

37 Jean Seznec, art. cit., *Jnl. Warburg and Courtauld Inst.*, p. 178.
38 g 226¹, fo. 160. Cf. *L'Artiste*, Jan–June 1841, pp. 255, 280. P.-A.-V.-F. Cassel, born Lyons 1801, exhibited in *Salons* 1824–48. 'Nina attendant' is quoted by Bénézit, Thieme and Becker, and by others as being among his representative successful works.
39 g 226¹, fo. 159. Cf. *L'Artiste*, 25 May 1840, p. 372. Joseph Bourdet, 1799–1869, exhibited in *Salons* from 1833 onwards.
40 g 226¹, fo. 160ᵛ. Cf. *L'Artiste*, 1841, p. 397. François-Claudius Compte-Calix exhibited in *Salons* from 1840 and was represented in the 1867 Exhibition.
41 J. Seznec, art. cit., *Jnl. Warburg and Courtauld Inst.* (see above, n. 19).
42 g 226¹, fo. 159. Cf. *L'Artiste*, 8 Mar. 1840. p. 180.
43 J. Seznec, art. cit., *Médecine de France*, pp. 37–40.
44 BHVP, CL¹², fos. 32ᵛ–35. Many critics have discussed the Fontainebleau episode in the novel by the side of these notes, and copious extracts have been published; a complete and accurate version is still needed (A. Dubuc's complete transcription, along with other Carnets, in *Les Amis de Flaubert*, XXXIV, May 1969, did not make use of the more correct readings in the extracts given by R. Dumesnil, Belles Lettres edition of *ES*, 1942, I.lxxxix ff., but the latter are incomplete even in relation to the passages discussed, and are conflated with another set of notes from the Conard edition. Cf. n. 8 above for the CHH edition.)

In his long mid-day pause at the inn at La Plâtrerie, 'A la bonne matelotte – Bertaud', Flaubert had already in mind the central functions of this key scene in his novel – Frédéric's moments of delight with Rosanette by the river in the evening form a deliberate pendant to his dreams of shared joy with Mme Arnoux on the river-steamer at the beginning ('La Plâtrerie rappelle à Fr. le voyage de Montereau'). For the combined delight and irony of this idyll of the everyday Flaubert then selects each detail of physical sensation to contribute to his effects, swiftly brushing in one of those potential paintings of the kind noted by Jean Seznec (art. cit., *Jnl. Warburg and Courtauld Inst.*, p. 182) among his immediate and characteristic reactions:

> en face: rideau ⟨clair⟩ d'arbres, ⟨prairie⟩ mamelon boisé – a g[auche] sur l'autre rive Héricy [.] église à toit de tuile bouquet de futaie sur la même rive Maisons ⟨au loin⟩ une à toit rouge se mire dans l'eau. Au 1er plan la Seine joncs, nénuphars bachots, boutiques à poisson – baigneurs ⟨hommes et fem.⟩ 2 ou 3. Filets sur des bâtons,

then notes the real pictures on the walls: 'Dans la salle de l'auberge, caricature de Bellangé, portraits de 1830. Lamennais Odilon Barrot.' (BHVP CL 12, fos. 34, 33ᵛ.)

There is a nice coincidence in that this very view from la Plâtrerie, opposite Valvins, was to be the scene of Mallarmé's long summers and later retreat only a few years afterwards.
45 The views of exotic cities, which initially hung in the hotel room where Emma and Léon met in Rouen (cf. Jean Seznec, art. cit., *Médecine de France*, p. 40), have been transferred to Frédéric's room. For Alfred de Dreux, and his function as suggesting frustrated aspirations, social or

emotional, cf. the passage from *Par les champs* quoted by Jean Seznec, art. cit., *Jnl. Warburg and Courtauld Inst.*, p. 180, n. 1, 'les sujets équestres d'Alfred de Dreux qu'on trouve chez les filles entretenues'.

46 Cf., in Baudelaire's art criticism, three brief remarks on the worth and limitations of Alfred de Dreux. For an interesting suggestion comparing another of Alfred de Dreux's paintings with a passage in *Madame Bovary*, cf.. Jean Pommier, in *Les Amis de Flaubert*, Nos. 2–3 (1951), p. 3.

24

Some patterns of suggestion in
L'Éducation sentimentale (1969)

'For I hold', wrote in 1934[1] a critic and scholar whose sensitive
insight has stimulated so many colleagues and students, 'that a work
of criticism should be to some extent a work of art.' So too, he
might agree, should be the act of reading.[2] Over the last hundred
years in particular, authors have sought to create forms which
consciously challenge the reader to an active form of creative
interpretation. Flaubert's *Éducation sentimentale*, now a century old,
works within an outwardly traditional form. Yet few novels can so
determinedly have summoned the reader to be himself the artist in
strenuously interpreting patterns of evocative and deliberately ambiguous detail. It is as if we had Proust's *A la recherche* with Frédéric
as the equivalent of the sensitive but ultimately inhibited dilettante
Swann, and were challenged at every turn to create for ourselves the
discoveries of an absent Marcel.[3]

This of course is not Flaubert's deficiency but Flaubert's intention. To him, the human hankering for clear-cut judgements is
pretentious and ineluctably comic; the abstract terms which are our
fallible means of expressing these judgements deform the full complexity of inner experience. The artist seeks not to impose facile
conclusions, but to 'faire rêver', 'amuser avec des idées'.[4] Voltaire's
Candide, with its rejection of metaphysical absolutes and its variable
interpretations of 'il faut cultiver notre jardin', was one of his
bedside books; he might have added *L'Histoire d'un bon bramin*, where
the basic paradox of: 'Je n'aurais pas voulu être heureux à condition
d'être imbécile' is followed by the infinite prolongation of: 'Il y a là
de quoi parler beaucoup.' His art is directed at once to involving the
reader particularly closely in the experience of senses, emotions and
intellect, and to detaching him sporadically and brutally from any
comfortable complicity with individuals or ideas: an art of endless

and deliberate exasperation, seeking to jolt us out of the fruitless and overweening search for the answer to the metaphysical 'why?' towards a fuller comprehension of the complex 'how?'[5] *Madame Bovary* suggests, at two extremes, cautionary cases of readers who oversimplify: Emma, in her emotional involvement, uses literature as a sentimental instrument to self-dramatization; Homais makes it a means to the smug superiority of stereotyped moral or social condescension.[6] Between these extremes there lies for Flaubert the delight of discovering and expressing, behind customarily simplified terminology or ideology, the suggestive patterns of unexpected analogy and contrast which both underlie and dislocate unexamined preconceptions.[7] Each invitation to immediate identification or rejection is intentionally countermanded by the suggestion of its opposite, in a special balance between critical virulence and bitterly tender comprehension.

Many probing and sensitive critics have given suggestive readings of *L'Éducation sentimentale.* Some have concentrated on its bitter vision of the disintegration of individuals and of a generation; others, seeking to salvage Flaubert's sense of the ineradicable worth of memory or dream, have idealized certain characters or scenes. The present article, owing much to many predecessors, will seek to show some further details in the working of Flaubert's technique for provoking a particular form of self-critical empathy. Our final judgement as readers is less a judgement of Flaubert, than of our perceptiveness. And it must needs be followed by the humble recognition that still 'Il y a là de quoi parler beaucoup'. I shall deliberately touch in passing on many aspects to which more systematic investigation could still be given.

The problems of a generation are seen through the eyes of Frédéric Moreau, and many critics have found him an inadequate sounding-board, a faulty non-conductor of social or aesthetic problems. Such criticism has generally been Anglo-Saxon, and in its serious concern with direct expression of moral or social significance has risked underestimating three kinds of suggestion.

The first is the creation of a poetic parallel between Frédéric's emotional aspirations and disillusions and those of a political movement[8] – all the more telling precisely because of his own careless detachment from the major social crises of his times. It is when Frédéric tosses aside or ignores the basic events of his day that he is ironically most significantly echoing in his own life their fundamental movement: if he unreflectingly neglects the summons to share in the key revolution of the century ('la poire est mûre') it is because he is breathlessly waiting in the rue Tronchet for the climactic and unfulfilled realization of his personal dreams, at just the moment when the Revolution embarks on its fruitless urge to the millennium; if at the next political turning-point he retreats to a snatched idyll at Fontainebleau, it is because his personal life reflects in detail the process through which post-insurrectionary activities have moved by way of chaos and compromise to the disillusioned desire to draw personal profit from immediate opportunity.

The second is part of a long tradition of the comic: and here we need a detailed study of Flaubert's treatment of both situation and expression. The reader is always made to see further than the hero, by very varying means. From the outset there is the amused epigrammatic summary:

Il trouvait que le bonheur mérité par l'excellence de son âme tardait à venir (p. 2),

or the direct speech in parody of romantic rhetoric:

Je suis de la race des déshérités, et je m'éteindrai avec un trésor qui était de strass ou de diamant, je n'en sais rien (p. 16).

Events show each enthusiasm culminating in an 'A quoi bon?' which is part spineless abandonment, part practical assessment: its sporadic intrusion invites both exasperated condemnation and rueful comprehension. The main technique is that of choosing the most everyday object or happening as a vehicle to reveal at once Frédéric's naïve ineptitude and his persistent idealization: the broken umbrella (that most prosaic of nineteenth-century objects) or the note of Arnoux's meeting with a mistress pinned round the wife's bouquet of roses from the garden. Frédéric is not the static *ingénu*, and as he gains in half-assimilated worldly-wisdom, so Flaubert's distancing technique gains in complexity. Amused indulgence for the romantic youth from the provinces bewildered by a first contact with Paris gives way to more direct and devastating comments ('l'homme de toutes les faiblesses') and variations on the theme of 'Frédéric n'y comprenait rien' grow into a refrain.[9] The mediocre and ubiquitous Martinon plods his tortoise-way to social supremacy, incurring at intervals the lordly pity of a Frédéric who will make nothing practical of his own more sensitive potentialities and understand nothing of Martinon's worming manœuvres.[10] To the end the would-be conqueror Frédéric remains the cat's paw, even serving as unconscious means of precipitating the sale of Mme Arnoux's last belongings: Mme Dambreuse sends him to Deslauriers when she intends to foreclose, and 'Frédéric fit naïvement sa commission'. (p. 409).

Events, then, are seen both through Frédéric's eyes and through a play on our own alert counter-interpretation of each smallest detail. Sometimes the tiniest objects serve as immediate suggestion of either Frédéric's blindness or his pusillanimity (the *mouton d'or* bracelet-charm as evidence of the sexual rivalry between Rosanette and Mlle Vatnaz in their relations with Delmar; the opal bracelet given by Cisy to Rosanette); sometimes, as with much great art, the full undertones can be savoured only on re-reading in the light of full knowledge of what comes later, as with the Dambreuse *soirée* in III 2 where each brief, trivial remark in dinner-conversation symphonically serves a hidden battle of wits and wills.

But the comic distancing from Frédéric, which constantly invites us to see beyond his experience (and would demand further detailed analysis) is set against a third form of suggestion: that which makes us share the human fallibility of his reactions to the major movements of his times. Flaubert's assessment of human beings as suggestive means for the artist shows him as preoccupied with three main aspects: against the insensitive and impervious thruster who succeeds or survives in the social conflict (Homais, Lheureux, Rodolphe, Martinon, Hussonnet) he sets on the one hand those who are animated by a questing and misled intensity, both admirable and ridiculous, and then those whose 'médiocres passions' will reveal the aspirations and insufficiencies of average humanity at their most complex.[11] Frédéric's very lack of commitment to the movements of the Revolution may provide a particularly suggestive form of sounding-board to the problems of his times; like the puzzled Fabrice at Waterloo, he registers not the mighty movements conventionally expected of a Hero in a Historic Event, but the peripheral oddities which make its substance, and the human inability to absorb the realities of sudden violence:

Les blessés qui tombaient, les morts étendus n'avaient pas l'air de vrais blessés, de vrais morts. (p. 289).

From his first dilettantism as observer of the Revolution – 'fasciné ... s'amusant extrêmement' – Frédéric moves to moments of emotional participation – in a movement which all the subsidiary details suggest as at the same time generous yet self-interested, idealistic yet crude and impractical. To interpret as an unadulterated satire on his naïveté his 'Moi, je trouve le peuple sublime' (p. 292) at the sack of the Tuileries would be a false simplification: it is indeed ironically juxtaposed with a spectacle of drunken vandalism (yet of a revolt whose suppressed causes are indicated and understood), is associated with his other impulses to abandon the struggle for intellectual discrimination in some unreflecting absorption, physical or emotional, and is given a critically mock-heroic introduction which yet moves into a certain serious participation:

> Frédéric, bien qu'il ne fût pas guerrier, sentit bondir son sang gaulois. Le magnétisme des foules enthousiastes l'avait pris. Il humait voluptueusement l'air orageux.... Il frissonnait sous les effluves d'un immense amour, d'un attendrissement suprême et universel, comme si le cœur de l'humanité tout entière avait battu dans sa poitrine. (pp. 293–4)

It is also deliberately contrasted with the rapid and frivolous responses of the perennially superficial Hussonnet ('Les héros ne sentent pas bon . . . Ce peuple me dégoûte'). As so often in Flaubert, no final absolute is indicated, but relative negatives are set at play to stimulate our own reflection. Two further key-scenes provoke conflicting reactions to a political involvement which is inextricably part generous, part self-interested, part naïve. First, the speech Frédéric reads to Dambreuse, summarizing so many progressive programmes, yet so inapposite both in immediate context and in wider practicability:[12]

> l'impôt sur la rente, l'impôt progressif, une fédération européenne, et l'instruction du peuple, des encouragements aux beaux-arts les plus larges. (p. 301)

Second, his later reflections on how republicanism had failed, culminating in the question:

> Le Progrès, peut-être, n'est réalisable que par une aristocratie ou par un homme? L'initiative vient toujours d'en haut! Le peuple est mineur, quoi qu'on prétende! (p. 370):

reflections which are deliberately punctured by the tiny, virulent parenthesis: 'il avait profité à l'hôtel Dambreuse' and by his later shocked recognition that the Sénécal whom he so hates gives an exaggerated exemplification of this point of view.

Frédéric, in fact, through his very nature as a mediocre sensibility, half carelessly detached and half impulsively involved, serves in a particularly provocative way as both a direct and an oblique reflector of the problems of his age. Round him, a group of individuals, chosen to represent a variety of social facets, follow the same chronological curve from aspiration to disillusion and provoke the same conflicting reflections. Deslauriers's famous plea for the scientific study of politics (pp. 177–8) has often, from its resemblance to passages from the *Correspondance*, been taken as Flaubert's own view: yet it is just when views most resemble his own that Flaubert most insinuates queries: it bears a serious criticism of revolutionary movements seen as unexamined pseudo-faiths, but its function in the novel must be interpreted at once chronologically (Deslauriers, like all others, moves into reaction), psychologically (his basic and impractical belief that scientific logic will solve any problem; his personal *déboires*) and with a comprehending irony (for he, like Frédéric, will remain suspended between aspiration and memory).

In this political drama, some commentators easily make of Sénécal the villain and, particularly, with a breath of relief, find a minor hero in Dussardier. In the pattern of the whole, Sénécal gives a systematic intensification of the logical, mathematical principles of Deslauriers; Dussardier an extension of the naïve sensibility of Frédéric. Neither is a schematic or one-sided puppet. Sénécal's desire for a mathematical egalitarianism and an impeccably logical efficiency is motivated by the personal embitterment of constantly renewed injustice and suffering, and is compounded with a puritan probity.[13] Dussardier's generosity of feeling is set against his touching and ignorant repetition of the slogans of the *autodidacte* – and his very love of justice sets him at one point ironically on the side he would not have wished to join. The reader's assessment is once again both through and beyond Frédéric's reactions: we are made both to share and to criticise Frédéric's resentment of Sénécal's personal and political influence on Deslauriers, and bitterly to understand the moment when Dussardier, having brought two friends together, is discarded as simply a useful subordinate.[14] Yet it is news of Dussardier's plight which brings Frédéric back in a generous impulse from Fontainebleau.

The problems of a generation are suggested through a number of crowd scenes. The parade through the Tuileries of the underprivileged unleashed in revolt is traced not simply satirically but with wryly retractile understanding, and is placed in suggestive contrast between the picnic atmosphere of the early days of insurrection and the grim suffering of the later barricades by night. The idiocies of concatenating theories in the 'Club de l'Intelligence' are set against the harsh realities of the 'Club de la Misère' where dilettante observers go fashionably to observe the outcome of the revolution. The 'Club de l'Intelligence' in itself becomes a deliberately heightened epic fantasy of the kind that most delighted Flaubert (could Ionesco have gone much further?): wild debates on linguistic, religious and aesthetic principles, bureaucratic quibbles, irrelevant interventions, spouting rhetoric, half-witted misinterpretations, all pushed to their *reductio ad absurdum*, culminate in resolutions to abolish poverty and prostitution by Governmental decree, to award University degrees by universal suffrage, and in a dazed worship of a speech from a foreign 'patriot' of which not one syllable is comprehensible. The babelesque and obsessive absurdity of the conclusion, like all details of the scene, is still tied to the dry insinuation of comprehensible human motives: the crowd reacts with insulted obstinacy to Frédéric's accusation that no word can be understood.

Opposite the demolition of the ignorant chaos of republican pseudo-faiths or personal aspirations stands the treatment of the reactionaries. Here, both in implications and in technique of presentation, the scales are not impartially balanced. The first chapter of Book III ends with le père Roque's brutal shooting of a starving prisoner through the bars; the event might speak for itself, but has added to it the deliberate *charge* of his weary sigh over supper: 'Je suis trop sensible'. During the rest of the third book the 'grande peur des bien-pensants' is anatomized through details of cliché and preconception. The luxuriant Dambreuse banquet stages the agape of relief now that 'Messieurs les républicains vont nous permettre de dîner' (p. 342). To Frédéric's observations as at first a relatively neutral sounding-board is added Flaubert's style of mock-heroic deflation; Frédéric watches

les *vieux ténors* du centre gauche, les *paladins* de la droite, les *burgraves* du juste-milieu; les éternels bonshommes de la comédie. Il fut stupéfait par leur exécrable langage, leurs petitesses, leurs rancunes, leur mauvaise foi. (pp. 363–4; my italics)

Then their very effect on Frédéric is made to serve as a double distancing device:

Le verbiage politique et la bonne chère engourdissaient sa moralité. Si médiocres que lui parussent ces personnages, il était fier de les connaître et intérieurement souhaitait la considération bourgeoise. (p. 364)[15]

And it is through· Frédéric's meditations by the deathbed of

Dambreuse that we modulate into the fiercest condemnation of the profiteer from all régimes: one brief sentence on the series of devastating tergiversations culminates in an epigram that bitingly combines fantastic illogic with serious suggestion:

Car il avait acclamé Napoléon, les Cosaques, Louis XVIII, 1830, les ouvriers, tous les régimes, chérissant le Pouvoir d'un tel amour qu'il aurait payé pour se vendre (p. 378).

But beyond Frédéric's reactions there are the moments of direct intervention on the part of the author, all the more significant in that they are contrary to his theoretical aesthetic. In III 1, the attitude of 'a plague on both your houses' and the caricatural images of meteor and cannibal still remain allusive:

Bien que ces théories, aussi neuves que le jeu d'oie, eussent été depuis quarante ans suffisamment débattues pour emplir des bibliothèques, elles épouvantèrent les bourgeois, comme une grêle d'aérolithes.... Alors, la Propriété monta dans les respects au niveau de la Religion et se confondit avec Dieu. Les attaques qu'on lui portait parurent du sacrilège, presque de l'anthropophagie. Malgré la législation la plus humaine qui fut jamais, le spectre de 93 reparut (p. 297).

Yet towards Roque, Dambreuse or the general brutality of the principle of reaction, Flaubert's implications are both virulent and sometimes explicit,[16] while to his bitter exposure of the naïveté or crudity of those in revolt he gives momentary, and again at times explicit, flashes of relative if limited values:

Çà et là, un éclair d'esprit dans ces nuages de sottise ... le droit formulé par un juron, et des fleurs d'éloquence aux lèvres d'un goujat (p. 302).

To George Sand he remarked, while writing the novel:

les réactionnaires, du reste, seront encore moins ménagés que les autres, car ils me semblent plus criminels (C v, 397).

That both insinuation and statement should tend to work through the interplay of a double negative may prove disconcerting alike to those looking for a more positive and predigested judgement and to those expecting theoretical impartiality. The oblique yet highly personal technique calls constantly on every alert response of the reader, both to the relative emphases of attack and to the subtle shades of expression.

To Frédéric, political ambitions are always secondary to personal feeling. Many critics have analysed aspects of the suggestive function, both social and individual, of the four women to whom he turns; some have perhaps unduly detached Mme Arnoux from the other three. Together, the four create a pattern of inter-related, conflicting and overlapping desires on several suggestive levels. At the centre are Mme Arnoux and Rosanette: the virtuous married woman and the 'lorette'; at the two extremes Louise, the naïve 'jeune fille', and Mme Dambreuse, the experienced 'grande dame'. Each serves to evoke both the physical background and the mental preconceptions of a representative social *milieu* (each in the flux of revolutionary pressures): that of the provincial emerging from doubtful origins (the Roque family); of the lesser bourgeoisie struggling to keep a precarious financial footing amid shift and change (the Arnoux); of the *demi-monde* with its combination of practical profiteering and sentimental carelessness of the morrow (Rosanette) and of the capitalist, scheming and domineering in its grasp on every personal safeguard (the Dambreuses). But above all, they serve to show four main aspects of desire and dream, familiar throughout the nineteenth century: the ideal (Mme Arnoux); the temptress – both contrast to and fallible substitute for the ideal (Rosanette); the might-have-been of youth, with the underlying suggestion that it could never have fully satisfied (Louise) and the social conquest (Mme Dambreuse).[17] But while each forms a representative focus, both personal and social, none is a fixed stereotype. Human mobility and complexity is suggested in several ways. First, chronologically: each constantly changes as her individual nature reacts to the book's central curves of circumstance. Second, analogically: beneath apparent contrasts are suggested many kinds of parallel. If Flaubert in the course of writing certainly softened some sardonic parallels between *bourgeoise* and *lorette* which made an initial focus in the *scénarios* published by Mme Durry,[18] he has yet left in all four women a passion whose origins lie in basic frustrations, and in all four has made jealousy the flash-point to either insight or action.[19] With each in turn Frédéric experiences, in very different tones, privileged moments of self-sufficient delight; to each in turn he extends in the aftermath a certain degree of pitying understanding. For all four, the reader is once again invited to go beyond Frédéric in combined criticism and comprehension.

In Frédéric's feelings for Louise, several strands conflict. The adoration given him by the tousled and freckled child with her red hair and jam-stained pinafore is a consolation in the provincial exile of I 6; she recalls Mme Arnoux's child and he plays with her in amused brotherly tenderness; yet leaves with scarcely a thought when given news of his fortune. As she grows up, they pause (II 5) in a shared experience of delight, Frédéric rejoicing in his memories of her childhood and his dreams of future travel; he and she enveloped, in one of Flaubert's most suggestive passages, in an aesthetic experience of the sensuous beauty of a transient world.[20] Behind this beauty, several insinuating forces play: on the one hand the practical lure of her fortune is set against the aesthetic shudder at her naïve provincial tastelessness; on the other, the sense of expansive joy because 'pour la première fois de sa vie, Frédéric se sentait aimé' is cut across by the instinctive terror before 'la vierge qui s'offre'[21] and by the flatly temporizing compromise in face of her demand. At the Dambreuse *soirée* (III 2) he sees her as the ridiculously rigged-out provincial, and temporizes still more crudely, preoccupied with Mme Arnoux; but finally (III 5), dazed and demolished by the failure of all his hopes, he rushes fruitlessly to the provinces to find Louise – again a substitute emotion, yet with a sense of the remembered freshness and peace of the restricted provincial background:

en haine du milieu factice où il avait tant souffert, il souhaita la fraîcheur de l'herbe, le repos de la province, une vie somnolente passée à l'ombre du toit natal, avec des cœurs ingénus.
— Elle m'aimait, celle-là! J'ai eu tort de ne pas saisir ce bonheur.... Elle était naïve, une paysanne, presque une sauvage, mais si bonne! (pp. 416–17)

What is the reader made to see of her beyond these conflicting impulses of Frédéric? First, the workings of a harsh causality: a deprived child, illegitimate product of domineering father and sensuous mother (p. 94); condemned with her clarity of mind and her physical needs to the deforming conventions of a petty provincial background. Second, that frank intensity of passion which to Flaubert constantly disrupts contemporary preconceptions dividing 'purity' from 'sensuality':

Toute petite, elle s'était prise d'un de ces amours d'enfant qui ont à la fois la pureté d'une religion et la violence d'un besoin. (p. 251)

Third, the stress laid on her candid and courageous intensity in pursuit of her aims ('Veux-tu être mon mari?', II 5), on her braving revolutionary Paris by night in her search for Frédéric (III 2), on her open suffering at the Dambreuse *soirée*, and on her clear-mindedness when faced with Frédéric's tergiversations: 'Louise tranchait tout,

d'un mot net' (p. 351). Fourth, her own individual following of the
chronological curves of the book as first, when all are compromising
politically or personally, she marries Frédéric's substitute,
Deslauriers; finally, leaving him as part of the scheme of unfulfilled
desires, and following her own nature, she 's'était enfuie avec un
chanteur' (III 7). This least developed of four women gives specially
suggestive insights both into the conflicting impulses of Frédéric – at
once tender and self-consolatory, critical and self-advancing – and
into her own nature where naïve tastelessness and sensuality interplay with intense suffering and intense longing.

With Rosanette, the same four threads of Frédéric's sensuous
delight, exasperated retraction, challenge to ambition, and human
pity will be more fully developed. Rosanette is both contrast with
and substitute for Mme Arnoux: once again we are made both to
share Frédéric's impulses, where ambition, pleasure, rejection and
pity interplay, and to see for ourselves beyond his own assessment.

For long she serves to counterpoint first Frédéric's naïveté and
then his pusillanimity, as he fails to comprehend or to seize her from
her multiple physical affairs, most stemming from money, some (e.g.
Delmar) from sentiment: the evening on which Cisy bribes her
highlights his weakness. When he does at last possess her, it is both
as a desperate attempt at consolation for, and a deliberately sacri-
legious gesture towards, his unfulfilled love for the Mme Arnoux
who did not come to the rendez-vous of the climax. Yet Rosanette
appeals to his feeling in her own right, and not simply as a symbol of
the sensuous substitute. The idyll at Fontainebleau superbly evokes
a period of enhanced joy when the whole stretch of human history
and the whole breadth and beauty of the natural world seem to add
their resonance to the individual's experience of a transient but
momentarily self-sufficient value. Behind it lies the interplay of
unspoken or half-hinted questions. Why should this sense of cosmic
harmony depend on the illusion of shared communion in a physical
relationship?[22] Rosanette's ignorance and triviality[23] are set against
her charm and her goodwill. To her, as to Louise, there is given a
background of causality, calling on comprehension all the more in
that she recounts her childhood poverty, seduction and attempted
suicide barely and unpretentiously. Yet the shared moment of
would-be total understanding between lovers rapidly disintegrates
into counter-pointing suggestions as Rosanette, creature of incoherent impulse, dismisses it with 'Ah! n'y pensons plus! ... Je t'aime,
je suis heureuse', while Frédéric is left to wonder in suspicion about

all that has not been told. They return to the gaiety of their flower-decked Paris balcony (parody of the *Vie de Bohême* idyll) and to the birth of their child, where Frédéric, as with Louise, feels both guilt and respect before the sheer intensity of a primitive emotion in the other:

Il se reprocha comme une monstruosité de trahir ce pauvre être, qui aimait et souffrait dans toute la franchise de sa nature (p. 386).

Yet three ironical facts come to undermine this: it is precisely the intensity of Rosanette's passion for Frédéric which makes her further prostitute herself so as not to 'spoil their love' by asking him for money; at the child's death she misinterprets Frédéric's grief, now all for Mme Arnoux; her very efforts towards a serious mould, clumsy and pretentious, alienate him as incongruous to the stereotyped image of 'lorette' in which he has cast her: 'Elle mentait à son rôle enfin' (p. 391).

Throughout the book she has served indirectly to highlight Frédéric's naïveté and impracticality, and the combined pusillanimity and suspect pleasure with which he shares any aspect of Arnoux's life as a substitute for possessing his wife; she has also been the clamant means of involving him in direct joy, pity, weariness, fury. Her own combination of practical profiteering from the highest bidder, sporadically abandoned under the impulse of sudden emotion, this in its turn shot through by exasperation, muddled efforts towards an efficient outcome, and her amalgam of treachery and fidelity – these at the same time destroy any romantic stereotype of the redeemed 'femme qui tombe', ironically reflect the different strands of Frédéric's own conflicting urges, and give a detailed picture of a human being in her own right. The last glimpse of her, in the symbolic retrospect of the last chapter, sixteen years later, contains one of Flaubert's most discreet means of double suggestion. Grown old and fat, she has married that recurrent protector, the ancient financier Oudry, whose existence Frédéric first weakly ignored then shruggingly accepted – but there is an echoing and significant train of suggestion in the brief and bare remark: 'tenant par la main un petit garçon qu'elle a adopté' (p. 425).

Mme Dambreuse is the necessary challenge to any post-Balzacian hero. But to see her as a mere symbol of social ambition would be to falsify both Frédéric's reactions and her own. If to Frédéric she is from the outset a Rastignac-image of the means to social advancement, she also stands for his delight in a delicate grace which, contrasting with the clumsy tastelessness of the provinces, the shift-less luxuries of the *demi-monde*, or the domestic practicalities of the strained *petit-bourgeois* background, represents certain civilized and aesthetic desires. She forms another yardstick to his ingenuousness as he blandly fails to comprehend both the degree to which con-ventional training gives to stereotyped etiquette the mask of per-sonal consideration, and the workings of her personal frustrations, desires and vengeances which lead to his startlingly easy conquest. His idyll with her is brief and sharply delimited, composed of the sensuous notation: 'la température embaumante des serres chaudes', and the mental: 'son cœur débordait d'orgueil' (pp. 367–8). With her his disillusions are more radical and cut more deeply (in keeping with what has been suggested above about Flaubert's implied attitude to the reactionary background of high finance). We have once again been allowed to see beyond Frédéric into the causes and sufferings that have made her as she is and have ironically caused her to turn to him: her bourgeois origins, and the insulting presence of her husband's illegitimate daughter, for whom her ambitious lover abandons her. Yet, whether through Frédéric's eyes or through oblique insinuations, she remains a figure of cold domination Direct commentary points out Frédéric's 'désillusion des sens' (p. 374). Rapid and pointed scenes suggest the crude calculations and practised hypocrisy that compose a social façade. Her own unguard-ed expression at a moment of crisis reveals her calculating egoism, and the author intervenes in the general comment:

Il échappe des fautes, même aux plus sages. Mme Dambreuse venait d'en faire une, par ce débordement de haine. Frédéric ... réfléchissait, scandalisé (p. 377).

Finally, if Frédéric abandons her when she insists on buying the 'petit coffret' that had belonged to Mme Arnoux, his gesture is no simple piece of idealism, but suggestively draws together many strands. Up to now, the demands of honour – both conventional and human – have made him overlook the three sides of sensuous disappointment, horror at harsh egoism, and practical loss of a vast inheritance. Now, against the babble of bidding, he makes his rapid appeal to her to desist: 'Mais, chère amie, c'est la première grâce que je vous demande', to be met by the coldly domineering 'Mais vous ne serez pas un mari aimable, savez-vous?' (p. 415). Frédéric's cold chill of final renunciation is in part a homage to his memory of Mme Arnoux; it is also the logical outcome of his sensuous, emotional and practical disillusion, brought to a head by a personal challenge.

Generous approaches to Mme Arnoux, partly with biography in mind, have tended to see in this unfulfilled love the persistent idealism and coherence which might redeem Frédéric's fruitless existence; others have interpreted his final renunciation as no more than a sterile cowardice. The deliberately mixed motives, so created as to demand the reader's intimate involvement and to encircle or break it with all the insinuated resources of indulgent comedy or virulent indignation, might still be further analysed.

The first chapter, as a symbol of the whole book, with its initial revelation on the river-steamer, has often been ably analysed. Certain details deserve further stress: among them Frédéric's way of giving to the ragged harp-player his last gold coin. This might have been a flamboyant gesture, consciously meant to impress: the insinuations of the expression are quite other:

Frédéric allongea vers la casquette sa main *fermée*, et, l'ouvrant *avec pudeur*, il y déposa un louis d'or (p. 6; my italics),

and there comes the rare authorial interpretation:

Ce n'était pas la vanité qui le poussait à faire cette aumône devant elle, mais une pensée de bénédiction où il l'associait, un mouvement de cœur presque religieux.[24]

Circumstances may chronologically and comically deflate the outcome of his action (while still leaving intact the naïve worship inherent in its initial if momentary impulse): the idiotic outcome of his leaving himself without the money to join her in a meal adumbrates the future conflicting claims of generosity and practicality on his finances. His isolated dream on deck (separated from her by generous impracticality, joined by receptivity to the tiniest sensuous detail) culminates in the final double reaction of his abandoning further pursuit (with a both practical and spineless 'A quoi bon?'), and contemplating his remembered impressions with 'une joie rêveuse et infinie'. The conflicting implications of this initial scene, with all that it suggests both of understanding and of criticism, will run throughout the book.

Frédéric is no conventionally consistent adorer – a first close reading of the text will force home the frequency of *les intermittences du cœur* in sporadic forgetfulness or in angry repudiation. After the *coup de foudre* of the first meeting blank months pass; it is after a disappointing visit to the Dambreuses and a purely chance glimpse of her husband's commercial sign that there occurs the revealing phrase: 'Comment n'avait-il pas songé à elle plus tôt?' (p. 21). (She for whom so many are to be substitute lovers here figures herself, ironically, as a substitute for other frustrations.) His first passion sets her in a romantic stereotype, as Andalusian or Creole, a vision to be drily deflated when later Arnoux remarks that her family hails from Chartres. He seems almost to idealize her surroundings more than herself, in a kind of Proustian curiosity for the absorption of every detail that surrounds the imagined or ungraspable life of the distant other; two puncturing moments occur when first he discovers that she does not live in the building to which he attached all his dreams, and later, when from provincial frustration and forgetfulness he returns breathless with memory of the past and hope for the future, to find all changed:

Frédéric s'était attendu à des spasmes de joie; – mais les passions s'étiolent quand on les dépayse, et, ne retrouvant plus Mme Arnoux dans le milieu où il l'avait connue, elle lui semblait avoir perdu quelque chose, porter confusément comme une dégradation, enfin n'être pas la même. Le calme de son cœur le stupéfiait (p. 109).

The *intermittences* stem both from his own fluctuations of feeling and from his sense of the impossibility of winning her: on this occasion he leaves with the furious and recurrent interjection: 'Quelle bourgeoise!'

For, throughout the story, she serves, as do the other women, at once as a means to our both sharing and criticizing Frédéric's vision or action, and as a complex being in her own right. In Frédéric are combined a marvelling worship and an inability to dare; yet neither side is simplified. Even in his own consciousness, the adoration of a madonna-figure of ideal probity is, whenever frustration intervenes, undercut by an incensed rejection: ('Eh bien! va te promener!'), while his seeming lack of initiative stems at the same time from his practical assessment that he might lose all by daring too much, and from the self-sufficient moments of an early love where the delight of recognition demands nothing further. In the idyllic days at Auteuil where she first admits her love (II 6): 'C'était une béatitude indéfinie, un tel enivrement qu'il en oubliait jusqu'à la possibilité d'un bonheur absolu', 'cette insouciance qui caractérise les grandes amours' – rapidly followed by bitter exasperation.

That the reader is constantly provoked to see further than Frédéric is obvious. There is the irony of the scene (II 5) when, as they drive back by night from the country, sensuously and tenderly close in the swaying carriage with the child stretched across their knees, Frédéric totally fails to realize the cause of her anguish or the means he might take to console her. Later (III 6), there comes a moment when at last he holds her in his arms and 'elle acceptait ses caresses, figée par la surprise et le ravissement'. Against his passionate declaration of love in the most absolute terms is set the phrase: 'L'expression bouleversée de sa figure l'arrêta', and one sentence is left to our own interpretation: 'Et Frédéric l'aimait tellement, qu'il sortit.' Delicacy or idiocy? We cannot but remember *Lucien Leuwen*, where the hero at last holds the loved woman in his arms, yet sees the appeal in her eyes, and the author writes simply 'Et il descendit', remarking in a note that 'Cette tournure exprime assez le blâme: plus serait indécent.'[25] Flaubert has deliberately added the 'Frédéric l'aimait tellement que ...'

And this raises a vital point about his technique. Precisely because of the ways in which he invites the reader to a special balance between participation and detachment, certain phrases which seem to be statements by the author are in fact, on close examination, added variations on *style indirect libre*, reflecting the particular experience or belief of an individual character.

The *style indirect libre* with which we have grown familiar functions usually through the imperfect tense as indicator of indirect inner experience.[26] Flaubert at times uses the past historic of apparently external and final statement simply as a means of putting the reader inside a personal and momentary experience, later to be changed or demolished. The *intermittences* of Frédéric's love for Mme Arnoux seem to culminate in an absolute external statement at the end of Book II: 'son amour disparut' (p. 283). But this will later be followed by his furious cry to Rosanette: 'Je n'ai jamais aimé qu'elle' (p. 411) and by the indirectly expressed reflection: 'Est-ce qu'elle ne faisait pas comme la substance de son cœur, le fond même de sa vie?' (p. 404).

Exasperation with Frédéric's rapid discouragement or lack of insight is deliberately balanced not only with a critically comprehending evocation of his marvelling worship, but with a third factor, the irony of circumstance. One of Flaubert's most suggestive instruments is the interplay of inner fatality and outer chance. The traditional tragic theme of man caught between personal flaw and pressures of fate has been developed in three ways: it is rooted in the logic of the most trivial events; it suggests at times the ironical way in which Frédéric's more generous impulses serve him least; and, in particular, the constant intervention of petty coincidence is pushed to a pitch of stylized crescendo. Two, three or four claims on Frédéric's money or his presence impinge always at the same moment; he has only to take any woman in his arms for a step to be heard in the corridor and the door to burst open. When at last (III 3) the double misunderstandings which had so long separated him from Mme Arnoux are explained in a shared moment of joy and tenderness, it is only to be shattered by the garish and pitiful intrusion of Rosanette: the most deliberately timed of coincidences and the logical result of a whole vacillating past. From now till the end of the book, he and Mme Arnoux will not see each other again.

For the conflicting suggestions which their unfulfilled love sets before the reader, two scenes are particularly suggestive. The major confrontation is placed structurally at the very centre of the book, and its brief dialogue has countless prolongations. Frédéric's stammering defence of passion is met by the uncompromising reply, bare and balanced: if one loves a woman, 'quand elle est à marier, on l'épouse; lorsqu'elle appartient à un autre, on s'éloigne'. The crux of the debate comes in Frédéric's question: 'la vertu ne serait donc que de la lâcheté?' and in her reply:

Dites de la clairvoyance, plutôt . . . Le simple bon sens peut suffire. L'égoïsme fait une base solide à la sagesse. (p. 199)

Further undertones are left to echo as Frédéric produces his angry rejoinder: 'Quelles maximes bourgeoises vous avez!' and she her tranquil reply: 'Mais je ne me vante pas d'être une grande dame.'

Their last meeting picks up, after sixteen years, all the threads of the past, to suggest the complexity of inextricably mixed motives. In Frédéric, a love stemming first from literary stereotypes and easily intoxicated by its own rhetoric, an intense physical desire, and an equally intense retraction from conquest, part practical and part deeply instinctive; a lasting devotion to memory and dream; impulses at once of delight, disillusion, practicality and pity. A joyous litany recalls their shared past (yet, as always, communication leaves the margin of the unstated – here in the lie over Rosanette's portrait). The apparently absolute statement from the narrator: 'Il ne regretta rien. Ses souffrances d'autrefois étaient payées' serves again as a kind of *style indirect libre* conveying the intensity of a momentary conviction, followed immediately by the demolishing shock of seeing her white hair. Frédéric's genuine and pitying attempt to hide his reaction betrays, in the imperfect tense and dubitative verb of his evocation of their past, his present change ('Vos moindres mouvements me semblaient ...'), yet gradually evokes an intensity of worship – followed by the succinct and bitter summary underlining a double irony:

Elle acceptait avec ravissement ces adorations pour la femme qu'elle n'était plus. Frédéric, se grisant par ses paroles, arrivait à croire ce qu'il disait.

In his last gesture of retreat, four contrasting and associated motives combine: intense sexual desire and obscure sexual retraction; practical fears and abstract idealism:

et il était repris par une convoitise plus forte que jamais, furieuse, enragée. Cependant, il sentait quelque chose d'inexprimable, une répulsion, et comme l'effroi d'un inceste. Une autre crainte l'arrêta, celle d'en avoir dégoût plus tard. D'ailleurs, quel embarras ce serait! – et tout à la fois par prudence et pour ne pas dégrader son idéal, il tourna sur ses talons et se mit à faire une cigarette.

Those who see in Frédéric simply the vacillating egoist may neglect both the violence of his desire and the underlying tenderness; those who over-easily idealize his renunciation (as does Mme Arnoux in her naïve and touching interpretation) may overlook both the everyday practicality and the fear of satiety (one of Flaubert's most fundamental themes) which underlie the general 'ne pas dégrader son idéal'. Flaubert's concern is with complex causality rather than facile categorisation; with the means of provoking prolonged resonances where sensitive understanding and detached criticism interplay in extended dialogue.[27]

It is significant that the scene should end in a stretch of prolonged silence. Throughout the book has been suggested the inadequacy of words ever fully to express feeling: the deepest urges have been conveyed by shared gestures or glances.[28] Between Frédéric and Mme Arnoux now falls the 'dernier quart d'heure' when they can neither separate nor speak; their long silence is woven of the joys, sufferings, misunderstandings and inarticulacies of the whole past. The narrator first sets us within a shared experience:

Tous deux ne trouvaient plus rien à se dire. Il y a un moment, dans les séparations, où la personne aimée n'est déjà plus avec nous,

then extends that silence to the rest of a lifetime in the four cutting monosyllables: 'Et ce fut tout.'[29]

To look back over the novel is to see how many-sided is the

presentation of Mme Arnoux. If in part we see her through Frédéric's eyes, she is far from being a sentimentally angelicized figure.[30] In keeping with the poetic patterns of the book as a whole, her peaceful and prosperous bourgeois background in Book I dissolves beneath financial and personal stress. The hostess singing by the piano to a gathering of artistic guests no longer holds such receptions; in place of the ideal mother-figure we see a harassed woman in straitened circumstances; children's clothes and medicines scatter the rooms; the daughter grows away from the mother; marital quarrels are heavy with reproach.[31]

Her central rejection of Frédéric's invitation to passion may represent at the same time a frank recognition of the nature of things, refusal of romantic dream, and yet also that most bourgeois of conventions: 'Count the cost.'[32] Nor is it fully sustained: her need to discover her husband's financial and sexual involvements first leads to an ambiguous complicity with Frédéric; later at Auteuil, she allows herself, against her own principles, long days of shared emotion, justifying them to herself and to Frédéric by the double shield of platonic safeguards and of the relative rights given by her past sufferings. In the evocation of these days at Auteuil, Flaubert's technique of critical empathy is at its most subtle.[33] Together they go through the eternal discoveries of frustrated lovers: shared memories, miraculous affinities ('Moi aussi ... Moi aussi!'); laments against the fate that prevented their earlier meeting, and visions of an ideal and absolute joy:

Et ils s'imaginaient une vie exclusivement amoureuse ... excédant toutes joies, défiant toutes les misères, où les heures auraient disparu dans un continuel épanchement d'eux-mêmes ... (pp. 272–3)

Those critics who idealize Mme Arnoux have perhaps overlooked how close here she is to Mme Bovary, while those who find Flaubert nihilistic risk neglecting the strength of the means by which he makes us share not only a permanent human experience, but the two extremes through which the fascination of phenomena is imprinted on the creative mind: on the one hand in their sheer physical delight (sunlight striking through the transparency of Mme Arnoux's fingers): on the other, through an abstract joy in a logical and patterned fulfilment:

Elle touchait au mois d'août des femmes, époque ... où ... l'être complet déborde de richesses dans l'harmonie de sa beauté (p. 273).

At several key moments there is a temporary but major shift in the angle of narration: instead of simply giving us the evidence available to Frédéric and insinuating further reflections, Flaubert allows us apparently direct vision in Frédéric's absence.[34] We see Mme Arnoux without Frédéric's vision at three significant moments: when she first realizes her love; at the central crisis of her child's illness; at a moment in the Dambreuse salon when the adoration in the eyes of Louise drives her to pitying and bitter reflections. For the central crisis there is the outright statement: 'Elle offrit à Dieu, comme un holocauste, le sacrifice de sa première passion, de sa seule faiblesse' (p. 283). We see her inner emotions: the sudden vision of a son in future shamed by his mother; the sense of divine punishment for guilt; – the inextricability of component motives (sensitivity, clarity, dramatic sacrifice, conventional sin) is left to our own reflections. Ironically, when she rejects Frédéric, she most resembles him: she has the same instinctive and hallucinating vision of an imagined scene that so often recurs in him, the same mingling of idealism – generous or sentimental – with practical fears; the same desire to worship or propitiate some mighty force outside the self. And in their final scene together, the ironic reversal whereby Frédéric turns away in an impulse which echoes her earlier 'l'expérience est trop coûteuse' has its parallel inversion in her last idealization of his retreat: 'Comme vous êtes délicat; il n'y a que vous . . .'[35] Two of her phrases in this last scene might indeed sum up Frédéric's whole experience: 'J'avais peur . . .' and 'J'aurais voulu . . .' Mme Arnoux's unpretentious dignity is in fact woven of many threads. To overlook the complexity of insinuation that rings her round is to miss the double delight of particular levels of both human comprehension and aesthetic pattern.

Frédéric's *alter ego*, Deslauriers, is clearly essential to all the resonances of the book. Two prime substances have been chosen on which to exercise the chemistry of experience. Deslauriers in the last instance functions as the best inhibiting instrument to immediate judgements on Frédéric's inadequacies: in contrast to sensitive sporadic idealism is set logical and persistent activity – both reaching the same end. Once again we share in causality: a harsh childhood and the determined struggle of the underprivileged man of parts. Serving at once as counterpoint and parallel to Frédéric, Deslauriers in a schematic pattern attempts to supplant Frédéric with each of four women in turn, urged on by jealous rivalry on the one hand, but on the other by a kind of distorted companionship which is highly suggestive:

se substituant à Frédéric et s'imaginant presque être lui, par une singulière évolution intellectuelle où il y avait à la fois de la vengeance et de la sympathie ... (p. 246)[36]

Through the constant *intermittences* of a friendship shot through by envy, resentment, financial squabbles, political disagreements, jealousy of each other's friends and pressure of circumstance, they are constantly reunited, half in genuine and generous warmth, half in self-seeking or momentary euphoria. Their final coda, and the suggestions it casts back over the book, has met many interpretations. That it suggests the joy of anticipation rather than fulfilment has often been brought out. What might still be further stressed is the implication of Flaubert's deliberate catching-up in this last chapter of an unelucidated allusion from the very beginning, to fuse both in a pervasive sense of the comedy of existence.[37] Against the periphrastic clichés by which respectable citizens avoid naming the unnameable: 'ce lieu de perdition', 'l'endroit que vous savez', is set the stiff naïveté of awkward boys with their inapposite bunches of flowers from mother's garden, Frédéric's symbolic combination of euphoric and undiscriminating contemplation and terrified retraction, and the final retreat. But what most rejoices the two friends in the early scene is the false judgement of the respectable, conventionally putting the worst construction on the matter: they are condemned for having done what they had run away from. With a flamboyant flourish of his hat Deslauriers remarks: 'Nous a-t-on assez calomniés pour ça, miséricorde' and 'Cette allusion à une aventure commune les mit en joie. Ils riaient très haut, dans les rues.' It is perhaps this gust of epic laughter which echoes at the end of the book: a laughter at human pretentiousness in presuming to judge through simplified categories events where it has understood neither motives nor results. 'Ce que nous avons eu de meilleur' amounts perhaps to that moment of detachment, godlike, comic or aesthetic, where the human being both shares and anatomises the mainsprings of individual aspiration and idiocy, and joyously rejects the ironies of more facile judgements.

This article has touched on only a few chosen aspects of Flaubert's insinuating art in a novel where every phrase counts. It has deliberately left aside the use of many minor characters, and of the figure of Arnoux. 'One or two general techniques might be briefly suggested in conclusion. The first is obvious: behind the amassing of richly documented detail, and the often rapid narration calculated to produce a surface of random impressionism, there lies a basic concern with complex geometrical patterns such as will combine apparently clear-cut contrast with ironical overlap or reversal. Four women are both clearly opposed and insidiously alike; Frédéric and Deslauriers from opposite extremes follow in individual ways the same course; Frédéric and Arnoux, conventionally contrasted as husband and lover, are drawn together in odd parallels and affinities.

Second, there is the amused aggrandisement of everyday detail in mock-heroic stylisation: the pushing of a multiplicity of authenticating facts to a pitch of obsessive hallucination. Frédéric in search of Mme Arnoux (like Voltaire's Ingénu constantly in pursuit of 'Ma chère Mlle de St Yves') follows an ever-absent Regimbart through an epically representative series of cafés, each in its petty detail intensifying hope or frustration. His return from Fontainebleau to Paris to find Dussardier, as he rockets from coach to carriage to train to arrest on the barricades, similarly heightens the epic obstacle-race of the individual to guignolesque proportions, yet sets it against a background all the more seriously representative for being only half-glimpsed by the individual in the grip of his personal obsession.

Third, the patterning of group-scenes, in particular those of celebration meals from which is worked out a symbolic ritual of contrasts and parallels between *milieux* of differing resources, taste, intent and outcome. At balanced intervals are held Frédéric's proud and prosperous house-warming; Cisy's entertainment of the influential nobility with the most delicate luxuries; Dussardier's celebration of the freeing of a friend, as he ranges his twelve bottles of beer on the chest-of-drawers between stalactite and coconut. Behind them lie the wider intertwinings of apparent contrast and insidious parallel in the comparison between the *idées reçues* of Frédéric's mother's provincial salon, the 'artistic' dinners of the Arnoux, the fancy-dress ball of La Maréchale (in itself a parodic epitome of human history and human stereotypes whether sentimental or comic) or the delicate and deathly conventionalism of the Dambreuse gatherings.

Effects here are produced rather by juxtaposition than by direct commentary. On other occasions the intervention of the author, whether obliquely or openly, has often been recognized: the two sides may be seen in concentrated and conflicting form in a remark on Dussardier:

Tout le mal répandu sur la terre, il l'attribuait *naïvement* au Pouvoir, et il le haïssait d'une haine essentielle, permanente, qui lui tenait tout le cœur et *raffinait sa sensibilité* (p. 233; my italics).

Beyond this, we still need a systematic examination of those moments when Flaubert moves into his generalized appeal to 'vous', 'on', or finally 'nous'. One of the most important sets going reflections around the idyll of Frédéric and Rosanette at Fontainebleau:

Car, au milieu des confidences les plus intimes, il y a toujours des restrictions, par fausse honte, délicatesse, pitié. On découvre chez l'autre ou dans soi-même des précipices ou des fanges qui empêchent de poursuivre; on sent, d'ailleurs, que l'on ne serait pas compris; il est difficile d'exprimer exactement quoi que ce soit ... (pp. 331–2)

If vanity and self-protection are here one side to motive, the other involves 'délicatesse, pitié' and the sheer problems of human inarticulacy.

And since the struggle for adequate expression, with its corresponding hatred of deforming cliché or verbiage, is the very centre of Flaubert, so certain of his oblique comments stress, through relative negatives, the quality of unpretentiousness. Mme Arnoux 'répondit sans aucune exagération de bêtise maternelle' (p. 154); 'elle ne s'exaltait point pour la littérature, mais son esprit charmait par des mots simples et pénétrants' (p. 145). We have already seen the function of moments of silence; behind certain silences may lie still other hypothetical or tentative values. In a would-be sophisticated discussion on women Dussardier blushingly remarks: 'Moi, je voudrais aimer la même, toujours' to be followed by the author's suggestion:

Cela fut dit d'une telle façon qu'il y eut un moment de silence, les uns étant surpris de cette candeur, et les autres y découvrant, peut-être, la secrète convoitise de leur âme. (p. 58)

From the difficulty of adequate expression come oblique indications of the worth of the struggle to express. Neither Frédéric nor the abortive theoretician of art, Pellerin, will achieve a work of art, but Frédéric has his glimpse of what that joy, whether an escapist or a creative absorption, might be:

Peu à peu, la sérénité du travail l'apaisa. En plongeant dans la personnalité des autres, il oublia la sienne, ce qui est la seule manière peut-être de n'en pas souffrir. (p. 185)

and on the tragi-comic Pellerin there is made one of the most suggestive remarks of all:

et il avait pour les maîtres une telle religion, qu'elle le montait presque jusqu'à eux (p. 38).

Words seem inadequate to feeling, yet the artist continues his struggle to shape their expressive potential. Theories, whether ideological or psychological, seem false stereotypes in face of the complexity of facts. Yet there is an equally firm insinuation of the insufficiency of sheer submission to things as they are: Regimbart, set against emotional revolutionary faiths, 'ne voyait que les faits', and impressed all with the promise of what would emerge from his taciturn contemplation: perpetually 'rien n'en sortait'. Once again a relative value, typically set against a negative, and culminating in a dying fall of bitter reservation, is insinuated in the passing observation of III 1:

cette haine que provoque l'avènement de toute idée parce que c'est une idée, exécration dont elle tire plus tard sa gloire, et qui fait que ses ennemis sont toujours au-dessous d'elle, si médiocre qu'elle puisse être (p. 297).

The novel sets at play an endless conflict of ideas, each inhibited by comic inadequacy, each deeply rooted in the substance of human aspiration. Behind the conflicting or faulty mental constructs of the characters is set our imaginative sharing of the experience of their senses. To the many stimulating analyses that have already been given,[38] one or two recurring points of emphasis might be added.

Sensuous experience in Flaubert is suggestive often just because it picks out not the dominating centre but the apparently peripheral detail. The tiniest impression may become either a symbol of stress or an ironic counterpoint to central preoccupations. To Cisy in terror before his duel 'la susurration des mouches se confondait avec le battement de ses artères', while in the peace of dawn 'on entendait, par moments, des lapins bondir' (p. 229).

Moments of joy or fear take their intensity not so much from central causes as from absorption in one tiny associated sensation. The hope and promise of the early evenings with Mme Arnoux is evoked by the touch of a door-knob:

la poignée, lisse au toucher, avait la douceur et comme l'intelligence d'une main dans la sienne (p. 38).

The delight in her person shines from the shape of a fingernail or pauses over the pattern of veins in her hand; her peaceful, intimate and bourgeois background is evoked by knitting-needles stuck through a ball of wool left lying, or the fragmentary dropped clippings of her sewing-silks.

Tiny and precise suggestions evoke moments of contemplation when the self is lost in the object; they also call up the flux and impermanence of flickering, momentary, impatient and subjective vision, as with the lights cast on fitful scenes in the coach journey when Frédéric returns to Paris by night (p. 101) or in the railway journey to Creil with its dancing and disappearing flakes of soot (p. 191).

Every range of sense-impression is subtly evoked, from depressive dankness to hot-house euphoria. Play of light, sensuous warmth, taste of exquisite food, touch of furs, silks, or human hands, scent of lavender or tar or of exotic flowers: all these and many more provide prolonged and suggestive associations. Perhaps certain infinitesimal sounds have a privileged position; sounds which both interrupt and echo. Again, they are chosen to be the most apparently insignificant and yet the most oddly evocative. When Frédéric is shut out from sharing Mme Arnoux's meal on the river steamer, he hears, as he watches her, the tinkle of a little medal hung to a gold chain on her wrist, which 'de temps à autre, sonnait contre son assiette' – just as, later, when he is excluded from her cares as a mother, he will hear from the sick-room the chink of spoon against medicine-glass.

While some sensations carry their suggestions through an allegorical intent (Flaubert is particularly drawn to the frail impermanent delicacy of the scurrying insects of a day on a surface of endlessly flowing water, or to the tenuous tendrils of wavering vegetation trailing in transient luxuriance over ancient or crumbling walls), others give simply the impact of the thing in itself – a random but intense object of perception at a moment of crisis (Frédéric at last receives his inheritance and while a whole magnificent future flashes before his imagination he contemplates the snow on the roofs 'et même il reconnut dans la cour un baquet à lessive, qui l'avait fait trébucher la veille au soir' (p. 98)), or a sudden and self-sufficient focus to ecstasy: as when the long days of joy at Fontainebleau find their moment of ecstatic culmination:

près de l'auberge, une fille en chapeau de paille tirait des seaux d'un puits; chaque fois qu'ils remontaient, Frédéric écoutait avec une jouissance inexprimable le grincement de la chaîne (p. 328).

Ideas set virulently at odds, each prolonged into its most absolute aspiration, each cruelly set against its equally absolute opposites or its inhibiting implications, sensations as the suggestive parallel or contrast to ideas and feelings, and as the sheer irreductible stuff of uncategorized experience: from these Flaubert creates a suggestive means making particular demands on the reader's resources of intelligence and sensitivity. No attempt at analysis can provide other than an arbitrary selection of points for discussion: every attempt will lay open to criticism not so much Flaubert as the commentator. In the end, we are left before the challenge of his own remark:[39]

Tout dépend de la perspective.

NOTES

1 *Towards Hérodiade*, by A. R. Chisholm, Melbourne University Press, 1934, p. 7.
2 The intention of the present article is to suggest some ways of interpreting a few central aspects in this rich and provocative novel. Considerations of space unfortunately prevent detailed discussion in footnotes of the very large body of previous criticism. Specialists will easily recognize where I am indebted to, or tentatively differ from, the basic works of criticism and scholarship to which readers owe so much. Among the most recent works, Professor Victor Brombert's *The Novels of Flaubert*, Princeton University Press, 1966, contains a stimulating chapter on *L'Éducation sentimentale* and a useful select bibliography. Certain individual articles will be mentioned here in relation to specific points in the text. References to Flaubert's texts will be taken, for the *Éducation sentimentale*, from the Garnier edition, and for the other works from the Conard edition, with the abbreviations C for the *Correspondance* and CS for the supplementary volumes. Ch. Carlut's *La Correspondance de Flaubert: Étude et Répertoire critique*, Nizet, 1968, now provides a useful attempt at thematic classification.
3 Cf. Enid Starkie, *Flaubert: the Making of the Master*, Weidenfeld and Nicolson, 1967, p. 357: 'Frédéric was what Flaubert might have been if he had not possessed genius and an overwhelming passion for art.'
4 C II, 329; III 53, 322; VII, 26, etc.
5 C IV, 244, etc. Peter Cortland's *The Sentimental Adventure*, The Hague, Mouton, 1967, though on the whole a very personal excursus around ideas raised by the novel, gives interesting remarks on some aspects of the reader's involvement. On others I would differ.
6 Cf. the quotations given in my brief *Flaubert: 'Madame Bovary'*, Arnold,

1962, pp. 17, 42, 45 and 65, and 'Flaubert et la Conscience du Réel' (see above, pp. 325–37).

7 Cf. *Novembre, Œuvres de Jeunesse*, II, Conard, 1910, p. 173: 'dans les actions humaines, j'y percevais tout à coup des rapports et des antithèses dont la précision lumineuse m'éblouissait moi-même'. J. Bruneau's *Les Débuts littéraires de Gustave Flaubert*, Armand Colin, 1962, has given much new insight into Flaubert's early writings: more remains to be done here. From very early there is the awareness of the difficulty of adequately presenting conflicting reactions: cf. *Souvenirs, notes et pensées intimes*, ed. L. Chevalley Sabatier, Buchet/Chastel, 1965, p. 104: 'Il se passe quelquefois des pensées opposées tandis qu'on écrit la même phrase.'

8 There are excellent remarks on this aspect in J. Proust, 'Structure et sens de *L'Éducation sentimentale*', *Revue des Sciences humaines*, mars 1967, pp. 67–100. This article, with many stimulating comments on the relation between political, personal and aesthetic preoccupations, over-simplifies Dussardier's role in particular, and some aspects of Frédéric.

9 Variations on this phrase and idea constantly recur (e.g., pp. 130, 134, 163, 366, 390). Cf. Charles Bovary. Even in his ecstasy as he first hears Mme Arnoux singing, Frédéric understands nothing of the Italian words. Nerval's *Voyage en Orient* has an amused treatment of the fascination exerted by hearing song in a language one does not understand, and its subsequent disillusion.

10 Those who succeed in this book are not the large-scale schemers, Homais or Lheureux, but the dull *bête à concours* Martinon, the frivolous scandal-sheet writer Hussonnet, and the ham-actor Delmar. When Martinon carries off the rich heiress despite the pretended news of her lack of fortune, Flaubert typically leaves open the question of his motives: p. 366 – 'ne croyant pas que cela fût vrai, ou trop avancé pour se dédire, ou par un de ces entêtements d'idiot qui sont des actes de génie'. His technique of inserting a 'peut-être' as if interpreting motives from the outside has been commented on by a number of critics. The adducing of alternative motives might be further examined.

11 C I, 417: 'nier l'existence des passions tièdes parce qu'elles sont tièdes, c'est nier le soleil tant qu'il n'est pas à midi'.

12 Many virulent comments in the *Correspondance* show Flaubert's own attitude to these, he would consider, doubtful dreams.

13 His uprightness and rigidity are constantly stressed. Though willing to profit from Frédéric's influence, he refuses proffered money. One piercing reaction of Frédéric to this 'homme de théories' (p. 197) with his hatred of individualism and his levelling egalitarianism is his simple 'Vous oubliez l'humanité' (p. 198). Frédéric is significantly shocked on several occasions by personal harshness in others (Deslaurier's treatment of his mistress; Mme Dambreuse's attitude to servants).

14 'Il y a des hommes, n'ayant pour mission parmi les autres que de servir d'intermédiaires; on les franchit comme des ponts, et l'on va plus loin' (p. 242).

15 Criticism of Flaubert as a 'bourgeois sans le savoir' (Sartrian or otherwise) has perhaps overlooked such remarks, just as it has not

sufficiently distinguished between reactions before and after 1870 and their relevance to works written earlier.

16 Cf. p. 338, and the caricatural but representative extension p. 390: 'haine contre les instituteurs primaires et contre les marchands de vin, contre les classes de philosophie, contre les cours d'histoire, contre les romans, les gilets rouges, les barbes longues....'

17 The echo and reversal of Balzacian types has been discussed by J. Vial: 'Flaubert émule et disciple émancipé de Balzac', *Revue d'Histoire littéraire de la France*, 1948, pp. 233–63. Interesting comparisons might be made with Nerval's contrasting and overlapping patterns in *Sylvie* – Adrienne the ideal, Aurélie its tempting and fallacious reflection, Sylvie the frank and freckled child, the might-have-been who yet ends as the village sophisticate – each oddly echoing the development of the others.

18 *Flaubert et ses Projets inédits*, Nizet, s.d., with penetrating comments on significant changes in plan and attitude.

19 To the 'entremetteuse' and insufferable theorist of feminism, la Vatnaz, is also given in certain passages a piercing and touching analysis of social and personal frustrations (p. 299, etc.). She becomes a fifth female figure serving to stress at once Frédéric's initial naïveté, his rigid, ridiculous, or self-interested theories, the wry comprehension of inhibited and intense desires, and even a sudden moment of physical lust for her (p. 256).

20 Cf. in a different tone, the final evening between Emma and Rodolphe, with its interplay of memory, ecstatic dream, and retreat.

21 Echoing, in a different range, his fear both of commitment and of profanation with Mme Arnoux. The nineteenth-century assumption of total contrast between 'pure' virgin or wife and the 'available' inhabitants of the *demi-monde* and the *haut-monde* is both exemplified and, finally, strenuously questioned.

22 Cf. the comment in *Madame Bovary* (III 5): 'Ce n'était pas la première fois qu'ils apercevaient des arbres, du ciel bleu, du gazon ... mais ils n'avaient sans doute jamais admiré tout cela, comme si la nature n'existait pas auparavant, ou qu'elle n'eût commencé à être belle que depuis l'assouvissement de leurs désirs.'

23 Her gasping effort to rise to the necessary Heights of History: 'Cela rappelle des souvenirs' goes back to a passage on *idées reçues* in *Par les Champs et par les Grèves*, Conard, 1910, p. 73.

24 Cf. Emma's last gesture of despair in tossing her final coin to the beggar, or the ironical remark on another occasion when Frédéric feels grateful to Providence for Mme Arnoux's existence: 'Il regardait autour de lui s'il n'y avait personne à secourir. Aucun misérable ne passait, et sa velléité de dévouement s'évanouit, car il n'était pas homme à en chercher au loin les occasions.'

25 Stendhal, *Romans et nouvelles*, Texte établi et annoté par Henri Martineau, Gallimard, Éditions de la Pléiade, Vol I, 1942, p. 1537.

26 Cf. the chapter in Stephen Ullmann: *Style in the French Novel*, Cambridge University Press, 1957.

27 A comparison with the analysis of *La Princesse de Clèves* in her renunciation scene would reveal a similar sense of many-sided motives, and a similar extension into the forgetfulness of time, beneath a different stress on tragic dignity.

28 An early silent walk with Mme Arnoux, and its memory, and a later inarticulate meeting in the street after long separation are among the moments of self-sufficient delight (pp. 67–8, 261); other mute gestures or wordless moments will unite them in a 'complicité silencieuse' (p. 270).

29 The initial version (Durry, op. cit., p. 175) suggests how much the smallest change of expression may count: this had read: 'Et tout fut fini.'

30 Pp. 150–1 in the *Scénarios* (Durry, op. cit.) represent of course a turning-point in the gradual discovery of particular focus. 'Il serait plus fort de ne pas faire baiser Mme Moreau [Mme Arnoux], qui, chaste, se rongerait d'amour. Elle aurait eu son moment de faiblesse que l'amant n'aurait pas vu, dont il n'aurait pas profité.'

31 Again the indication of the *Scénarios* (Durry, op. cit., p. 163), that this is to become a 'ménage querelleur, plutôt de la part de la femme que du mari', has been softened in the novel, but is still present; we move from the silent suffering in I 5 to the bitter quarrel over the shawl, both wife and husband battling in incongruous pseudo-logic, as she, so hurt by infidelity, asserts that it is only his lies she minds, and he, caught in irrational tergiversations, replies with the inapposite retort: 'Du moment qu'on s'emporte et qu'il n'y a pas moyen de raisonner!'

32 It is worth recalling the note in the *Scénarios* (Durry, op. cit., p. 150) where she is spoken of as having 'doucement basé son refus sur la Vertu, les devoirs', the *doucement* being a pencil addition.

33 Peter Cortland (op. cit.) has looked closely at the expression of their ideal longings on pp. 272–3 (so close to Mme Bovary's final appeal to Rodolphe) and noted how the expression seems critically directed. V. Brombert's remark (op. cit., p. 153) on their final scene might well be applied here: 'It is not the first time that Flaubert places the banal in the service of intense emotion.' See also as part-parallel, part-contrast, *Madame Bovary*, III 1.

34 It would be worth systematically examining which other characters and which occasions are temporarily seen in this direct light. Deslauriers and Louise immediately come to mind.

35 The *Scénarios* contain the remark (Durry, op. cit., p. 174) 'ne pas la rendre ridicule. Il en a pitié.'

36 Flaubert's both schematic and psychological use of the contrasting, quarrelling yet constantly united friends runs from Jules and Henry to Bouvard and Pécuchet. If there is nothing of the fantastic and magical undertones of the fashionable *Doppelgänger* theme of the period, it would yet be interesting to compare his treatment of the friend or 'double' with for example Nerval's constant use of it; beneath a very different tone run similar intertwining patterns around a double who is at once companion and usurper, opponent and *alter ego*.

37 V. Brombert (op. cit., pp. 126–8) makes some interesting remarks here. I suggest another point of emphasis.

38 Cf. particularly, from different points of view, J. Pommier, 'Sensations et images chez Flaubert', reprinted in *Dialogues avec le Passé*, Nizet, 1967, and J.-P. Richard, 'La création de la forme chez Flaubert', in *Littérature et sensation*, Éditions du Seuil, 1954.

39 *L'Éducation sentimentale*, Version de 1845, Conard, 1910, p. 227.

25

Pellerin et le thème de l'art dans *L'Éducation sentimentale* (1969)[1]

Derrière la complexité infinie qu'offrent les personnages principaux de *L'Éducation sentimentale* se rangent les comparses, chacun imbriqué avec une précision à la fois géométrique et poétique dans la structure et dans l'effet suggestif de l'ensemble. Hussonnet, Cisy, Regimbart et ainsi de suite – on a tendance à les voir comme autant de pantins schématiques. D'ailleurs, Flaubert le premier se serait réjoui devant l'idée de les envisager en tant que pantins: car, parmi les tentations les plus séduisantes qu'offre le Diable à son saint Antoine, se trouve cette phrase si riche de conséquences:

Je te mènerai aux marionnettes, à la meilleure place, entends-tu? sur la première banquette, petit, à côté des lampions, de manière à bien voir tous les bonshommes *et les doigts du machiniste à travers la toile.*[2]

Dès l'enfance s'imposent cette double vision et cette double jouissance: celle de se complaire et de s'identifier à un spectacle, et celle d'examiner avec une joie esthétique et critique le jeu de ficelles que comporte toute technique créatrice. C'est donc Flaubert lui-même qui nous invite à saisir en même temps la fonction schématique et la complexité humaine de ses pantins, destinés qu'ils sont à la double fonction de nous «faire rêver» du point de vue humain et, du point de vue intellectuel, de nous «amuser avec des idées».

Parmi ces pantins, j'ai choisi le personnage de Pellerin, pour plusieurs raisons. D'abord, comme moyen de voir chez un personnage secondaire ce sens de la structure dont M. Cellier a analysé les grandes lignes,[3] ensuite comme représentant de son époque, finalement comme le foyer où se concentrent certaines des convictions, des doutes ou des hantises qui se reflètent à travers toute l'œuvre de Flaubert, et devant lesquels, pour citer un mot de ce Voltaire qu'il admirait tellement, «il y a là de quoi parler beaucoup». Le choix d'un peintre comme personnage symptomatique comporte déjà plusieurs résonances. L'auteur tiraillé par le problème de l'insuffisance des mots serait peut-être enclin à envier à la peinture ou à la musique des ressources qui sembleraient offrir des moyens de communication moins contaminés par la contingence, plus directs. La totale absorption de Flaubert devant certains tableaux, ses efforts pour en consigner tous les détails dans ses *Notes de Voyage*, ont été commentés par M. Pommier.[4] Bien des personnages, bien des décors de ses romans pourraient se caractériser simplement selon les tableaux ou les gravures accrochés aux murs: M. Seznec en a fait une étude passionnante en ce qui concerne certains examples dans *Madame Bovary*.[5] Ce personnage du peintre permet à Flaubert de distancer certaines de ses propres réflexions sur les problèmes et la nature de l'art, et de combiner la représentation, la caricature et de multiples sous-entendus.

Il est d'abord évident que Pellerin sert à représenter tous ceux qui, croyant d'une façon béate à l'infaillibilité des théories, montrent leur ineptie devant les faits, leur incapacité d'atteindre à une réalisation pratique:

Pellerin lisait tous les ouvrages d'esthétique pour découvrir la véritable théorie du Beau, convaincu, quand il l'aurait trouvée, de faire des chefs-d'œuvre (p. 37).

Déclamant avec une conviction inébranlable les théories les plus intransigeantes et quelquefois les plus inconséquentes, il reparaît à intervalles fixes, chaque fois certain d'avoir trouvé le principe absolu; son Eurêka se répète dans des exclamations enthousiastes: «J'ai découvert le secret! ... J'ai découvert le secret, vous voyez!» (p. 118). Au milieu du livre il ambitionne d'être nommé à une chaire d'Esthétique (p. 140); dans la troisième partie il participe à une députation qui réclame au Gouvernement «la création d'un Forum de l'Art, une espèce de Bourse où l'on débattrait les intérêts de l'Esthétique» (p. 296) – et ces marchands de majuscules et d'abstractions se trouvent symboliquement intercalés entre les députations des tailleurs de pierre et du commerce de la volaille. Le résumé, au dernier chapitre, des quinze années après le coup d'État précipite ce malheureux de façon vertigineuse à travers des théories encore plus disparates et encore plus infructueuses:

Pellerin, après avoir donné dans le fouriérisme, l'homéopathie, les tables tournantes, l'art gothique et la peinture humanitaire, était devenu photographe (p. 424).

Bêtise d'une aveugle croyance à des théories simplistes; bêtise aussi d'un «défaut de méthode». On pense tout de suite à Bouvard et Pécuchet: «Leur défaut est à la fois théorique et expérimental».[6] Bêtise aussi qui ressort des habitudes d'une imitation enthousiaste. Au lieu de pouvoir se créer une vision individuelle, Pellerin ne fait que singer les maîtres. Son portrait de Rosanette est un effort exagéré pour faire du Titien, relevé par quelques détails pris à Véronèse (pp. 150, 215); pour le portrait de l'enfant mort il s'en réfère complaisamment à Corrège, Vélasquez, Reynolds et Lawrence (p. 402).

Quant aux résultats, ils sont risibles. Frédéric, entrant pour la première fois dans l'atelier, se trouve devant deux toiles parsemées de taches de couleur et d'un réseau de lignes à la craie; impossible d'y rien comprendre.

Pellerin expliqua le sujet de ces deux compositions en indiquant avec le pouce les parties qui manquaient (p. 37).

Pour la fête de Mme Arnoux, il offre «un fusain, représentant une espèce de danse macabre, hideuse fantaisie d'une exécution médiocre» (p. 81). Le portrait de Rosanette, gâté par d'infinies retouches, est d'un effet «abominable» (p. 267); le grand tableau historique, où se combinent, au lieu d'une conception individuelle et harmonieuse, les clichés les plus disparates – le Christ, debout sur une locomotive et qui fraye son chemin à travers une forêt vierge – est une «turpitude» (300); le portrait de l'enfant mort est «une chose hideuse, presque dérisoire» (p. 407). Mais Flaubert ne sème pas de vagues adjectifs de condamnation; il fournit de brèves mais pénétrantes analyses qui permettent de voir les éléments qui détonnent, que ce soit dans des efforts trop poussés pour atteindre à un clair-obscur subtil (portrait de Rosanette), ou dans les couleurs criardes qui résultent de la tentative d'éviter toute ressemblance avec la nature (portrait de l'enfant).

Ce pantin qu'est Pellerin sert aussi, évidemment, à représenter les défauts d'une génération particulière, où tous les personnages suivent les mêmes courbes chronologiques. Les modes artistiques, partant d'un individualisme échevelé (et lui-même de seconde main) subissent tour à tour des impulsions néo-classiques (Pellerin admire Phidias et Winckelmann, p. 38; ou blâme Frédéric de n'avoir pas

choisi, pour son appartement, plutôt le style néo-grec, p. 141);
ensuite le fol enthousiasme d'un art révolutionnaire et engagé (pp.
87, 300); finalement la rechute dans une réaction stéréotypée: «Ce
qu'il y avait de plus favorable pour les arts», selon le Pellerin du
troisième livre, «c'était une monarchie bien entendue» (p. 346).

Il sert, en plus, à la satire des égoïsmes et des intérêts qui sous-
tendent des théories en apparence idéalistes. L'idée de la chaire
d'Esthétique est le produit de déboires et d'ambitions personnelles;
autour du portrait de Rosanette se tisse tout un réseau de calculs où
s'enchevêtrent des questions d'argent, d'ambition ou de vengeance.

Et pourtant ... Car, pour peu qu'il soit attentif ou sensible, le
lecteur de Flaubert, chaque fois qu'il essaiera d'adopter un
jugement tranchant, se trouvera toujours acculé à un «pourtant»
inéluctable, tout comme il reconnaîtra la valeur significative de ce
«cependant» dont Flaubert ponctue sa narration. Ce pantin qu'est
Pellerin est pourtant doué d'un nom symbolique; ce serait en fait le
pèlerin qui chemine à la recherche de l'absolu, suggérant certes la
bêtise, mais aussi les valeurs et les souffrances que comporte cette
aspiration en même temps démesurée et digne.

Ses théories sont loin d'être simplement celles que Flaubert
voudrait démolir sans pitié. Pellerin servirait plutôt de porte-parole à
certaines convictions ou tentations qui représentent à la fois les plus
intimes impulsions de l'auteur, et son auto-critique la plus
rigoureuse. Derrière chaque phrase déclamatoire sur les principes
artistiques on pourrait dresser une longue liste de passages
parallèles, même de citations presque textuelles, provenant de la
Correspondance.[7] Refus d'un réalisme étroitement conçu:

Laissez-moi tranquille avec votre hideuse réalité! Qu'est-ce que cela veut
dire, la réalité? Les uns voient noir, d'autres bleu ... (p. 47). Eh! je me
moque de la ressemblance! A bas le Réalisme! (p. 402);

définition du but de l'art «qui est de nous causer une exaltation
impersonnelle»[8] (p. 47); admiration pour l'excessif et l'intense:

le plus crâne monument, ce sera toujours les Pyramides. Mieux vaut
l'exubérance que le goût, le désert qu'un trottoir, et un sauvage qu'un coiffeur
(p. 48),[9]

autant de convictions auxquelles Flaubert dans sa correspondance
s'est pleinement adonné: pour dresser constamment en face d'elles
d'autres questions et d'autres hypothèses. Si ce qui fait l'intérêt de

cette correspondance, et la difficulté pour ceux qui voudraient en tirer une esthétique cohérente, réside précisément dans la combinaison d'un certain absolutisme de formules avec une inépuisable kyrielle de questions et de points de vue opposés, le personnage de Pellerin montre à quel point Flaubert était pleinement conscient et des contradictions que comporte toute contemplation de principes esthétiques, et des valeurs qui pourraient ressortir, malgré la Babel des théories, de la forte personnalité d'un artiste souverain.

Même dans des détails minimes, Pellerin fait écho à son créateur: au début il s'essaie aux grands sujets historiques (p. 37), et son «Incendie de Rome par Néron» choisit un sujet qui a hanté Flaubert toute sa vie;[10] si c'est le Titien qu'il imite pour le portrait de Rosanette, ses observations rappellent les notes détaillées faites par Flaubert pendant ses voyages. Mais surtout, dans le personnage de Pellerin, se retrouvent les grandes discussions du siècle: la Couleur contre la Ligne; l'Idée contre la Forme; la Beauté et l'Unité contre le Caractère et la Diversité[11] (p. 118). Lui-même sombre devant l'incohérence qui résulte de trop d'enthousiasmes successifs, et surtout devant l'inhibition qui s'interpose entre ambition et réalisation. Ses aspirations ne sont aucunement un simple objet de satire; leur outrecuidance et leurs contradictions mêmes les relient aux impulsions les plus fondamentales et de Flaubert et du lecteur. Et si Flaubert démolit certaines prétentions, son attaque n'est point celle du narrateur qui se tiendrait au-dessus et en dehors du problème; sa prétendue cruauté s'exerce surtout pour mettre à l'épreuve la substance essentielle de ses plus intimes convictions personnelles, qu'elles soient fondées sur l'intelligence, sur la sensibilité, ou sur une culture traditionnelle.[12]

Chez Pellerin d'ailleurs se présentent aussi les faux-fuyants ridicules et les souffrances authentiques qu'entraînent les *affres du style*. Dans le résumé du début c'est le ton satirique qui domine: les excuses du velléitaire s'accumulent d'une façon superbe:

il s'entourait de tous les auxiliaires imaginables, dessins, plâtres, modèles, gravures; et il cherchait, se rongeait; il accusait le temps, ses nerfs, son atelier, sortait dans la rue pour rencontrer l'inspiration, tressaillait de l'avoir saisie, puis abandonnait son œuvre et en rêvait une autre qui devait être plus belle . . . (p. 37).[13]

Beaucoup plus tard, il examine, avant de la compléter, son portrait de Rosanette:

Alors avait commencé l'ère des doutes, tiraillements de la pensée qui provoquent les crampes d'estomac, les insomnies, la fièvre, le dégoût de soi-même. (p. 215).

Pantin et pèlerin, provoquant à la fois de francs éclats de rire et des mouvements de sympathie d'autant plus pénétrants qu'ils se limitent à des suggestions sous-jacentes et intermittentes, ce personnage a encore d'autres fonctions à remplir. Dès sa première apparition, il suggère de façon pitoyable le rôle subalterne que décernera à l'artiste une société bourgeoise. Devant la commande d'Arnoux, il rougit mais s'incline:

Il me faudrait deux dessus de porte, à deux cent cinquante la pièce, genre Boucher, est-ce convenu? (p. 37);

quinze jours plus tard, Arnoux lui-même vend ces copies à un Espagnol pour deux mille francs. Dambreuse achètera le grand tableau révolutionnaire et s'en débarrassera selon les besoins politiques.

Ses soi-disant œuvres d'art permettent aussi de juger du goût et des critères de ceux qui cherchent à se poser en critiques. Frédéric, jeune, ne se permet pas de jugements au moment de sa première visite à l'atelier, où il reste bouche bée; un Frédéric plus âgé jugera immédiatement de la valeur du tableau «révolutionnaire» avec l'exclamation: «quelle turpitude!» (p. 300). Dambreuse, au contraire, cherchant à faire figure d'expert en la matière, ne jugera que selon l'à-propos du sujet dans un contexte politique. La pauvre Rosanette voudra surtout, qu'il s'agisse de son propre portrait ou de celui de son enfant mort, «que ce soit ressemblant» (p. 402). Le père Roque sera incapable de distinguer entre une piètre imitation et «un tableau gothique» (p. 345). Devant «la lithographie célèbre représentant toute la famille royale livrée à des occupations édifiantes» et dont Flaubert fait pour nous une joyeuse esquisse satirique:

Louis-Philippe tenait un code, la reine un paroissien, les princesses brodaient, le duc de Nemours ceignait un sabre, M. de Joinville montrait une carte géographique à ses jeunes frères; on apercevait, dans le fond, un lit à deux compartiments

Sénécal juge uniquement selon le principe de «la moralisation des masses»; pour Pellerin «ça dépend de l'exécution» (p. 52). Et ce Pellerin, qui ne voudrait juger que selon les principes esthétiques, découvre le rôle néfaste, à l'égard des arts, des régimes les plus opposés. Sous la monarchie on a osé raccourcir ou rallonger les toiles de Delacroix et de Gros; au Louvre on a, de façon désastreuse, «restauré, gratté et tripoté» toutes les toiles (p. 139); tandis que sous la Révolution on a détruit le Musée espagnol.[14]

Ce n'est pourtant pas simplement comme type de l'artiste ni comme pierre de touche pour les réactions esthétiques des autres que Pellerin figure dans l'histoire. Il a son rôle à jouer dans l'intrigue et son tour d'esprit personnel. Au cœur même du livre, le portrait de Rosanette est comme entouré de tout un réseau d'ambitions et de déceptions. Frédéric commande ce portrait sous l'impulsion d'une «idée machiavélique»: pouvoir profiter des séances pour séduire Rosanette; plus tard il s'en désintéresse totalement; plus tard encore la vengeance de Pellerin, faisant exposer le tableau d'une belle courtisane avec l'inscription «appartenant à M. Frédéric Moreau», et les discussions suscitées chez les Dambreuse serviront à provoquer une jalousie désespérée chez Mme Arnoux et chez Louise Roque. La personnalité de Pellerin en tant qu'individu joue aussi un rôle souvent inaperçu et pourtant essentiel dans le développement des événements. C'est l'«homme qui sait tout», espèce de confident fournissant à Frédéric ses renseignements sur les autres personnages. Dès le début c'est lui qui, devant les questions d'un Frédéric singeant le ton cynique, résume la nature de Mme Arnoux: «Pas du tout! elle est honnête!» (p. 38); au bal chez la Maréchale c'est lui qui campe de façon alerte et anecdotique les personnages que Frédéric ne connaît pas; c'est lui qui le premier fait savoir à Frédéric la situation financière embarrassée d'Arnoux: «on prétend qu'il branle dans le manche?» (p. 141); vers la fin c'est lui qui, pendant qu'il fait le portrait de l'enfant mort, laisse tomber comme par hasard le renseignement qu'Arnoux est finalement «perdu ... peut-être coffré» (p. 402–3). Il y a sans doute une ironie voulue à faire de l'artiste, qu'on s'attendrait à voir enfermé dans sa tour d'ivoire, l'équivalent du journaliste du «Tout-Paris», toujours «à la page», et de le faire s'exprimer par les expressions les plus quotidiennes.

Ses connaissances des faits anecdotiques et ses obsessions esthétiques servent d'ailleurs à souligner maints effets ironiques. D'abord, ses efforts pour se documenter ne contribuent en rien à la réussite de son art. Ensuite, perdu dans ses propres préoccupations, il néglige totalement l'effet que peuvent produire sur d'autres les faits ou les idées qu'il énonce à tort et à travers. Devant le cadavre de l'enfant il construit ses phrases qui passent du ton cru au ton sonore pour suggérer une vérité fondamentale:

D'ailleurs, peut-on trouver rien de plus charmant que ces crapauds-là! Le type du sublime (Raphaël l'a prouvé par ses madones) c'est peut-être une mère avec son enfant, sans s'apercevoir que la pauvre mère en suffoque (p. 402); devant l'angoisse de Frédéric à qui il vient de faire savoir le triste sort des Arnoux, il répète des questions sur la réussite de son tableau: «Regardez un peu. Est-ce ça?» Le triple effet de cette scène est exceptionnel pour les suggestions qu'elle suscite en tant que conflit intellectuel, humain, esthétique: douleur déchirante de la mère qui ne s'exprime qu'à travers des poses et des conventions; remords et préoccupations du père; obsessions de l'artiste raté qui passe à côté des souffrances des autres, et à qui sont réservées les souffrances que provoqueront ses propres insuffisances. Et Flaubert tire une ironie de plus du fait qu'il y a un hideux parallèle entre les couleurs criardes et disparates du mauvais tableau et les tons que produit la pourriture de la chair humaine.

Ineptie et ironie, soit. Pellerin montre pourtant, quelles que soient les limites de sa capacité, quelque étincelle de ce feu sacré qui ferait le vrai artiste. Le faux artiste lui sert de contre-partie essentielle – dans le personnage de ce Delmar qui, tout le long du roman, sait tirer son profit des circonstances personnelles, politiques, artistiques. Pour comprendre les réflexions suscitées par n'importe quel personnage de Flaubert, il importerait souvent de chercher le compagnon qui lui sert ou de «double» ou de «revers de la médaille». Henry et Jules, Frédéric et Deslauriers, Bouvard et Pécuchet: ces frères ennemis font tout de suite reconnaître les parallèles et les antithèses d'où naissent en même temps le plaisir d'un schéma mathématique et la joie d'une prolifération de suggestions poétiques.[15] Les personnages secondaires également montrent les structures géométriques qui président à leur invention, les «parallélismes renversés» dont parle une note dans ces *Projets inédits* dont nous a dotés Mme Durry,[16] parallélismes qui seront enrichis par toute une gamme de résonances individuelles.

En face de Pellerin, Delmar représente, sans ambages, le faux artiste. C'est celui qui tire son profit personnel des modes les plus superficielles. Vu d'abord comme «pop-singer» de l'époque, «il gémit une romance» dans une boîte de nuit. Avec le temps, il devient l'acteur à la mode du siècle et en adopte le jargon prétentieux (dont Flaubert nous donne des exemples précis):

émaillant son discours de mots peu intelligibles pour lui-même, et qu'il affectionnait, tels que morbidezza, analogue et homogénéité (p. 122);

après la Révolution il trouve le rôle qui lui permettra, en variant à l'infini les idées reçues, de faire fortune:

sa fonction, maintenant, consistait à bafouer les monarques de tous les pays.

Brasseur anglais, il invectivait Charles Ier; étudiant de Salamanque, maudissait Philippe II; ou, père sensible, s'indignait contre la Pompadour, c'était le plus beau ... Il avait une mission, il devenait Christ (pp. 174–5).

C'est en fait la «television personality» incarnée; pendant la Révolution il se fait fort de calmer une émeute par un moyen très simple: «N'ayez pas peur! je leur montrerai ma tête». Ce faux artiste est l'homme à bonnes fortunes qui profite des femmes; Rosanette et la Vatnaz se disputent ses faveurs. Pellerin au contraire vit dans un état d'ascétisme (qu'il s'agisse de son intérieur ou de ses rapports avec les femmes (p. 37)) mi-comique, mi-digne, où toute préoccupation se subordonne à celle de son art. Quant aux femmes il dit leur préférer les tigres; d'ailleurs la femme est pour lui «inférieure dans la hiérarchie esthétique», faisant appel aux sens et non pas à l'Idée (p. 57). Caricature de certaines poses à la mode du jour; suggestion aussi de certaines impulsions inhérentes à la nature de Flaubert lui-même là où il s'agit de la primauté de l'art.

Vers le milieu du livre se place la scène où le personnage de Pellerin, loin d'être comme Delmar un simple objet de satire, sert à suggérer à la fois les puissances de l'imagination cherchant à transformer en une beauté idéale les détails d'une existence prosaïque et aussi cet écart qui sépare aspiration et réalisation (p. 151). Pellerin fait poser Rosanette pour le portrait où elle sera entourée de tout un choix d'accessoires «pohétiques»: architecture vénitienne, massifs d'orangers, plat d'argent, chapelet d'ambre, poignard et «coffret de vieil ivoire un peu jaune dégorgeant des sequins d'or». Pour figurer ces objets précieux, il dispose une caisse, un tabouret, sa vareuse, un couteau, un paquet de plumes – et finalement, une boîte de sardines et une douzaine de gros sous. «Imaginez-vous que ces choses-là sont des richesses, des présents splendides». Scène qui comporte de multiples résonances. Car ces objets suffisent à provoquer chez Pellerin une glorieuse vision des splendeurs de la Renaissance: «Pendant une heure, il rêva tout haut»; cependant, le portrait sera immanquablement raté. Une boîte à sardines aura servi en même temps à susciter et à démolir les rêves. Et cela parce que cet artiste, capable de voir plus loin que ce qui est devant son nez, aura cependant voulu moudre la réalité contemporaine pour l'adapter aux besoins de principes conventionnels et traditionnels, donc n'aura pas su découvrir sa façon individuelle de transformer et d'illuminer les choses.[17] La vraie beauté de Rosanette ressortira non point du portrait qui la déguisera en vénitienne, mais du moment où Frédéric, pourtant exaspéré par sa sentimentalité et ses bêtises,

ses inconséquences et sa frivolité, se réjouira devant une vision momentanée de son charmant minois tout barbouillé de sucre de pâtissier. Ce que Pellerin n'aura pu capter, l'auteur lui-même, de par les yeux de ses personnages, nous le suggérera. L'échec de Pellerin comportera bien des ambitions généreuses et bien des souffrances authentiques; cet échec est dû en dernière analyse au fait qu'il se précipite toujours sur des critères abstraits et de seconde main, au lieu d'aboutir à la découverte que fait Jules dans la première *Éducation:*

chaque œuvre d'art a sa poétique spéciale en vertu de laquelle elle est faite et elle subsiste (p. 258).

Avant de conclure, je voudrais tâcher très brièvement de situer Pellerin dans les thèmes du roman flaubertien en général. Pour l'écrivain du 19ᵉ ou du 20ᵉ siècle, devant le désarroi des principes métaphysiques et des systèmes politiques, prendre l'artiste comme héros offre la plus insidieuse des tentations. Tentation qui comporte un triple danger et un triple défi. Danger d'abord de présenter un cas trop exceptionnel qui n'entraînerait pas l'adhésion du lecteur – et pour Flaubert «le premier venu est plus intéressant que M. G. Flaubert»;[18] danger, de l'autre côté, de faire appel, de par un personnage de convention, à une complicité sentimentale entre un auteur et un lecteur également désireux de se féliciter de leur profonde sensibilité; difficulté finalement de présenter *dans* le roman même ce qui ferait vivre le génie du héros: c'est-à-dire, son œuvre. A ces problèmes un Gide et surtout un Proust apporteront leurs solutions individuelles.

Flaubert s'était déjà essayé au roman de l'artiste, dont M. Brombert nous a fait ce matin une analyse passionnante. Mais si Jules, dans la première *Éducation*, a découvert et sa vocation et celle de Flaubert, le roman en lui-même, malgré son énorme intérêt, ne cherche pas à faire vivre devant nous le personnage d'un grand artiste qui aurait déjà produit des œuvres d'une haute valeur: devant les phrases de la fin: «il est devenu un grave et grand artiste ... C'est la concision de son style qui le rend si mordant ...» même le lecteur le plus attiré par ce «Portrait of the Artist as a Young Man» mesurera la distance qui sépare intentions et résultats.

La satire dans l'œuvre de Flaubert s'est de bonne heure attaquée aux faux artistes, et ils foisonnent. Le Ternande de la première *Éducation*, comme l'a noté M. Bruneau dans son livre magistral sur les *Œuvres de Jeunesse*,[19] fait figure d'un Delmar avant la lettre.

Même il laisse prévoir le procédé stylistique par lequel Flaubert résume et dégonfle les triomphes de l'artiste populaire; nous avons déjà entendu le crescendo de phrases scandées qui servent à transformer en idole le médiocre Delmar: «il avait une mission; il devenait Christ». Ternande, à la fin de sa carrière, «s'adonne exclusivement au portrait, il gagne beaucoup d'argent, c'est une célébrité». (p. 315). Le Binet de *Madame Bovary* a trouvé son tour – ou plutôt sa tour d'ivoire, lui permettant de fignoler des ronds de serviette:

perdu dans un de ces bonheurs complets, n'appartenant sans doute qu'aux occupations médiocres, qui amusent l'intelligence par des difficultés faciles, et l'assouvissent en une réalisation au-delà de laquelle il n'y a pas à rêver.

L'Éducation sentimentale est non seulement le roman des vocations manquées en général, mais un livre qui peint toute une galerie de personnages représentant les efforts infructueux pour réaliser leurs aspirations par le moyen des beaux-arts. Nombreux sont ceux qui s'essaient à la peinture, à commencer évidemment par Frédéric (qui, sous l'influence de Pellerin, se détourne bientôt vers le projet d'une grandiose histoire de l'esthétique). Au centre du livre se place la conception comique et désespérante de l'Art Industriel où se combinent les aspirations artistiques et l'esprit terre-à-terre de Jacques Arnoux; chez ce personnage s'unissent certaines échappées vers la recherche de l'absolu à la mode balzacienne et tous les compromis d'un mauvais goût qui passera par les enjolivements bourgeois pour en arriver aux ridicules et pathétiques bondieuseries. Et dans quelques grandes scènes, du genre des pièces de résistance, mais provoquant les plus intimes espérances ou remords de tant d'individus, surgit une représentation épique de la prétention et de l'incongruité de l'époque en matière artistique: tel l'Alhambra vers le début: boîte de nuit combinant des aspects moresques, gothiques, chinois, vénitiens, classiques et ainsi de suite (p. 70); ou vers la fin, le cimetière où est enterré Dambreuse – «colonnes brisées, pyramides, temples, dolmens, obélisques, caveaux étrusques à porte de bronze . . . boudoirs funèbres, avec des fauteuils rustiques et des pliants» (p. 382).

Pellerin, comme tant d'autres dans cette comédie – j'espère l'avoir suggéré – est loin d'être un simple objet de satire. La même ambiguïté qui fera pour les fervents l'intérêt exceptionnel de *Bouvard et Pécuchet* l'anime. Comme pour beaucoup de personnages flaubertiens, la création de ce personnage comporte et la

représentation d'une tradition et le plaisir de faire naître des
contrastes ou des variations. Les échos du *Chef-d'œuvre inconnu* de
Balzac me semblent être choisis exprès: scène du jeune homme
impressionné par sa première visite à l'atelier; objurgations du vieil
artiste: «La mission de l'art n'est pas de copier la nature, mais de
l'exprimer», discussions poussées sur la ligne et la couleur,
admiration pour les effets de clair-obscur dont le Titien serait
maître, analyse détaillée des retouches qui gâtent inéluctablement
le portrait de la femme idéale vue par Frenhofer; échos, même dans
l'expression, des mêmes impulsions (Le «Paf! paf! paf! voilà comment
cela se beurre, jeune homme! venez, mes petites touches . . . allons
donc! Pon! pon! pon!» de l'artiste au travail se reproduit dans les
explications de méthode et d'intentions que profère Pellerin non pas
devant un tableau mais au bal: «de l'indigo sous les yeux, une
plaque de cinabre à la joue, du bistre sur les tempes: pif! paf!»).
L'écho comporte évidemment la contre-indication: là où le
Frenhofer de Balzac exprime des théories que sont censés partager
auteur et lecteur, se fait adorer par les trois personnages
secondaires, et montre, derrière sa tragique recherche de l'absolu, la
griffe du génie, dans l'exquis pied de femme qui résiste à ses
retouches, Pellerin au contraire sera le porte-parole de théories à la
fois pénétrantes et contestées, et ne produira aucune trace du chef-
d'œuvre tant désiré. S'il compte parmi ses ancêtres le Frenhofer de
Balzac, il descend aussi du velléitaire Wenceslas.

Trois qualités pourtant le protègent. D'abord la simple aspiration
dont Flaubert a si souvent fait le plus essentiel des critères de
valeur.[20] Ensuite, ses «affres» – nous avons vu ses doutes, ses crampes
d'estomac et ses fièvres, et ces doutes ressortent précisément du fait
qu'au lieu de se pavaner dans la suffisance d'un Delmar ou d'un
Ternande

Il avait été revoir les Titien, avait compris la distance, reconnu sa faute (p.
215).

Même, dans un aperçu psychologique où se retrouvent en même
temps l'ironie et la compréhension intime de l'auteur, nous avons le
commentaire sur ses efforts pour tirer un profit monétaire du
portrait de Rosanette:

S'il eût cru à l'excellence de son œuvre, il n'eût pas songé, peut-être, à
l'exploiter (p. 216).

– il cherche à le bien vendre parce qu'une grosse somme serait un démenti non seulement aux critiques mais à ses propres doutes intérieurs. Et cette indication d'une auto-critique nous ramène devant le fait essentiel. A la fin de la première *Éducation* nous voyons dans la personne de Ternande le faux artiste devenu célèbre.

Il regarde les anciens maîtres comme des braves gens sans idées, et les modernes comme des barbouilleurs sans talents (p. 315).

Une minuscule phrase sur Pellerin comporte de tout autres conséquences:

Et il avait pour les maîtres une telle religion, qu'elle le montait presque jusqu'à eux (p. 38).

Le «presque» est bien de Flaubert. La phrase elle-même pourrait peut-être figurer comme l'humble devise de tous ceux qui se réunissent ici: «Il avait pour les maîtres une telle religion ...». Pantins ou pèlerins, nous restons devant le paradoxe (et Pellerin aimait les paradoxes (p. 37)): un livre qui refuse de représenter la réussite de l'artiste sera en lui-même l'éclatante preuve de la victoire de l'art.

NOTES

1 Texte d'une communication faite au Colloque Flaubert (Rouen, avril 1969) et publiée dans *Europe* 485–7, septembre–octobre–novembre 1969, pp. 38–51. Pour les citations de *L'Education sentimentale*, je donne dans le texte la pagination selon l'édition par Édouard Maynial, Garnier, 1961. Pour la première *Éducation* et pour la *Correspondance*, la pagination de l'édition Conard. J'ai, dans le texte, fait allusion à certains travaux d'érudits auxquels tout flaubertien est reconnaissant: les limites d'une communication de ce genre ne permettent évidemment pas de discuter tous les travaux qui ont touché à cette question.

2 *Œuvres complètes*, préface de Jean Bruneau, présentation et notes de Bernard Masson, Éditions du Seuil (L'Intégrale), 1964, Vol. I, p. 422.

3 L. Cellier: *Études de structure*, Minard, 1964. Voir aussi Jacques Proust: «Structure et sens de *L'Éducation sentimentale*», *Revue des Sciences humaines*, janv–mars 1967, pp. 67–100.

4 *Dialogues avec le passé*, Nizet, 1967, p. 315.

5 Jean Seznec: «*Madame Bovary* et la puissance des images», *Médecine de France*, N^e VIII, 1949.

6 *Bouvard et Pécuchet*, Édition critique par Alberto Cento, précédée des scénarios inédits, Nizet, 1964, p. 71.

7 *Corr.* V, 92; VII, 224, 309, 351; Suppl. IV, 52, etc. *L'Étude et Répertoire critique de la Correspondance de Flaubert* par Charles Carlut, qui vient de

paraître, Nizet, 1968, rendra service; on souhaiterait un index plus détaillé on une autre disposition des rubriques.

8 *Corr.* V 260: le «but de l'art qui est l'exaltation vague».

9 *Corr.* III, 28–31: «Je suis un homme d'excès en tout ... Quand on ne fait pas le Parthénon, il faut accumuler des pyramides.» Ici on pourrait multiplier les références. Le coiffeur sert souvent de symbole du prosaïque chez Flaubert; cependant lui aussi, dans *Madame Bovary*, est ironiquement en proie à des rêves outrecuidants.

10 Voir *Rome et les Césars*, éd. L'Intégrale, I, p. 219 et l'index de la *Correspondance*.

11 Pour ses discussions sur la légitimité des monstres ou ses questions «où est le type?» «qu'est-ce que le beau?» on pourrait encore multiplier les références à la *Correspondance*.

12 Cf. *Corr.* II, p. 378: «il n'est pas de choses, faits, sentiments ou gens, sur lesquels je n'aie passé naïvement ma bouffonnerie ... C'est une bonne méthode. On voit ensuite ce qui en reste. Il est trois fois enraciné dans vous le sentiment que vous y laissez, en plein vent, sans tuteur ni fil de fer ...» etc.

13 Quand il sort dans la rue, c'est souvent pour assister à des funérailles, tâchant comme Flaubert de faire de toute expérience une matière artistique (p. 55).

14 Voir, pour la fureur suscitée chez Flaubert par ces procédés, *Corr.* I, p. 111, etc., et ci-dessus pp. 364–5 et notes 33 et 34.

15 C'est une des grandes découvertes de Jules dans la première *Éducation*: «je percevais tout à coup des rapports et des antithèses dont la précision lumineuse m'éblouissait». (p. 173) Cf. «Flaubert et la Conscience du Réel» (voir ci-dessus, pp. 325–37).

16 Marie-Jeanne Durry: *Flaubert et ses Projets inédits*, Nizet, s.d.

17 Voir *Corr.* IV, p. 205 (à Baudelaire) etc.

18 *Corr.* V, p. 253.

19 Jean Bruneau: *Les Débuts littéraires de Gustave Flaubert*, Armand Colin, 1962, pp. 419 et 491.

20 *Corr.* IV, 346: «Or nous ne valons quelque chose que par nos aspirations»; III, 201: «une âme se mesure à la dimension de son désir»; III 158, etc.

26

Sentiments et sensations chez Flaubert (1974)[1]

— Ah! dit-elle.

Ce monosyllabe constitue à lui seul la première réponse de Félicité à Théodore, à un moment qui marquera pourtant un tournant dans sa vie (p. 8). Et si Félicité est évidemment moins douée pour la parole que les autres personnages de Flaubert, leurs conversations à eux, aux moments critiques, servent également à souligner, de façon ironique, l'écart qui existe entre sentiments et expression. Léon part pour Paris sans que ni lui ni Emma n'aient pu soulager en l'exprimant le trop-plein de leur cœur:

> — Il va pleuvoir, dit Emma.
> — J'ai un manteau, répondit-il.
> — Ah! (p. 122).

Frédéric, après une longue absence, se trouve ébloui et extasié en rencontrant Mme Arnoux dans la rue:

> — Comment se porte Arnoux?
> — Je vous remercie!
> — Et vos enfants?
> — Ils vont très bien!
> — Ah! ... ah! ... Quel beau temps nous avons, n'est-ce pas?
> — Magnifique, c'est vrai!
> — Vous faites des courses?
> — Oui (p. 261).

Ce ne sera évidemment pas le dialogue qui sera chargé chez Flaubert de communiquer de façon directe l'intensité et la complexité des sentiments qui sous-tendent les paroles. D'excellentes études ont analysé certaines causes et conséquences de ce fait, examiné les ressources du style indirect libre, évoqué «les silences de Flaubert» et la façon dont des gestes ou des regards désespérés ou avides se substituent aux mots, montré comment chez Flaubert narration, dialogue, analyse ont tendance à faire place à un art qui suggère les événements psychologiques à travers les sensations provoquées par les objets minimes que perçoivent les personnages, ou que, souvent, ils négligent.[2] Je ne m'attarderai donc pas sur ce côté de la question, que d'autres ont étudié avec pertinence et avec finesse: chaque page de Flaubert pourrait servir d'exemple. L'extase de Frédéric qui ne sait que «balbutier au hasard les premières paroles venues» se transmet par le détail de sensations visuelles:

Le soleil l'entourait [il s'agit de Mme Arnoux; le choix de ce verbe ferait croire que le soleil le fait exprès, se dirige sur elle seule, crée autour d'elle un nimbe]; – et sa figure ovale, ... son châle de dentelle noire, moulant la forme de ses épaules, sa robe de soie gorge-de-pigeon ... tout lui parut d'une splendeur extraordinaire. Une suavité infinie s'épanchait de ses beaux yeux ... (p. 261).

Quant à Félicité, la promesse ironique d'une joie riche, paisible, naturelle se suggère ainsi:

Du bras gauche Théodore lui entourait la taille; elle marchait soutenue de son étreinte; ils se ralentirent. Le vent était mou, les étoiles brillaient, l'énorme charretée de foin oscillait devant eux ... (p. 9).

Je voudrais simplement ajouter aux considérations de mes prédécesseurs certaines questions que suggère le rapport très complexe qui existe chez Flaubert entre sentiments, sensations et expression.

D'abord, si les paroles, les sentiments ou les idées des personnages nous détachent souvent d'eux, les sensations sont un moyen inéluctable de nous faire participer à leur destinée. On ne critique pas une sensation, matière première de l'expérience: la critique ne peut porter que sur les fausses interprétations qu'y attachent les personnages, cherchant, à cause des convenances, à dissocier sensation et émotion, à vivre dans un monde de pur sentiment. Le thème de la sensation, cause partielle mais inavouée du sentiment, thème fondamental dans *Madame Bovary*,[3] court en filigrane à travers les détails de maintes scènes de tendresse ou d'extase: Frédéric et Deslauriers, avec un sentiment de bonheur ineffable, renouent leur amitié interrompue, en déjeunant chez Véfour: le soleil éblouissant, la bonne chère, une molle tiédeur comme de serre chaude les entourent et les hypnotisent (p. 112); Emma et Rodolphe retrouvent «la tendresse des anciens jours» dans la splendeur d'une nuit d'été (p. 203); Bouvard et Pécuchet sortent du désordre de leur propriété dévastée et de leur tentative de suicide manquée, pour trouver soudain dans l'église, au moment de la messe de minuit, une sorte d'explosion de lumière, une chaleur enveloppante, et la beauté d'un rituel ordonné (p. 497).[4]

La banalité voulue de certains dialogues n'est d'ailleurs pas (comme on l'a quelquefois soutenu) une ressource simplement satirique. L'insuffisance de la parole humaine pour exprimer les sentiments qui la sous-tendent donne lieu, on le sait, à quelques-unes des interventions les plus explicites de la part de l'auteur, à commencer par l'observation faite à propos de l'erreur de Rodolphe, «cet homme si plein de pratique», incapable pourtant de distinguer les différences essentielles qui se cachent sous «les mêmes formes et le même langage». Comme pour dérouter les lecteurs trop avisés qui risqueraient, tel Rodolphe, de reléguer Emma dans une catégorie trop simplifiée, Flaubert a inséré le commentaire si souvent cité, et à juste titre, où personnages, auteur et lecteur s'unissent devant le même dilemme fondamental:

comme si la plénitude de l'âme ne débordait pas quelquefois par les métaphores les plus vides, puisque personne, jamais, ne peut donner l'exacte mesure de ses besoins, ni de ses conceptions, ni de ses douleurs, et que la parole humaine est comme un chaudron fêlé où nous battons des mélodies à faire danser les ours, quand on voudrait attendrir les étoiles (p. 196).

Mais a-t-on assez remarqué la fréquence et la force des passages où ce thème est, non pas simplement suggéré, mais souligné, comme ici, de façon très explicite, et analysé dans ses causes et ses conséquences? Emma et Léon se promènent en proférant des banalités à propos de danseurs espagnols; une description des plus subtiles et des plus délicates évoque les infimes détails du paysage qu'ils méprisent ou qu'ils négligent, et crée en même temps une riche atmosphère de plénitude et d'attente. Flaubert souligne exprès le contraste, commente la lacune entre paroles et émotions: «N'avaient-ils rien autre chose à se dire?», en analyse les causes:

ils sentaient une même langueur les envahir tous les deux; c'était comme un murmure de l'âme, profond, continu, qui dominait celui des voix. Surpris de cette suavité nouvelle, ils ne songeaient pas à s'en raconter la sensation ou à en découvrir la cause,[5]

et enfin fait peu à peu participer le lecteur à une expérience généralisée: celle où, en méditant sur «les bonheurs futurs [...] on s'assoupit dans cet enivrement» (p. 97–8). Dès le début de *Bouvard et Pécuchet*, il avait noté dans ses plans:

Vide de leurs discours. (– Mais les grands sentiments n'ont pas besoin de paroles. La moindre chose suffit pour l'épanchement quand le cœur est plein) (p. 20-1).

Et si les efforts des deux bonshommes en tant qu'interprètes de la Littérature sont aussi maladroits que leur conversation est plate, ces efforts provoquent encore une fois un commentaire direct d'une importance capitale: la veuve Bordin

éprouvait une surprise, un charme qui venait de la Littérature. L'Art, en de certaines occasions, ébranle les esprits médiocres, – et des horizons infinis peuvent être révélés par ses interprètes les plus lourds (p. 403).

Enfin, s'il y eut jamais des dialogues de sourds, ce sont certes ceux qui se tiennent entre Félicité et son perroquet – et là encore, l'évocation qu'en fait Flaubert est construite pour culminer, presque sans qu'on s'aperçoive du léger changement de registre, en un commentaire succinct:

Ils avaient des dialogues, lui, débitant à satiété les trois phrases de son répertoire, et elle, y répondant par des mots sans plus de suite, *mais où son cœur s'épanchait* (p. 57).[6]

Le thème de l'insuffisance des paroles, on l'aura déjà noté, est susceptible de prendre chez Flaubert des formes très différentes: téméraire celui qui essayerait de porter des jugements tranchés sur les sentiments en ne tenant compte que de la superficie de l'expression chez les personnages. Si mutisme, bégaiement, simplicité ou platitude peuvent indiquer la force de sentiments cachés, on n'en peut point conclure qu'une phraséologie prétentieuse soit inévitablement un indice de fausseté ou de médiocrité foncière – témoin Rodolphe, convaincu à tort que «les discours exagérés cachent les affections médiocres» (p. 196). Plus troublant encore est le cas de celui qui, en cherchant à exprimer de façon adéquate les sentiments qu'il voudrait éprouver, arrivera momentanément, tel l'Adolphe de Benjamin Constant, à s'en convaincre lui-même. Emma et Léon, se retrouvant à Rouen, se racontent en un dialogue d'un comique savoureux leurs années de séparation:

C'est ainsi qu'ils auraient voulu avoir été, l'un et l'autre se faisant un idéal sur lequel ils ajustaient à présent leur vie passée. D'ailleurs, la parole est un laminoir qui allonge toujours les sentiments (p. 239).

Et Frédéric, dans sa dernière scène avec Mme Arnoux, «se grisant par ses paroles, arrivait à croire ce qu'il disait» (p. 422).[7] De plus, il y a la possibilité d'une fausse simplicité feinte à dessein: Frédéric, entreprenant la conquête de Mme Dambreuse, exprime la crainte de paraître charlatan:

[Les femmes] se moquent de nous quand on leur dit qu'on les aime, simplement! Moi, je trouve ces hyperboles où elles s'amusent une profanation de l'amour vrai; si bien qu'on ne sait plus comment l'exprimer ... (p. 367).

Paroles en même temps fausses et vraies, comportant dans le contexte une triple ironie.[8]

Le double registre, de critique et de compréhension, que Flaubert soumet au lecteur, dépend donc de multiples sous-entendus et de techniques extrêmement variées; la fonction et la valeur de l'analyse directe et du commentaire explicite sont plus importantes qu'on n'a quelquefois voulu le croire. Un dernier exemple, faisant suite aux conversations que tiennent Frédéric et Rosanette à Fontainebleau: Frédéric invente un passé et Rosanette cache une partie du sien,

car, au milieu des confidences les plus intimes, il y a toujours des restrictions, par fausse honte, délicatesse, pitié. On découvre chez l'autre ou dans soi-même des précipices ...; on sent, d'ailleurs, que l'on ne serait pas compris; il est difficile d'exprimer exactement quoi que ce soit (p. 331–2).[9]

Les insuffisances d'expression que commente cette généralisation résultent non pas simplement de la lâcheté ou de la fausse honte, mais comportent aussi, comme le feront les paroles exagérées de Frédéric dans sa dernière scène avec Mme Arnoux, des éléments de pitié et de délicatesse.

«Il est difficile d'exprimer exactement quoi que ce soit.» Difficile, non seulement à cause de l'insuffisance des mots, mais à cause de la complexité des sentiments. Constant l'avait déjà dit de façon lapidaire:

Les sentiments de l'homme sont confus et mélangés, et presque jamais personne n'est tout à fait sincère ni tout à fait de mauvaise foi.[10]

S'il y a un problème qui a hanté les romanciers les plus intelligents du XIXe siècle, c'est sans doute celui de l'authenticité de nos émotions les plus intimes: ce que nous croyons éprouver avec le plus d'intensité ne serait-ce qu'un amalgame résultant de conventions sociales, littéraires ou linguistiques? L'artiste d'ailleurs se sent acculé au problème si souvent formulé par un Nerval: «Vous ne m'aimez pas! ... vous cherchez un drame, voilà tout.»[11] Flaubert dans sa

Correspondance demande:

Avons-nous seulement la certitude de nos désirs et de nos répulsions? à qui n'est-il pas arrivé de douter de son affection la plus profonde et de se demander s'il ne prenait pas le change? (B I, p. 455).

De là l'intérêt qu'il porte à la gageure de représenter ce qu'il appelle «les sentiments tièdes». Certaines conventions de son époque – auxquelles (ou à leur équivalent) on donnerait sans doute de nos jours le qualificatif de «codes», faute de dire tout simplement «l'attente du lecteur moyen» – ces conventions ne reconnaissaient comme sentiments valables que des émotions simples, intenses, univoques. Pour Flaubert,

nier l'existence des sentiments tièdes parce qu'ils sont tièdes, c'est nier le soleil tant qu'il n'est pas à midi.... Ce ne sont pas les grands malheurs qui font le malheur, ni les grands bonheurs qui font le bonheur, mais c'est le tissu fin et imperceptible de mille détails ténus, qui composent toute une vie de calme radieux ou d'agitation infernale.... Les piqûres d'épingle réitérées peuvent blesser autant que les grands coups d'épée (B I, p. 415, 447; cf. p. 387, 453, 468, 746, etc.).

Le sentiment qu'éprouve Léon pour Emma est «d'autant plus difficile à peindre qu'il est à la fois timide et profond» (II, p. 351): ce sentiment a pourtant suscité des jugements critiques plutôt simplistes, tant sont tenaces ces mêmes conventions.

D'ailleurs, quand nous croyons aimer, est-ce à une personne dans son unicité que s'adressent nos sentiments, ou ne serait-ce qu'à toute une ambiance représentée par elle? Dans les plans de *Madame Bovary*, Emma devait se croire amoureuse d'un jeune beau rencontré au bal, et Flaubert de commenter: «Mais ce qu'elle aimait à vrai dire ... c'est l'entourage, la vie dorée» (P.L., p. 8). Frédéric aimera à tel point «tout ce qui dépendait de Mme Arnoux, ses meubles, ses domestiques, sa maison, sa rue», y attachera tellement de rêves, que la femme elle-même, redécouverte dans une autre ambiance, ne sera plus adorée comme avant:

les passions s'étiolent quand on les dépayse, et, ne retrouvant plus Mme Arnoux dans le milieu où il l'avait connue, elle lui semblait avoir perdu quelque chose, porter confusément comme une dégradation, enfin n'être pas la même (p. 109).

Et à travers le livre, sa «curiosité douloureuse qui n'avait pas de limites» (p. 5), ses souvenirs et ses rêves, seront formés du tissu de sensations suscitées par les moindres objets de sa vie journalière –

les brindilles de soie qu'elle laisse tomber en cousant, le tintement d'une cuiller contre un verre, ses aiguilles à tricoter en ivoire ...

Ce désir, si proustien, de savoir le moindre détail sur l'autre, c'est foncièrement le désir imaginatif de l'artiste. Ces besoins de l'imagination se manifestent aussi à travers le désir de se substituer à un autre, d'assumer sa vie. Contrairement à ce qu'on attendrait des sentiments selon les conventions, le mari n'est plus jaloux de l'amant, ni l'amant du mari. On se sent, de façon paradoxale mais logique, attiré vers le rival; on voudrait, de toutes les forces de l'imagination, s'emparer de son existence. Charles, éclairé enfin sur l'adultère d'Emma, se trouve en présence de Rodolphe:

Charles se perdait en rêveries devant cette figure qu'elle avait aimée. Il lui semblait revoir quelque chose d'elle. C'était un émerveillement. Il aurait voulu être cet homme (p. 355).

Et quand il s'agit d'Arnoux, Frédéric

(cela tenait sans doute à des ressemblances profondes) éprouvait un certain entraînement pour sa personne. Il se reprochait cette faiblesse, trouvant qu'il aurait dû le haïr, au contraire (p. 173, cf. p. 69, 114).

Plus complexe encore est le cas de Deslauriers, qui cherche à remplacer Frédéric auprès de chacune des quatre femmes qui comptent dans la vie de celui-ci: là, encore une fois, une analyse directe et pénétrante vient empêcher toute interprétation simpliste qui n'y verrait que bassesse ou envie:

... se substituant à Frédéric et s'imaginant presque être lui, par une singulière évolution intellectuelle où il y avait à la fois de la vengeance et de la sympathie, de l'imitation et de l'audace (p. 246).

Si Flaubert a refusé la tentation (si typique du XIXe siècle et si dangereuse dans ses possibilités de complicité sentimentale) d'incarner dans un héros de roman la figure de l'artiste, il a pourtant suggéré en sourdine, par des personnages nullement idéalisés, les impulsions imaginatives qui poussent l'artiste à vouloir se mettre dans la peau des autres.

Deux incidents, entre autres, suggèrent l'intensité de ce besoin de sentir par procuration, et montrent en même temps le contraste paradoxal qui existe entre le sentiment directement éprouvé et la participation imaginative: celle-ci serait-elle la plus forte? Bouvard et Pécuchet, par curiosité, suivent la foule qui se présente à la messe de minuit. «Tous priaient, absorbés dans la même joie profonde», de sorte que:

Cette foi des autres touchait Bouvard en dépit de sa raison et Pécuchet malgré la dureté de son cœur.... Alors éclata un chant d'allégresse, qui conviait le monde au pied du Roi des Anges. Bouvard et Pécuchet involontairement s'y mêlèrent; et ils sentaient comme une aurore se lever dans leur âme (p. 497).

Ce qu'ils éprouveront plus tard, quand ils iront eux-mêmes communier, ne sera aucunement comparable à cette joie imaginative qu'ils ont ressentie à travers l'expérience des autres.[12] Et ce contraste est encore plus évident en ce qui concerne Félicité, dans *Un Cœur simple*. En assistant à la première communion de Virginie,

avec l'imagination que donnent les vraies tendresses, il lui sembla qu'elle était elle-même cette enfant; sa figure devenait la sienne, sa robe l'habillait, son cœur lui battait dans la poitrine; au moment d'ouvrir la bouche, en fermant les paupières, elle manqua s'évanouir (p. 28).

Un bref paragraphe succède: quand Félicité se présente elle-même pour prendre l'hostie, «elle la reçut dévotement, mais n'y goûta pas les mêmes délices».

L'intensité des sensations suscitées dans l'imagination de Félicité a provoqué chez elle un effet hallucinant. On a souvent fait remarquer[13] que, dans les monologues intérieurs où les personnages de Flaubert imaginent l'avenir ou se souviennent du passé, l'auteur déploie une précision dans le détail, une hyperacuité dans l'évocation des sensations, qui donnent au rêve une qualité hallucinatoire; ce qui n'existe que dans l'imagination prend une netteté de définition qui surpasse même celle de la vie réelle. L'avenir se présente moins sous forme d'abstractions intellectuelles ou sentimentales que dans des scènes d'une richesse et d'une exactitude exceptionnelles, faisant appel à tous les sens; ces scènes sont introduites le plus souvent, non par un verbe qui indiquerait une supposition, mais par l'expression «il aperçut ...».[14] La crainte tout autant que l'espoir peut les susciter: Mme Arnoux, saisie par un sentiment de culpabilité devant la maladie de son enfant, «aperçut son fils jeune homme, blessé dans une rencontre, rapporté sur un brancard ...» (p. 283). Quant aux souvenirs, provoqués souvent par le hasard d'une sensation – Emma lit la lettre de son père:

On avait séché l'écriture avec les cendres du foyer, car un peu de poussière grise glissa de la lettre sur sa robe, et elle crut presque apercevoir son père se courbant vers l'âtre pour saisir les pincettes,

– si quelquefois ces souvenirs reprennent des détails que nous avions déjà vus dans le passé, très souvent ils servent à ajouter à nos connaissances de ce passé en même temps une nouvelle richesse d'atmosphère et un nouveau sens de l'illusion de celui qui se souvient.[15] Emma pense à sa jeunesse, aux soirs d'été tout pleins de soleil:

Les poulains hennissaient quand on passait, et galopaient, galopaient . . . Il y avait sous sa fenêtre une ruche à miel, et quelquefois les abeilles, tournoyant dans la lumière, frappaient contre les carreaux comme des balles d'or rebondissantes. Quel bonheur dans ce temps-là! . . . (p. 177).

– nous n'avions vu au début ni la fillette sur son escabeau tisonnant à côté de son père, ni les sensations de joie et de liberté dans une campagne paisible – car Emma méprisait cette même campagne quand elle l'habitait, toute tendue dans son désir d'échapper pour trouver une vie plus large. Précision et illusion de désir sans cesse dirigé vers l'avenir ou le passé; c'est à travers l'acuité des sensations que Flaubert crée l'emprise des désirs sur l'expérience qu'ils déforment et qu'ils transforment.

Même après beaucoup d'études intelligentes et fines, la place reste ouverte pour ceux qui voudront examiner dans le détail les différentes gammes de sensations chez Flaubert et leurs fonctions différentes. Fonctions représentatives, fonctions suggestives, fonctions symboliques et fonctions pour ainsi dire gratuites. J'aurais voulu faire aujourd'hui une analyse plus poussée surtout des sensations auditives, dont certaines au moins sont moins facilement réductibles que ne le sont les autres sensations aux besoins ou aux dangers d'une symbolisation rigoureuse. Un son isolé, en lui-même, ne comporte pas nécessairement un équivalent conceptuel ou sentimental. Comment interpréter avec certitude ce moment de délice dans l'expérience d'Emma:

Alors, elle entendit tout au loin, au delà du bois, sur les autres collines, un cri vague et prolongé, une voix qui se traînait, et elle l'écoutait silencieusement, se mêlant comme une musique aux dernières vibrations de ses nerfs émus (p. 165–6).[16]

Une voix qui chante peut même paraître d'autant plus magique qu'on ne comprend pas les paroles: ainsi pour Frédéric écoutant celle de Mme Arnoux (p. 49).[17]

Que des sons provenant d'objets familiers, ou se rattachant à des traditions séculaires, offrent à l'écrivain de riches possibilités suggestives et symboliques, cela va sans dire. Bruits réguliers et sonores de la vie quotidienne qui ponctuent les moments de bonheur, de terreur ou d'ennui – tels les marteaux des calfats tamponnant les carènes qu'entendent Emma et Léon pendant le soir de leur «lune de miel» à Rouen, et Félicité pendant les longs jours d'été à Trouville; ou le marteau du savetier pendant l'ennui de l'été que subit Frédéric à Paris. Roulement sourd de voitures au loin dans la nuit, entendu par Emma qui rêve dans le silence de son dortoir de couvent, ou par Fréderic veillant dans la chambre mortuaire de Dambreuse.[18] Musique en même temps mélancolique et grinçante, mécanique et porteuse de rêves: l'orgue de Barbarie dans le paysage normand ou les romances du harpiste à bord du vapeur. Notations de son d'une extrême délicatesse: dans les rues désertes, l'été, «on entendait toutes sortes de bruits paisibles, des battements d'ailes dans des cages» (p. 65); dans la pureté du matin, quand Cisy terrorisé avançait en titubant sur le terrain du duel, «on entendait, par moments, des lapins bondir» et «la susurration des mouches se confondait avec le battement de ses artères» (p. 229); dans le palais de *Saint Julien*, «partout un tel silence que l'on entendait le frôlement d'une écharpe ou l'écho d'un soupir» (p. 106).[19]

Mais il y a un genre de son qui surtout semble hanter Flaubert: le tintement métallique. S'il s'en sert parfois comme moyen simple et naturel de représentation, il l'associe très souvent à des moments de bonheur, en un réseau d'effets à peine perceptibles et pourtant indéniables. Je n'en choisis que les exemples les plus remarquables. Ayant reçu la nouvelle de son héritage,

Avec la netteté d'une hallucination, Frédéric s'aperçut auprès de [Mme Arnoux]; il entendait piaffer son cheval, et le bruit de la gourmette se confondait avec le murmure de leurs baisers (p. 98).

La diligence de la réalité l'emporte vers elle: «les chaînettes de fer sonnaient» (p. 101). Mais la sensation la plus aiguë et la plus délicate dans ce genre, Frédéric l'a éprouvée dès le début, le jour du coup de foudre, en contemplant Marie Arnoux comme elle mangeait a bord du bateau:

elle cassait un peu de croûte entre ses doigts; le médaillon de lapis-lazuli, attaché par une chaînette d'or à son poignet, de temps à autre sonnait contre son assiette (p. 7).

Sensation sans équivalence symbolique: délice pour ainsi dire gratuit.

Et, beaucoup plus tard, dans un des moments d'illusion, ou des moments privilégiés, les plus intenses, le soir au bord de la rivière avec Rosanette, Frédéric, comblé, comme l'était Emma Bovary avec Rodolphe, en même temps par l'amour physique et par la paisible beauté du paysage, concentre toute sa joie et tout son émerveillement en la perception d'un son réitéré:

Près de l'auberge, une fille en chapeau de paille tirait des seaux d'un puits; – chaque fois qu'ils remontaient, Frédéric écoutait avec une jouissance inexprimable le grincement de la chaîne (p. 328).

Flaubert avait noté dans ses *Carnets*, en allant recueillir à Fontainebleau les détails très précis qu'il destinait à ces pages, que la scène idyllique à l'auberge des Plâtreries devait rappeler à Frédéric le voyage du début et sa vision de bonheur en contemplant Mme Arnoux.[20] Dans le roman, aucun rappel spécifique, mais tout un réseau de suggestions.[21]

Je n'épuiserai pas – ce qui risquerait, en isolant trop le motif, de devenir d'un comique involontaire – le catalogue des chaînes ou chaînettes qui figurent dans l'histoire de Frédéric: chaînes de montre, de bracelet, de voiture ... ; je laisserai également de côté la chaînette symbole érotique dans *Salammbô*, et la grotesque chaîne Pulver-macher, symbole de la Science, qui s'entortille autour du digne corps de M. Homais. Mais je signalerai, et c'est par là que je terminerai, dans l'histoire de Félicité, la persistance chez Flaubert de ce schéma secret selon lequel le tintement d'une chaînette s'associerait à des moments d'illusion et de béatitude. Dans un plan, sans doute l'un des premiers en date, plan retrouvé par le regretté Alberto Cento parmi les dossiers de *Bouvard et Pécuchet*, la vie de Félicité qui, mourant au moment de la Fête-Dieu, a une vision extatique du Saint-Esprit descendant sous la forme de Loulou, son perroquet empaillé et mité, se termine en un dialogue avec le prêtre:

Il m'a semblé que les chaînettes des encensoirs étaient le bruit de sa chaîne
– est-ce un péché, mon père.
– non mon enfant
& elle expira.[22]

La version définitive a exclu la justification, trop explicite en son expression du sentiment de la pitié. Elle a coupé aussi l'explication qui ramène l'origine de l'extase à une correspondance entre sensations (Félicité d'ailleurs subit finalement le pire des isolements, celui de la surdité). Elle a pourtant laissé, au troisième chapitre, les phrases qui décrivent l'arrivée de Loulou vivant, «avec le bâton, la chaîne et le cadenas» (p. 51), et, à la fin, celles qui évoquent la procession devant les reposoirs, où «les encensoirs, allant à pleine volée, glissaient sur leurs chaînettes» (p. 72), et Félicité s'éteint en un mouvement de «sensualité mystique». C'est ainsi que, de toutes les ressources variées de son art, tantôt en commentant ou en analysant, tantôt en suggérant, Flaubert crée l'union la plus étroite et la plus complexe entre ces aspects de l'expérience humaine où nos nomenclatures traditionnelles érigent des divisions souvent trompeuses.

NOTES

1 Texte d'une communication faite au XXVe Congrès de l'Association Internationale des Études Françaises, le 27 juillet 1973 et publiée dans les *Cahiers* de l'Association, N° 26, 1974, pp. 233–49 (voir aussi la discussion pp. 343–6). Les références qui suivent les citations dans le texte se rapportent aux éditions suivantes: *Madame Bovary*, éd. C. Gothot-Mersch, Garnier, 1971; *L'Éducation sentimentale*, éd. E. Maynial, Garnier, 1961; *Trois Contes*, éd. É. Maynial, Garnier, 1961; *Bouvard et Pécuchet*, éd. A. Cento, Nizet, 1964; *Correspondance*, édition Conard, sauf quand la référence est précédée de «B», indiquant la nouvelle édition par J. Bruneau, Vol. I, Pléiade, 1973. P. L. signifie *Madame Bovary, nouvelle version*, textes établis par J. Pommier et G. Leleu, Corti, 1949.

2 Il serait évidemment impossible de discuter ou même de signaler dans le détail ici les passages se rapportant à notre sujet dans des ouvrages de base qui sont entre toutes les mains (Auerbach, Bollème, Brombert, Bruneau, Cento, Cigada, Descharmes, Digeon, Dumesnil, Durry, Genette, Gothot-Mersch, Lubbock, Naaman, Nadeau, Pommier, Raimond, Richard, Rousset, Sarraute, Sartre, Sherrington, Thibaudet, Ullmann . . .). Sur «Le Dialogue dans l'Œuvre de Flaubert», voir C. Gothot-Mersch, *Europe*, Sept.–Nov., 1969; cf. G. Genette, «Silences de Flaubert», dans *Figures*, Seuil, 1966, et deux excellents articles par R. Debray-Genette: «Les figures du récit dans *Un Cœur simple*», *Poétique*, 1970, n° 3, et «Du mode narratif dans les *Trois Contes*», *Littérature*, mai 1971.

3 Ici comme ailleurs, cause concomitante plutôt que déterminante. (Cf., dans les Scénarios, P.L. p. 9, «le sentiment l'a portée aux sens, les sens la portent au sentiment».)

4 Dans toutes ces scènes, et dans bien d'autres, l'hypnotisme par une lumière éblouissante mériterait une étude poussée.

5 Cf. dans la première *Éducation* (L'Intégrale, I, 284): «Ils étaient déjà un peu amis, non pas par ce qu'ils s'étaient dit, mais par le ton dont ils se l'étaient dit.»

6 Comme l'on tend depuis quelque temps à s'intéresser surtout aux techniques qui font oublier la figure du narrateur omniscient, ou qui remplacent la narration par la contemplation, j'ai tenu à souligner le rôle essentiel que tiennent l'analyse et le commentaire. Sur certaines

techniques par lesquelles Flaubert cherche à «coïncider avec l'intériorité du personnage, tout en ayant une position en surplomb», cf. M. Raimond, «Réalisme subjectif dans *L'Education sentimentale*», *C.A.I.E.F.*, n° 23, mai 1971, p. 299–310; voir aussi C. Gothot-Mersch, «Le Point de vue dans *Madame Bovary*», *ibid.*, p. 243–59; les remarques de V. Brombert dans *Flaubert par lui-même*, Seuil, 1971, p. 114 etc.; A. Fairlie, «Flaubert et la Conscience du Réel» (voir ci-dessus, pp. 325–37).

7 Cf. la première *Éducation* (Intégrale, I, 296): «Peut-être se dupent-ils eux-mêmes et leur passion n'est-elle qu'un sujet de rhétorique qu'ils prennent au sérieux», et *Corr.*, B I, 380 et 489.

8 Différentes analyses de la dernière scène entre Frédéric et Mme Arnoux ont tendance ou à prendre pour argent comptant les phrases imagées qui évoquent leur passé, ou à n'y voir que des clichés romanesques. V. Brombert, *op. cit.*, p. 59, a bien posé le problème: «Rien ne serait plus difficile que d'établir une ligne de démarcation bien précise entre la caricature des rêves romantiques et la compassion du romancier [ne pourrait-on peut-être lire «compréhension» ou «participation» au lieu de «compassion»?] ... le langage de la banalité se trouve à la fois ridiculisé et transmué en poésie.»

9 Dans *Corr.*, II, 323, Flaubert cite de mémoire une phrase de la première *Éducation*: «Dans les confidences les plus intimes, il y a toujours quelque chose qu'on ne dit pas.» Cette pensée trouve deux formes différentes dans les deux romans. Voici celle du roman de jeunesse: «Comme il reste toujours, même dans les confidences les plus sincères, quelque chose qu'on ne dit pas, il est probable qu'elle avait plus éprouvé dans la vie qu'elle n'en avait raconté, mais fut-ce la pudeur, l'amour ou l'inexpérience à parler de ces matières qui l'avait empêchée d'en dire davantage?» (I, 324). Dans la seconde *Éducation*, la participation morale est diminuée par la substitution d'«intime» au lieu de «sincère», tandis que l'explication, au lieu de poser une question vue de l'extérieur, engage le lecteur («on découvre», «on sent») et comporte, entre autres choses, le souci d'épargner les susceptibilités de l'autre.

10 *Adolphe*, éd. J.-H. Bornecque, Garnier, 1955, p. 30.

11 *Sylvie*, dans *Œuvres*, éd. A. Béguin et J. Richer, Pléiade, Vol. I, 1966, p. 271. Cf. *Voyage en Orient*, Vol. II, 1956, p. 350: «Ah! je crois être amoureux, ah! je crois être malade, n'est-ce pas? Mais, si je crois l'être, je le suis!» Et Flaubert, dans la première *Éducation* (Intégrale, I, 314): «Puisqu'ils se croyaient heureux, ils l'étaient en effet, le bonheur ne dépendant que de l'idée qu'on s'en forme.»

12 Cf., pour Frédéric aux Tuileries, le double effet des sensations physiques (tourbillon de fumée et d'étincelles, violente sonnerie des cloches, bruit des armes qu'on décharge) et de l'identification avec la cohue: «Le magnétisme des foules enthousiastes l'avait pris. Il humait voluptueusement l'air orageux,... frissonnait sous les effluves d'un immense amour, d'un attendrissement suprême et universel, comme si le cœur de l'humanité tout entière avait battu dans sa poitrine» (p. 293–4); ou, quand il travaille à son *Histoire de la Renaissance*: «En plongeant dans la personnalité des autres, il oublia la sienne, ce qui est la seule manière peut-être de n'en pas souffrir» (p. 185). Aucune idéalisation:

ridicule de Frédéric qui «sentit bondir son sang gaulois» ou qui abandonnera vite ses travaux d'historien velléitaire – mais participation momentanée à un élan imaginatif.

13 Voir l'excellent choix d'exemples que donne G. Genette, *op. cit.*, p. 226 *sqq.* Ne serait-ce pas, cependant, l'acuité de l'expression, plutôt que l'invraisemblance d'avoir attribué aux personnages une telle précision dans leurs rêves, qui témoignerait de la présence de l'auteur?

14 Voir par exemple *E.S.*, p. 98, 143, 162, 316, 360.

15 Comme exemples de cette technique de retours en arrière se présentant jusqu'au bout du roman, pour rappeler des scènes dont nous n'avions aucune conscience (pour ajouter de nouveaux points de vue et de nouvelles précisions), voir par exemple dans *Madame Bovary* les souvenirs du père Rouault sur les sensations les plus infimes qu'il éprouvait à se promener à cheval avec sa femme en croupe pendant les premiers mois de leur mariage (p. 32); les souvenirs de Léon à Rouen, racontant tous les détails d'une promenade où, il y a des années, il avait suivi Emma de loin (p. 240), ou, d'une ironie plus navrante, la réaction mécanique de l'enfant Berthe, apportée moitié endormie près du lit de mort de sa mère, et s'attendant à y recevoir ses étrennes du jour de l'an dans son soulier (p. 325).

16 Voir la note de C. Gothot-Mersch dans son édition, sur la substitution *délicieusement/silencieusement*.

17 Cf. *Corr.*, B I, pp. 6–7 (Flaubert en Égypte). Ce thème des rêveries suggérées par une voix qui chante des paroles incompréhensibles se trouve à plusieurs reprises dans le *Voyage en Orient* de Nerval.

18 Ces effets d'ouverture sur le lointain à partir de l'étroitesse d'une chambre close, que J. Rousset retrace (*Forme et Signification*, Corti, 1962) dans le domaine visuel, trouvent ici leur équivalent auditif.

19 Pour quelques exemples intéressants de «bruits ténus annonciateurs de jouissance», voir J.-P. Duquette, *Flaubert ou l'Architecture du Vide*, Montréal, Presses de l'Université, 1972, pp. 27–8.

20 Bibliothèque Historique de la Ville de Paris, «Carnet de lecture» n° 12, F° 33: «une des servantes, blonde, charmante, a des traits fins me sert en chapeau de paille / un[e] autre, tout à l'heure, me tirait de l'eau d'un puits.» F° 33 V°: «La Plâtrerie rappelle à Frédéric le voyage de Montereau.»

21 Le tintement métallique semblerait combiner de façon privilégiée trois qualités: le simple plaisir de la sensation en elle-même, qui suspend le temps dans la joie de l'instant; puis le double effet d'une précision momentanée et d'une résonance qui se dissipe en vibrations lointaines. On aura noté que le tintement de la clochette à la messe de minuit fait partie de l'extase passagère de Bouvard et Pécuchet. Un autre son métallique hante Flaubert dans sa correspondance: le bruit annonciateur du loquet en fer qui ouvre la grille du jardin à Croisset (B I, pp. 537, 700, etc.).

J'ai indiqué un réseau où des sons de ce genre s'associent au bonheur, mais ici encore il n'y a aucune symbolisation rigoureuse. M. R. Bismut m'a fait observer que, vers la fin de *Madame Bovary*, Emma lance au loin les boutons de manchette de Rodolphe «dont la chaîne d'or se rompit en cognant contre la muraille» (p. 318). Et, dans une autre gamme de bruits métalliques, quand Emma se ranime après la nuit sordide de la Mi-Carême, en pensant à la chambre paisible où dort son enfant, «une charrette pleine de longs rubans de fer passa, en jetant contre le mur des maisons une vibration métallique assourdissante» (p. 298) (cf. la note 18 ci-dessus).

22 Bibliothèque Municipale de Rouen, MS g 226⁸, F° 195. Je n'ai pu tenir compte, dans la présente communication, de l'étude subtile et détaillée de Pierre Danger: *Sensations et objets dans le roman de Flaubert*, Armand Colin, 1973.

27

La Contradiction créatrice: quelques remarques sur la genèse d'*Un Cœur simple* (1979)

Profitons de la faiblesse des autres pour n'y pas tomber.[1]
Je t'assure que, comme style, les gens que je déteste le plus m'ont peut-être plus servi que les autres. (C II 409)

C'est Baudelaire qui, le premier, a vu combien chez Flaubert l'acte d'écrire trouve sa genèse dans un esprit de contradiction créatrice. Contradiction qui, selon Baudelaire, se baserait tant sur une analyse des théories critiques les plus récentes et les plus rebattues (et partant les plus «vagues», les plus «élastiques» et les plus «puéril[e]s») que sur le choix, comme sujet, de la «donnée la plus usée, la plus prostituée, l'orgue de Barbarie le plus éreinté».[2] Le but de ce bref article sera de suggérer, à partir de documents dont certains sont peu connus, comment déjà dans les premières années 1850, une ou deux œuvres littéraires spécifiques ont constitué pour Flaubert un défi, mettant en branle un mouvement qui devait aboutir, bien plus tard, à la création en 1876 d'*Un Cœur simple*. J'examinerai trois points principaux: d'abord, l'élaboration par Flaubert de sa conclusion: la mort, au point culminant de l'été, et la vision béatifique mais illusoire, d'une vieille campagnarde après une vie de servitude supportée avec patience; ensuite, certains problèmes esthétiques apparentés découlant du défi que provoque le stéréotype littéraire de la servante;[3] enfin, quelques détails du texte de Flaubert et des variantes qui contribuent à l'ambiguïté voulue de ce conte qu'on a interprété de façons si différentes.[4]

En septembre 1852, Louise Colet avait déjà entrepris une suite projetée de six longues narrations en vers sous le titre général et volontairement provocateur: *Le Poème de la Femme*. (C III 21) Ces récits étaient destinés à pleurer tour à tour le triste sort de *La Paysanne*, *La Princesse*, *La Prostituée*, *La Femme Supérieure*, *La Servante* et *La Bourgeoise*. En novembre, elle apporta le brouillon de *La Paysanne* au rendez-vous de Mantes (C III 48); tout au long des deux mois suivants, Flaubert, avec Bouilhet le dimanche, passa et repassa au crible chaque détail de narration et d'expression.[5] Lettre après lettre, Flaubert donne des conseils pour le remaniement de l'intrigue et des proportions, des parties narratives et descriptives; il en vient à centrer de plus en plus ses observations sur ce problème: comment présenter (dans le cinquième des six chants de *La Paysanne*), contre la toile de fond d'un décor naturel riche et trempé de soleil, la mort et la dernière vision d'une vieille paysanne dont la vie, après une courte idylle amoureuse, n'a été qu'une longue souffrance.

La Paysanne, telle qu'elle fut publiée en 1853, est un récit en vers de plus de 800 décasyllabes, divisé en six sections.[6] Dans la première, une femme âgée, squelettique et en sueur, va glanant aux champs; de sa bouche édentée sort le refrain d'une plainte séculaire sur un amant perdu.[7] Qui devinerait qu'elle fut jadis «l'accorte Jeanneton»? Ainsi sommes-nous reportés à sa dure enfance, fille sans mère d'un pauvre pêcheur du Rhône. Elle a pourtant son idylle adolescente avec Jean, fils du jardinier d'un château splendide; lorsque son père ivrogne est noyé, elle est adoptée par la famille de Jean comme sa femme future. Juste quand les bans vont être publiés, Jean doit partir, conscrit dans l'armée napoléonienne; il laisse Jeanneton enceinte.

Les sections médianes n'ont guère de rapports étroits avec le conte de Flaubert. Les conscrits partent; Jean donne à Jeanneton en la quittant un anneau et un petit cœur d'or, jurant qu'il reviendra; le père de Jean meurt, et Jeanneton se trouve sans ressources. Dans la section III, chacun a envoyé à l'autre une lettre par intermédiaire (ni l'un ni l'autre ne sait écrire); Jean enjoint tendrement à Jeanneton d'avoir soin de leur fils – il l'épousera à son retour. Aucune autre lettre n'arrive; l'enfant meurt, et, dans la section IV, le malotru Gros-Pierre, ayant causé la mort de sa femme en lui infligeant des grossesses annuelles, viole la petite servante de dix-huit ans; le curé et la rumeur publique la convainquent que le régiment de Jean a été massacré à Saragosse et que la morale lui dicte d'épouser Gros-Pierre.

Les sections V et VI ont attiré le plus de commentaires détaillés de la part de Flaubert, mais surtout la section V où, après de longues années passées à traîner patiemment le boulet conjugal, et après une vieillesse misérable, Jeanneton meurt, seule dans le paysage inondé de soleil, ayant dans ses derniers instants une vision intense de son idylle lointaine et fugitive avec Jean. Dans la section VI, Jean devenu vieux revient, en traversant toute l'Europe, de ses longues années comme prisonnier de guerre en Sibérie, devient le fossoyeur du village, et, dans une conclusion macabre, trouve un jour dans un tas d'ossements son unique lettre et son gage d'amour. C'est à partir de sa lettre de dix-neuf pages datée du 28 novembre 1852 (F^{os} 15-24), que Flaubert discute longuement le brouillon de ces deux sections. Rappelons-nous d'abord le début et la fin du chapitre v d'*Un Cœur simple:*

> Les herbages envoyaient l'odeur de l'été; des mouches bourdonnaient; le soleil faisait luire la rivière, chauffait les ardoises.

Suit la procession de la Fête-Dieu et l'agonie de Félicité. Finalement:

> Le prêtre gravit lentement les marches, et posa sur la dentelle son grand soleil d'or qui rayonnait. Tous s'agenouillèrent. Il se fit un grand silence. Et les encensoirs, allant à pleine volée, glissaient sur leurs chaînettes.
> Une vapeur d'azur monta dans la chambre de Félicité. Elle avança les narines, en la humant avec une sensualité mystique; puis ferma les paupières. Ses lèvres souriaient. Les mouvements de son cœur se ralentirent un à un, plus vagues chaque fois, plus doux, comme une fontaine s'épuise, comme un écho disparaît; et, quand elle exhala son dernier souffle, elle crut voir, dans les cieux entr'ouverts, un perroquet gigantesque, planant au-dessus de sa tête.

La mort de Jeanneton est dès le début très différente. Lorsqu'elle s'éteint, seule au bord du fleuve, sous le soleil ardent, elle voit à l'horizon la serre du vieux château, théâtre de son idylle de jeunesse, imaginaire souvenir du réel, non pas vision imaginaire. Flaubert désapprouve la phrase: «des parfums en sortaient». «Mais non, *il lui semble* que des parfums en sortent . . . elle ouvre les narines» (F^o 21^v). L'impression sensorielle et la vision illusoire à la mort de Félicité («Elle avança les narines, en la humant avec une sensualité mystique . . . elle crut voir . . . un perroquet gigantesque») auront, cela va de soi, une toute autre portée suggestive et significative. Flaubert trouve beaucoup trop exagérés les gestes de Jeanneton moribonde:

Je voudrais quelque chose de moins dramatique comme action personnelle de son corps, quelque chose de plus faible, de plus éteint, qui fût mou. Ce doit presque être de l'idiotisme, un vague souvenir, quelque chose dont elle ne se rendît pas compte à elle-même (F^o 21^v).[8]

et l'on pense déjà à cette phrase extraordinaire de Flaubert qu'on vient de lire, évoquant la vie qui s'éteint. On songe aussi à la manière dont Flaubert développera l'«idiotisme» de Félicité, et à l'écart qu'il créera entre ce dont le lecteur a conscience et la relative inconscience du personnage.

Quant à la section VI, il insiste sur le fait qu'elle a reçu un développement trop étendu, ruinant ainsi la concentration d'intérêt sur Jeanneton, et donnant l'impression de redites. Louise avait montré Jean rêvant à son pays natal lorsqu'il y retourne à travers l'Europe:

Ce souvenir du pays natal lui arrivant au cœur avec un parfum agreste est trop poétique. Jean revient dans son pays tout bonnement parce que c'est le pays et qu'il ne sait pas où aller (F° 22ᵛ).⁹

Ces parfums et autres détails sensoriels de l'arrière-fond naturel, attribués au souvenir de Jean, devraient être transposés à la mort de Jeanneton,

que je ferais plus ample, avec les sonnettes des chèvres, le bruit des eaux du Rhône, les bruyères roussies, un paysage immense et calme – et au milieu une pauvre vieille crevant tout doucement (F° 22ᵛ).

Déjà la relation réciproque entre la splendeur naturelle et la simplicité humaine commence à prendre forme; déjà les détails physiques se précisent; et déjà la conscience de la beauté ambiante doit fonctionner, non pas à travers l'expérience intérieure d'un personnage, mais à travers l'analogie que percevra le lecteur entre le calme et l'immensité du paysage, et la douceur et la dignité de la mort.

Dans la section VI, Flaubert veut aussi voir développer la conclusion macabre:

Il faut qu'on voie, dans la terre grasse, des cheveux sur lesquels le soleil passe, de la viande autour des vertèbres, que ce soit enfin Shakespearien, hideux de vérité de de froid (F° 23ʳ);

et il ébauche des détails, comme le fossoyeur, la pipe à la bouche, qui déterre les restes, le cœur d'or «bosselé et cassé», et la lettre maculée et moisissante.¹⁰ Mais avant tout, il faut laisser parler ces choses elles-mêmes, sans que l'auteur souligne l'effet par aucun commentaire:

Et surtout pas de *pris d'un frisson* – le fait *seul* (F° 23ʳ).

D'ailleurs, la découverte faite par Jean doit être totalement subordonnée au thème central de la vie et de la mort de Jeanneton.

La lettre du 19 décembre 1852 (F°ˢ 25–6) insiste de nouveau sur la nécessité d'enlever au récit de la mort de Jeanneton toute expansion lyrique, tout commentaire explicatif, et tout plat énoncé des faits:

Le mouvement lyrique: «Comme l'on voit quand» etc. coupe l'action ... Il est à enlever *complètement* malgré les deux admirables vers ... (F° 26ʳ).[11]

D'un autre passage:

C'est de l'*explication*, ça; il faut que nous voyons [*sic*] l'explication et qu'on ne nous la dise pas (F° 26ʳ).

Finalement, commentant la scène de la mort:

Après le tintement des sonnettes, et le Rhône au loin fuyant, il faut *qu'on voie* Jeannette mourir, et non se contenter d'un vers, appuyer davantage sur la situation et faire la description de son agonie encadrée dans le paysage.

Le 3 janvier 1853, Flaubert revient sur les dernières sections du poème (F°ˢ 28–32). L'auteur ne doit pas devenir un «participant du tableau». Flaubert prend comme exemple l'emploi de l'adjectif *sinistre* pour qualifier le travail des vers dans la scène du cimetière (v. 810):

Enlève-moi donc *sinistre* et mets *tranquille* .... Ce seul mot de sentiment et d'appréciation morale me gâte mon impression. *Je voyais* les vers, et ici, avec sinistre, *j'entends* qu'on parle d'eux. Sinistre me rappelle l'auteur, il me remet dans la littérature, quand j'étais dans la nature (F° 29ᵛ).

A propos de la mort de Jeanneton, il s'élève encore une fois contre l'intervention lyrique et les commentaires; il critique divers détails d'expression:

«C'est le bonheur qui l'appelle là-bas» – Vulgaire, expression de la Grande Opéra [*sic*];

ensuite il imagine lui-même la manière dont il faudrait suggérer une telle mort:

Or, voici ce que je propose. Continue après «les souvenirs par degrés remontaient», les moutons qui paissaient, le tintement des chèvres, le gazouillis de l'eau du Rhône, des flocons de laine ou mieux des brins de bruyère, rasant le sol au vent du soir – et puis Jeanneton s'affaisse, s'affaisse, son œil se ferme, elle veut parler, ses vieux cheveux blancs tombent sur les romarins, un sourire passe sur sa bouche, de petites convulsions de ses membres maigris, et elle expire, doucement, au bruit ... (F° 32ʳ).[12]

Ici Flaubert propose que Louise trouve quelque bruit aigu et évocateur, typique du paysage provençal, comme l'était la scène (pour nous, maladroitement insérée) du pressoir aux olives dans la section VI. L'équivalent normand serait «le cri du coucou, pendant que cette femme meurt par terre». (Pour Félicité, dès le premier plan, le son qui suggère sa vision sera celui des chaînettes des encensoirs, rappelant la chaîne du perroquet).[13] Flaubert insiste encore

une fois sur la nécessité de ne pas dramatiser la mort: «Il faut faire
cette fin en queue de rat, que ce soit aminci, éteint, baigné de calme
et de grandes ombres bleues»,[14] contrastant avec la découverte finale
faite par Jean (F° 32ʳ). Enfin, une note marginale d'une importance
capitale indique que Louise, au lieu d'expliquer, dans des commentaires abstraits, les sentiments de Jeanneton, doit chercher à les
suggérer exclusivement à travers les expressions changeantes du
visage mourant:

Montrer par sa physionomie ce que tu as voulu mettre dans le mouvement
«Oh, c'est l'amour», et parbleu on le devine bien, son sentiment, donc il ne
faut pas le dire, mais le *montrer*.

Montrer et non dire: cent ans plus tard, cette distinction deviendra
célèbre et courante, dans les théories anglo-saxonnes ultérieures sur le
roman.[15]

D'autres scènes que les dernières suggèrent des détails sur lesquels
Flaubert méditera et dont il tirera plus tard des effets d'une
concision et d'une discrétion toutes différentes. D'abord la structure
du début – contraste entre la vieillesse présente et l'idylle passée.
Chez Louise, c'est d'abord le tableau de la Victime où le grotesque
est poussé jusqu'à son dernier point («sa main décharnée» ... «ainsi
qu'une araignée», «noire poitrine», poils au menton «comme à
celui des chèvres», «dents de loup», «peau ridée comme un égout où
s'amassait sa sueur»), ensuite (fleur de rhétorique) l'interrogation:
«Comment deviner qu'elle fut jeune et belle?»

Chez Flaubert, la brave domestique est vue à travers les actions de
sa vie journalière qui l'ont fait admirer pendant un demi-siècle par
toutes les bourgeoises, et qui cependant en font «une femme en bois,
fonctionnant d'une manière automatique»; on passe directement à
la constatation présentée comme allant de soi: «Elle avait eu, *comme
une autre*, son histoire d'amour». Ensuite l'idylle, développée par
Louise à travers 140 vers: pour Flaubert, pas de «beau château»
(expression dont Louise abusait, note-t-il), ni de participation aux
joyeuses danses villageoises (sa Félicité se tient stupéfaite devant le
bruit assourdissant et la lumière aveuglante de «cette masse de
monde sautant à la fois»); surtout, absence de dialogue sentimental
entre les amants et de commentaires abstraits sur leur amour.[16])

Pour Jeanneton comme pour Félicité, la conscription met fin à
l'espoir – mais de façon combien différente. Jean aime sa Jeanneton
mais part parce qu'il le faut, en criant: «Vive l'Empereur!»;

Théodore, épouvanté par la guerre et trop pauvre pour «s'acheter un homme», se marie à la riche Mme Lehoussais.[17] Rien ne remplacera Jean dans le cœur de Jeanneton, et à partir de son départ sa vie ne sera que souffrances – viol mélodramatique, dureté ou incompréhension de l'Église qui lui conseille le mariage avec son ravisseur, servitude prolongée – là où Félicité après chaque perte s'accroche à un nouvel être aimé, et trouve en chemin des moments privilégiés sans cesse renouvelés, sans cesse reperdus.

En pensant à l'effet général que devrait produire *La Paysanne*, Flaubert fit remarquer:

Il plaira aux artistes qui y verront le style et aux bourgeois qui y verront le sentiment (C III 50).

D'innombrables passages dans ses commentaires insistent sur le fait que c'est précisément l'expression explicite et abstraite qui empêche la communication des sentiments au lecteur:

toujours peindre ou émouvoir, et *jamais déclamer* (C IV 10)
C'est avec la tête qu'on écrit (C III 50).

Une autre histoire de servitude, très populaire dans ces années, est souvent citée en avertissement, à cause de ses personnages idéalisés, de ses cas exceptionnels et de ses dissertations sentimentales: *La Case de l'Oncle Tom*. Pourtant, en dernière analyse, «j'aime mieux le mauvais goût que la sécheresse» (F° 29ᵛ); et la lettre du 3 janvier 1853, après un éclat de fureur contre le manque de sentiment chez Augier et d'autres, insiste sur ce point:

Cette foi dont parlait Jésus, qui suffit à remuer les montagnes, est la même chose qui fait les grandes choses partout. La Sainteté n'est qu'une croyance, et la Poésie qui est *une manière de voir* n'arrive à ses résultats extérieurs que par une conviction enthousiaste du Vrai (F° 30ᵛ).

Les chansons populaires, qui saisissent par leur perfection dans leur genre, peuvent résulter du sentiment pénétrant de ceux qui sont «bêtes» ou «imbéciles»:

Il faut sentir. Eh bien, est-ce que tu n'as, au plus profond de toi (car ce n'est ni dans le cœur, ni dans la tête, mais plus loin, plus haut), comme un grand lac où tout se reflète, où tout miroite, un murmure perpétuel qui veut s'épandre, une fluidité qui veut sortir? (F° 30ᵛ).[18]

Ce sentiment est évidemment celui de l'artiste devant ses matériaux, et non pas l'émotion à l'état brut et immédiat (on songe au «Moi pur» de Valéry). Et Flaubert devait constamment opposer par la suite le second récit du *Poème de la Femme*, *La Servante* (basé effrontément en partie sur des épisodes de la vie de Musset dont elle avait été témoin), à *La Paysanne*, où l'auteur aurait cherché à créer, par la force de l'imagination, le général et le typique. Mariette, héroïne de *La Servante*, est trop exceptionnelle, trop douée:

Pense le plus possible à toutes les servantes.
Il faut que ton héroïne soit *médiocre*. Ce que je reproche à Mariette c'est que c'est une femme supérieure (C III 402).

Quelques passages visent sans doute à représenter les familles typiques dans lesquelles une servante peut souffrir (pp. 82 sqq; plusieurs d'entre elles semblent être des portraits satiriques de certains contemporains, des transpositions transparentes). Mais on trouve, dans ce conte mélodramatique, avec sa tentative de suicide, et la scène grotesque de la folie à la Salpêtrière qui la termine,[19] peu d'éléments qui suggéreraient une vie moyenne quelconque de servante.

Flaubert relève aussi avec raison, dans *La Servante*, l'obsession excessive de «l'impureté», et suggère qu'il serait salutaire à Louise d'écrire une œuvre

où il ne soit pas question d'amour, une œuvre in-sexuelle, in-passionnelle (C III 402);

pour *La Religieuse* qu'elle projetait, il l'avertit:

point d'amour, et surtout point de déclamation contre les prêtres ni la religion!

(Hélas! ce poème tombera dans ces deux excès).[20]

A mesure qu'il s'exaspère de plus en plus fortement, de plus en plus ouvertement, devant les efforts successifs de Louise pour représenter les frustrations de la Femme, il rappelle par contraste ce qu'au moins il aurait voulu voir *La Paysanne* représenter. Sous une forme condensée, Louise a traité, dit-il,

une histoire commune et dont le fond est à tout le monde. Et c'est là, pour moi, la vraie marque de la force en littérature. Le lieu commun n'est manié que par les imbéciles ou par les très grands (C III 262).[21]

Le résultat en était

parfaitement composé, simple et poétique à la fois, deux qualités presque contradictoires... Où est la force, c'est d'avoir tiré d'un sujet commun une histoire touchante et *pas canaille* (C III 87).[22]

Structure, simplicité, expression. Dans sa poursuite de ces trois

La Genèse d'Un Cœur simple 445

qualités fondamentales, Flaubert avait connu d'autres luttes avec le stéréotype de la servante. Que sa propre Berthe, dans *Rage et Impuissance*, écrit à l'âge de quinze ans, annonce Félicité, on l'a souvent signalé:

> la vieille Berthe se retraçait ainsi toute sa vie, qui s'était passée monotone et uniforme, dans son village, et qui, dans un cercle si étroit, avait eu aussi ses passions, ses angoisses et ses douleurs (OJ i 149).

Mais elle et le chien Fox, seuls compagnons fidèles du maître solitaire qui souffre, proviennent très directement de la servante Marthe et du chien bien-aimé Fido dans le *Jocelyn* de Lamartine qui parut cette même année 1836.[23]

L'attachement passionné à un maître, l'accomplissement impeccable des tâches journalières, la proximité au monde animal avec sa fidélité analogue et inconditionnelle: l'adolescent Flaubert absorbe avec sérieux tous ces traits de la servante idéale. Mais dans les années 1850, lorsque Louise (fortement influencée elle-même), lui impose continuellement la lecture de Lamartine, il y a de fortes raisons pour les réactions carrément critiques de Flaubert. Si, dans sa poésie, Lamartine avait déjà depuis quelque temps adopté des buts humanitaires, c'est à partir de 1849 que dans ses récits en prose il se lance dans des théories sur le genre de littérature qui conviendrait réellement au peuple; ses théories comme sa pratique horripilent Flaubert.

Dans sa correspondance avec Louise (celle-ci visiblement enthousiaste), Flaubert s'acharne contre les trois récits en prose: *Geneviève (Histoire d'une Servante)*, *Graziella* et *Raphaël*. Le premier de ces récits est le plus pertinent ici, mais avant d'examiner l'incitation négative qu'il a pu apporter, rappelons brièvement la réaction de Flaubert devant *Graziella*, qu'il lut en avril 1852:

> Le malheureux! Quelle belle histoire il a gâtée là (C ii 389).
> C'est un ouvrage médiocre, quoique la meilleure chose que Lamartine ait faite en prose (C ii 396).

Attitudes conventionnelles, personnages-marionnettes, idées reçues, «messages pour dames», suppression ou falsification de la sexualité, création de stéréotypes sociaux par une opposition factice entre «les classes pauvres» et «les classes aisées» et, bien entendu, par-dessus tout, manque d'un style approprié – ses critiques sont multiples. Encore une fois, ce n'est pas l'excès de sentiment, mais l'incapacité de l'exprimer avec justesse, qui est au centre de ses griefs. Il manque à Lamartine ce coup d'œil médical de la vie, cette vue du Vrai, enfin, qui est le seul moyen d'arriver à de grands effets d'émotion (C II 398).

Pourtant il relève dans ce roman des notations physiques aiguës, des personnages, des thèmes généraux, qui lui sont restés dans la mémoire, qui auraient dû produire leur effet:[24]

Rien dans ce livre ne vous prend aux entrailles.
Il y aurait eu moyen de faire pleurer avec Cecco, le cousin dédaigné (C II 397).
Il y aurait eu moyen de faire un beau livre avec cette histoire . . .: un jeune homme à Naples, par hasard, au milieu de ses autres distractions, couchant avec la fille d'un pêcheur et l'envoyant promener ensuite, laquelle ne meurt pas, mais se console, ce qui est plus ordinaire et plus amer (C II 398).

L'impulsion à remanier, à récrire, ressort continuellement:

Oui, je le répète, il y avait là de quoi faire un beau livre, pourtant (C III 398).

Sur *Raphaël*, sur *Jocelyn* relu, et sur les œuvres critiques ou politiques de Lamartine, il s'exprime avec acerbité; il frappe d'anathème la fausse idéalisation:

Je le déclare même sale, quand il veut faire de l'amour éthéré (C III 175).[25]

Deux grands écrivains, très différents, s'opposent à Lamartine: Voltaire dans la pénétration dépourvue de sentimentalité de *Candide*; La Fontaine dans son expression, soit des détails de l'amour physique dans les *Contes*, soit d'une tendresse subtilement suggérée dans certaines *Fables*:

La fable des deux pigeons m'a toujours plus ému que tout Lamartine (C IV 62).

Ce fut à Alexandrie, en 1850, que Flaubert lut pour la première fois, dans *Le Constitutionnel*, des extraits de *Geneviève, Histoire d'une Servante*: il écrivit à Bouilhet:

Il y a dans la préface une revue des grands livres que je te recommande. C'est de la folie arrivée à l'idiotisme (C II 221).

Cette Préface du récit qui inaugurait en 1849 ce que Lamartine appela une «série de récits et de dialogues à l'usage du peuple de la ville et des campagnes», se présente sous la forme d'un étonnant dialogue entre Lamartine et une couturière-poète, Reine Garde, sur la Littérature pour le Peuple; presque toutes les grandes œuvres du passé sont rejetées comme étant ou trop altières ou sans rapport avec les besoins des humbles − ce qu'il faut, selon Reine, ce sont des histoires simples et touchantes sur des Gens comme Nous.

Que Lamartine ait vu le sujet de son propre récit comme étant d'une nouveauté et d'une pertinence provocantes – l'histoire des humbles racontée aux humbles – c'est ce qui ressort avec une évidence surabondante de la forme même du récit. Le narrateur, après avoir dépeint les détails banals du labeur quotidien de Geneviève («véritable» nom de Marthe, la vieille servante dans *Jocelyn*), l'interroge peu à peu sur sa vie passée; elle refuse à plusieurs reprises de croire que l'existence d'une pauvre servante puisse avoir un intérêt quelconque; lui, avec une ahurissante condescendance, l'assure qu'il s'intéresse à l'existence des créatures les plus infimes – une fourmi, un grillon, une araignée même.[26] Dans cette œuvre dont le but est de «glorifier la domesticité», bon nombre des multiples incidents ont été manifestement choisis pour être typiques des origines et des vicissitudes d'une servante: Geneviève est successivement une petite tâcheronne patiente qui soigne sa mère mourante, une orpheline qui fait vivre sa sœur cadette, ensuite, pendant un court laps de temps, l'heureuse promise d'un jeune montagnard; plus tard, après avoir été injustement emprisonnée, une domestique dans une suite de familles, cruelles ou bienveillantes; enfin, la servante dévouée corps et âme du curé Jocelyn.

Pourtant trois aspects de l'histoire vont à l'encontre de tous les principes qu'élaborera Flaubert. Les complications inouïes de l'intrigue, avec une prolifération de coïncidences dont l'artifice éclate (mariage clandestin et mort en couches de la sœur de Geneviève, fuites à travers la campagne, y compris celle où Geneviève se cache, fugitive déguenillée, dans l'étable précisément de la jeune et belle femme de son ex-fiancée, épilogue où le petit neveu, enlevé tôt après sa naissance, est rendu non seulement à Geneviève mais aux parents redécouverts de son père); la nature exceptionnelle et supérieure de Geneviève (dès le début, à l'encontre de Jeanneton ou de Félicité, toutes deux illettrées, Geneviève, appelée «la sérieuse» par les autres enfants, apprend à lire auprès de sa mère et se rend tous les jours à la messe du matin; la perfection de sa conduite s'étalera à travers tout le récit); enfin, et surtout, le style (Cf. C ii 399, 434; iii 158–159, 175).

Quand il a à peindre les choses vulgaires de la vie, il est au-dessous du commun (C iii 198, sur *Jocelyn*).

(Et la réussite relative de *La Paysanne*, qui fait un vif contraste avec Lamartine, serait d'avoir su

dire proprement et simplement des choses vulgaires (F° 30ʳ)).

C'est d'ailleurs dans les années où il critique *La Paysanne* et lit ou relit Lamartine que Flaubert, peinant sur *Madame Bovary*, est hanté par le problème du dialogue dans la vie de personnages médiocres:

Comment faire du dialogue trivial qui soit bien écrit? (C III 20; cf. III 24 etc, etc).[27]

Le double danger du «mauvais plat» et du «mauvais recherché» (F° 25^v) ne se montre que trop dans les vers de Louise. Jeanneton pleure son père noyé:

> O Rhône ingrat! O Rhône déloyal!!
> Non! non! jamais je ne te fis de mal.
> Oh! sois clément, Rhône! rends-moi mon père ... (144 sqq.)

combien différente de Félicité, proférant une seule phrase «caractéristique»: «Pauvre petit gars! pauvre petit gars!» tandis que l'auteur exprime la profondeur de sa douleur par le son des coups de battoir au bord de la rivière, là où les grandes herbes vertes traînant dans l'eau rappellent des cheveux de noyé. Dans les longs monologues de *Geneviève* et de sa Préface, platitude et prétention dans l'expression alternent d'une façon même plus déconcertante:

«Oh mon bon ange! couvrez-moi de vos ailes et rendez-moi invisible, et dérobez ma misère et mon humiliation à celle qui jouit justement de la richesse, de la bonne renommée et du bonheur que j'ai eus sous la main, et que j'ai perdus en trahissant Cyprien.» (209)

Peut-on cependant discerner un rapport quelconque entre le méli-mélo plein de bonnes intentions de Lamartine et le récit de Flaubert, concentré, discret et suggestif? Les indications qui suivent sont proposées seulement à titre d'hypothèse, mais, prises dans leur ensemble (et si l'on se souvient de la façon dont Flaubert utilise «Le Lac» dans *Madame Bovary*, et de sa prédilection pour des effets parodiques généraux ou de menues allusions satiriques), elles concordent avec la délectation qu'il éprouvait à faire écho aux clichés de l'époque, à les renverser, à les transformer radicalement.

On a vu plus haut sa colère devant la Préface: là, mise à part la condamnation sans appel des grands auteurs, une discussion se prolonge sur les animaux et les oiseaux en tant que compagnons chéris de ceux qui sont rejetés par la société. L'oiseau de Reine est mort: «Nous nous parlions tant, nous nous fêtions tous les deux!»[28] Son oiseau à elle était un chardonneret, mais elle se plaint de ce qu'il ne fût pas un perroquet, puisque ceux-ci vivent le plus longtemps. Cependant, raisonne-t-elle, les oiseaux apprivoisés ont sûrement une place au Ciel:

Bah! bah! laissons dire les savants, j'espère bien qu'il y aura des arbres et des oiseaux en Paradis . . . Est-ce que le bon Dieu nous tromperait? Est-ce qu'il nous ferait aimer ce qui ne serait que mort et illusion? (p. 13 sqq).

(cette dernière phrase serait certainement suggestive par rapport à la dernière vision de Félicité). Lamartine souligne l'espoir qu'a Reine «de revoir au ciel son oiseau» et rappelle «son cœur où l'amour d'un oiseau tenait une si grande place» (19, 20).[29]

Dans le récit même, certains moments sérieux et relativement réussis ont pu contribuer au choix par Flaubert de certains effets et à son traitement si différent: le résumé de *Geneviève* «elle avait besoin de servir quelqu'un et d'aimer celui qu'elle servait» (66); les nombreuses descriptions de l'accomplissement machinal des tâches journalières, surtout après la douleur ou le deuil (par ex. 58, 60, 66, 225, 229); les conséquences de la conscription pour les pauvres qui ne peuvent acheter un remplaçant (82); l'attachement intense aux endroits et aux choses (le thème de la vente des objets domestiques familiers, qui revient si souvent et avec des accents si amers chez Flaubert, est présenté à travers les yeux de la servante après la mort du curé); et le Flaubert qui évoquera avec tant de netteté les objets hétéroclites si chargés de souvenirs dans la chambre de Félicité aurait fort bien pu se réjouir devant les trésors du «coffre de bois» de Geneviève, y compris un «beau chapelet en noix de cerises, sculpté à jour par un chartreux» (69);[30] enfin, le sentiment de solidarité qui existe parmi les pauvres, apportant leur secours avec la pensée simplement exprimée: «nous pourrions bien être comme cela demain».[31]

Finalement, Flaubert aurait-il semé exprès des indices pour signaler certaines allusions? On pourrait, sous toutes réserves, en proposer trois. D'abord, le titre: le narrateur de Lamartine fait remarquer: «Je craignais de remuer plus longtemps dans ce *cœur simple* les souvenirs», et ailleurs: «dans ces *cœurs simples*, l'amitié. . .» (228, 203; c'est moi qui souligne).[32] Ensuite, les noms Paul et Virginie auraient-ils été choisis parce que le livre de Bernardin de Saint-Pierre est un des très rares ouvrages auxquels Lamartine accorde la faveur de plaire à toutes les classes sociales (le seul dans *Graziella*)? Enfin, le compagnon de Geneviève le plus chéri (et qui est abattu de la manière la plus mélodramatique (187), là où Félicité ne fait qu'imaginer le «meurtre» du perroquet par Fabu) – il est vrai qu'il s'agit ici d'un chien – ce compagnon porte le petit nom de Loulou.

Vers la fin de 1852, donc, les mois passés à essayer de refondre *La*

Paysanne, et les discussions sur Lamartine entre autres, semblent avoir suscité chez Flaubert des réflexions soutenues sur les problèmes que comporte une histoire de servante. Plus de treize ans plus tard, juste au moment où il entreprend la rédaction d'*Un Cœur simple*, il apprend la mort de Louise:

Son souvenir ainsi ravivé m'a fait remonter le cours de ma vie (C VII 291).[33]

Nous ignorons évidemment à quel moment le perroquet et la vieille servante se sont rejoints dans le premier plan conservé de Flaubert, association offrant ses multiples possibilités d'harmoniques et tendres et satiriques. Commentant une pièce de théâtre projetée par Louise en 1852, *L'Institutrice*, il note l'effet de ridicule insoutenable que produirait sur la scène un perroquet empaillé (C II 388). Nous ignorons également à quel moment aura été ajoutée, à l'idée centrale d'une vieille mourant parmi les sons et les parfums de l'été, celle de la procession de la Fête-Dieu, moyen infiniment suggestif d'unir autour du reposoir toute la solennité d'une cérémonie séculaire. Déjà par la narration de Maria dans le récit de jeunesse *Novembre*, Flaubert avait évoqué les réactions intenses d'une jeune fille de la campagne devant la procession solennelle, les riches tapis, les fleurs amoncelées (OJ II 217-8). Déjà dans *Par les Champs et par les Grèves* sont annoncés les thèmes de la servante et de la Fête-Dieu.[34] En juin 1852, lorsque «aujourd'hui Rouen a été pleine de processions, de reposoirs», il réfléchit en même temps sur la tristesse obsédante du «carillon des processions que nous entendions au loin» (C II 434), sur la bêtise d'une fausse idéalisation du peuple et sur les fondements de la religion qui se situent à un niveau bien plus profond que le dogme:

La superstition est le fond de la religion, la seule vraie, celle qui survit sous toutes les autres. Le dogme est une affaire d'invention humaine. Mais la superstition est un sentiment éternel de l'âme et dont on ne se débarrasse pas (C II 433).[35]

«Pour de pareilles âmes, le surnaturel est tout simple»: c'est là un des commentaires du narrateur sur Félicité (commentaires moins rares qu'on n'a quelquefois coutume de le dire); ou encore: «Quant aux dogmes, elle n'y comprenait rien, ne tâcha même pas de comprendre». A l'encontre de ces effusions d'une religiosité peu appropriée qu'il avait critiquées chez Louise, ou de la foi idéaliste de Geneviève, Flaubert a suggéré, chez Félicité, deux impulsions tout à fait différentes: la simplicité des affinités avec le monde animal; la tendresse imaginative qui lui fait éprouver l'extase à travers la

première communion de l'enfant Virginie plutôt qu'une participation mystique quand plus tard elle communie elle-même.

A la différence des intrigues épisodiques ou mélodramatiques
qu'ont bâties d'autres sur les souffrances de la servante, celle de
Flaubert va concentrer le «besoin d'aimer» de Félicité dans cinquante ans passés au service d'une même famille, avec un crescendo
savamment construit[36] de pertes et de substitutions, allant de ce qui
est le plus intimement personnel (le projet de mariage avec
Théodore), en passant par la famille adoptée et le neveu adoré,
jusqu'aux pratiques charitables les plus vastes (et les plus typiques
des «engouements» de l'époque): envers l'armée, les exilés polonais,
les victimes du choléra. Les commentaires du narrateur soulignent,
de façon discrète mais explicite, les deux thèmes: d'un côté «la bonté
de son cœur se développa» et «avec l'imagination que donnent les
vraies tendresses»,[37] et de l'autre «tant son esprit était borné» et «le
petit cercle de ses idées se rétrécit encore». Mais nous sommes à
égale distance d'une fausse idéalisation et d'une satire exagérée.[38]
Nullement ingénue, elle se méfie longtemps des intentions dont
Théodore fait état – méfiance due cette fois à la «raison» et à
«l'instinct»,[39] mais qui plus tard tourne au ridicule dans les soupçons
qu'elle manifeste à l'égard du rempailleur ou dans l'invention du
«crime» de Fabu. Si elle réfléchit peu sur elle-même, et ne se rend
pas compte de son héroïsme dans la scène du taureau, elle n'est
aucunement la créature inconsciente que certains commentateurs
ont cru voir; elle ressent une indignation momentanée devant
l'injustice de Mme Aubain (p. 36) et, comme d'autres personnages
majeurs de Flaubert, elle connaît le moment critique où l'amertume
de son existence tout entière l'inonde en un flot de souvenirs précis
(p. 60). C'est cependant dans la seconde partie, lorsque la surdité et
la vieillesse l'isolent du monde extérieur, qu'elle trouve la paix
totale, seule avec les illusions qu'elle se crée autour de son perroquet
mort et empaillé, se rappelant tous les détails du passé, «sans
douleur, pleine de tranquillité». Et c'est en marge d'une esquisse de
ce passage que Flaubert a écrit dans ses brouillons: «Son genre de
bonheur. Son calme. Pour que ce soit la moralité de l'histoire, qu'on
ait envie de l'imiter» (f° 447) – remarque qui pourrait bien com-
porter un élément sardonique mais qui reste significative. Car
Félicité, qui va de la douleur, des deuils, du sens parfois de
l'injustice, jusqu'à son acceptation finale, inconditionnelle et quasi
inconsciente de la nature de la vie et de la mort, et qui éprouve sa
propre forme d'extase par l'intense contemplation imaginative du

perroquet,[40] est à coup sûr, dans un mode différent, très proche de saint Antoine avec son désir final: se fondre dans la création, «être la matière».[41]

Aux très nombreuses analyses qui essaient de dégager le rapport entre ironie et sérénité, je voudrais ajouter ici simplement trois suggestions, fondées sur le texte lui-même et sur quelques-unes des variantes qui l'ont précédé. D'abord, le rôle de certains personnages secondaires dans leur rapports avec Félicité. Théodore l'abandonne; Paul, une fois grandi, la néglige dans sa vieillesse; Bourais, espèce d'Homais au petit pied, est le mauvais génie de la famille Aubain; surtout, Félicité subit le cruel coup de fouet du cocher. Mais elle est loin d'être traitée en éternelle victime, moyen facile de provoquer l'attendrissement ou l'amertume. Même Mme Aubain, arrogante et dure, qui considère les divisions sociales comme allant de soi («Votre neveu?...» ou «Comme vous êtes bête!») a néanmoins, à un point culminant, le geste soudain de l'union dans la douleur, lorsque Félicité réclame comme mémorial le petit chapeau de peluche de Virginie morte depuis longtemps:

Leurs yeux se fixèrent l'une sur l'autre, s'emplirent de larmes; enfin la maîtresse ouvrit ses bras, la servante s'y jeta; et elles s'étreignirent, satisfaisant leur douleur dans un baiser qui les égalisait. (49)

Dès le plan le plus ancien, la fonction du Curé (nullement un Bournisien)[42] avait été envisagée comme bienveillante, et il permet d'emblée et sans se choquer que l'on place sur l'autel Loulou pourrissant. (D'ailleurs, en ce qui concerne l'Église, les variantes des brouillons montrent un adoucissement dans les détails: lorsque Félicité arrive au couvent, où elle va apprendre, à travers le cliché «elle vient de passer», la mort de Virginie, on lisait d'abord: «Eh bien, dit très vite la religieuse», puis «la bonne sœur répondit d'*un ton béat et parfaitement insensible*» (F° 365ʳ, cf. 359, 371; c'est moi qui souligne) – là où on trouve dans le texte définitif: «La bonne sœur, avec un air de componction, dit...» (p. 43)). Plus tard, lorsque Félicité soigne dans sa maladie atroce le hideux père Colmiche,

Le pauvre vieux, en bavant et en tremblant, la remerciait de sa voix éteinte, craignait de la perdre, allongeait les mains dès qu'il la voyait s'éloigner (50).

Et lorsqu'elle meurt elle-même, elle est soignée pendant toute la longue journée d'été par la Simonne, qui place Loulou sur le reposoir («Allons, dites-lui adieu») et qu'on voit plus tard dans une des phrases les plus significatives du conte:

Une sueur froide mouillait les tempes de Félicité. La Simonne l'épongeait avec un linge, en se disant qu'un jour il lui faudrait passer par là.

Deuxième point. Le père Colmiche et le perroquet empaillé Loulou marquent le point culminant de toute une série d'images apparentées, autour du thème de la décomposition et de son dépassement.[43] Le triple schéma – beauté riche et ironique de l'été à son comble; objet pourrissant; tendresse transcendante – se répète avec des variations discrètes. De tout l'amas hétéroclite des trésors de Félicité, le plus précieux est le «petit chapeau de peluche» de Virginie: un jour où

> l'air était chaud et bleu, un merle gazouillait, tout semblait vivre dans une douceur profonde (48–9),

les deux femmes retirent de l'armoire les vêtements de l'enfant morte depuis longtemps, et retrouvent le petit chapeau «tout mangé de vermine». Le désir ardent qu'éprouve Félicité de conserver ce souvenir rongé des mites provoque la scène centrale que nous venons de voir et où se déclare une compréhension humaine, momentanée, silencieuse et intense, entre maîtresse et servante. Le père Colmiche, avec sa réputation sinistre («passant pour avoir fait des horreurs en 93»), son taudis actuel («les décombres d'une porcherie») et son corps purulent et ulcéreux (équivalent de celui du lépreux dans *Saint Julien*), est soigné et placé «au soleil sur une botte de paille» (50); outre sa propre reconnaissance de mourant, il y a le «miracle» de l'arrivée de Loulou le jour même où Félicité fait dire une messe pour le repos de son âme. Point minime mais peut-être significatif: Félicité, imaginant la naissance du Christ, la voit s'accomplir, non sur la paille d'une crèche, mais ainsi:

> lui qui ... avait voulu, par douceur, naître sur le fumier d'une étable (26).

Et au dernier chapitre, les odeurs et les sons d'été répandent, autour de la mort de Félicité, leur beauté et leur majesté. La procession est à la fois solennelle et inéluctablement ridicule, avec ses splendeurs locales (pompiers, suisse, bedeau, instituteur, religieuse, petites filles «frisées comme des anges», diacres, encensoirs, fusillades des postillons).[44] Le perroquet empaillé, offrande suprême de Félicité, est depuis longtemps une épave en pleine décomposition:

> Les vers le dévoraient; une de ses ailes était cassée, l'étoupe lui sortait du ventre (69).

Mais sur l'autel, placé parmi l'étalage hétérogène de trésors bourgeois, étincelants et bizarrement touchants (un sucrier de vermeil, des pendeloques en pierres d'Alençon, deux écrans chinois …), et entouré par les riches gerbes de fleurs estivales (tournesols, lis, pivoines, digitales, hortensias), il ne manifeste plus que sa beauté:

Loulou, caché sous des roses, ne laissait voir que son front bleu pareil à une plaque de lapis (72).

Enfin, les multiples harmoniques du paragraphe final. Pour décrire le dernier souffle de Félicité, humant la vapeur de l'encens, Flaubert, dans des versions successives, avait essayé bien des mots qui pourraient exprimer l'intensité de sa béatitude – «délectation», «volupté», «joie», «joie sensuelle», «avec toute la sensualité d'une âme mystique» – pour finir par river ensemble deux notions qu'on croit d'habitude diamétralement opposées: «en la humant avec une sensualité mystique». Pour la dernière phrase, il avait prévu un seul mouvement prolongé, partant de la vie qui s'en va, pour aboutir à la vision finale; il esquisse le contraste et le rythme qu'il faudra:

Et quand elle exhala son dernier souffle … quand (une phrase très longue) cette vie terrestre s'éteignit … elle crut voir le Perroquet … comme un Saint-Esprit, planant au-dessus de sa tête (F° 349^r).

D'innombrables efforts jalonneront la conquête du ton exact. Pour suggérer l'illusion, «Elle voyait» devient «elle croyait voir» ou «elle crut voir» (F^{os} 340^v, 349^v). Des notations religieuses trop spécifiques – non seulement «comme un Saint-Esprit» mais «entre Jésus et le Père» (F° 349^v) ou «entre des nuages d'or, à droite du fils, à gauche de Dieu» (F° 352^r) – sont enlevées, ce qui donne, au lieu d'un dernier effet de choc pour heurter les croyances traditionnelles, une sorte d'expansion mythologique. Mais la «phrase très longue» pour exprimer la fin d'une vie reste encore à trouver. La sueur froide, l'agonie, le râle sont terminés.[45] Pour les derniers moments, les brouillons montrent des images telles que «quand s'éteignit cette vie terrestre», «quand le dernier lien de la vie se rompit» (F° 340^v), «pendant que se cassaient (ou «se déliaient» ou «rompant») les derniers ressorts» (ou «tous les ressorts») de la vie», ou «pendant la rupture de l'âme et du corps» (F° 352^r) – que remplacent les expressions plus directes et plus simples: «les mouvements de son cœur s'affaiblissaient ⟩ se ralentissaient ⟩ se ralentirent un à un» (F° 353^r). Flaubert essaie différents adjectifs – «plus longs chaque fois, plus lents», finalement «plus vagues»; surtout «plus faibles» devient «plus doux». Il essaie des images développées:

comme les vibrations d'une corde d'argent sur laquelle on a joué ou bien l'écho tombant au fond d'un précipice (Fº 353ʳ),

dont il reconnaît le caractère trop décoratif ou trop dramatique et qu'il transforme peu à peu en une musique plus tranquille et plus équilibrée: «comme une fontaine s'épuise, comme un écho disparaît».

La mort et le rêve, comme tout le reste de la vie de Félicité, avec ses frustrations, ses préoccupations pratiques, ses gestes de résignation et ses élans d'imagination, sont exprimés avec une dignité et une discrétion foncières.[46]

Dans les *Contes* de Voltaire, que Flaubert relisait si souvent «pour la centième» ou «pour la millième fois», se trouve la question toujours ouverte qui sous-tend l'histoire de Félicité:

Je n'aurais pas voulu être heureux à condition d'être imbécile . . . . Mais, après y avoir réfléchi, il paraît que de préférer la raison à la félicité, c'est être très insensé . . . Il y a là de quoi parler beaucoup.[47]

Provoqué en partie par les stéréotypes et les sentimentalisations de sa propre époque, Flaubert a recréé ce dilemme dans un conte où l'ironie fondamentale devient une partie intégrante et nécessaire de «cette imagination que donnent les vraies tendresses».[48]

NOTES

1 Lettre à Louise Colet, BN N. a. fr. 23825 Fº 2ᵛ.
Je me sers ici (en même temps que des textes imprimés) de deux fonds manuscrits. (A) BN N. a. fr. 23825 (papiers Descharmes) (sigle: D) contient des lettres à Louise Colet dont celles d'avant avril, 1851 (qui ne nous concernent pas ici) ont été publiées par Jean Bruneau (*Correspondance*, Tome I, Bibliothèque de la Pléiade, 1973), et d'autres par Jacques Suffel (*Figaro Littéraire*, 21/12/1957 et 11/8/62). Plusieurs d'entre celles qui se rapportent à *La Paysanne* de Louise Colet semblaient être demeurées inédites au moment où j'ai entrepris le présent article (sauf le facsimilé d'une page, Suffel 11/8/62). Elles figurent maintenant dans le tome 13 des *Œuvres complètes* de Flaubert, procurées par le Club de l'Honnête Homme (sigle CHH). Étant donné les coquilles et les lectures douteuses ou fausses qui déparent malheureusement cette édition ('métaphysiquement' pour 'métaphoriquement', omissions de mots ou de phrases, fausses citations de *La Paysanne*, etc.) je cite directement les manuscrits, en normalisant la ponctuation. (Il faut noter d'ailleurs, devant la mention 'inédite' que donne CHH, que la lettre du 3/1/1853 a été publiée par J. Suffel dans *Les Amis de Flaubert*, Nº 36.) Dans l'édition CHH, deux lettres mal datées dans l'édition Conard (14/1/52 et 17/1/52) sont datées correctement: 12/1/53 et 15/1/53.) (B) BN N. a. fr. 23663: manuscrits et brouillons des *Trois Contes*. Certains extraits qui ont paru dans les éditions Conard, Belles Lettres, CHH, ou dans

l'intéressant article de Colin Burns: 'The Manuscripts of Flaubert's *Trois Contes*', *French Studies*, VIII, 4 (Oct. 1954), mis à part les lacunes, comportent quelques erreurs de lecture ('Culte du stupide' pour 'Culte du St. Esprit'; 'le poète miraculeux' pour 'la pêche miraculeuse'; 'Décadence. Progression' pour 'Décadence physique', etc.), erreurs reprises par d'autres; je cite donc le manuscrit.

Pour *Un Cœur simple* (sigle CS), je donne la pagination de l'édition procurée par Édouard Maynial chez Garnier, éd. de 1961. Pour les autres œuvres de Flaubert, sauf avis contraire, l'édition Conard (Sigles: OJ = *Œuvres de Jeunesse*, 3 vols.; PCG = *Par les Champs et par les Grèves*; C = *Correspondance*, 9 vols.; C Su = *Supplément à la Correspondance*, 4 vols.).

2 Baudelaire, *Œuvres complètes*, Pléiade, 1961, p. 651.

3 La thématique de la servante dans la littérature du 19e siècle mériterait évidemment un examen plus général; je n'analyse ici que deux cas particuliers. R. Debray-Genette, dans son admirable article: 'Du Mode narratif dans les *Trois Contes*', *Littérature* N° 2, mai 1971, indique (p. 40, n. 4) qu'elle a l'intention d'étudier les rapports avec *Eugénie Grandet*. Il faudrait tenir compte de *Germinie Lacerteux*, de l'œuvre de Hugo, de Tourgueneff, de George Sand, etc.

4 On ne saurait évidemment donner ici une liste exhaustive des travaux consacrés à la question de l'ambiguïté dans ce conte; je me bornerai à relever certaines références particulièrement pertinentes pour les problèmes que je soulève ici.

5 Pour les lettres où Bouilhet souligne les opinions de Flaubert («*moi* c'est *lui*, et vice versa») voir Louis Bouilhet: *Lettres à Louise Colet*, introduction et commentaires par Marie-Claire Bancquart, Publications de l'Université de Rouen, s.d., pp. 116–32.

6 *Le Poème de la Femme. 1er Récit. La Paysanne*, Paris, Perrotin, 1853, sans nom d'auteur. Louise incorpora des suggestions de Flaubert, tout en en négligeant obstinément beaucoup d'autres. Ce ne sera qu'au moment où le poème est presque terminé que Flaubert dira: «Ne choisis plus ce mètre . . .; je le trouve peu musical, de soi-même». (C III 87)

7 Elle reprendra ce refrain juste avant sa mort (v. 615). Rappelons la chanson de l'aveugle dans *Madame Bovary*, les remarques de Flaubert sur les chansons populaires (citées ci-dessus, p. 443) et le fait que la commission Fortoul sur les chansons populaires date de 1852.

8 Cf. Bouilhet, *op. cit.*, p. 123.

9 Même si le rêve de Jean sur son pays natal est conforme à «la vérité réelle», dit Flaubert, «la vérité artistique et idéale» demande des sacrifices pour qu'on arrive à concentrer les effets en subordonnant les détails.

10 Flaubert et Bouilhet tous deux cherchent à «motiver son introduction [celle de Jean] dans le cimetière» (Bouilhet, 6/12/52, *op. cit.*, p. 123); on décide finalement que c'est à la suite d'une épidémie qu'il deviendra fossoyeur. Le choléra comme événement-type de l'époque figure chez Lamartine (voir ci-dessous) et se retrouvera dans CS (p. 49); renversant exprès les proportions habituelles, Flaubert résuma trois thèmes majeurs de la littérature humanitaire dans trois courtes phrases). Pour la pipe dans la bouche du fossoyeur, cf. *Rage et impuissance* (1836), OJ I, 156.

11 Ces vers: Et l'homme accourt, malgré sa lassitude,
    Les bras tendus aux ombres d'autrefois.

12 Cf. pour Félicité: «puis ferma les paupières. Ses lèvres souriaient». Voir les discussions détaillées au sujet du sourire de Jeanneton, C II 341, 349, et cf. les brouillons d'*Un Cœur simple*.

13 Cf. la sonnette des chèvres dans les citations qu'on vient de lire. Le premier plan d'*Un Cœur simple* a été publié par A. Cento dans *Studi francesi*, 5 (1961), et repris par d'autres depuis. Voir aussi A. Fairlie «Sentiments et sensations chez Flaubert» (ci-dessus, pp. 422–36).

14 Cf., dans les brouillons, différentes versions où Flaubert évoque «le ciel pur», et, dans le texte, la «vapeur d'azur» qui entoure Félicité mourante.

15 Cf., par exemple, R. Debray-Genette, *art. cit.*, p. 42.

16 Cf. *id., ibid.*, p. 43, et A. Fairlie, ci-dessus, p. 422 sqq. Voir dans les brouillons les versions successives de la phrase «l'énorme charretée de foins oscillait devant eux» et cf. dans les OJ les nombreux passages où l'odeur des foins s'associe à la naissance de la passion (en particulier, *Novembre*, OJ II, 215–6). Le thème du début se reprend à la fin: au lieu de souvenirs de l'idylle chez Félicité, nous avons: «Les herbages envoyaient l'odeur de l'été». Sur d'autres rapports subtils qui unissent les moments privilégiés de Félicité, cf. H. Cockerham: «Sur la structure d'*Un Cœur simple*», *Travaux de Linguistique et de Littérature*, Strasbourg, VIII 2.

17 Flaubert a deux objections à faire au dialogue des villageoises sur la conscription. D'abord, elles devraient parler «de l'événement et non pas de l'amour (comme feraient des philosophes ou des artistes). La situation est ici plus large». Ensuite: «ça ne se formulait pas comme ça dans leurs têtes». Chez les conscrits il verrait, lui, une «exaltation moitié factice, moitié vraie» (F° 18ᵛ).

18 Cette même lettre contient un passage fondamental en ce qui concerne les croyances de Flaubert: «je suis aussi athée que toi en médecine, et plus. Mais non pas en médecins. Je ne crois pas à la science qui est (dans son état moderne) toute d'analogie et d'instinct. Mais je crois au *sens* spécial de certains hommes qui sont *nés pour ça*, et ont pioché. J'ai vu mon père guérir bien des gens où d'autres avaient manqué et dire qu'il ne savait pas pourquoi, que ce qui sauvait l'un tuait l'autre, etc.»

19 Cf. la folie et le suicide de la vieille servante, devenue «Berthe la folle», dans *Rage et impuissance*, OJ I 160, et *La Paysanne*: «Dans le village on la traite de folle» parce qu'elle va chantant sans cesse son vieux refrain (une Ophélie vieillie?).

20 Deux thèmes cependant en parallèle avec CS: les offrandes bizarres et touchantes amassées sur l'autel (p. 125); les soins donnés par la religieuse à différentes victimes (p. 127).

21 Cf. C III 174: «Tu as écrit l'histoire [non pas de la Femme mais] de Jean et de Jeanneton, tout bonnement, et il s'est trouvé qu'en écrivant l'histoire de Jean et de Jeanneton tu as écrit l'histoire de la *Paysanne*, parce que toute individualité idéale, fortement rendue, résume. Mais il ne faut pas vouloir résumer».

22 J. F. Jackson, dans *Louise Colet et ses amis littéraires*, Yale, 1937, p. 189 sqq, s'étonne devant les louanges que décernent Flaubert et Bouilhet à

La Paysanne. Il n'avait pas accès aux lettres où la critique détaillée se poursuit souvent avec âpreté. Mais, mis à part la situation personnelle, ce qui ressort des documents, c'est d'abord que Flaubert était conscient d'une tradition littéraire où la paysanne ou la servante figurait d'habitude comme un élément grotesque; essayer de traiter ce sujet «trivial» de façon sérieuse et émouvante, c'était là déjà un pas en avant; ensuite, qu'il voyait dans *La Paysanne* une réussite au moins relative en comparaison avec *La Servante* ou avec la *Geneviève* de Lamartine.

23 J'ajoute ici des renseignements qui compléteront le travail de Jean Bruneau dans son ouvrage de base *Les Débuts littéraires de Gustave Flaubert 1821–1845*. Pour *Rage et impuissance*, voir les détails dans *Jocelyn*, vers 47 *sqq*, et la IXe époque.

24 «Le vieux pêcheur couché sur le dos avec les hirondelles qui rasent ses tempes» (C II 396), détail repris dans *La Paysanne*.

25 Cf. C II 405, 438, III 159, 176, 182–3, 194, 199, 343, D F° 26^v, etc.

26 *Geneviève. Histoire d'une Servante*, Introduction de Pierre Emmanuel, 1972, p. 71.

27 Parmi d'excellentes discussions sur l'art du dialogue chez Flaubert, rappelons C. Gothot-Mersch, «Le Dialogue dans l'Œuvre de Flaubert», *Europe*, Sept.–Nov., 1969; R. Debray-Genette, *art. cit.*, et «Les Figures du récit dans *Un Cœur simple*», *Poétique*, 3, 1970. Je me propose d'étudier ailleurs certains aspects de ce problème en ce qui concerne *Un Cœur simple*.

28 Elle avait même écrit un long poème sur son oiseau; quelques vers suffiront pour en donner le ton: «Oh! qu'ensemble nous étions bien!/Le peu qu'il nous fallait pour notre nourriture/Je le gagnais à la couture/Je pensais: mon pain est le sien!»

29 Le trio de compagnons dans la souffrance, chien, oiseau, servante, est tiré de *Robinson Crusoé* (là encore le thème du perroquet), un des quatre ouvrages que la préface trouve appropriés au peuple (avec *Paul et Virginie*, *Télémaque* et la *Vie des Saints*).

30 Cf. le «bénitier en noix de coco» de Félicité, et, dans *L'Éducation sentimentale*, les objets fignolés en noix de coco dans la chambre de Dussardier. Sur la chambre de Félicité, voir l'admirable analyse par A. W. Raitt, *The Art of Criticism*, ed. P. H. Nurse, Edinburgh, 1969, pp. 206–15. Voir aussi, du même auteur, «Flaubert and the art of the short story», *Essays by diverse hands*, Vol. XXXVIII.

31 Cf. ci-dessous, p. 452–3 (La Simonne).

32 Cf. cependant R. Debray-Genette, à propos d'*Eugénie Grandet* (art. cit. n. 2).

33 On sait que les origines de *Saint Julien l'Hospitalier* remontent à l'année 1856, et sans doute jusqu'aux années 1840. En ce qui concerne CS, on cite d'habitude *Rage et impuissance*, une lettre du 14/11/50, et les figures de servantes dans *Madame Bovary*.

34 Cf. aussi *Une Nuit de Don Juan* (Éditions du Seuil, II, 721–2). D. L. Demorest, *L'expression figurée et symbolique dans l'œuvre de Gustave Flaubert*, (Conard, 1937, p. 583 sqq.) a signalé l'importance pour CS de la magnifique évocation de la Fête-Dieu dans PCPG 187–90. Cf. aussi, dans le même texte, sur l'amoncellement des fleurs sur l'autel, sur le

mélange de désirs sensuels et mystiques, et les vitraux qui font rêver, le passage évocateur, ironique et tendre, pp. 196–7; sur la monotonie d'une existence passée dans une petite ville de province, p. 11 sqq; («on se plaît à rêver ... quelque profonde et grande histoire intime ... amour de vieille fille dévote ...»); sur le triste sort des servantes, p. 171–2 («fille ... de visage âpre et d'une tenue rigide, avec son bonnet blanc ... et son bavolet carré.... Voilà donc les deux sociétés face à face») et sur leurs rêves, p. 306; sur les «acheteurs d'hommes», p. 232. Pour divers aspects de la reprise de ses propres thèmes par Flaubert, voir les articles pénétrants de S. Cigada.

35 Cf. C IV 170: «Je n'aime point les philosophes qui n'ont vu là que jonglerie et sottise. J'y découvre, moi, nécessité et instinct; aussi je respecte le nègre baisant son fétiche autant que le catholique aux pieds du Sacré-Cœur». Voir aussi, s.v. Religion, C. Carlut, *La Correspondance de Flaubert, Etude et Répertoire critique*, Nizet, 1968.

36 Un plan parmi les brouillons (F° 381ᵛ, reproduit avec quelques erreurs CHH 469–70) insère, à la fin des événements résumés dans les différentes sections, le mot abstrait désignant les qualités dont témoigne Félicité: Ch. I: «automatique»; II: «sensible, pudique, tendre», «pleine de respect, et de douceur», «brave». III: «sa dévotion», «maternelle», «patiente, résignée, vertueuse»; IV: «charitable», «amour filial»; puis, à partir du «cadeau du perroquet», «heureuse».

37 A noter la différence essentielle entre la phrase des brouillons (F° 302ᵛ): «Et par l'espèce d'imagination que donnait sa tendresse» et celle du texte définitif: «avec l'imagination que donnent les vraies tendresses».

38 Félicité ne succombera pas à la corruption du milieu, comme le fait enfin la Jeanneton de Louise. Ses insuffisances résulteront de la *reductio ad absolutum* de ses qualités mêmes. De son innocence d'ailleurs ressort le thème comique et touchant de celle qui, au confessionnal, cherche à se faire absoudre de péchés inexistants (cf., là encore, OJ).

39 Résumé abstrait de la part du narrateur. A comparer avec la scène dans *L'Éducation sentimentale* où Mme Arnoux suggère à Frédéric que le bon sens suffit pour les empêcher de consommer leur amour – et où Frédéric rejette ces «maximes bourgeoises».

40 Cf. les causes physiques de l'espèce d'hypnotisme qu'elle subit comme le soleil, tombant sur l'œil de verre, l'éblouit.

41 Cf. dans les deux textes le rôle du soleil, qui prend des proportions mythologiques, rappelant une célébration du solstice. (Voir P. Nykrog: «Les *Trois Contes* dans l'évolution de la structure thématique chez Flaubert», *Romantisme*, 6, 1973). Cf. aussi, dans une tonalité toute différente, la fin des *Funérailles du Dr Mathurin*, OJ II 142–3.

On sait que Flaubert disait avoir écrit CS pour plaire à George Sand; c'est le 8/12/75 qu'elle lui parle du «bonheur, c'est-à-dire l'acceptation de la vie quelle qu'elle soit». Flaubert d'ailleurs sera toute sa vie tiraillé entre cette acceptation de la part de l'artiste (Jules à la fin de la première *Éducation sentimentale*) et la conviction que sans nos aspirations nous serions «plus bêtes que les oiseaux».

42 Cf. les rôles de curé dans *La Paysanne* et dans *La Servante*.

43 Cf., sur «la thématique de la pourriture», M. Issacharoff, «*Trois Contes*

et le problème de la non-linéarité», *Littérature*, n° 15, Oct. 1974, p. 34.

44 Cf. D. L. Demorest, *op. cit.*, p. 583 sqq.; j'ajoute certaines lectures de brouillons et quelques hypothèses quant à l'interprétation.

45 Au lieu de la notation des brouillons (F° 347ʳ) «Bourdonnement d'une grosse mouche qui se pose sur les narines de Félicité», Flaubert laisse simplement «des mouches bourdonnaient».

46 Je ne discute pas ici la question de savoir si CS aurait marqué un changement profond dans l'attitude ou la technique de Flaubert, comme ont tendance à le croire bien des commentateurs; je serais plutôt de l'avis de ceux qui voient dans ce conte la même ambiguïté voulue qui sous-tend toute l'œuvre de Flaubert.

47 *Histoire d'un bon bramin.* Voltaire, *Romans et Contes.* Bibliothèque de la Pléiade, 1938, pp. 124–6.

48 Depuis la rédaction de cet article ont paru des travaux importants, notamment *Plans, Notes et Scénarios de «Un Cœur simple»* par François Fleury (Lecerf, Rouen, 1977), *The Dossier of Flaubert's «Un Cœur simple»* by G. Willenbrink (Rodopi, Amsterdam, 1976). Ce n'est également qu'en 1976 (mon article étant déjà entre les mains de l'éditeur) que j'ai pu consulter l'ouvrage de S. Douyère «*Un Cœur simple*» (Pensée universelle, Paris, 1974) où sont étudiés les rapports avec *Geneviève* de Lamartine. Parmi les articles, signalons ceux de Shoshana Felman, de Michael Issacharoff et, en particulier, ceux de Raymonde Debray-Genette.

Select bibliography of the works of
ALISON FAIRLIE
compiled by L. J. Austin

ABBREVIATIONS

AJFS   *Australian Journal of French Studies*
CAIEF   *Cahiers de l'Association Internationale des Études françaises*
CR   *Cambridge Review*
EFL   *Essays in French Literature*, Perth, WA
FMLS   *Forum for Modern Language Studies*
FS   *French Studies*
MLR   *The Modern Language Review*
RHLF   *Revue d'Histoire Littéraire de la France*
RSH   *Revue des sciences humaines*
TLS   *Times Literary Supplement*

CUP   Cambridge University Press
EA   Edward Arnold

1947

Leconte de Lisle's Poems on the Barbarian Races (CUP), xv + 426 pp.

1952

'Some Remarks on Baudelaire's *Poème du Haschisch*.' In *The French Mind, Studies in Honour of Gustave Rudler* (Oxford: The Clarendon Press), pp. 291–317.
Review:
Irving Putter, *Leconte de Lisle and his contemporaries*, FS VI, 83.

1953

Reviews:
Wallace Fowlie, *Rimbaud's Illuminations*, CR LXXV, 92–4.
Wallace Fowlie, *Mallarmé*, *Ibid*.
P. Mansell Jones, *Baudelaire*, FS VII, 172.

1954

Reviews:
Jean Prévost, *Baudelaire*, FS VIII, 76.
Martin Turnell, *Baudelaire*, *ibid*., 278.

1955

Reviews:
Enid Starkie, *Petrus Borel*, FS IX, 80.
Enid Starkie, *Arthur Rimbaud*, *ibid*., 84.
Pierre Flottes, *Leconte de Lisle*, *ibid*., 277.
Irving Putter, *The Pessimism of Leconte de Lisle*, *ibid*., 277.

1956

Reviews:
René Huyghe, *L'esthétique de l'individualisme à travers Delacroix et Baudelaire*, FS X, 273.
Claude Pichois, *Le vrai visage du général Aupick*, *ibid*., 366.

1957

Review:
Lloyd James Austin, *L'Univers poétique de Baudelaire*, FS XI, 180.

1958

'Nerval et Richelet', RSH, pp. 397–400.
Reviews:
Lloyd James Austin, *L'Univers poétique de Baudelaire*, RSH, 430–2.
Baudelaire devant ses contemporains (ed. Bandy and Pichois), FS XII, 276.
Jacques Crépet, *Propos sur Baudelaire*, *ibid*., 276.
Enid Starkie, *Baudelaire*, *ibid*., 276.
Ch. Baudelaire, *La Fanfarlo* (éd. Cl. Pichois), *ibid*., 382.

1959

Reviews:
Daniel Vouga, *Baudelaire et Joseph de Maistre*, FS XIII, 77.
Pierre Jean Jouve, *Tombeau de Baudelaire*, *ibid*., 84.
The Centennial Celebration of Baudelaire's 'Fleurs du Mal', *ibid*., 179.

1960

Baudelaire: 'Les Fleurs du Mal' (Studies in French Literature, 6) (London: EA), 64 pp.
Reviews:
Œuvres complémentaires de Gérard de Nerval. I. *La Vie des Lettres* (éd. J. Richer), MLR, LV, 286.
D. P. Scales, *Alphonse Karr, sa vie et son œuvre*, *ibid*., 464.

1961

'An approach to Nerval'. In *Studies in Modern French Literature presented to P. Mansell Jones* (Manchester: University Press), 87–103.

Reviews:
Charles Baudelaire, *Les Fleurs du Mal* (éd. A. Adam), FS XV, 178.
Charles Baudelaire, *Petits Poèmes en Prose* (éd. H. Lemaitre), *ibid.*, 178.
Cl. Pichois et Fr. Ruchon, *Iconographie de Charles Baudelaire, ibid.*, 272.
D. J. Mossop, *Baudelaire's Tragic Hero, The Listener*, 27.7.61, 142.

1962

Flaubert: 'Madame Bovary' (Studies in French Literature, 8) (London: EA), 89 pp.
Review:
D. J. Mossop, *Baudelaire's Tragic Hero*, FS XVI, 190.

1963

Review:
Irving Putter, *The Pessimism of Leconte de Lisle*, FS XVII, 273.

1964

Reviews:
Jean Seznec, *Literature and the Visual Arts in Nineteenth-Century France*, FS XVIII, 274.
L. Bopp, *Psychologie des 'Fleurs du Mal'*, Vol. I, *ibid.*, 395.

1965

'Literary History and Literary Criticism in relation to Constant's *Adolphe*.' In *Literary History and Literary Criticism*. Acta of the Ninth Congress International Federation for Modern Languages & Literatures, held at New York University, 25–31 August 1963 (New York: University Press), pp. 245–6 (summary of a paper: full text unpublished).

Reviews:
Gérard de Nerval, *L'Académie ou Les Membres introuvables* (éd. M. Françon), FS, XIX, 74.
Baudelaire, *Curiosités esthétiques, l'Art romantique* (éd. H. Lemaitre), *ibid.*, 77.

1966

'The art of Constant's *Adolphe*: creation of character', FMLS II, pp. 253–63.
'The art of Constant's *Adolphe*: structure and style', FS XX, pp. 226–42.
Reviews:
Jean Seznec, *John Martin en France*, FS XX, 86.

M. Easton, *Artists and Writers in Paris: the Bohemian Idea, 1803–1867, ibid.*, 198.
Baudelaire as a literary critic (ed. Lois B. Hyslop and F. E. Hyslop, Jr), *ibid.*, 201.
L. Bopp, *Psychologie des 'Fleurs du Mal'*, Vol.II, *ibid.*, 202.
Benjamin Constant, *Adolphe*, ed. Carlo Cordié, MLR LXI, 519.
Richard et Cosima Wagner, *Lettres à Judith Gautier* (éd. Léon Guichard), *ibid.*, 523.

1967

'The art of Constant's *Adolphe*: the stylization of experience,' MLR, LXII, pp. 31–47.
'Observations sur les *Petits poèmes en prose*', RSH, pp. 449–60.
'Flaubert et la conscience du réel'. In EFL 4, pp. 1–12 (Résumé in *Le Réel dans la littérature et la langue*. Actes du Xe congrès de la Fédération Internationale des Langues et Littératures Modernes. Strasbourg 29 août – 3 septembre 1966 (Paris: Klincksieck), p. 214.)
Reviews:
   Flaubert: a collection of critical essays (ed. R. Giraud), FS XXI, 73.
   P. Moreau, *Sylvie et ses sœurs nervaliennes, ibid.*, 174.
   A. Pohle, *Das Gedicht 'Qaïn' von Leconte de Lisle, ibid.*, 175.
   P. Deguise, *Benjamin Constant méconnu: Le Livre 'De la Religion', ibid.*, 251.
   B. Constant, *Wallstein* (éd, J.-R. Derré), *ibid.*, 253.
   Eugène Fromentin, *Dominique* (ed. Barbara Wright), MLR LXIII, 534.

1968

'Flaubert and the authors of the French Renaissance.' In *The French Renaissance and its Heritage. Essays presented to Alan Boase* (London: Methuen), pp. 43–62.
'L'Individu et l'ordre social dans *Adolphe*', Europe, 467, pp. 30–8.
'Quelques remarques sur les *Petits poèmes en prose*' (Colloque Baudelaire de Nice, 25–7 mai 1967). Actes, dans *Annales de la Faculté des Lettres et Sciences Humaines de Nice*, 4–5, pp. 89–97.
'Constant romancier: le problème de l'expression.' In *Benjamin Constant: Actes du congrès de Lausanne*, octobre 1967. (Histoire des idées et critique littéraire, 91) (Genève: Droz), pp. 161–9.
Reviews:
   B. F. Bart, *Flaubert*, FS XXII, 170.
   J. Senelier, *Un amour inconnu de Gérard de Nerval, ibid.*, 346.
   C. Mauron, *Le dernier Baudelaire, ibid.*, 348.
   Charles Baudelaire, *Petits poèmes en prose* (ed. M. Zimmermann), *ibid.*, 348.
   Charles Baudelaire, *L'Art romantique – Littérature et Musique* (ed. L. J. Austin), *ibid.*, 350.
   S. Buck, *Gustave Flaubert*, RHLF LXVIII, 150–1.

1969

'Pellerin et le thème de l'art dans *L'Éducation sentimentale*' (Colloque Flaubert, Centenaire de *L'Éducation sentimentale*, Rouen, avril 1969). Dans *Europe* 485–7, pp. 38–51.

'Some Patterns of Suggestion in *L'Éducation sentimentale*', AJFS 6, pp. 266–93. (Special number in honour of Professor A. R. Chisholm.)

Reviews:

L. Bouilhet, *Lettres à Louise Colet* (éd. Marie-Claire Bancquart), FS XXIII, 87.

Benjamin Constant, *Adolphe* (éd. W. A. Oliver), *ibid*, 187.

Charles Baudelaire, *Les Fleurs du Mal* [facs. of first edn], *ibid.*, 190.

J. Pommier, *Autour de l'édition originale des 'Fleurs du Mal'*, *ibid.*, 190.

J. Fletcher, *A critical commentary on Flaubert's 'Trois contes'*, *ibid.*, 304.

Irving Putter, *La dernière illusion de Leconte de Lisle. Lettres inédites à Emilie Forestier*, *ibid.*, 422.

Victor Brombert, *The Novels of Flaubert*, RHLF LXIX, 1051–2.

Ch. Baudelaire, *Les Fleurs du Mal*[...] avec certaines images qui ont pu inspirer le poète, éd. J. Pommier et Claude Pichois, *Deux années d'études baudelairiennes* (juillet 1966–juin 1968). Supplément au n° 39 des *Studi francesi*, 15–16.

Claude Pichois, *Baudelaire à Paris*, *ibid.*, 28–9.

1970

'Le mythe d'Orphée dans l'œuvre de Nerval', *CAIEF* 22, pp. 153–68, 299–300.

Dr Enid Starkie (1897–1970), FS XXIV, 439–40.

Reviews:

Ross Chambers, *Gérard de Nerval et la poétique du voyage*, FS XXIV, 74.

Gérard de Nerval, *Pandora*, (ed. J. Guillaume), *ibid.*, 74.

J. Villas, *Gérard de Nerval: a critical bibliography*, *ibid.*, 74.

Charles Baudelaire, *Les Fleurs du Mal* (éd. Crépet–Blin–Pichois), *ibid.*, 191.

Charles Baudelaire, *Petits poèmes en prose* (éd. R. Kopp), *ibid.*, 191.

Charles Baudelaire, *Œuvres complètes*, (éd. M. Ruff), *ibid.*, 191.

R. T. Cargo, *Baudelaire Criticism 1950–1967*, *ibid.*, 191.

E. J. Mickel, Jr, *The Artificial Paradises in French Literature. I. The Influence of Opium and Hashish*, *ibid.*, 302.

Max Milner, *Baudelaire, enfer ou ciel, qu'importe?* RHLF LXX, 1090–1.

Chateaubriand, *Voyage en Italie* (éd. J.-M. Gautier), MLR LXV, 906.

Jean-Pierre Richard, *Paysage de Chateaubriand*, *ibid.*, 907.

1971

'Journée Gustave Flaubert', CAIEF, pp. 367 (introduction), 367–84 (discussion).

'Romantic sensibilia [Jean-Pierre Richard: *Études sur le romantisme*]', TLS 23.7.71, 854.

Reviews:

Madame de Staël et l'Europe. Colloque de Coppet (1966), FS XXV, 93.

Flaubert, *L'Éducation sentimentale* (éd. J. Suffel), *ibid.*, 98.

R. J. Sherrington, *Three Novels by Flaubert, ibid.*, 221.

J.-L. Douchin, *Le Sentiment de l'absurde chez Flaubert, ibid.*, 343.

P. Bénichou, *Nerval et la chanson folklorique, ibid.*, 475.

Baudelaire as a Love Poet and other essays (ed. Lois B. Hyslop), *ibid.*, 477.

1972

'Constant's *Adolphe* read by Balzac and Nerval.' In *Balzac and the Nineteenth Century. Studies in French literature presented to Herbert J. Hunt* (Leicester: University Press), pp. 209–24.

'Aspects of Expression in Baudelaire's Art Criticism.' In *French 19th Century Painting and Literature* (ed. Ulrich Finke) (Manchester: University Press), pp. 40–64.

Reviews:

Beatrice W. Jasinski, *L'Engagement de Benjamin Constant: Amour et politique,* FS XXVI, 83.

A. Oliver, *Benjamin Constant: écriture et conquête du moi, ibid.*, 83.

French Literature and its Background (ed. J. Cruickshank), 4. *The Early Nineteenth Century, ibid.*, 209.

E. L. Gans, *The Discovery of Illusion. Flaubert's Early Works, ibid.*, 216.

P.-G. Castex, *Baudelaire critique d'art, ibid.*, 345.

Flaubert, *Madame Bovary* (éd. Cl. Gothot-Mersch), *ibid.*, 464.

F. W. Leakey, *Baudelaire and Nature*, RHLF LXXII, 144–8.

1973

'Reflections on the successive versions of "Une gravure fantastique".' Dans *Mélanges offerts au Professeur W. T. Bandy pour son soixante-dixième anniversaire* (Etudes baudelairiennes, 3) (Neuchâtel: A la Baconnière), pp. 217–31.

'"Mène-t-on la foule dans les ateliers?" Some remarks on Baudelaire's Variants.' In *Order and Adventure in French Poetry. Essays presented to C. A. Hackett* (Oxford: Blackwell), pp. 17–37.

(with Anne Green.) 'Deciphering Flaubert's manuscripts. The "Club de l'honnête homme" edition', FS XXVII, pp. 287–315.

Reviews:

Concordance to Baudelaire's 'Petits poèmes en prose', compiled by R. T. Cargo, FS XXVII, 87.

G. Flaubert, *The Sentimental Education*, translated by Perdita Burlingame, *ibid.*, 345.

R. T. Denommé, *The French Parnassian Poets, ibid.*, 464.

Joanna Richardson, *Enid Starkie, The Times Higher Education Supplement,* 30.11.73.

D. J. Mossop, *Pure Poetry*, TLS 12.10.73, 1248.

1974

'Sentiments et sensations chez Flaubert', CAIEF XXVI, pp. 233–49; 343–6.

'Flaubert and some painters of his time.' In *The Artist and the Writer in France. Essays in Honour of Jean Seznec* (Oxford: Clarendon Press), pp. 111–25.

'The Procrastinations of a Poet [*Correspondance de Baudelaire* (éd. Cl. Pichois)]', TLS LXXIII, 688–90.

Text of an address given at the memorial service of Dr May Wallas, in *Newnham College Roll Letter*, pp. 45–48.

Reviews:

Benjamin Constant, *De la Justice politique*, ed. Burton R. Pollin, FS XXVIII, 85.

Madame de Duras, *Olivier ou le secret* (éd. Denise Vivieux) *ibid.*, 86.

Flaubert, *Correspondance.* T. I. (éd. J. Bruneau), *ibid.*, 97.

R. Winiker, *Madame de Charrière*, *ibid.*, 201.

Gérard de Nerval, *Aurélia*. Prolégomènes à une édition critique par J. Guillaume SJ, *ibid.*, 216.

Gérard de Nerval, *Lettres à Franz Liszt* (éd. J. Guillaume et Cl. Pichois), *ibid.*, 216.

Gérard de Nerval, *Les Chimères* (ed. Norma Rinsler), *ibid.*, 217.

Norma Rinsler, *Gérard de Nerval*, *ibid.*, 217.

J. P. Houston, *The Demonic Imagination*, *ibid.*, 336.

J. P. Houston, *Fictional Technique in France 1802–1827*, *ibid.*, 336.

Dorothy M. Di Orio, *Leconte de Lisle: A hundred and twenty years of criticism*, *ibid.*, 476.

R. Galand, *Baudelaire – poétique et poésie*, *ibid.*, 477.

J.-J. Mayoux, *L'Humour et l'absurde: attitudes anglo-saxonnes, attitudes françaises*, *ibid.*, 489.

J. Smith, *Shakespearian and other Essays*, *ibid.*, 490.

Roland Bourneuf et Réal Ouellet, *L'Univers du roman*, *ibid.*, 490.

Molière, stage and study. Essays in Honour of W. G. Moore. Journal of European Studies IV, 301.

Pierre Danger, *Sensations et objets dans le roman de Flaubert*, TLS 3.5.74, 478.

1975

Réception à l'Hôtel de ville de Paris, le 26 juillet 1974. Réponse au Vice-Président, CAIEF XXVII, pp. 472–3.

Reviews:

R. T. Denommé, *Leconte de Lisle*, FS XXIX, 102.

P. Barbéris, «*René*» *de Chateaubriand, un nouveau roman*, *ibid.*, 204.

Chateaubriand, *Atala* (éd. J.-M. Gautier), *ibid.*, 204.

Chateaubriand, *René* (éd. J.-M. Gautier), *ibid.*, 204.

J.-P. Duquette, *Flaubert ou l'Architecture du vide: une lecture de «L'Éducation sentimentale»*, *ibid.*, 215.

P. Bénichou, *Le Sacre de l'Écrivain 1750–1870*, *ibid.*, 467.

J. Cruickshank, *Benjamin Constant, ibid.*, 470.

Hamlet-Metz, Mario, *La Critique littéraire de Lamartine, ibid.*, 472.

Stendhal, *Le Rouge et le Noir* (éd. P.-G. Castex), RHLF LXXV, 464–6.

1976

'Observations sur les *Petits poèmes en prose.*' In *Baudelaire: herausgegeben von Alfred Noyer-Weidner.* (Wege der Forschung, 283) (Darmstadt: Wissenchaftliche Buchgesellschaft), pp. 394–409. (Already published in RSH, 1967, pp. 449–60.))

'Forthcoming Retirements: The Mistress of Girton', CR 30.1.76, 98–9.

Reviews:

E. Pich, *Leconte de Lisle et sa Création poétique*, FS XXX, 82.

Gérard de Nerval, *Poésies et souvenirs* (éd. J. Richer), *ibid.*, 223.

Théophile Gautier, *Poésies (1830).* (ed. H. Cockerham), *ibid.*, 225.

H. Verhoeff, '*Adolphe' et Constant, une étude psychocritique, ibid.* 329.

Marie J. Diamond, *Flaubert, ibid.*, 337.

R. Mortier, *La Poétique des ruines en France, ibid.*, 353.

Alison and Sonia Landes, *Pariswalks, ibid.*, 356.

Morten Nøjgard, *Élévation et expansion. Les deux dimensions de Baudelaire,* MLR LXXI, 676.

1977

'The Ambitions of Baudelaire [*Œuvres complètes de Baudelaire*, t.I et II, (ed. Cl. Pichois)]', TLS LXXVI, 567.

Reviews:

H. Corbat, *Hantise et Imagination chez Aloysius Bertrand*, FS XXXI, 87.

Théophile Gautier, *Voyage pittoresque en Algérie* (éd. Madeleine Cottin),) *ibid.*, 89.

Richard B. Grant, *Théophile Gautier, ibid.*, 90.

Edouard Guitton, *Jacques Delille, ibid.*, 206.

Charles Baudelaire, *Un Mangeur d'Opium* (éd. Michèle Stäuble-Lipman Wulf), *ibid.*, 221.

Armand Moss, *Baudelaire et Madame Sabatier, ibid.*, 346.

Études baudelairiennes VIII, *ibid.*, 347.

Graham Chesters, *Some Functions of Sound-Repetition in 'Les Fleurs du Mal', ibid.*, 348.

Œuvres de Leconte de Lisle. I. *Poèmes antiques*. II. *Poèmes barbares* (éd. Edgard Pich), *ibid.*, 469.

R. A. Lewis, '*La Cloche fêlée'. An Essay in the Analysis of a Poem, ibid.*, 471.

Tamara Bassim, *La Femme dans l'œuvre de Baudelaire*, MLR LXXII, 450.

1978

Dr W. G. Moore (1905–1978). FS XXXII, pp. 247–8.

Reviews:

Le Groupe de Coppet. Actes et Documents du deuxième Colloque de Coppet, FS XXXII, 83.

Benjamin Constant, *Lettres à Madame Récamier (1807–1830)* (éd. E. Harpaz), *ibid.*, 84.
La Production du sens chez Flaubert. Colloque de Cerisy, ibid., 91.
Langages de Flaubert. Actes du Colloque de London (Canada) 1973, ibid., 93.
David H. T. Scott, *Sonnet Theory and Practice in Nineteenth-century France, ibid.*, 200.
Chateaubriand, *Mémoires de ma vie* (éd. J.-M. Gautier), *ibid.*, 201.
Benjamin Constant, *Adolphe* (éd. P. Delbouille), *ibid.*, 340.
Gustave Flaubert, *Plans, notes et scénarios de 'Un cœur simple'* (éd. François Fleury), *ibid.*, 474.
George A. Willenbrink, *The Dossier of Flaubert's 'Un Cœur simple', ibid.*, 474.

1979

'La Contradiction créatrice. Quelques remarques sur la genèse d'*Un Cœur simple*' in *Essais sur Flaubert en l'honneur du professeur Don Demorest* (Paris: Nizet, pp. 203–31).
'Framework as a suggestive art in Constant's *Adolphe* (with remarks on its relation to Chateaubriand's *René*) AJFS, Special No. 16, Parts I and II: *Studies in Memory of R. F. Jackson* (eds. Wallace Kirsop and Jacques Birnberg), 6–16.
Reviews:
   Leconte de Lisle, *Œuvres*, t. III. *Poèmes tragiques. Derniers Poèmes* (éd. Edgard Pich), FS XXXIII, 94.
   Maxime Du Camp, *Lettres inédites à Gustave Flaubert* (ed. G. Bonaccorso and Rose Maria de Stefano), *ibid.*, 95.
   Dora Wiebenson, *The Picturesque Garden in France, ibid.*, 205.
   Baudelaire, *Les Fleurs du Mal* (ed. Max Milner), *ibid.*, 352.
   Simone Balayé, *Madame de Staël, ibid.*, 455.
   Madelyn Gutwirth, *Madame de Staël, Novelist, ibid.*, 455.
   Madame de Staël, *Des Circonstances actuelles qui peuvent terminer la Révolution* (éd. L. Omacini). *ibid.*, 455.
   Dominique Rincé, *La Littérature française du XIXe siècle, ibid.*, 453.
   Dominique Rincé, *La Poésie française du XIXe siècle, ibid.*, 453.
   Giovanni Bonaccorso, *Sul testo di 'Madame Bovary', ibid.*, 466.
   Ch. Carlut, P.-H. Dubé, J. R. Dugan, *A Concordance to Flaubert's 'Madame Bovary', ibid.*, 467.
   Ch. Carlut, P.-H. Dubé, J. R. Dugan, *A Concordance to Flaubert's 'L'Éducation sentimentale', ibid.*, 467.

1980

'The Shaping of *Adolphe*. Some remarks on Variants', in *Mélanges de littérature française moderne. Offerts à Garnet Rees* (ed. C. E. Pickford) (Paris: Minard), pp. 145–64.
'Suggestions on the art of the novelist in Constant's *Cécile*', in *Literature and Society. Studies in Nineteenth and Twentieth-Century French Literature presented to R. J. North* (ed. C. A. Burns) Birmingham: John Goodman, pp. 29–37.

Reviews:
Gustave Flaubert, *L'Éducation sentimentale*. Texte présenté et commenté par Alan Raitt, FS XXXIV, 212–13.
Charles Carlut, P.-H. Dubé, J. R. Dugan, *A Concordance to Flaubert's 'Salammbô', ibid.*, 214.
Charles Carlut, P.-H. Dubé, J. R. Dugan, *A Concordance to Flaubert's 'Trois Contes', ibid.*, 214.
Charles Carlut, P.-H. Dubé, J. R. Dugan, *A Concordance to Flaubert's 'La Tentation de Saint Antoine', ibid.*, 353.
Baudelaire, *Le Spleen de Paris. Petits Poèmes en prose*. Texte présenté et commenté par Max Milner, *ibid.*, 460–1.

1981

'La quête de la femme à travers la ville chez Flaubert' (Colloquium 'Flaubert, la femme, la ville', Paris, 26 November 1980, organized by the Institute de Français de l'Université de Paris X-Nanterre).
'Aspects de l'histoire de l'art dans *L'Éducation sentimentale*' (Colloquium 'Flaubert', Paris, 28 November 1980, organized by the Société d'Histoire Littéraire de la France).
Review:
Michel Jeanneret, *La Lettre perdue. Écriture et folie dans l'œuvre de Nerval*, MLR LXXVI.

Index